Defect
Detect

Windows Debugging[4]

Accelerated

Version 4.0

Dmitry Vostokov
Software Diagnostics Services

Published by OpenTask, Republic of Ireland

Product and company names mentioned in this book may be trademarks of their owners.

OpenTask books and magazines are available through booksellers and distributors worldwide. For further information or comments, send requests to press@opentask.com.

A CIP catalog record for this book is available from the British Library.

ISBN-l3: 978-1912636-72-3 (Paperback)

Revision 4.00 (February 2024)

Contents

About the Author

Dmitry Vostokov is an internationally recognized expert, speaker, educator, scientist, inventor, and author. He founded the pattern-oriented software diagnostics, forensics, and prognostics discipline (Systematic Software Diagnostics) and Software Diagnostics Institute (DA+TA: DumpAnalysis.org + TraceAnalysis.org). Vostokov has also authored over 50 books on software diagnostics, anomaly detection and analysis, software and memory forensics, root cause analysis and problem solving, memory dump analysis, debugging, software trace and log analysis, reverse engineering, and malware analysis. He has over 25 years of experience in software architecture, design, development, and maintenance in various industries, including leadership, technical, and people management roles. Dmitry also founded Syndromatix, Anolog.io, BriteTrace, DiaThings, Logtellect, OpenTask Iterative and Incremental Publishing (OpenTask.com), Software Diagnostics Technology and Services (former Memory Dump Analysis Services) PatternDiagnostics.com, and Software Prognostics. In his spare time, he presents various topics on Debugging.TV and explores Software Narratology, its further development as Narratology of Things and Diagnostics of Things (DoT), Software Pathology, and Quantum Software Diagnostics. His current interest areas are theoretical software diagnostics and its mathematical and computer science foundations, application of formal logic, artificial intelligence, machine learning and data mining to diagnostics and anomaly detection, software diagnostics engineering and diagnostics-driven development, diagnostics workflow and interaction. Recent interest areas also include cloud native computing, security, automation, functional programming, applications of category theory to software development and big data, and diagnostics of artificial intelligence.

Presentation Slides and Transcript

Hello, everyone, my name is Dmitry Vostokov, and I teach this training course. In the beginning, we go through a few introductory slides.

Prerequisites

◉ Debugging in Visual Studio

or

◉ Basic crash dump analysis

To get most of this training, you are expected to have basic Visual Studio debugging or crash dump analysis experience.

Why WinDbg/WinDbg Classic?

◉ Easy to install (WinDbg)

◉ Production debugging

◉ Redistributable (WinDbg Classic)

◉ Kernel mode debugging

◉ Time Travel Debugging (WinDbg)

Suppose you deployed your application or service to production computers and need to debug them because you cannot reproduce the problem on your development machine. You need a lightweight debugger there. Here, the WinDbg app comes in handy as it can be easily installed. Debugging Tools for Windows that have WinDbg Classic and other tools can also be easily redistributed and deployed. Plus, to do kernel mode debugging on a target machine, you don't need to install anything[1]. Also, with WinDbg, you can record the application execution history and later replay it on another machine, seeing all memory changes, which has an advantage over postmortem debugging using static memory dumps.

---

[1] If you debug via a serial port. For faster debugging using KDNET you need to copy some files from Debugging Tools for Windows.

Training Goals

◉ Review fundamentals

◉ Learn live debugging techniques

◉ See how software diagnostics is used during debugging

Our primary goal is to learn live debugging in an accelerated fashion. So, first, we review the essential fundamentals necessary for debugging using WinDbg[2]. Then, we learn how to debug different scenarios and, in the process, learn how pattern-oriented software diagnostics is used and influences the choice of various debugging techniques.

---

[2] WinDbg is a modern GUI version of WinDbg from Debugging Tools for Windows.

Training Principles

⦿ Talk only about what I can show

⦿ Lots of pictures

⦿ Lots of examples

⦿ Original content and examples

There were many training formats to consider, and I decided that the best way is to concentrate on hands-on exercises. Specifically, for this training, I developed 16 of them.

Course Idea

Chemistry[3]: Introducing Inorganic, Organic, and Physical Chemistry book

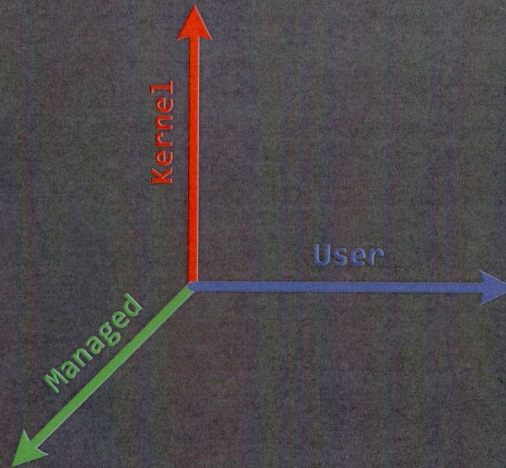

I took the course idea from the book **Chemistry[3]**, which I bought in 2012, to refresh my knowledge[3]. I quickly realized the potential of the same multidimensional format to cover all different debugging spaces to show their interrelationship.

---

[3] My first professional education was in Chemistry.

14

Debugging TV

- www.debugging.tv (more than 40 episodes)

- PDB Symbols: episodes 0x01 – 0x04

- Kernel debugging setup: episode 0x25

Due to time constraints, we don't cover everything from Windows debugging. I already covered some topics, such as debugging symbols, in several episodes of Debugging TV Frames (www.debugging.tv). I decided not to repeat that in this training.

Schedule Summary

Day 1

- Debugging Fundamentals and x64 Disassembly Review (1 hour)
- User Mode Debugging (30 minutes)

Day 2/3

- User Mode Debugging (3 hours)

Day 4

- Kernel Debugging (1 hour 30 minutes)

Day 5

- Managed Debugging (30 minutes)
- Time-Travel Debugging (30 minutes)
- Rust Debugging (30 minutes)

This is a roughly planned schedule. You are welcome to type your questions during the training, and I will do my best to answer them immediately. However, if some questions require preparation time, I postpone their answers and send them after the training sessions.

Part 1: Fundamentals

Now, I will show you some pictures.

Memory Space[3]

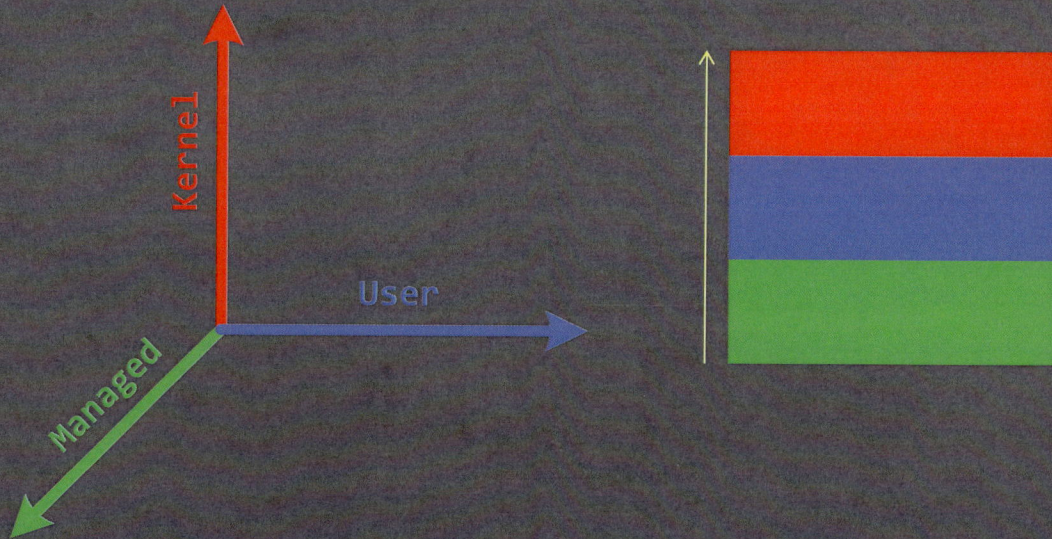

We divided memory space into 3 areas: kernel, process user space, and managed space. Managed .NET space is a fictitious space. It is a part of the process user space, but we consider it a separate space due to specialized analysis extensions and analysis differences. Abstractly, we can see it as .NET code (from managed space) that uses Windows API (for example, windowing and graphics, DLLs from process user space). Windows API is located in user space DLLs such as *user32* and *kernel32,* and they forward requests to *ntdll.dll*[4] and from there to kernel space where a graphics subsystem such as *win32k.sys* is located. The yellow arrow on the right shows the approximate stack trace direction in the output of WinDbg commands.

---

[4] Windows 10 and 11 uses *win32u.dll* and *ntdll.dll*.

Execution Mode[3]

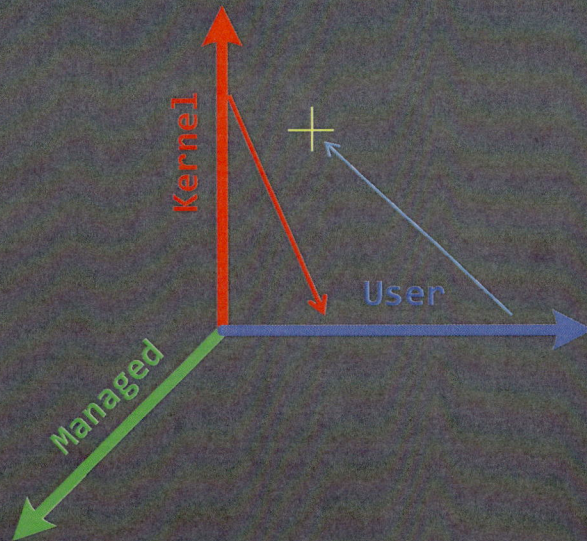

Please note that the CPU execution mode differs from the memory space partition. We can have kernel drivers accessing user space in kernel mode, for example, when they need application buffers to write data to a disk.

Code³

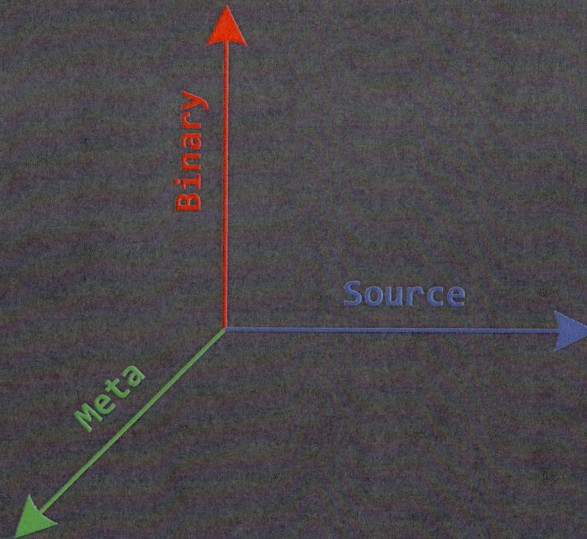

Debugging is usually considered as fixing source code defects. However, it is also important that some problems can be fixed by adjusting code generation parameters (which we call meta-code), especially when porting legacy code or due to a platform change. We would see that in one of our exercises.

Live Debugging Technique[3]

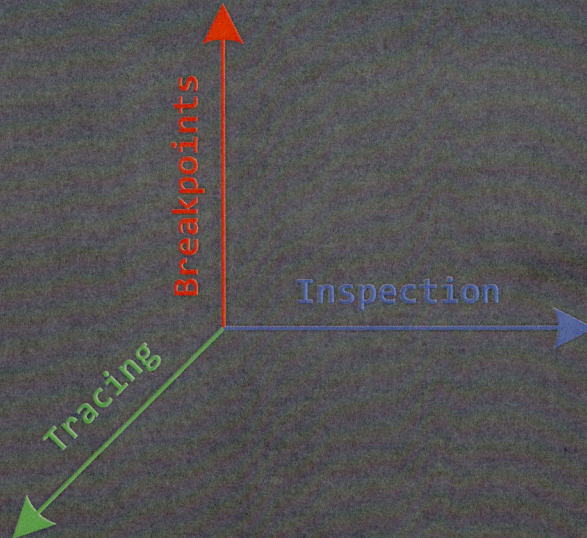

In this training, we also cover 3 important debugging techniques: setting appropriate data and code breakpoints, tracing source code, and inspecting data either structured by source code symbol files or just binary.

Pattern³

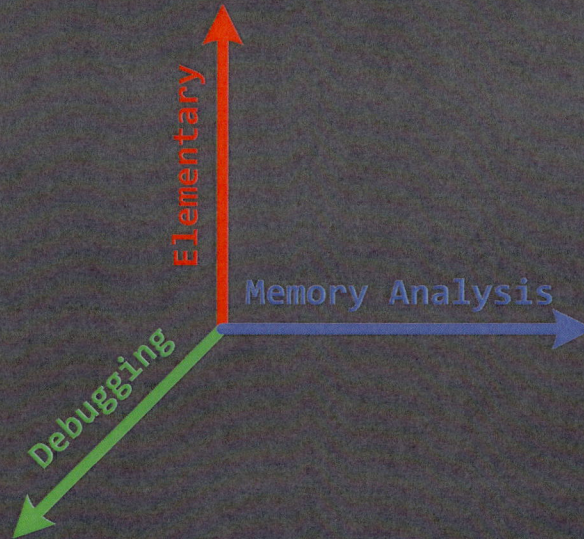

Here is a diagram for the pattern catalogs we use in this training. There are many different catalogs, and we selected only three: **Elementary Software Diagnostics** patterns, **Memory Analysis** patterns, and **Debugging Implementation** patterns. Their difference is explained in the next slide.

Debugging Paradigm[3]

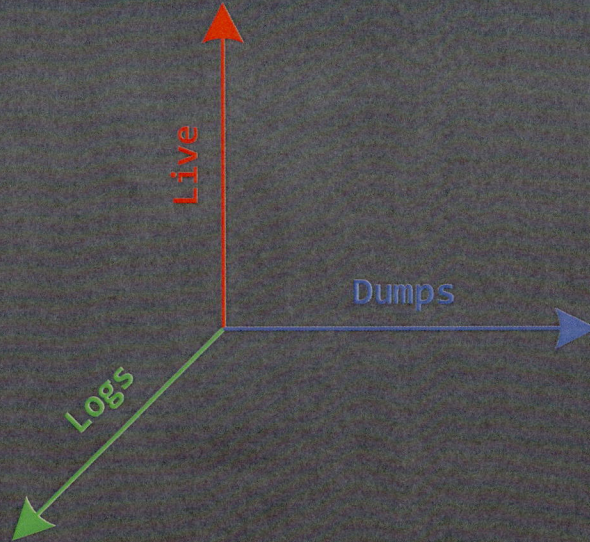

Traditionally, there are three debugging paradigms: dumps (postmortem debugging), logs, and live (debugging).

Debugging Paradigm[4]

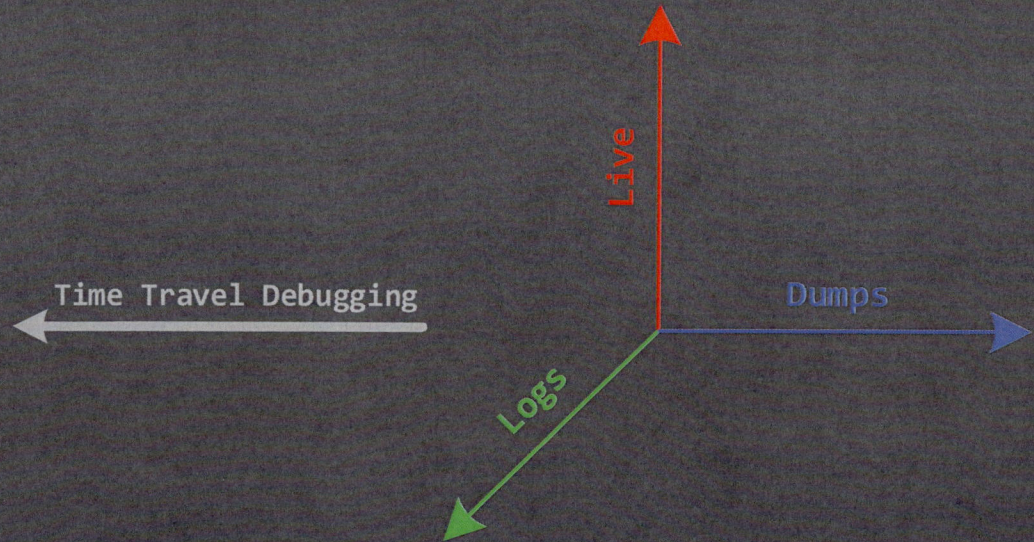

To them, Microsoft added the 4th paradigm, time travel debugging[5] (TTD).

---

[5] https://docs.microsoft.com/en-us/windows-hardware/drivers/debugger/time-travel-debugging-overview

Memory Spacetime

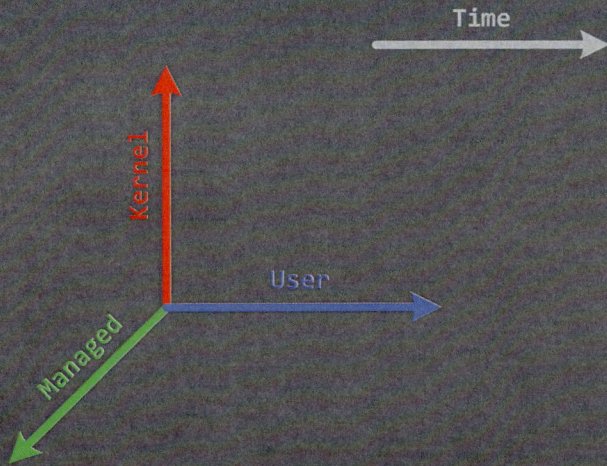

© 2024 Software Diagnostics Services

We can also apply the metaphor of spacetime from relativity theories in physics to memory spaces and their changes in time. Both TDD and memory spacetime inspired the Debugging[4] or Debugging 4D course title.

Debugging Paradigm^5

Idea: Kaluza-Klein Theory of a microscopic 5th dimension

Because we do kernel debugging of guest VM 4D space from the separate host machine 4D space we can also apply the metaphor a microscopic 5th dimension.

Kaluza-Klein Theory
https://en.wikipedia.org/wiki/Kaluza%E2%80%93Klein_theory

Pattern Mapping

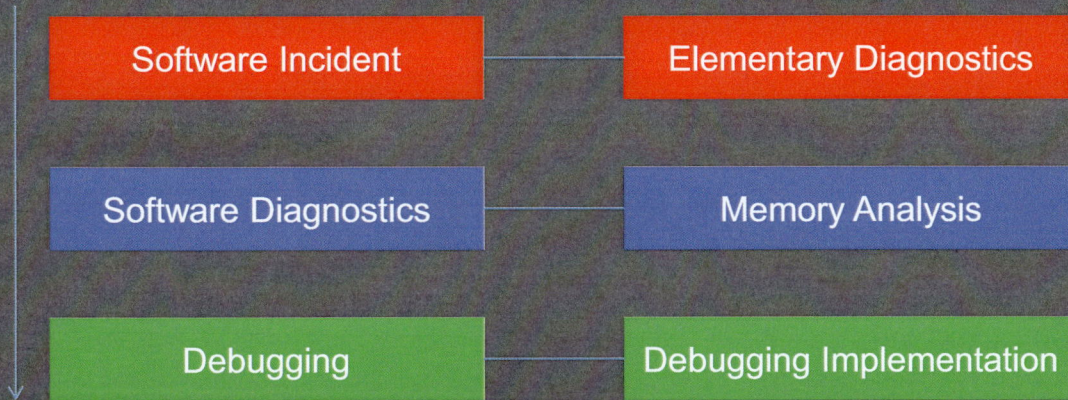

Upon a software incident described by elementary software diagnostics patterns, we perform some software diagnostics activities such as memory analysis (be it live memory or postmortem memory dump analysis or software trace and log analysis) and finally come to some debugging strategy covered by debugging implementation patterns.

Elementary Diagnostics

- ⊚ Functional
  - Use-case Deviation

- ⊚ Non-functional
  - Crash
  - Hang (includes delays)
  - Counter Value (includes resource leaks, CPU spikes)
  - Error Message

What are **Elementary Software Diagnostics** patterns? These are patterns of abnormal software behavior that affect software users and trigger the application of pattern-oriented software diagnostics and debugging if necessary. On this slide, you see the initial list of relevant elementary patterns we cover in this training.

Analysis Patterns

- [Memory Analysis catalog](#)

- [Software Trace and Log Analysis catalog](#)

Analysis patterns allow us to reuse memory dump and software trace and log analysis pattern catalogs from the Software Diagnostics Library[6]. In this training, we only cover relevant memory analysis patterns. At the end of this training, I put a slide with links to their description and additional examples.

Memory Analysis catalog
https://www.dumpanalysis.org/blog/index.php/crash-dump-analysis-patterns/

Software Trace and Log Analysis catalog
https://www.dumpanalysis.org/blog/index.php/trace-analysis-patterns/

---

[6] Also available in **Memory Dump Analysis Anthology (Diagnomicon)** volumes, **Encyclopedia of Crash Dump Analysis Patterns**, and **Trace, Log, Text, Narrative, Data** books.

Pattern-Oriented Diagnostic Analysis

Diagnostic Pattern: a common recurrent identifiable problem together with a set of recommendations and possible solutions to apply in a specific context.

Diagnostic Problem: a set of indicators (symptoms, signs) describing a problem.

Diagnostic Analysis Pattern: a common recurrent analysis technique and method of diagnostic pattern identification in a specific context.

Diagnostics Pattern Language: common names of diagnostic and diagnostic analysis patterns. The same language for any operating system: Windows, Mac OS X, Linux, ...

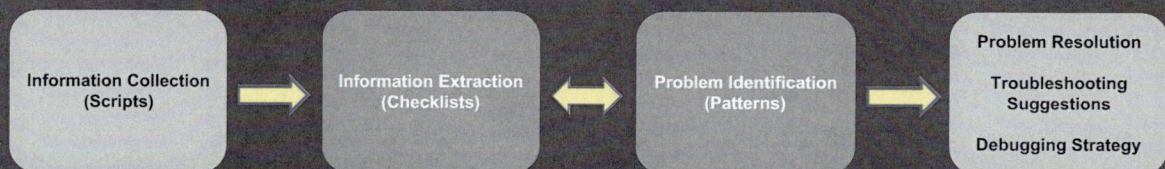

Information Collection (Scripts)	→	Information Extraction (Checklists)	↔	Problem Identification (Patterns)	→	Problem Resolution Troubleshooting Suggestions Debugging Strategy

Checklist: http://www.dumpanalysis.org/windows-memory-analysis-checklist

© 2024 Software Diagnostics Services

A few words about logs, checklists, and patterns: memory analysis is usually an analysis of a text for the presence of patterns. We run commands, they output text, and then we look at that textual output, and when we find something suspicious, we execute more commands. Here, checklists can be very useful. One such checklist is provided as a link. In some cases (such as physical memory), it is beneficial to collect information into one log file by running several commands at once (like a script) and then doing the first-order analysis.

Checklist

https://www.dumpanalysis.org/windows-memory-analysis-checklist

Unified Debugging Patterns

- Analysis (software diagnostics)

- Architecture/Design of debugging

- Implementation of debugging

- Usage/presentation of debugging (for example, Watch dialog)

Debugging Implementation patterns come from a unified debugging pattern approach[7] like the pattern-oriented approach in software construction with its architecture and design phases, implementation, usage, and presentation patterns[8]. In this training, we only cover implementation patterns as they are basically core debugging techniques. The full unified pattern stack is still being developed at the time of this writing.

---

[7] Memory Dump Analysis Anthology, Volume 6, and Volume 7

[8] See also **Pattern-Oriented Debugging Process**: https://www.dumpanalysis.org/pattern-oriented-debugging-process

Full Debugging Patterns Catalog

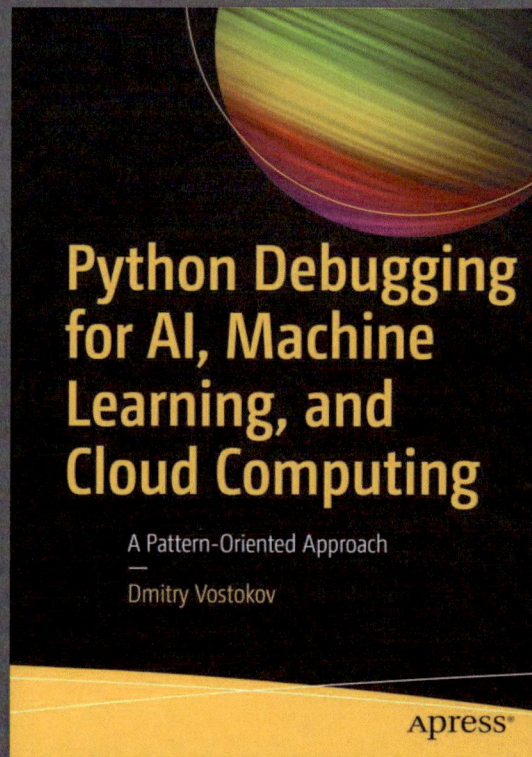

The full unified pattern stack is described in **Python Debugging for AI, Machine Learning, and Cloud Computing: A Pattern-Oriented Approach**[9] book.

---

[9] https://link.springer.com/book/10.1007/978-1-4842-9745-2

Space Review (x86)

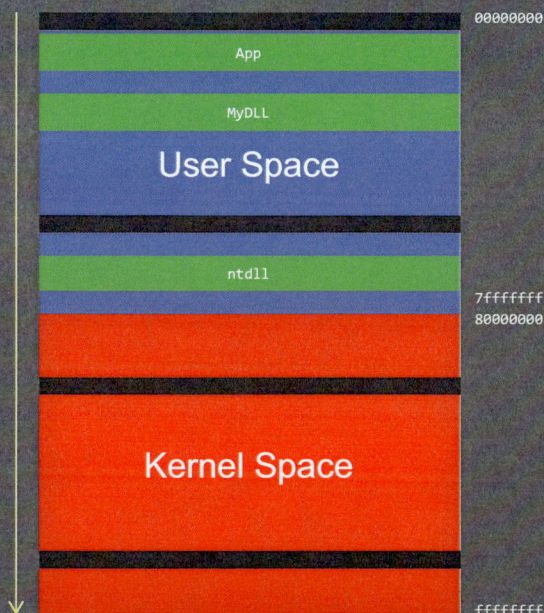

```
0:000> lm
start    end      module name
00ed0000 00f0e000 App
0f450000 0f530000 MyDLL
638d0000 63b2d000 CoreUIComponents
63b30000 63bbb000 CoreMessaging
642d0000 64435000 twinapi_appcore
6beb0000 6c0b4000 comctl32
6d7e0000 6d803000 dwmapi
6d930000 6d9ac000 uxtheme
6d9c0000 6da96000 WinTypes
6dac0000 6dce8000 iertutil
6dcf0000 6de8c000 urlmon
700b0000 70230000 propsys
70230000 7029c000 winspool
702a0000 702f6000 oleacc
70530000 70559000 ntmarta
70af0000 70b08000 mpr
74080000 74099000 bcrypt
74280000 742b0000 IPHLPAPI
746a0000 746aa000 CRYPTBASE
746b0000 746d0000 sspicli
74870000 74892000 gdi32
749a0000 74b2d000 user32
74b60000 74c1f000 msvcrt
74c20000 74c98000 advapi32
74ca0000 74d28000 SHCore
74d30000 74f14000 KERNELBASE
74f20000 7517c000 combase
75180000 75260000 kernel32
75260000 752e3000 clbcatq
752f0000 75434000 msctf
75440000 7678a000 shell32
767a0000 767f8000 bcryptPrimitives
76800000 7691e000 ucrtbase
76920000 769e0000 rpcrt4
769e0000 769f7000 win32u
76a00000 76a39000 cfgmgr32
76ee0000 76ee8000 fltLib
76f00000 76f45000 powrprof
76f50000 76f95000 shlwapi
76fa0000 77036000 oleaut32
77200000 77218000 profapi
77310000 77354000 sechost
773c0000 77524000 gdi32full
77590000 775b6000 imm32
775e0000 776b6000 comdlg32
776c0000 77c7a000 windows_storage
77c80000 77cfd000 msvcp_win
77df0000 77f80000 ntdll
```

© 2024 Software Diagnostics Services

Now, we briefly review memory spaces. Most of you are familiar with the 32-bit process address space mapping, especially if you attended the **Accelerated Windows Memory Dump Analysis** course or read its book. I just briefly repeat that when we run an application or service, its executable file is loaded into memory, and if it references other DLLs, they are loaded too at some addresses in memory. There may be gaps between them, like black regions in this picture. Some memory is also allocated for additional working regions needed for process execution, such as process heap or .NET heap, stack regions, mapped files, and large virtual address regions. It usually has a 2 GB range, and we see addresses where modules are loaded using the **lm** command.

Space Review (x64)

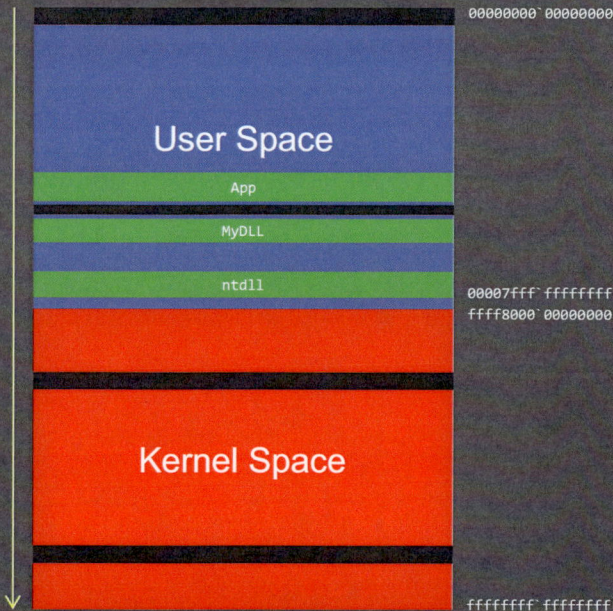

User Space

App

MyDLL

ntdll

Kernel Space

```
00000000`00000000



00007fff`ffffffff
ffff8000`00000000




ffffffff`ffffffff
```

```
0:000> lm
start             end               module name
00007ff7`73080000 00007ff7`7330f000 App
00007ff8`44990000 00007ff8`44a27000 MyDLL
00007ff8`46ad0000 00007ff8`46d39000 comctl32
00007ff8`56d70000 00007ff8`56ddb000 oleacc
00007ff8`56de0000 00007ff8`56f7a000 GdiPlus
00007ff8`58dd0000 00007ff8`58e54000 winspool
00007ff8`5c6b0000 00007ff8`5c9ce000 CoreUIComponents
00007ff8`5ca10000 00007ff8`5ca75000 ninput
00007ff8`5ce40000 00007ff8`5cf8d000 WinTypes
00007ff8`5db50000 00007ff8`5dd04000 propsys
00007ff8`5ec10000 00007ff8`5ec3a000 winmmbase
00007ff8`5ec40000 00007ff8`5ec63000 winmm
00007ff8`5ee10000 00007ff8`5ee17000 msimg32
00007ff8`5f210000 00007ff8`5f2ea000 CoreMessaging
00007ff8`5f590000 00007ff8`5f628000 uxtheme
00007ff8`5f820000 00007ff8`5f849000 dwmapi
00007ff8`601c0000 00007ff8`601f1000 ntmarta
00007ff8`606d0000 00007ff8`60708000 IPHLPAPI
00007ff8`60c30000 00007ff8`60c55000 bcrypt
00007ff8`610d0000 00007ff8`6111c000 powrprof
00007ff8`61120000 00007ff8`6112a000 fltLib
00007ff8`61150000 00007ff8`61161000 kernel_appcore
00007ff8`61170000 00007ff8`6118f000 profapi
00007ff8`61190000 00007ff8`6128a000 ucrtbase
00007ff8`61290000 00007ff8`612d9000 cfgmgr32
00007ff8`612e0000 00007ff8`61472000 gdi32full
00007ff8`61480000 00007ff8`614a0000 win32u
00007ff8`616f0000 00007ff8`61dfd000 windows_storage
00007ff8`61e00000 00007ff8`61e7a000 bcryptPrimitives
00007ff8`61e80000 00007ff8`61f1f000 msvcp_win
00007ff8`61f20000 00007ff8`62193000 KERNELBASE
00007ff8`62250000 00007ff8`622ab000 sechost
00007ff8`622d0000 00007ff8`63710000 shell32
00007ff8`63710000 00007ff8`637d2000 oleaut32
00007ff8`637e0000 00007ff8`63881000 advapi32
00007ff8`63890000 00007ff8`638bd000 imm32
00007ff8`638c0000 00007ff8`63a50000 user32
00007ff8`63ae0000 00007ff8`63c55000 msctf
00007ff8`63ce0000 00007ff8`63d08000 gdi32
00007ff8`63d20000 00007ff8`63dbe000 msvcrt
00007ff8`63fc0000 00007ff8`64069000 SHCore
00007ff8`64070000 00007ff8`64194000 rpcrt4
00007ff8`641a0000 00007ff8`641f1000 shlwapi
00007ff8`642f0000 00007ff8`64613000 combase
00007ff8`64620000 00007ff8`64771000 ole32
00007ff8`64820000 00007ff8`648d2000 kernel32
00007ff8`64dc0000 00007ff8`64fa1000 ntdll
```

Here, we provide a picture of process space in 64-bit Windows. The user space is no longer restricted to 2 or 3 GB. DLLs are loaded at higher addresses[10].

---

[10] In earlier Windows x64 versions some DLLs were still loaded in 2 GB address range.

Thread Stack Trace

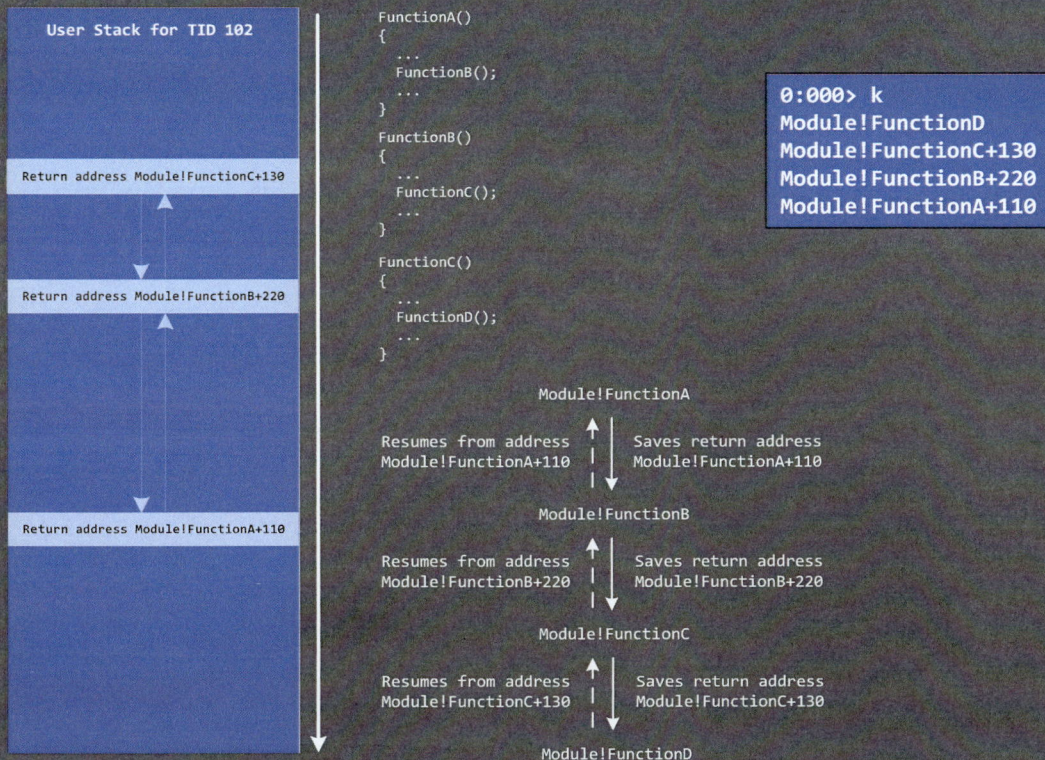

```
User Stack for TID 102


Return address Module!FunctionC+130



Return address Module!FunctionB+220




Return address Module!FunctionA+110
```

```
FunctionA()
{
  ...
  FunctionB();
  ...
}
FunctionB()
{
  ...
  FunctionC();
  ...
}
FunctionC()
{
  ...
  FunctionD();
  ...
}
```

```
0:000> k
Module!FunctionD
Module!FunctionC+130
Module!FunctionB+220
Module!FunctionA+110
```

```
                    Module!FunctionA
Resumes from address  ↑ |  Saves return address
Module!FunctionA+110  | ↓  Module!FunctionA+110
                    Module!FunctionB
Resumes from address  ↑ |  Saves return address
Module!FunctionB+220  | ↓  Module!FunctionB+220
                    Module!FunctionC
Resumes from address  ↑ |  Saves return address
Module!FunctionC+130  | ↓  Module!FunctionC+130
                    Module!FunctionD
```

I assume you are familiar with stack traces from Visual Studio debugging or crash dump analysis experience. I just briefly review them here from the WinDbg perspective. Suppose we have source code where *FunctionA* calls *FunctionB* at some point, *FunctionB* calls *FunctionC,* and so on. This is a thread of execution. If *FunctionA* calls *FunctionB*, you expect the execution thread to return to the same place where it left and resume from there. This is achieved by saving a return address in a thread stack region. Every return address is saved and then restored during thread execution. Although the memory addresses grow from top to bottom, in this picture, return addresses are saved from bottom to top (the stack grows from higher to lower addresses in memory). This might seem counter-intuitive to all previous pictures, but this is how you would see the output from WinDbg commands. What WinDbg does when you instruct it to dump a stack trace from a given thread is to analyze thread raw stack data and figure out return addresses, map them to symbolic form according to symbol files, and show them from top to bottom. Note that *FunctionD* is not present in the raw stack data on the left because it is currently being executed after being called from *FunctionC*. However, *FunctionC* called *FunctionD*, and the return address of *FunctionC* was saved. In the blue box on the right, we see the results of the WinDbg **k** command.

Thread Stack Trace (no PDB)

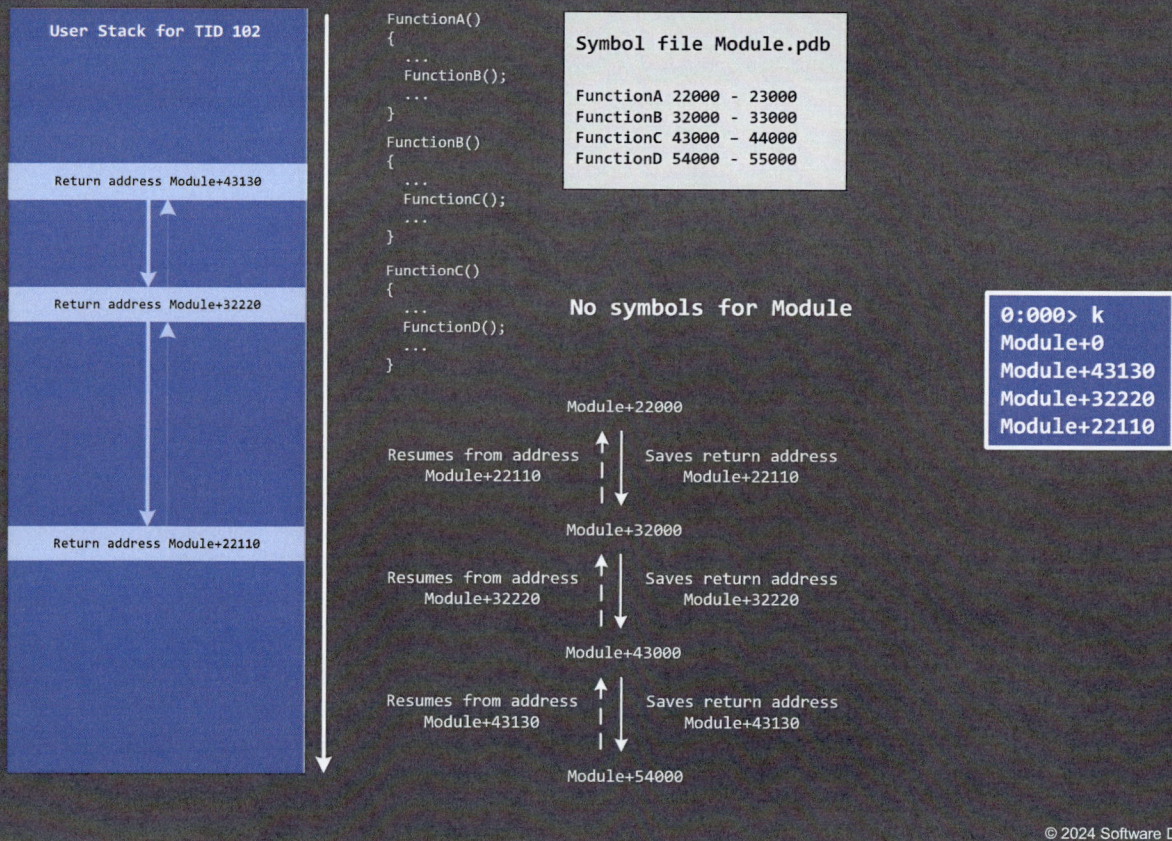

Here, I'd like to show you why symbol files are important and what stack traces you get without them. Symbol files provide mappings between memory address ranges and associated symbolic names. In the absence of symbols, we are left with bare module names. .NET code is much better because .NET modules usually include full code description inside.

Thread Raw Stack Data

```
void main()
{
    foo();
    crash();
}

void foo()
{
    char sz[256] = "Some String";
    bar();
}

void bar()
{
    do();
}

void crash()
{
    WER();
}
```

```
0:000> k
module!crash+30
module!main+10
```

Stack memory region (bottom to top):
- module!bar+20
- Some String
- module!crash+30
- module!main+10

© 2024 Software Diagnostics Services

Each thread of execution has its own region in user space called a stack. We also call it raw stack to differentiate it from the stack trace. Every function call stores a return address. Sometimes, such return addresses are overwritten by subsequent execution, and sometimes they survive. We call this the **Execution Residue** pattern. We can also see ASCII and UNICODE string fragments there if they survived. For example, in the output of the WinDbg **k** command on the right after the *crash()* function execution that calls exception processing code, we see a stack trace, but there is also surviving execution residue of the *bar()* because of a pre-allocated buffer. Please note again that the stack grows towards lower addresses during function calls, as shown by blue arrows on the left of the stack memory region box.

First vs. Second Chance

⊚ **First chance exceptions**

WinDbg is notified of an exception, you can ignore it

⊚ **Second chance exceptions**

If the exception wasn't handled (for example, by a catch block) WinDbg is notified again

⊚ **Relation to crash dumps**

Another important concept is the difference between the first and second chance exceptions. For example, if there is an exception, such as invalid memory access, a debugger is notified of its occurrence before your code has any chance to handle it. You can ignore it in WinDbg (for example, by continuing), and if it is not handled, the debugger gets the second notification. We would see that in our practical exercises. For postmortem debugging purposes, we can save a memory dump at any stage, and this is illustrated with some diagrams in three articles from the Software Diagnostics Library I put a reference to below[11].

Relation to crash dumps

https://www.dumpanalysis.org/blog/index.php/first-chance-exceptions-explained/

---

[11] Also available in Memory Dump Analysis Anthology, Volume 1 (p. 109), Volume 2 (p. 129), and Volume 5 (p. 335).

Review of x64 Disassembly

Part 2: x64 Disassembly

This section provides an overview of disassembly for the x64 platform. Linux developers who know the x64 assembly language may benefit because we use a different flavor than the default in Linux GDB.

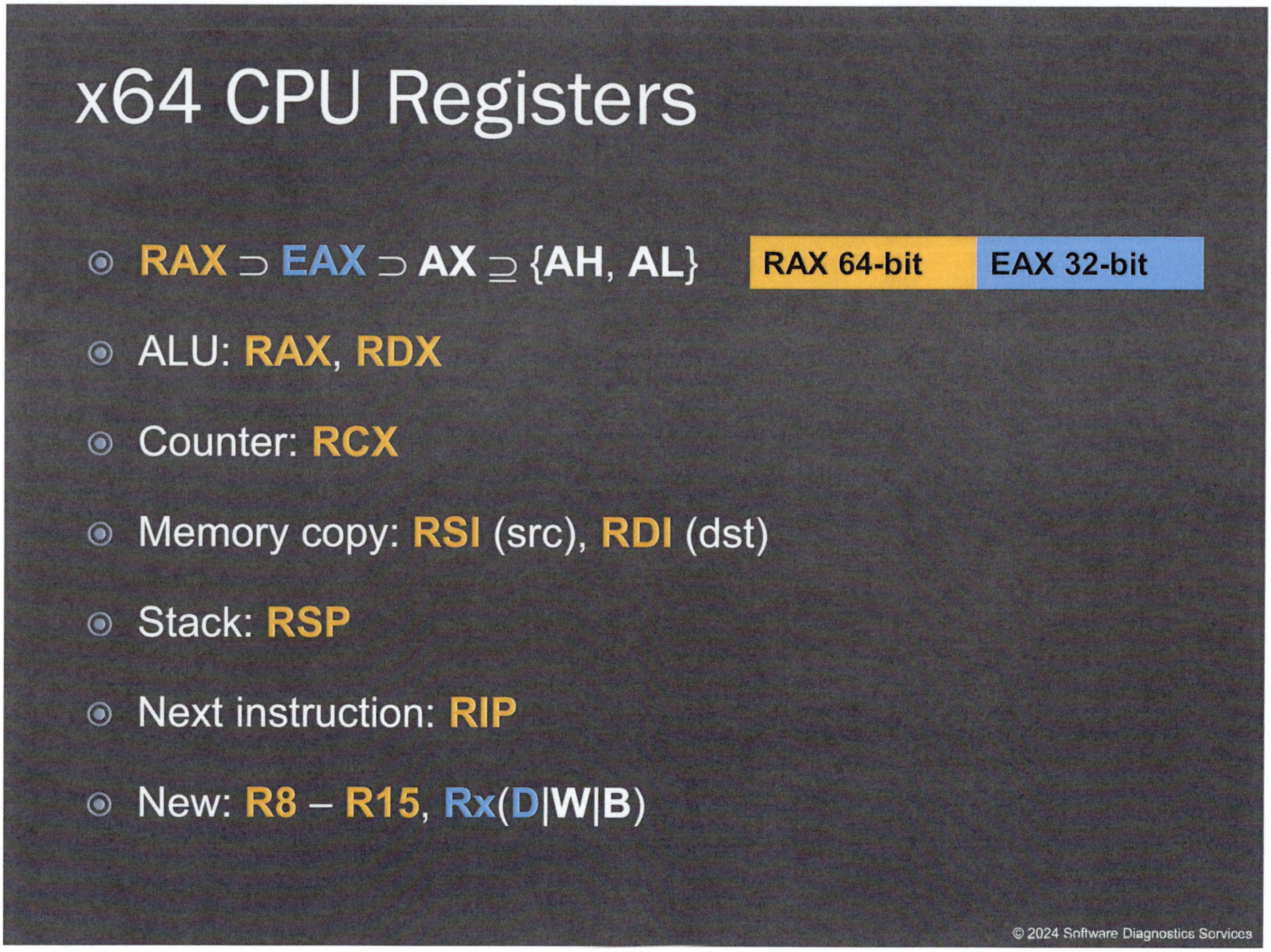

x64 CPU Registers
RAX ⊃ EAX ⊃ AX ⊇ {AH, AL}
RAX 64-bit
EAX 32-bit
ALU: RAX, RDX
Counter: RCX
Memory copy: RSI (src), RDI (dst)
Stack: RSP
Next instruction: RIP
New: R8 – R15, Rx(D|W|B)
© 2024 Software Diagnostics Services

There are familiar 32-bit CPU register names, such as **EAX,** that are extended to 64-bit names, such as **RAX**. Most of them are traditionally specialized, such as ALU, counter, and memory copy registers. Although, now they all can be used as general-purpose registers. There is, of course, a stack pointer, **RSP**, and it also takes the role of a frame pointer, which is also used to address local variables and saved parameters. It can be used for stack reconstruction. In Microsoft compiler code generation implementations, **RBP** is also used as a general-purpose register. An instruction pointer **RIP** is saved in the stack memory region with every function call, then restored on return from the called function. In addition, the x64 platform features another eight general-purpose registers, from **R8** to **R15**.

Instructions and Registers

◎ Opcode DST, SRC

◎ Examples:

```
mov    rax, 10h        ; RAX ← 0x10
mov    r13, rdx        ; R13 ← RDX
add    r10, 10h        ; R10 ← R10 + 0x10
imul   edx, ecx        ; EDX ← EDX * ECX
call   rdx             ; RDX already contains
                       ;     the address of func (&func)
                       ; PUSH RIP; &func → RIP
sub    rsp, 30h        ; RSP ← RSP-0x30
                       ; make room for local variables
```

This slide shows a few examples of CPU instructions involving operations with registers, such as moving a value and doing arithmetic. The direction of operands is opposite to the AT&T x64 disassembly flavor if you are accustomed to default GDB disassembly on Linux.

Memory and Stack Addressing

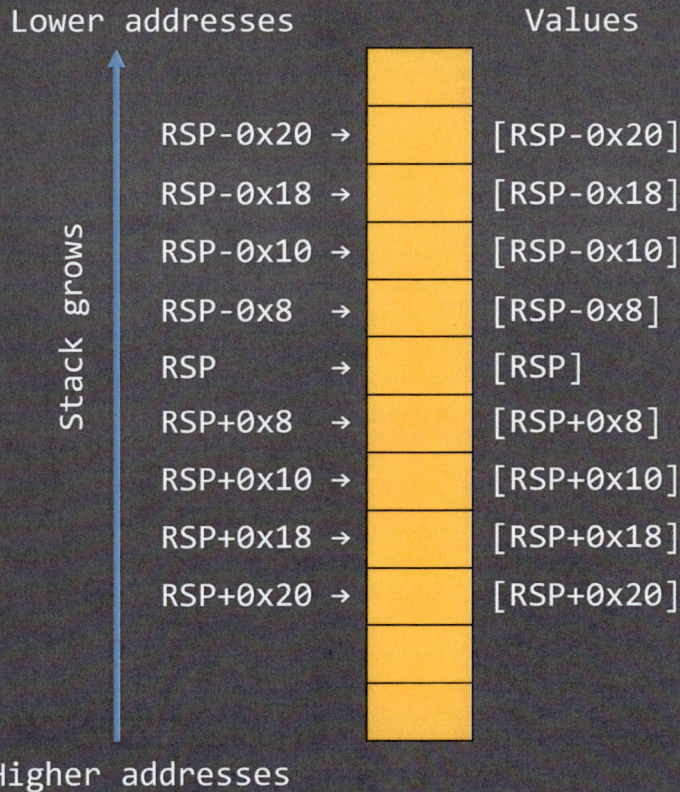

```
         Lower addresses                    Values

         RSP-0x20 →    ┌──────┐         [RSP-0x20]
                       ├──────┤
         RSP-0x18 →    ├──────┤         [RSP-0x18]
                       ├──────┤
    s    RSP-0x10 →    ├──────┤         [RSP-0x10]
    w                  ├──────┤
    o    RSP-0x8  →    ├──────┤         [RSP-0x8]
    r                  ├──────┤
    g    RSP      →    ├──────┤         [RSP]
                       ├──────┤
    k    RSP+0x8  →    ├──────┤         [RSP+0x8]
    c                  ├──────┤
    a    RSP+0x10 →    ├──────┤         [RSP+0x10]
    t                  ├──────┤
    S    RSP+0x18 →    ├──────┤         [RSP+0x18]
                       ├──────┤
         RSP+0x20 →    ├──────┤         [RSP+0x20]
                       ├──────┤
                       ├──────┤
                       └──────┘

         Higher addresses
```

Before we look at operations with memory, let's look at a graphical representation of memory addressing where, for simplicity, I use 64-bit (or 8-byte) memory cells. A thread stack is just any other memory region, so instead of **RSP,** any other register can be used. Please note that the stack grows towards lower addresses, so to access the previously pushed values, you need to use positive offsets from **RSP**.

Memory Cell Sizes

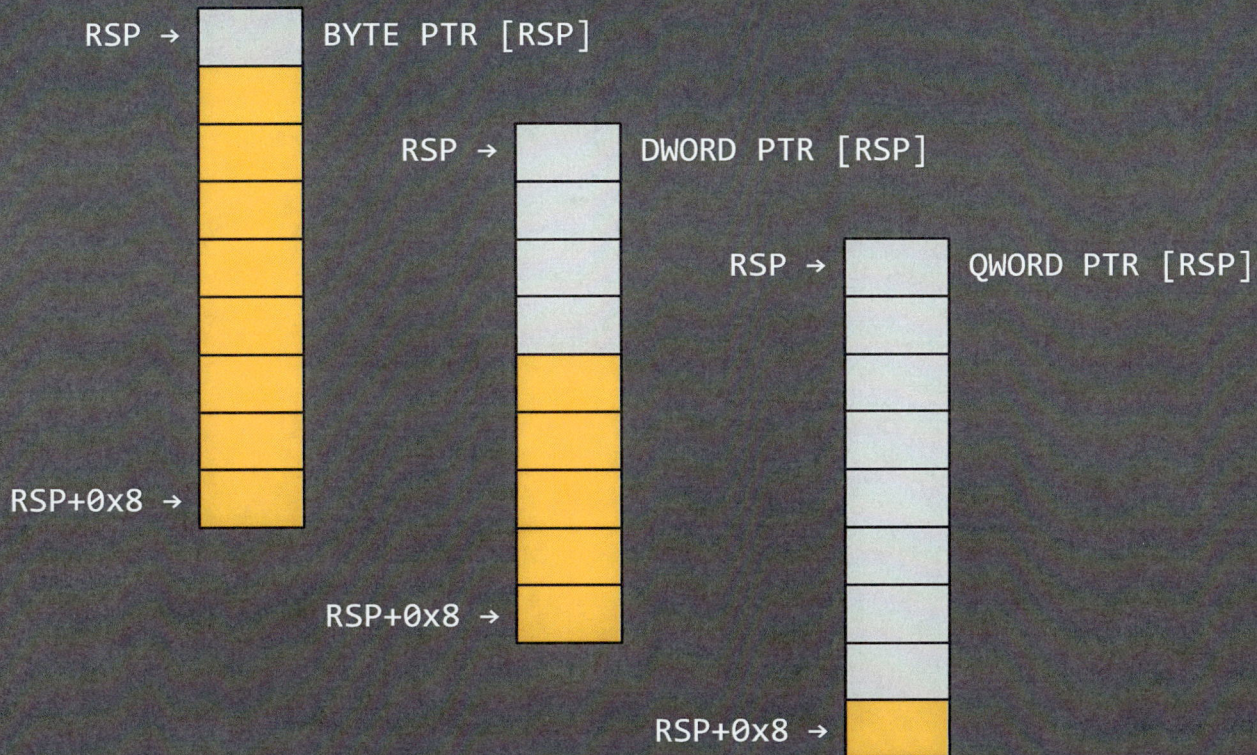

Here, each memory cell is 8-bit (or one byte). When we have a register pointing to memory, and we want to work with the value at that address, we need to specify the size of memory cells to work with, for example, **BYTE PTR** if we want to work with a byte, **DWORD PTR** if we want to work with 32-bit double words, and **QWORD PTR** if we want to work with 64-bit quad words. There's also **WORD PTR** for 16-bit values. This notation is different from Linux GDB, where we have bytes, half-words, words, and double words.

Memory Load Instructions

- Opcode DST, PTR [SRC+Offset]

- Opcode DST

- Examples:

```
mov   rax, qword ptr [rsp+10h] ; RAX ←
                              ; 64-bit value at address RSP+0x10
mov   ecx, dword ptr [20]     ; ECX ←
                              ; 32-bit value at address 0x20
pop   rdi                     ; RDI ← value at address RSP
                              ; RSP ← RSP + 8
lea   r8, [rsp+20h]           ; R8 ← address RSP+0x20
```

Constants are encoded in instructions, but if we need arbitrary values, we must get them from memory. Square brackets show memory access relative to an address stored in a register.

Memory Store Instructions

- Opcode PTR [DST+Offset], SRC

- Opcode DST|SRC

- Examples:

```
mov    qword ptr [rbp-20h], rcx ; 64-bit value at address RBP-0x20
                                 ;    ← RCX
mov    byte ptr [0], 1           ; 8-bit value at address 0 ← 1
push   rsi                       ; RSP ← RSP - 8
                                 ; value at address RSP ← RSI
inc    dword ptr [rcx]           ; 32-bit value at address RCX ←
                                 ;   1 + 32-bit value at address RCX
```

Storing is similar to loading.

Flow Instructions

- Opcode DST

- Opcode PTR [DST]

- Examples:

```
jmp    00007ff6`9ef2f008    ; RIP ← 0x7ff69ef2f008
                            ; (goto 0x7ff69ef2f008)
jmp    qword ptr [rax+10h]  ; RIP ← value at address RAX+0x10
call   00007ff6`9ef21400    ; RSP ← RSP - 8
00007ff6`9ef21057:          ; value at address RSP ← 0x7ff69ef21057
                            ; RIP ← 0x7ff69ef21400
                            ; (goto 0x7ff69ef21400)
```

Goto (an unconditional jump) is implemented via the **JMP** instruction. Function calls are implemented via **CALL** instruction. For conditional branches, please look at the official Intel documentation. We don't use these instructions in our exercises.

Windows API Parameters

- x86: Right to left PUSH

   `Args to Child are parameters`

- x64: Left to right RCX, RDX, R8, R9, stack

   `Args to Child are not parameters`

```
WinDbg Commands

0:000> kv
 # Child-SP    RetAddr    : Args to Child   : Call Site
...
```

Additional calling convention explanation slides are available from the "Accelerated Windows API for Software Diagnostics" presentation:
https://www.patterndiagnostics.com/Training/Accelerated-Windows-API-Slides.pdf

Practice Exercises

Part 3: Practice Exercises

Now we come to practice. The goal is to show you important commands and techniques and how they help in debugging.

Links

- **Applications:**

  Download links are in exercises UD0 and KD0.

- **Exercise Transcripts:**

  Included in this book.

Warning

Because of live debugging, due to differences in actual systems and ASLR (Address Space Layout Randomization), when you launch applications, actual addresses and even the number and order of threads in WinDbg command output may differ from those shown in exercise transcripts.

Here is a warning if you see differences in the output from your system and what is shown in exercise transcripts.

Exercise UD0

- **Goal:** Download and verify your WinDbg installation

- **Memory Analysis Patterns:** Stack Trace; Incorrect Stack Trace

- \AWD4\Exercise-UD0-Download-WinDbg.pdf

Exercise UD0

Goal: Download and verify your WinDbg installation.

Memory Analysis Patterns: Stack Trace; Incorrect Stack Trace.

1.   Download course files if you haven't done that already and unpack the archive:

https://www.patterndiagnostics.com/Training/AWD4/AWD4-Projects.zip

You can also download the course files from this repository instead:

https://bitbucket.org/softwarediagnostics/awd4

2.   Install WinDbg (or upgrade existing WinDbg Preview) from https://learn.microsoft.com/en-gb/windows-hardware/drivers/debugger. Run WinDbg.

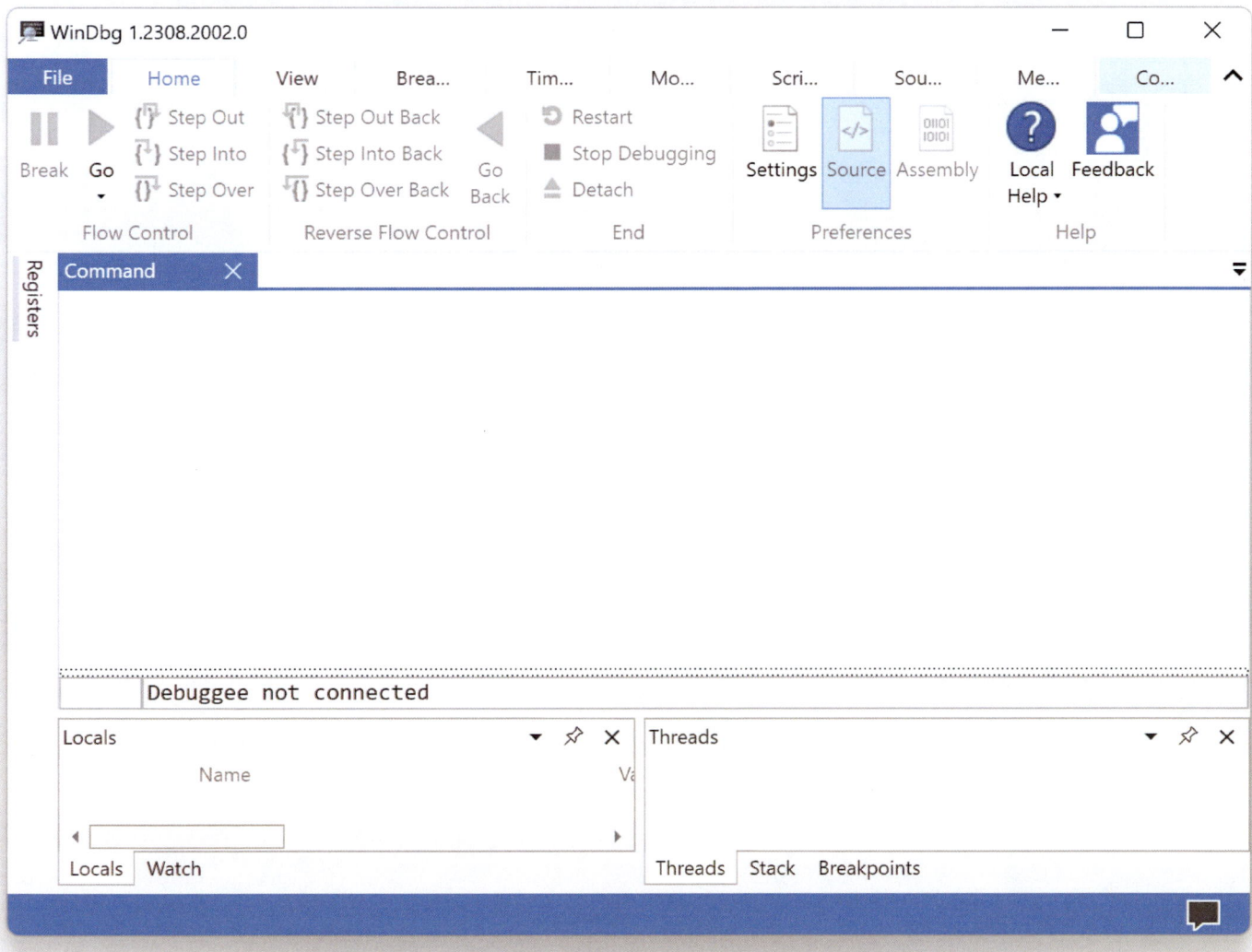

3.   Launch the WordPad app.

4. Choose *File \ Attach to process* menu option:

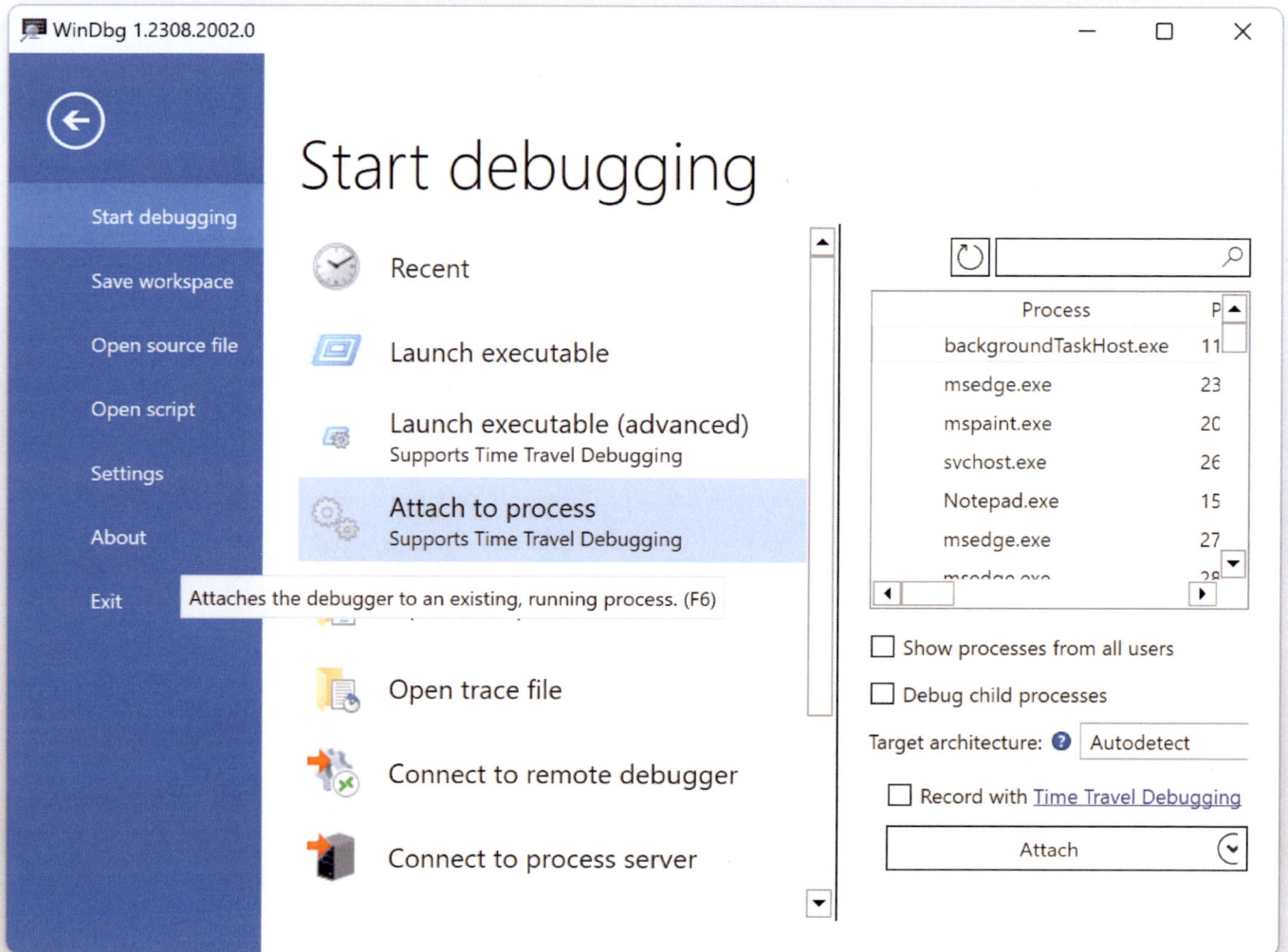

5.   Select the *wordpad.exe* process and use the *Attach* button:

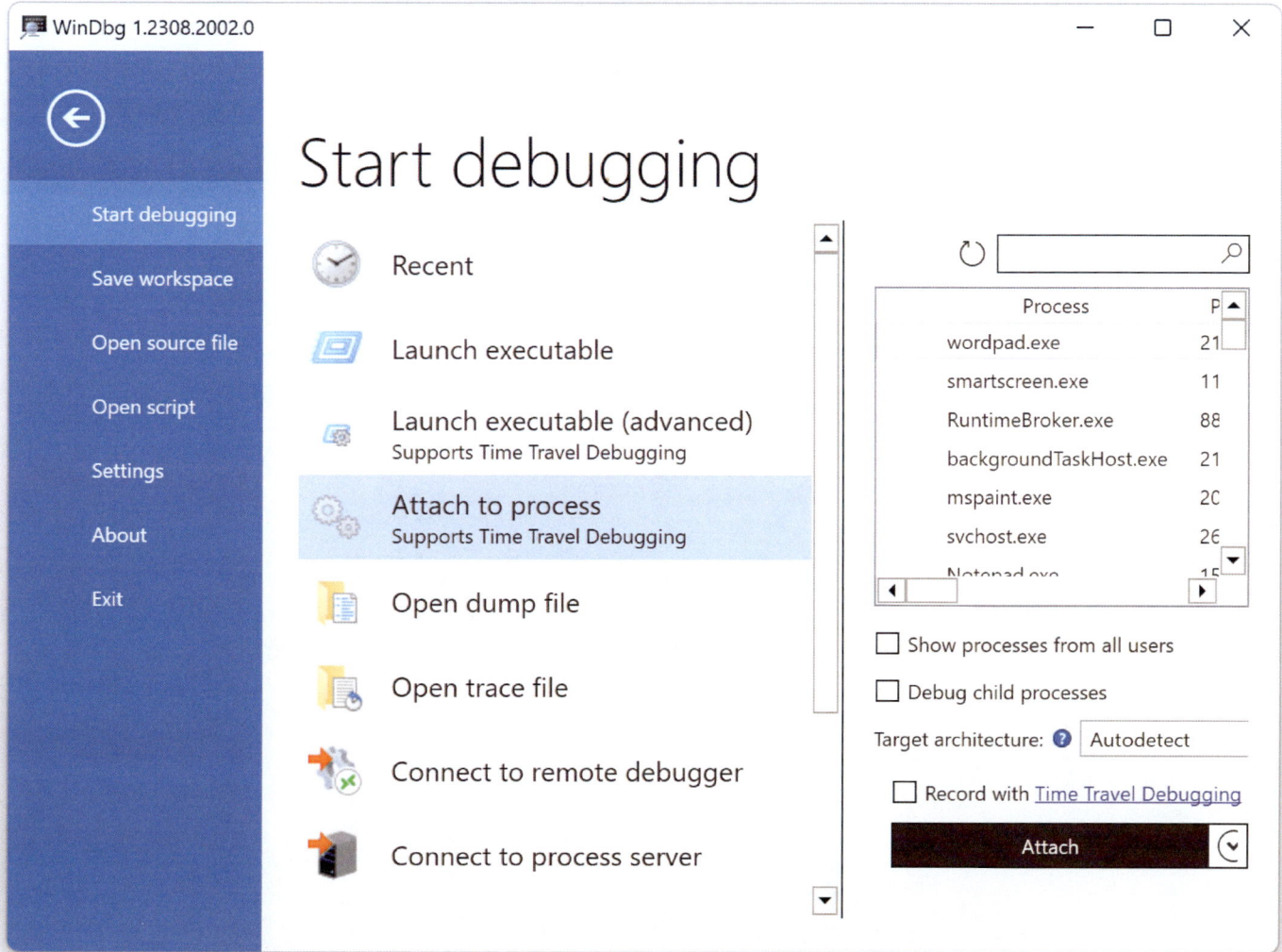

6. You get the WinDbg debugger attached to the *wordpad.exe* process:

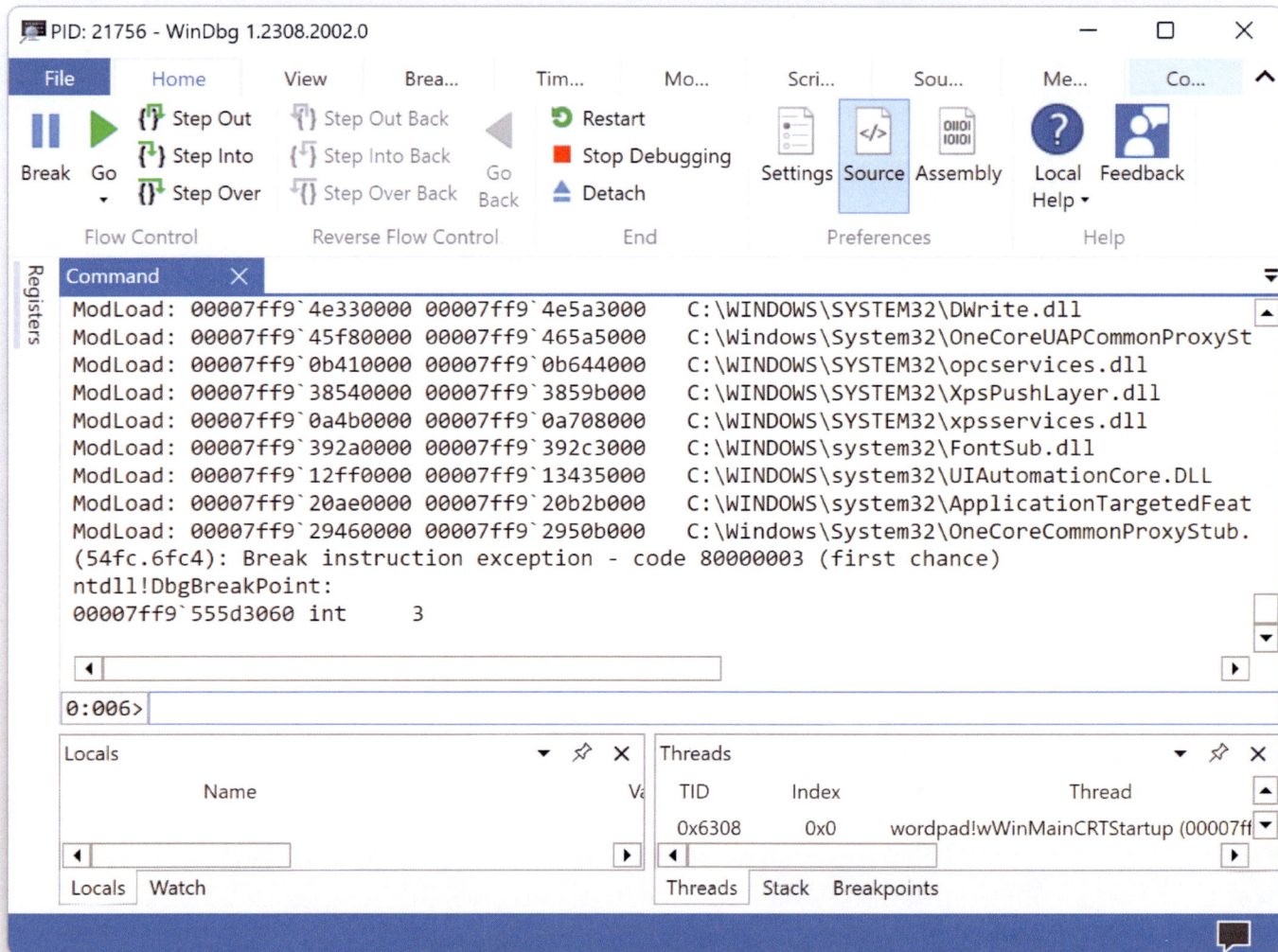

7.   Type **~0k** command to verify the correctness of the main *WordPad* thread (**~0**) stack trace (**k**):

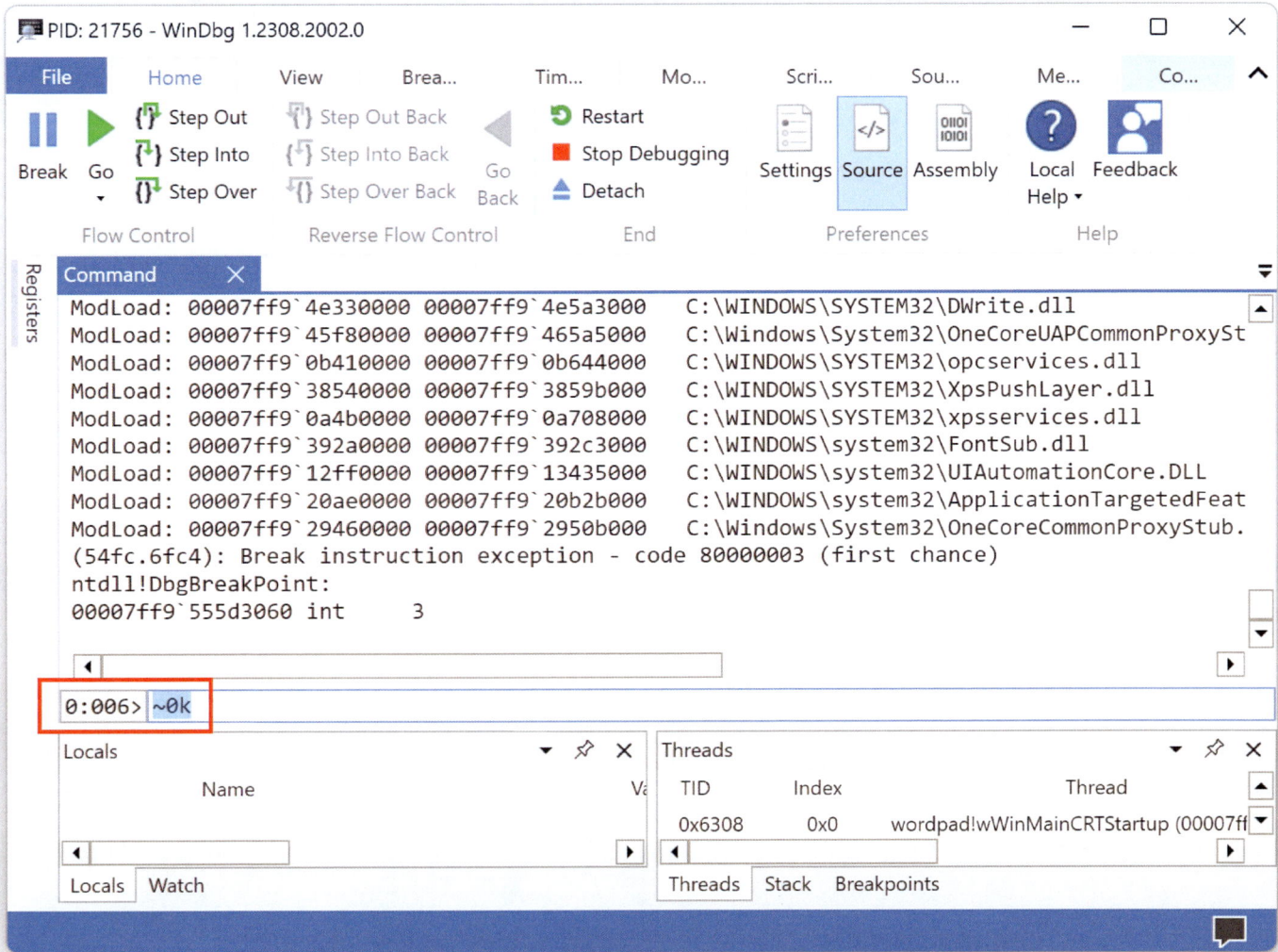

PID: 21756 - WinDbg 1.2308.2002.0   —   □   ✕

| File | Home | View | Brea... | Tim... | Mo... | Scri... | Sou... | Me... | Co... | ^ |

Break   Go   {↑} Step Out   {↑} Step Out Back   ◄   ↺ Restart
             {↓} Step Into   {↓} Step Into Back   Go   ■ Stop Debugging   Settings Source Assembly   Local Feedback
             {} Step Over   {} Step Over Back Back   ▲ Detach   Help ▾

Flow Control   Reverse Flow Control   End   Preferences   Help

Command   ✕

```
ModLoad: 00007ff9`4e330000 00007ff9`4e5a3000    C:\WINDOWS\SYSTEM32\DWrite.dll
ModLoad: 00007ff9`45f80000 00007ff9`465a5000    C:\Windows\System32\OneCoreUAPCommonProxySt
ModLoad: 00007ff9`0b410000 00007ff9`0b644000    C:\WINDOWS\SYSTEM32\opcservices.dll
ModLoad: 00007ff9`38540000 00007ff9`3859b000    C:\WINDOWS\SYSTEM32\XpsPushLayer.dll
ModLoad: 00007ff9`0a4b0000 00007ff9`0a708000    C:\WINDOWS\SYSTEM32\xpsservices.dll
ModLoad: 00007ff9`392a0000 00007ff9`392c3000    C:\WINDOWS\system32\FontSub.dll
ModLoad: 00007ff9`12ff0000 00007ff9`13435000    C:\WINDOWS\system32\UIAutomationCore.DLL
ModLoad: 00007ff9`20ae0000 00007ff9`20b2b000    C:\WINDOWS\system32\ApplicationTargetedFeat
ModLoad: 00007ff9`29460000 00007ff9`2950b000    C:\Windows\System32\OneCoreCommonProxyStub.
(54fc.6fc4): Break instruction exception - code 80000003 (first chance)
ntdll!DbgBreakPoint:
00007ff9`555d3060 int     3
```

`0:006>` ~0k

Locals	▾ 📌 ✕	Threads	▾ 📌 ✕
Name	Va	TID	Index	Thread
		0x6308	0x0	wordpad!wWinMainCRTStartup (00007ff

| Locals | Watch | | Threads | Stack | Breakpoints |

8.   We get the following output:

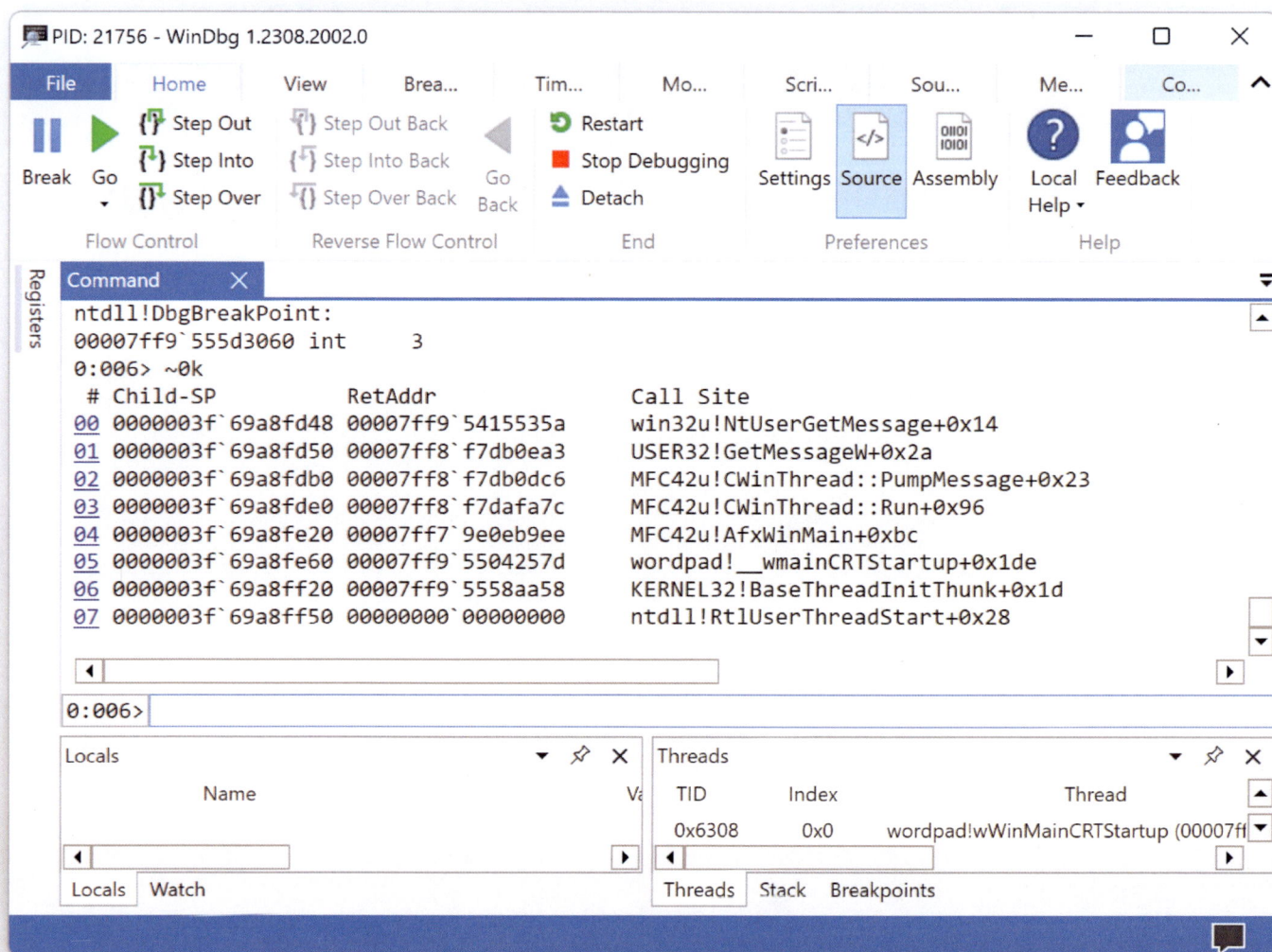

9.   The **Call Site** column output of the command should be similar to this:

```
0:006> ~0k
 # Child-SP          RetAddr           Call Site
00 0000003f`69a8fd48 00007ff9`5415535a win32u!NtUserGetMessage+0x14
01 0000003f`69a8fd50 00007ff8`f7db0ea3 USER32!GetMessageW+0x2a
02 0000003f`69a8fdb0 00007ff8`f7db0dc6 MFC42u!CWinThread::PumpMessage+0x23
03 0000003f`69a8fde0 00007ff8`f7dafa7c MFC42u!CWinThread::Run+0x96
04 0000003f`69a8fe20 00007ff7`9e0eb9ee MFC42u!AfxWinMain+0xbc
05 0000003f`69a8fe60 00007ff9`5504257d wordpad!__wmainCRTStartup+0x1de
06 0000003f`69a8ff20 00007ff9`5558aa58 KERNEL32!BaseThreadInitThunk+0x1d
07 0000003f`69a8ff50 00000000`00000000 ntdll!RtlUserThreadStart+0x28
```

If it has this form below with a large offset, then your symbol files were not set up correctly – **Incorrect Stack Trace** pattern:

```
0:000> k
# Child-SP          RetAddr               Call Site
00 000000a5`cd5bf578 00007ff9`8997464e   win32u!NtUserGetMessage+0x14
01 000000a5`cd5bf580 00007ff9`4e800813   user32!GetMessageW+0x2e
02 000000a5`cd5bf5e0 00007ff9`4e800736   mfc42u!Ordinal5730+0x23
03 000000a5`cd5bf610 00007ff9`4e7ff2bc   mfc42u!Ordinal6054+0x96
04 000000a5`cd5bf650 00007ff7`c3fbbcfd   mfc42u!Ordinal11584+0xbc
05 000000a5`cd5bf690 00007ff9`883454e0   wordpad+0xbcfd
06 000000a5`cd5bf750 00007ff9`89da485b   kernel32!BaseThreadInitThunk+0x10
07 000000a5`cd5bf780 00000000`00000000   ntdll!RtlUserThreadStart+0x2b
```

If you find any symbol problems, please use the Contact form on www.patterndiagnostics.com to report them.

10.   We recommend exiting WinDbg after each exercise.

User Mode Debugging

Exercises UD1 – UD8

I use Windows 11 x64 Professional to run applications compiled under Visual Studio 2022 build tools. Most of the applications are 64-bit.

Exercise UD1

- **Goal:** Learn how code generation parameters can influence process execution behavior

- **Elementary Diagnostics Patterns:** Error Message or Crash

- **Memory Analysis Patterns:** Message Box or Exception Stack Trace; Constant Subtrace

- **Debugging Implementation Patterns:** Break-in; Scope; Variable Value; Type Structure; Code Breakpoint

- \AWD4\Exercise-UD1.pdf

Exercise UD1

Goal: Learn how code generation parameters can influence process execution behavior.

Elementary Diagnostics Patterns: Error Message or Crash.

Memory Analysis Patterns: Message Box or Exception Stack Trace; Constant Subtrace.

Debugging Implementation Patterns: Break-in; Scope; Variable Value; Type Structure; Code Breakpoint.

1.   Launch WinDbg.

2.   Open *\AWD4\AppD1A\x64\Release\AppD1A.exe* executable by choosing *File \ Launch executable* menu option:

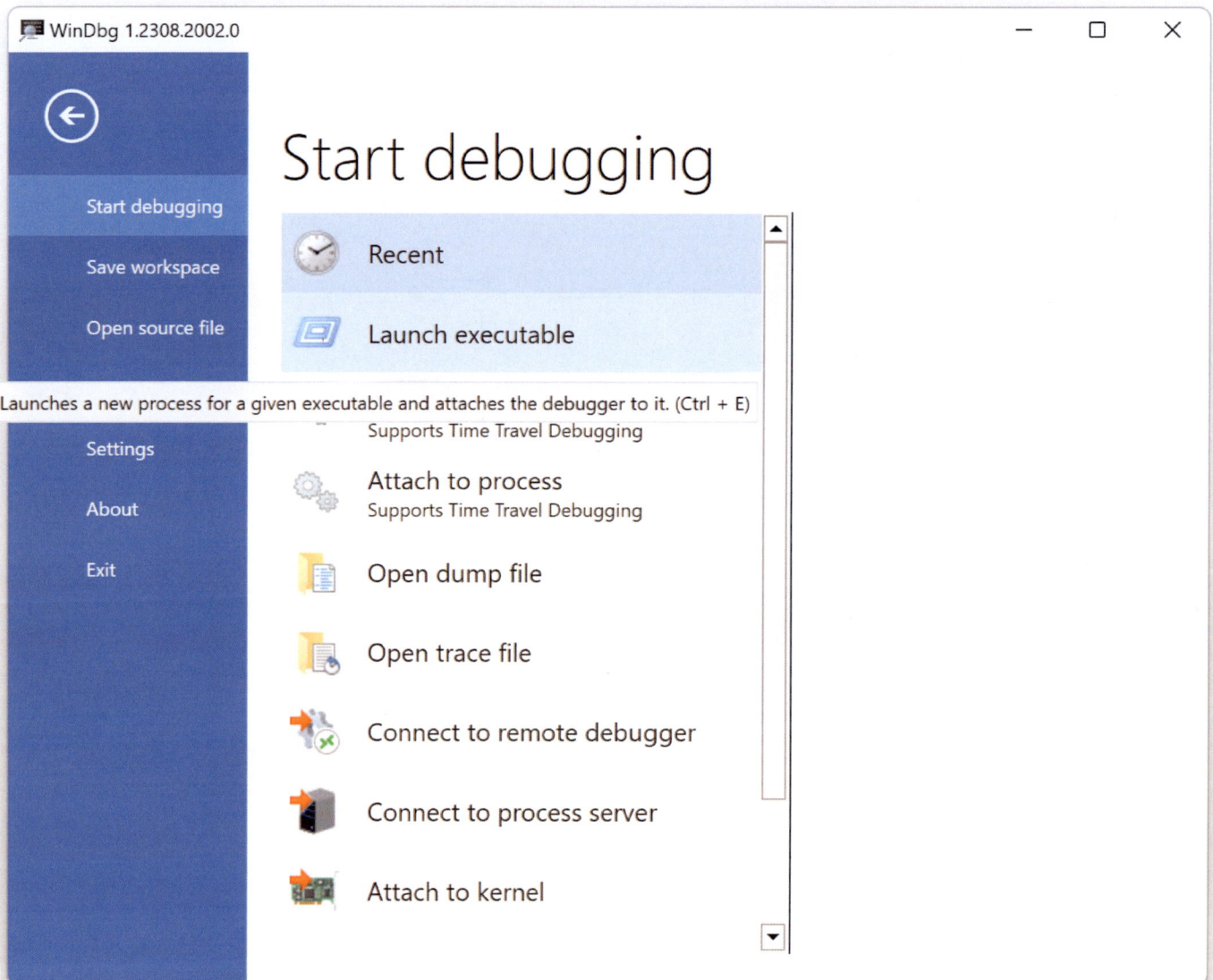

3.   We get the executable file loaded and ready for a debugging session:

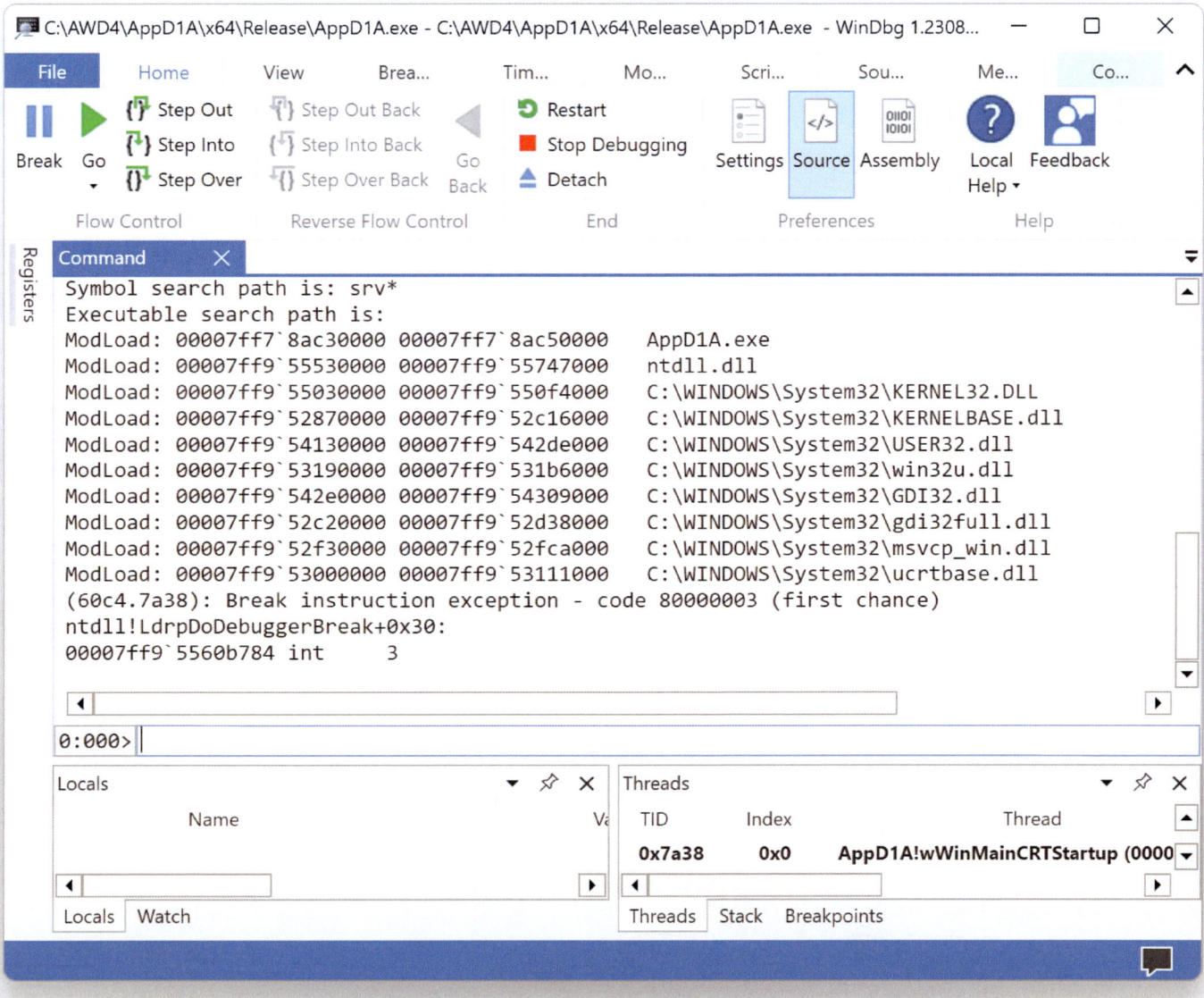

WinDbg 1.2308... window — C:\AWD4\AppD1A\x64\Release\AppD1A.exe

Command window output:

```
Symbol search path is: srv*
Executable search path is:
ModLoad: 00007ff7`8ac30000 00007ff7`8ac50000   AppD1A.exe
ModLoad: 00007ff9`55530000 00007ff9`55747000   ntdll.dll
ModLoad: 00007ff9`55030000 00007ff9`550f4000   C:\WINDOWS\System32\KERNEL32.DLL
ModLoad: 00007ff9`52870000 00007ff9`52c16000   C:\WINDOWS\System32\KERNELBASE.dll
ModLoad: 00007ff9`54130000 00007ff9`542de000   C:\WINDOWS\System32\USER32.dll
ModLoad: 00007ff9`53190000 00007ff9`531b6000   C:\WINDOWS\System32\win32u.dll
ModLoad: 00007ff9`542e0000 00007ff9`54309000   C:\WINDOWS\System32\GDI32.dll
ModLoad: 00007ff9`52c20000 00007ff9`52d38000   C:\WINDOWS\System32\gdi32full.dll
ModLoad: 00007ff9`52f30000 00007ff9`52fca000   C:\WINDOWS\System32\msvcp_win.dll
ModLoad: 00007ff9`53000000 00007ff9`53111000   C:\WINDOWS\System32\ucrtbase.dll
(60c4.7a38): Break instruction exception - code 80000003 (first chance)
ntdll!LdrpDoDebuggerBreak+0x30:
00007ff9`5560b784 int     3
```

0:000>

Locals / Threads panes:

TID	Index	Thread
0x7a38	0x0	AppD1A!wWinMainCRTStartup (0000

From now on, we only show the output from the command window unless we need another view.

```
Microsoft (R) Windows Debugger Version 10.0.25921.1001 AMD64
Copyright (c) Microsoft Corporation. All rights reserved.

CommandLine: C:\AWD4\AppD1A\x64\Release\AppD1A.exe

************* Path validation summary **************
Response                         Time (ms)      Location
Deferred                                        srv*
Symbol search path is: srv*
Executable search path is:
ModLoad: 00007ff7`8ac30000 00007ff7`8ac50000   AppD1A.exe
ModLoad: 00007ff9`55530000 00007ff9`55747000   ntdll.dll
ModLoad: 00007ff9`55030000 00007ff9`550f4000   C:\WINDOWS\System32\KERNEL32.DLL
ModLoad: 00007ff9`52870000 00007ff9`52c16000   C:\WINDOWS\System32\KERNELBASE.dll
ModLoad: 00007ff9`54130000 00007ff9`542de000   C:\WINDOWS\System32\USER32.dll
ModLoad: 00007ff9`53190000 00007ff9`531b6000   C:\WINDOWS\System32\win32u.dll
ModLoad: 00007ff9`542e0000 00007ff9`54309000   C:\WINDOWS\System32\GDI32.dll
ModLoad: 00007ff9`52c20000 00007ff9`52d38000   C:\WINDOWS\System32\gdi32full.dll
ModLoad: 00007ff9`52f30000 00007ff9`52fca000   C:\WINDOWS\System32\msvcp_win.dll
ModLoad: 00007ff9`53000000 00007ff9`53111000   C:\WINDOWS\System32\ucrtbase.dll
(60c4.7a38): Break instruction exception - code 80000003 (first chance)
ntdll!LdrpDoDebuggerBreak+0x30:
00007ff9`5560b784 int         3
```

4.   Open a log file (useful when the output doesn't fit into the buffer and we need to search for something):

```
0:000> .logopen C:\AWD4\D1A.log
Opened log file 'C:\AWD4\D1A.log'
```

5.   The **lm** command lists loaded modules and their addresses (it also shows whether symbols files are loaded):

```
0:000> lm
start             end               module name
00007ff7`8ac30000 00007ff7`8ac50000   AppD1A   C (private pdb symbols)
C:\ProgramData\Dbg\sym\AppD1A.pdb\926ED291EC994719BD0DFB167D2EB42E1\AppD1A.pdb
00007ff9`52870000 00007ff9`52c16000   KERNELBASE   (deferred)
00007ff9`52c20000 00007ff9`52d38000   gdi32full    (deferred)
00007ff9`52f30000 00007ff9`52fca000   msvcp_win    (deferred)
00007ff9`53000000 00007ff9`53111000   ucrtbase     (deferred)
00007ff9`53190000 00007ff9`531b6000   win32u       (deferred)
00007ff9`54130000 00007ff9`542de000   USER32       (deferred)
00007ff9`542e0000 00007ff9`54309000   GDI32        (deferred)
00007ff9`55030000 00007ff9`550f4000   KERNEL32     (deferred)
00007ff9`55530000 00007ff9`55747000   ntdll        (pdb symbols)
C:\ProgramData\Dbg\sym\ntdll.pdb\58A282C24AEE7E03A8CF8CB0A782CE0C1\ntdll.pdb
```

6.   We continue process execution using the **g** command. We may get an error message box:

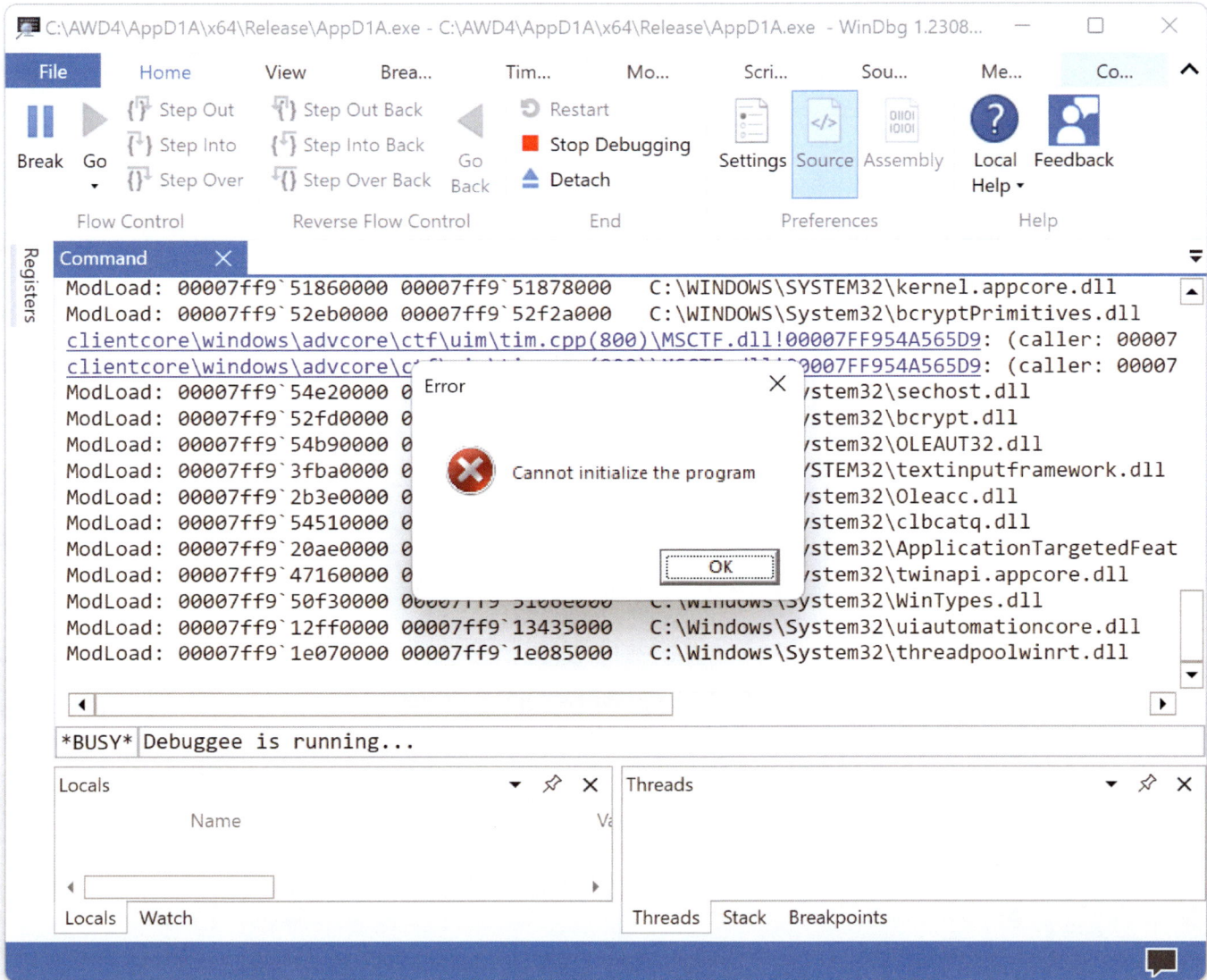

Note: Instead of an error message box, we may get exceptions. In such a case, we have to ignore any first chance exceptions until we come to a second chance exception (the crash scenario), for example:

```
0:000> g
ModLoad: 00007ff9`6caf0000 00007ff9`6cb21000   C:\WINDOWS\System32\IMM32.DLL
(1588.7e98): Access violation - code c0000005 (first chance)
First chance exceptions are reported before any exception handling.
This exception may be expected and handled.
USER32!StringDuplicateW+0x20:
00007ff9`6dfd4864 66392c41        cmp     word ptr [rcx+rax*2],bp ds:0bc8acf0`00000000=????

0:000> g
(1588.7e98): Access violation - code c0000005 (!!! second chance !!!)
USER32!StringDuplicateW+0x20:
00007ff9`6dfd4864 66392c41        cmp     word ptr [rcx+rax*2],bp ds:0bc8acf0`00000000=????
```

There, we see that the crash happens in the **USER32** module with the following CPU state:

```
0:000> r
rax=0000000000000000 rbx=000000cc248ff4c0 rcx=0bc8acf000000000
rdx=0bc8acf000000000 rsi=000000cc248ff450 rdi=0bc8acf000000000
rip=00007ff96dfd4864 rsp=000000cc248ff350 rbp=0000000000000000
 r8=000000cc248ff4c0  r9=0000000000000080 r10=000001d56e280000
r11=0000000000000000 r12=0000000000000000 r13=0000000000000000
r14=0000000000000000 r15=0000000000000000
iopl=0         nv up ei pl zr ac po nc
cs=0033  ss=002b  ds=002b  es=002b  fs=0053  gs=002b             efl=00010254
USER32!StringDuplicateW+0x20:
00007ff9`6dfd4864 66392c41        cmp     word ptr [rcx+rax*2],bp ds:0bc8acf0`00000000=????
```

7.   In the case of an error message box, we break in using the *Break* button:

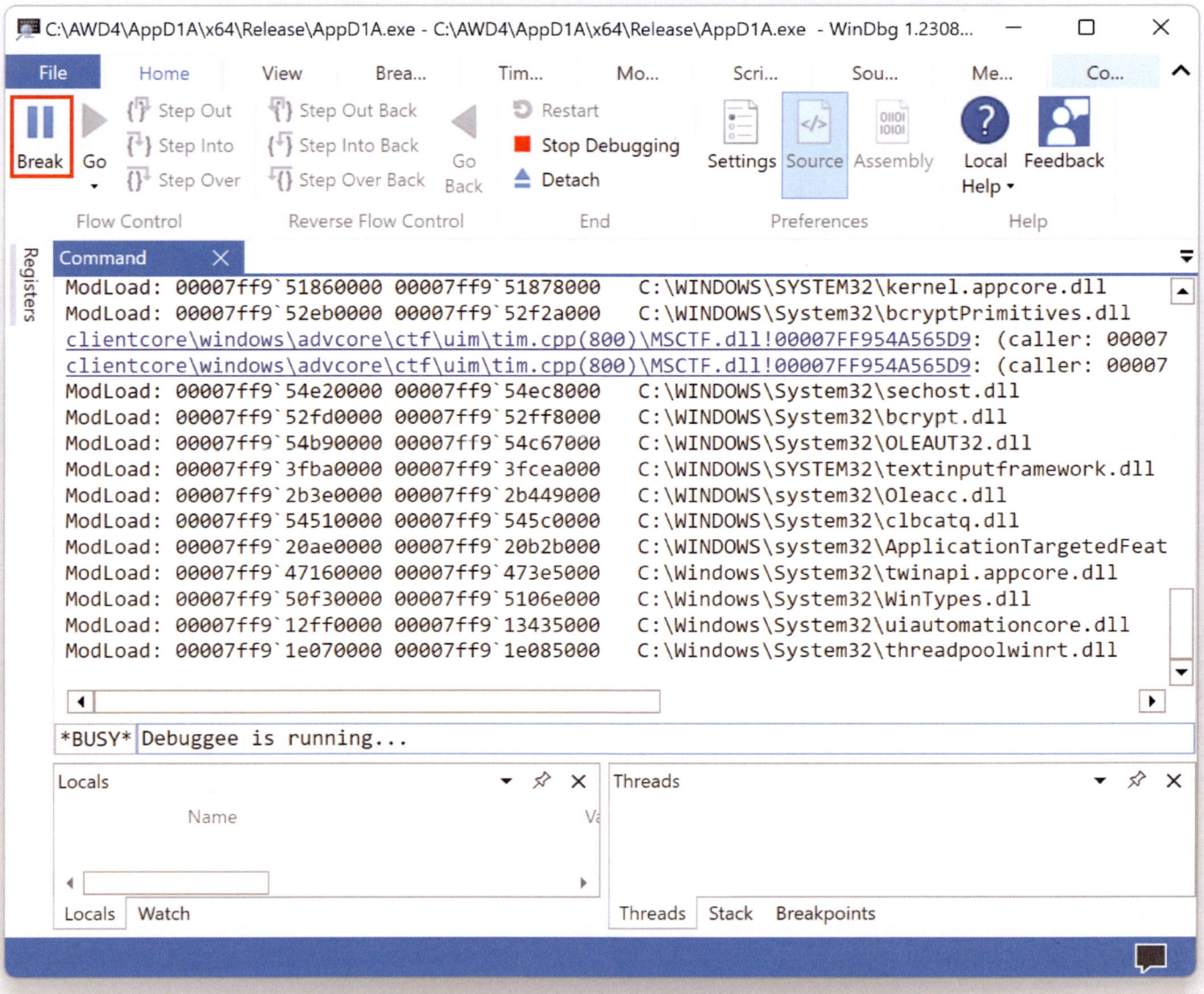

```
(60c4.356c): Break instruction exception - code 80000003 (first chance)
ntdll!DbgBreakPoint:
00007ff9`555d3060 int     3
```

8. We switch to the original thread #0 and check its stack trace:

```
0:001> ~0s
win32u!NtUserWaitMessage+0x14:
00007ff9`531915f4 ret
```

```
0:000> kL
 # Child-SP          RetAddr               Call Site
00 000000e9`d54ff5a8 00007ff9`541316c6     win32u!NtUserWaitMessage+0x14
01 000000e9`d54ff5b0 00007ff9`5413152b     USER32!DialogBox2+0x172
02 000000e9`d54ff660 00007ff9`541aa666     USER32!InternalDialogBox+0x127
03 000000e9`d54ff6c0 00007ff9`541a8fc9     USER32!SoftModalMessageBox+0x826
04 000000e9`d54ff800 00007ff9`541a9da8     USER32!MessageBoxWorker+0x341
05 000000e9`d54ff9b0 00007ff9`541a9e2e     USER32!MessageBoxTimeoutW+0x198
06 000000e9`d54ffab0 00007ff7`8ac3107f     USER32!MessageBoxW+0x4e
07 000000e9`d54ffaf0 00007ff7`8ac3168a     AppD1A!wWinMain+0x7f
08 (Inline Function) --------`--------     AppD1A!invoke_main+0x21
09 000000e9`d54ffb50 00007ff9`5504257d     AppD1A!__scrt_common_main_seh+0x106
0a 000000e9`d54ffb90 00007ff9`5558aa58     KERNEL32!BaseThreadInitThunk+0x1d
0b 000000e9`d54ffbc0 00000000`00000000     ntdll!RtlUserThreadStart+0x28
```

9. We also set the source search path:

```
0:000> .srcpath+ C:\AWD4\AppD1A\AppD1A
Source search path is: SRV*;C:\AWD4\AppD1A\AppD1A

************* Path validation summary **************
Response                    Time (ms)      Location
Deferred                                   SRV*
OK                                         C:\AWD4\AppD1A\AppD1A
```

Note: If you get a second chance exception (the crash scenario) instead of an error message box, then the default analysis command gives us the source code:

```
0:000> !analyze -v
*******************************************************************************
*                                                                    *
*                        Exception Analysis                          *
*                                                                    *
*******************************************************************************

KEY_VALUES_STRING: 1

    Key  : AV.Fault
    Value: Read

    Key  : Analysis.CPU.mSec
    Value: 1093

    Key  : Analysis.DebugAnalysisManager
    Value: Create

    Key  : Analysis.Elapsed.mSec
    Value: 1811

    Key  : Analysis.Init.CPU.mSec
    Value: 2749

    Key  : Analysis.Init.Elapsed.mSec
    Value: 1229233

    Key  : Analysis.Memory.CommitPeak.Mb
    Value: 89

    Key  : Timeline.OS.Boot.DeltaSec
    Value: 698874

    Key  : Timeline.Process.Start.DeltaSec
    Value: 1228

    Key  : WER.OS.Branch
    Value: co_release
```

71

    Key : WER.OS.Timestamp
    Value: 2021-06-04T16:28:00Z

    Key : WER.OS.Version
    Value: 10.0.22000.1

NTGLOBALFLAG: 470

PROCESS_BAM_CURRENT_THROTTLED: 0

PROCESS_BAM_PREVIOUS_THROTTLED: 0

APPLICATION_VERIFIER_FLAGS: 0

EXCEPTION_RECORD: (.exr -1)
ExceptionAddress: 00007ff96dfd4864 (USER32!StringDuplicateW+0x0000000000000020)
   ExceptionCode: c0000005 (Access violation)
  ExceptionFlags: 00000000
NumberParameters: 2
   Parameter[0]: 0000000000000000
   Parameter[1]: ffffffffffffffff
Attempt to read from address ffffffffffffffff

FAULTING_THREAD: 00007e98

PROCESS_NAME: AppD1A.exe

READ_ADDRESS: ffffffffffffffff

ERROR_CODE: (NTSTATUS) 0xc0000005 - The instruction at 0x%p referenced memory at 0x%p. The memory could not be %s.

EXCEPTION_CODE_STR: c0000005

EXCEPTION_PARAMETER1: 0000000000000000

EXCEPTION_PARAMETER2: ffffffffffffffff

STACK_TEXT:
000000cc`248ff350 00007ff9`6dfd7fda   : 000000cc`248ff4c0 0bc8acf0`00000000 000000cc`248ff450 00000000`00000000 : USER32!StringDuplicateW+0x20
000000cc`248ff380 00007ff9`6dfd7d6b   : 000000cc`248ff760 000000cc`248ff4d0 00000000`00000000 00007ff9`6dff5a00 : USER32!InitClsMenuNameW+0x76
000000cc`248ff3d0 00007ff9`6dfd7c49   : 000000cc`248ff810 00000000`00000000 00000000`00000000 00000000`00000000 : USER32!RegisterClassExWOWW+0x113
000000cc`248ff730 00007ff6`0bc7116d   : 00000000`00000000 00000000`00000000 00000000`00000000 00000000`00000000 : USER32!RegisterClassW+0x59
000000cc`248ff7c0 00007ff6`0bc7105c   : 00007ff6`0bc70000 00000000`00000000 00000000`00000000 00000000`00000000 : AppD1A!MyRegisterClass+0x8d
000000cc`248ff840 00007ff6`0bc7166a   : 00007ff6`0bc70000 00000000`00000000 000001d5`6deb529e 00000000`0000000a : AppD1A!wWinMain+0x5c
000000cc`248ff8a0 00007ff9`6d8c54e0   : 00000000`00000000 00000000`00000000 00000000`00000000 00000000`00000000 : AppD1A!__scrt_common_main_seh+0x106
000000cc`248ff8e0 00007ff9`6e44485b   : 00000000`00000000 00000000`00000000 00000000`00000000 00000000`00000000 : KERNEL32!BaseThreadInitThunk+0x10
000000cc`248ff910 00000000`00000000   : 00000000`00000000 00000000`00000000 00000000`00000000 00000000`00000000 : ntdll!RtlUserThreadStart+0x2b

STACK_COMMAND: ~0s ; .cxr ; kb

FAULTING_SOURCE_LINE: C:\AWD3\AppD1A\AppD1A\AppD1A.cpp

FAULTING_SOURCE_FILE: C:\AWD3\AppD1A\AppD1A\AppD1A.cpp

FAULTING_SOURCE_LINE_NUMBER: 84

FAULTING_SOURCE_CODE:
    80:     wc.lpszMenuName   = MAKEINTRESOURCE(IDC_APPD1A);
    81:     wc.lpszClassName   = szWindowClass;
    82:
    83:     return RegisterClass(&wc);
>   84: }
    85:
    86: //
    87: //   FUNCTION: InitInstance(HINSTANCE, int)
    88: //
    89: //   PURPOSE: Saves instance handle and creates main window

SYMBOL_NAME: appd1a!MyRegisterClass+8d

MODULE_NAME: AppD1A

IMAGE_NAME: AppD1A.exe

FAILURE_BUCKET_ID: INVALID_POINTER_READ_c0000005_AppD1A.exe!MyRegisterClass

OS_VERSION: 10.0.22000.1

BUILDLAB_STR: co_release

OSPLATFORM_TYPE: x64

OSNAME: Windows 10

FAILURE_ID_HASH: {0e59b433-475d-53b5-9229-de642189649b}

Followup: MachineOwner
----

10. In the case of an error message box, we switch to the *WinMain* thread stack frame:

```
0:000> .frame 7
07 000000e9`d54ffaf0 00007ff7`8ac3168a     AppD1A!wWinMain+0x7f [C:\AWD4\AppD1A\AppD1A\AppD1A.cpp @ 44]
```

Note: We see a source code window immediately to the left of the command window:

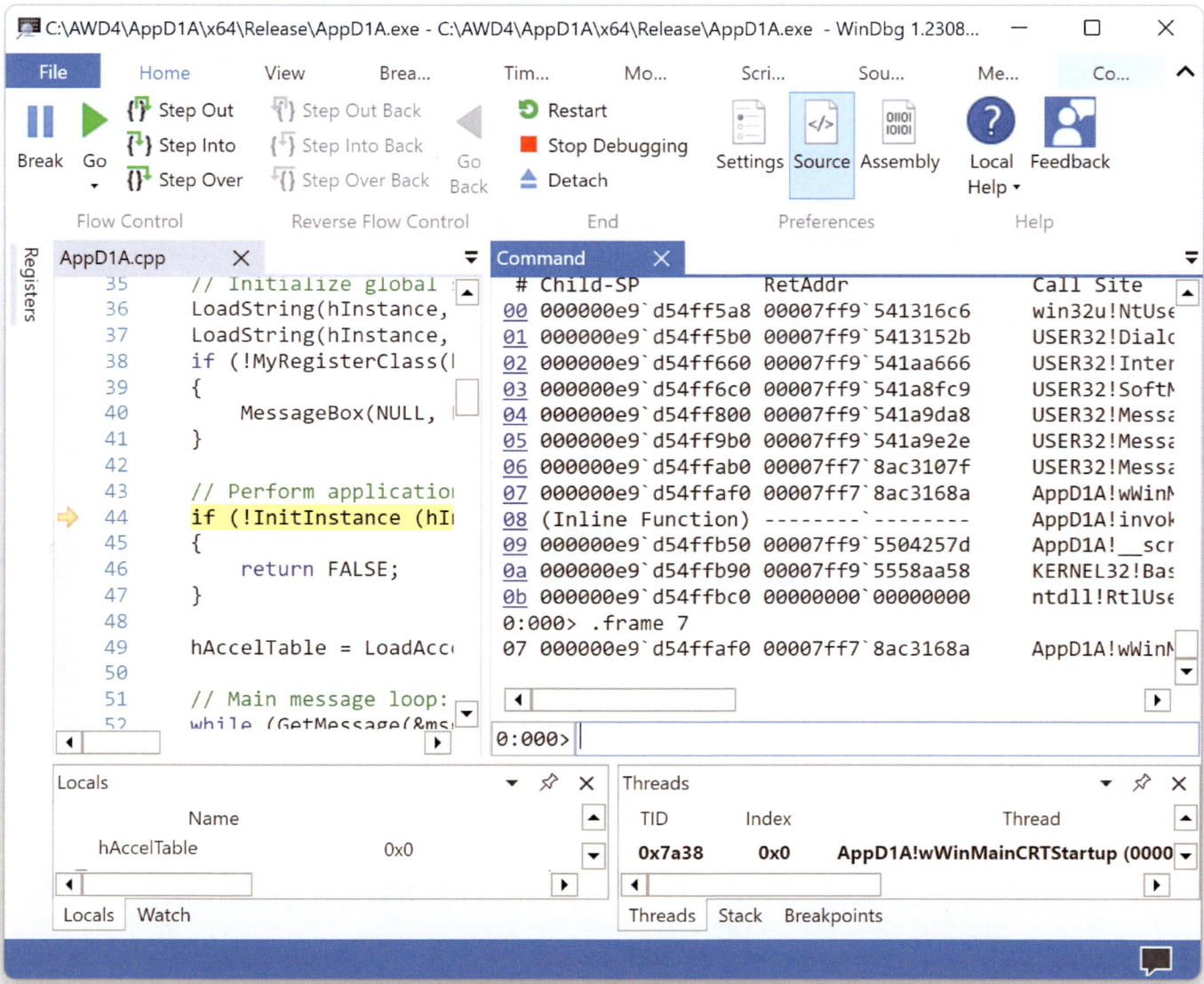

Note: In the case of a second-chance exception (the crash scenario), we get a similar stack trace and also set the appropriate stack frame in our code that called Windows API:

```
0:000> k
 # Child-SP          RetAddr           Call Site
00 000000cc`248ff350 00007ff9`6dfd7fda USER32!StringDuplicateW+0x20
01 000000cc`248ff380 00007ff9`6dfd7d6b USER32!InitClsMenuNameW+0x76
02 000000cc`248ff3d0 00007ff9`6dfd7c49 USER32!RegisterClassExWOWW+0x113
03 000000cc`248ff730 00007ff6`0bc7116d USER32!RegisterClassW+0x59
04 000000cc`248ff7c0 00007ff6`0bc7105c AppD1A!MyRegisterClass+0x8d [C:\AWD3\AppD1A\AppD1A\AppD1A.cpp @ 84]
05 000000cc`248ff840 00007ff6`0bc7166a AppD1A!wWinMain+0x5c [C:\AWD3\AppD1A\AppD1A\AppD1A.cpp @ 41]
06 (Inline Function) --------`-------- AppD1A!invoke_main+0x21
[d:\a01\_work\43\s\src\vctools\crt\vcstartup\src\startup\exe_common.inl @ 118]
```

```
07 000000cc`248ff8a0 00007ff9`6d8c54e0    AppD1A!__scrt_common_main_seh+0x106
[d:\a01\_work\43\s\src\vctools\crt\vcstartup\src\startup\exe_common.inl @ 288]
08 000000cc`248ff8e0 00007ff9`6e44485b    KERNEL32!BaseThreadInitThunk+0x10
09 000000cc`248ff910 00000000`00000000    ntdll!RtlUserThreadStart+0x2b
```

```
0:000> .frame 4
04 000000cc`248ff7c0 00007ff6`0bc7105c    AppD1A!MyRegisterClass+0x8d [C:\AWD3\AppD1A\AppD1A\AppD1A.cpp @ 84]
```

11.   The yellow source code highlighting points to the next line to be executed if we dismiss the message box. Therefore, we need to investigate the previous call to the *MyRegisterClass* function. Inside, it returns the result of the *RegisterClass* Windows API call:

```
ATOM MyRegisterClass(HINSTANCE hInstance)
{
    WNDCLASS wc;

    wc.style          = CS_HREDRAW | CS_VREDRAW;
    wc.lpfnWndProc    = WndProc;
    wc.cbClsExtra     = 0;
    wc.cbWndExtra     = 0;
    wc.hInstance      = hInstance;
    wc.hIcon          = LoadIcon(hInstance, MAKEINTRESOURCE(IDI_APPD1A));
    wc.hCursor        = LoadCursor(NULL, IDC_ARROW);
    wc.hbrBackground  = (HBRUSH)(COLOR_WINDOW+1);
    wc.lpszMenuName   = MAKEINTRESOURCE(IDC_APPD1A);
    wc.lpszClassName  = szWindowClass;

    return RegisterClass(&wc);
}
```

We put a code breakpoint at the line number #86 (right-click or F9):

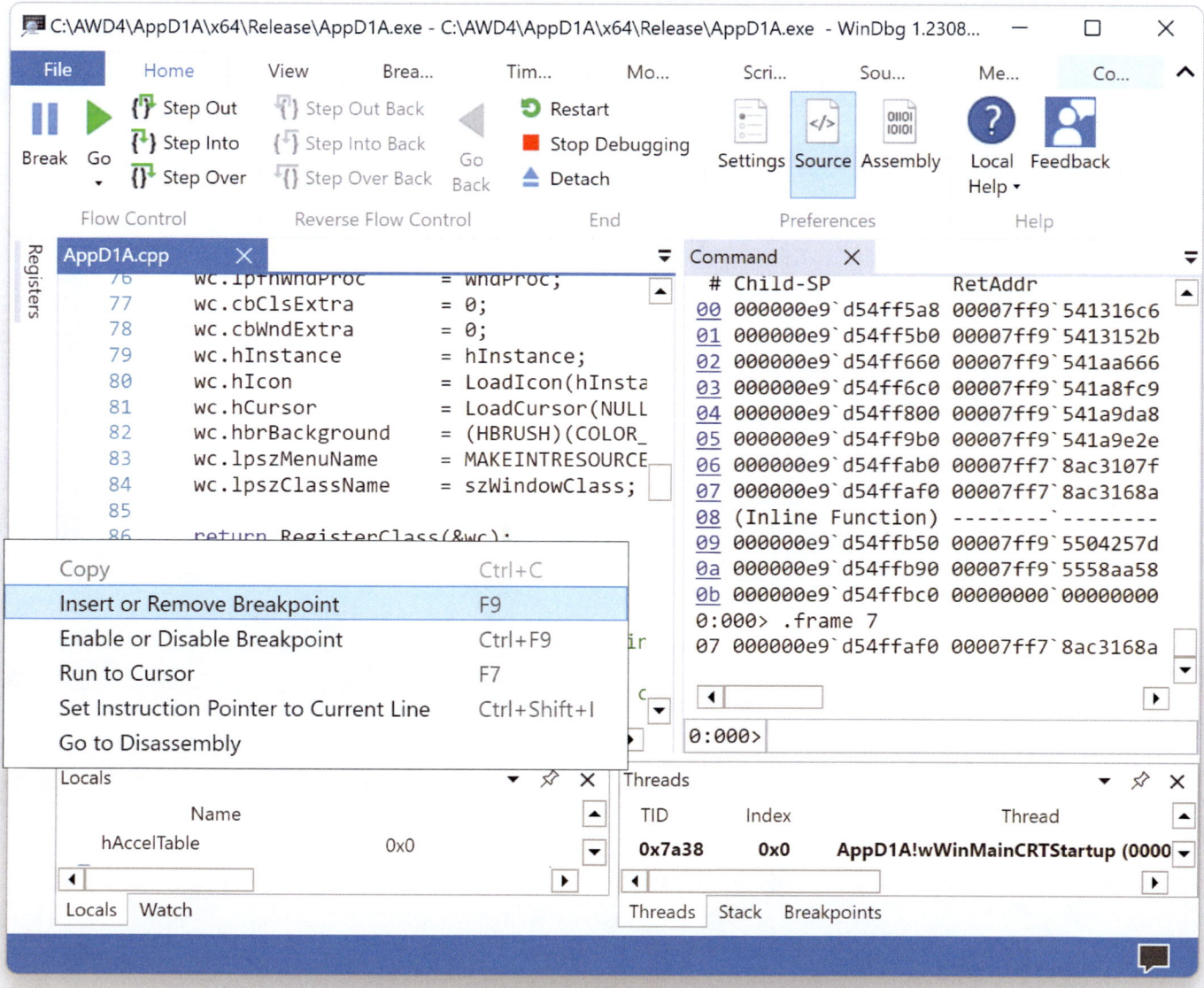

Then we restart our debugging session:

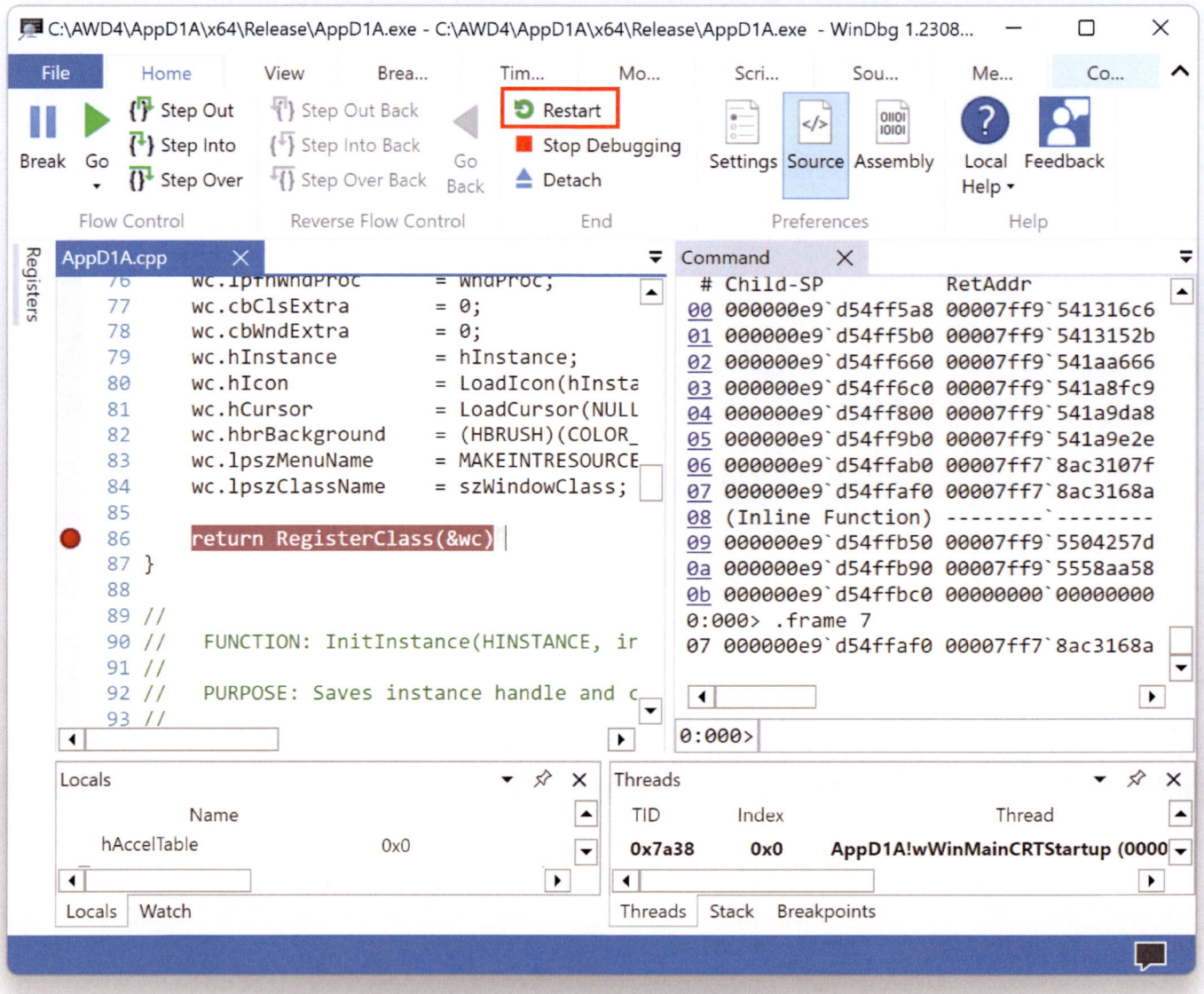

```
Microsoft (R) Windows Debugger Version 10.0.25921.1001 AMD64
Copyright (c) Microsoft Corporation. All rights reserved.

CommandLine: C:\AWD4\AppD1A\x64\Release\AppD1A.exe

************** Path validation summary **************
Response                        Time (ms)     Location
Deferred                                      srv*
Symbol search path is: srv*
Executable search path is:
ModLoad: 00007ff7`8ac30000 00007ff7`8ac50000   AppD1A.exe
ModLoad: 00007ff9`55530000 00007ff9`55747000   ntdll.dll
ModLoad: 00007ff9`55030000 00007ff9`550f4000   C:\WINDOWS\System32\KERNEL32.DLL
ModLoad: 00007ff9`52870000 00007ff9`52c16000   C:\WINDOWS\System32\KERNELBASE.dll
ModLoad: 00007ff9`54130000 00007ff9`542de000   C:\WINDOWS\System32\USER32.dll
ModLoad: 00007ff9`53190000 00007ff9`531b6000   C:\WINDOWS\System32\win32u.dll
ModLoad: 00007ff9`542e0000 00007ff9`54309000   C:\WINDOWS\System32\GDI32.dll
ModLoad: 00007ff9`52c20000 00007ff9`52d38000   C:\WINDOWS\System32\gdi32full.dll
```

```
ModLoad: 00007ff9`52f30000 00007ff9`52fca000   C:\WINDOWS\System32\msvcp_win.dll
ModLoad: 00007ff9`53000000 00007ff9`53111000   C:\WINDOWS\System32\ucrtbase.dll
(6b40.93ec): Break instruction exception - code 80000003 (first chance)
ntdll!LdrpDoDebuggerBreak+0x30:
00007ff9`5560b784 int        3
```

12.   We then resume execution until we hit the breakpoint:

```
0:000> g
ModLoad: 00007ff9`53ef0000 00007ff9`53f21000   C:\WINDOWS\System32\IMM32.DLL
Breakpoint 1 hit
AppD1A!MyRegisterClass+0x82:
00007ff7`8ac31182 lea        rcx,[rsp+20h]
```

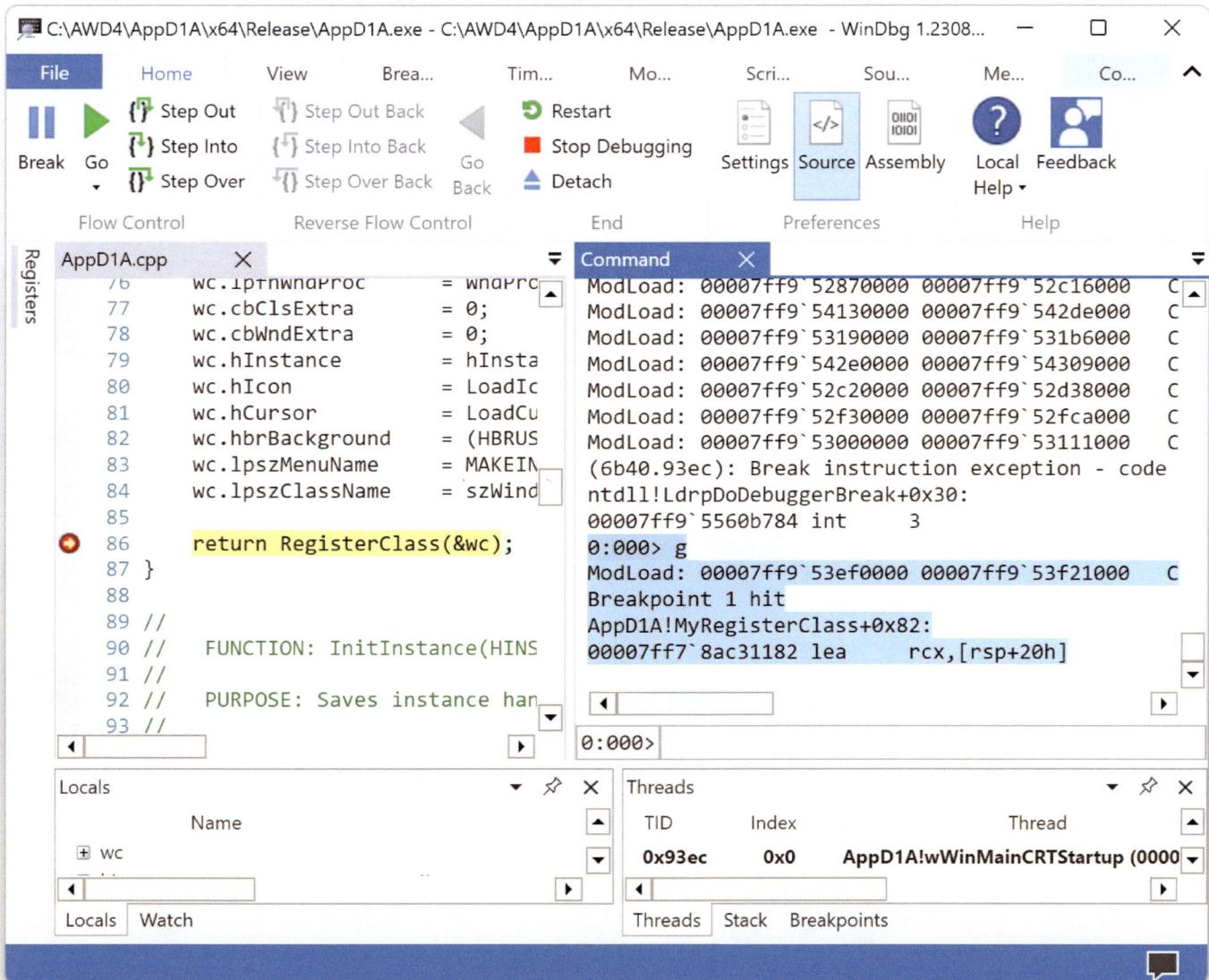

13. We can now expand local structures in the *Locals* window (for example, *wc*):

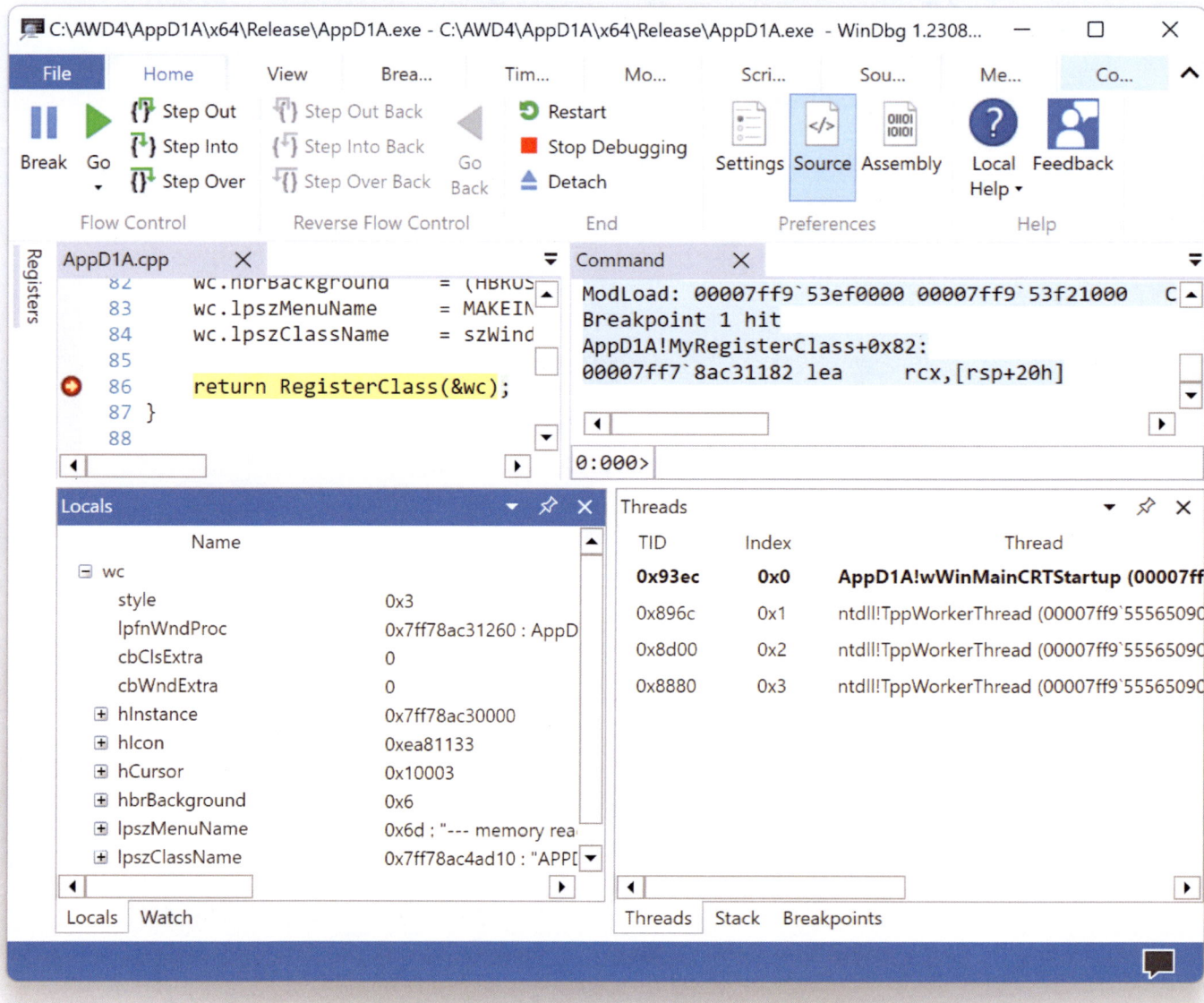

We can also dump this variable using type information:

```
0:000> dt wc
Local var @ 0xe17d2ff760 Type tagWNDCLASSW
   +0x000 style          : 3
   +0x004 lpfnWndProc    : 0x00007ff7`8ac31260        int64  AppD1A!WndProc+0
   +0x00c cbClsExtra     : 0n0
   +0x010 cbWndExtra     : 0n0
   +0x014 hInstance      : 0x00007ff7`8ac30000 HINSTANCE__
   +0x01c hIcon          : 0x00000000`0ea81133 HICON__
   +0x024 hCursor        : 0x00000000`00010003 HICON__
   +0x02c hbrBackground  : 0x00000000`00000006 HBRUSH__
   +0x034 lpszMenuName   : 0x00000000`0000006d  "--- memory read error at address 0x00000000`0000006d -
--"
   +0x03c lpszClassName  : 0x00007ff7`8ac4ad10  "APPD1A"
```

14.   We can also list all other local variables and parameters for the current frame:

```
0:000> dv /i /V
prv param   000000e1`7d2ff7c0 @rsp+0x0080        hInstance = 0x00007ff7`8ac30000
prv local   000000e1`7d2ff760 @rsp+0x0020              wc = struct tagWNDCLASSW
```

Note: Since all structure members seem to be valid (*lpszMenuName* read error can be ignored because in the source code, it is specified as an integer resource index), let's compare it with another application that doesn't crash.

15.   Launch another instance of WinDbg and launch *\AWD4\AppD1B\x64\Release\AppD1B.exe* executable. We get the following output:

```
Microsoft (R) Windows Debugger Version 10.0.25921.1001 AMD64
Copyright (c) Microsoft Corporation. All rights reserved.

CommandLine: C:\AWD4\AppD1B\x64\Release\AppD1B.exe

************* Path validation summary **************
Response                      Time (ms)     Location
Deferred                                    srv*
Symbol search path is: srv*
Executable search path is:
ModLoad: 00007ff6`bcc80000 00007ff6`bcca0000   AppD1B.exe
ModLoad: 00007ff9`55530000 00007ff9`55747000   ntdll.dll
ModLoad: 00007ff9`55030000 00007ff9`550f4000   C:\WINDOWS\System32\KERNEL32.DLL
ModLoad: 00007ff9`52870000 00007ff9`52c16000   C:\WINDOWS\System32\KERNELBASE.dll
ModLoad: 00007ff9`54130000 00007ff9`542de000   C:\WINDOWS\System32\USER32.dll
ModLoad: 00007ff9`53190000 00007ff9`531b6000   C:\WINDOWS\System32\win32u.dll
ModLoad: 00007ff9`542e0000 00007ff9`54309000   C:\WINDOWS\System32\GDI32.dll
ModLoad: 00007ff9`52c20000 00007ff9`52d38000   C:\WINDOWS\System32\gdi32full.dll
ModLoad: 00007ff9`52f30000 00007ff9`52fca000   C:\WINDOWS\System32\msvcp_win.dll
ModLoad: 00007ff9`53000000 00007ff9`53111000   C:\WINDOWS\System32\ucrtbase.dll
(2228.62e4): Break instruction exception - code 80000003 (first chance)
ntdll!LdrpDoDebuggerBreak+0x30:
00007ff9`5560b784 int     3
```

16.   We open a new log file:

```
0:000> .logopen C:\AWD4\D1B.log
Opened log file 'C:\AWD4\D1B.log'
```

17.   If we run it via the **g** command, we don't get any exceptions. We also see that the Debuggee (our program) is running):

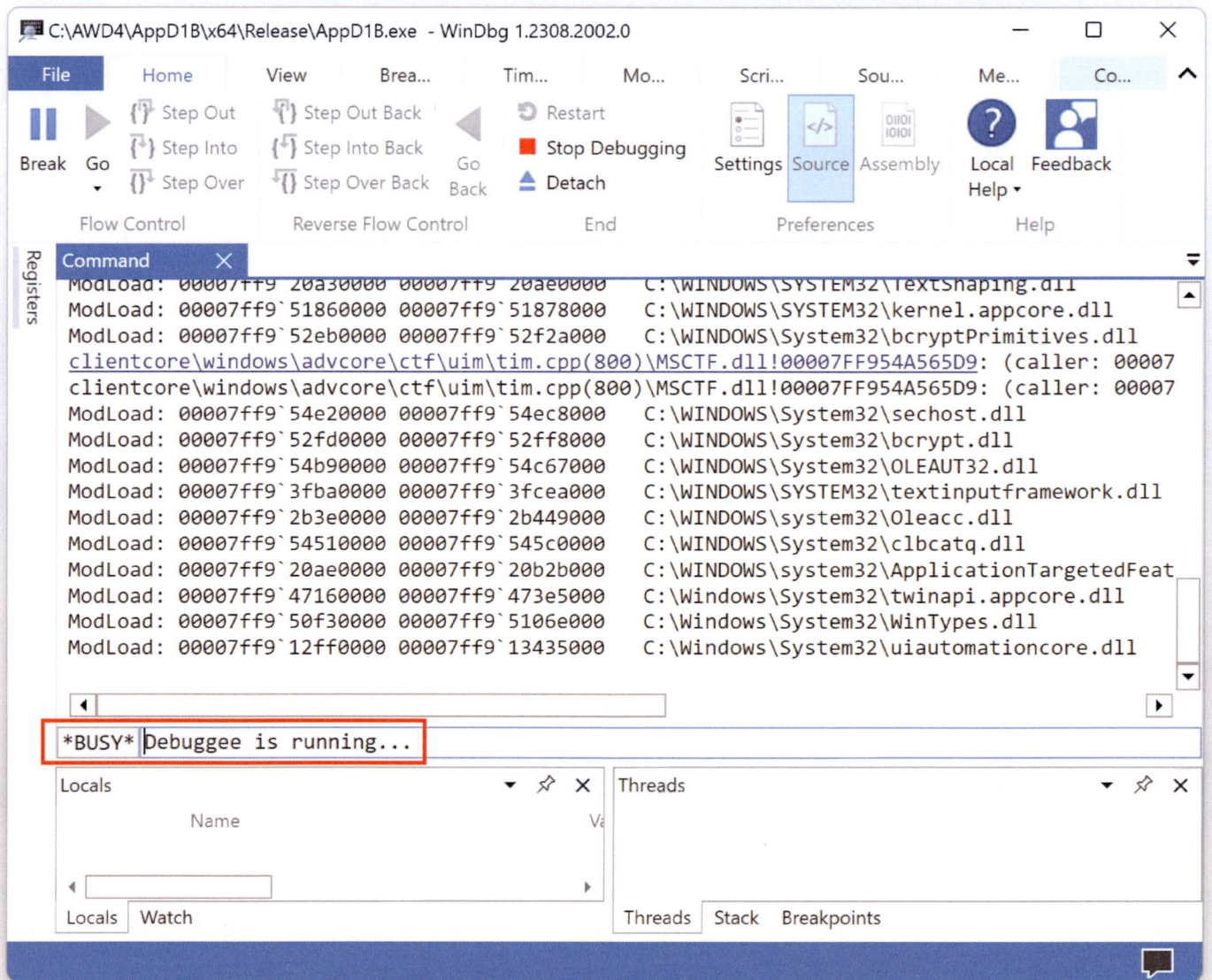

80

18.   So we click on the *Home \ Break* button:

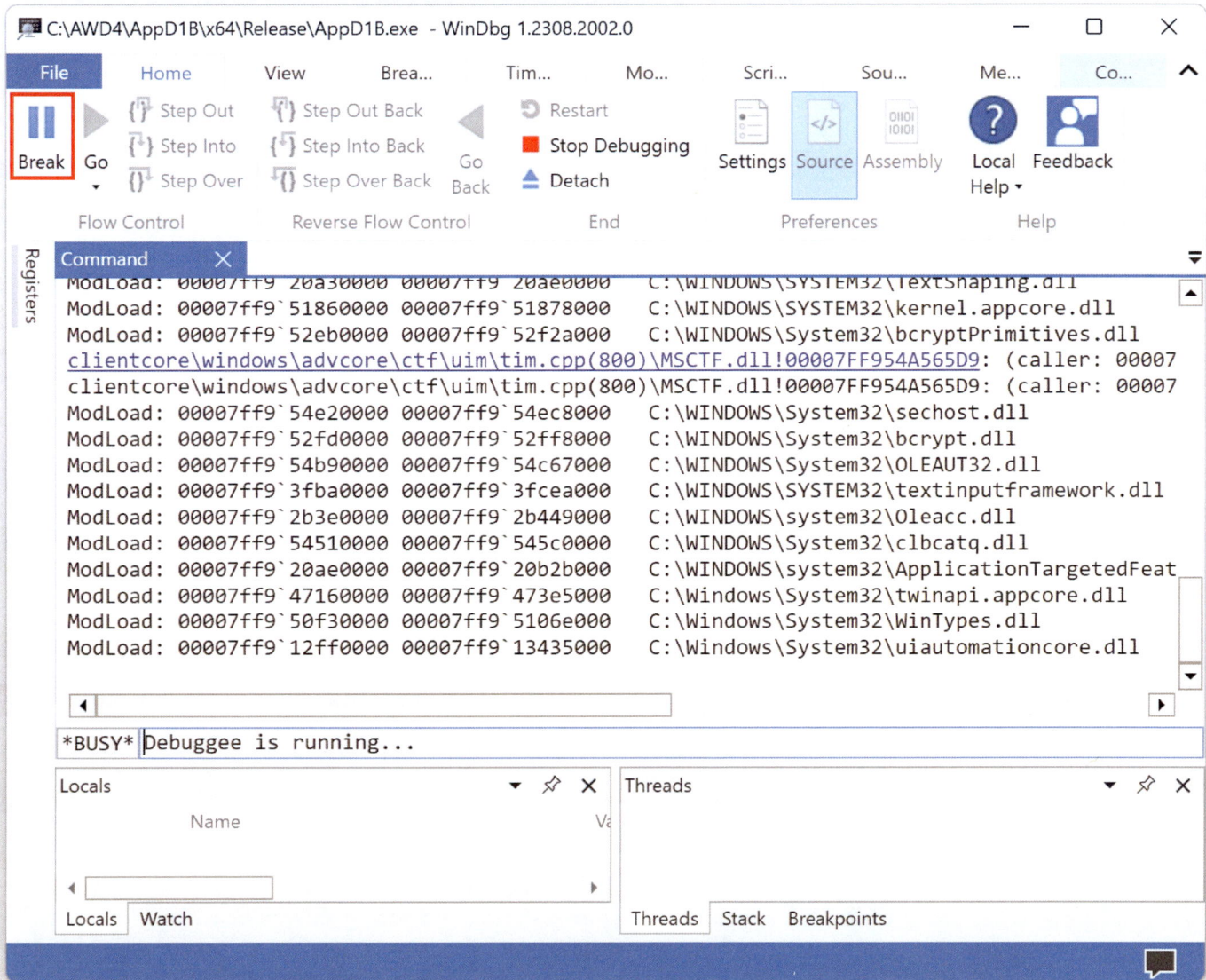

19.   And then on *Home \ Restart* (or the **.restart** command):

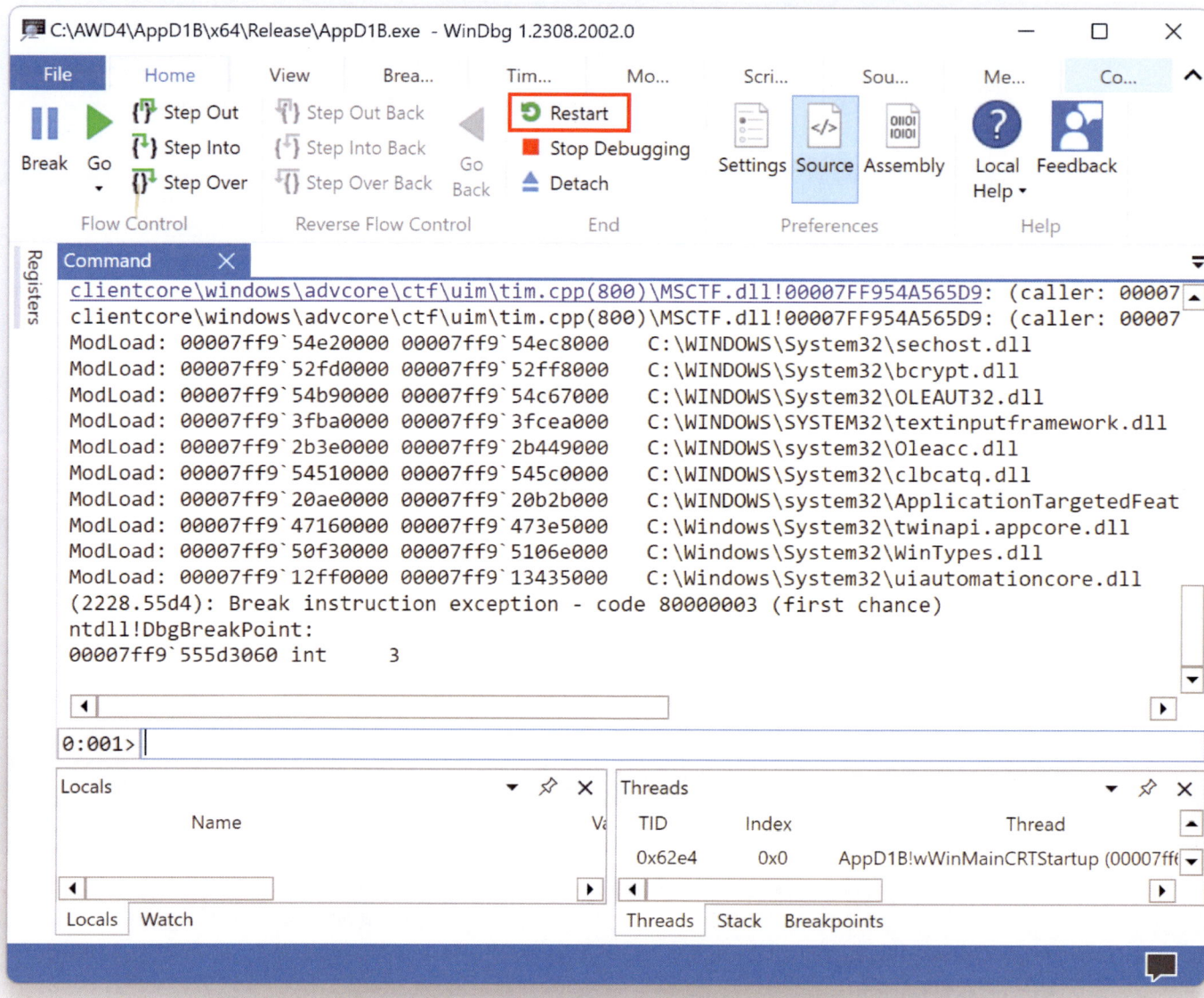

20.   We get the following output:

```
0:000> g
ModLoad: 00007ff9`53ef0000 00007ff9`53f21000    C:\WINDOWS\System32\IMM32.DLL
ModLoad: 00007ff9`4f920000 00007ff9`4f9cb000    C:\WINDOWS\system32\uxtheme.dll
ModLoad: 00007ff9`53b60000 00007ff9`53ee9000    C:\WINDOWS\System32\combase.dll
ModLoad: 00007ff9`543d0000 00007ff9`544e7000    C:\WINDOWS\System32\RPCRT4.dll
ModLoad: 00007ff9`54a40000 00007ff9`54b90000    C:\WINDOWS\System32\MSCTF.dll
ModLoad: 00007ff9`55100000 00007ff9`551a7000    C:\WINDOWS\System32\msvcrt.dll
ModLoad: 00007ff9`20a30000 00007ff9`20ae0000    C:\WINDOWS\SYSTEM32\TextShaping.dll
ModLoad: 00007ff9`51860000 00007ff9`51878000    C:\WINDOWS\SYSTEM32\kernel.appcore.dll
ModLoad: 00007ff9`52eb0000 00007ff9`52f2a000    C:\WINDOWS\System32\bcryptPrimitives.dll
clientcore\windows\advcore\ctf\uim\tim.cpp(800)\MSCTF.dll!00007FF954A565D9: (caller:
00007FF954A5720C) LogHr(1) tid(62e4) 8007029C An assertion failure has occurred.
clientcore\windows\advcore\ctf\uim\tim.cpp(800)\MSCTF.dll!00007FF954A565D9: (caller:
00007FF954A5720C) LogHr(2) tid(62e4) 8007029C An assertion failure has occurred.
ModLoad: 00007ff9`54e20000 00007ff9`54ec8000    C:\WINDOWS\System32\sechost.dll
ModLoad: 00007ff9`52fd0000 00007ff9`52ff8000    C:\WINDOWS\System32\bcrypt.dll
```

```
ModLoad: 00007ff9`54b90000 00007ff9`54c67000    C:\WINDOWS\System32\OLEAUT32.dll
ModLoad: 00007ff9`3fba0000 00007ff9`3fcea000    C:\WINDOWS\SYSTEM32\textinputframework.dll
ModLoad: 00007ff9`2b3e0000 00007ff9`2b449000    C:\WINDOWS\system32\Oleacc.dll
ModLoad: 00007ff9`54510000 00007ff9`545c0000    C:\WINDOWS\System32\clbcatq.dll
ModLoad: 00007ff9`20ae0000 00007ff9`20b2b000
C:\WINDOWS\system32\ApplicationTargetedFeatureDatabase.dll
ModLoad: 00007ff9`47160000 00007ff9`473e5000    C:\Windows\System32\twinapi.appcore.dll
ModLoad: 00007ff9`50f30000 00007ff9`5106e000    C:\Windows\System32\WinTypes.dll
ModLoad: 00007ff9`12ff0000 00007ff9`13435000    C:\Windows\System32\uiautomationcore.dll
(2228.55d4): Break instruction exception - code 80000003 (first chance)
ntdll!DbgBreakPoint:
00007ff9`555d3060 int     3
```

```
0:001> .restart
```

NatVis script unloaded from 'C:\Program
Files\WindowsApps\Microsoft.WinDbg_1.2308.2002.0_x64__8wekyb3d8bbwe\amd64\Visualizers\atlmfc.na
tvis'
NatVis script unloaded from 'C:\Program
Files\WindowsApps\Microsoft.WinDbg_1.2308.2002.0_x64__8wekyb3d8bbwe\amd64\Visualizers\Objective
C.natvis'
NatVis script unloaded from 'C:\Program
Files\WindowsApps\Microsoft.WinDbg_1.2308.2002.0_x64__8wekyb3d8bbwe\amd64\Visualizers\concurren
cy.natvis'
NatVis script unloaded from 'C:\Program
Files\WindowsApps\Microsoft.WinDbg_1.2308.2002.0_x64__8wekyb3d8bbwe\amd64\Visualizers\cpp_rest.
natvis'
NatVis script unloaded from 'C:\Program
Files\WindowsApps\Microsoft.WinDbg_1.2308.2002.0_x64__8wekyb3d8bbwe\amd64\Visualizers\stl.natvi
s'
NatVis script unloaded from 'C:\Program
Files\WindowsApps\Microsoft.WinDbg_1.2308.2002.0_x64__8wekyb3d8bbwe\amd64\Visualizers\Windows.D
ata.Json.natvis'
NatVis script unloaded from 'C:\Program
Files\WindowsApps\Microsoft.WinDbg_1.2308.2002.0_x64__8wekyb3d8bbwe\amd64\Visualizers\Windows.D
evices.Geolocation.natvis'
NatVis script unloaded from 'C:\Program
Files\WindowsApps\Microsoft.WinDbg_1.2308.2002.0_x64__8wekyb3d8bbwe\amd64\Visualizers\Windows.D
evices.Sensors.natvis'
NatVis script unloaded from 'C:\Program
Files\WindowsApps\Microsoft.WinDbg_1.2308.2002.0_x64__8wekyb3d8bbwe\amd64\Visualizers\Windows.M
edia.natvis'
NatVis script unloaded from 'C:\Program
Files\WindowsApps\Microsoft.WinDbg_1.2308.2002.0_x64__8wekyb3d8bbwe\amd64\Visualizers\windows.n
atvis'
NatVis script unloaded from 'C:\Program
Files\WindowsApps\Microsoft.WinDbg_1.2308.2002.0_x64__8wekyb3d8bbwe\amd64\Visualizers\winrt.nat
vis'

Microsoft (R) Windows Debugger Version 10.0.25921.1001 AMD64
Copyright (c) Microsoft Corporation. All rights reserved.

CommandLine: C:\AWD4\AppD1B\x64\Release\AppD1B.exe

************* Path validation summary **************
Response   Time (ms)   Location
Deferred   srv*
Symbol search path is: srv*
Executable search path is:
ModLoad: 00007ff6`bcc80000 00007ff6`bcca0000   AppD1B.exe

```
ModLoad: 00007ff9`55530000 00007ff9`55747000   ntdll.dll
ModLoad: 00007ff9`55030000 00007ff9`550f4000   C:\WINDOWS\System32\KERNEL32.DLL
ModLoad: 00007ff9`52870000 00007ff9`52c16000   C:\WINDOWS\System32\KERNELBASE.dll
ModLoad: 00007ff9`54130000 00007ff9`542de000   C:\WINDOWS\System32\USER32.dll
ModLoad: 00007ff9`53190000 00007ff9`531b6000   C:\WINDOWS\System32\win32u.dll
ModLoad: 00007ff9`542e0000 00007ff9`54309000   C:\WINDOWS\System32\GDI32.dll
ModLoad: 00007ff9`52c20000 00007ff9`52d38000   C:\WINDOWS\System32\gdi32full.dll
ModLoad: 00007ff9`52f30000 00007ff9`52fca000   C:\WINDOWS\System32\msvcp_win.dll
ModLoad: 00007ff9`53000000 00007ff9`53111000   C:\WINDOWS\System32\ucrtbase.dll
(7738.8430): Break instruction exception - code 80000003 (first chance)
ntdll!LdrpDoDebuggerBreak+0x30:
00007ff9`5560b784 int     3
```

21.   Since we want to compare the same behavior of the *RegisterClassW* function, we need to put a breakpoint to break in when this function is about to be executed. Then, we would see the *WNDCLASS* structure passed to it. We set a pattern-matching breakpoint using the **bm** command:

```
0:000> bm *!RegisterClassW
  0: 00007ff9`529f6a50 @!"KERNELBASE!RegisterClassW"
  1: 00007ff9`5413f130 @!"USER32!RegisterClassW"
```

22.   Indeed, we hit the breakpoint immediately:

```
0:000> g
ModLoad: 00007ff9`53ef0000 00007ff9`53f21000   C:\WINDOWS\System32\IMM32.DLL
Breakpoint 1 hit
USER32!RegisterClassW:
00007ff9`5413f130 push    rbx
```

We get an identical stack trace prior to *RegisterClassW* when we compare it with the previously running instance of *AppD1A.exe* (**kL** command omits source code references, **; *** is for comments):

```
0:000> kL; * AppD1B
 # Child-SP          RetAddr               Call Site
00 0000006f`c2defc48 00007ff6`bcc8118d     USER32!RegisterClassW
01 0000006f`c2defc50 00007ff6`bcc8105c     AppD1B!MyRegisterClass+0x8d
02 0000006f`c2defcd0 00007ff6`bcc8168a     AppD1B!wWinMain+0x5c
03 (Inline Function) --------`--------     AppD1B!invoke_main+0x21
04 0000006f`c2defd40 00007ff9`5504257d     AppD1B!__scrt_common_main_seh+0x106
05 0000006f`c2defd80 00007ff9`5558aa58     KERNEL32!BaseThreadInitThunk+0x1d
06 0000006f`c2defdb0 00000000`00000000     ntdll!RtlUserThreadStart+0x28
```

```
0:000> kL; * AppD1A
 # Child-SP          RetAddr               Call Site
00 000000e1`7d2ff740 00007ff7`8ac3105c     AppD1A!MyRegisterClass+0x82
01 000000e1`7d2ff7c0 00007ff7`8ac3168a     AppD1A!wWinMain+0x5c
02 (Inline Function) --------`--------     AppD1A!invoke_main+0x21
03 000000e1`7d2ff820 00007ff9`5504257d     AppD1A!__scrt_common_main_seh+0x106
04 000000e1`7d2ff860 00007ff9`5558aa58     KERNEL32!BaseThreadInitThunk+0x1d
05 000000e1`7d2ff890 00000000`00000000     ntdll!RtlUserThreadStart+0x28
```

Note: In the case of an AppD1A crash, we have to execute the **.cxr** command to reset the current stack frame to #0 before executing the **kL** command.

23.   We choose frame #1, which called the *RegisterClassW* function, and immediately get access to the *wc* variable (we also note that the function *MyRegisterClass* source code is identical to *AppD1A*):

```
0:000> .frame 1
01 0000006f`c2defc50 00007ff6`bcc8105c     AppD1B!MyRegisterClass+0x8d [C:\AWD4\AppD1B\AppD1B\AppD1B.cpp @ 87]
```

```
0:000> dt wc * AppD1B
Local var @ 0x6fc2defc70 Type tagWNDCLASSW
   +0x000 style   : 3
   +0x008 lpfnWndProc : 0x00007ff6`bcc81260     int64  AppD1B!WndProc+0
   +0x010 cbClsExtra : 0n0
   +0x014 cbWndExtra : 0n0
   +0x018 hInstance : 0x00007ff6`bcc80000 HINSTANCE__
   +0x020 hIcon   : 0x00000000`0425127a HICON__
   +0x028 hCursor : 0x00000000`00010003 HICON__
   +0x030 hbrBackground : 0x00000000`00000006 HBRUSH__
   +0x038 lpszMenuName : 0x00000000`0000006d  "--- memory read error at address 0x00000000`0000006d ---"
   +0x040 lpszClassName : 0x00007ff6`bcc9ad10  "APPD1B"
```

24.   But if we look at the AppD1A structure variant, we see its members have different offsets:

```
0:000> dt wc * AppD1A
Local var @ 0xe17d2ff760 Type tagWNDCLASSW
   +0x000 style   : 3
   +0x004 lpfnWndProc : 0x00007ff7`8ac31260     int64  AppD1A!WndProc+0
   +0x00c cbClsExtra : 0n0
   +0x010 cbWndExtra : 0n0
   +0x014 hInstance : 0x00007ff7`8ac30000 HINSTANCE__
   +0x01c hIcon   : 0x00000000`0ea81133 HICON__
   +0x024 hCursor : 0x00000000`00010003 HICON__
   +0x02c hbrBackground : 0x00000000`00000006 HBRUSH__
   +0x034 lpszMenuName : 0x00000000`0000006d  "--- memory read error at address 0x00000000`0000006d ---"
   +0x03c lpszClassName : 0x00007ff7`8ac4ad10  "APPD1A"
```

Note: In the case of an AppD1A crash scenario, we have to switch to frame #4 first.

25.   We close logs in both WinDbg instances:

```
0:000> .logclose * AppD1A
Closing open log file C:\AWD4\D1A.log
```

```
0:000> .logclose * AppD1B
Closing open log file C:\AWD4\D1B.log
```

Note: We recommend exiting WinDbg after each exercise to avoid possible confusion and glitches.

26.   The problem was partially fixed without changing alignment by using a different, bigger *WNDCLASSEX* structure and the *RegisterClassExW* Win32 API function. We launch *\AWD4\AppD1C\x64\Release\AppD1C.exe* in another WinDbg instance:

```
Microsoft (R) Windows Debugger Version 10.0.25921.1001 AMD64
Copyright (c) Microsoft Corporation. All rights reserved.

CommandLine: C:\AWD4\AppD1C\x64\Release\AppD1C.exe

************* Path validation summary **************
Response                        Time (ms)     Location
Deferred                                      srv*
Symbol search path is: srv*
Executable search path is:
ModLoad: 00007ff6`d0d30000 00007ff6`d0d50000     AppD1C.exe
```

```
ModLoad: 00007ff9`55530000 00007ff9`55747000   ntdll.dll
ModLoad: 00007ff9`55030000 00007ff9`550f4000   C:\WINDOWS\System32\KERNEL32.DLL
ModLoad: 00007ff9`52870000 00007ff9`52c16000   C:\WINDOWS\System32\KERNELBASE.dll
ModLoad: 00007ff9`54130000 00007ff9`542de000   C:\WINDOWS\System32\USER32.dll
ModLoad: 00007ff9`53190000 00007ff9`531b6000   C:\WINDOWS\System32\win32u.dll
ModLoad: 00007ff9`542e0000 00007ff9`54309000   C:\WINDOWS\System32\GDI32.dll
ModLoad: 00007ff9`52c20000 00007ff9`52d38000   C:\WINDOWS\System32\gdi32full.dll
ModLoad: 00007ff9`52f30000 00007ff9`52fca000   C:\WINDOWS\System32\msvcp_win.dll
ModLoad: 00007ff9`53000000 00007ff9`53111000   C:\WINDOWS\System32\ucrtbase.dll
(8b48.7758): Break instruction exception - code 80000003 (first chance)
ntdll!LdrpDoDebuggerBreak+0x30:
00007ff9`5560b784 int        3
```

```
0:000> bm *!RegisterClassExW
  0: 00007ff9`529f6a20 @!"KERNELBASE!RegisterClassExW"
  1: 00007ff9`5413ef30 @!"USER32!RegisterClassExW"
```

```
0:000> g
ModLoad: 00007ff9`53ef0000 00007ff9`53f21000   C:\WINDOWS\System32\IMM32.DLL
Breakpoint 1 hit
USER32!RegisterClassExW:
00007ff9`5413ef30 sub        rsp,38h
```

```
0:000> kL
 # Child-SP          RetAddr               Call Site
00 00000052`c21ef7e8 00007ff6`d0d311aa     USER32!RegisterClassExW
01 00000052`c21ef7f0 00007ff6`d0d3105c     AppD1C!MyRegisterClass+0xaa
02 00000052`c21ef870 00007ff6`d0d3169a     AppD1C!wWinMain+0x5c
03 (Inline Function) --------`--------     AppD1C!invoke_main+0x21
04 00000052`c21ef8d0 00007ff9`5504257d     AppD1C!__scrt_common_main_seh+0x106
05 00000052`c21ef910 00007ff9`5558aa58     KERNEL32!BaseThreadInitThunk+0x1d
06 00000052`c21ef940 00000000`00000000     ntdll!RtlUserThreadStart+0x28
```

```
0:000> .frame 1
01 00000052`c21ef7f0 00007ff6`d0d3105c     AppD1C!MyRegisterClass+0xaa [C:\AWD4\AppD1C\AppD1C\AppD1C.cpp @ 87]
```

```
0:000> dv /i /V
prv param  00000052`c21ef870 @rsp+0x0080            hInstance = 0x00007ff6`d0d30000
prv local  00000052`c21ef810 @rsp+0x0020                 wcex = struct tagWNDCLASSEXW
```

Note: Adding a new extra member in the new structure shifts the remaining members and sets the same layout as in *AppD1B*:

```
0:000> dt wcex * AppD1C
Local var @ 0x52c21ef810 Type tagWNDCLASSEXW
   +0x000 cbSize : 0x50
   +0x004 style  : 3
   +0x008 lpfnWndProc : 0x00007ff6`d0d31270      int64  AppD1C!WndProc+0
   +0x010 cbClsExtra : 0n0
   +0x014 cbWndExtra : 0n0
   +0x018 hInstance : 0x00007ff6`d0d30000 HINSTANCE__
   +0x020 hIcon  : 0x00000000`00b11998 HICON__
   +0x028 hCursor : 0x00000000`00010003 HICON__
   +0x030 hbrBackground : 0x00000000`00000006 HBRUSH__
   +0x038 lpszMenuName : 0x00000000`0000006d  "--- memory read error at address 0x00000000`0000006d ---"
   +0x040 lpszClassName : 0x00007ff6`d0d4ad10  "APPD1C"
   +0x048 hIconSm : 0x00000000`00ec19f2 HICON__
```

```
0:000> dt wc * AppD1B
Local var @ 0x6fc2defc70 Type tagWNDCLASSW
   +0x000 style    : 3
   +0x008 lpfnWndProc : 0x00007ff6`bcc81260       int64  AppD1B!WndProc+0
   +0x010 cbClsExtra : 0n0
   +0x014 cbWndExtra : 0n0
   +0x018 hInstance : 0x00007ff6`bcc80000 HINSTANCE__
   +0x020 hIcon    : 0x00000000`0425127a HICON__
   +0x028 hCursor  : 0x00000000`00010003 HICON__
   +0x030 hbrBackground : 0x00000000`00000006 HBRUSH__
   +0x038 lpszMenuName : 0x00000000`0000006d    "--- memory read error at address 0x00000000`0000006d ---"
   +0x040 lpszClassName : 0x00007ff6`bcc9ad10  "APPD1B"
```

Note: *AppD1A* wasn't working because of structure member alignment. This models an old Windows 3.x project that was ported to x64. It had the minimum alignment in the past to reduce memory consumption:

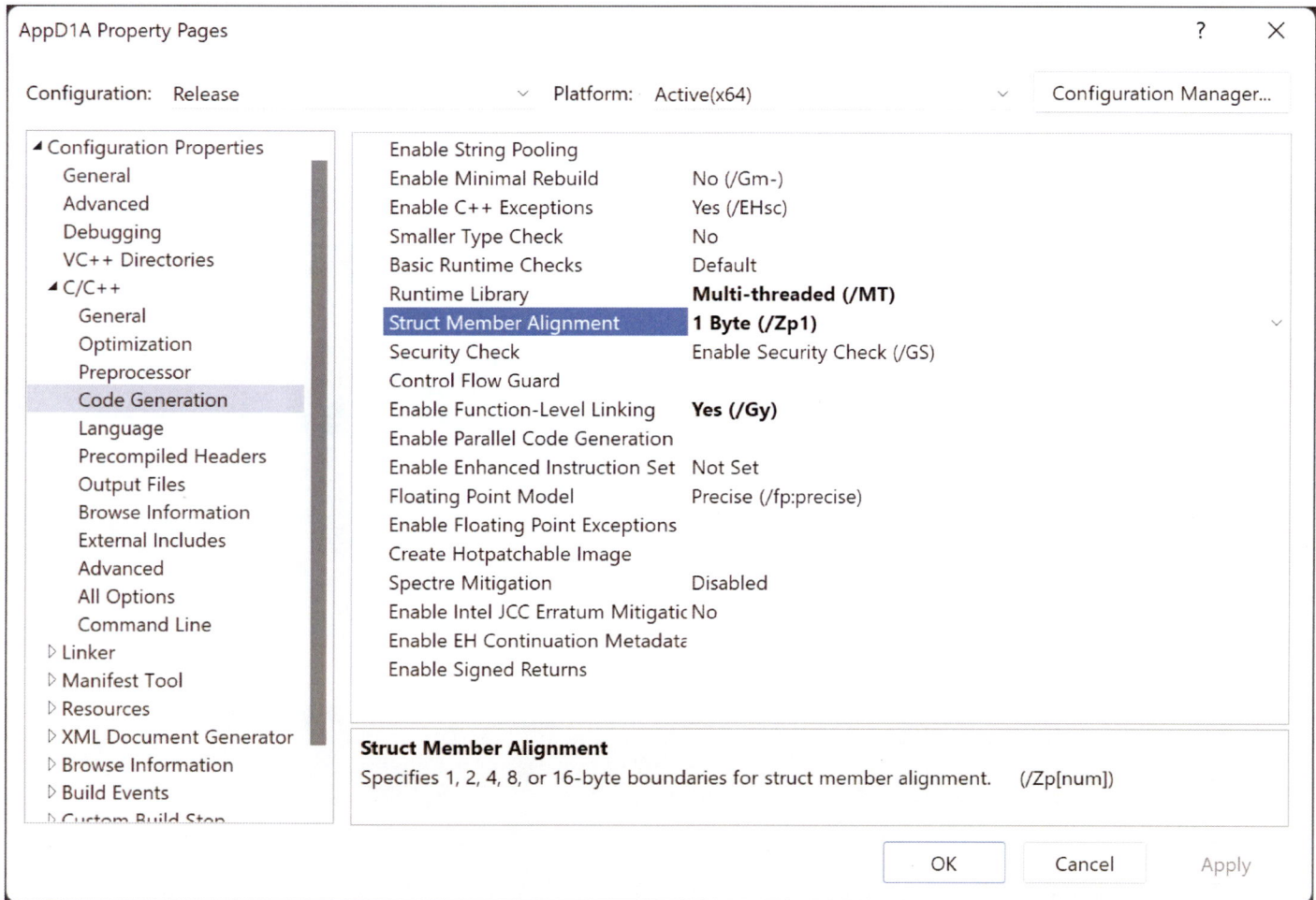

AppD1A Property Pages		? ✕
Configuration: Release	Platform: Active(x64) ⌄	Configuration Manager...

◢ Configuration Properties	Enable String Pooling	
General	Enable Minimal Rebuild	No (/Gm-)
Advanced	Enable C++ Exceptions	Yes (/EHsc)
Debugging	Smaller Type Check	No
VC++ Directories	Basic Runtime Checks	Default
◢ C/C++	Runtime Library	**Multi-threaded (/MT)**
General	**Struct Member Alignment**	**1 Byte (/Zp1)** ⌄
Optimization	Security Check	Enable Security Check (/GS)
Preprocessor	Control Flow Guard	
Code Generation	Enable Function-Level Linking	**Yes (/Gy)**
Language	Enable Parallel Code Generation	
Precompiled Headers	Enable Enhanced Instruction Set	Not Set
Output Files	Floating Point Model	Precise (/fp:precise)
Browse Information	Enable Floating Point Exceptions	
External Includes	Create Hotpatchable Image	
Advanced	Spectre Mitigation	Disabled
All Options	Enable Intel JCC Erratum Mitigatic	No
Command Line	Enable EH Continuation Metadata	
▷ Linker	Enable Signed Returns	
▷ Manifest Tool		
▷ Resources		
▷ XML Document Generator	**Struct Member Alignment**	
▷ Browse Information	Specifies 1, 2, 4, 8, or 16-byte boundaries for struct member alignment. (/Zp[num])	
▷ Build Events		
▷ Custom Build Step		

| | OK | Cancel | Apply |

Note: *AppD1B* was working because the alignment was changed to default. *AppD1C* still used the same 1-byte alignment, but because the bigger structure shifted members of the substructure, it didn't fail the Windows API call (or didn't crash).

Exercise UD2

- **Goal:** Learn how to use hardware breakpoints to catch data corruption

- **Elementary Diagnostics Patterns:** Counter Value

- **Memory Analysis Patterns:** Unloaded Module; Memory Leak (Process Heap); Corrupt Structure; Abnormal Value (*from trace analysis patterns*)

- **Debugging Implementation Patterns:** Break-in; Code Breakpoint; Scope; Variable Value; Data Breakpoint

- \AWD4\Exercise-UD2.pdf

Exercise UD2

Goal: Learn how to use hardware breakpoints to catch data corruption.

Elementary Diagnostics Patterns: Counter Value.

Memory Analysis Patterns: Unloaded Module; Memory Leak (Process Heap); Corrupt Structure; Abnormal Value *(from trace analysis patterns)*.

Debugging Implementation Patterns: Break-in; Code Breakpoint; Scope; Variable Value; Data Breakpoint.

1.   Problem history:

An application *AppD2* starts consuming memory after some time. We want to find out the root cause.

2.   Launch *\AWD4\AppD2\x64\Release\AppD2.exe* executable. Launch Task Manager. *Choose File \ Start* in AppD2. We see approximately this memory consumption:

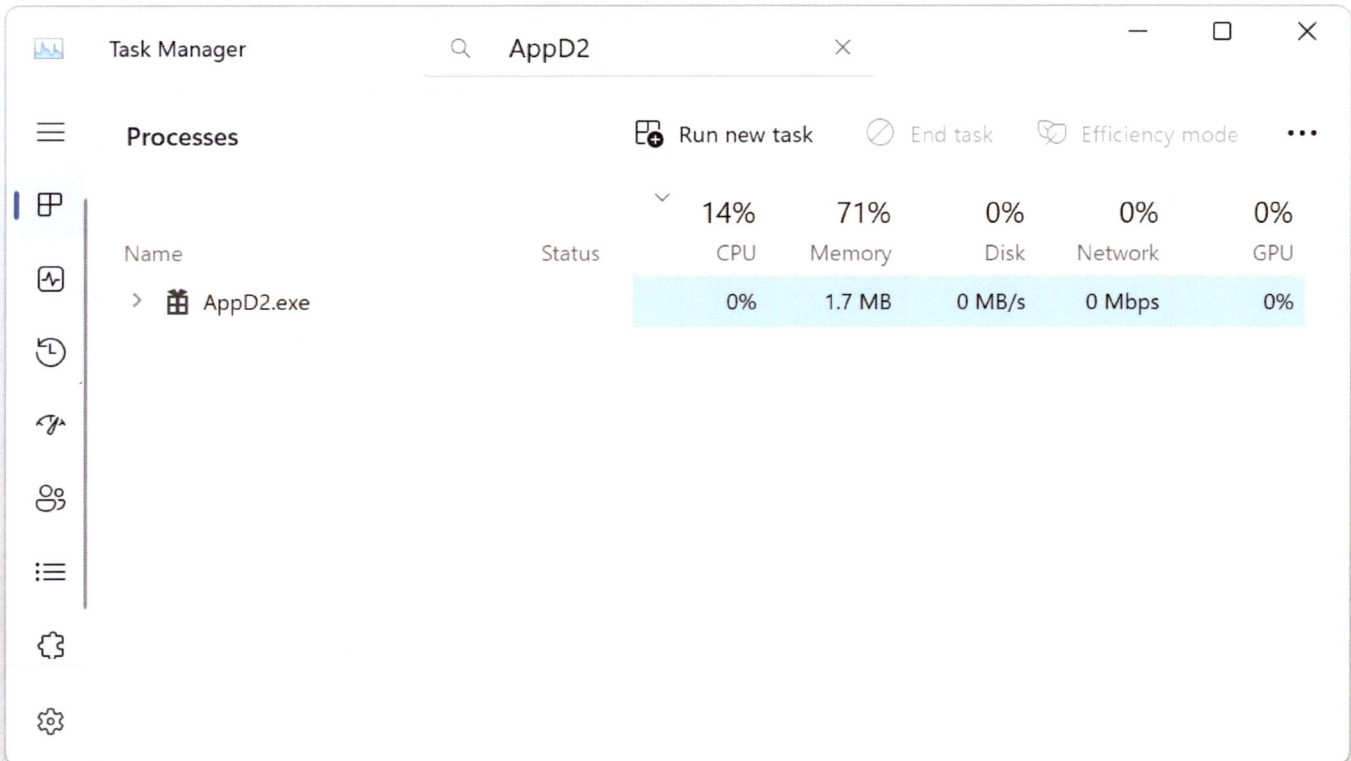

Task Manager		AppD2	✕		—	☐	✕
Processes			🗗 Run new task	⊘ End task	🗭 Efficiency mode		•••
			14%	71%	0%	0%	0%
Name		Status	CPU	Memory	Disk	Network	GPU
> 🎁 AppD2.exe			0%	1.7 MB	0 MB/s	0 Mbps	0%

3. After a minute, memory starts growing:

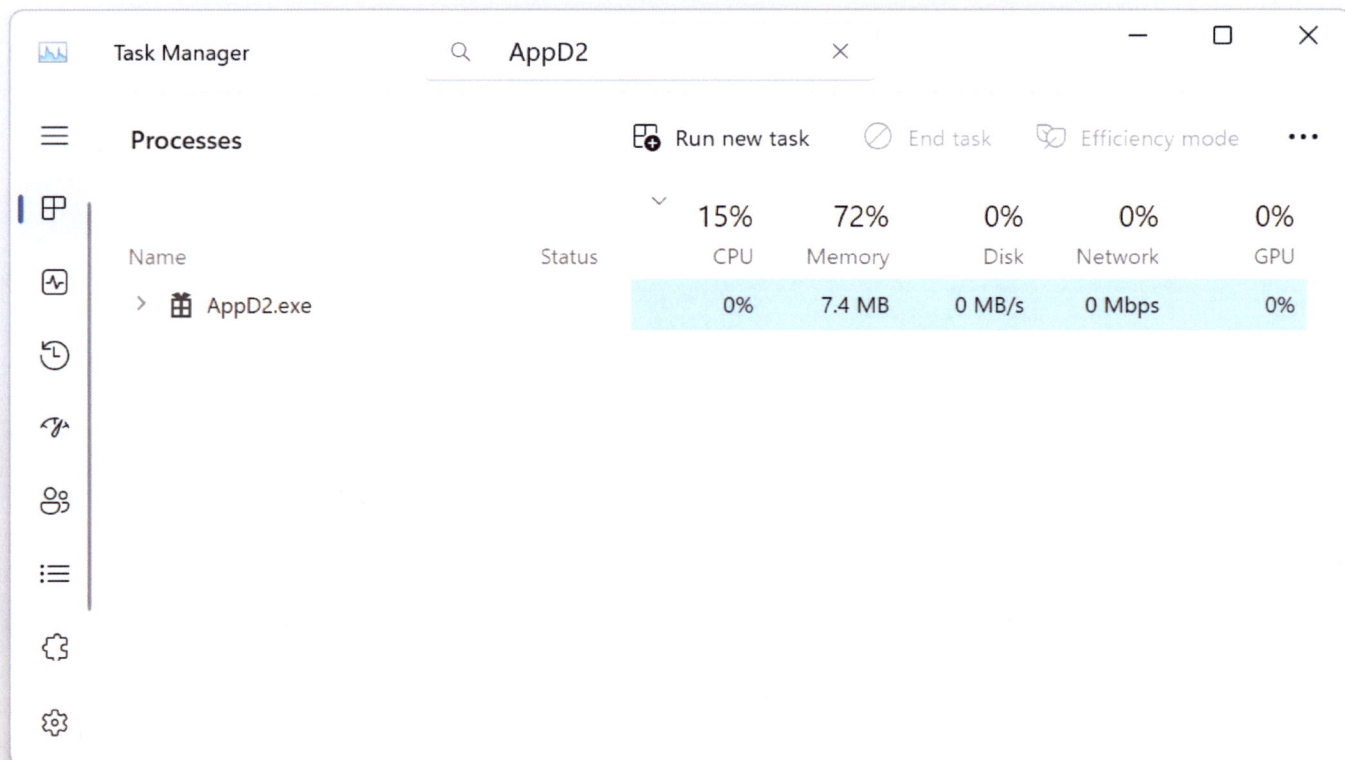

4. Wait for another 2-3 minutes and launch WinDbg. Then, choose *File \ Attach to process* and select *AppD2.exe*.

5. You get WinDbg attached to *AppD2.exe*:

```
Microsoft (R) Windows Debugger Version 10.0.25921.1001 AMD64
Copyright (c) Microsoft Corporation. All rights reserved.

*** wait with pending attach

************* Path validation summary **************
Response                        Time (ms)      Location
Deferred                                       srv*
Symbol search path is: srv*
Executable search path is:
ModLoad: 00007ff7`36760000 00007ff7`36780000   C:\AWD4\AppD2\x64\Release\AppD2.exe
ModLoad: 00007ff9`55530000 00007ff9`55747000   C:\WINDOWS\SYSTEM32\ntdll.dll
ModLoad: 00007ff9`55030000 00007ff9`550f4000   C:\WINDOWS\System32\KERNEL32.DLL
ModLoad: 00007ff9`52870000 00007ff9`52c16000   C:\WINDOWS\System32\KERNELBASE.dll
ModLoad: 00007ff9`54130000 00007ff9`542de000   C:\WINDOWS\System32\USER32.dll
ModLoad: 00007ff9`53190000 00007ff9`531b6000   C:\WINDOWS\System32\win32u.dll
ModLoad: 00007ff9`542e0000 00007ff9`54309000   C:\WINDOWS\System32\GDI32.dll
ModLoad: 00007ff9`52c20000 00007ff9`52d38000   C:\WINDOWS\System32\gdi32full.dll
ModLoad: 00007ff9`52f30000 00007ff9`52fca000   C:\WINDOWS\System32\msvcp_win.dll
ModLoad: 00007ff9`53000000 00007ff9`53111000   C:\WINDOWS\System32\ucrtbase.dll
ModLoad: 00007ff9`53ef0000 00007ff9`53f21000   C:\WINDOWS\System32\IMM32.DLL
ModLoad: 00007ff9`4f920000 00007ff9`4f9cb000   C:\WINDOWS\system32\uxtheme.dll
ModLoad: 00007ff9`53b60000 00007ff9`53ee9000   C:\WINDOWS\System32\combase.dll
```

```
ModLoad: 00007ff9`543d0000 00007ff9`544e7000   C:\WINDOWS\System32\RPCRT4.dll
ModLoad: 00007ff9`54a40000 00007ff9`54b90000   C:\WINDOWS\System32\MSCTF.dll
ModLoad: 00007ff9`55100000 00007ff9`551a7000   C:\WINDOWS\System32\msvcrt.dll
ModLoad: 00007ff9`20a30000 00007ff9`20ae0000   C:\WINDOWS\SYSTEM32\TextShaping.dll
ModLoad: 00007ff9`51860000 00007ff9`51878000   C:\WINDOWS\SYSTEM32\kernel.appcore.dll
ModLoad: 00007ff9`52eb0000 00007ff9`52f2a000   C:\WINDOWS\System32\bcryptPrimitives.dll
ModLoad: 00007ff9`54e20000 00007ff9`54ec8000   C:\WINDOWS\System32\sechost.dll
ModLoad: 00007ff9`52fd0000 00007ff9`52ff8000   C:\WINDOWS\System32\bcrypt.dll
ModLoad: 00007ff9`3fba0000 00007ff9`3fcea000   C:\WINDOWS\SYSTEM32\textinputframework.dll
ModLoad: 00007ff9`54b90000 00007ff9`54c67000   C:\WINDOWS\System32\OLEAUT32.dll
ModLoad: 00007ff9`4f470000 00007ff9`4f5a4000   C:\WINDOWS\SYSTEM32\CoreMessaging.dll
ModLoad: 00007ff9`49070000 00007ff9`493dc000   C:\WINDOWS\SYSTEM32\CoreUIComponents.dll
ModLoad: 00007ff9`50f30000 00007ff9`5106e000   C:\WINDOWS\SYSTEM32\wintypes.dll
ModLoad: 00007ff9`54310000 00007ff9`543c3000   C:\WINDOWS\System32\advapi32.dll
ModLoad: 00007ff9`51ed0000 00007ff9`51edc000   C:\WINDOWS\SYSTEM32\CRYPTBASE.DLL
ModLoad: 00007ff9`2b3e0000 00007ff9`2b449000   C:\WINDOWS\system32\Oleacc.dll
ModLoad: 00007ff9`54510000 00007ff9`545c0000   C:\WINDOWS\System32\clbcatq.dll
ModLoad: 00007ff9`20ae0000 00007ff9`20b2b000
C:\WINDOWS\system32\ApplicationTargetedFeatureDatabase.dll
ModLoad: 00007ff9`47160000 00007ff9`473e5000   C:\Windows\System32\twinapi.appcore.dll
ModLoad: 00007ff9`12ff0000 00007ff9`13435000   C:\Windows\System32\uiautomationcore.dll
ModLoad: 00007ff9`4fb50000 00007ff9`4fb7b000   C:\Windows\system32\dwmapi.dll
ModLoad: 00007ff9`1e070000 00007ff9`1e085000   C:\Windows\System32\threadpoolwinrt.dll
(7d60.32ec): Break instruction exception - code 80000003 (first chance)
ntdll!DbgBreakPoint:
00007ff9`555d3060 int     3
```

6.   Open a log file:

```
0:011> .logopen C:\AWD4\D2.log
Opened log file 'C:\AWD4\D2.log'
```

7.   There are 12 threads (the number can be different on your system), and the current one, #11 (numbering starts from 0), has a thread stack trace related to a breakpoint:

```
0:011> ~
   0  Id: 7d60.593c Suspend: 1 Teb: 000000e6`f2ce2000 Unfrozen
   1  Id: 7d60.515c Suspend: 1 Teb: 000000e6`f2cee000 Unfrozen
   2  Id: 7d60.68c4 Suspend: 1 Teb: 000000e6`f2cf0000 Unfrozen
   3  Id: 7d60.5d54 Suspend: 1 Teb: 000000e6`f2cf4000 Unfrozen
   4  Id: 7d60.86f8 Suspend: 1 Teb: 000000e6`f2cf6000 Unfrozen
   5  Id: 7d60.656c Suspend: 1 Teb: 000000e6`f2cf8000 Unfrozen
   6  Id: 7d60.7b9c Suspend: 1 Teb: 000000e6`f2cfa000 Unfrozen
   7  Id: 7d60.cac Suspend: 1 Teb: 000000e6`f2cfc000 Unfrozen
   8  Id: 7d60.734c Suspend: 1 Teb: 000000e6`f2cfe000 Unfrozen
   9  Id: 7d60.4ec Suspend: 1 Teb: 000000e6`f2d00000 Unfrozen
  10  Id: 7d60.86d4 Suspend: 1 Teb: 000000e6`f2d02000 Unfrozen
. 11  Id: 7d60.32ec Suspend: 1 Teb: 000000e6`f2d04000 Unfrozen

0:0011> k
# Child-SP          RetAddr               Call Site
00 000000e6`f2fff7f8 00007ff9`556069ae     ntdll!DbgBreakPoint
01 000000e6`f2fff800 00007ff9`5504257d     ntdll!DbgUiRemoteBreakin+0x4e
02 000000e6`f2fff830 00007ff9`5558aa58     KERNEL32!BaseThreadInitThunk+0x1d
03 000000e6`f2fff860 00000000`00000000     ntdll!RtlUserThreadStart+0x28
```

8. We can list all threads using **~*k** (or **~*kL** to omit source code references) command:

```
0:011> ~*kL

   0  Id: 7d60.593c Suspend: 1 Teb: 000000e6`f2ce2000 Unfrozen
 # Child-SP          RetAddr               Call Site
00 000000e6`f2effd78 00007ff9`5415535a     win32u!NtUserGetMessage+0x14
01 000000e6`f2effd80 00007ff7`367610d5     USER32!GetMessageW+0x2a
02 000000e6`f2effde0 00007ff7`3676180a     AppD2!wWinMain+0xd5
03 (Inline Function) --------`--------     AppD2!invoke_main+0x21
04 000000e6`f2effe50 00007ff9`5504257d     AppD2!__scrt_common_main_seh+0x106
05 000000e6`f2effe90 00007ff9`5558aa58     KERNEL32!BaseThreadInitThunk+0x1d
06 000000e6`f2effec0 00000000`00000000     ntdll!RtlUserThreadStart+0x28

   1  Id: 7d60.515c Suspend: 1 Teb: 000000e6`f2cee000 Unfrozen
 # Child-SP          RetAddr               Call Site
00 000000e6`f34ff6d8 00007ff9`5556537e     ntdll!NtWaitForWorkViaWorkerFactory+0x14
01 000000e6`f34ff6e0 00007ff9`5504257d     ntdll!TppWorkerThread+0x2ee
02 000000e6`f34ff9c0 00007ff9`5558aa58     KERNEL32!BaseThreadInitThunk+0x1d
03 000000e6`f34ff9f0 00000000`00000000     ntdll!RtlUserThreadStart+0x28

   2  Id: 7d60.68c4 Suspend: 1 Teb: 000000e6`f2cf0000 Unfrozen
 # Child-SP          RetAddr               Call Site
00 000000e6`f33ffa28 00007ff9`528cffe9     ntdll!NtWaitForMultipleObjects+0x14
01 000000e6`f33ffa30 00007ff9`528cfeee     KERNELBASE!WaitForMultipleObjectsEx+0xe9
02 000000e6`f33ffd10 00007ff9`1304df7d     KERNELBASE!WaitForMultipleObjects+0xe
03 000000e6`f33ffd50 00007ff9`1304daf9     uiautomationcore!OverlappedIOManager::IoThreadProc+0x47d
04 000000e6`f33ffdc0 00007ff9`5504257d     uiautomationcore!OverlappedIOManager::StaticIoThreadProc+0x9
05 000000e6`f33ffdf0 00007ff9`5558aa58     KERNEL32!BaseThreadInitThunk+0x1d
06 000000e6`f33ffe20 00000000`00000000     ntdll!RtlUserThreadStart+0x28

   3  Id: 7d60.5d54 Suspend: 1 Teb: 000000e6`f2cf4000 Unfrozen
 # Child-SP          RetAddr               Call Site
00 000000e6`f36ffa48 00007ff9`5556537e     ntdll!NtWaitForWorkViaWorkerFactory+0x14
01 000000e6`f36ffa50 00007ff9`5504257d     ntdll!TppWorkerThread+0x2ee
02 000000e6`f36ffd30 00007ff9`5558aa58     KERNEL32!BaseThreadInitThunk+0x1d
03 000000e6`f36ffd60 00000000`00000000     ntdll!RtlUserThreadStart+0x28

   4  Id: 7d60.86f8 Suspend: 1 Teb: 000000e6`f2cf6000 Unfrozen
 # Child-SP          RetAddr               Call Site
00 000000e6`f37ff808 00007ff9`5556537e     ntdll!NtWaitForWorkViaWorkerFactory+0x14
01 000000e6`f37ff810 00007ff9`5504257d     ntdll!TppWorkerThread+0x2ee
02 000000e6`f37ffaf0 00007ff9`5558aa58     KERNEL32!BaseThreadInitThunk+0x1d
03 000000e6`f37ffb20 00000000`00000000     ntdll!RtlUserThreadStart+0x28

   5  Id: 7d60.656c Suspend: 1 Teb: 000000e6`f2cf8000 Unfrozen
 # Child-SP          RetAddr               Call Site
00 000000e6`f38ff698 00007ff9`541552f7     win32u!NtUserMsgWaitForMultipleObjectsEx+0x14
01 000000e6`f38ff6a0 00007ff9`130e880f     USER32!MsgWaitForMultipleObjects+0x57
02 000000e6`f38ff6e0 00007ff9`132d15e1
uiautomationcore!WorkerThread<WinEventsManager::ThreadState>::ThreadProc+0x18b
03 000000e6`f38ff850 00007ff9`53029363
uiautomationcore!std::thread::_Invoke<std::tuple<<lambda_d869f02c39f35682526e1a41b8686bac> >,0>+0x11
04 000000e6`f38ff880 00007ff9`5504257d     ucrtbase!thread_start<unsigned int (__cdecl*)(void *),1>+0x93
05 000000e6`f38ff8b0 00007ff9`5558aa58     KERNEL32!BaseThreadInitThunk+0x1d
06 000000e6`f38ff8e0 00000000`00000000     ntdll!RtlUserThreadStart+0x28

   6  Id: 7d60.7b9c Suspend: 1 Teb: 000000e6`f2cfa000 Unfrozen
 # Child-SP          RetAddr               Call Site
00 000000e6`f39ff5c8 00007ff9`5556537e     ntdll!NtWaitForWorkViaWorkerFactory+0x14
01 000000e6`f39ff5d0 00007ff9`5504257d     ntdll!TppWorkerThread+0x2ee
02 000000e6`f39ff8b0 00007ff9`5558aa58     KERNEL32!BaseThreadInitThunk+0x1d
03 000000e6`f39ff8e0 00000000`00000000     ntdll!RtlUserThreadStart+0x28
```

```
   7  Id: 7d60.cac Suspend: 1 Teb: 000000e6`f2cfc000 Unfrozen
 # Child-SP          RetAddr               Call Site
00 000000e6`f3aff998 00007ff9`555851b3     ntdll!NtDelayExecution+0x14
01 000000e6`f3aff9a0 00007ff9`528b506d     ntdll!RtlDelayExecution+0x43
02 000000e6`f3aff9d0 00007ff7`36761554     KERNELBASE!SleepEx+0x7d
03 000000e6`f3affa50 00007ff9`5504257d     AppD2!ThreadProcA+0x14
04 000000e6`f3affa80 00007ff9`5558aa58     KERNEL32!BaseThreadInitThunk+0x1d
05 000000e6`f3affab0 00000000`00000000     ntdll!RtlUserThreadStart+0x28

   8  Id: 7d60.734c Suspend: 1 Teb: 000000e6`f2cfe000 Unfrozen
 # Child-SP          RetAddr               Call Site
00 000000e6`f3bffdd8 00007ff9`555851b3     ntdll!NtDelayExecution+0x14
01 000000e6`f3bffde0 00007ff9`528b506d     ntdll!RtlDelayExecution+0x43
02 000000e6`f3bffe10 00007ff7`3676158f     KERNELBASE!SleepEx+0x7d
03 000000e6`f3bffe90 00007ff9`5504257d     AppD2!ThreadProcB+0x2f
04 000000e6`f3bffec0 00007ff9`5558aa58     KERNEL32!BaseThreadInitThunk+0x1d
05 000000e6`f3bffef0 00000000`00000000     ntdll!RtlUserThreadStart+0x28

   9  Id: 7d60.4ec Suspend: 1 Teb: 000000e6`f2d00000 Unfrozen
 # Child-SP          RetAddr               Call Site
00 000000e6`f3cff818 00007ff9`555851b3     ntdll!NtDelayExecution+0x14
01 000000e6`f3cff820 00007ff9`528b506d     ntdll!RtlDelayExecution+0x43
02 000000e6`f3cff850 00007ff7`367615dc     KERNELBASE!SleepEx+0x7d
03 000000e6`f3cff8d0 00007ff9`5504257d     AppD2!ThreadProcC+0x2c
04 000000e6`f3cff900 00007ff9`5558aa58     KERNEL32!BaseThreadInitThunk+0x1d
05 000000e6`f3cff930 00000000`00000000     ntdll!RtlUserThreadStart+0x28

  10  Id: 7d60.86d4 Suspend: 1 Teb: 000000e6`f2d02000 Unfrozen
 # Child-SP          RetAddr               Call Site
00 000000e6`f3dff9f8 00007ff9`5556537e     ntdll!NtWaitForWorkViaWorkerFactory+0x14
01 000000e6`f3dffa00 00007ff9`5504257d     ntdll!TppWorkerThread+0x2ee
02 000000e6`f3dffce0 00007ff9`5558aa58     KERNEL32!BaseThreadInitThunk+0x1d
03 000000e6`f3dffd10 00000000`00000000     ntdll!RtlUserThreadStart+0x28

# 11  Id: 7d60.32ec Suspend: 1 Teb: 000000e6`f2d04000 Unfrozen
 # Child-SP          RetAddr               Call Site
00 000000e6`f2fff7f8 00007ff9`556069ae     ntdll!DbgBreakPoint
01 000000e6`f2fff800 00007ff9`5504257d     ntdll!DbgUiRemoteBreakin+0x4e
02 000000e6`f2fff830 00007ff9`5558aa58     KERNEL32!BaseThreadInitThunk+0x1d
03 000000e6`f2fff860 00000000`00000000     ntdll!RtlUserThreadStart+0x28
```

9.   The **lm** command lists modules (notice an unloaded module **DllD2**):

```
0:011> lm
start             end               module name
00007ff7`36760000 00007ff7`36780000     AppD2    C (private pdb symbols)
C:\ProgramData\Dbg\sym\AppD2.pdb\2F7B31C4BAED4DE88A0B4ED2E41935721\AppD2.pdb
00007ff9`12ff0000 00007ff9`13435000     uiautomationcore   (pdb symbols)
C:\ProgramData\Dbg\sym\UIAutomationCore.pdb\E5C936DDADB8B31CA37BAE8422B99F6D1\UIAutomationCore.
pdb
00007ff9`1e070000 00007ff9`1e085000     threadpoolwinrt   (deferred)
00007ff9`20a30000 00007ff9`20ae0000     TextShaping   (deferred)
00007ff9`20ae0000 00007ff9`20b2b000     ApplicationTargetedFeatureDatabase    (deferred)
00007ff9`2b3e0000 00007ff9`2b449000     Oleacc    (deferred)
00007ff9`3fba0000 00007ff9`3fcea000     textinputframework   (deferred)
00007ff9`47160000 00007ff9`473e5000     twinapi_appcore   (deferred)
00007ff9`49070000 00007ff9`493dc000     CoreUIComponents   (deferred)
00007ff9`4f470000 00007ff9`4f5a4000     CoreMessaging   (deferred)
00007ff9`4f920000 00007ff9`4f9cb000     uxtheme   (deferred)
00007ff9`4fb50000 00007ff9`4fb7b000     dwmapi   (deferred)
00007ff9`50f30000 00007ff9`5106e000     wintypes   (deferred)
00007ff9`51860000 00007ff9`51878000     kernel_appcore   (deferred)
```

```
00007ff9`51ed0000 00007ff9`51edc000   CRYPTBASE    (deferred)
00007ff9`52870000 00007ff9`52c16000   KERNELBASE   (pdb symbols)
C:\ProgramData\Dbg\sym\kernelbase.pdb\F4B4FFF5878CAD6B2D379D9403C5E78D1\kernelbase.pdb
00007ff9`52c20000 00007ff9`52d38000   gdi32full    (deferred)
00007ff9`52eb0000 00007ff9`52f2a000   bcryptPrimitives   (deferred)
00007ff9`52f30000 00007ff9`52fca000   msvcp_win    (deferred)
00007ff9`52fd0000 00007ff9`52ff8000   bcrypt       (deferred)
00007ff9`53000000 00007ff9`53111000   ucrtbase     (pdb symbols)
C:\ProgramData\Dbg\sym\ucrtbase.pdb\A18B58F2E2DD692A4591DD05331782BA1\ucrtbase.pdb
00007ff9`53190000 00007ff9`531b6000   win32u       (pdb symbols)
C:\ProgramData\Dbg\sym\win32u.pdb\0E51DC7F3B252A04573226AFF596E6E71\win32u.pdb
00007ff9`53b60000 00007ff9`53ee9000   combase      (deferred)
00007ff9`53ef0000 00007ff9`53f21000   IMM32        (deferred)
00007ff9`54130000 00007ff9`542de000   USER32       (pdb symbols)
C:\ProgramData\Dbg\sym\user32.pdb\90972EEAF432ADAB1D81C603DB571A751\user32.pdb
00007ff9`542e0000 00007ff9`54309000   GDI32        (deferred)
00007ff9`54310000 00007ff9`543c3000   advapi32     (deferred)
00007ff9`543d0000 00007ff9`544e7000   RPCRT4       (deferred)
00007ff9`54510000 00007ff9`545c0000   clbcatq      (deferred)
00007ff9`54a40000 00007ff9`54b90000   MSCTF        (deferred)
00007ff9`54b90000 00007ff9`54c67000   OLEAUT32     (deferred)
00007ff9`54e20000 00007ff9`54ec8000   sechost      (deferred)
00007ff9`55030000 00007ff9`550f4000   KERNEL32     (pdb symbols)
C:\ProgramData\Dbg\sym\kernel32.pdb\6F7660385E7D8D33ED9B5A39B03822F01\kernel32.pdb
00007ff9`55100000 00007ff9`551a7000   msvcrt       (deferred)
00007ff9`55530000 00007ff9`55747000   ntdll        (pdb symbols)
C:\ProgramData\Dbg\sym\ntdll.pdb\58A282C24AEE7E03A8CF8CB0A782CE0C1\ntdll.pdb

Unloaded modules:
00007ff9`38fe0000 00007ff9`38fff000   DllD2.dll
```

10.   We suspect process heap leak and print heap statistics:

```
0:011> !heap -s

*****************************************************************************************
                             NT HEAP STATS BELOW
*****************************************************************************************
LFH Key                 : 0x60d8413397718e0f
Termination on corruption : ENABLED
          Heap     Flags   Reserv  Commit   Virt   Free  List   UCR  Virt  Lock  Fast
                            (k)     (k)      (k)    (k) length        blocks cont. heap
-------------------------------------------------------------------------------------------
000001ebf8d10000 00000002   48940   47708   48740   118    71     7     0     5   LFH
000001ebf8ae0000 00008000      64       4      64     2     1     1     0     0
000001ebfa7f0000 00001002     260      32      60     1     4     1     0     0   LFH
000001ebfa6f0000 00001002    1280     100    1080    17     9     2     0     0   LFH
-------------------------------------------------------------------------------------------
```

Then we resume via the *Go* button (or **g** command):

Then we wait for 2-3 minutes and break in via the *Break* button:

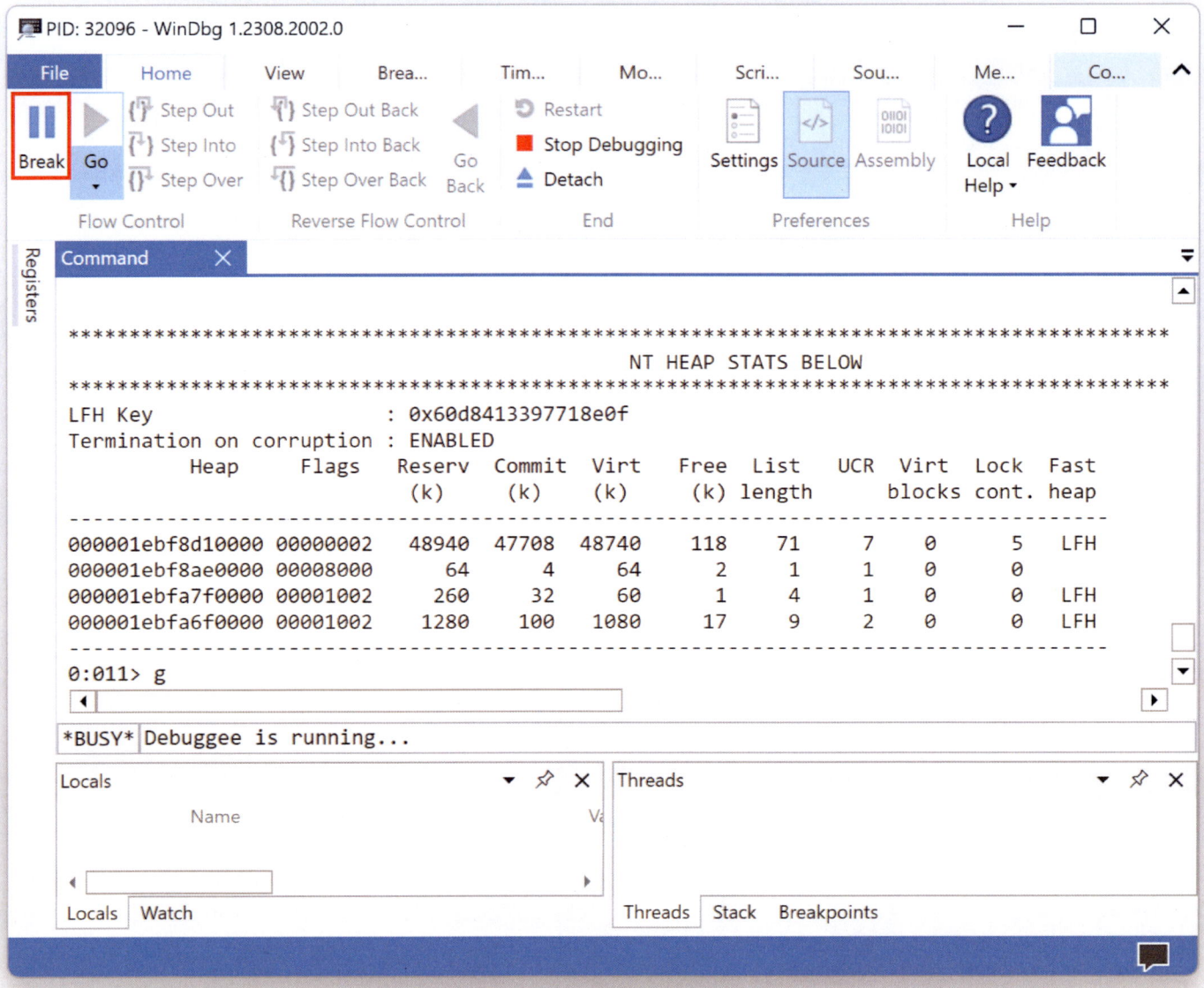

and print heap stats again:

```
0:012> g
(7d60.38bc): Break instruction exception - code 80000003 (first chance)
ntdll!DbgBreakPoint:
00007ff9`555d3060 int        3

0:012> !heap -s

*****************************************************************************
                           NT HEAP STATS BELOW
*****************************************************************************
LFH Key                    : 0x60d8413397718e0f
Termination on corruption : ENABLED
          Heap     Flags   Reserv  Commit  Virt   Free  List   UCR  Virt  Lock  Fast
                            (k)     (k)     (k)    (k) length       blocks cont. heap
          -------------------------------------------------------------------------
```

```
000001ebf8d10000 00000002    81316   78704   81116     138     73     9     0     5   LFH
000001ebf8ae0000 00008000       64       4      64       2      1     1     0     0
000001ebfa7f0000 00001002      260      32      60       1      4     1     0     0   LFH
000001ebfa6f0000 00001002     1280     100    1080      16      8     2     0     0   LFH
-------------------------------------------------------------------------------------
```

Note: We see an increase in process heap memory usage.

11.   Let's put a breakpoint on the *RtlAllocateHeap* function (usually, even if we use *malloc* or *new* in C++, allocations go through that function) and inspect a stack trace when the breakpoint is hit (there may be some delay when downloading symbol files):

```
0:012> bm *!RtlAllocateHeap*
  0: 00007ff9`5504ffe4 @!"KERNEL32!RtlAllocateHeap"
  1: 00007ff9`5556c610 @!"ntdll!RtlAllocateHeap"
```

```
0:012> g
Breakpoint 1 hit
ntdll!RtlAllocateHeap:
00007ff9`5556c610 mov      qword ptr [rsp+8],rbx ss:000000e6`f3bffe60=0000000000000000
```

```
0:008> kL
 # Child-SP          RetAddr               Call Site
00 000000e6`f3bffe58 00007ff7`367669f0     ntdll!RtlAllocateHeap
01 000000e6`f3bffe60 00007ff7`3676157d     AppD2!_malloc_base+0x44
02 000000e6`f3bffe90 00007ff9`5504257d     AppD2!ThreadProcB+0x1d
03 000000e6`f3bffec0 00007ff9`5558aa58     KERNEL32!BaseThreadInitThunk+0x1d
04 000000e6`f3bffef0 00000000`00000000     ntdll!RtlUserThreadStart+0x28
```

Note: If we get a different stack trace, we may need to repeat the **g**, **kL** command sequence until we get a stack trace involving "malloc".

12.   Let's now set the source code path and switch to the appropriate frame that calls *malloc*:

```
0:008> .srcpath+ C:\AWD4\AppD2\AppD2
Source search path is: C:\AWD4\AppD2\AppD2
```

```
************* Path validation summary **************
Response                     Time (ms)   Location
OK                                       C:\AWD4\AppD2\AppD2
```

```
0:008> .frame 2
02 000000e6`f3bffe90 00007ff9`5504257d     AppD2!ThreadProcB+0x1d [C:\AWD3\AppD2\AppD2\AppD2.cpp @ 231]
```

13.   Let's examine our source code fragments related to using *malloc* and *free*:

```
typedef struct
{
    DWORD dwAllocSize;
    BOOL  bKeep;
    BYTE *allocData;
} ALLOCMGR;

ALLOCMGR allocManager;
void StartModeling (void)
{
```

```
        allocManager.dwAllocSize = 64;
        allocManager.bKeep = false;

        CreateThread(NULL, 0, ThreadProcA, NULL, 0, NULL);
        CreateThread(NULL, 0, ThreadProcB, NULL, 0, NULL);
        CreateThread(NULL, 0, ThreadProcC, NULL, 0, NULL);
}

DWORD WINAPI ThreadProcB(LPVOID)
{
        while (1)
        {
                allocManager.allocData = (BYTE *)malloc(allocManager.dwAllocSize);
                Sleep(100);  // do some work
                if (!allocManager.bKeep)
                {
                        free(allocManager.allocData);
                }
        }

        return 0;
}
```

According to the source code, every allocation should be freed after some work.

14.   Let's now examine the *allocManager* structure:

```
0:008> dt allocManager
AppD2!allocManager
   +0x000 dwAllocSize      : 0x454c
   +0x004 bKeep            : 0n19265
   +0x008 allocData        : 0x000001eb`81d3a180  "P???"

0:008> dc allocManager
00007ff7`3677acf0  0000454c 00004b41 81d3a180 000001eb  LE..AK..........
00007ff7`3677ad00  38fe0000 00007ff9 36760000 00007ff7  ...8......v6....
00007ff7`3677ad10  00500041 00440050 00000032 00000000  A.P.P.D.2.......
00007ff7`3677ad20  00000000 00000000 00000000 00000000  ................
00007ff7`3677ad30  00000000 00000000 00000000 00000000  ................
00007ff7`3677ad40  00000000 00000000 00000000 00000000  ................
00007ff7`3677ad50  00000000 00000000 00000000 00000000  ................
00007ff7`3677ad60  00000000 00000000 00000000 00000000  ................
```

Note: We see the corruption effect: *dwAllocSize* is no longer 64 (0x40), *bKeep* is no longer 0, and the latter prevents *free* according to the source code.

15.   To catch the moment of corruption, we need to stop debugging the process:

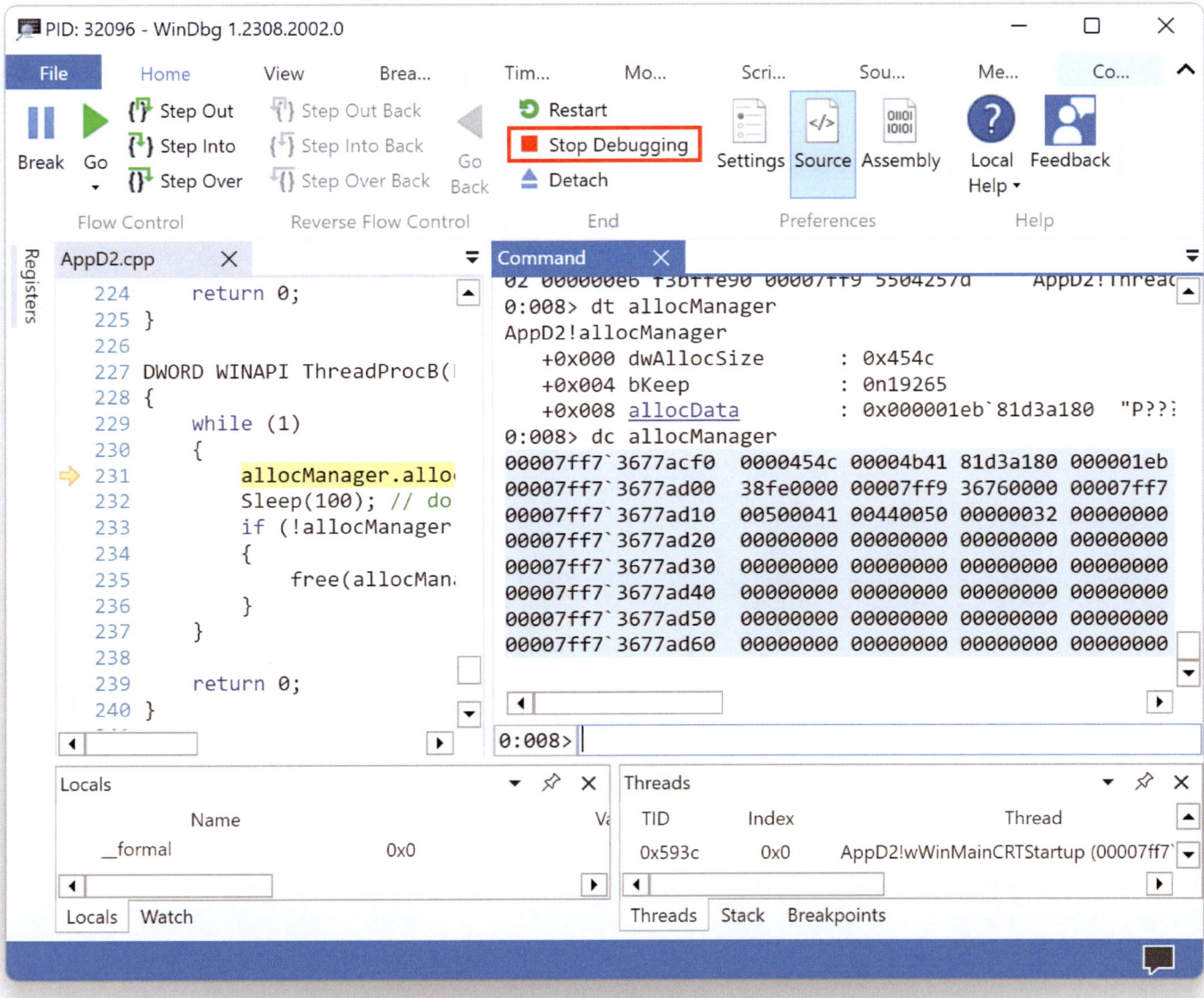

Then we use *File \ Launch executable*, choose *AppD2.exe*, and put a hardware breakpoint (**ba**) on that structure:

```
NatVis script unloaded from 'C:\Program
Files\WindowsApps\Microsoft.WinDbg_1.2308.2002.0_x64__8wekyb3d8bbwe\amd64\Visualizers\atlmfc.na
tvis'
NatVis script unloaded from 'C:\Program
Files\WindowsApps\Microsoft.WinDbg_1.2308.2002.0_x64__8wekyb3d8bbwe\amd64\Visualizers\Objective
C.natvis'
NatVis script unloaded from 'C:\Program
Files\WindowsApps\Microsoft.WinDbg_1.2308.2002.0_x64__8wekyb3d8bbwe\amd64\Visualizers\concurren
cy.natvis'
NatVis script unloaded from 'C:\Program
Files\WindowsApps\Microsoft.WinDbg_1.2308.2002.0_x64__8wekyb3d8bbwe\amd64\Visualizers\cpp_rest.
natvis'
NatVis script unloaded from 'C:\Program
Files\WindowsApps\Microsoft.WinDbg_1.2308.2002.0_x64__8wekyb3d8bbwe\amd64\Visualizers\stl.natvi
s'
```

```
Microsoft (R) Windows Debugger Version 10.0.25921.1001 AMD64
Copyright (c) Microsoft Corporation. All rights reserved.

CommandLine: C:\AWD4\AppD2\x64\Release\AppD2.exe

************* Path validation summary **************
Response                        Time (ms)       Location
Deferred                                        srv*
Symbol search path is: srv*
Executable search path is:
ModLoad: 00007ff7`36760000 00007ff7`36780000   AppD2.exe
ModLoad: 00007ff9`55530000 00007ff9`55747000   ntdll.dll
ModLoad: 00007ff9`55030000 00007ff9`550f4000   C:\WINDOWS\System32\KERNEL32.DLL
ModLoad: 00007ff9`52870000 00007ff9`52c16000   C:\WINDOWS\System32\KERNELBASE.dll
ModLoad: 00007ff9`54130000 00007ff9`542de000   C:\WINDOWS\System32\USER32.dll
ModLoad: 00007ff9`53190000 00007ff9`531b6000   C:\WINDOWS\System32\win32u.dll
ModLoad: 00007ff9`542e0000 00007ff9`54309000   C:\WINDOWS\System32\GDI32.dll
ModLoad: 00007ff9`52c20000 00007ff9`52d38000   C:\WINDOWS\System32\gdi32full.dll
ModLoad: 00007ff9`52f30000 00007ff9`52fca000   C:\WINDOWS\System32\msvcp_win.dll
ModLoad: 00007ff9`53000000 00007ff9`53111000   C:\WINDOWS\System32\ucrtbase.dll
(2c28.74ec): Break instruction exception - code 80000003 (first chance)
ntdll!LdrpDoDebuggerBreak+0x30:
00007ff9`5560b784 int     3
```

```
0:000> dt AppD2!allocManager
   +0x000 dwAllocSize       : 0
   +0x004 bKeep             : 0n0
   +0x008 allocData         : (null)
```

```
0:000> ba w 8 AppD2!allocManager
```

Note: We use 8 to cover 8 affected bytes in the structure. If you get the following error:

```
0:000> ba w 8 AppD2!allocManager
          ^ Unable to set breakpoint error
The system resets thread contexts after the process
breakpoint so hardware breakpoints cannot be set.
Go to the executable's entry point and set it then.
```

```
'ba w 8 AppD2!allocManager'
```

step out a few times (**gu** command) and repeat **ba** command.

Note: to check that the breakpoint was set correctly, use the **bl** command:

```
0:000> bl
     0 e Disable Clear  00007ff7`3677acf0 w 8 0001 (0001)  0:**** AppD2!allocManager
```

16.   Now we resume execution (**g**) and choose *File \ Start* in the *AppD2* menu:

```
0:000> g
ModLoad: 00007ff9`53ef0000 00007ff9`53f21000   C:\WINDOWS\System32\IMM32.DLL
ModLoad: 00007ff9`3b140000 00007ff9`3b15f000   C:\AWD4\AppD2\x64\Release\DllD2.dll
ModLoad: 00007ff9`4f920000 00007ff9`4f9cb000   C:\WINDOWS\system32\uxtheme.dll
ModLoad: 00007ff9`53b60000 00007ff9`53ee9000   C:\WINDOWS\System32\combase.dll
ModLoad: 00007ff9`543d0000 00007ff9`544e7000   C:\WINDOWS\System32\RPCRT4.dll
ModLoad: 00007ff9`54a40000 00007ff9`54b90000   C:\WINDOWS\System32\MSCTF.dll
ModLoad: 00007ff9`55100000 00007ff9`551a7000   C:\WINDOWS\System32\msvcrt.dll
ModLoad: 00007ff9`20a30000 00007ff9`20ae0000   C:\WINDOWS\SYSTEM32\TextShaping.dll
ModLoad: 00007ff9`51860000 00007ff9`51878000   C:\WINDOWS\SYSTEM32\kernel.appcore.dll
ModLoad: 00007ff9`52eb0000 00007ff9`52f2a000   C:\WINDOWS\System32\bcryptPrimitives.dll
clientcore\windows\advcore\ctf\uim\tim.cpp(800)\MSCTF.dll!00007FF954A565D9: (caller: 00007FF954A5720C) LogHr(1)
tid(74ec) 8007029C An assertion failure has occurred.
clientcore\windows\advcore\ctf\uim\tim.cpp(800)\MSCTF.dll!00007FF954A565D9: (caller: 00007FF954A5720C) LogHr(2)
tid(74ec) 8007029C An assertion failure has occurred.
ModLoad: 00007ff9`54e20000 00007ff9`54ec8000   C:\WINDOWS\System32\sechost.dll
ModLoad: 00007ff9`52fd0000 00007ff9`52ff8000   C:\WINDOWS\System32\bcrypt.dll
ModLoad: 00007ff9`54b90000 00007ff9`54c67000   C:\WINDOWS\System32\OLEAUT32.dll
ModLoad: 00007ff9`3fba0000 00007ff9`3fcea000   C:\WINDOWS\SYSTEM32\textinputframework.dll
ModLoad: 00007ff9`2b3e0000 00007ff9`2b449000   C:\WINDOWS\system32\Oleacc.dll
ModLoad: 00007ff9`54510000 00007ff9`545c0000   C:\WINDOWS\System32\clbcatq.dll
ModLoad: 00007ff9`20ae0000 00007ff9`20b2b000   C:\WINDOWS\system32\ApplicationTargetedFeatureDatabase.dll
ModLoad: 00007ff9`47160000 00007ff9`473e5000   C:\Windows\System32\twinapi.appcore.dll
ModLoad: 00007ff9`50f30000 00007ff9`5106e000   C:\Windows\System32\WinTypes.dll
ModLoad: 00007ff9`12ff0000 00007ff9`13435000   C:\Windows\System32\uiautomationcore.dll
ModLoad: 00007ff9`4f470000 00007ff9`4f5a4000   C:\WINDOWS\SYSTEM32\CoreMessaging.dll
ModLoad: 00007ff9`49070000 00007ff9`493dc000   C:\WINDOWS\SYSTEM32\CoreUIComponents.dll
ModLoad: 00007ff9`54310000 00007ff9`543c3000   C:\WINDOWS\System32\advapi32.dll
ModLoad: 00007ff9`51ed0000 00007ff9`51edc000   C:\WINDOWS\SYSTEM32\CRYPTBASE.DLL
ModLoad: 00007ff9`4fb50000 00007ff9`4fb7b000   C:\WINDOWS\system32\dwmapi.dll
ModLoad: 00007ff9`1e070000 00007ff9`1e085000   C:\Windows\System32\threadpoolwinrt.dll
(2c28.6850): C++ EH exception - code e06d7363 (first chance)
(2c28.6850): C++ EH exception - code e06d7363 (first chance)
(2c28.6850): C++ EH exception - code e06d7363 (first chance)
(2c28.6850): C++ EH exception - code e06d7363 (first chance)
(2c28.6850): C++ EH exception - code e06d7363 (first chance)
(2c28.6850): C++ EH exception - code e06d7363 (first chance)
Breakpoint 0 hit
AppD2!StartModeling+0xe:
00007ff7`367614be mov     dword ptr [AppD2!allocManager+0x4 (00007ff7`3677acf4)],0 ds:00007ff7`3677acf4=00000000
```

```
0:000> kL
 # Child-SP          RetAddr               Call Site
00 000000c5`45dffba0 00007ff7`36761341     AppD2!StartModeling+0xe
01 000000c5`45dffbe0 00007ff9`54148241     AppD2!WndProc+0xb1
02 000000c5`45dffca0 00007ff9`54147d01     USER32!UserCallWinProcCheckWow+0x2d1
03 000000c5`45dffe00 00007ff7`36761108     USER32!DispatchMessageWorker+0x1f1
04 000000c5`45dffe80 00007ff7`3676180a     AppD2!wWinMain+0x108
05 (Inline Function) --------`--------     AppD2!invoke_main+0x21
06 000000c5`45dffef0 00007ff9`5504257d     AppD2!__scrt_common_main_seh+0x106
07 000000c5`45dfff30 00007ff9`5558aa58     KERNEL32!BaseThreadInitThunk+0x1d
08 000000c5`45dfff60 00000000`00000000     ntdll!RtlUserThreadStart+0x28
```

```
0:000> dt AppD2!allocManager
   +0x000 dwAllocSize     : 0x40
   +0x004 bKeep           : 0n0
   +0x008 allocData       : (null)
```

Note: the first and the second hits are normal as they are related to structure initialization:

```
0:000> g
Breakpoint 0 hit
AppD2!StartModeling+0x18:
00007ff7`367614c8 mov     qword ptr [rsp+28h],0 ss:000000c5`45dffbc8=0000000080006010
```

```
0:000> kL
# Child-SP          RetAddr               Call Site
00 000000c5`45dffba0 00007ff7`36761341     AppD2!StartModeling+0x18
01 000000c5`45dffbe0 00007ff9`54148241     AppD2!WndProc+0xb1
02 000000c5`45dffca0 00007ff9`54147d01     USER32!UserCallWinProcCheckWow+0x2d1
03 000000c5`45dffe00 00007ff7`36761108     USER32!DispatchMessageWorker+0x1f1
04 000000c5`45dffe80 00007ff7`3676180a     AppD2!wWinMain+0x108
05 (Inline Function) --------`--------     AppD2!invoke_main+0x21
06 000000c5`45dffef0 00007ff9`5504257d     AppD2!__scrt_common_main_seh+0x106
07 000000c5`45dfff30 00007ff9`5558aa58     KERNEL32!BaseThreadInitThunk+0x1d
08 000000c5`45dfff60 00000000`00000000     ntdll!RtlUserThreadStart+0x28
```

```
0:000> dt AppD2!allocManager
   +0x000 dwAllocSize     : 0x454c
   +0x004 bKeep           : 0n0
   +0x008 allocData       : (null)
```

Note: However, we may already see some corruption going on.

17.   The 3rd and the 4th hits show the structure access from another *DllD2* module and thread:

```
0:000> g
(2c28.5fac): Single step exception - code 80000004 (first chance)
First chance exceptions are reported before any exception handling.
This exception may be expected and handled.
DllD2!ThreadProcD+0x25:
00007ff9`3b1410a5 mov     rax,qword ptr [DllD2!lpData (00007ff9`3b15abe0)]
ds:00007ff9`3b15abe0={AppD2!allocManager (00007ff7`3677acf0)}
```

```
0:004> kL
 # Child-SP          RetAddr               Call Site
00 000000c5`463ffaa0 00007ff9`5504257d     DllD2!ThreadProcD+0x25
01 000000c5`463ffad0 00007ff9`5558aa58     KERNEL32!BaseThreadInitThunk+0x1d
02 000000c5`463ffb00 00000000`00000000     ntdll!RtlUserThreadStart+0x28
```

```
0:004> dt AppD2!allocManager
   +0x000 dwAllocSize     : 0x454c
   +0x004 bKeep           : 0n0
   +0x008 allocData       : (null)
```

```
0:004> g
Breakpoint 0 hit
DllD2!ThreadProcD+0x37:
00007ff9`3b1410b7 33c0            xor     eax,eax
```

```
0:004> dt AppD2!allocManager
   +0x000 dwAllocSize    : 0x454c
   +0x004 bKeep          : 0n19265
   +0x008 allocData      : (null)
```

```
0:004> kL
 # Child-SP          RetAddr               Call Site
00 000000c5`463ffaa0 00007ff9`5504257d     DllD2!ThreadProcD+0x37
01 000000c5`463ffad0 00007ff9`5558aa58     KERNEL32!BaseThreadInitThunk+0x1d
02 000000c5`463ffb00 00000000`00000000     ntdll!RtlUserThreadStart+0x28
```

Note: It can also be just one hit with both structure members corrupt.

18.   We can even modify the structure contents (**eq** writes 8 bytes) to eliminate the leak:

```
0:004> eq AppD2!allocManager 40
```

```
0:004> dt AppD2!allocManager
   +0x000 dwAllocSize    : 0x40
   +0x004 bKeep          : 0n0
   +0x008 allocData      : 0x000002b6`1f8a5c00  ".???"
```

Note: If we continue execution (*Detach* button or **.detach** command), we don't see any leaks anymore:

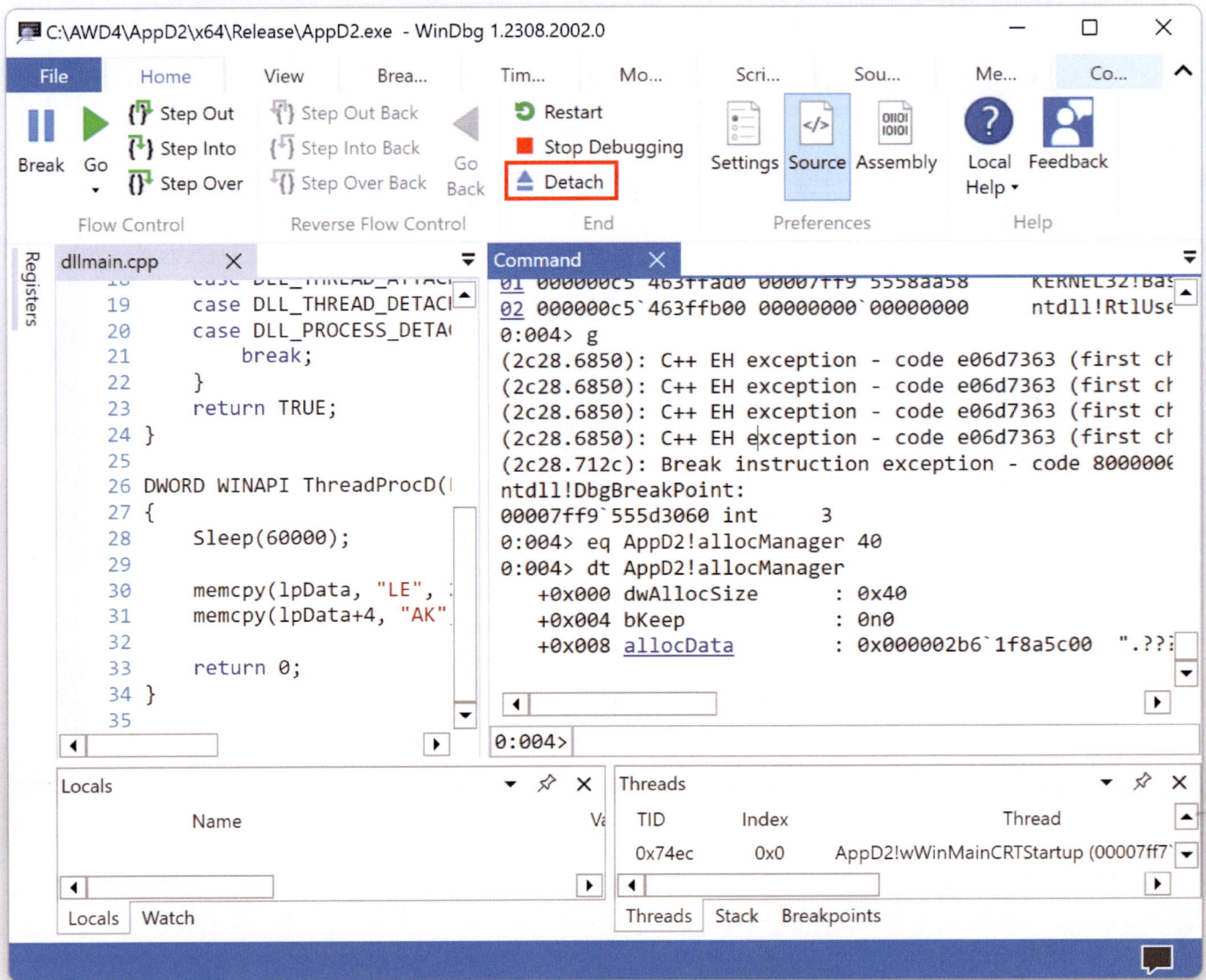

```
0:004> .detach
Detached
```

19.   We can now close the log if we have used the **.detach** command.

```
NoTarget> .logclose
WARNING: The debugger does not have a current process or thread
WARNING: Many commands will not work
Closing open log file C:\AWD4\D2.log
```

Exercise UD3

- **Goal:** Learn how to navigate parameters, static and local variables, and data structures

- **Elementary Diagnostics Patterns:** Crash

- **Memory Analysis Patterns:** Exception Stack Trace; Stack Overflow (User Mode); String Parameter; Module Variable

- **Debugging Implementation Patterns:** Break-in; Scope; Variable Value; Type Structure

- \AWD4\Exercise-UD3.pdf

Goal: Learn how to navigate parameters, static and local variables, and data structures.

Elementary Diagnostics Patterns: Crash.

Memory Analysis Patterns: Exception Stack Trace; Stack Overflow (User Mode); String Parameter; Module Variable.

Debugging Implementation Patterns: Break-in; Scope; Variable Value; Type Structure.

1.   Launch ·\AWD4\AppD3\x64\Release\AppD3.exe executable.

2.   Launch WinDbg. Choose File \ Attach to process and select AppD3.exe.

3.   You get WinDbg attached to AppD3.exe:

```
Microsoft (R) Windows Debugger Version 10.0.25921.1001 AMD64
Copyright (c) Microsoft Corporation. All rights reserved.

*** wait with pending attach

************* Path validation summary **************
Response                        Time (ms)     Location
Deferred                                      srv*
Symbol search path is: srv*
Executable search path is:
ModLoad: 00007ff6`21760000 00007ff6`2178a000   C:\AWD4\AppD3\x64\Release\AppD3.exe
ModLoad: 00007ff9`55530000 00007ff9`55747000   C:\WINDOWS\SYSTEM32\ntdll.dll
ModLoad: 00007ff9`55030000 00007ff9`550f4000   C:\WINDOWS\System32\KERNEL32.DLL
ModLoad: 00007ff9`52870000 00007ff9`52c16000   C:\WINDOWS\System32\KERNELBASE.dll
ModLoad: 00007ff9`4f780000 00007ff9`4f817000   C:\WINDOWS\SYSTEM32\apphelp.dll
ModLoad: 00007ff9`54130000 00007ff9`542de000   C:\WINDOWS\System32\USER32.dll
ModLoad: 00007ff9`53190000 00007ff9`531b6000   C:\WINDOWS\System32\win32u.dll
ModLoad: 00007ff9`542e0000 00007ff9`54309000   C:\WINDOWS\System32\GDI32.dll
ModLoad: 00007ff9`52c20000 00007ff9`52d38000   C:\WINDOWS\System32\gdi32full.dll
ModLoad: 00007ff9`52f30000 00007ff9`52fca000   C:\WINDOWS\System32\msvcp_win.dll
ModLoad: 00007ff9`53000000 00007ff9`53111000   C:\WINDOWS\System32\ucrtbase.dll
ModLoad: 00007ff9`53ef0000 00007ff9`53f21000   C:\WINDOWS\System32\IMM32.DLL
ModLoad: 00007ff9`4f920000 00007ff9`4f9cb000   C:\WINDOWS\system32\uxtheme.dll
ModLoad: 00007ff9`53b60000 00007ff9`53ee9000   C:\WINDOWS\System32\combase.dll
ModLoad: 00007ff9`543d0000 00007ff9`544e7000   C:\WINDOWS\System32\RPCRT4.dll
ModLoad: 00007ff9`54a40000 00007ff9`54b90000   C:\WINDOWS\System32\MSCTF.dll
ModLoad: 00007ff9`55100000 00007ff9`551a7000   C:\WINDOWS\System32\msvcrt.dll
ModLoad: 00007ff9`20a30000 00007ff9`20ae0000   C:\WINDOWS\SYSTEM32\TextShaping.dll
ModLoad: 00007ff9`51860000 00007ff9`51878000   C:\WINDOWS\SYSTEM32\kernel.appcore.dll
ModLoad: 00007ff9`52eb0000 00007ff9`52f2a000   C:\WINDOWS\System32\bcryptPrimitives.dll
ModLoad: 00007ff9`54e20000 00007ff9`54ec8000   C:\WINDOWS\System32\sechost.dll
ModLoad: 00007ff9`52fd0000 00007ff9`52ff8000   C:\WINDOWS\System32\bcrypt.dll
ModLoad: 00007ff9`3fba0000 00007ff9`3fcea000   C:\WINDOWS\SYSTEM32\textinputframework.dll
ModLoad: 00007ff9`54b90000 00007ff9`54c67000   C:\WINDOWS\System32\OLEAUT32.dll
ModLoad: 00007ff9`4f470000 00007ff9`4f5a4000   C:\WINDOWS\SYSTEM32\CoreMessaging.dll
ModLoad: 00007ff9`49070000 00007ff9`493dc000   C:\WINDOWS\SYSTEM32\CoreUIComponents.dll
ModLoad: 00007ff9`50f30000 00007ff9`5106e000   C:\WINDOWS\SYSTEM32\wintypes.dll
ModLoad: 00007ff9`54310000 00007ff9`543c3000   C:\WINDOWS\System32\advapi32.dll
ModLoad: 00007ff9`51ed0000 00007ff9`51edc000   C:\WINDOWS\SYSTEM32\CRYPTBASE.DLL
```

```
ModLoad: 00007ff9`2b3e0000 00007ff9`2b449000   C:\WINDOWS\system32\Oleacc.dll
ModLoad: 00007ff9`54510000 00007ff9`545c0000   C:\WINDOWS\System32\clbcatq.dll
ModLoad: 00007ff9`20ae0000 00007ff9`20b2b000
C:\WINDOWS\system32\ApplicationTargetedFeatureDatabase.dll
ModLoad: 00007ff9`47160000 00007ff9`473e5000   C:\Windows\System32\twinapi.appcore.dll
ModLoad: 00007ff9`12ff0000 00007ff9`13435000   C:\Windows\System32\uiautomationcore.dll
(78dc.88e8): Break instruction exception - code 80000003 (first chance)
ntdll!DbgBreakPoint:
00007ff9`555d3060 int       3
```

4.   Open a log file:

```
0:010> .logopen C:\AWD4\D3.log
Opened log file 'C:\AWD4\D3.log'
```

5.   Continue execution using the **g** command, switch to the *AppD3.exe* process, and choose *File \ Start*. We get
a first chance exception:

```
0:010> g
ModLoad: 00007ff9`4fb50000 00007ff9`4fb7b000   C:\WINDOWS\system32\dwmapi.dll
ModLoad: 00007ff9`1e070000 00007ff9`1e085000   C:\Windows\System32\threadpoolwinrt.dll
(78dc.6314): C++ EH exception - code e06d7363 (first chance)
(78dc.6314): C++ EH exception - code e06d7363 (first chance)
(78dc.6314): C++ EH exception - code e06d7363 (first chance)
(78dc.6314): C++ EH exception - code e06d7363 (first chance)
(78dc.6314): C++ EH exception - code e06d7363 (first chance)
(78dc.6314): C++ EH exception - code e06d7363 (first chance)
(78dc.74c): Stack overflow - code c00000fd (first chance)
First chance exceptions are reported before any exception handling.
This exception may be expected and handled.
AppD3!bar+0x40:
00007ff6`21762470 rep movs byte ptr [rdi],byte ptr [rsi]
```

Note: From the source code, it looks like the problem happened during memory copy:

```
void bar(int param1, LPSTR param2, LPWSTR param3)
{
        wchar_t local[1024] = L"Local wide character array";

        if (param1)
                bar(++param1, param2, param3);
}
```

6.   If we continue execution, we get a second chance exception at the same exception point:

```
0:000> g
(78dc.74c): Stack overflow - code c00000fd (!!! second chance !!!)
AppD3!bar+0x40:
00007ff6`21762470 rep movs byte ptr [rdi],byte ptr [rsi]
```

7.   If we try to see a stack trace, we get only 256 frames for this stack overflow:

```
0:000> k
 # Child-SP          RetAddr           Call Site
00 000000ee`68c03f00 00007ff6`217624b9  AppD3!bar+0x40 [C:\AWD3\AppD3\AppD3\AppD3.cpp @ 347]
01 000000ee`68c04750 00007ff6`217624b9  AppD3!bar+0x89 [C:\AWD3\AppD3\AppD3\AppD3.cpp @ 351]
```

```
02 000000ee`68c04fa0 00007ff6`217624b9    AppD3!bar+0x89 [C:\AWD3\AppD3\AppD3\AppD3.cpp @ 351]
03 000000ee`68c057f0 00007ff6`217624b9    AppD3!bar+0x89 [C:\AWD3\AppD3\AppD3\AppD3.cpp @ 351]
04 000000ee`68c06040 00007ff6`217624b9    AppD3!bar+0x89 [C:\AWD3\AppD3\AppD3\AppD3.cpp @ 351]
05 000000ee`68c06890 00007ff6`217624b9    AppD3!bar+0x89 [C:\AWD3\AppD3\AppD3\AppD3.cpp @ 351]
06 000000ee`68c070e0 00007ff6`217624b9    AppD3!bar+0x89 [C:\AWD3\AppD3\AppD3\AppD3.cpp @ 351]
07 000000ee`68c07930 00007ff6`217624b9    AppD3!bar+0x89 [C:\AWD3\AppD3\AppD3\AppD3.cpp @ 351]
08 000000ee`68c08180 00007ff6`217624b9    AppD3!bar+0x89 [C:\AWD3\AppD3\AppD3\AppD3.cpp @ 351]
09 000000ee`68c089d0 00007ff6`217624b9    AppD3!bar+0x89 [C:\AWD3\AppD3\AppD3\AppD3.cpp @ 351]
0a 000000ee`68c09220 00007ff6`217624b9    AppD3!bar+0x89 [C:\AWD3\AppD3\AppD3\AppD3.cpp @ 351]
0b 000000ee`68c09a70 00007ff6`217624b9    AppD3!bar+0x89 [C:\AWD3\AppD3\AppD3\AppD3.cpp @ 351]
0c 000000ee`68c0a2c0 00007ff6`217624b9    AppD3!bar+0x89 [C:\AWD3\AppD3\AppD3\AppD3.cpp @ 351]
0d 000000ee`68c0ab10 00007ff6`217624b9    AppD3!bar+0x89 [C:\AWD3\AppD3\AppD3\AppD3.cpp @ 351]
0e 000000ee`68c0b360 00007ff6`217624b9    AppD3!bar+0x89 [C:\AWD3\AppD3\AppD3\AppD3.cpp @ 351]
0f 000000ee`68c0bbb0 00007ff6`217624b9    AppD3!bar+0x89 [C:\AWD3\AppD3\AppD3\AppD3.cpp @ 351]
10 000000ee`68c0c400 00007ff6`217624b9    AppD3!bar+0x89 [C:\AWD3\AppD3\AppD3\AppD3.cpp @ 351]
[...]
f0 000000ee`68c80a00 00007ff6`217624b9    AppD3!bar+0x89 [C:\AWD3\AppD3\AppD3\AppD3.cpp @ 351]
f1 000000ee`68c81250 00007ff6`217624b9    AppD3!bar+0x89 [C:\AWD3\AppD3\AppD3\AppD3.cpp @ 351]
f2 000000ee`68c81aa0 00007ff6`217624b9    AppD3!bar+0x89 [C:\AWD3\AppD3\AppD3\AppD3.cpp @ 351]
f3 000000ee`68c822f0 00007ff6`217624b9    AppD3!bar+0x89 [C:\AWD3\AppD3\AppD3\AppD3.cpp @ 351]
f4 000000ee`68c82b40 00007ff6`217624b9    AppD3!bar+0x89 [C:\AWD3\AppD3\AppD3\AppD3.cpp @ 351]
f5 000000ee`68c83390 00007ff6`217624b9    AppD3!bar+0x89 [C:\AWD3\AppD3\AppD3\AppD3.cpp @ 351]
f6 000000ee`68c83be0 00007ff6`217624b9    AppD3!bar+0x89 [C:\AWD3\AppD3\AppD3\AppD3.cpp @ 351]
f7 000000ee`68c84430 00007ff6`217624b9    AppD3!bar+0x89 [C:\AWD3\AppD3\AppD3\AppD3.cpp @ 351]
f8 000000ee`68c84c80 00007ff6`217624b9    AppD3!bar+0x89 [C:\AWD3\AppD3\AppD3\AppD3.cpp @ 351]
f9 000000ee`68c854d0 00007ff6`217624b9    AppD3!bar+0x89 [C:\AWD3\AppD3\AppD3\AppD3.cpp @ 351]
fa 000000ee`68c85d20 00007ff6`217624b9    AppD3!bar+0x89 [C:\AWD3\AppD3\AppD3\AppD3.cpp @ 351]
fb 000000ee`68c86570 00007ff6`217624b9    AppD3!bar+0x89 [C:\AWD3\AppD3\AppD3\AppD3.cpp @ 351]
fc 000000ee`68c86dc0 00007ff6`217624b9    AppD3!bar+0x89 [C:\AWD3\AppD3\AppD3\AppD3.cpp @ 351]
fd 000000ee`68c87610 00007ff6`217624b9    AppD3!bar+0x89 [C:\AWD3\AppD3\AppD3\AppD3.cpp @ 351]
fe 000000ee`68c87e60 00007ff6`217624b9    AppD3!bar+0x89 [C:\AWD3\AppD3\AppD3\AppD3.cpp @ 351]
ff 000000ee`68c886b0 00007ff6`217624b9    AppD3!bar+0x89 [C:\AWD3\AppD3\AppD3\AppD3.cpp @ 351]
```

Note: The source code path in the output of the **k** command is the original path where the app was built; in our case, it was *C:\AWD3* where we modified and recompiled source code from the previous edition, not the current source code search location, which is *C:\AWD4* or your own location if you downloaded project files into a different folder.

8.   Let's increase the number of shown frames:

```
0:000> .kframes 0xfff
Default stack trace depth is 0n4095 frames
```

```
0:000> k
 # Child-SP          RetAddr               Call Site
00 000000ee`68c03f00 00007ff6`217624b9    AppD3!bar+0x40 [C:\AWD3\AppD3\AppD3\AppD3.cpp @ 347]
01 000000ee`68c04750 00007ff6`217624b9    AppD3!bar+0x89 [C:\AWD3\AppD3\AppD3\AppD3.cpp @ 351]
02 000000ee`68c04fa0 00007ff6`217624b9    AppD3!bar+0x89 [C:\AWD3\AppD3\AppD3\AppD3.cpp @ 351]
03 000000ee`68c057f0 00007ff6`217624b9    AppD3!bar+0x89 [C:\AWD3\AppD3\AppD3\AppD3.cpp @ 351]
04 000000ee`68c06040 00007ff6`217624b9    AppD3!bar+0x89 [C:\AWD3\AppD3\AppD3\AppD3.cpp @ 351]
05 000000ee`68c06890 00007ff6`217624b9    AppD3!bar+0x89 [C:\AWD3\AppD3\AppD3\AppD3.cpp @ 351]
06 000000ee`68c070e0 00007ff6`217624b9    AppD3!bar+0x89 [C:\AWD3\AppD3\AppD3\AppD3.cpp @ 351]
07 000000ee`68c07930 00007ff6`217624b9    AppD3!bar+0x89 [C:\AWD3\AppD3\AppD3\AppD3.cpp @ 351]
08 000000ee`68c08180 00007ff6`217624b9    AppD3!bar+0x89 [C:\AWD3\AppD3\AppD3\AppD3.cpp @ 351]
09 000000ee`68c089d0 00007ff6`217624b9    AppD3!bar+0x89 [C:\AWD3\AppD3\AppD3\AppD3.cpp @ 351]
0a 000000ee`68c09220 00007ff6`217624b9    AppD3!bar+0x89 [C:\AWD3\AppD3\AppD3\AppD3.cpp @ 351]
0b 000000ee`68c09a70 00007ff6`217624b9    AppD3!bar+0x89 [C:\AWD3\AppD3\AppD3\AppD3.cpp @ 351]
0c 000000ee`68c0a2c0 00007ff6`217624b9    AppD3!bar+0x89 [C:\AWD3\AppD3\AppD3\AppD3.cpp @ 351]
0d 000000ee`68c0ab10 00007ff6`217624b9    AppD3!bar+0x89 [C:\AWD3\AppD3\AppD3\AppD3.cpp @ 351]
0e 000000ee`68c0b360 00007ff6`217624b9    AppD3!bar+0x89 [C:\AWD3\AppD3\AppD3\AppD3.cpp @ 351]
0f 000000ee`68c0bbb0 00007ff6`217624b9    AppD3!bar+0x89 [C:\AWD3\AppD3\AppD3\AppD3.cpp @ 351]
10 000000ee`68c0c400 00007ff6`217624b9    AppD3!bar+0x89 [C:\AWD3\AppD3\AppD3\AppD3.cpp @ 351]
[...]
1d0 000000ee`68cf5000 00007ff6`217624b9    AppD3!bar+0x89 [C:\AWD3\AppD3\AppD3\AppD3.cpp @ 351]
```

```
1d1 000000ee`68cf5850 00007ff6`217624b9          AppD3!bar+0x89 [C:\AWD3\AppD3\AppD3\AppD3.cpp @ 351]
1d2 000000ee`68cf60a0 00007ff6`217624b9          AppD3!bar+0x89 [C:\AWD3\AppD3\AppD3\AppD3.cpp @ 351]
1d3 000000ee`68cf68f0 00007ff6`217624b9          AppD3!bar+0x89 [C:\AWD3\AppD3\AppD3\AppD3.cpp @ 351]
1d4 000000ee`68cf7140 00007ff6`217624b9          AppD3!bar+0x89 [C:\AWD3\AppD3\AppD3\AppD3.cpp @ 351]
1d5 000000ee`68cf7990 00007ff6`217624b9          AppD3!bar+0x89 [C:\AWD3\AppD3\AppD3\AppD3.cpp @ 351]
1d6 000000ee`68cf81e0 00007ff6`217624b9          AppD3!bar+0x89 [C:\AWD3\AppD3\AppD3\AppD3.cpp @ 351]
1d7 000000ee`68cf8a30 00007ff6`217624b9          AppD3!bar+0x89 [C:\AWD3\AppD3\AppD3\AppD3.cpp @ 351]
1d8 000000ee`68cf9280 00007ff6`217624b9          AppD3!bar+0x89 [C:\AWD3\AppD3\AppD3\AppD3.cpp @ 351]
1d9 000000ee`68cf9ad0 00007ff6`217624b9          AppD3!bar+0x89 [C:\AWD3\AppD3\AppD3\AppD3.cpp @ 351]
1da 000000ee`68cfa320 00007ff6`217624b9          AppD3!bar+0x89 [C:\AWD3\AppD3\AppD3\AppD3.cpp @ 351]
1db 000000ee`68cfab70 00007ff6`217624b9          AppD3!bar+0x89 [C:\AWD3\AppD3\AppD3\AppD3.cpp @ 351]
1dc 000000ee`68cfb3c0 00007ff6`217624b9          AppD3!bar+0x89 [C:\AWD3\AppD3\AppD3\AppD3.cpp @ 351]
1dd 000000ee`68cfbc10 00007ff6`217624b9          AppD3!bar+0x89 [C:\AWD3\AppD3\AppD3\AppD3.cpp @ 351]
1de 000000ee`68cfc460 00007ff6`217624b9          AppD3!bar+0x89 [C:\AWD3\AppD3\AppD3\AppD3.cpp @ 351]
1df 000000ee`68cfccb0 00007ff6`217624b9          AppD3!bar+0x89 [C:\AWD3\AppD3\AppD3\AppD3.cpp @ 351]
1e0 000000ee`68cfd500 00007ff6`217624b9          AppD3!bar+0x89 [C:\AWD3\AppD3\AppD3\AppD3.cpp @ 351]
1e1 000000ee`68cfdd50 00007ff6`217624b9          AppD3!bar+0x89 [C:\AWD3\AppD3\AppD3\AppD3.cpp @ 351]
1e2 000000ee`68cfe5a0 00007ff6`217624b9          AppD3!bar+0x89 [C:\AWD3\AppD3\AppD3\AppD3.cpp @ 351]
1e3 000000ee`68cfedf0 00007ff6`2176241d          AppD3!bar+0x89 [C:\AWD3\AppD3\AppD3\AppD3.cpp @ 351]
1e4 000000ee`68cff640 00007ff6`21762371          AppD3!foo+0x5d [C:\AWD3\AppD3\AppD3\AppD3.cpp @ 343]
1e5 000000ee`68cff680 00007ff6`21761851          AppD3!StartModeling+0x191 [C:\AWD3\AppD3\AppD3\AppD3.cpp @
332]
1e6 000000ee`68cffa30 00007ff9`54148241          AppD3!WndProc+0xb1 [C:\AWD3\AppD3\AppD3\AppD3.cpp @ 153]
1e7 000000ee`68cffaf0 00007ff9`54147d01          USER32!UserCallWinProcCheckWow+0x2d1
1e8 000000ee`68cffc50 00007ff6`21761620          USER32!DispatchMessageWorker+0x1f1
1e9 000000ee`68cffcd0 00007ff6`21766552          AppD3!wWinMain+0xd0 [C:\AWD3\AppD3\AppD3\AppD3.cpp @ 64]
1ea (Inline Function) --------`--------          AppD3!invoke_main+0x21
[d:\a01\_work\43\s\src\vctools\crt\vcstartup\src\startup\exe_common.inl @ 118]
1eb 000000ee`68cffd40 00007ff9`5504257d          AppD3!__scrt_common_main_seh+0x106
[d:\a01\_work\43\s\src\vctools\crt\vcstartup\src\startup\exe_common.inl @ 288]
1ec 000000ee`68cffd80 00007ff9`5558aa58          KERNEL32!BaseThreadInitThunk+0x1d
1ed 000000ee`68cffdb0 00000000`00000000          ntdll!RtlUserThreadStart+0x28
```

9.   Since our goal is data navigation, we switch into each frame one by one and inspect data there. Let's start with frame **1e3**:

```
0:000> .frame 1e3
1e3 000000ee`68cfedf0 00007ff6`2176241d          AppD3!bar+0x89 [C:\AWD3\AppD3\AppD3\AppD3.cpp @ 351]
```

```
0:000> dv /i /V
prv param  000000ee`68cff640 @rsp+0x0850          param1 = 0n2
prv param  000000ee`68cff648 @rsp+0x0858          param2 = 0x00007ff6`2177d9d8 "Hello World!"
prv param  000000ee`68cff650 @rsp+0x0860          param3 = 0x00007ff6`2177d9e8 "Hello World Wide!"
prv local  000000ee`68cfee10 @rsp+0x0020           local = wchar_t [1024] "Local wide character array"
```

Notice the distance between the *param3* and the *local* variable. This is because of the large local array, and its space was allocated on stack by the **sub** instruction. Also, despite parameters being passed by **ecx**, **rdx**, and **r8** registers (the first was passed by 32-bit **ecx** and not by 64-bit **rcx** because it is a 32-bit **int** parameter), they were saved on the stack, and this is why we are able to get them:

```
0:000> uf bar
AppD3!bar [C:\AWD3\AppD3\AppD3\AppD3.cpp @ 346]:
  346 00007ff6`21762430 mov     qword ptr [rsp+18h],r8
  346 00007ff6`21762435 mov     qword ptr [rsp+10h],rdx
  346 00007ff6`2176243a mov     dword ptr [rsp+8],ecx
  346 00007ff6`2176243e push    rsi
  346 00007ff6`2176243f push    rdi
  346 00007ff6`21762440 sub     rsp,838h
  346 00007ff6`21762447 mov     rax,qword ptr [AppD3!__security_cookie (00007ff6`21781008)]
  346 00007ff6`2176244e xor     rax,rsp
  346 00007ff6`21762451 mov     qword ptr [rsp+820h],rax
```

```
347 00007ff6`21762459 lea      rax,[rsp+20h]
347 00007ff6`2176245e lea      rcx,[AppD3!std::piecewise_construct+0x5a (00007ff6`2177da40)]
347 00007ff6`21762465 mov      rdi,rax
347 00007ff6`21762468 mov      rsi,rcx
347 00007ff6`2176246b mov      ecx,36h
347 00007ff6`21762470 rep movs byte ptr [rdi],byte ptr [rsi]
347 00007ff6`21762472 lea      rax,[rsp+56h]
347 00007ff6`21762477 mov      rdi,rax
347 00007ff6`2176247a xor      eax,eax
347 00007ff6`2176247c mov      ecx,7CAh
347 00007ff6`21762481 rep stos byte ptr [rdi]
349 00007ff6`21762483 cmp      dword ptr [rsp+850h],0
349 00007ff6`2176248b je       AppD3!bar+0x89 (00007ff6`217624b9)  Branch

AppD3!bar+0x5d [C:\AWD3\AppD3\AppD3\AppD3.cpp @ 350]:
  350 00007ff6`2176248d mov      eax,dword ptr [rsp+850h]
  350 00007ff6`21762494 inc      eax
  350 00007ff6`21762496 mov      dword ptr [rsp+850h],eax
  350 00007ff6`2176249d mov      r8,qword ptr [rsp+860h]
  350 00007ff6`217624a5 mov      rdx,qword ptr [rsp+858h]
  350 00007ff6`217624ad mov      ecx,dword ptr [rsp+850h]
  350 00007ff6`217624b4 call     AppD3!bar (00007ff6`21762430)

AppD3!bar+0x89 [C:\AWD3\AppD3\AppD3\AppD3.cpp @ 351]:
  351 00007ff6`217624b9 mov      rcx,qword ptr [rsp+820h]
  351 00007ff6`217624c1 xor      rcx,rsp
  351 00007ff6`217624c4 call     AppD3!__security_check_cookie (00007ff6`21766080)
  351 00007ff6`217624c9 add      rsp,838h
  351 00007ff6`217624d0 pop      rdi
  351 00007ff6`217624d1 pop      rsi
  351 00007ff6`217624d2 ret
```

10.   Let's look at three variables:

```
prv param  000000ee`68cff640 @rsp+0x0850      param1 = 0n2
prv param  000000ee`68cff648 @rsp+0x0858      param2 = 0x00007ff6`2177d9d8 "Hello World!"
prv param  000000ee`68cff650 @rsp+0x0860      param3 = 0x00007ff6`2177d9e8 "Hello World Wide!"
```

Green numbers are the stack region addresses where they are located. The first one is an integer and can be directly inspected by the simple data dumping command **dd**:

```
0:000> dd param1 L1
000000ee`68cff640  00000002
```

```
0:000> dd 000000ee`68cff640 L1
000000ee`68cff640  00000002
```

```
0:000> dd @rsp+0x0850 L1
000000ee`68c04750  000001e4
```

Notice that we cannot use registers such as **rsp** as they are from the current exception frame 0 and have never been saved. We can take **rsp** from stack trace, though:

```
#   Child-SP          RetAddr           Call Site
...
1e3 000000ee`68cfedf0 00007ff6`2176241d AppD3!bar+0x89 [C:\AWD3\AppD3\AppD3\AppD3.cpp @ 351]
1e4 000000ee`68cff640 00007ff6`21762371 AppD3!foo+0x5d [C:\AWD3\AppD3\AppD3\AppD3.cpp @ 343]
...
```

```
0:000> dd 000000ee`68cfedf0+0x0850 L1
000000ee`68cff640  00000002
```

11.   For **param2** and **param3**, the stack region contains pointer values. We can use character dumping commands for ASCII and UNICODE strings (**da** and **du**):

```
0:000> dq param2 L1
000000ee`68cff648  00007ff6`2177d9d8

0:000> dq param3 L1
000000ee`68cff650  00007ff6`2177d9e8

0:000> dc 00007ff6`2177d9d8
00007ff6`2177d9d8  6c6c6548 6f57206f 21646c72 00000000  Hello World!....
00007ff6`2177d9e8  00650048 006c006c 0020006f 006f0057  H.e.l.l.o. .W.o.
00007ff6`2177d9f8  006c0072 00200064 00690057 00650064  r.l.d. .W.i.d.e.
00007ff6`2177da08  00000021 00656e6f 006f7774 65726874  !...one.two.thre
00007ff6`2177da18  00000065 00656e6f 0079004d 00530057  e...one.M.y.W.S.
00007ff6`2177da28  00720074 006e0069 00000067 006f7774  t.r.i.n.g...two.
00007ff6`2177da38  65726874 00000065 006f004c 00610063  three...L.o.c.a.
00007ff6`2177da48  0020006c 00690077 00650064 00630020  l. .w.i.d.e. .c.

0:000> da 00007ff6`2177d9d8
00007ff6`2177d9d8  "Hello World!"

0:000> dc 00007ff6`2177d9e8
00007ff6`2177d9e8  00650048 006c006c 0020006f 006f0057  H.e.l.l.o. .W.o.
00007ff6`2177d9f8  006c0072 00200064 00690057 00650064  r.l.d. .W.i.d.e.
00007ff6`2177da08  00000021 00656e6f 006f7774 65726874  !...one.two.thre
00007ff6`2177da18  00000065 00656e6f 0079004d 00530057  e...one.M.y.W.S.
00007ff6`2177da28  00720074 006e0069 00000067 006f7774  t.r.i.n.g...two.
00007ff6`2177da38  65726874 00000065 006f004c 00610063  three...L.o.c.a.
00007ff6`2177da48  0020006c 00690077 00650064 00630020  l. .w.i.d.e. .c.
00007ff6`2177da58  00610068 00610072 00740063 00720065  h.a.r.a.c.t.e.r.

0:000> du 00007ff6`2177d9e8
00007ff6`2177d9e8  "Hello World Wide!"
```

Note: Here, we can also use dumping commands for pointers, such as **dpa** and **dpu**:

```
0:000> dpa param2 L1
000000ee`68cff648  00007ff6`2177d9d8 "Hello World!"

0:000> dpu param3 L1
000000ee`68cff650  00007ff6`2177d9e8 "Hello World Wide!"
```

Note: We can also use a C++ evaluation operator **??** and **dx** command. The latter displays a C++ expression using the NatVis extension model:

```
0:000> ?? param1
int 0n2

0:000> ?? param2
char * 0x00007ff6`2177d9d8
 "Hello World!"
```

```
0:000> ?? param3
wchar_t * 0x00007ff6`2177d9e8
 "Hello World Wide!"
```

```
0:000> ?? local
wchar_t [1024] 0x000000ee`68cfee10
0x4c 'L'
```

```
0:000> dx param1
param1            : 2 [Type: int]
```

```
0:000> dx param2
param2                   : 0x7ff62177d9d8 : "Hello World!" [Type: char *]
    72 'H' [Type: char]
```

```
0:000> dx param3
param3                   : 0x7ff62177d9e8 : "Hello World Wide!" [Type: wchar_t *]
    72 'H' [Type: wchar_t]
```

```
0:000> dx local
local                    : "Local wide character array" [Type: wchar_t [1024]]
```

12.   Let's now move to the next frame **1e4**:

```
0:000> .frame 1e4
1e4 000000ee`68cff640 00007ff6`21762371    AppD3!foo+0x5d [C:\AWD3\AppD3\AppD3\AppD3.cpp @ 343]
```

The associated source code:

```
void foo(MYSTRUCT& refStruct, MYSTRUCT * pStruct, const MYCLASS& refClass, MYCLASS * pClass,
MYSUBCLASS& refSubClass, MYSUBCLASS * pSubClass)
{
        LPSTR lpString = pClass->getData().lpString;
        LPWSTR lpwString = pSubClass->getData().lpwString;

        bar(1, lpString, lpwString);
}
```

```
0:000> dv /i /V
prv param  000000ee`68cff680 @rsp+0x0040            refStruct = 0x000000ee`68cff740
prv param  000000ee`68cff688 @rsp+0x0048              pStruct = 0x00000225`22ab0e30
prv param  000000ee`68cff690 @rsp+0x0050             refClass = 0x000000ee`68cff710
prv param  000000ee`68cff698 @rsp+0x0058               pClass = 0x00000225`22aadd10
prv param  000000ee`68cff6a0 @rsp+0x0060          refSubClass = 0x000000ee`68cff720
prv param  000000ee`68cff6a8 @rsp+0x0068            pSubClass = 0x00000225`22aad810
prv local  000000ee`68cff660 @rsp+0x0020            lpwString = 0x00007ff6`2177d9e8 "Hello World Wide!"
prv local  000000ee`68cff668 @rsp+0x0028             lpString = 0x00007ff6`2177d9d8 "Hello World!"
```

Note: We are interested in 6 parameters, either references or pointers to structures and C++ classes. Remember that in C++, a structure is the same as a class regarding its data layout. Also, even if a variable is passed as a reference, it is internally passed as a pointer:

```
0:000> ?? refStruct
struct MyStruct * 0x000000ee`68cff740
    +0x000 lpString          : 0x00007ff6`2177d9d8  "Hello World!"
    +0x008 lpwString         : 0x00007ff6`2177d9e8  "Hello World Wide!"
    +0x010 dwArray           : [10] 0
    +0x038 pdwArray          : [10] 0x00000225`22ab1660  -> 0
```

```
    +0x088 ppdwArray        : [10] 0x00000225`22a9ec10   -> 0x00000225`22ab16a0   -> 0
    +0x0d8 dwArray2         : [10] [10] 0
    +0x268 pSubStruct       : 0x000000ee`68cff9b0 MySubStruct
    +0x270 subStruct        : MySubStruct
    +0x2c8 pList            : 0x00000225`22aade50 MyDList
```

```
0:000> dx refStruct
refStruct                       [Type: MyStruct]
    [+0x000] lpString          : 0x7ff62177d9d8 : "Hello World!" [Type: char *]
    [+0x008] lpwString         : 0x7ff62177d9e8 : "Hello World Wide!" [Type: wchar_t *]
    [+0x010] dwArray           [Type: unsigned long [10]]
    [+0x038] pdwArray          [Type: unsigned long * [10]]
    [+0x088] ppdwArray         [Type: unsigned long * * [10]]
    [+0x0d8] dwArray2          [Type: unsigned long [10][10]]
    [+0x268] pSubStruct        : 0xee68cff9b0 [Type: MySubStruct *]
    [+0x270] subStruct         [Type: MySubStruct]
    [+0x2c8] pList             : 0x22522aade50 [Type: MyDList *]
```

```
0:000> ?? pStruct
struct MyStruct * 0x00000225`22ab0e30
    +0x000 lpString         : 0x00007ff6`2177d9d8  "Hello World!"
    +0x008 lpwString        : 0x00007ff6`2177d9e8  "Hello World Wide!"
    +0x010 dwArray          : [10] 0
    +0x038 pdwArray         : [10] 0x00000225`22ab1b90   -> 0
    +0x088 ppdwArray        : [10] 0x00000225`22a9ef70   -> 0x00000225`22ab2070   -> 0
    +0x0d8 dwArray2         : [10] [10] 0
    +0x268 pSubStruct       : 0x00000225`22ab10a0 MySubStruct
    +0x270 subStruct        : MySubStruct
    +0x2c8 pList            : 0x00000225`22aad870 MyDList
```

```
0:000> dx pStruct
pStruct                         : 0x22522ab0e30 [Type: MyStruct *]
    [+0x000] lpString          : 0x7ff62177d9d8 : "Hello World!" [Type: char *]
    [+0x008] lpwString         : 0x7ff62177d9e8 : "Hello World Wide!" [Type: wchar_t *]
    [+0x010] dwArray           [Type: unsigned long [10]]
    [+0x038] pdwArray          [Type: unsigned long * [10]]
    [+0x088] ppdwArray         [Type: unsigned long * * [10]]
    [+0x0d8] dwArray2          [Type: unsigned long [10][10]]
    [+0x268] pSubStruct        : 0x22522ab10a0 [Type: MySubStruct *]
    [+0x270] subStruct         [Type: MySubStruct]
    [+0x2c8] pList             : 0x22522aad870 [Type: MyDList *]
```

The associated source code:

```
typedef struct MyStruct
{
    LPSTR lpString;
    LPWSTR lpwString;
    DWORD dwArray[10];
    DWORD *pdwArray[10];
    DWORD **ppdwArray[10];
    DWORD dwArray2[10][10];
    MYSUBSTRUCT *pSubStruct;
    MYSUBSTRUCT subStruct;
    PMYDLIST pList;
} MYSTRUCT;
```

```
0:000> ?? refClass
class MYCLASS * 0x000000f9`6ef0f540
```

```
    +0x000 __VFN_table : 0x00007ff7`a13cdab8
    +0x008 m_refMyStruct   : 0x000000f9`6ef0f570 MyStruct

0:000> dx refClass
refClass          [Type: MYCLASS (derived from MYCLASS)]
    [+0x008] m_refMyStruct     : 0xf96ef0f570 [Type: MyStruct &]

0:000> ?? pClass
class MYCLASS * 0x00000258`c2cbaaf0
    +0x000 __VFN_table : 0x00007ff7`a13cdab8
    +0x008 m_refMyStruct   : 0x00000258`c2cc2ec0 MyStruct

0:000> dx pClass
pClass                   : 0x258c2cbaaf0 [Type: MYCLASS *]
    [+0x008] m_refMyStruct     : 0x258c2cc2ec0 [Type: MyStruct &]
```

The associated source code:

```
class MYCLASS
{
public:
      MYCLASS(MYSTRUCT& _refMyStruct) : m_refMyStruct(_refMyStruct) {}

      virtual ~MYCLASS() {}
      virtual MYSTRUCT& getData() { return m_refMyStruct; }

private:
      MYSTRUCT& m_refMyStruct;
};
```

```
0:000> ?? refSubClass
class MYSUBCLASS * 0x000000ee`68cff720
    +0x000 __VFN_table : 0x00007ff6`2177daa0
    +0x008 m_refMyStruct   : 0x000000ee`68cff740 MyStruct
    +0x010 m_pszName       : 0x00007ff6`2177d9c8  "Derived Class"

0:000> dx refSubClass
refSubClass             [Type: MYSUBCLASS]
    [+0x008] m_refMyStruct     : 0xee68cff740 [Type: MyStruct &]
    [+0x010] m_pszName         : 0x7ff62177d9c8 : "Derived Class" [Type: char *]

0:000> ?? pSubClass
class MYSUBCLASS * 0x00000225`22aad810
    +0x000 __VFN_table : 0x00007ff6`2177daa0
    +0x008 m_refMyStruct   : 0x00000225`22ab0e30 MyStruct
    +0x010 m_pszName       : 0x00007ff6`2177d9c8  "Derived Class"

0:000> dx pSubClass
pSubClass                : 0x22522aad810 [Type: MYSUBCLASS *]
    [+0x008] m_refMyStruct     : 0x22522ab0e30 [Type: MyStruct &]
    [+0x010] m_pszName         : 0x7ff62177d9c8 : "Derived Class" [Type: char *]
```

The associated source code:

```
class MYSUBCLASS : public MYCLASS
{
public:
```

```
        MYSUBCLASS(MYSTRUCT& _refMyStruct) : MYCLASS(_refMyStruct) { m_pszName = "Derived
Class"; }

private:
        const char *m_pszName;
};
```

13.   We can also check any member of a structure or a class (you need to use -> for **??** and . for **dx**):

```
0:000> ?? refStruct->pSubStruct
struct MySubStruct * 0x000000ee`68cff9b0
   +0x000 iVec               : std::vector<int,std::allocator<int> >
   +0x018 wStr               :
std::basic_string<wchar_t,std::char_traits<wchar_t>,std::allocator<wchar_t> >
   +0x038 sLst               :
std::list<std::basic_string<char,std::char_traits<char>,std::allocator<char>
>,std::allocator<std::basic_string<char,std::char_traits<char>,std::allocator<char> > > >
   +0x048 isMap              :
std::map<int,std::basic_string<char,std::char_traits<char>,std::allocator<char>
>,std::less<int>,std::allocator<std::pair<int const
,std::basic_string<char,std::char_traits<char>,std::allocator<char> > > > >
```

```
0:000> dx refStruct.pSubStruct
refStruct.pSubStruct                     : 0xee68cff9b0 [Type: MySubStruct *]
    [+0x000] iVec            : { size=3 } [Type: std::vector<int,std::allocator<int> >]
    [+0x018] wStr            : "MyWString" [Type:
std::basic_string<wchar_t,std::char_traits<wchar_t>,std::allocator<wchar_t> >]
    [+0x038] sLst            : { size=0x3 } [Type:
std::list<std::basic_string<char,std::char_traits<char>,std::allocator<char>
>,std::allocator<std::basic_string<char,std::char_traits<char>,std::allocator<char> > > >]
    [+0x048] isMap           : { size=0x3 } [Type:
std::map<int,std::basic_string<char,std::char_traits<char>,std::allocator<char>
>,std::less<int>,std::allocator<std::pair<int const
,std::basic_string<char,std::char_traits<char>,std::allocator<char> > > > >]
```

The associated source code:

```
typedef struct MySubStruct
{
        vector<int> iVec;
        wstring wStr;
        list<string> sLst;
        map<int, string> isMap;
} MYSUBSTRUCT;
```

```
0:000> ?? refStruct->pList
struct MyDList * 0x00000225`22aade50
   +0x000 data               : 1.1000000000000000888
   +0x008 pNext              : 0x00000225`22aadc30 MyDList
   +0x010 pPrev              : (null)
```

```
0:000> dx refStruct.pList
refStruct.pList                 : 0x22522aade50 [Type: MyDList *]
    [+0x000] data            : 1.100000 [Type: double]
    [+0x008] pNext           : 0x22522aadc30 [Type: MyDList *]
    [+0x010] pPrev           : 0x0 [Type: MyDList *]
```

The associated source code:

```
typedef struct MyDList
{
        double data;
        struct MyDList *pNext;
        struct MyDList *pPrev;
} MYDLIST, *PMYDLIST;
```

```
0:000> ?? refClass->m_refMyStruct
struct MyStruct * 0x000000ee`68cff740
   +0x000 lpString         : 0x00007ff6`2177d9d8  "Hello World!"
   +0x008 lpwString        : 0x00007ff6`2177d9e8  "Hello World Wide!"
   +0x010 dwArray          : [10] 0
   +0x038 pdwArray         : [10] 0x00000225`22ab1660  -> 0
   +0x088 ppdwArray        : [10] 0x00000225`22a9ec10  -> 0x00000225`22ab16a0  -> 0
   +0x0d8 dwArray2         : [10] [10] 0
   +0x268 pSubStruct       : 0x000000ee`68cff9b0 MySubStruct
   +0x270 subStruct        : MySubStruct
   +0x2c8 pList            : 0x00000225`22aade50 MyDList
```

```
0:000> dx refClass.m_refMyStruct
refClass.m_refMyStruct                    [Type: MyStruct]
    [+0x000] lpString     : 0x7ff62177d9d8 : "Hello World!" [Type: char *]
    [+0x008] lpwString    : 0x7ff62177d9e8 : "Hello World Wide!" [Type: wchar_t *]
    [+0x010] dwArray      [Type: unsigned long [10]]
    [+0x038] pdwArray     [Type: unsigned long * [10]]
    [+0x088] ppdwArray    [Type: unsigned long * * [10]]
    [+0x0d8] dwArray2     [Type: unsigned long [10][10]]
    [+0x268] pSubStruct   : 0xee68cff9b0 [Type: MySubStruct *]
    [+0x270] subStruct    [Type: MySubStruct]
    [+0x2c8] pList        : 0x22522aade50 [Type: MyDList *]
```

```
0:000> ?? refStruct->dwArray2[3][3]
unsigned long 9
```

```
0:000> dx refStruct.dwArray2[3][3]
refStruct.dwArray2[3][3] : 0x9 [Type: unsigned long]
```

Note: There is also a global variable that can be found by examining symbols using a pattern:

```
0:000> x *!*MyStruct
00007ff6`21782fe0 AppD3!g_MyStruct = struct MyStruct
00007ff6`21761c40 AppD3!InitializeMyStruct (struct MyStruct *)
00007ff6`217621c0 AppD3!InitializeMyStruct (struct MyStruct *)
00007ff6`21761c10 AppD3!MyStruct::~MyStruct (void)
00007ff6`21761b10 AppD3!MyStruct::MyStruct (void)
```

```
0:000> ?? g_MyStruct
struct MyStruct
   +0x000 lpString         : 0x00007ff6`2177d9d8  "Hello World!"
   +0x008 lpwString        : 0x00007ff6`2177d9e8  "Hello World Wide!"
   +0x010 dwArray          : [10] 0
   +0x038 pdwArray         : [10] 0x00000225`22aa2e10  -> 0
   +0x088 ppdwArray        : [10] 0x00000225`22a9ea90  -> 0x00000225`22aa2e70  -> 0
   +0x0d8 dwArray2         : [10] [10] 0
   +0x268 pSubStruct       : 0x00007ff6`21783250 MySubStruct
   +0x270 subStruct        : MySubStruct
```

```
   +0x2c8 pList              : 0x00000225`22aadbf0 MyDList
```

```
0:000> dx g_MyStruct
g_MyStruct                       [Type: MyStruct]
    [+0x000] lpString            : 0x7ff62177d9d8 : "Hello World!" [Type: char *]
    [+0x008] lpwString           : 0x7ff62177d9e8 : "Hello World Wide!" [Type: wchar_t *]
    [+0x010] dwArray             [Type: unsigned long [10]]
    [+0x038] pdwArray            [Type: unsigned long * [10]]
    [+0x088] ppdwArray           [Type: unsigned long * * [10]]
    [+0x0d8] dwArray2            [Type: unsigned long [10][10]]
    [+0x268] pSubStruct          : 0x7ff621783250 [Type: MySubStruct *]
    [+0x270] subStruct           [Type: MySubStruct]
    [+0x2c8] pList               : 0x22522aadbf0 [Type: MyDList *]
```

Note: In case there are similar names in different modules, use module qualification:

```
0:000> ?? AppD3!g_MyStruct.lpString
char * 0x00007ff6`2177d9d8
 "Hello World!
```

```
0:000> dx AppD3!g_MyStruct.lpString
AppD3!g_MyStruct.lpString                    : 0x7ff62177d9d8 : "Hello World!" [Type: char *]
    72 'H' [Type: char]
```

14.   We can also check for data types and associated variables that exist globally using the **dt** command. Since the output is very big, we restrict it to "**My**" structures and classes:

```
0:000> dt AppD3!*My*
          AppD3!PMYDLIST
          AppD3!_Mybase
          AppD3!MYSTRUCT
          AppD3!MYDLIST
          AppD3!MYSUBSTRUCT
          AppD3!std::_Nontrivial_dummy_type
          AppD3!std::_Iosb<int>::_Dummy_enum
          AppD3!MYSUBCLASS
          AppD3!MYSUBCLASS
          AppD3!MYCLASS
          AppD3!MYCLASS
          AppD3!MyStruct
          AppD3!MyStruct
          AppD3!MyDList
          AppD3!MySubStruct
          AppD3!MySubStruct
00007ff621776330  AppD3!g_MyClass$initializer$
00007ff62177dab8  AppD3!MYCLASS::`vftable'
00007ff621782fe0  AppD3!g_MyStruct
00007ff62177daa0  AppD3!MYSUBCLASS::`vftable'
00007ff621776338  AppD3!g_MySubClass$initializer$
00007ff621776328  AppD3!g_MyStruct$initializer$
00007ff6217832b0  AppD3!g_MyClass
00007ff621782fc8  AppD3!g_MySubClass
00007ff621761630  AppD3!MyRegisterClass
00007ff621761bc0  AppD3!MySubStruct::~MySubStruct
00007ff621761000  AppD3!`dynamic initializer for 'g_MyStruct''
00007ff621761060  AppD3!`dynamic initializer for 'g_MySubClass''
00007ff6217754a0  AppD3!`dynamic atexit destructor for 'g_MySubClass''
```

```
00007ff6217619f0    AppD3!MYCLASS::~MYCLASS
00007ff621775480    AppD3!`dynamic atexit destructor for 'g_MyClass''
00007ff621761af0    AppD3!MYSUBCLASS::~MYSUBCLASS
00007ff621774cd6    AppD3!`InitializeMyStruct'::`1'::dtor$2
00007ff621774cbb    AppD3!`InitializeMyStruct'::`1'::dtor$1
00007ff621774ca0    AppD3!`InitializeMyStruct'::`1'::dtor$0
00007ff6217619c0    AppD3!MYCLASS::MYCLASS
00007ff621761030    AppD3!`dynamic initializer for 'g_MyClass''
00007ff621761b40    AppD3!MySubStruct::MySubStruct
00007ff621761ab0    AppD3!MYSUBCLASS::`scalar deleting destructor'
00007ff621774c50    AppD3!`MySubStruct::MySubStruct'::`1'::dtor$0
00007ff621774c68    AppD3!`MySubStruct::MySubStruct'::`1'::dtor$1
00007ff621774c84    AppD3!`MySubStruct::MySubStruct'::`1'::dtor$2
00007ff621775460    AppD3!`dynamic atexit destructor for 'g_MyStruct''
00007ff621761a10    AppD3!MYCLASS::getData
00007ff621761c40    AppD3!InitializeMyStruct
00007ff6217621c0    AppD3!InitializeMyStruct
00007ff621761a60    AppD3!MYSUBCLASS::MYSUBCLASS
00007ff621763280    AppD3!std::_String_val<std::_Simple_types<char> >::_Myptr
00007ff621761c10    AppD3!MyStruct::~MyStruct
00007ff621762ed0    AppD3!std::_String_val<std::_Simple_types<wchar_t> >::_Myptr
00007ff621761a20    AppD3!MYCLASS::`scalar deleting destructor'
00007ff621761b10    AppD3!MyStruct::MyStruct
```

15.   With the **dt** command, we can see a bigger picture:

```
0:000> dt AppD3!MYSTRUCT
   +0x000 lpString           : Ptr64 Char
   +0x008 lpwString          : Ptr64 Wchar
   +0x010 dwArray            : [10] Uint4B
   +0x038 pdwArray           : [10] Ptr64 Uint4B
   +0x088 ppdwArray          : [10] Ptr64 Ptr64 Uint4B
   +0x0d8 dwArray2           : [10] [10] Uint4B
   +0x268 pSubStruct         : Ptr64 MySubStruct
   +0x270 subStruct          : MySubStruct
   +0x2c8 pList              : Ptr64 MyDList
```

```
0:000> dt AppD3!MYSUBCLASS
   +0x000 __VFN_table : Ptr64
   +0x008 m_refMyStruct      : Ptr64 MyStruct
   +0x010 m_pszName          : Ptr64 Char
```

Note: With the **-v** switch, we can get more information, including associated constructors and destructors for C++:

```
0:000> dt -v AppD3!MYSTRUCT
struct MyStruct, 16 elements, 0x2d0 bytes
   +0x000 lpString           : Ptr64 to Char
   +0x008 lpwString          : Ptr64 to Wchar
   +0x010 dwArray            : [10] Uint4B
   +0x038 pdwArray           : [10] Ptr64 to Uint4B
   +0x088 ppdwArray          : [10] Ptr64 to Ptr64 to Uint4B
   +0x0d8 dwArray2           : [10] [10] Uint4B
   +0x268 pSubStruct         : Ptr64 to struct MySubStruct, 11 elements, 0x58 bytes
   +0x270 subStruct          : struct MySubStruct, 11 elements, 0x58 bytes
   +0x2c8 pList              : Ptr64 to struct MyDList, 3 elements, 0x18 bytes
   <function> MyStruct       void (
      MyStruct*)
   <function> MyStruct       void (
```

```
        MyStruct*)
    <function> MyStruct::MyStruct      void ( void )
    <function> MyStruct::~MyStruct      void ( void )
    <function> operator=      MyStruct* (
        MyStruct*)
    <function> operator=      MyStruct* (
        MyStruct*)
    <function> __vecDelDtor      void* (
        unsigned int)
```

```
0:000> dt -v AppD3!MYSUBCLASS
class MYSUBCLASS, 7 elements, 0x18 bytes
   +0x000 __BaseClass class MYCLASS, 7 elements, 0x10 bytes
   +0x000 __VFN_table : Ptr64 to 2 entries
   <function> MYCLASS      void (
        MYCLASS*)
   <function> MYCLASS::MYCLASS      void (
        MyStruct*)
   <function> MYCLASS::~MYCLASS      void ( void )
   <function> MYCLASS::getData      MyStruct* ( void )
   +0x008 m_refMyStruct    : Ptr64 to struct MyStruct, 16 elements, 0x2d0 bytes
   <function> __vecDelDtor      void* (
        unsigned int)
   <function> MYSUBCLASS      void (
        MYSUBCLASS*)
   <function> MYSUBCLASS      void (
        MYSUBCLASS*)
   <function> MYSUBCLASS::MYSUBCLASS      void (
        MyStruct*)
   +0x010 m_pszName          : Ptr64 to Char
   <function> MYSUBCLASS::~MYSUBCLASS      void ( void )
   <function> __vecDelDtor      void* (
        unsigned int)
```

Note: To print substructures and subclasses, we can use the **-r** (recursion) switch:

```
0:000> dt -r AppD3!MYSTRUCT
   +0x000 lpString       : Ptr64 Char
   +0x008 lpwString      : Ptr64 Wchar
   +0x010 dwArray        : [10] Uint4B
   +0x038 pdwArray       : [10] Ptr64 Uint4B
   +0x088 ppdwArray      : [10] Ptr64 Ptr64 Uint4B
   +0x0d8 dwArray2       : [10] [10] Uint4B
   +0x268 pSubStruct     : Ptr64 MySubStruct
      +0x000 iVec           : std::vector<int,std::allocator<int> >
         +0x000 _Mypair        : std::_Compressed_pair<std::allocator<int>,std::_Vector_val<std::_Simple_types<int> >,1>
      +0x018 wStr           : std::basic_string<wchar_t,std::char_traits<wchar_t>,std::allocator<wchar_t> >
         +0x000 _Mypair        : std::_Compressed_pair<std::allocator<wchar_t>,std::_String_val<std::_Simple_types<wchar_t> >,1>
      +0x038 sLst           : std::list<std::basic_string<char,std::char_traits<char>,std::allocator<char>
>,std::allocator<std::basic_string<char,std::char_traits<char>,std::allocator<char> > > >
         +0x000 _Mypair        : std::_Compressed_pair<std::allocator<std::_List_node<std::basic_string<char,std::char_traits<char>,std::allocator<char>
>,void *> >,std::_List_val<std::_List_simple_types<std::basic_string<char,std::char_traits<char>,std::allocator<char> > > >,1>
      +0x048 isMap          : std::map<int,std::basic_string<char,std::char_traits<char>,std::allocator<char> >,std::less<int>,std::allocator<std::pair<int
const ,std::basic_string<char,std::char_traits<char>,std::allocator<char> > > > >
         +0x000 _Mypair        : std::_Compressed_pair<std::less<int>,std::_Compressed_pair<std::allocator<std::_Tree_node<std::pair<int const
,std::basic_string<char,std::char_traits<char>,std::allocator<char> > > >,void *> >,std::_Tree_val<std::_Tree_simple_types<std::pair<int const
,std::basic_string<char,std::char_traits<char>,std::allocator<char> > > > >,1>,1>
   +0x270 subStruct      : MySubStruct
      +0x000 iVec           : std::vector<int,std::allocator<int> >
         +0x000 _Mypair        : std::_Compressed_pair<std::allocator<int>,std::_Vector_val<std::_Simple_types<int> >,1>
      +0x018 wStr           : std::basic_string<wchar_t,std::char_traits<wchar_t>,std::allocator<wchar_t> >
         +0x000 _Mypair        : std::_Compressed_pair<std::allocator<wchar_t>,std::_String_val<std::_Simple_types<wchar_t> >,1>
      +0x038 sLst           : std::list<std::basic_string<char,std::char_traits<char>,std::allocator<char>
>,std::allocator<std::basic_string<char,std::char_traits<char>,std::allocator<char> > > >
         +0x000 _Mypair        : std::_Compressed_pair<std::allocator<std::_List_node<std::basic_string<char,std::char_traits<char>,std::allocator<char>
>,void *> >,std::_List_val<std::_List_simple_types<std::basic_string<char,std::char_traits<char>,std::allocator<char> > > >,1>
      +0x048 isMap          : std::map<int,std::basic_string<char,std::char_traits<char>,std::allocator<char> >,std::less<int>,std::allocator<std::pair<int
const ,std::basic_string<char,std::char_traits<char>,std::allocator<char> > > > >
         +0x000 _Mypair        : std::_Compressed_pair<std::less<int>,std::_Compressed_pair<std::allocator<std::_Tree_node<std::pair<int const
,std::basic_string<char,std::char_traits<char>,std::allocator<char> > > >,void *> >,std::_Tree_val<std::_Tree_simple_types<std::pair<int const
,std::basic_string<char,std::char_traits<char>,std::allocator<char> > > > >,1>,1>
   +0x2c8 pList          : Ptr64 MyDList
      +0x000 data           : Float
```

```
        +0x008 pNext            : Ptr64 MyDList
          +0x000 data           : Float
          +0x008 pNext          : Ptr64 MyDList
          +0x010 pPrev          : Ptr64 MyDList
        +0x010 pPrev            : Ptr64 MyDList
          +0x000 data           : Float
          +0x008 pNext          : Ptr64 MyDList
          +0x010 pPrev          : Ptr64 MyDList
```

```
0:000> dt -r AppD3!MYSUBCLASS
   +0x000 __VFN_table : Ptr64
   +0x008 m_refMyStruct     : Ptr64 MyStruct
      +0x000 lpString       : Ptr64 Char
      +0x008 lpwString      : Ptr64 Wchar
      +0x010 dwArray        : [10] Uint4B
      +0x038 pdwArray       : [10] Ptr64 Uint4B
      +0x088 ppdwArray      : [10] Ptr64 Ptr64 Uint4B
      +0x0d8 dwArray2       : [10] [10] Uint4B
      +0x268 pSubStruct     : Ptr64 MySubStruct
         +0x000 iVec        : std::vector<int,std::allocator<int> >
         +0x018 wStr        : std::basic_string<wchar_t,std::char_traits<wchar_t>,std::allocator<wchar_t> >
         +0x038 sLst        : std::list<std::basic_string<char,std::char_traits<char>,std::allocator<char>
>,std::allocator<std::basic_string<char,std::char_traits<char>,std::allocator<char> > >
         +0x048 isMap       : std::map<int,std::basic_string<char,std::char_traits<char>,std::allocator<char>
>,std::less<int>,std::allocator<std::pair<int const ,std::basic_string<char,std::char_traits<char>,std::allocator<char> > > >
      +0x270 subStruct      : MySubStruct
         +0x000 iVec        : std::vector<int,std::allocator<int> >
         +0x018 wStr        : std::basic_string<wchar_t,std::char_traits<wchar_t>,std::allocator<wchar_t> >
         +0x038 sLst        : std::list<std::basic_string<char,std::char_traits<char>,std::allocator<char>
>,std::allocator<std::basic_string<char,std::char_traits<char>,std::allocator<char> > >
         +0x048 isMap       : std::map<int,std::basic_string<char,std::char_traits<char>,std::allocator<char>
>,std::less<int>,std::allocator<std::pair<int const ,std::basic_string<char,std::char_traits<char>,std::allocator<char> > > >
      +0x2c8 pList          : Ptr64 MyDList
         +0x000 data        : Float
         +0x008 pNext       : Ptr64 MyDList
         +0x010 pPrev       : Ptr64 MyDList
   +0x010 m_pszName     : Ptr64 Char
```

16.   We can supply a variable address to the **dt** command as well, for example:

```
00007ff6`21782fe0 AppD3!g_MyStruct = struct MyStruct * from the previous x output above
```

```
0:000> dt -r MYSTRUCT 00007ff6`21782fe0
AppD3!MYSTRUCT
   +0x000 lpString      : 0x00007ff6`2177d9d8  "Hello World!"
   +0x008 lpwString     : 0x00007ff6`2177d9e8  "Hello World Wide!"
   +0x010 dwArray       : [10] 0
   +0x038 pdwArray      : [10] 0x00000225`22aa2e10 -> 0
   +0x088 ppdwArray     : [10] 0x00000225`22a9ea90 -> 0x00000225`22aa2e70  -> 0
   +0x0d8 dwArray2      : [10] [10] 0
   +0x268 pSubStruct    : 0x00007ff6`21783250 MySubStruct
      +0x000 iVec       : std::vector<int,std::allocator<int> >
         +0x000 _Mypair      : std::_Compressed_pair<std::allocator<int>,std::_Vector_val<std::_Simple_types<int> >,1>
      +0x018 wStr       : std::basic_string<wchar_t,std::char_traits<wchar_t>,std::allocator<wchar_t> >
         +0x000 _Mypair      : std::_Compressed_pair<std::allocator<wchar_t>,std::_String_val<std::_Simple_types<wchar_t> >,1>
      +0x038 sLst       : std::list<std::basic_string<char,std::char_traits<char>,std::allocator<char>
>,std::allocator<std::basic_string<char,std::char_traits<char>,std::allocator<char> > >
         +0x000 _Mypair      : std::_Compressed_pair<std::allocator<std::_List_node<std::basic_string<char,std::char_traits<char>,std::allocator<char>
>,void *> >,std::_List_val<std::_List_simple_types<std::basic_string<char,std::char_traits<char>,std::allocator<char> > > >,1>
      +0x048 isMap      : std::map<int,std::basic_string<char,std::char_traits<char>,std::allocator<char> >,std::less<int>,std::allocator<std::pair<int
const ,std::basic_string<char,std::char_traits<char>,std::allocator<char> > > >
         +0x000 _Mypair      : std::_Compressed_pair<std::less<int>,std::_Compressed_pair<std::allocator<std::_Tree_node<std::pair<int const
,std::basic_string<char,std::char_traits<char>,std::allocator<char> > >,void *> >,std::_Tree_val<std::_Tree_simple_types<std::pair<int const
,std::basic_string<char,std::char_traits<char>,std::allocator<char> > > > >,1>,1>
      +0x270 subStruct   : MySubStruct
      +0x000 iVec       : std::vector<int,std::allocator<int> >
         +0x000 _Mypair      : std::_Compressed_pair<std::allocator<int>,std::_Vector_val<std::_Simple_types<int> >,1>
      +0x018 wStr       : std::basic_string<wchar_t,std::char_traits<wchar_t>,std::allocator<wchar_t> >
         +0x000 _Mypair      : std::_Compressed_pair<std::allocator<wchar_t>,std::_String_val<std::_Simple_types<wchar_t> >,1>
      +0x038 sLst       : std::list<std::basic_string<char,std::char_traits<char>,std::allocator<char>
>,std::allocator<std::basic_string<char,std::char_traits<char>,std::allocator<char> > >
         +0x000 _Mypair      : std::_Compressed_pair<std::allocator<std::_List_node<std::basic_string<char,std::char_traits<char>,std::allocator<char>
>,void *> >,std::_List_val<std::_List_simple_types<std::basic_string<char,std::char_traits<char>,std::allocator<char> > > >,1>
      +0x048 isMap      : std::map<int,std::basic_string<char,std::char_traits<char>,std::allocator<char> >,std::less<int>,std::allocator<std::pair<int
const ,std::basic_string<char,std::char_traits<char>,std::allocator<char> > > >
         +0x000 _Mypair      : std::_Compressed_pair<std::less<int>,std::_Compressed_pair<std::allocator<std::_Tree_node<std::pair<int const
,std::basic_string<char,std::char_traits<char>,std::allocator<char> > >,void *> >,std::_Tree_val<std::_Tree_simple_types<std::pair<int const
,std::basic_string<char,std::char_traits<char>,std::allocator<char> > > > >,1>,1>
      +0x2c8 pList       : 0x00000225`22aadbf0 MyDList
         +0x000 data     : 1.1000000000000000888
         +0x008 pNext    : 0x00000225`22aad9b0 MyDList
            +0x000 data  : 2.2000000000000001776
            +0x008 pNext : 0x00000225`22aaddb0 MyDList
            +0x010 pPrev : 0x00000225`22aad9b0 MyDList
         +0x010 pPrev    : (null)
```

17.   We can also view local variables and parameters in the *Locals* tab:

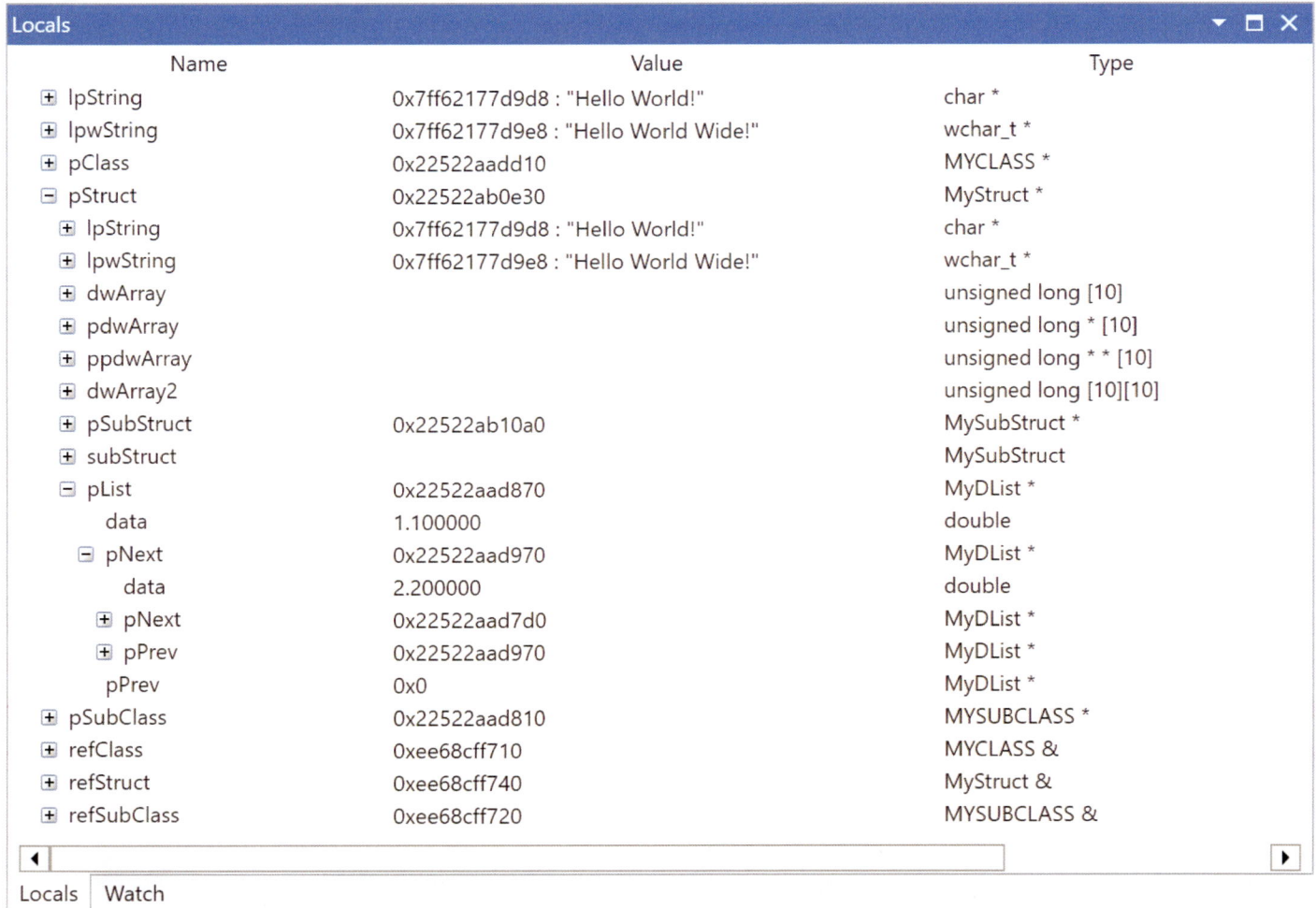

Name	Value	Type
⊞ lpString	0x7ff62177d9d8 : "Hello World!"	char *
⊞ lpwString	0x7ff62177d9e8 : "Hello World Wide!"	wchar_t *
⊞ pClass	0x22522aadd10	MYCLASS *
⊟ pStruct	0x22522ab0e30	MyStruct *
⊞ lpString	0x7ff62177d9d8 : "Hello World!"	char *
⊞ lpwString	0x7ff62177d9e8 : "Hello World Wide!"	wchar_t *
⊞ dwArray		unsigned long [10]
⊞ pdwArray		unsigned long * [10]
⊞ ppdwArray		unsigned long * * [10]
⊞ dwArray2		unsigned long [10][10]
⊞ pSubStruct	0x22522ab10a0	MySubStruct *
⊞ subStruct		MySubStruct
⊟ pList	0x22522aad870	MyDList *
data	1.100000	double
⊟ pNext	0x22522aad970	MyDList *
data	2.200000	double
⊞ pNext	0x22522aad7d0	MyDList *
⊞ pPrev	0x22522aad970	MyDList *
pPrev	0x0	MyDList *
⊞ pSubClass	0x22522aad810	MYSUBCLASS *
⊞ refClass	0xee68cff710	MYCLASS &
⊞ refStruct	0xee68cff740	MyStruct &
⊞ refSubClass	0xee68cff720	MYSUBCLASS &

Locals   Watch

Name	Value	Type
⊞ lpString	0x7ff62177d9d8 : "Hello World!"	char *
⊞ lpwString	0x7ff62177d9e8 : "Hello World Wide!"	wchar_t *
⊞ pClass	0x22522aadd10	MYCLASS *
⊟ pStruct	0x22522ab0e30	MyStruct *
⊞ lpString	0x7ff62177d9d8 : "Hello World!"	char *
⊞ lpwString	0x7ff62177d9e8 : "Hello World Wide!"	wchar_t *
⊞ dwArray		unsigned long [10]
⊞ pdwArray		unsigned long * [10]
⊞ ppdwArray		unsigned long * * [10]
⊟ dwArray2		unsigned long [10][10]
⊞ [0]		unsigned long [10]
⊞ [1]		unsigned long [10]
⊞ [2]		unsigned long [10]
⊟ [3]		unsigned long [10]
[0]	0x0	unsigned long
[1]	0x3	unsigned long
[2]	0x6	unsigned long
[3]	0x9	unsigned long
[4]	0xc	unsigned long
[5]	0xf	unsigned long
[6]	0x12	unsigned long
[7]	0x15	unsigned long
[8]	0x18	unsigned long
[9]	0x1b	unsigned long
⊞ [4]		unsigned long [10]
⊞ [5]		unsigned long [10]
⊞ [6]		unsigned long [10]
⊞ [7]		unsigned long [10]
⊞ [8]		unsigned long [10]
⊞ [9]		unsigned long [10]
⊞ pSubStruct	0x22522ab10a0	MySubStruct *
⊞ subStruct		MySubStruct
⊞ pList	0x22522aad870	MyDList *
⊞ pSubClass	0x22522aad810	MYSUBCLASS *
⊞ refClass	0xee68cff710	MYCLASS &
⊞ refStruct	0xee68cff740	MyStruct &
⊞ refSubClass	0xee68cff720	MYSUBCLASS &

Locals | Watch

Note: We can convert any data displayed as hexadecimal to other formats, for example:

```
0:000> ? 1b
Evaluate expression: 27 = 00000000`0000001b
```

```
0:000> ? 0n27
Evaluate expression: 27 = 00000000`0000001b
```

```
0:000> .formats 1b
Evaluate expression:
  Hex:     00000000`0000001b
  Decimal: 27
  Octal:   0000000000000000000033
  Binary:  00000000 00000000 00000000 00000000 00000000 00000000 00000000 00011011
  Chars:   ........
  Time:    Wed Dec 31 16:00:27 1969
  Float:   low 3.78351e-044 high 0
  Double:  1.33398e-322
```

18.   If we go two frames up (towards higher stack addresses), we can see locals from our window procedure:

```
0:000> .frame 1e5
1e5 000000ee`68cff680 00007ff6`21761851     AppD3!StartModeling+0x191 [C:\AWD3\AppD3\AppD3\AppD3.cpp @ 332]
```

```
0:000> .frame 1e6
1e6 000000ee`68cffa30 00007ff9`54148241     AppD3!WndProc+0xb1 [C:\AWD3\AppD3\AppD3\AppD3.cpp @ 153]
```

```
0:000> dv /i /V
prv param  000000ee`68cffaf0 @rsp+0x00c0             hWnd = 0x00000000`003917ee
prv param  000000ee`68cffaf8 @rsp+0x00c8          message = 0x111
prv param  000000ee`68cffb00 @rsp+0x00d0           wParam = 0x8003
prv param  000000ee`68cffb08 @rsp+0x00d8           lParam = 0n0
prv local  000000ee`68cffa68 @rsp+0x0038             wmId = 0n32771
prv local  000000ee`68cffa6c @rsp+0x003c          wmEvent = 0n0
prv local  000000ee`68cffa80 @rsp+0x0050               ps = struct tagPAINTSTRUCT
prv local  000000ee`68cffa70 @rsp+0x0040              hdc = 0x00000000`00000000
```

19.   There is also a possibility to watch variables during program tracing via the *Watch* tab:

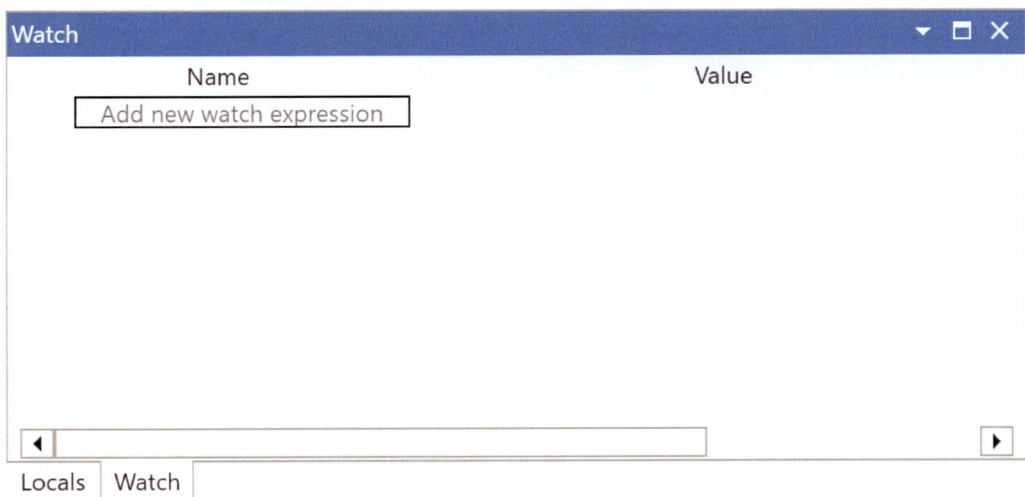

To try this out, we stop our debugging session, launch *AppD3.exe* again, and attach WinDbg:

```
Microsoft (R) Windows Debugger Version 10.0.25921.1001 AMD64
Copyright (c) Microsoft Corporation. All rights reserved.

*** wait with pending attach

************** Path validation summary **************
Response                        Time (ms)    Location
Deferred                                     srv*
Symbol search path is: srv*
Executable search path is:
ModLoad: 00007ff6`21760000 00007ff6`2178a000   C:\AWD4\AppD3\x64\Release\AppD3.exe
ModLoad: 00007ff9`55530000 00007ff9`55747000   C:\WINDOWS\SYSTEM32\ntdll.dll
ModLoad: 00007ff9`55030000 00007ff9`550f4000   C:\WINDOWS\System32\KERNEL32.DLL
ModLoad: 00007ff9`52870000 00007ff9`52c16000   C:\WINDOWS\System32\KERNELBASE.dll
ModLoad: 00007ff9`54130000 00007ff9`542de000   C:\WINDOWS\System32\USER32.dll
ModLoad: 00007ff9`53190000 00007ff9`531b6000   C:\WINDOWS\System32\win32u.dll
ModLoad: 00007ff9`542e0000 00007ff9`54309000   C:\WINDOWS\System32\GDI32.dll
ModLoad: 00007ff9`52c20000 00007ff9`52d38000   C:\WINDOWS\System32\gdi32full.dll
ModLoad: 00007ff9`52f30000 00007ff9`52fca000   C:\WINDOWS\System32\msvcp_win.dll
ModLoad: 00007ff9`53000000 00007ff9`53111000   C:\WINDOWS\System32\ucrtbase.dll
ModLoad: 00007ff9`53ef0000 00007ff9`53f21000   C:\WINDOWS\System32\IMM32.DLL
ModLoad: 00007ff9`4f920000 00007ff9`4f9cb000   C:\WINDOWS\system32\uxtheme.dll
ModLoad: 00007ff9`53b60000 00007ff9`53ee9000   C:\WINDOWS\System32\combase.dll
ModLoad: 00007ff9`543d0000 00007ff9`544e7000   C:\WINDOWS\System32\RPCRT4.dll
ModLoad: 00007ff9`54a40000 00007ff9`54b90000   C:\WINDOWS\System32\MSCTF.dll
ModLoad: 00007ff9`55100000 00007ff9`551a7000   C:\WINDOWS\System32\msvcrt.dll
ModLoad: 00007ff9`20a30000 00007ff9`20ae0000   C:\WINDOWS\SYSTEM32\TextShaping.dll
ModLoad: 00007ff9`51860000 00007ff9`51878000   C:\WINDOWS\SYSTEM32\kernel.appcore.dll
ModLoad: 00007ff9`52eb0000 00007ff9`52f2a000   C:\WINDOWS\System32\bcryptPrimitives.dll
ModLoad: 00007ff9`54e20000 00007ff9`54ec8000   C:\WINDOWS\System32\sechost.dll
ModLoad: 00007ff9`52fd0000 00007ff9`52ff8000   C:\WINDOWS\System32\bcrypt.dll
ModLoad: 00007ff9`3fba0000 00007ff9`3fcea000   C:\WINDOWS\SYSTEM32\textinputframework.dll
ModLoad: 00007ff9`54b90000 00007ff9`54c67000   C:\WINDOWS\System32\OLEAUT32.dll
ModLoad: 00007ff9`4f470000 00007ff9`4f5a4000   C:\WINDOWS\SYSTEM32\CoreMessaging.dll
ModLoad: 00007ff9`49070000 00007ff9`493dc000   C:\WINDOWS\SYSTEM32\CoreUIComponents.dll
ModLoad: 00007ff9`50f30000 00007ff9`5106e000   C:\WINDOWS\SYSTEM32\wintypes.dll
ModLoad: 00007ff9`54310000 00007ff9`543c3000   C:\WINDOWS\System32\advapi32.dll
ModLoad: 00007ff9`51ed0000 00007ff9`51edc000   C:\WINDOWS\SYSTEM32\CRYPTBASE.DLL
ModLoad: 00007ff9`2b3e0000 00007ff9`2b449000   C:\WINDOWS\system32\Oleacc.dll
ModLoad: 00007ff9`54510000 00007ff9`545c0000   C:\WINDOWS\System32\clbcatq.dll
ModLoad: 00007ff9`20ae0000 00007ff9`20b2b000
C:\WINDOWS\system32\ApplicationTargetedFeatureDatabase.dll
ModLoad: 00007ff9`47160000 00007ff9`473e5000   C:\Windows\System32\twinapi.appcore.dll
ModLoad: 00007ff9`12ff0000 00007ff9`13435000   C:\Windows\System32\uiautomationcore.dll
(6fdc.8934): Break instruction exception - code 80000003 (first chance)
ntdll!DbgBreakPoint:
00007ff9`555d3060 int        3
```

Then, we put a breakpoint on the *StartModeling* function:

```
0:009> bp AppD3!StartModeling
```

We can see breakpoints in the *Breakpoints* tab:

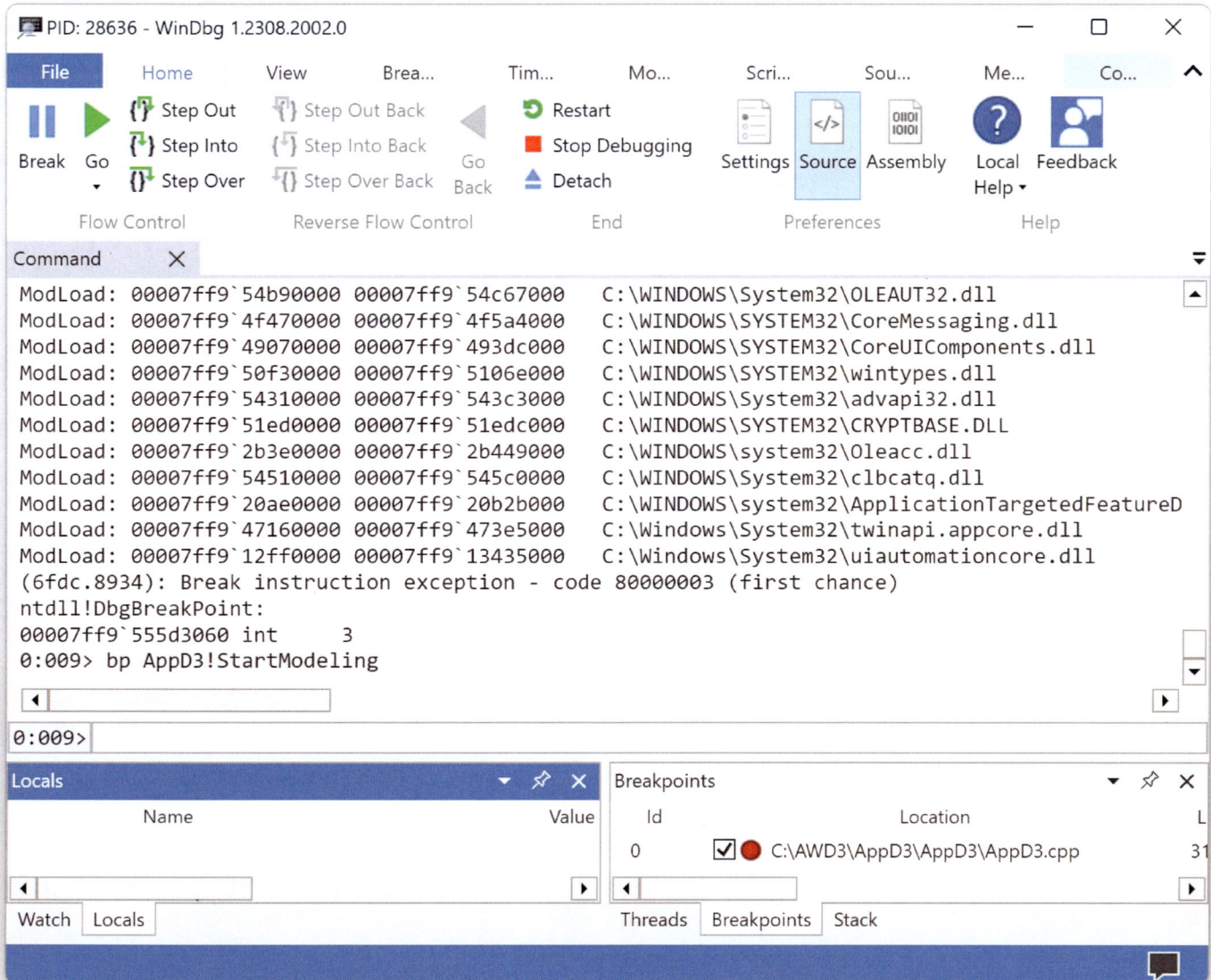

```
0:009> bl
    0 e Disable Clear  00007ff6`217621e0  [C:\AWD3\AppD3\AppD3\AppD3.cpp @ 318]    0001 (0001)  0:**** AppD3!StartModeling

0:004> g
```

We then switch to *AppD3* and choose *File \ Start* and then switch to WinDbg and add *AppD3!g_MyStruct* to the *Watch* tab (*Add new watch expression*):

```
ModLoad: 00007ff9`4fb50000 00007ff9`4fb7b000     C:\WINDOWS\system32\dwmapi.dll
ModLoad: 00007ff9`1e070000 00007ff9`1e085000     C:\Windows\System32\threadpoolwinrt.dll
Breakpoint 0 hit
AppD3!StartModeling:
00007ff6`217621e0 sub       rsp,3A8h
```

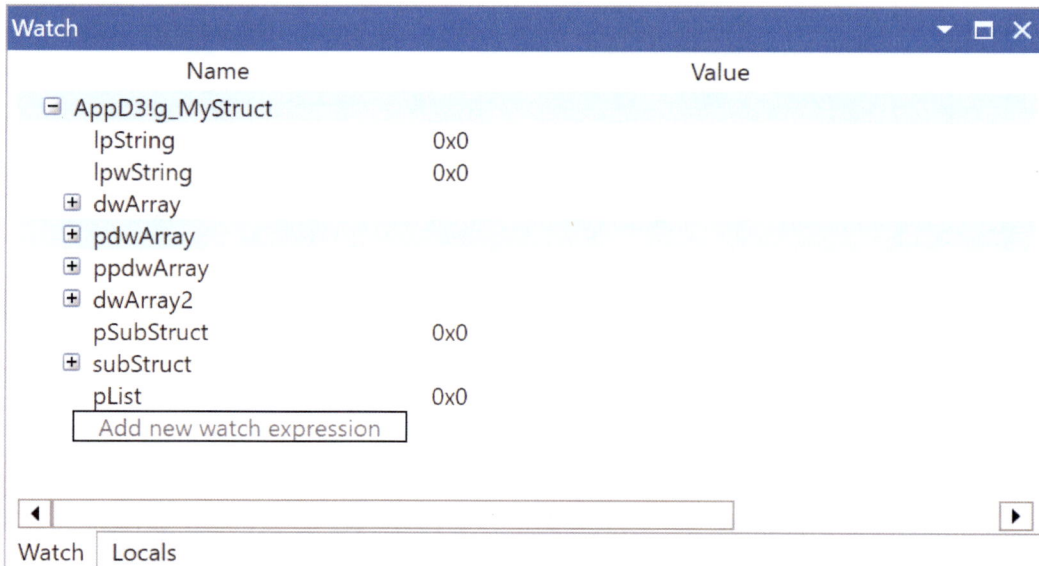

We then step (*Step Over*) through source code (**p** command, also F10 key) until we pass over *g_MyStruct* initialization (please note that the trace **t** command (*Step Into*) may enter into a function and even into a hidden function such as a constructor if you do that accidentally then you need to do *Step Out*, **gu** or Shift-F11 key):

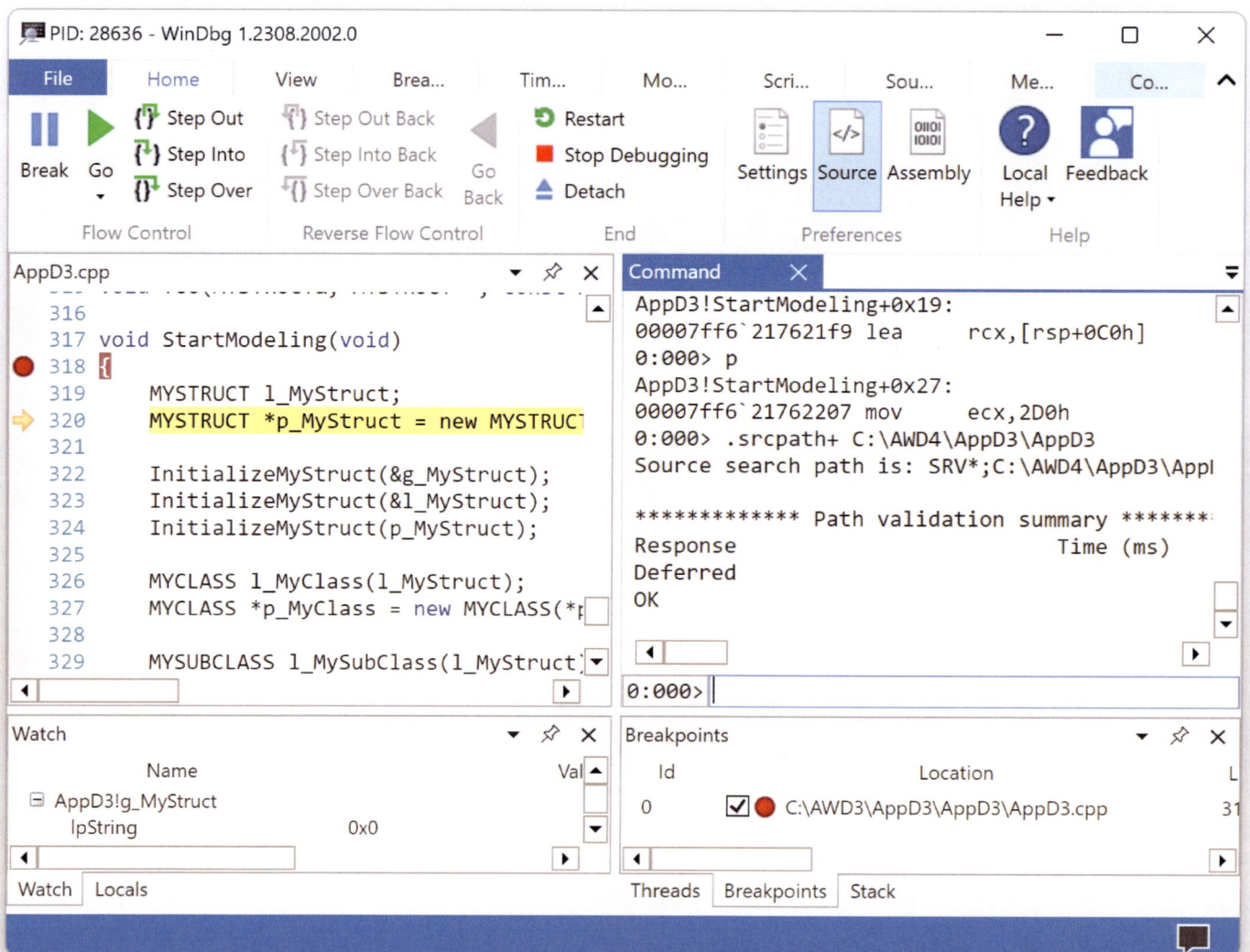

If you don't see the source code, add its path using the **.srcpath+** command. **t, p**, and **gu** commands are illustrated below:

```
0:000> p
AppD3!StartModeling+0x19:
00007ff6`217621f9 lea        rcx,[rsp+0C0h]

0:000> p
AppD3!StartModeling+0x27:
00007ff6`21762207 mov        ecx,2D0h

0:000> .srcpath+ C:\AWD4\AppD3\AppD3
Source search path is: SRV*;C:\AWD4\AppD3\AppD3

************* Path validation summary **************
Response                        Time (ms)      Location
Deferred                                       SRV*
OK                                             C:\AWD4\AppD3\AppD3

0:000> t
*** The C++ standard library and CRT step filter can be enabled to skip this function. Run
.settings set Sources.SkipCrtCode = true to enable it. ***
AppD3!operator new:
00007ff6`217660d4 push       rbx

0:000> t
AppD3!operator new+0x9:
00007ff6`217660dd jmp        AppD3!operator new+0x1a (00007ff6`217660ee)

0:000> gu
AppD3!StartModeling+0x31:
00007ff6`21762211 mov        qword ptr [rsp+38h],rax ss:000000e6`1556f608=00007ff94f93ede9

0:000> p
AppD3!StartModeling+0x6c:
00007ff6`2176224c lea        rcx,[AppD3!g_MyStruct (00007ff6`21782fe0)]

0:000> p
AppD3!StartModeling+0x78:
00007ff6`21762258 lea        rcx,[rsp+0C0h]
```

The associated source code and *Watch* tab:

```
void StartModeling(void)
{
        MYSTRUCT l_MyStruct;
        MYSTRUCT *p_MyStruct = new MYSTRUCT;

        InitializeMyStruct(&g_MyStruct);
>>>     InitializeMyStruct(&l_MyStruct);
        InitializeMyStruct(p_MyStruct);

        MYCLASS l_MyClass(l_MyStruct);
        MYCLASS *p_MyClass = new MYCLASS(*p_MyStruct);

        MYSUBCLASS l_MySubClass(l_MyStruct);
        MYSUBCLASS *p_MySubClass = new MYSUBCLASS(*p_MyStruct);
```

```
        foo(l_MyStruct, p_MyStruct, l_MyClass, p_MyClass, l_MySubClass, p_MySubClass);
}
```

```
AppD3.cpp                                                    ▼ □ ✕

  316
  317  void StartModeling(void)
● 318  {
  319      MYSTRUCT l_MyStruct;
  320      MYSTRUCT *p_MyStruct = new MYSTRUCT;
  321
  322      InitializeMyStruct(&g_MyStruct);
⇨ 323      InitializeMyStruct(&l_MyStruct);
  324      InitializeMyStruct(p_MyStruct);
  325
  326      MYCLASS l_MyClass(l_MyStruct);
  327      MYCLASS *p_MyClass = new MYCLASS(*p_MyStruct);
  328
  329      MYSUBCLASS l_MySubClass(l_MyStruct);
  330      MYSUBCLASS *p_MySubClass = new MYSUBCLASS(*p_MyStruct);
  331
```

```
Watch                                                        ▼ □ ✕

           Name                                 Value
  ⊟ AppD3!g_MyStruct
    ⊞ dwArray
    ⊞ pdwArray
    ⊞ ppdwArray
    ⊞ dwArray2
    ⊞ subStruct
    ⊞ lpString            0x7ff62177d9d8 : "Hello World!"
    ⊞ lpwString           0x7ff62177d9e8 : "Hello World Wide!"
    ⊞ pSubStruct          0x7ff621783250
    ⊞ pList               0x2e5565defd0
      Add new watch expression

  ◄                                                          ►
  Watch   Locals
```

Exercise UD4

- **Goal:** Learn how to use conditional breakpoints to log behavior

- **Elementary Diagnostics Patterns:** Use-case Deviation

- **Memory Analysis Patterns:** -

- **Debugging Implementation Patterns:** Break-in; Code Breakpoint; Breakpoint Action

- \AWD4\Exercise-UD4.pdf

Goal: Learn how to use conditional breakpoints to log behavior.

Elementary Diagnostics Patterns: Use-case Deviation.

Memory Analysis Patterns: -

Debugging Implementation Patterns: Break-in; Code Breakpoint; Breakpoint Action.

1. Launch *\AWD4\AppD4\x64\Release\AppD4.exe* executable.

2. Launch WinDbg. Choose *File \ Attach to process* and select *AppD4.exe*.

3. We get WinDbg attached to *AppD4.exe*:

```
Microsoft (R) Windows Debugger Version 10.0.25921.1001 AMD64
Copyright (c) Microsoft Corporation. All rights reserved.

*** wait with pending attach

************* Path validation summary **************
Response                        Time (ms)     Location
Deferred                                      srv*
Symbol search path is: srv*
Executable search path is:
ModLoad: 00007ff6`599f0000 00007ff6`59a10000   C:\AWD4\AppD4\x64\Release\AppD4.exe
ModLoad: 00007ff9`55530000 00007ff9`55747000   C:\WINDOWS\SYSTEM32\ntdll.dll
ModLoad: 00007ff9`55030000 00007ff9`550f4000   C:\WINDOWS\System32\KERNEL32.DLL
ModLoad: 00007ff9`52870000 00007ff9`52c16000   C:\WINDOWS\System32\KERNELBASE.dll
ModLoad: 00007ff9`4f780000 00007ff9`4f817000   C:\WINDOWS\SYSTEM32\apphelp.dll
ModLoad: 00007ff9`54130000 00007ff9`542de000   C:\WINDOWS\System32\USER32.dll
ModLoad: 00007ff9`53190000 00007ff9`531b6000   C:\WINDOWS\System32\win32u.dll
ModLoad: 00007ff9`542e0000 00007ff9`54309000   C:\WINDOWS\System32\GDI32.dll
ModLoad: 00007ff9`52c20000 00007ff9`52d38000   C:\WINDOWS\System32\gdi32full.dll
ModLoad: 00007ff9`52f30000 00007ff9`52fca000   C:\WINDOWS\System32\msvcp_win.dll
ModLoad: 00007ff9`53000000 00007ff9`53111000   C:\WINDOWS\System32\ucrtbase.dll
ModLoad: 00007ff9`53ef0000 00007ff9`53f21000   C:\WINDOWS\System32\IMM32.DLL
ModLoad: 00007ff9`4f920000 00007ff9`4f9cb000   C:\WINDOWS\system32\uxtheme.dll
ModLoad: 00007ff9`53b60000 00007ff9`53ee9000   C:\WINDOWS\System32\combase.dll
ModLoad: 00007ff9`543d0000 00007ff9`544e7000   C:\WINDOWS\System32\RPCRT4.dll
ModLoad: 00007ff9`54a40000 00007ff9`54b90000   C:\WINDOWS\System32\MSCTF.dll
ModLoad: 00007ff9`55100000 00007ff9`551a7000   C:\WINDOWS\System32\msvcrt.dll
ModLoad: 00007ff9`20a30000 00007ff9`20ae0000   C:\WINDOWS\SYSTEM32\TextShaping.dll
ModLoad: 00007ff9`51860000 00007ff9`51878000   C:\WINDOWS\SYSTEM32\kernel.appcore.dll
ModLoad: 00007ff9`52eb0000 00007ff9`52f2a000   C:\WINDOWS\System32\bcryptPrimitives.dll
ModLoad: 00007ff9`54e20000 00007ff9`54ec8000   C:\WINDOWS\System32\sechost.dll
ModLoad: 00007ff9`52fd0000 00007ff9`52ff8000   C:\WINDOWS\System32\bcrypt.dll
ModLoad: 00007ff9`3fba0000 00007ff9`3fcea000   C:\WINDOWS\SYSTEM32\textinputframework.dll
ModLoad: 00007ff9`54b90000 00007ff9`54c67000   C:\WINDOWS\System32\OLEAUT32.dll
ModLoad: 00007ff9`4f470000 00007ff9`4f5a4000   C:\WINDOWS\SYSTEM32\CoreMessaging.dll
ModLoad: 00007ff9`49070000 00007ff9`493dc000   C:\WINDOWS\SYSTEM32\CoreUIComponents.dll
ModLoad: 00007ff9`50f30000 00007ff9`5106e000   C:\WINDOWS\SYSTEM32\wintypes.dll
ModLoad: 00007ff9`54310000 00007ff9`543c3000   C:\WINDOWS\System32\advapi32.dll
ModLoad: 00007ff9`51ed0000 00007ff9`51edc000   C:\WINDOWS\SYSTEM32\CRYPTBASE.DLL
```

```
ModLoad: 00007ff9`2b3e0000 00007ff9`2b449000   C:\WINDOWS\system32\Oleacc.dll
ModLoad: 00007ff9`54510000 00007ff9`545c0000   C:\WINDOWS\System32\clbcatq.dll
ModLoad: 00007ff9`20ae0000 00007ff9`20b2b000
C:\WINDOWS\system32\ApplicationTargetedFeatureDatabase.dll
ModLoad: 00007ff9`47160000 00007ff9`473e5000   C:\Windows\System32\twinapi.appcore.dll
ModLoad: 00007ff9`12ff0000 00007ff9`13435000   C:\Windows\System32\uiautomationcore.dll
(1368.8468): Break instruction exception - code 80000003 (first chance)
ntdll!DbgBreakPoint:
00007ff9`555d3060 int       3
```

4.   Open a log file:

```
0:010> .logopen C:\AWD4\D4.log
Opened log file 'C:\AWD4\D4.log'
```

5.   Our task is to log any characters that can be typed inside the *AppD4* main window. For this, we need to put a breakpoint on a window procedure. First, let's open a source file via the *Source \ Open Source File...* dialog and choose *\AWD4\AppD4\AppD4\AppD4.cpp*.

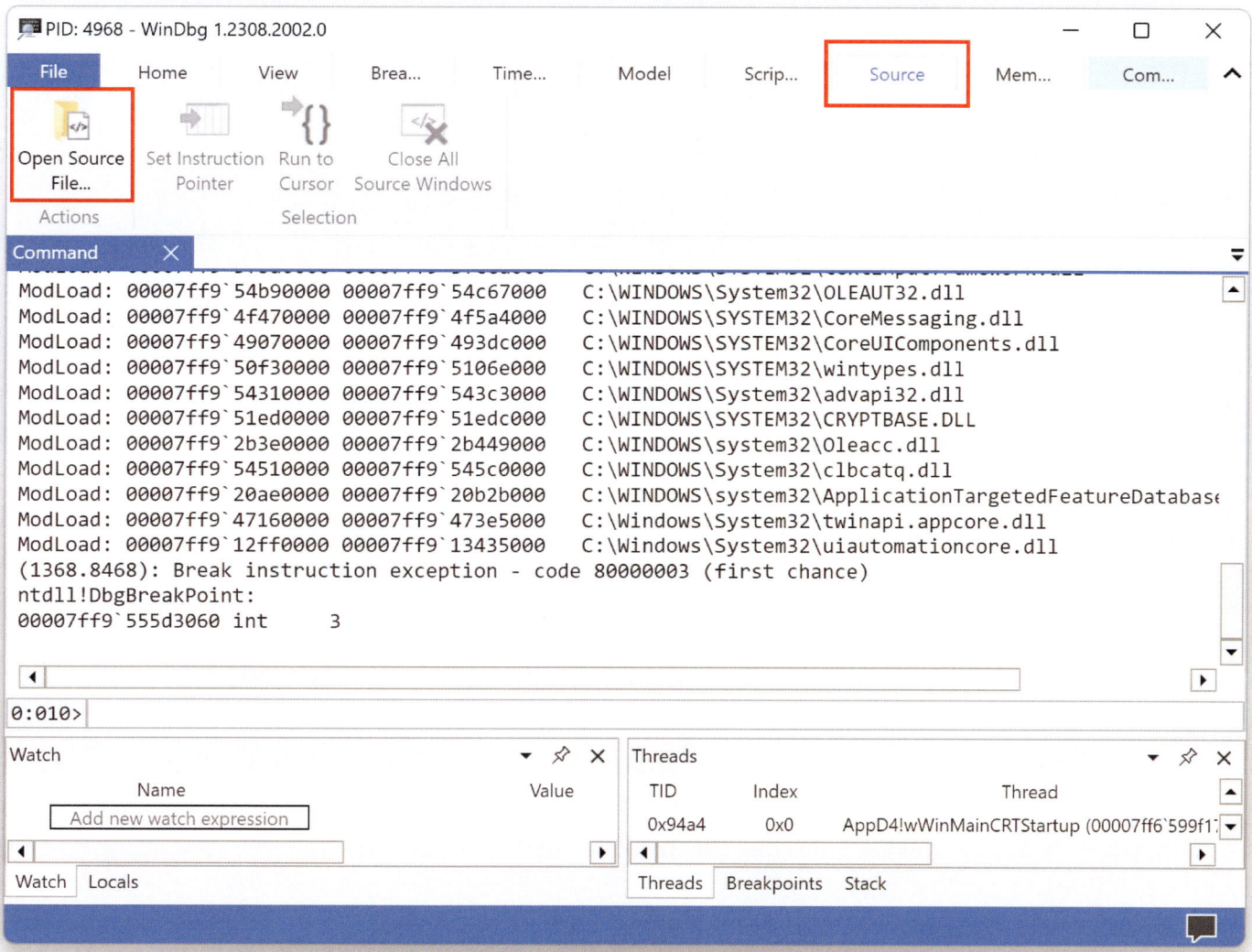

In the source code window, scroll until you see *WndProc*:

```
//
//   FUNCTION: WndProc(HWND, UINT, WPARAM, LPARAM)
//
//   PURPOSE:  Processes messages for the main window.
//
//   WM_COMMAND      - process the application menu
//   WM_PAINT - Paint the main window
//   WM_DESTROY      - post a quit message and return
//
//
LRESULT CALLBACK WndProc(HWND hWnd, UINT message, WPARAM wParam, LPARAM lParam)
{
        int wmId, wmEvent;
        PAINTSTRUCT ps;
        HDC hdc;

        switch (message)
        {
        case WM_COMMAND:
                wmId    = LOWORD(wParam);
                wmEvent = HIWORD(wParam);
                // Parse the menu selections:
                switch (wmId)
                {
                case ID_FILE_START:
                        StartModeling();
                        break;
                case IDM_ABOUT:
                        DialogBox(hInst, MAKEINTRESOURCE(IDD_ABOUTBOX), hWnd, About);
                        break;
                case IDM_EXIT:
                        DestroyWindow(hWnd);
                        break;
                default:
                        return DefWindowProc(hWnd, message, wParam, lParam);
                }
                break;
        case WM_PAINT:
                hdc = BeginPaint(hWnd, &ps);
                // TODO: Add any drawing code here...
                EndPaint(hWnd, &ps);
                break;
        case WM_DESTROY:
                PostQuitMessage(0);
                break;
        default:
                return DefWindowProc(hWnd, message, wParam, lParam);
        }
        return 0;
}
```

Move a text caret to "switch (message)" line #136.

6.   Now, we put a breakpoint on *AppD4.cpp* line 136 (we can also use right mouse click, *Insert or Remove Breakpoint* or F9):

```
0:010> bp `AppD4.cpp:136`
```

```
0:010> bl
     0 e Disable Clear   00007ff6`599f127c   [C:\AWD3\AppD4\AppD4\AppD4.cpp @ 136]      0001 (0001)  0:**** AppD4!WndProc+0x2c
```

The line is immediately highlighted:

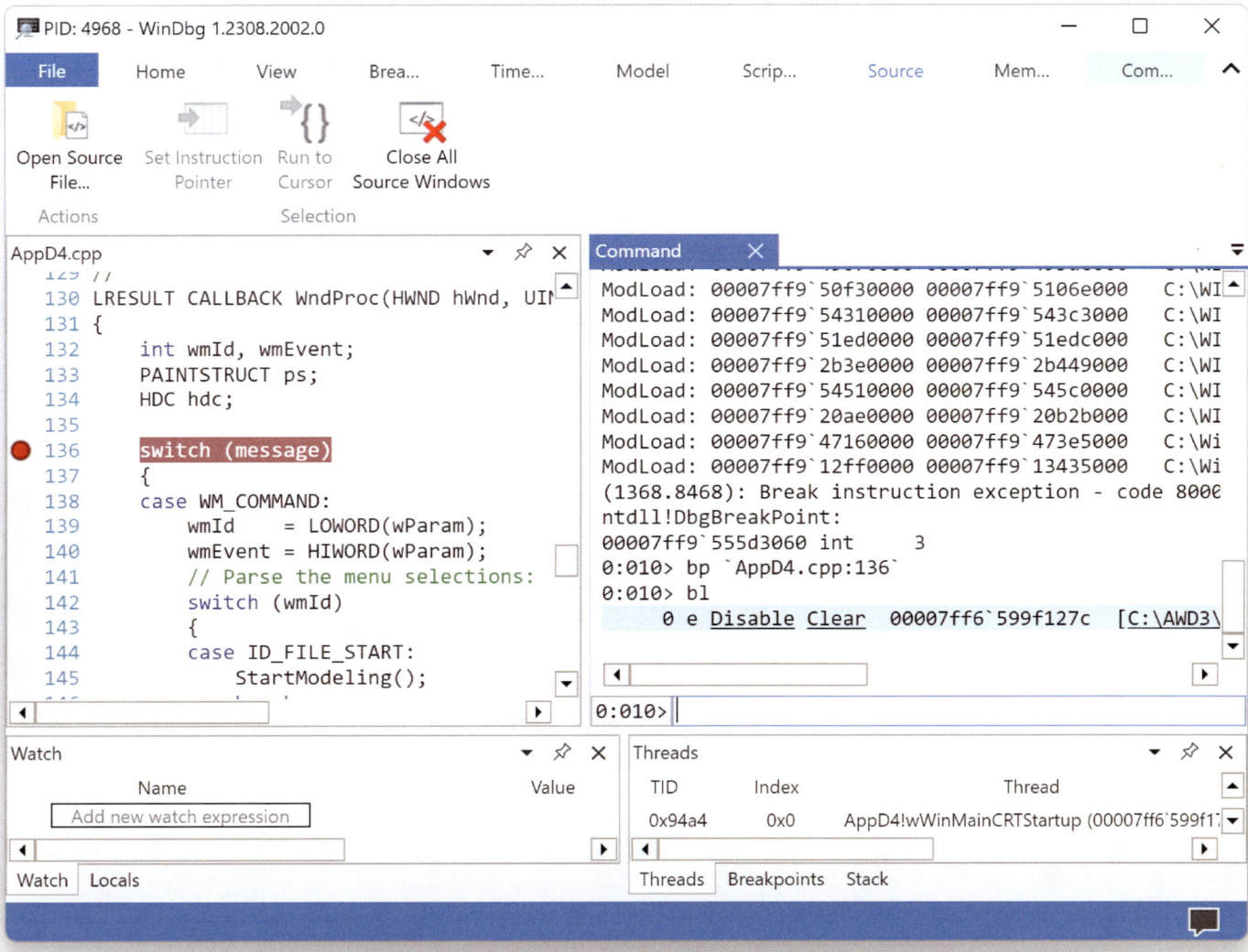

7.   To log typed characters, we need to intercept the WM_CHAR message. Its value is 0x0102 (from *WinUser.h*). We can add a script to a **conditional** breakpoint that compares *message* value (UINT, dword) and only logs WM_CHAR. Because this breakpoint is hit quite often, we gradually refine it. We first print the message value only when the message equals 0x102 and ignore all other messages:

```
0:010> bp AppD4!WndProc+0x2c "j (dwo(message)=102) '.printf \"message: %p\", dwo(message); .echo';gc"
breakpoint 0 redefined
```

If we continue execution, we switch to the *AppD4* window and press some key, for example, 'h', then we get a breakpoint hit:

```
0:010> g
ModLoad: 00007ff9`54c70000 00007ff9`54e10000   C:\WINDOWS\System32\ole32.dll
message: 0000000000000102
AppD4!WndProc+0x2c:
00007ff6`599f127c mov        eax,dword ptr [rsp+0C8h] ss:0000008e`f00ff778=00000102
```

Note: we use the **dwo** command to get the message value because the *message* symbol is an address for that value:

```
0:000> ? message
Evaluate expression: 613912934264 = 0000008e`f00ff778

0:000> dd message L1
0000008e`f00ff778  00000102

0:000> ? dwo(message)
Evaluate expression: 258 = 00000000`00000102

0:000> ?? message
unsigned int 0x102

0:000> dx message
message          : 0x102 [Type: unsigned int]
```

Note: We also use **\"** to insert **"** into an already existing string, and we use **.echo** for a new line. The **gc** command is the "else" branch to resume execution from a conditional breakpoint. Also, for 64-bit values such as *long long* or *pointers,* we should use **poi** instead of **dwo**.

8.   *wParam* (64-bit) of this message contains the character code. We modify our breakpoint to print this instead (we use **poi** here for *wParam*):

```
0:000> dx wParam
wParam           : 0x68 [Type: unsigned __int64]

0:000> ?? wParam
unsigned int64 0x68

0:000> bp AppD4!WndProc+0x2c "j (dwo(message)=102) '.printf \"wParam: %p\", poi(wParam); .echo';gc"
breakpoint 0 redefined

0:000> g
wParam: 0000000000000068
AppD4!WndProc+0x2c:
00007ff6`599f127c mov        eax,dword ptr [rsp+0C8h] ss:0000008e`f00ff778=00000102
```

9.   Now, since our goal is to print typed characters, we remove extra output such as a prompt:

```
0:000> .prompt_allow
Allow the following information to be displayed at the prompt:
(Other settings can affect whether the information is actually displayed)
   sym - Symbol for current instruction
   dis - Disassembly of current instruction
    ea - Effective address for current instruction
   src - Source info for current instruction
Do not allow the following information to be displayed at the prompt:
   reg - Register state
```

```
0:000> .prompt_allow -sym -dis -ea -src
Allow the following information to be displayed at the prompt:
(Other settings can affect whether the information is actually displayed)
  None
Do not allow the following information to be displayed at the prompt:
   sym - Symbol for current instruction
   dis - Disassembly of current instruction
    ea - Effective address for current instruction
   reg - Register state
   src - Source info for current instruction
```

```
0:000> g
wParam: 0000000000000068
```

10.   Actually, 0000000000000068 looks like a NULL terminated string: 0000000000000068. This is because 68 is located at a lower address due to little-endian notation. So we can use the **%ma** format specifier in the **.printf**, but then we need to remove **poi** and pass only this value address, just wParam:

```
0:000> bp AppD4!WndProc+0x2c "j (dwo(message)=102) '.printf \"wParam: %ma\", wParam; .echo ';gc"
breakpoint 0 redefined
```

```
0:000> g
wParam: h
```

11.   Now we leave only **\"%ma\"**, replace **.echo** with **gc**, and after redefining the breakpoint and **g**, switch to *AppD4* and type 'Hello World!' in the *AppD4* window:

```
0:000> bp AppD4!WndProc+0x2c "j (dwo(message)=102) '.printf \"%ma\", wParam;gc';gc"
breakpoint 0 redefined
```

```
0:000> g
Hello World!
```

12.   We now break in and close logging:

```
(1368.5398): Break instruction exception - code 80000003 (first chance)
```

```
0:012> .logclose
Closing open log file C:\AWD4\D4.log
```

Exercise UD5

- **Goal:** Learn how to debug multiple processes and their deadlock

- **Elementary Diagnostics Patterns:** Crash; Hang

- **Memory Analysis Patterns:** Exception Stack Trace; Constant Subtrace; NULL Pointer (Data); Main Thread; Execution Residue (Unmanaged Space, User); Hidden Exception (User Space); Handled Exception (User Space); Wait Chain (Mutex Objects); Deadlock (Objects, User Space)

- **Debugging Implementation Patterns:** Break-in

- \AWD4\Exercise-UD5.pdf

Exercise UD5

Goal: Learn how to debug multiple processes and their deadlock.

Elementary Diagnostics Patterns: Crash; Hang.

Memory Analysis Patterns: Exception Stack Trace; Constant Subtrace; NULL Pointer (Data); Main Thread; Execution Residue (Unmanaged Space, User); Hidden Exception (User Space); Handled Exception (User Space); Wait Chain (Mutex Objects); Deadlock (Objects, User Space).

Debugging Implementation Patterns: Break-in.

1.   Launch *\AWD4\AppD5A\x64\Release\AppD5A.exe* executable.

2.   Launch *\AWD4\AppD5B\x64\Release\AppD5B.exe* executable.

3.   Switch to *AppD5A* and choose *File \ Start*. Next, switch to *AppD5B* and choose *File \ Start*. The applications do not respond for less than 30 seconds and then start responding again. This is normal expected behavior (from these applications) as they mutually wait while doing some work (modeled by *Sleep*).

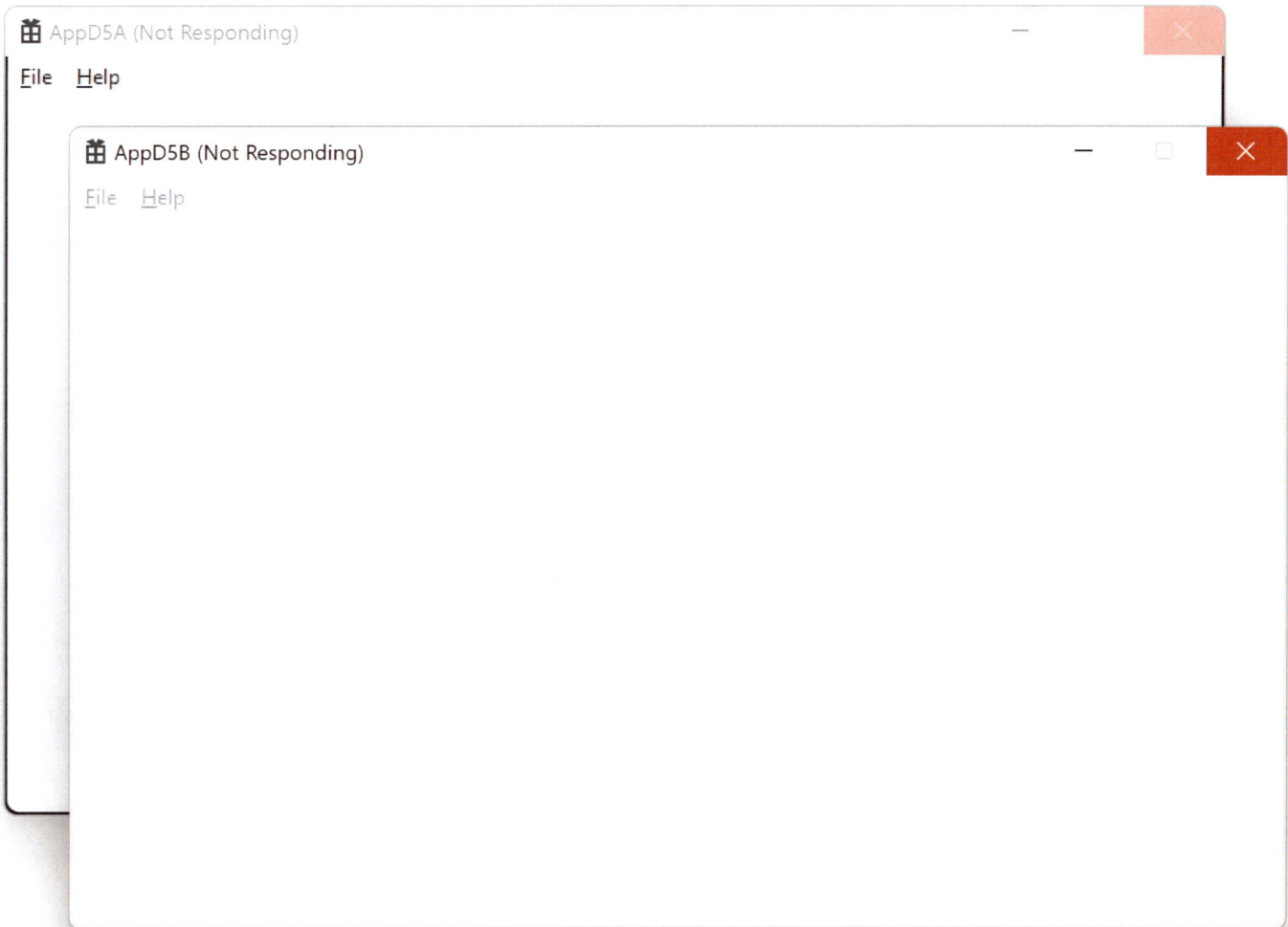

The source code for the *AppD5A* part:

```
void StartModeling(void)
{
        HANDLE hMutexA = CreateMutex(NULL, TRUE, L"AppD5_MutexA");

        Sleep(20000); // some work

        HANDLE hMutexB = OpenMutex(SYNCHRONIZE, FALSE, L"AppD5_MutexB");

        if (hMutexB)
        {
                WaitForSingleObject(hMutexB,INFINITE);
        }

        Sleep(10000); // some more work

        ReleaseMutex(hMutexB);
        ReleaseMutex(hMutexA);
}
```

The source code for the *AppD5B* part:

```
void StartModeling(void)
{
        HANDLE hMutexB  = CreateMutex(NULL, TRUE, L"AppD5_MutexB");

        Sleep(10000); // some work

        ReleaseMutex(hMutexB);

        HANDLE hMutexA = OpenMutex(SYNCHRONIZE, FALSE, L"AppD5_MutexA");

        if (hMutexA)
        {
                WaitForSingleObject(hMutexA,INFINITE);
        }

        Sleep(10000); // some more work

        ReleaseMutex(hMutexA);
}
```

Note: Although we have 2 synchronization objects, the code is deadlock-free as we acquire and release them in ABBA order and hold their ownership for a limited time.

4.   Check the following registry key under *HKEY_LOCAL_MACHINE\Software\Microsoft\Windows\Windows Error Reporting*:

```
DontShowUI = 0
DWORD
```

If it doesn't exist, then create it and set its value to 0. This is to enable crashing applications to display "... has stopped working" WER dialog necessary for the rest of this exercise.

5.   Quit *AppD5A* and *AppD5B*. Launch *AppD5A* again and then launch *\AWD4\AppD5BV2\x64\Release\AppD5BV2.exe* executable. The new feature was added to *AppD5B* (now Version 2):

```
void StartModeling(void)
{
        HANDLE hMutexB  = CreateMutex(NULL, TRUE, L"AppD5_MutexB");

        Sleep(10000); // some work

        NewFeature();
        ReleaseMutex(hMutexB);

        HANDLE hMutexA = OpenMutex(SYNCHRONIZE, FALSE, L"AppD5_MutexA");

        if (hMutexA)
        {
                WaitForSingleObject(hMutexA,INFINITE);
        }

        Sleep(10000); // some more work

        ReleaseMutex(hMutexA);
}
```

6.   We switch to AppD5A and choose *File \ Start*. Then switch to AppD5BV2 and choose *File \ Start*. After that, AppD5BV2 should crash (**do not cancel or close WER dialogs**):

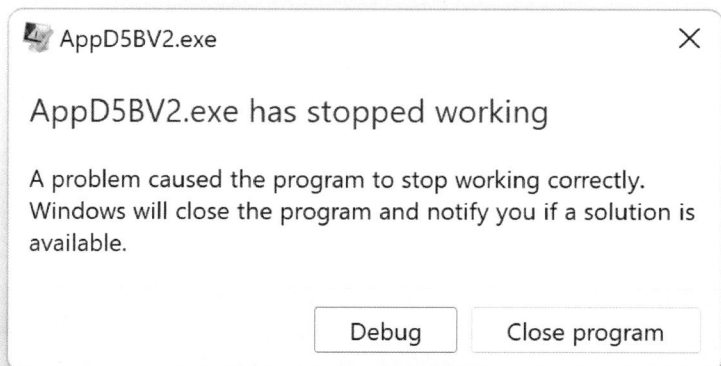

AppD5A window is not responding, so we attached WinDbg to it:

```
Microsoft (R) Windows Debugger Version 10.0.25921.1001 AMD64
Copyright (c) Microsoft Corporation. All rights reserved.

*** wait with pending attach

************* Path validation summary **************
Response                         Time (ms)      Location
Deferred                                        srv*
Symbol search path is: srv*
Executable search path is:
ModLoad: 00007ff7`f0350000 00007ff7`f0370000   C:\AWD4\AppD5A\x64\Release\AppD5A.exe
ModLoad: 00007ff9`55530000 00007ff9`55747000   C:\WINDOWS\SYSTEM32\ntdll.dll
ModLoad: 00007ff9`55030000 00007ff9`550f4000   C:\WINDOWS\System32\KERNEL32.DLL
ModLoad: 00007ff9`52870000 00007ff9`52c16000   C:\WINDOWS\System32\KERNELBASE.dll
ModLoad: 00007ff9`54130000 00007ff9`542de000   C:\WINDOWS\System32\USER32.dll
ModLoad: 00007ff9`53190000 00007ff9`531b6000   C:\WINDOWS\System32\win32u.dll
ModLoad: 00007ff9`542e0000 00007ff9`54309000   C:\WINDOWS\System32\GDI32.dll
ModLoad: 00007ff9`52c20000 00007ff9`52d38000   C:\WINDOWS\System32\gdi32full.dll
ModLoad: 00007ff9`52f30000 00007ff9`52fca000   C:\WINDOWS\System32\msvcp_win.dll
ModLoad: 00007ff9`53000000 00007ff9`53111000   C:\WINDOWS\System32\ucrtbase.dll
ModLoad: 00007ff9`53ef0000 00007ff9`53f21000   C:\WINDOWS\System32\IMM32.DLL
ModLoad: 00007ff9`4f920000 00007ff9`4f9cb000   C:\WINDOWS\system32\uxtheme.dll
ModLoad: 00007ff9`53b60000 00007ff9`53ee9000   C:\WINDOWS\System32\combase.dll
ModLoad: 00007ff9`543d0000 00007ff9`544e7000   C:\WINDOWS\System32\RPCRT4.dll
ModLoad: 00007ff9`54a40000 00007ff9`54b90000   C:\WINDOWS\System32\MSCTF.dll
ModLoad: 00007ff9`55100000 00007ff9`551a7000   C:\WINDOWS\System32\msvcrt.dll
ModLoad: 00007ff9`20a30000 00007ff9`20ae0000   C:\WINDOWS\SYSTEM32\TextShaping.dll
ModLoad: 00007ff9`51860000 00007ff9`51878000   C:\WINDOWS\SYSTEM32\kernel.appcore.dll
ModLoad: 00007ff9`52eb0000 00007ff9`52f2a000   C:\WINDOWS\System32\bcryptPrimitives.dll
ModLoad: 00007ff9`54e20000 00007ff9`54ec8000   C:\WINDOWS\System32\sechost.dll
ModLoad: 00007ff9`52fd0000 00007ff9`52ff8000   C:\WINDOWS\System32\bcrypt.dll
ModLoad: 00007ff9`3fba0000 00007ff9`3fcea000   C:\WINDOWS\SYSTEM32\textinputframework.dll
ModLoad: 00007ff9`54b90000 00007ff9`54c67000   C:\WINDOWS\System32\OLEAUT32.dll
ModLoad: 00007ff9`4f470000 00007ff9`4f5a4000   C:\WINDOWS\SYSTEM32\CoreMessaging.dll
ModLoad: 00007ff9`49070000 00007ff9`493dc000   C:\WINDOWS\SYSTEM32\CoreUIComponents.dll
ModLoad: 00007ff9`50f30000 00007ff9`5106e000   C:\WINDOWS\SYSTEM32\wintypes.dll
ModLoad: 00007ff9`54310000 00007ff9`543c3000   C:\WINDOWS\System32\advapi32.dll
ModLoad: 00007ff9`51ed0000 00007ff9`51edc000   C:\WINDOWS\SYSTEM32\CRYPTBASE.DLL
ModLoad: 00007ff9`2b3e0000 00007ff9`2b449000   C:\WINDOWS\system32\Oleacc.dll
ModLoad: 00007ff9`54510000 00007ff9`545c0000   C:\WINDOWS\System32\clbcatq.dll
ModLoad: 00007ff9`20ae0000 00007ff9`20b2b000
C:\WINDOWS\system32\ApplicationTargetedFeatureDatabase.dll
ModLoad: 00007ff9`47160000 00007ff9`473e5000   C:\Windows\System32\twinapi.appcore.dll
ModLoad: 00007ff9`12ff0000 00007ff9`13435000   C:\Windows\System32\uiautomationcore.dll
ModLoad: 00007ff9`4fb50000 00007ff9`4fb7b000   C:\Windows\system32\dwmapi.dll
ModLoad: 00007ff9`1e070000 00007ff9`1e085000   C:\Windows\System32\threadpoolwinrt.dll
(95b4.2e4): Break instruction exception - code 80000003 (first chance)
ntdll!DbgBreakPoint:
00007ff9`555d3060 int     3
```

7.   We open a log file :

```
0:008> .logopen C:\AWD4\D5V2.log
Opened log file 'C:\AWD4\D5V2.log'
```

8.   We switch to the main thread and examine its stack trace:

```
0:008> ~0s
ntdll!NtWaitForSingleObject+0x14:
00007ff9`555cf3f4 ret
```

```
0:000> kL
 # Child-SP          RetAddr               Call Site
00 000000cc`362ff758 00007ff9`528a44ee     ntdll!NtWaitForSingleObject+0x14
01 000000cc`362ff760 00007ff7`f03514c9     KERNELBASE!WaitForSingleObjectEx+0x8e
02 000000cc`362ff800 00007ff7`f0351301     AppD5A!StartModeling+0x59
03 000000cc`362ff840 00007ff9`54148241     AppD5A!WndProc+0xb1
04 000000cc`362ff900 00007ff9`54147d01     USER32!UserCallWinProcCheckWow+0x2d1
05 000000cc`362ffa60 00007ff7`f03510d0     USER32!DispatchMessageWorker+0x1f1
06 000000cc`362ffae0 00007ff7`f035170a     AppD5A!wWinMain+0xd0
07 (Inline Function) --------`--------     AppD5A!invoke_main+0x21
08 000000cc`362ffb50 00007ff9`5504257d     AppD5A!__scrt_common_main_seh+0x106
09 000000cc`362ffb90 00007ff9`5558aa58     KERNEL32!BaseThreadInitThunk+0x1d
0a 000000cc`362ffbc0 00000000`00000000     ntdll!RtlUserThreadStart+0x28
```

We see it is waiting for some synchronization object. When we choose frame #2, we see the source code:

```
0:000> .srcfix
Source search path is: SRV*
```

```
0:000> .srcpath+ C:\AWD4\AppD5A\AppD5A
Source search path is: SRV*;C:\AWD4\AppD5A\AppD5A

************ Path validation summary **************
Response                      Time (ms)     Location
Deferred                                    SRV*
OK                                          C:\AWD4\AppD5A\AppD5A
```

```
0:000> .frame 2
02 00000028`5fb1fb80 00007ff6`ff771301     AppD5A!StartModeling+0x59
[C:\AWD3\AppD5A\AppD5A\AppD5A.cpp @ 204]
```

Note: What is highlighted in yellow is a return line, which we return to if *WaitForSingleObject* returns.

File   Home   View   Brea...   Time...   Model   Scri...   Sou...   Me...   Com...

Break Go   Step Out   Step Out Back   Go Back   Restart   Settings Source Assembly   Local Help   Feedback
        Step Into   Step Into Back   Stop Debugging
        Step Over   Step Over Back   Detach

Flow Control   Reverse Flow Control   End   Preferences   Help

AppD5A.cpp

```
193    HANDLE hMutexA = CreateMutex(NULL,
194
195    Sleep(20000); // some work
196
197    HANDLE hMutexB = OpenMutex(SYNCHROI
198
199    if (hMutexB)
200    {
201        WaitForSingleObject(hMutexB,INF
202    }
203
204    Sleep(10000); // some more work
205
206    ReleaseMutex(hMutexB);
207    ReleaseMutex(hMutexA);
208  }
209
```

Command

```
Response                        Time (ms)      Lo
Deferred                                       SR
OK                                             C:
0:000> .srcfix
Source search path is: SRV*
0:000> .srcpath+ C:\AWD4\AppD5A\AppD5A
Source search path is: SRV*;C:\AWD4\AppD5A\AppD5A

************* Path validation summary ***********
Response                        Time (ms)      Lo
Deferred                                       SR
OK                                             C:
0:000> .frame 2
02 000000cc`362ff800 00007ff7`f0351301      AppD5A

0:000>
```

Watch

Name	Value
Add new watch expression	

Watch Locals

Threads

TID	Index	Thread
0x9734	0x0	AppD5A!wWinMainCRTStartup (00007ff7

Threads Breakpoints Stack

9.   Let's now launch another instance of WinDbg and attach it to the *AppD5BV2* process from your session while it shows the error message box. We should get this output:

```
Microsoft (R) Windows Debugger Version 10.0.25921.1001 AMD64
Copyright (c) Microsoft Corporation. All rights reserved.

*** wait with pending attach

************* Path validation summary **************
Response                        Time (ms)       Location
Deferred                                        srv*
Symbol search path is: srv*
Executable search path is:
ModLoad: 00007ff6`56450000 00007ff6`56470000    C:\AWD4\AppD5BV2\x64\Release\AppD5BV2.exe
ModLoad: 00007ff9`55530000 00007ff9`55747000    C:\WINDOWS\SYSTEM32\ntdll.dll
ModLoad: 00007ff9`55030000 00007ff9`550f4000    C:\WINDOWS\System32\KERNEL32.DLL
ModLoad: 00007ff9`52870000 00007ff9`52c16000    C:\WINDOWS\System32\KERNELBASE.dll
ModLoad: 00007ff9`4f780000 00007ff9`4f817000    C:\WINDOWS\SYSTEM32\apphelp.dll
ModLoad: 00007ff9`54130000 00007ff9`542de000    C:\WINDOWS\System32\USER32.dll
ModLoad: 00007ff9`53190000 00007ff9`531b6000    C:\WINDOWS\System32\win32u.dll
ModLoad: 00007ff9`542e0000 00007ff9`54309000    C:\WINDOWS\System32\GDI32.dll
ModLoad: 00007ff9`52c20000 00007ff9`52d38000    C:\WINDOWS\System32\gdi32full.dll
ModLoad: 00007ff9`52f30000 00007ff9`52fca000    C:\WINDOWS\System32\msvcp_win.dll
ModLoad: 00007ff9`53000000 00007ff9`53111000    C:\WINDOWS\System32\ucrtbase.dll
ModLoad: 00007ff9`53ef0000 00007ff9`53f21000    C:\WINDOWS\System32\IMM32.DLL
ModLoad: 00007ff9`4f920000 00007ff9`4f9cb000    C:\WINDOWS\system32\uxtheme.dll
ModLoad: 00007ff9`53b60000 00007ff9`53ee9000    C:\WINDOWS\System32\combase.dll
ModLoad: 00007ff9`543d0000 00007ff9`544e7000    C:\WINDOWS\System32\RPCRT4.dll
ModLoad: 00007ff9`54a40000 00007ff9`54b90000    C:\WINDOWS\System32\MSCTF.dll
ModLoad: 00007ff9`55100000 00007ff9`551a7000    C:\WINDOWS\System32\msvcrt.dll
ModLoad: 00007ff9`20a30000 00007ff9`20ae0000    C:\WINDOWS\SYSTEM32\TextShaping.dll
ModLoad: 00007ff9`51860000 00007ff9`51878000    C:\WINDOWS\SYSTEM32\kernel.appcore.dll
ModLoad: 00007ff9`52eb0000 00007ff9`52f2a000    C:\WINDOWS\System32\bcryptPrimitives.dll
ModLoad: 00007ff9`54e20000 00007ff9`54ec8000    C:\WINDOWS\System32\sechost.dll
ModLoad: 00007ff9`52fd0000 00007ff9`52ff8000    C:\WINDOWS\System32\bcrypt.dll
ModLoad: 00007ff9`3fba0000 00007ff9`3fcea000    C:\WINDOWS\SYSTEM32\textinputframework.dll
ModLoad: 00007ff9`54b90000 00007ff9`54c67000    C:\WINDOWS\System32\OLEAUT32.dll
ModLoad: 00007ff9`4f470000 00007ff9`4f5a4000    C:\WINDOWS\SYSTEM32\CoreMessaging.dll
ModLoad: 00007ff9`49070000 00007ff9`493dc000    C:\WINDOWS\SYSTEM32\CoreUIComponents.dll
ModLoad: 00007ff9`50f30000 00007ff9`5106e000    C:\WINDOWS\SYSTEM32\wintypes.dll
ModLoad: 00007ff9`54310000 00007ff9`543c3000    C:\WINDOWS\System32\advapi32.dll
ModLoad: 00007ff9`51ed0000 00007ff9`51edc000    C:\WINDOWS\SYSTEM32\CRYPTBASE.DLL
ModLoad: 00007ff9`2b3e0000 00007ff9`2b449000    C:\WINDOWS\system32\Oleacc.dll
ModLoad: 00007ff9`54510000 00007ff9`545c0000    C:\WINDOWS\System32\clbcatq.dll
ModLoad: 00007ff9`20ae0000 00007ff9`20b2b000
C:\WINDOWS\system32\ApplicationTargetedFeatureDatabase.dll
ModLoad: 00007ff9`47160000 00007ff9`473e5000    C:\Windows\System32\twinapi.appcore.dll
ModLoad: 00007ff9`12ff0000 00007ff9`13435000    C:\Windows\System32\uiautomationcore.dll
ModLoad: 00007ff9`4fb50000 00007ff9`4fb7b000    C:\Windows\system32\dwmapi.dll
ModLoad: 00007ff9`1e070000 00007ff9`1e085000    C:\Windows\System32\threadpoolwinrt.dll
(5070.65c8): Break instruction exception - code 80000003 (first chance)
ntdll!DbgBreakPoint:
00007ff9`555d3060 int     3
```

10.   We open an existing log file to append any output:

```
0:009> .logappend C:\AWD4\D5V2.log
```

```
Opened log file 'C:\AWD4\D5V2.log'
```

11.   We switch to the main thread and examine its stack trace:

```
0:009> ~0s
ntdll!NtWaitForMultipleObjects+0x14:
00007ff9`555cfec4 ret
```

```
0:000> kL
 # Child-SP          RetAddr               Call Site
00 00000044`d2dde3e8 00007ff9`528cffe9     ntdll!NtWaitForMultipleObjects+0x14
01 00000044`d2dde3f0 00007ff9`528cfeee     KERNELBASE!WaitForMultipleObjectsEx+0xe9
02 00000044`d2dde6d0 00007ff9`550a27f7     KERNELBASE!WaitForMultipleObjects+0xe
03 00000044`d2dde710 00007ff9`550a2236     KERNEL32!WerpReportFaultInternal+0x587
04 00000044`d2dde830 00007ff9`529ccafb     KERNEL32!WerpReportFault+0xbe
05 00000044`d2dde870 00007ff9`555d8abd     KERNELBASE!UnhandledExceptionFilter+0x3db
06 00000044`d2dde990 00007ff9`555bf197     ntdll!RtlUserThreadStart$filt$0+0xac
07 00000044`d2dde9d0 00007ff9`555d441f     ntdll!_C_specific_handler+0x97
08 00000044`d2ddea40 00007ff9`5554e466     ntdll!RtlpExecuteHandlerForException+0xf
09 00000044`d2ddea70 00007ff9`555d340e     ntdll!RtlDispatchException+0x286
0a 00000044`d2ddf1c0 00007ff6`56451510     ntdll!KiUserExceptionDispatch+0x2e
0b 00000044`d2ddf940 00007ff6`5645149d     AppD5BV2!NewFeature+0x10
0c 00000044`d2ddf960 00007ff6`56451301     AppD5BV2!StartModeling+0x2d
0d 00000044`d2ddf9a0 00007ff9`54148241     AppD5BV2!WndProc+0xb1
0e 00000044`d2ddfa60 00007ff9`54147d01     USER32!UserCallWinProcCheckWow+0x2d1
0f 00000044`d2ddfbc0 00007ff6`564510d0     USER32!DispatchMessageWorker+0x1f1
10 00000044`d2ddfc40 00007ff6`5645173a     AppD5BV2!wWinMain+0xd0
11 (Inline Function) --------`--------     AppD5BV2!invoke_main+0x21
12 00000044`d2ddfcb0 00007ff9`5504257d     AppD5BV2!__scrt_common_main_seh+0x106
13 00000044`d2ddfcf0 00007ff9`5558aa58     KERNEL32!BaseThreadInitThunk+0x1d
14 00000044`d2ddfd20 00000000`00000000     ntdll!RtlUserThreadStart+0x28
```

A large part of the stack trace above is exception processing calls (in green) calling Windows Error Reporting (WER) functions. We now switch to our frame **0b**:

```
0:000> .srcfix
Source search path is: SRV*
```

```
0:000> .srcpath+ C:\AWD4\AppD5BV2\AppD5BV2
Source search path is: SRV*;C:\AWD4\AppD5BV2\AppD5BV2
```

```
************* Path validation summary **************
Response                        Time (ms)    Location
Deferred                                     SRV*
OK                                           C:\AWD4\AppD5BV2\AppD5BV2
```

```
0:000> .frame b
0b 00000044`d2ddf940 00007ff6`5645149d     AppD5BV2!NewFeature+0x10
[C:\AWD3\AppD5BV2\AppD5BV2\NewFeature.cpp @ 7]
```

Source code should also be highlighted:

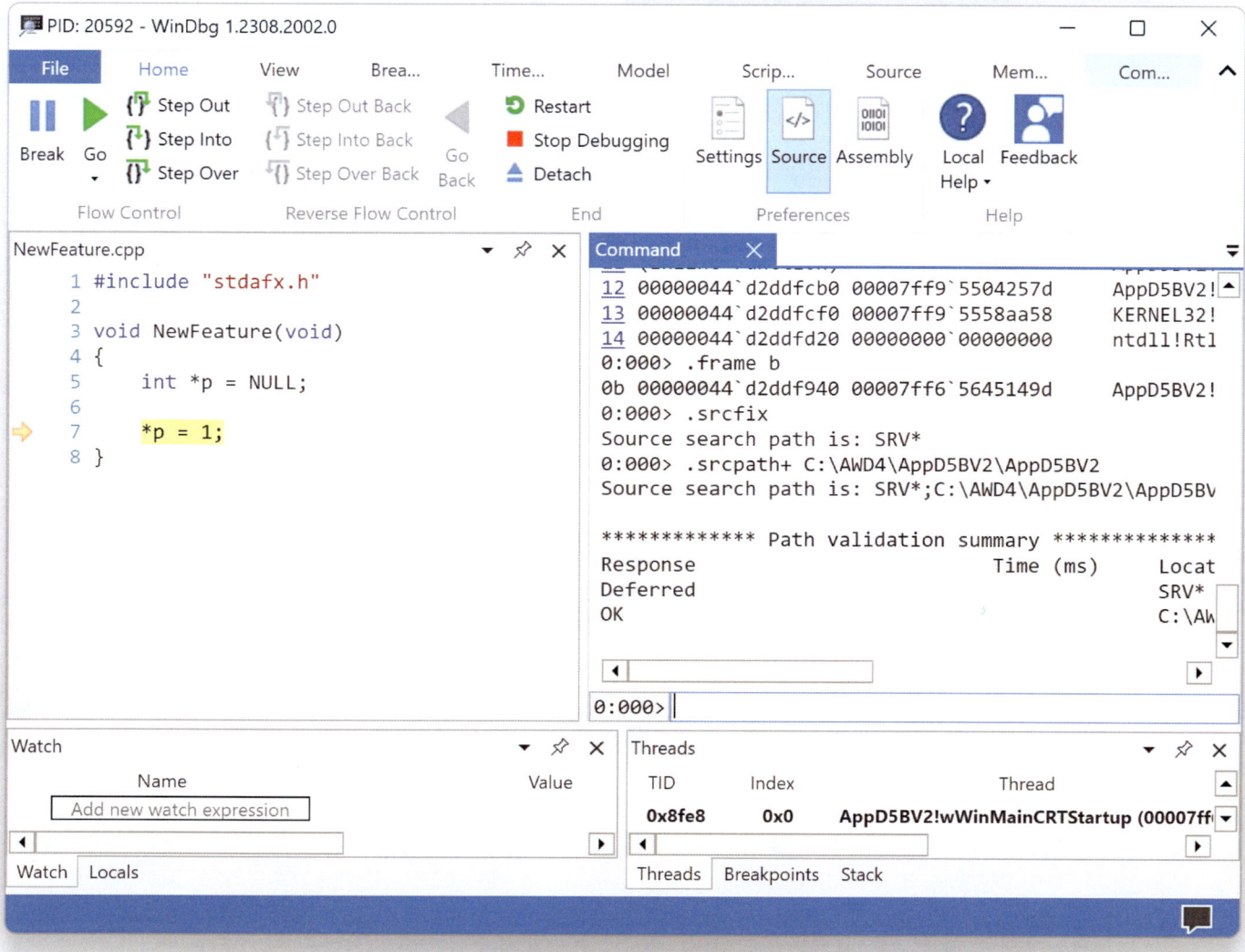

12.	We now want to see only the stack trace prior to the exception and ignore exception processing. For that, we need to set the new exception context: change CPU registers to values existing at the time of the exception. One of the values on a stack region below the *KiUserExceptionDispatch* return address is a pointer to such a context. So, we inspect the stack trace and choose one of the stack pointer values in the first column:

```
0:000> kL
 # Child-SP          RetAddr           Call Site
00 00000044`d2dde3e8 00007ff9`528cffe9 ntdll!NtWaitForMultipleObjects+0x14
01 00000044`d2dde3f0 00007ff9`528cfeee KERNELBASE!WaitForMultipleObjectsEx+0xe9
02 00000044`d2dde6d0 00007ff9`550a27f7 KERNELBASE!WaitForMultipleObjects+0xe
03 00000044`d2dde710 00007ff9`550a2236 KERNEL32!WerpReportFaultInternal+0x587
04 00000044`d2dde830 00007ff9`529ccafb KERNEL32!WerpReportFault+0xbe
05 00000044`d2dde870 00007ff9`555d8abd KERNELBASE!UnhandledExceptionFilter+0x3db
06 00000044`d2dde990 00007ff9`555bf197 ntdll!RtlUserThreadStart$filt$0+0xac
07 00000044`d2dde9d0 00007ff9`555d441f ntdll!_C_specific_handler+0x97
08 00000044`d2ddea40 00007ff9`5554e466 ntdll!RtlpExecuteHandlerForException+0xf
09 00000044`d2ddea70 00007ff9`555d340e ntdll!RtlDispatchException+0x286
0a 00000044`d2ddf1c0 00007ff6`56451510 ntdll!KiUserExceptionDispatch+0x2e
0b 00000044`d2ddf940 00007ff6`5645149d AppD5BV2!NewFeature+0x10
```

```
0c 00000044`d2ddf960 00007ff6`56451301     AppD5BV2!StartModeling+0x2d
0d 00000044`d2ddf9a0 00007ff9`54148241     AppD5BV2!WndProc+0xb1
0e 00000044`d2ddfa60 00007ff9`54147d01     USER32!UserCallWinProcCheckWow+0x2d1
0f 00000044`d2ddfbc0 00007ff6`564510d0     USER32!DispatchMessageWorker+0x1f1
10 00000044`d2ddfc40 00007ff6`5645173a     AppD5BV2!wWinMain+0xd0
11 (Inline Function) --------`--------     AppD5BV2!invoke_main+0x21
12 00000044`d2ddfcb0 00007ff9`5504257d     AppD5BV2!__scrt_common_main_seh+0x106
13 00000044`d2ddfcf0 00007ff9`5558aa58     KERNEL32!BaseThreadInitThunk+0x1d
14 00000044`d2ddfd20 00000000`00000000     ntdll!RtlUserThreadStart+0x28

0:000> .cxr 00000044`d2ddf1c0
rax=0000000000000000 rbx=0000000000000000 rcx=00007ff9555cf9f4
rdx=0000000000000000 rsi=0000000080006010 rdi=0000000000000001
rip=00007ff656451510 rsp=00000044d2ddf940 rbp=0000000000000000
 r8=00000044d2ddf8a8  r9=0000000000000000 r10=0000000000000000
r11=00000044d2ddf950 r12=0000000000000000 r13=0000000000000000
r14=0000000000000111 r15=0000000000000000
iopl=0         nv up ei pl nz na pe nc
cs=0033  ss=002b  ds=002b  es=002b  fs=0053  gs=002b             efl=00010202
AppD5BV2!NewFeature+0x10:
00007ff6`56451510 mov     dword ptr [rax],1        ds:00000000`00000000=????????

0:000> kL
  *** Stack trace for last set context - .thread/.cxr resets it
 # Child-SP          RetAddr           Call Site
00 00000044`d2ddf940 00007ff6`5645149d     AppD5BV2!NewFeature+0x10
01 00000044`d2ddf960 00007ff6`56451301     AppD5BV2!StartModeling+0x2d
02 00000044`d2ddf9a0 00007ff9`54148241     AppD5BV2!WndProc+0xb1
03 00000044`d2ddfa60 00007ff9`54147d01     USER32!UserCallWinProcCheckWow+0x2d1
04 00000044`d2ddfbc0 00007ff6`564510d0     USER32!DispatchMessageWorker+0x1f1
05 00000044`d2ddfc40 00007ff6`5645173a     AppD5BV2!wWinMain+0xd0
06 (Inline Function) --------`--------     AppD5BV2!invoke_main+0x21
07 00000044`d2ddfcb0 00007ff9`5504257d     AppD5BV2!__scrt_common_main_seh+0x106
08 00000044`d2ddfcf0 00007ff9`5558aa58     KERNEL32!BaseThreadInitThunk+0x1d
09 00000044`d2ddfd20 00000000`00000000     ntdll!RtlUserThreadStart+0x28
```

13.   We now close both instances of WinDbg (logs should close automatically). Also, dismiss WER dialogs, if any.

14.   To compare with live debugging without WER dialog boxes, we now launch *AppD5BV2* again but under WinDbg:

```
Microsoft (R) Windows Debugger Version 10.0.25921.1001 AMD64
Copyright (c) Microsoft Corporation. All rights reserved.

CommandLine: C:\AWD4\AppD5BV2\x64\Release\AppD5BV2.exe

************* Path validation summary **************
Response                        Time (ms)     Location
Deferred                                      srv*
Symbol search path is: srv*
Executable search path is:
ModLoad: 00007ff6`56450000 00007ff6`56470000     AppD5BV2.exe
ModLoad: 00007ff9`55530000 00007ff9`55747000     ntdll.dll
ModLoad: 00007ff9`55030000 00007ff9`550f4000     C:\WINDOWS\System32\KERNEL32.DLL
ModLoad: 00007ff9`52870000 00007ff9`52c16000     C:\WINDOWS\System32\KERNELBASE.dll
ModLoad: 00007ff9`54130000 00007ff9`542de000     C:\WINDOWS\System32\USER32.dll
ModLoad: 00007ff9`53190000 00007ff9`531b6000     C:\WINDOWS\System32\win32u.dll
ModLoad: 00007ff9`542e0000 00007ff9`54309000     C:\WINDOWS\System32\GDI32.dll
```

```
ModLoad: 00007ff9`52c20000 00007ff9`52d38000   C:\WINDOWS\System32\gdi32full.dll
ModLoad: 00007ff9`52f30000 00007ff9`52fca000   C:\WINDOWS\System32\msvcp_win.dll
ModLoad: 00007ff9`53000000 00007ff9`53111000   C:\WINDOWS\System32\ucrtbase.dll
(2e68.5164): Break instruction exception - code 80000003 (first chance)
ntdll!LdrpDoDebuggerBreak+0x30:
00007ff9`5560b784 int     3
```

15.   We open a log file in append mode:

```
0:000> .logappend C:\AWD4\D5V2.log
Opened log file 'C:\AWD4\D5V2.log'
```

16.   We continue execution (**g**):

```
ModLoad: 00007ff9`53ef0000 00007ff9`53f21000   C:\WINDOWS\System32\IMM32.DLL
ModLoad: 00007ff9`4f920000 00007ff9`4f9cb000   C:\WINDOWS\system32\uxtheme.dll
ModLoad: 00007ff9`53b60000 00007ff9`53ee9000   C:\WINDOWS\System32\combase.dll
ModLoad: 00007ff9`543d0000 00007ff9`544e7000   C:\WINDOWS\System32\RPCRT4.dll
ModLoad: 00007ff9`54a40000 00007ff9`54b90000   C:\WINDOWS\System32\MSCTF.dll
ModLoad: 00007ff9`55100000 00007ff9`551a7000   C:\WINDOWS\System32\msvcrt.dll
ModLoad: 00007ff9`20a30000 00007ff9`20ae0000   C:\WINDOWS\SYSTEM32\TextShaping.dll
ModLoad: 00007ff9`51860000 00007ff9`51878000   C:\WINDOWS\SYSTEM32\kernel.appcore.dll
ModLoad: 00007ff9`52eb0000 00007ff9`52f2a000   C:\WINDOWS\System32\bcryptPrimitives.dll
clientcore\windows\advcore\ctf\uim\tim.cpp(800)\MSCTF.dll!00007FF954A565D9: (caller:
00007FF954A5720C) LogHr(1) tid(5164) 8007029C An assertion failure has occurred.
clientcore\windows\advcore\ctf\uim\tim.cpp(800)\MSCTF.dll!00007FF954A565D9: (caller:
00007FF954A5720C) LogHr(2) tid(5164) 8007029C An assertion failure has occurred.
ModLoad: 00007ff9`54e20000 00007ff9`54ec8000   C:\WINDOWS\System32\sechost.dll
ModLoad: 00007ff9`52fd0000 00007ff9`52ff8000   C:\WINDOWS\System32\bcrypt.dll
ModLoad: 00007ff9`54b90000 00007ff9`54c67000   C:\WINDOWS\System32\OLEAUT32.dll
ModLoad: 00007ff9`3fba0000 00007ff9`3fcea000   C:\WINDOWS\SYSTEM32\textinputframework.dll
ModLoad: 00007ff9`2b3e0000 00007ff9`2b449000   C:\WINDOWS\system32\Oleacc.dll
ModLoad: 00007ff9`12ff0000 00007ff9`13435000   C:\Windows\System32\uiautomationcore.dll
ModLoad: 00007ff9`54510000 00007ff9`545c0000   C:\WINDOWS\System32\clbcatq.dll
ModLoad: 00007ff9`20ae0000 00007ff9`20b2b000
C:\WINDOWS\system32\ApplicationTargetedFeatureDatabase.dll
ModLoad: 00007ff9`47160000 00007ff9`473e5000   C:\Windows\System32\twinapi.appcore.dll
ModLoad: 00007ff9`50f30000 00007ff9`5106e000   C:\Windows\System32\WinTypes.dll
```

Then we launch *AppD5A* again and choose *File \ Start*, switch to *AppD5BV2* and choose *File \ Start,* and switch to
WinDbg. After some time, we should see a first chance exception pointing to a NULL pointer access violation:

```
ModLoad: 00007ff9`4f470000 00007ff9`4f5a4000   C:\WINDOWS\SYSTEM32\CoreMessaging.dll
ModLoad: 00007ff9`49070000 00007ff9`493dc000   C:\WINDOWS\SYSTEM32\CoreUIComponents.dll
ModLoad: 00007ff9`54310000 00007ff9`543c3000   C:\WINDOWS\System32\advapi32.dll
ModLoad: 00007ff9`51ed0000 00007ff9`51edc000   C:\WINDOWS\SYSTEM32\CRYPTBASE.DLL
ModLoad: 00007ff9`4fb50000 00007ff9`4fb7b000   C:\WINDOWS\system32\dwmapi.dll
ModLoad: 00007ff9`1e070000 00007ff9`1e085000   C:\Windows\System32\threadpoolwinrt.dll
(2e68.4d24): C++ EH exception - code e06d7363 (first chance)
(2e68.4d24): C++ EH exception - code e06d7363 (first chance)
(2e68.4d24): C++ EH exception - code e06d7363 (first chance)
(2e68.4d24): C++ EH exception - code e06d7363 (first chance)
(2e68.4d24): C++ EH exception - code e06d7363 (first chance)
(2e68.4d24): C++ EH exception - code e06d7363 (first chance)
(2e68.877c): C++ EH exception - code e06d7363 (first chance)
(2e68.877c): C++ EH exception - code e06d7363 (first chance)
(2e68.877c): C++ EH exception - code e06d7363 (first chance)
```

```
(2e68.877c): C++ EH exception - code e06d7363 (first chance)
(2e68.5164): Access violation - code c0000005 (first chance)
First chance exceptions are reported before any exception handling.
This exception may be expected and handled.
AppD5BV2!NewFeature+0x10:
00007ff6`56451510 mov        dword ptr [rax],1        ds:00000000`00000000=????????
```

We continue and get a second chance exception pointing to the same location:

```
0:000> g
(2e68.5164): Access violation - code c0000005 (!!! second chance !!!)
AppD5BV2!NewFeature+0x10:
00007ff6`56451510 mov        dword ptr [rax],1        ds:00000000`00000000=????????

0:000> r
rax=0000000000000000 rbx=0000000000000000 rcx=00007ff9555cf9f4
rdx=0000000000000000 rsi=0000000080006010 rdi=0000000000000001
rip=00007ff656451510 rsp=000000237a1df4f0 rbp=0000000000000000
 r8=000000237a1df458  r9=0000000000000000 r10=0000000000000000
r11=000000237a1df500 r12=0000000000000000 r13=0000000000000000
r14=0000000000000111 r15=0000000000000000
iopl=0         nv up ei pl nz na po nc
cs=0033  ss=002b  ds=002b  es=002b  fs=0053  gs=002b            efl=00010204
AppD5BV2!NewFeature+0x10:
00007ff6`56451510 mov        dword ptr [rax],1        ds:00000000`00000000=????????
```

17.   The stack trace points to the *NewFeature* function called from *StartModeling*:

```
0:000> kL
 # Child-SP          RetAddr           Call Site
00 00000023`7a1df4f0 00007ff6`5645149d AppD5BV2!NewFeature+0x10
01 00000023`7a1df510 00007ff6`56451301 AppD5BV2!StartModeling+0x2d
02 00000023`7a1df550 00007ff9`54148241 AppD5BV2!WndProc+0xb1
03 00000023`7a1df610 00007ff9`54147d01 USER32!UserCallWinProcCheckWow+0x2d1
04 00000023`7a1df770 00007ff6`564510d0 USER32!DispatchMessageWorker+0x1f1
05 00000023`7a1df7f0 00007ff6`5645173a AppD5BV2!wWinMain+0xd0
06 (Inline Function) --------`-------- AppD5BV2!invoke_main+0x21
07 00000023`7a1df860 00007ff9`5504257d AppD5BV2!__scrt_common_main_seh+0x106
08 00000023`7a1df8a0 00007ff9`5558aa58 KERNEL32!BaseThreadInitThunk+0x1d
09 00000023`7a1df8d0 00000000`00000000 ntdll!RtlUserThreadStart+0x28
```

18.   We now close the logging and quit WinDbg (the *AppD5BV2* process disappears, but we exit the AppD5A process, too):

```
0:000> .logclose
Closing open log file C:\AWD4\D5V2.log

0:000> q
```

19.   An inexperienced developer tried to fix it by enclosing a portion of the code into a *try/catch* block and produced *AppD5V3.exe*:

```
void StartModeling(void)
{
        HANDLE hMutexB  = CreateMutex(NULL, TRUE, L"AppD5_MutexB");

        Sleep(10000); // some work
```

```
        try
        {
                NewFeature();
                ReleaseMutex(hMutexB);
        }
        catch (...)
        {
                // ignore
        }
```

```
        HANDLE hMutexA = OpenMutex(SYNCHRONIZE, FALSE, L"AppD5_MutexA");

        if (hMutexA)
        {
                WaitForSingleObject(hMutexA,INFINITE);
        }

        Sleep(10000); // some more work

        ReleaseMutex(hMutexA);
}
```

20.   We launch *\AWD4\AppD5BV3\x64\Release\AppD5BV3.exe* executable, launch *AppD5A* and choose *File \ Start,* and then switch to *AppD5BV3* and choose *File \ Start*. Then we wait for a minute or more, and both windows are still not responding:

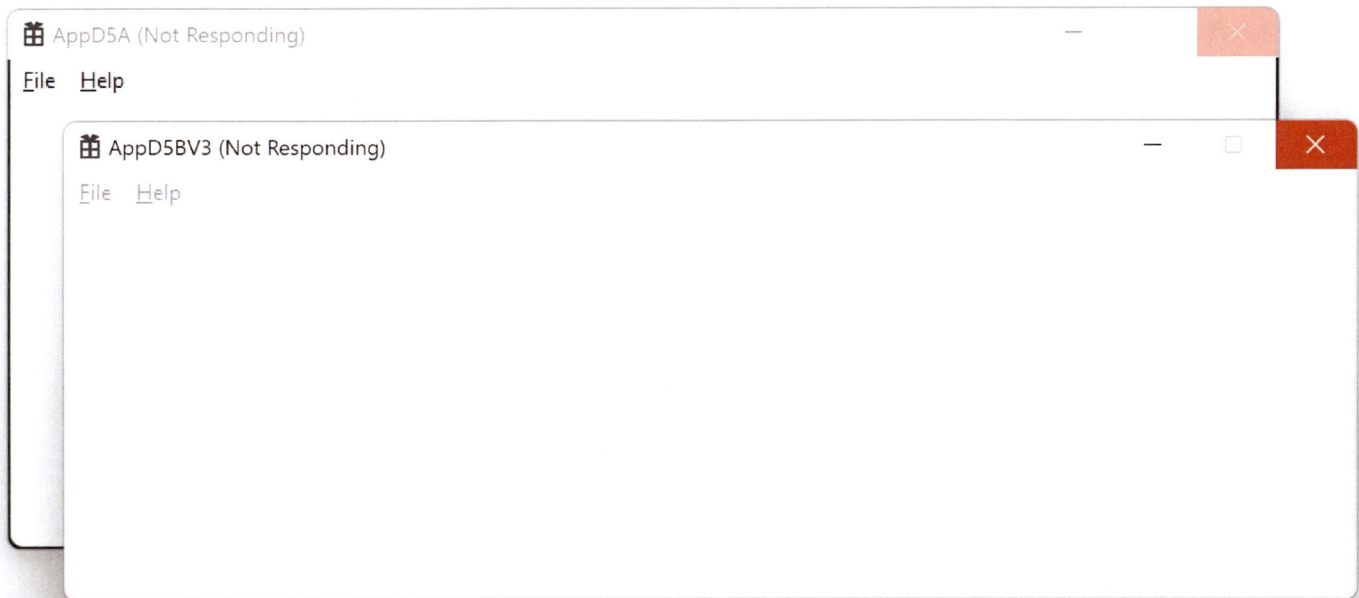

21.   We now attach WinDbg to the *AppD5BV3* process and open a log file:

```
Microsoft (R) Windows Debugger Version 10.0.25921.1001 AMD64
Copyright (c) Microsoft Corporation. All rights reserved.

*** wait with pending attach

************* Path validation summary **************
Response                        Time (ms)       Location
Deferred                                        srv*
```

```
Symbol search path is: srv*
Executable search path is:
ModLoad: 00007ff7`04210000 00007ff7`04233000   C:\AWD4\AppD5BV3\x64\Release\AppD5BV3.exe
ModLoad: 00007ff9`55530000 00007ff9`55747000   C:\WINDOWS\SYSTEM32\ntdll.dll
ModLoad: 00007ff9`55030000 00007ff9`550f4000   C:\WINDOWS\System32\KERNEL32.DLL
ModLoad: 00007ff9`52870000 00007ff9`52c16000   C:\WINDOWS\System32\KERNELBASE.dll
ModLoad: 00007ff9`4f780000 00007ff9`4f817000   C:\WINDOWS\SYSTEM32\apphelp.dll
ModLoad: 00007ff9`54130000 00007ff9`542de000   C:\WINDOWS\System32\USER32.dll
ModLoad: 00007ff9`53190000 00007ff9`531b6000   C:\WINDOWS\System32\win32u.dll
ModLoad: 00007ff9`542e0000 00007ff9`54309000   C:\WINDOWS\System32\GDI32.dll
ModLoad: 00007ff9`52c20000 00007ff9`52d38000   C:\WINDOWS\System32\gdi32full.dll
ModLoad: 00007ff9`52f30000 00007ff9`52fca000   C:\WINDOWS\System32\msvcp_win.dll
ModLoad: 00007ff9`53000000 00007ff9`53111000   C:\WINDOWS\System32\ucrtbase.dll
ModLoad: 00007ff9`53ef0000 00007ff9`53f21000   C:\WINDOWS\System32\IMM32.DLL
ModLoad: 00007ff9`4f920000 00007ff9`4f9cb000   C:\WINDOWS\system32\uxtheme.dll
ModLoad: 00007ff9`53b60000 00007ff9`53ee9000   C:\WINDOWS\System32\combase.dll
ModLoad: 00007ff9`543d0000 00007ff9`544e7000   C:\WINDOWS\System32\RPCRT4.dll
ModLoad: 00007ff9`54a40000 00007ff9`54b90000   C:\WINDOWS\System32\MSCTF.dll
ModLoad: 00007ff9`55100000 00007ff9`551a7000   C:\WINDOWS\System32\msvcrt.dll
ModLoad: 00007ff9`20a30000 00007ff9`20ae0000   C:\WINDOWS\SYSTEM32\TextShaping.dll
ModLoad: 00007ff9`51860000 00007ff9`51878000   C:\WINDOWS\SYSTEM32\kernel.appcore.dll
ModLoad: 00007ff9`52eb0000 00007ff9`52f2a000   C:\WINDOWS\System32\bcryptPrimitives.dll
ModLoad: 00007ff9`54e20000 00007ff9`54ec8000   C:\WINDOWS\System32\sechost.dll
ModLoad: 00007ff9`52fd0000 00007ff9`52ff8000   C:\WINDOWS\System32\bcrypt.dll
ModLoad: 00007ff9`3fba0000 00007ff9`3fcea000   C:\WINDOWS\SYSTEM32\textinputframework.dll
ModLoad: 00007ff9`54b90000 00007ff9`54c67000   C:\WINDOWS\System32\OLEAUT32.dll
ModLoad: 00007ff9`4f470000 00007ff9`4f5a4000   C:\WINDOWS\SYSTEM32\CoreMessaging.dll
ModLoad: 00007ff9`49070000 00007ff9`493dc000   C:\WINDOWS\SYSTEM32\CoreUIComponents.dll
ModLoad: 00007ff9`50f30000 00007ff9`5106e000   C:\WINDOWS\SYSTEM32\wintypes.dll
ModLoad: 00007ff9`54310000 00007ff9`543c3000   C:\WINDOWS\System32\advapi32.dll
ModLoad: 00007ff9`51ed0000 00007ff9`51edc000   C:\WINDOWS\SYSTEM32\CRYPTBASE.DLL
ModLoad: 00007ff9`2b3e0000 00007ff9`2b449000   C:\WINDOWS\system32\Oleacc.dll
ModLoad: 00007ff9`54510000 00007ff9`545c0000   C:\WINDOWS\System32\clbcatq.dll
ModLoad: 00007ff9`20ae0000 00007ff9`20b2b000
C:\WINDOWS\system32\ApplicationTargetedFeatureDatabase.dll
ModLoad: 00007ff9`47160000 00007ff9`473e5000   C:\Windows\System32\twinapi.appcore.dll
ModLoad: 00007ff9`12ff0000 00007ff9`13435000   C:\Windows\System32\uiautomationcore.dll
ModLoad: 00007ff9`4fb50000 00007ff9`4fb7b000   C:\WINDOWS\system32\dwmapi.dll
ModLoad: 00007ff9`1e070000 00007ff9`1e085000   C:\Windows\System32\threadpoolwinrt.dll
(96e8.762c): Break instruction exception - code 80000003 (first chance)
ntdll!DbgBreakPoint:
00007ff9`555d3060 int       3
```

```
0:010> .logopen c:\AWD4\D5V3.log
Opened log file 'c:\AWD4\D5V3.log'
```

22.   We now switch to the main thread and examine its stack trace:

```
0:010> ~0s
ntdll!NtWaitForSingleObject+0x14:
00007ff9`555cf3f4 ret
```

```
0:000> kL
 # Child-SP          RetAddr               Call Site
00 000000cb`e06ff458 00007ff9`528a44ee     ntdll!NtWaitForSingleObject+0x14
01 000000cb`e06ff460 00007ff7`042114dd     KERNELBASE!WaitForSingleObjectEx+0x8e
02 000000cb`e06ff500 00007ff7`04211301     AppD5BV3!StartModeling+0x6d
03 000000cb`e06ff540 00007ff9`54148241     AppD5BV3!WndProc+0xb1
```

```
04 000000cb`e06ff600 00007ff9`54147d01     USER32!UserCallWinProcCheckWow+0x2d1
05 000000cb`e06ff760 00007ff7`042110d0     USER32!DispatchMessageWorker+0x1f1
06 000000cb`e06ff7e0 00007ff7`0421173a     AppD5BV3!wWinMain+0xd0
07 (Inline Function) --------`--------     AppD5BV3!invoke_main+0x21
08 000000cb`e06ff850 00007ff9`5504257d     AppD5BV3!__scrt_common_main_seh+0x106
09 000000cb`e06ff890 00007ff9`5558aa58     KERNEL32!BaseThreadInitThunk+0x1d
0a 000000cb`e06ff8c0 00000000`00000000     ntdll!RtlUserThreadStart+0x28
```

23.   Since we do not expect a wait (we assume *NewFeature* code is complex), we look at raw stack data to find any anomalies, such as hidden and handled exceptions. This is done by finding the stack region boundaries from the Thread Environment Block (TEB) using the **!teb** command, then dumping that region (**dps**), looking for the *KiUserExceptionDispatch* symbol reference, and trying a stack pointer address below that line as the exception record (**.cxr**):

```
0:000> !teb
TEB at 000000cbe0552000
    ExceptionList:         0000000000000000
    StackBase:             000000cbe0700000
    StackLimit:            000000cbe06fa000
    SubSystemTib:          0000000000000000
    FiberData:             0000000000001e00
    ArbitraryUserPointer:  0000000000000000
    Self:                  000000cbe0552000
    EnvironmentPointer:    0000000000000000
    ClientId:              00000000000096e8 . 0000000000006ea8
    RpcHandle:             0000000000000000
    Tls Storage:           000001e1a106bd70
    PEB Address:           000000cbe0551000
    LastErrorValue:        0
    LastStatusValue:       c0000034
    Count Owned Locks:     0
    HardErrorMode:         0
```

```
0:000> dps 000000cbe06fa000 000000cbe0700000
000000cb`e06fa000  00000000`00000000
000000cb`e06fa008  00000000`00000000
000000cb`e06fa010  00000000`00000000
000000cb`e06fa018  00000000`00000000
[...]
000000cb`e06fed20  00000000`00000001
000000cb`e06fed28  00000000`80006010
000000cb`e06fed30  00000000`00000000
000000cb`e06fed38  00007ff9`555d340e ntdll!KiUserExceptionDispatch+0x2e
000000cb`e06fed40  00000000`00000000
000000cb`e06fed48  00000000`00000001
000000cb`e06fed50  00000000`00000000
000000cb`e06fed58  000001e1`a2a80be0
000000cb`e06fed60  00000000`00000000
000000cb`e06fed68  00000000`80006010
000000cb`e06fed70  00001f80`0010005f
000000cb`e06fed78  0053002b`002b0033
000000cb`e06fed80  00010202`002b002b
000000cb`e06fed88  00000000`00000000
000000cb`e06fed90  00000000`00000000
000000cb`e06fed98  00000000`00000000
000000cb`e06feda0  00000000`00000000
000000cb`e06feda8  00000000`00000000
000000cb`e06fedb0  00000000`00000000
000000cb`e06fedb8  00000000`00000000
000000cb`e06fedc0  00007ff9`555cf9f4 ntdll!NtDelayExecution+0x14
000000cb`e06fedc8  00000000`00000000
000000cb`e06fedd0  00000000`00000000
```

```
000000cb`e06fedd8  000000cb`e06ff4e0
000000cb`e06fede0  00000000`00000000
000000cb`e06fede8  00000000`80006010
000000cb`e06fedf0  00000000`00000001
000000cb`e06fedf8  000000cb`e06ff448
000000cb`e06fee00  00000000`00000000
000000cb`e06fee08  00000000`00000000
000000cb`e06fee10  000000cb`e06ff4f0
000000cb`e06fee18  00000000`00000000
000000cb`e06fee20  00000000`00000000
000000cb`e06fee28  00000000`00000111
000000cb`e06fee30  00000000`00000000
000000cb`e06fee38  00007ff7`04211510 AppD5BV3!NewFeature+0x10 [C:\AWD3\AppD5BV3\AppD5BV3\NewFeature.cpp @ 7]
000000cb`e06fee40  00000000`0000027f
000000cb`e06fee48  00000000`00000000
000000cb`e06fee50  00000000`00000000
000000cb`e06fee58  0000ffff`00001f80
[...]
```

24.   If we switch to that exception context, we would see a hidden NULL pointer exception that was caught and ignored:

```
0:000> .cxr 000000cb`e06fed40
rax=0000000000000000 rbx=0000000000000000 rcx=00007ff9555cf9f4
rdx=0000000000000000 rsi=0000000080006010 rdi=0000000000000001
rip=00007ff704211510 rsp=000000cbe06ff4e0 rbp=0000000000000000
 r8=000000cbe06ff448  r9=0000000000000000 r10=0000000000000000
r11=000000cbe06ff4f0 r12=0000000000000000 r13=0000000000000000
r14=0000000000000111 r15=0000000000000000
iopl=0         nv up ei pl nz na pe nc
cs=0033  ss=002b  ds=002b  es=002b  fs=0053  gs=002b            efl=00010202
AppD5BV3!NewFeature+0x10:
00007ff7`04211510 mov     dword ptr [rax],1        ds:00000000`00000000=????????
```

```
0:000> kL
  *** Stack trace for last set context - .thread/.cxr resets it
 # Child-SP          RetAddr           Call Site
00 000000cb`e06ff4e0 00007ff7`042114dd AppD5BV3!NewFeature+0x10
01 000000cb`e06ff500 00007ff7`04211301 AppD5BV3!StartModeling+0x6d
02 000000cb`e06ff540 00007ff9`54148241 AppD5BV3!WndProc+0xb1
03 000000cb`e06ff600 00007ff9`54147d01 USER32!UserCallWinProcCheckWow+0x2d1
04 000000cb`e06ff760 00007ff7`042110d0 USER32!DispatchMessageWorker+0x1f1
05 000000cb`e06ff7e0 00007ff7`0421173a AppD5BV3!wWinMain+0xd0
06 (Inline Function) --------`-------- AppD5BV3!invoke_main+0x21
07 000000cb`e06ff850 00007ff9`5504257d AppD5BV3!__scrt_common_main_seh+0x106
08 000000cb`e06ff890 00007ff9`5558aa58 KERNEL32!BaseThreadInitThunk+0x1d
09 000000cb`e06ff8c0 00000000`00000000 ntdll!RtlUserThreadStart+0x28
```

25.   We now close WinDbg and the *AppD5A* process window.

Expected Behavior

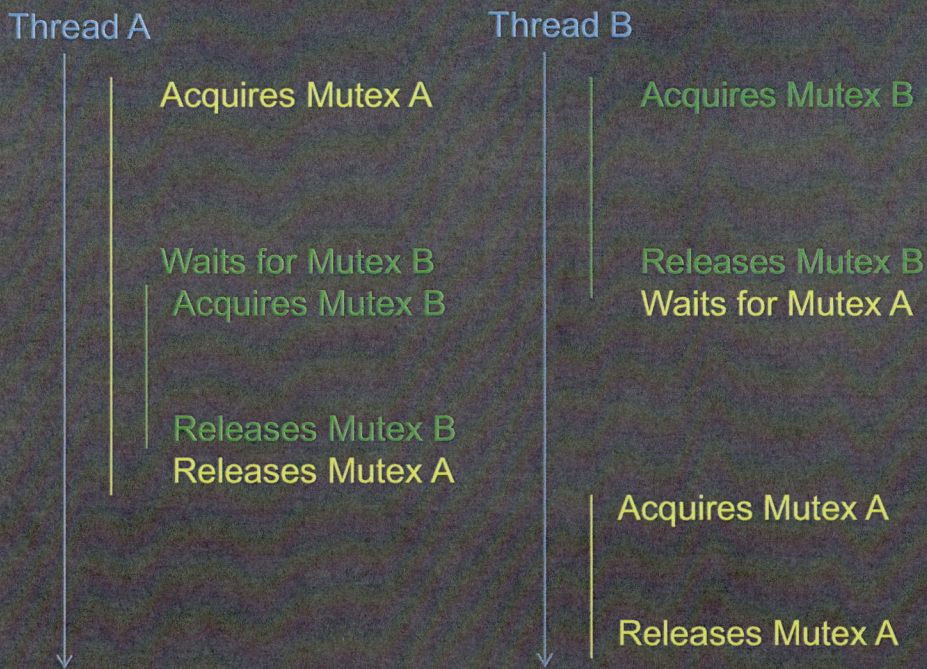

Thread A	Thread B
Acquires Mutex A	Acquires Mutex B
Waits for Mutex B	Releases Mutex B
Acquires Mutex B	Waits for Mutex A
Releases Mutex B	
Releases Mutex A	
	Acquires Mutex A
	Releases Mutex A

The diagram shows the expected behavior for *AppD5A* and *AppD5B* applications.

Deadlock

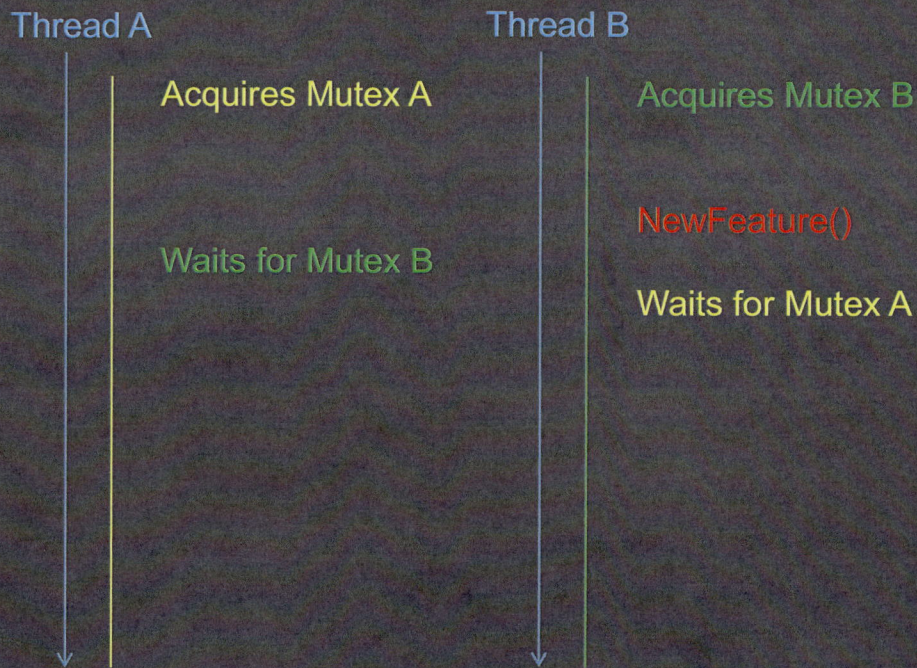

Thread A

Acquires Mutex A

Waits for Mutex B

Thread B

Acquires Mutex B

NewFeature()

Waits for Mutex A

The diagram shows the abnormal behavior for *AppD5BV3* after the problem new feature was introduced in *AppD5BV2* and incorrectly fixed.

Exercise UD6

- **Goal:** Learn how to recognize when we need kernel level debugging

- **Elementary Diagnostics Patterns:** Hang; Counter Value

- **Memory Analysis Patterns:** Abnormal Value (*from trace analysis patterns*); Spiking Thread

- **Debugging Implementation Patterns:** Break-in; Code Breakpoint; Data Breakpoint; Code Trace

- \AWD4\Exercise-UD6.pdf

Goal: Learn how to recognize when we need kernel level debugging.

Elementary Diagnostics Patterns: Hang; Counter Value.

Memory Analysis Patterns: Abnormal Value (*from trace analysis patterns*); Spiking Thread.

Debugging Implementation Patterns: Break-in; Code Breakpoint; Data Breakpoint; Code Trace.

1.   Launch *\AWD4\AppD6\x64\Release\AppD6.exe* executable, choose *File \ Start* and wait about 30 seconds until an application becomes **responsive**.

2.   Here's the source code:

```
void StartModeling(void)
{
        volatile unsigned int *pint = NULL;

        AllocateStorage(&pint); // allocates a memory for pint

        *pint = 5000;

        Sleep(30000);

        while (--(*pint))
        {
                Sleep(0); // do some work
        }

        DeAllocateStorage(pint);
}
```

The application is not supposed to hang after 30 seconds and, subsequently, shouldn't have CPU consumption.

3.   Now launch *\AWD4\DriverEmulator\x64\Release\DriverEmulator.exe* executable, switch to *AppD6*, choose *File \ Start,* **in less than 30 seconds,** switch to *DriverEmulator* and choose *File \ Start.* Next, launch Task Manager and select *AppD6* there; wait for about 30 seconds until *AppD6* starts consuming CPU:

Processes   Run new task   End task   Efficiency mode   •••

Name	Status	38% CPU	66% Memory	0% Disk	0% Network	3% GPU
> ▦ AppD6.exe		29.9%	1.8 MB	0 MB/s	0 Mbps	0%

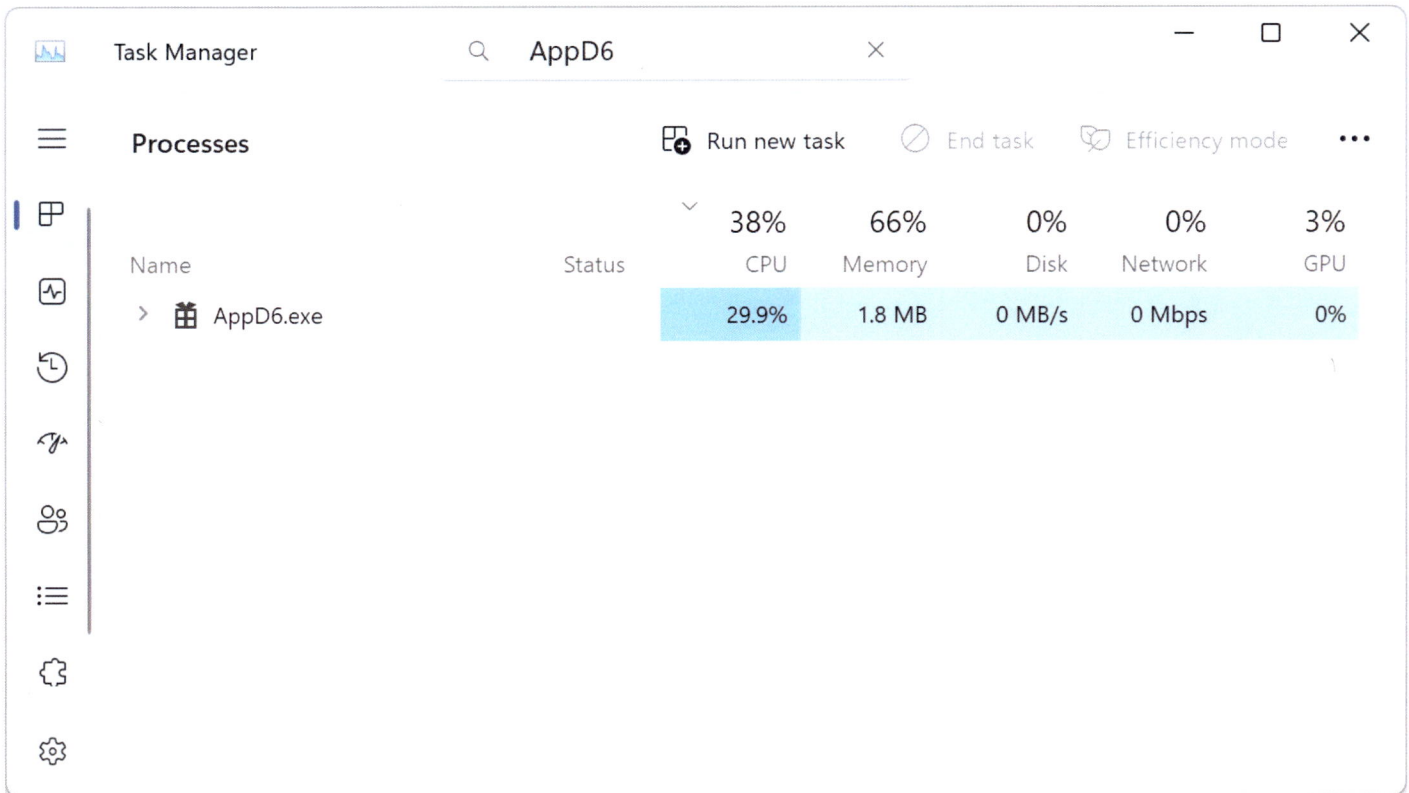

4.   Quickly launch WinDbg, attach it to the *AppD6* process, and open a log file:

```
Microsoft (R) Windows Debugger Version 10.0.25921.1001 AMD64
Copyright (c) Microsoft Corporation. All rights reserved.

*** wait with pending attach

************* Path validation summary **************
Response                        Time (ms)       Location
Deferred                                        srv*
Symbol search path is: srv*
Executable search path is:
ModLoad: 00007ff6`8a7f0000 00007ff6`8a810000    C:\AWD4\AppD6\x64\Release\AppD6.exe
ModLoad: 00007ff9`55530000 00007ff9`55747000    C:\WINDOWS\SYSTEM32\ntdll.dll
ModLoad: 00007ff9`55030000 00007ff9`550f4000    C:\WINDOWS\System32\KERNEL32.DLL
ModLoad: 00007ff9`52870000 00007ff9`52c16000    C:\WINDOWS\System32\KERNELBASE.dll
ModLoad: 00007ff9`4f780000 00007ff9`4f817000    C:\WINDOWS\System32\apphelp.dll
ModLoad: 00007ff9`54130000 00007ff9`542de000    C:\WINDOWS\System32\USER32.dll
ModLoad: 00007ff9`53190000 00007ff9`531b6000    C:\WINDOWS\System32\win32u.dll
ModLoad: 00007ff9`542e0000 00007ff9`54309000    C:\WINDOWS\System32\GDI32.dll
ModLoad: 00007ff9`52c20000 00007ff9`52d38000    C:\WINDOWS\System32\gdi32full.dll
ModLoad: 00007ff9`52f30000 00007ff9`52fca000    C:\WINDOWS\System32\msvcp_win.dll
ModLoad: 00007ff9`53000000 00007ff9`53111000    C:\WINDOWS\System32\ucrtbase.dll
ModLoad: 00007ff9`53ef0000 00007ff9`53f21000    C:\WINDOWS\System32\IMM32.DLL
ModLoad: 00007ff9`4f920000 00007ff9`4f9cb000    C:\WINDOWS\system32\uxtheme.dll
ModLoad: 00007ff9`53b60000 00007ff9`53ee9000    C:\WINDOWS\System32\combase.dll
ModLoad: 00007ff9`543d0000 00007ff9`544e7000    C:\WINDOWS\System32\RPCRT4.dll
ModLoad: 00007ff9`54a40000 00007ff9`54b90000    C:\WINDOWS\System32\MSCTF.dll
ModLoad: 00007ff9`55100000 00007ff9`551a7000    C:\WINDOWS\System32\msvcrt.dll
ModLoad: 00007ff9`20a30000 00007ff9`20ae0000    C:\WINDOWS\SYSTEM32\TextShaping.dll
ModLoad: 00007ff9`51860000 00007ff9`51878000    C:\WINDOWS\SYSTEM32\kernel.appcore.dll
ModLoad: 00007ff9`52eb0000 00007ff9`52f2a000    C:\WINDOWS\System32\bcryptPrimitives.dll
```

```
ModLoad: 00007ff9`54e20000 00007ff9`54ec8000    C:\WINDOWS\System32\sechost.dll
ModLoad: 00007ff9`52fd0000 00007ff9`52ff8000    C:\WINDOWS\System32\bcrypt.dll
ModLoad: 00007ff9`3fba0000 00007ff9`3fcea000    C:\WINDOWS\SYSTEM32\textinputframework.dll
ModLoad: 00007ff9`54b90000 00007ff9`54c67000    C:\WINDOWS\System32\OLEAUT32.dll
ModLoad: 00007ff9`4f470000 00007ff9`4f5a4000    C:\WINDOWS\SYSTEM32\CoreMessaging.dll
ModLoad: 00007ff9`49070000 00007ff9`493dc000    C:\WINDOWS\SYSTEM32\CoreUIComponents.dll
ModLoad: 00007ff9`50f30000 00007ff9`5106e000    C:\WINDOWS\SYSTEM32\wintypes.dll
ModLoad: 00007ff9`54310000 00007ff9`543c3000    C:\WINDOWS\System32\advapi32.dll
ModLoad: 00007ff9`51ed0000 00007ff9`51edc000    C:\WINDOWS\SYSTEM32\CRYPTBASE.DLL
ModLoad: 00007ff9`2b3e0000 00007ff9`2b449000    C:\WINDOWS\system32\Oleacc.dll
ModLoad: 00007ff9`54510000 00007ff9`545c0000    C:\WINDOWS\System32\clbcatq.dll
ModLoad: 00007ff9`20ae0000 00007ff9`20b2b000
C:\WINDOWS\system32\ApplicationTargetedFeatureDatabase.dll
ModLoad: 00007ff9`47160000 00007ff9`473e5000    C:\Windows\System32\twinapi.appcore.dll
ModLoad: 00007ff9`12ff0000 00007ff9`13435000    C:\Windows\System32\uiautomationcore.dll
ModLoad: 00007ff9`4fb50000 00007ff9`4fb7b000    C:\WINDOWS\system32\dwmapi.dll
ModLoad: 00007ff9`1e070000 00007ff9`1e085000    C:\Windows\System32\threadpoolwinrt.dll
(3858.42f8): Break instruction exception - code 80000003 (first chance)
ntdll!DbgBreakPoint:
00007ff9`555d3060 int        3
```

```
0:007> .logopen c:\AWD4\D6.log
Opened log file 'c:\AWD4\D6.log'
```

5.   Switch to the main thread, list its stack trace, select frame #2, and then inspect the value of *pint*:

```
0:007> ~0s
ntdll!NtDelayExecution+0x14:
00007ff9`555cf9f4 ret
```

```
0:000> kL
 # Child-SP          RetAddr               Call Site
00 0000004e`80aff488 00007ff9`555851b3     ntdll!NtDelayExecution+0x14
01 0000004e`80aff490 00007ff9`528b506d     ntdll!RtlDelayExecution+0x43
02 0000004e`80aff4c0 00007ff6`8a7f14c0     KERNELBASE!SleepEx+0x7d
03 0000004e`80aff540 00007ff6`8a7f1301     AppD6!StartModeling+0x50
04 0000004e`80aff580 00007ff9`54148241     AppD6!WndProc+0xb1
05 0000004e`80aff640 00007ff9`54147d01     USER32!UserCallWinProcCheckWow+0x2d1
06 0000004e`80aff7a0 00007ff6`8a7f10d0     USER32!DispatchMessageWorker+0x1f1
07 0000004e`80aff820 00007ff6`8a7f17aa     AppD6!wWinMain+0xd0
08 (Inline Function) --------`--------     AppD6!invoke_main+0x21
09 0000004e`80aff890 00007ff9`5504257d     AppD6!__scrt_common_main_seh+0x106
0a 0000004e`80aff8d0 00007ff9`5558aa58     KERNEL32!BaseThreadInitThunk+0x1d
0b 0000004e`80aff900 00000000`00000000     ntdll!RtlUserThreadStart+0x28
```

```
0:000> .frame 3
03 0000004e`80aff540 00007ff6`8a7f1301     AppD6!StartModeling+0x50 [C:\AWD3\AppD6\AppD6\AppD6.cpp @ 207]
```

```
0:000> ?? *pint
unsigned int 0xfa3c00f0
```

```
0:000> dx *pint
*pint            : 0xfa3c00f0 [Type: unsigned int]
```

Note: Its value is not the expected 0 or less than 5000.

6.	To find when it is changed, we quit our session, quit and again launch *DriverEmulator,* and launch *AppD6* again under WinDbg:

```
0:000> q
NatVis script unloaded from 'C:\Program
Files\WindowsApps\Microsoft.WinDbg_1.2308.2002.0_x64__8wekyb3d8bbwe\amd64\Visualizers\atlmfc.na
tvis'
NatVis script unloaded from 'C:\Program
Files\WindowsApps\Microsoft.WinDbg_1.2308.2002.0_x64__8wekyb3d8bbwe\amd64\Visualizers\Objective
C.natvis'
NatVis script unloaded from 'C:\Program
Files\WindowsApps\Microsoft.WinDbg_1.2308.2002.0_x64__8wekyb3d8bbwe\amd64\Visualizers\concurren
cy.natvis'
NatVis script unloaded from 'C:\Program
Files\WindowsApps\Microsoft.WinDbg_1.2308.2002.0_x64__8wekyb3d8bbwe\amd64\Visualizers\cpp_rest.
natvis'
NatVis script unloaded from 'C:\Program
Files\WindowsApps\Microsoft.WinDbg_1.2308.2002.0_x64__8wekyb3d8bbwe\amd64\Visualizers\stl.natvi
s'
NatVis script unloaded from 'C:\Program
Files\WindowsApps\Microsoft.WinDbg_1.2308.2002.0_x64__8wekyb3d8bbwe\amd64\Visualizers\Windows.D
ata.Json.natvis'
NatVis script unloaded from 'C:\Program
Files\WindowsApps\Microsoft.WinDbg_1.2308.2002.0_x64__8wekyb3d8bbwe\amd64\Visualizers\Windows.D
evices.Geolocation.natvis'
NatVis script unloaded from 'C:\Program
Files\WindowsApps\Microsoft.WinDbg_1.2308.2002.0_x64__8wekyb3d8bbwe\amd64\Visualizers\Windows.D
evices.Sensors.natvis'
NatVis script unloaded from 'C:\Program
Files\WindowsApps\Microsoft.WinDbg_1.2308.2002.0_x64__8wekyb3d8bbwe\amd64\Visualizers\Windows.M
edia.natvis'
NatVis script unloaded from 'C:\Program
Files\WindowsApps\Microsoft.WinDbg_1.2308.2002.0_x64__8wekyb3d8bbwe\amd64\Visualizers\windows.n
atvis'
NatVis script unloaded from 'C:\Program
Files\WindowsApps\Microsoft.WinDbg_1.2308.2002.0_x64__8wekyb3d8bbwe\amd64\Visualizers\winrt.nat
vis'

Microsoft (R) Windows Debugger Version 10.0.25921.1001 AMD64
Copyright (c) Microsoft Corporation. All rights reserved.

CommandLine: C:\AWD4\AppD6\x64\Release\AppD6.exe

************* Path validation summary **************
Response                        Time (ms)       Location
Deferred                                        srv*
Symbol search path is: srv*
Executable search path is:
ModLoad: 00007ff6`8a7f0000 00007ff6`8a810000   AppD6.exe
ModLoad: 00007ff9`55530000 00007ff9`55747000   ntdll.dll
ModLoad: 00007ff9`55030000 00007ff9`550f4000   C:\WINDOWS\System32\KERNEL32.DLL
ModLoad: 00007ff9`52870000 00007ff9`52c16000   C:\WINDOWS\System32\KERNELBASE.dll
ModLoad: 00007ff9`54130000 00007ff9`542de000   C:\WINDOWS\System32\USER32.dll
ModLoad: 00007ff9`53190000 00007ff9`531b6000   C:\WINDOWS\System32\win32u.dll
ModLoad: 00007ff9`542e0000 00007ff9`54309000   C:\WINDOWS\System32\GDI32.dll
ModLoad: 00007ff9`52c20000 00007ff9`52d38000   C:\WINDOWS\System32\gdi32full.dll
ModLoad: 00007ff9`52f30000 00007ff9`52fca000   C:\WINDOWS\System32\msvcp_win.dll
ModLoad: 00007ff9`53000000 00007ff9`53111000   C:\WINDOWS\System32\ucrtbase.dll
```

```
(89ac.66dc): Break instruction exception - code 80000003 (first chance)
ntdll!LdrpDoDebuggerBreak+0x30:
00007ff9`5560b784 int     3
```

```
0:000> .logappend C:\AWD4\D6.log
Opened log file 'C:\AWD4\D6.log'
```

We put a breakpoint on the *StartModeling* function and continue:

```
0:000> bp AppD6!StartModeling
```

```
0:000> g
ModLoad: 00007ff9`53ef0000 00007ff9`53f21000   C:\WINDOWS\System32\IMM32.DLL
ModLoad: 00007ff9`4f920000 00007ff9`4f9cb000   C:\WINDOWS\system32\uxtheme.dll
ModLoad: 00007ff9`53b60000 00007ff9`53ee9000   C:\WINDOWS\System32\combase.dll
ModLoad: 00007ff9`543d0000 00007ff9`544e7000   C:\WINDOWS\System32\RPCRT4.dll
ModLoad: 00007ff9`54a40000 00007ff9`54b90000   C:\WINDOWS\System32\MSCTF.dll
ModLoad: 00007ff9`55100000 00007ff9`551a7000   C:\WINDOWS\System32\msvcrt.dll
ModLoad: 00007ff9`20a30000 00007ff9`20ae0000   C:\WINDOWS\SYSTEM32\TextShaping.dll
ModLoad: 00007ff9`51860000 00007ff9`51878000   C:\WINDOWS\SYSTEM32\kernel.appcore.dll
ModLoad: 00007ff9`52eb0000 00007ff9`52f2a000   C:\WINDOWS\System32\bcryptPrimitives.dll
clientcore\windows\advcore\ctf\uim\tim.cpp(800)\MSCTF.dll!00007FF954A565D9: (caller:
00007FF954A5720C) LogHr(1) tid(66dc) 8007029C An assertion failure has occurred.
clientcore\windows\advcore\ctf\uim\tim.cpp(800)\MSCTF.dll!00007FF954A565D9: (caller:
00007FF954A5720C) LogHr(2) tid(66dc) 8007029C An assertion failure has occurred.
ModLoad: 00007ff9`54e20000 00007ff9`54ec8000   C:\WINDOWS\System32\sechost.dll
ModLoad: 00007ff9`52fd0000 00007ff9`52ff8000   C:\WINDOWS\System32\bcrypt.dll
ModLoad: 00007ff9`54b90000 00007ff9`54c67000   C:\WINDOWS\System32\OLEAUT32.dll
ModLoad: 00007ff9`3fba0000 00007ff9`3fcea000   C:\WINDOWS\SYSTEM32\textinputframework.dll
ModLoad: 00007ff9`2b3e0000 00007ff9`2b449000   C:\WINDOWS\system32\Oleacc.dll
ModLoad: 00007ff9`54510000 00007ff9`545c0000   C:\WINDOWS\System32\clbcatq.dll
ModLoad: 00007ff9`20ae0000 00007ff9`20b2b000
C:\WINDOWS\system32\ApplicationTargetedFeatureDatabase.dll
ModLoad: 00007ff9`47160000 00007ff9`473e5000   C:\Windows\System32\twinapi.appcore.dll
ModLoad: 00007ff9`50f30000 00007ff9`5106e000   C:\Windows\System32\WinTypes.dll
ModLoad: 00007ff9`12ff0000 00007ff9`13435000   C:\Windows\System32\uiautomationcore.dll
```

We then switch to the *AppD6* window and choose *File \ Start*. After that, we switch back to WinDbg and see the breakpoint hit:

```
ModLoad: 00007ff9`4f470000 00007ff9`4f5a4000   C:\WINDOWS\SYSTEM32\CoreMessaging.dll
ModLoad: 00007ff9`49070000 00007ff9`493dc000   C:\WINDOWS\SYSTEM32\CoreUIComponents.dll
ModLoad: 00007ff9`54310000 00007ff9`543c3000   C:\WINDOWS\System32\advapi32.dll
ModLoad: 00007ff9`51ed0000 00007ff9`51edc000   C:\WINDOWS\SYSTEM32\CRYPTBASE.DLL
ModLoad: 00007ff9`4fb50000 00007ff9`4fb7b000   C:\WINDOWS\system32\dwmapi.dll
ModLoad: 00007ff9`1e070000 00007ff9`1e085000   C:\Windows\System32\threadpoolwinrt.dll
(89ac.dfc): C++ EH exception - code e06d7363 (first chance)
(89ac.dfc): C++ EH exception - code e06d7363 (first chance)
(89ac.dfc): C++ EH exception - code e06d7363 (first chance)
(89ac.dfc): C++ EH exception - code e06d7363 (first chance)
(89ac.dfc): C++ EH exception - code e06d7363 (first chance)
(89ac.dfc): C++ EH exception - code e06d7363 (first chance)
Breakpoint 0 hit
AppD6!StartModeling:
00007ff6`8a7f1470 sub     rsp,38h
```

7.   We then step over until the storage for the *pint* variable is allocated:

```
0:000> .srcfix
Source search path is: SRV*

0:000> .srcpath+ C:\AWD4\AppD6\AppD6
Source search path is: SRV*;C:\AWD4\AppD6\AppD6


...
OK                                                      C:\AWD4\AppD6\AppD6


0:000> p
AppD6!StartModeling+0x4:
00007ff6`8a7f1474 mov     qword ptr [rsp+20h],0 ss:0000009e`a04ff770=0000000100000000


0:000> p
AppD6!StartModeling+0xd:
00007ff6`8a7f147d lea     rcx,[rsp+20h]


0:000> p
AppD6!StartModeling+0x17:
00007ff6`8a7f1487 mov     rax,qword ptr [rsp+20h] ss:0000009e`a04ff770=0000000012340000
```

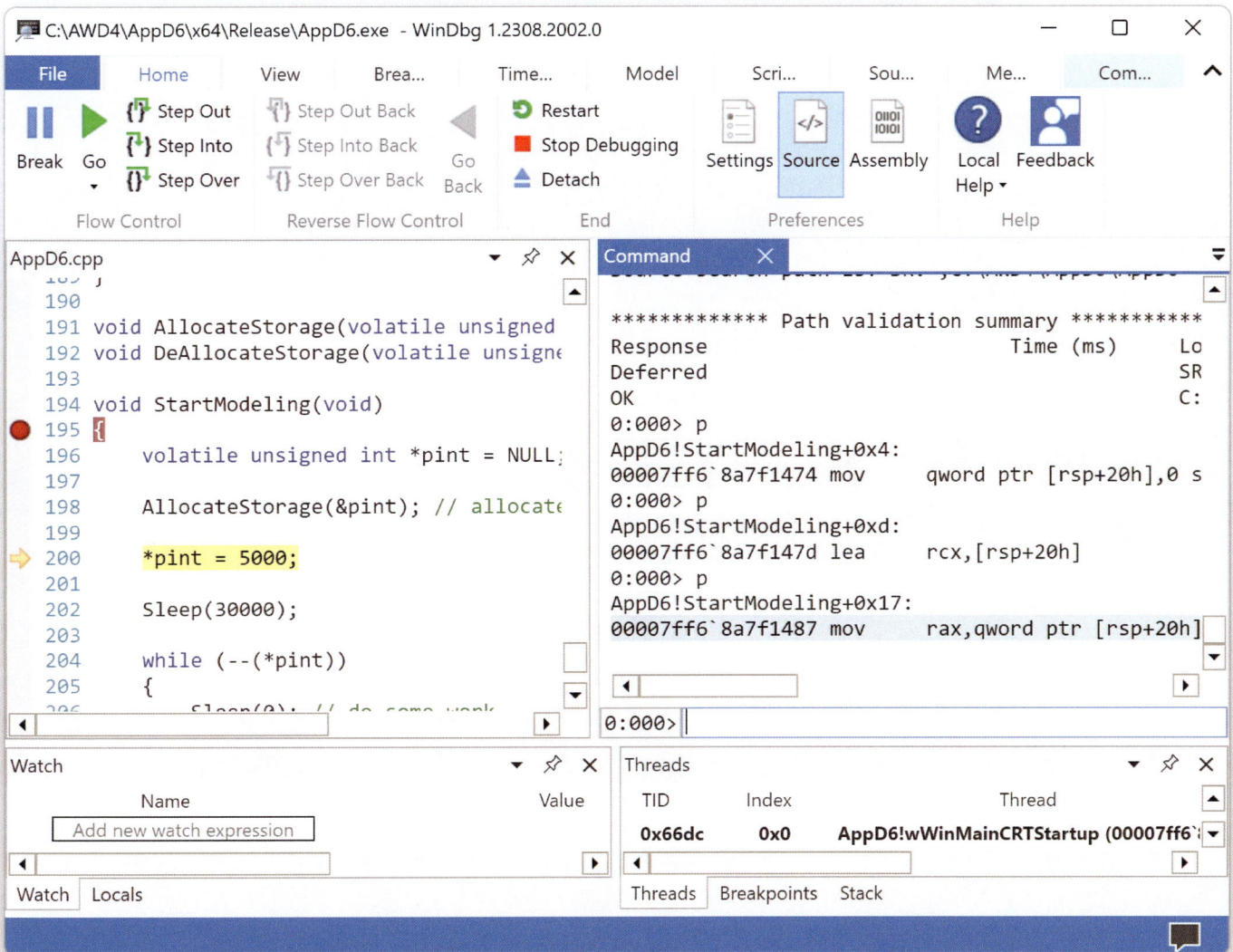

8.   We now put a write hardware breakpoint for 4 bytes (int) on the value of pint:

```
0:000> ?? pint
unsigned int * 0x00000000`12340000

0:000> dx pint
pint                : 0x12340000 : 0x0 [Type: unsigned int *]
    0x0 [Type: unsigned int]

0:000> ba w 4 0x00000000`12340000

0:000> bl
     0 e Disable Clear  00007ff6`8a7f1470  [C:\AWD3\AppD6\AppD6\AppD6.cpp @ 195]    0001 (0001)  0:**** AppD6!StartModeling
     1 e Disable Clear  00000000`12340000 w 4 0001 (0001)  0:****
```

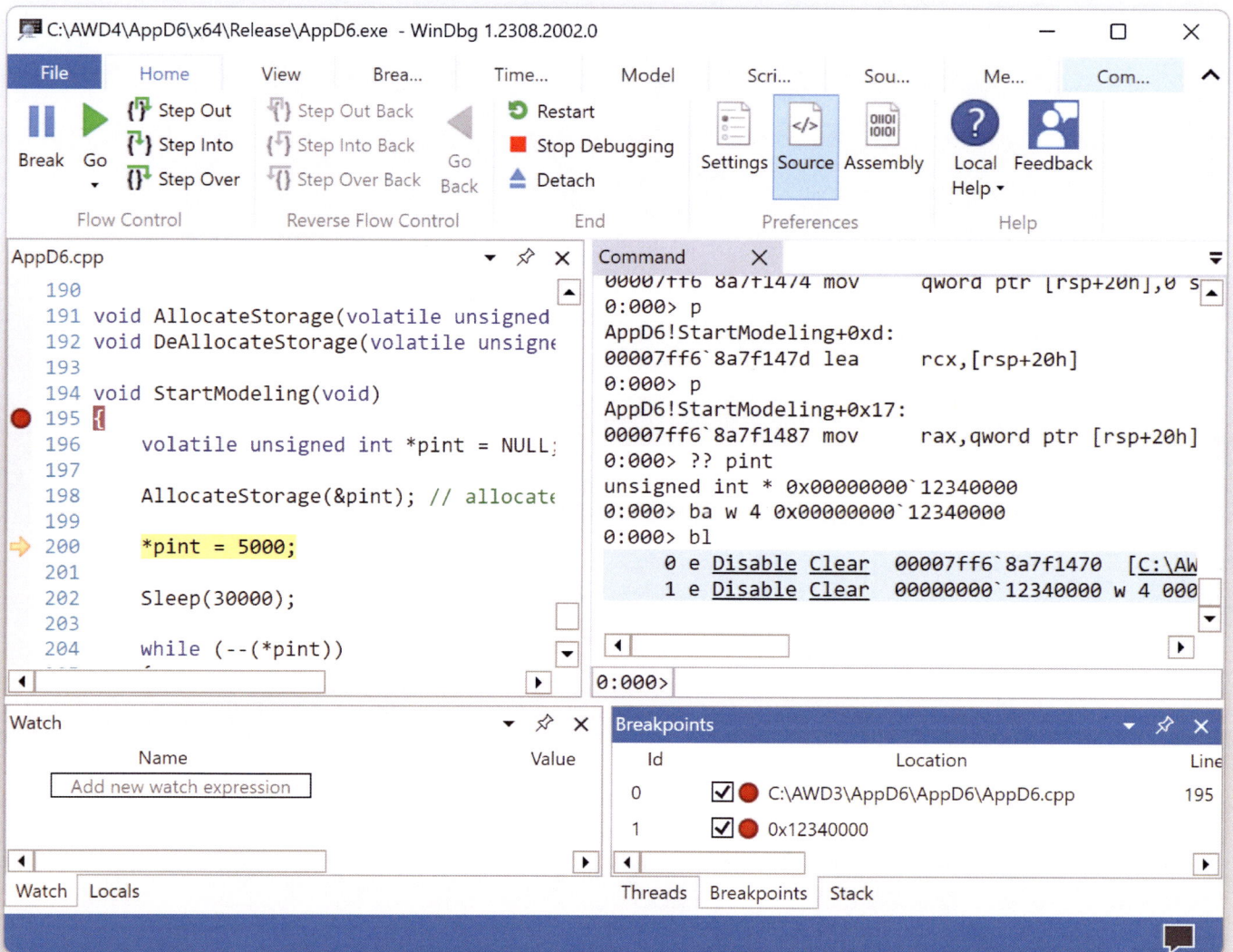

If we continue, we get the first hit where we change the value to 5000 as expected:

```
0:000> g
Breakpoint 1 hit
AppD6!StartModeling+0x22:
00007ff6`8a7f1492 mov      ecx,7530h
```

```
0:000> ?? *pint
unsigned int 0x1388
```

```
0:000> dx *pint
*pint            : 0x1388 [Type: unsigned int]
```

```
0:000> ? 0x1388
Evaluate expression: 5000 = 00000000`00001388
```

9.   We then resume and switch to the *DriverEmulator* window, choose *File \ Start* (we have no more than 30 seconds to do that!), and wait:

```
0:000> g
(89ac.dfc): C++ EH exception - code e06d7363 (first chance)
(89ac.21a8): C++ EH exception - code e06d7363 (first chance)
(89ac.dfc): C++ EH exception - code e06d7363 (first chance)
(89ac.dfc): C++ EH exception - code e06d7363 (first chance)
(89ac.21a8): C++ EH exception - code e06d7363 (first chance)
(89ac.dfc): C++ EH exception - code e06d7363 (first chance)
(89ac.dfc): C++ EH exception - code e06d7363 (first chance)
(89ac.dfc): C++ EH exception - code e06d7363 (first chance)
(89ac.21a8): C++ EH exception - code e06d7363 (first chance)
(89ac.dfc): C++ EH exception - code e06d7363 (first chance)
(89ac.21a8): C++ EH exception - code e06d7363 (first chance)
(89ac.dfc): C++ EH exception - code e06d7363 (first chance)
(89ac.dfc): C++ EH exception - code e06d7363 (first chance)
(89ac.dfc): C++ EH exception - code e06d7363 (first chance)
(89ac.dfc): C++ EH exception - code e06d7363 (first chance)
(89ac.dfc): C++ EH exception - code e06d7363 (first chance)
(89ac.dfc): C++ EH exception - code e06d7363 (first chance)
(89ac.dfc): C++ EH exception - code e06d7363 (first chance)
(89ac.dfc): C++ EH exception - code e06d7363 (first chance)
(89ac.dfc): C++ EH exception - code e06d7363 (first chance)
Breakpoint 1 hit
AppD6!StartModeling+0x3d:
00007ff6`8a7f14ad mov     rax,qword ptr [rsp+20h] ss:0000009e`a04ff770=0000000012340000
```

```
0:000> ?? *pint
unsigned int 0xfffffffe
```

```
0:000> dx *pint
*pint            : 0xfffffffe [Type: unsigned int]
```

```
0:000> kL
 # Child-SP          RetAddr               Call Site
00 0000009e`a04ff750 00007ff6`8a7f1301     AppD6!StartModeling+0x3d
01 0000009e`a04ff790 00007ff9`54148241     AppD6!WndProc+0xb1
02 0000009e`a04ff850 00007ff9`54147d01     USER32!UserCallWinProcCheckWow+0x2d1
03 0000009e`a04ff9b0 00007ff6`8a7f10d0     USER32!DispatchMessageWorker+0x1f1
04 0000009e`a04ffa30 00007ff6`8a7f17aa     AppD6!wWinMain+0xd0
05 (Inline Function) --------`--------     AppD6!invoke_main+0x21
06 0000009e`a04ffaa0 00007ff9`5504257d     AppD6!__scrt_common_main_seh+0x106
07 0000009e`a04ffae0 00007ff9`5558aa58     KERNEL32!BaseThreadInitThunk+0x1d
08 0000009e`a04ffb10 00000000`00000000     ntdll!RtlUserThreadStart+0x28
```

Note: Unfortunately, the next hit only happened when we started the loop, which modifies *pint* in each iteration, and we were unable to catch the moment when the variable value was changed from 0n5000 to 0xffffffff. We try to debug such corruption in kernel mode debugging.

```
AppD6.cpp                                               ▼  ☐  ✕
   192 void DeAllocateStorage(volatile unsigned int *);
   193
   194 void StartModeling(void)
●  195 {
   196     volatile unsigned int *pint = NULL;
   197
   198     AllocateStorage(&pint); // allocates a memory for pint
   199
   200     *pint = 5000;
   201
   202     Sleep(30000);
   203
⇨  204     while (--(*pint))
   205     {
   206         Sleep(0); // do some work
   207     }
```

10.   Now we clear all breakpoints, continue for some time, and then break in again:

```
0:000> bc *
```

```
0:000> bl
```

```
0:000> g
(89ac.75bc): Break instruction exception - code 80000003 (first chance)
ntdll!DbgBreakPoint:
00007ff9`555d3060 int     3
```

Now we can check CPU consumption via the **!runaway** command:

```
0:012> !runaway f
User Mode Time
  Thread       Time
   0:66dc      0 days 0:00:14.359
   3:21a8      0 days 0:00:00.015
  12:406c      0 days 0:00:00.000
  11:7144      0 days 0:00:00.000
  10:6850      0 days 0:00:00.000
   9:8ee8      0 days 0:00:00.000
   8:3ab0      0 days 0:00:00.000
   7:6210      0 days 0:00:00.000
   6:751c      0 days 0:00:00.000
   5:389c      0 days 0:00:00.000
   4:dfc       0 days 0:00:00.000
   2:1bfc      0 days 0:00:00.000
   1:9434      0 days 0:00:00.000
Kernel Mode Time
  Thread       Time
   0:66dc      0 days 0:00:10.421
  12:406c      0 days 0:00:00.000
```

```
11:7144      0 days 0:00:00.000
10:6850      0 days 0:00:00.000
 9:8ee8      0 days 0:00:00.000
 8:3ab0      0 days 0:00:00.000
 7:6210      0 days 0:00:00.000
 6:751c      0 days 0:00:00.000
 5:389c      0 days 0:00:00.000
 4:dfc       0 days 0:00:00.000
 3:21a8      0 days 0:00:00.000
 2:1bfc      0 days 0:00:00.000
 1:9434      0 days 0:00:00.000
Elapsed Time
 Thread      Time
 0:66dc      0 days 0:29:13.580
 5:389c      0 days 0:27:55.250
 4:dfc       0 days 0:27:55.229
 7:6210      0 days 0:27:55.219
 8:3ab0      0 days 0:27:55.216
 9:8ee8      0 days 0:27:55.187
 1:9434      0 days 0:26:59.701
 2:1bfc      0 days 0:26:57.800
 3:21a8      0 days 0:26:57.776
11:7144      0 days 0:08:49.626
10:6850      0 days 0:08:25.141
 6:751c      0 days 0:02:23.411
12:406c      0 days 0:00:01.567
```

Note: Although we loop in user mode, kernel mode also consumes CPU because *Sleep* incurs thread scheduling.

11.   We now close WinDbg (the log should close automatically) and *DriverEmulator*.

Exercise UD7

- **Goal:** Learn how to manipulate threads to debug race conditions

- **Elementary Diagnostics Patterns:** Crash

- **Memory Analysis Patterns:** Exception Stack Trace; NULL Pointer (Data)

- **Debugging Implementation Patterns:** Frozen Thread

- \AWD4\Exercise-UD7.pdf

Exercise UD7

Goal: Learn how to manipulate threads to debug race conditions.

Elementary Diagnostics Patterns: Crash.

Memory Analysis Patterns: Exception Stack Trace; NULL Pointer (Code).

Debugging Implementation Patterns: Frozen Thread.

1.   Launch *\AWD4\AppD7\x64\Release\AppD7.exe* executable, and choose *File \ Start*. It should crash shortly.

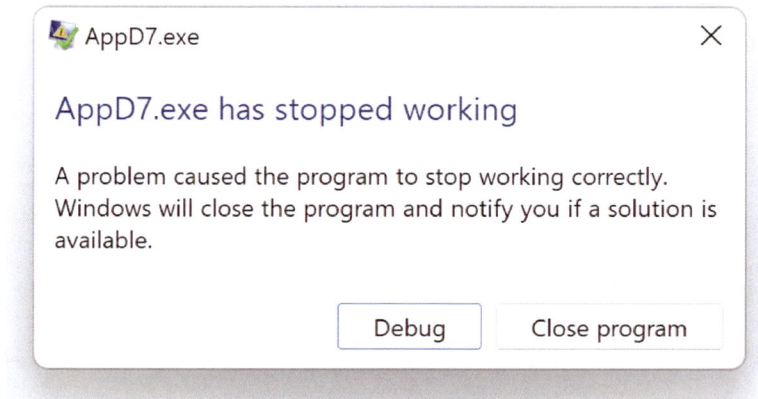

```
AppD7.exe                               ×

AppD7.exe has stopped working

A problem caused the program to stop working correctly.
Windows will close the program and notify you if a solution is
available.

                      Debug        Close program
```

2.   Now launch it under WinDbg and continue:

```
Microsoft (R) Windows Debugger Version 10.0.25921.1001 AMD64
Copyright (c) Microsoft Corporation. All rights reserved.

CommandLine: C:\AWD4\AppD7\x64\Release\AppD7.exe

************* Path validation summary **************
Response                        Time (ms)       Location
Deferred                                        srv*
Symbol search path is: srv*
Executable search path is:
ModLoad: 00007ff7`3c6e0000 00007ff7`3c700000   AppD7.exe
ModLoad: 00007ff9`55530000 00007ff9`55747000   ntdll.dll
ModLoad: 00007ff9`55030000 00007ff9`550f4000   C:\WINDOWS\System32\KERNEL32.DLL
ModLoad: 00007ff9`52870000 00007ff9`52c16000   C:\WINDOWS\System32\KERNELBASE.dll
ModLoad: 00007ff9`54130000 00007ff9`542de000   C:\WINDOWS\System32\USER32.dll
ModLoad: 00007ff9`53190000 00007ff9`531b6000   C:\WINDOWS\System32\win32u.dll
ModLoad: 00007ff9`542e0000 00007ff9`54309000   C:\WINDOWS\System32\GDI32.dll
ModLoad: 00007ff9`52c20000 00007ff9`52d38000   C:\WINDOWS\System32\gdi32full.dll
ModLoad: 00007ff9`52f30000 00007ff9`52fca000   C:\WINDOWS\System32\msvcp_win.dll
ModLoad: 00007ff9`53000000 00007ff9`53111000   C:\WINDOWS\System32\ucrtbase.dll
(7d00.5880): Break instruction exception - code 80000003 (first chance)
ntdll!LdrpDoDebuggerBreak+0x30:
00007ff9`5560b784 int     3

0:000> .logopen c:\AWD4\D7.log
Opened log file 'c:\AWD4\D7.log'
```

```
0:000> g
ModLoad: 00007ff9`53ef0000 00007ff9`53f21000    C:\WINDOWS\System32\IMM32.DLL
ModLoad: 00007ff9`4f920000 00007ff9`4f9cb000    C:\WINDOWS\system32\uxtheme.dll
ModLoad: 00007ff9`53b60000 00007ff9`53ee9000    C:\WINDOWS\System32\combase.dll
ModLoad: 00007ff9`543d0000 00007ff9`544e7000    C:\WINDOWS\System32\RPCRT4.dll
ModLoad: 00007ff9`54a40000 00007ff9`54b90000    C:\WINDOWS\System32\MSCTF.dll
ModLoad: 00007ff9`55100000 00007ff9`551a7000    C:\WINDOWS\System32\msvcrt.dll
ModLoad: 00007ff9`20a30000 00007ff9`20ae0000    C:\WINDOWS\SYSTEM32\TextShaping.dll
ModLoad: 00007ff9`51860000 00007ff9`51878000    C:\WINDOWS\SYSTEM32\kernel.appcore.dll
ModLoad: 00007ff9`52eb0000 00007ff9`52f2a000    C:\WINDOWS\System32\bcryptPrimitives.dll
clientcore\windows\advcore\ctf\uim\tim.cpp(800)\MSCTF.dll!00007FF954A565D9: (caller:
00007FF954A5720C) LogHr(1) tid(5880) 8007029C An assertion failure has occurred.
clientcore\windows\advcore\ctf\uim\tim.cpp(800)\MSCTF.dll!00007FF954A565D9: (caller:
00007FF954A5720C) LogHr(2) tid(5880) 8007029C An assertion failure has occurred.
ModLoad: 00007ff9`54e20000 00007ff9`54ec8000    C:\WINDOWS\System32\sechost.dll
ModLoad: 00007ff9`52fd0000 00007ff9`52ff8000    C:\WINDOWS\System32\bcrypt.dll
ModLoad: 00007ff9`54b90000 00007ff9`54c67000    C:\WINDOWS\System32\OLEAUT32.dll
ModLoad: 00007ff9`3fba0000 00007ff9`3fcea000    C:\WINDOWS\SYSTEM32\textinputframework.dll
ModLoad: 00007ff9`2b3e0000 00007ff9`2b449000    C:\WINDOWS\system32\Oleacc.dll
ModLoad: 00007ff9`54510000 00007ff9`545c0000    C:\WINDOWS\System32\clbcatq.dll
ModLoad: 00007ff9`20ae0000 00007ff9`20b2b000
C:\WINDOWS\system32\ApplicationTargetedFeatureDatabase.dll
ModLoad: 00007ff9`47160000 00007ff9`473e5000    C:\Windows\System32\twinapi.appcore.dll
ModLoad: 00007ff9`50f30000 00007ff9`5106e000    C:\Windows\System32\WinTypes.dll
ModLoad: 00007ff9`12ff0000 00007ff9`13435000    C:\Windows\System32\uiautomationcore.dll
```

Note: After choosing *File \ Start,* it doesn't crash. So, it looks like the WinDbg debugger influenced program behavior.

3.   Let's look at the source code of the *StartModeling* function:

```
void StartModeling (void)
{
        CreateThread(NULL, 0, ThreadProcA, NULL, 0, NULL);
        CreateThread(NULL, 0, ThreadProcB, NULL, 0, NULL);
}
```

We put breakpoints after breaking into *AppD7* and restarting it:

```
(7d00.1360): C++ EH exception - code e06d7363 (first chance)
(7d00.1360): C++ EH exception - code e06d7363 (first chance)
(7d00.1360): C++ EH exception - code e06d7363 (first chance)
(7d00.1360): C++ EH exception - code e06d7363 (first chance)
(7d00.1360): C++ EH exception - code e06d7363 (first chance)
(7d00.1360): C++ EH exception - code e06d7363 (first chance)
(7d00.1360): C++ EH exception - code e06d7363 (first chance)
(7d00.1360): C++ EH exception - code e06d7363 (first chance)
(7d00.1360): C++ EH exception - code e06d7363 (first chance)
(7d00.1d38): Break instruction exception - code 80000003 (first chance)
ntdll!DbgBreakPoint:
00007ff9`555d3060 int     3
```

```
0:006> .restart
NatVis script unloaded from 'C:\Program
Files\WindowsApps\Microsoft.WinDbg_1.2308.2002.0_x64__8wekyb3d8bbwe\amd64\Visualizers\atlmfc.na
tvis'
```

NatVis script unloaded from 'C:\Program
Files\WindowsApps\Microsoft.WinDbg_1.2308.2002.0_x64__8wekyb3d8bbwe\amd64\Visualizers\Objective
C.natvis'
NatVis script unloaded from 'C:\Program
Files\WindowsApps\Microsoft.WinDbg_1.2308.2002.0_x64__8wekyb3d8bbwe\amd64\Visualizers\concurren
cy.natvis'
NatVis script unloaded from 'C:\Program
Files\WindowsApps\Microsoft.WinDbg_1.2308.2002.0_x64__8wekyb3d8bbwe\amd64\Visualizers\cpp_rest.
natvis'
NatVis script unloaded from 'C:\Program
Files\WindowsApps\Microsoft.WinDbg_1.2308.2002.0_x64__8wekyb3d8bbwe\amd64\Visualizers\stl.natvi
s'
NatVis script unloaded from 'C:\Program
Files\WindowsApps\Microsoft.WinDbg_1.2308.2002.0_x64__8wekyb3d8bbwe\amd64\Visualizers\Windows.D
ata.Json.natvis'
NatVis script unloaded from 'C:\Program
Files\WindowsApps\Microsoft.WinDbg_1.2308.2002.0_x64__8wekyb3d8bbwe\amd64\Visualizers\Windows.D
evices.Geolocation.natvis'
NatVis script unloaded from 'C:\Program
Files\WindowsApps\Microsoft.WinDbg_1.2308.2002.0_x64__8wekyb3d8bbwe\amd64\Visualizers\Windows.D
evices.Sensors.natvis'
NatVis script unloaded from 'C:\Program
Files\WindowsApps\Microsoft.WinDbg_1.2308.2002.0_x64__8wekyb3d8bbwe\amd64\Visualizers\Windows.M
edia.natvis'
NatVis script unloaded from 'C:\Program
Files\WindowsApps\Microsoft.WinDbg_1.2308.2002.0_x64__8wekyb3d8bbwe\amd64\Visualizers\windows.n
atvis'
NatVis script unloaded from 'C:\Program
Files\WindowsApps\Microsoft.WinDbg_1.2308.2002.0_x64__8wekyb3d8bbwe\amd64\Visualizers\winrt.nat
vis'

Microsoft (R) Windows Debugger Version 10.0.25921.1001 AMD64
Copyright (c) Microsoft Corporation. All rights reserved.

CommandLine: C:\AWD4\AppD7\x64\Release\AppD7.exe

************* Path validation summary **************
Response   Time (ms)   Location
Deferred   srv*
Symbol search path is: srv*
Executable search path is:
ModLoad: 00007ff7`3c6e0000 00007ff7`3c700000   AppD7.exe
ModLoad: 00007ff9`55530000 00007ff9`55747000   ntdll.dll
ModLoad: 00007ff9`55030000 00007ff9`550f4000   C:\WINDOWS\System32\KERNEL32.DLL
ModLoad: 00007ff9`52870000 00007ff9`52c16000   C:\WINDOWS\System32\KERNELBASE.dll
ModLoad: 00007ff9`54130000 00007ff9`542de000   C:\WINDOWS\System32\USER32.dll
ModLoad: 00007ff9`53190000 00007ff9`531b6000   C:\WINDOWS\System32\win32u.dll
ModLoad: 00007ff9`542e0000 00007ff9`54309000   C:\WINDOWS\System32\GDI32.dll
ModLoad: 00007ff9`52c20000 00007ff9`52d38000   C:\WINDOWS\System32\gdi32full.dll
ModLoad: 00007ff9`52f30000 00007ff9`52fca000   C:\WINDOWS\System32\msvcp_win.dll
ModLoad: 00007ff9`53000000 00007ff9`53111000   C:\WINDOWS\System32\ucrtbase.dll
(7d1c.11f0): Break instruction exception - code 80000003 (first chance)
ntdll!LdrpDoDebuggerBreak+0x30:
00007ff9`5560b784 int   3

0:000> **bp** AppD7!ThreadProcA

0:000> **bp** AppD7!ThreadProcB

4.　We now continue execution, switch to the *AppD7* window, choose *File \ Start,* and wait until we break in:

```
0:000> g
ModLoad: 00007ff9`53ef0000 00007ff9`53f21000    C:\WINDOWS\System32\IMM32.DLL
ModLoad: 00007ff9`4f920000 00007ff9`4f9cb000    C:\WINDOWS\system32\uxtheme.dll
ModLoad: 00007ff9`53b60000 00007ff9`53ee9000    C:\WINDOWS\System32\combase.dll
ModLoad: 00007ff9`543d0000 00007ff9`544e7000    C:\WINDOWS\System32\RPCRT4.dll
ModLoad: 00007ff9`54a40000 00007ff9`54b90000    C:\WINDOWS\System32\MSCTF.dll
ModLoad: 00007ff9`55100000 00007ff9`551a7000    C:\WINDOWS\System32\msvcrt.dll
ModLoad: 00007ff9`20a30000 00007ff9`20ae0000    C:\WINDOWS\SYSTEM32\TextShaping.dll
ModLoad: 00007ff9`51860000 00007ff9`51878000    C:\WINDOWS\SYSTEM32\kernel.appcore.dll
ModLoad: 00007ff9`52eb0000 00007ff9`52f2a000    C:\WINDOWS\System32\bcryptPrimitives.dll
clientcore\windows\advcore\ctf\uim\tim.cpp(800)\MSCTF.dll!00007FF954A565D9: (caller:
00007FF954A5720C) LogHr(1) tid(11f0) 8007029C An assertion failure has occurred.
clientcore\windows\advcore\ctf\uim\tim.cpp(800)\MSCTF.dll!00007FF954A565D9: (caller:
00007FF954A5720C) LogHr(2) tid(11f0) 8007029C An assertion failure has occurred.
ModLoad: 00007ff9`54e20000 00007ff9`54ec8000    C:\WINDOWS\System32\sechost.dll
ModLoad: 00007ff9`52fd0000 00007ff9`52ff8000    C:\WINDOWS\System32\bcrypt.dll
ModLoad: 00007ff9`54b90000 00007ff9`54c67000    C:\WINDOWS\System32\OLEAUT32.dll
ModLoad: 00007ff9`3fba0000 00007ff9`3fcea000    C:\WINDOWS\SYSTEM32\textinputframework.dll
ModLoad: 00007ff9`2b3e0000 00007ff9`2b449000    C:\WINDOWS\system32\Oleacc.dll
ModLoad: 00007ff9`54510000 00007ff9`545c0000    C:\WINDOWS\System32\clbcatq.dll
ModLoad: 00007ff9`20ae0000 00007ff9`20b2b000
C:\WINDOWS\system32\ApplicationTargetedFeatureDatabase.dll
ModLoad: 00007ff9`47160000 00007ff9`473e5000    C:\Windows\System32\twinapi.appcore.dll
ModLoad: 00007ff9`50f30000 00007ff9`5106e000    C:\Windows\System32\WinTypes.dll
ModLoad: 00007ff9`12ff0000 00007ff9`13435000    C:\Windows\System32\uiautomationcore.dll
ModLoad: 00007ff9`4f470000 00007ff9`4f5a4000    C:\WINDOWS\SYSTEM32\CoreMessaging.dll
ModLoad: 00007ff9`49070000 00007ff9`493dc000    C:\WINDOWS\SYSTEM32\CoreUIComponents.dll
ModLoad: 00007ff9`54310000 00007ff9`543c3000    C:\WINDOWS\System32\advapi32.dll
ModLoad: 00007ff9`51ed0000 00007ff9`51edc000    C:\WINDOWS\SYSTEM32\CRYPTBASE.DLL
ModLoad: 00007ff9`4fb50000 00007ff9`4fb7b000    C:\WINDOWS\system32\dwmapi.dll
ModLoad: 00007ff9`1e070000 00007ff9`1e085000    C:\Windows\System32\threadpoolwinrt.dll
(7d1c.4be0): C++ EH exception - code e06d7363 (first chance)
(7d1c.4be0): C++ EH exception - code e06d7363 (first chance)
(7d1c.4be0): C++ EH exception - code e06d7363 (first chance)
(7d1c.4be0): C++ EH exception - code e06d7363 (first chance)
(7d1c.4be0): C++ EH exception - code e06d7363 (first chance)
(7d1c.4be0): C++ EH exception - code e06d7363 (first chance)
Breakpoint 0 hit
AppD7!ThreadProcA:
00007ff7`3c6e14d0 mov     qword ptr [rsp+8],rcx ss:0000009b`3a3ffcc0=0000000000000000
```

Note: If we hit *ThreadProcB* instead, do **.restart** and **g** again until we hit *ThreadProcA.*

```
0:011> kL
 # Child-SP          RetAddr           Call Site
00 0000009b`3a3ffcb8 00007ff9`5504257d AppD7!ThreadProcA
01 0000009b`3a3ffcc0 00007ff9`5558aa58 KERNEL32!BaseThreadInitThunk+0x1d
02 0000009b`3a3ffcf0 00000000`00000000 ntdll!RtlUserThreadStart+0x28
```

5.　We freeze this thread using the **~f** command:

```
0:011> ~
   0  Id: 7d1c.11f0 Suspend: 1 Teb: 0000009b`39784000 Unfrozen
   1  Id: 7d1c.286c Suspend: 1 Teb: 0000009b`39786000 Unfrozen
   2  Id: 7d1c.9594 Suspend: 1 Teb: 0000009b`39788000 Unfrozen
   3  Id: 7d1c.4be0 Suspend: 1 Teb: 0000009b`3978e000 Unfrozen
```

```
    4  Id: 7d1c.7458 Suspend: 1 Teb: 0000009b`3978c000 Unfrozen
    5  Id: 7d1c.898c Suspend: 1 Teb: 0000009b`39790000 Unfrozen
    6  Id: 7d1c.8b84 Suspend: 1 Teb: 0000009b`39792000 Unfrozen
    7  Id: 7d1c.8220 Suspend: 1 Teb: 0000009b`39794000 Unfrozen
    8  Id: 7d1c.41c Suspend: 1 Teb: 0000009b`39796000 Unfrozen
    9  Id: 7d1c.67a8 Suspend: 1 Teb: 0000009b`39798000 Unfrozen
   10  Id: 7d1c.14fc Suspend: 1 Teb: 0000009b`3979a000 Unfrozen
.  11  Id: 7d1c.5e90 Suspend: 1 Teb: 0000009b`3979c000 Unfrozen
   12  Id: 7d1c.8de8 Suspend: 1 Teb: 0000009b`3979e000 Unfrozen

0:011> ~f

0:011> ~
    0  Id: 7d1c.11f0 Suspend: 1 Teb: 0000009b`39784000 Unfrozen
    1  Id: 7d1c.286c Suspend: 1 Teb: 0000009b`39786000 Unfrozen
    2  Id: 7d1c.9594 Suspend: 1 Teb: 0000009b`39788000 Unfrozen
    3  Id: 7d1c.4be0 Suspend: 1 Teb: 0000009b`3978e000 Unfrozen
    4  Id: 7d1c.7458 Suspend: 1 Teb: 0000009b`3978c000 Unfrozen
    5  Id: 7d1c.898c Suspend: 1 Teb: 0000009b`39790000 Unfrozen
    6  Id: 7d1c.8b84 Suspend: 1 Teb: 0000009b`39792000 Unfrozen
    7  Id: 7d1c.8220 Suspend: 1 Teb: 0000009b`39794000 Unfrozen
    8  Id: 7d1c.41c Suspend: 1 Teb: 0000009b`39796000 Unfrozen
    9  Id: 7d1c.67a8 Suspend: 1 Teb: 0000009b`39798000 Unfrozen
   10  Id: 7d1c.14fc Suspend: 1 Teb: 0000009b`3979a000 Unfrozen
.  11  Id: 7d1c.5e90 Suspend: 1 Teb: 0000009b`3979c000 Frozen
   12  Id: 7d1c.8de8 Suspend: 1 Teb: 0000009b`3979e000 Unfrozen
```

6.   We then continue execution, and upon the next breakpoint hit, freeze the newly created thread:

```
0:011> g
Breakpoint 0 will not be deferred because of changes in the context. Breakpoint may hit again.
System 0: 1 of 13 threads are frozen
System 0: 1 of 14 threads were frozen
System 0: 1 of 14 threads are frozen
System 0: 1 of 14 threads were frozen
Breakpoint 1 hit
AppD7!ThreadProcB:
00007ff7`3c6e1510 mov     qword ptr [rsp+8],rcx ss:0000009b`3a4ffc70=0000000000000000

0:012> ~
    0  Id: 7d1c.11f0 Suspend: 1 Teb: 0000009b`39784000 Unfrozen
    1  Id: 7d1c.286c Suspend: 1 Teb: 0000009b`39786000 Unfrozen
    2  Id: 7d1c.9594 Suspend: 1 Teb: 0000009b`39788000 Unfrozen
    3  Id: 7d1c.4be0 Suspend: 1 Teb: 0000009b`3978e000 Unfrozen
    4  Id: 7d1c.7458 Suspend: 1 Teb: 0000009b`3978c000 Unfrozen
    5  Id: 7d1c.898c Suspend: 1 Teb: 0000009b`39790000 Unfrozen
    6  Id: 7d1c.8b84 Suspend: 1 Teb: 0000009b`39792000 Unfrozen
    7  Id: 7d1c.8220 Suspend: 1 Teb: 0000009b`39794000 Unfrozen
    8  Id: 7d1c.41c Suspend: 1 Teb: 0000009b`39796000 Unfrozen
    9  Id: 7d1c.67a8 Suspend: 1 Teb: 0000009b`39798000 Unfrozen
   10  Id: 7d1c.14fc Suspend: 1 Teb: 0000009b`3979a000 Unfrozen
   11  Id: 7d1c.5e90 Suspend: 1 Teb: 0000009b`3979c000 Frozen
.  12  Id: 7d1c.8de8 Suspend: 1 Teb: 0000009b`3979e000 Unfrozen
   13  Id: 7d1c.2df0 Suspend: 1 Teb: 0000009b`397a0000 Unfrozen

0:012> ~f

0:012> ~
    0  Id: 7d1c.11f0 Suspend: 1 Teb: 0000009b`39784000 Unfrozen
```

```
  1  Id: 7d1c.286c Suspend: 1 Teb: 0000009b`39786000 Unfrozen
  2  Id: 7d1c.9594 Suspend: 1 Teb: 0000009b`39788000 Unfrozen
  3  Id: 7d1c.4be0 Suspend: 1 Teb: 0000009b`3978e000 Unfrozen
  4  Id: 7d1c.7458 Suspend: 1 Teb: 0000009b`3978c000 Unfrozen
  5  Id: 7d1c.898c Suspend: 1 Teb: 0000009b`39790000 Unfrozen
  6  Id: 7d1c.8b84 Suspend: 1 Teb: 0000009b`39792000 Unfrozen
  7  Id: 7d1c.8220 Suspend: 1 Teb: 0000009b`39794000 Unfrozen
  8  Id: 7d1c.41c Suspend: 1 Teb: 0000009b`39796000 Unfrozen
  9  Id: 7d1c.67a8 Suspend: 1 Teb: 0000009b`39798000 Unfrozen
 10  Id: 7d1c.14fc Suspend: 1 Teb: 0000009b`3979a000 Unfrozen
 11  Id: 7d1c.5e90 Suspend: 1 Teb: 0000009b`3979c000 Frozen
. 12  Id: 7d1c.8de8 Suspend: 1 Teb: 0000009b`3979e000 Frozen
 13  Id: 7d1c.2df0 Suspend: 1 Teb: 0000009b`397a0000 Unfrozen
```

7.   We then continue execution, break in again, examine threads, switch to thread #12, and unfreeze it (the **~u** command):

```
0:012> g
Breakpoint 1 will not be deferred because of changes in the context. Breakpoint may hit again.
System 0: 2 of 14 threads are frozen
System 0: 2 of 13 threads were frozen
System 0: 2 of 13 threads are frozen
System 0: 2 of 14 threads were frozen
System 0: 2 of 14 threads are frozen
(7d1c.4be0): C++ EH exception - code e06d7363 (first chance)
System 0: 2 of 14 threads were frozen
System 0: 2 of 14 threads are frozen
(7d1c.4be0): C++ EH exception - code e06d7363 (first chance)
System 0: 2 of 14 threads were frozen
System 0: 2 of 14 threads are frozen
(7d1c.4be0): C++ EH exception - code e06d7363 (first chance)
System 0: 2 of 14 threads were frozen
System 0: 2 of 14 threads are frozen
(7d1c.4be0): C++ EH exception - code e06d7363 (first chance)
System 0: 2 of 14 threads were frozen
System 0: 2 of 14 threads are frozen
System 0: 2 of 15 threads were frozen
System 0: 2 of 15 threads are frozen
System 0: 2 of 15 threads were frozen
(7d1c.92c0): Break instruction exception - code 80000003 (first chance)
ntdll!DbgBreakPoint:
00007ff9`555d3060 int     3

0:014> ~
  0  Id: 7d1c.11f0 Suspend: 1 Teb: 0000009b`39784000 Unfrozen
  1  Id: 7d1c.286c Suspend: 1 Teb: 0000009b`39786000 Unfrozen
  2  Id: 7d1c.9594 Suspend: 1 Teb: 0000009b`39788000 Unfrozen
  3  Id: 7d1c.4be0 Suspend: 1 Teb: 0000009b`3978e000 Unfrozen
  4  Id: 7d1c.7458 Suspend: 1 Teb: 0000009b`3978c000 Unfrozen
  5  Id: 7d1c.9078 Suspend: 1 Teb: 0000009b`397a2000 Unfrozen
  6  Id: 7d1c.8b84 Suspend: 1 Teb: 0000009b`39792000 Unfrozen
  7  Id: 7d1c.8220 Suspend: 1 Teb: 0000009b`39794000 Unfrozen
  8  Id: 7d1c.41c Suspend: 1 Teb: 0000009b`39796000 Unfrozen
  9  Id: 7d1c.67a8 Suspend: 1 Teb: 0000009b`39798000 Unfrozen
 10  Id: 7d1c.14fc Suspend: 1 Teb: 0000009b`3979a000 Unfrozen
 11  Id: 7d1c.5e90 Suspend: 1 Teb: 0000009b`3979c000 Frozen
 12  Id: 7d1c.8de8 Suspend: 1 Teb: 0000009b`3979e000 Frozen
 13  Id: 7d1c.2df0 Suspend: 1 Teb: 0000009b`397a0000 Unfrozen
```

```
.  14   Id: 7d1c.92c0 Suspend: 1 Teb: 0000009b`397a4000 Unfrozen
```

```
0:014> ~12s
AppD7!ThreadProcB:
00007ff7`3c6e1510 mov    qword ptr [rsp+8],rcx ss:0000009b`3a4ffc70=0000000000000000
```

```
0:012> ~u
```

8.   We then continue execution, skip the breakpoint on *ThreadProcB,* and resume again. Shortly, we see a first chance exception:

```
0:012> g
System 0: 1 of 15 threads are frozen
System 0: 1 of 15 threads were frozen
Breakpoint 1 hit
AppD7!ThreadProcB:
00007ff7`3c6e1510 mov    qword ptr [rsp+8],rcx ss:0000009b`3a4ffc70=0000000000000000
```

```
0:012> g
System 0: 1 of 15 threads are frozen
System 0: 1 of 14 threads were frozen
System 0: 1 of 14 threads are frozen
System 0: 1 of 14 threads were frozen
System 0: 1 of 14 threads are frozen
System 0: 1 of 15 threads were frozen
System 0: 1 of 15 threads are frozen
(7d1c.628): Access violation - code c0000005 (first chance)
System 0: 1 of 15 threads were frozen
First chance exceptions are reported before any exception handling.
This exception may be expected and handled.
00000000`00000000 ???
```

9.   We switch to thread #11, unfreeze it, continue, skip the breakpoint hit on *ThreadProcA* if there is any, and continue again until we hit a second chance exception:

```
0:014> ~11s
AppD7!ThreadProcA:
00007ff7`3c6e14d0 mov    qword ptr [rsp+8],rcx ss:0000009b`3a3ffcc0=0000000000000000
```

```
0:011> ~u
```

```
0:011> g
(7d1c.628): Access violation - code c0000005 (!!! second chance !!!)
00000000`00000000 ???
```

Stack trace shows that another newly created thread was called with NULL thread function:

```
0:014> kL
 # Child-SP          RetAddr               Call Site
00 0000009b`39dffd78 00007ff9`5504257d    0x0
01 0000009b`39dffd80 00007ff9`5558aa58    KERNEL32!BaseThreadInitThunk+0x1d
02 0000009b`39dffdb0 00000000`00000000    ntdll!RtlUserThreadStart+0x28
```

Source code inspection shows a race condition with initialization of *g_sharedData.lpProc,* which under debugger was masked by the extra delay in *SimulateDelay:*

```
DWORD WINAPI ThreadProcA(LPVOID)
{
        Sleep(100); // some work
        g_sharedData.lpProc = ThreadProcC;
        Sleep(10000);
        return 0;
}

DWORD WINAPI ThreadProcB(LPVOID)
{
        SimulateDelay(); // some work
        CreateThread(NULL, 0, g_sharedData.lpProc, NULL, 0, NULL);
        Sleep(10000);
        return 0;
}

void SimulateDelay(void)
{
        if (IsDebuggerPresent())
                Sleep(1000);
}
```

10.   We now close WinDbg (the log should close automatically).

Exercise UD8

- **Goal:** Learn how to inspect heap for signs of corruption

- **Elementary Diagnostics Patterns:** Crash

- **Memory Analysis Patterns:** Dynamic Memory Corruption (Process Heap); Module Variable; Exception Stack Trace

- **Debugging Implementation Patterns:** Break-in

- \AWD4\Exercise-UD8.pdf

Goal: Learn how to inspect the heap for signs of corruption.

Elementary Diagnostics Patterns: Crash.

Memory Analysis Patterns: Dynamic Memory Corruption (Process Heap); Module Variable; Exception Stack Trace.

Debugging Implementation Patterns: Break-in.

1.   Launch \AWD4\AppD8\Release\AppD8.exe executable, and choose File \ Start. Nothing happens, although if we inspect the source code of the StartModeling function, we see a corruption attempt:

```
void StartModeling (void)
{
    char *pc = (char *)malloc(100);

    free(pc+50);
}
```

Note: if you want to build a legacy x86 AppD8 project, you need to install Windows SDK for Windows 7 from the SDK archive[12] because Visual Studio Community 2022 platform toolset Visual Studio 2015 - Windows XP (v140_xp) requires it. Use GET THE DVD ISO installation type and choose x64 image (GRMSDKX_EN_DVD.iso), but during setup, choose C:\Program Files (x86)\Microsoft SDKs\Windows\v7.1A as SDK destination folder. You also need to download and install Visual Studio Community 2015 with Update 3, where, during installation, you need to select the Windows XP Support for C++ option.

2.   We attach WinDbg to this 32-bit application (its target architecture is autodetected):

```
Microsoft (R) Windows Debugger Version 10.0.25921.1001 X86
Copyright (c) Microsoft Corporation. All rights reserved.

*** wait with pending attach

************* Path validation summary **************
Response                        Time (ms)      Location
Deferred                                       srv*
Symbol search path is: srv*
Executable search path is:
ModLoad: 004e0000 004f8000   C:\AWD4\AppD8\Release\AppD8.exe
ModLoad: 775a0000 77751000   C:\WINDOWS\SYSTEM32\ntdll.dll
ModLoad: 772f0000 773e0000   C:\WINDOWS\System32\KERNEL32.DLL
ModLoad: 75e00000 76074000   C:\WINDOWS\System32\KERNELBASE.dll
ModLoad: 74d80000 74e26000   C:\WINDOWS\SYSTEM32\apphelp.dll
ModLoad: 773e0000 77588000   C:\WINDOWS\System32\USER32.dll
ModLoad: 772d0000 772ea000   C:\WINDOWS\System32\win32u.dll
ModLoad: 76d00000 76d23000   C:\WINDOWS\System32\GDI32.dll
ModLoad: 758b0000 75992000   C:\WINDOWS\System32\gdi32full.dll
ModLoad: 75480000 754f9000   C:\WINDOWS\System32\msvcp_win.dll
ModLoad: 75360000 75472000   C:\WINDOWS\System32\ucrtbase.dll
ModLoad: 76490000 764b5000   C:\WINDOWS\System32\IMM32.DLL
```

---

[12] https://developer.microsoft.com/en-gb/windows/downloads/sdk-archive/

```
ModLoad: 70620000 7069f000    C:\WINDOWS\system32\uxtheme.dll
ModLoad: 76df0000 7706d000    C:\WINDOWS\System32\combase.dll
ModLoad: 75750000 7580a000    C:\WINDOWS\System32\RPCRT4.dll
ModLoad: 771d0000 772cc000    C:\WINDOWS\System32\MSCTF.dll
ModLoad: 76520000 765e4000    C:\WINDOWS\System32\msvcrt.dll
ModLoad: 55d50000 55de5000    C:\WINDOWS\SYSTEM32\TextShaping.dll
ModLoad: 73490000 734a3000    C:\WINDOWS\SYSTEM32\kernel.appcore.dll
ModLoad: 76380000 763e2000    C:\WINDOWS\System32\bcryptPrimitives.dll
ModLoad: 763f0000 76475000    C:\WINDOWS\System32\sechost.dll
ModLoad: 75de0000 75dfa000    C:\WINDOWS\System32\bcrypt.dll
ModLoad: 70520000 70619000    C:\WINDOWS\SYSTEM32\textinputframework.dll
ModLoad: 75810000 758ac000    C:\WINDOWS\System32\OLEAUT32.dll
ModLoad: 6bd10000 6bdde000    C:\WINDOWS\SYSTEM32\CoreMessaging.dll
ModLoad: 6b700000 6b991000    C:\WINDOWS\SYSTEM32\CoreUIComponents.dll
ModLoad: 734f0000 735b7000    C:\WINDOWS\SYSTEM32\wintypes.dll
ModLoad: 76300000 7637f000    C:\WINDOWS\System32\advapi32.dll
ModLoad: 73090000 7309b000    C:\WINDOWS\SYSTEM32\CRYPTBASE.DLL
ModLoad: 73d40000 73d94000    C:\WINDOWS\system32\Oleacc.dll
ModLoad: 75220000 752a2000    C:\WINDOWS\System32\clbcatq.dll
ModLoad: 64080000 643cc000    C:\Windows\System32\uiautomationcore.dll
ModLoad: 70ff0000 71014000    C:\WINDOWS\system32\dwmapi.dll
ModLoad: 5a390000 5a3a1000    C:\Windows\System32\threadpoolwinrt.dll
(6b18.7670): Break instruction exception - code 80000003 (first chance)
eax=00682000 ebx=00000000 ecx=776540e0 edx=776540e0 esi=776540e0 edi=776540e0
eip=77618b80 esp=051ff7d8 ebp=051ff804 iopl=0         nv up ei pl zr na pe nc
cs=0023  ss=002b  ds=002b  es=002b  fs=0053  gs=002b             efl=00000246
ntdll!DbgBreakPoint:
77618b80 int        3
```

```
0:011> .logopen c:\AWD4\D8.log
Opened log file 'c:\AWD4\D8.log'
```

3.   The heap verification command shows a corruption attempt:

```
0:011> !heap -s -v

*****************************************************************************************
                              NT HEAP STATS BELOW
*****************************************************************************************
*****************************************************************
*                                                               *
*              HEAP ERROR DETECTED                              *
*                                                               *
*****************************************************************


Details:

Heap address:  008f0000
Error address: 0095a05a
Error type: HEAP_FAILURE_INVALID_ARGUMENT
Details:    The caller tried to a free a block at an invalid
            (unaligned) address.
Follow-up:  Check the error's stack trace to find the culprit.

Stack trace:
Stack trace at 0x776cb948
    7769ce9b: ntdll!RtlpLogHeapFailure+0x43
    7762fe53: ntdll!RtlpFreeHeapInternal+0x10c
    775ef036: ntdll!RtlFreeHeap+0x46
```

177

```
*** WARNING: Unable to verify checksum for C:\AWD4\AppD8\Release\AppD8.exe
    004e39cd: AppD8!_free_base+0x1c
    004e134d: AppD8!StartModeling+0x1d
    004e121a: AppD8!WndProc+0x7a
    77412e53: USER32!_InternalCallWinProc+0x2b
    77403c26: USER32!UserCallWinProcCheckWow+0x4c6
    774024e5: USER32!DispatchMessageWorker+0x4a5
    77402030: USER32!DispatchMessageW+0x10
    004e109d: AppD8!wWinMain+0x9d
    004e1519: AppD8!__scrt_common_main_seh+0xf6
    77307ba9: KERNEL32!BaseThreadInitThunk+0x19
    7760bd2b: ntdll!__RtlUserThreadStart+0x2b
    7760bcaf: ntdll!_RtlUserThreadStart+0x1b
```

```
LFH Key                    : 0x7d78ab9a
Termination on corruption : DISABLED
  Heap     Flags    Reserv  Commit  Virt  Free  List   UCR  Virt   Lock  Fast
                     (k)     (k)    (k)   (k) length      blocks cont. heap
-----------------------------------------------------------------------------
.008f0000 00000002   1128    468    464    25    36    1    0      0    LFH
.02710000 00001002    168     32     60     4     4    1    0      0    LFH
.026f0000 00001002    168     64     60     9     4    1    0      0    LFH
-----------------------------------------------------------------------------
```

4.   Please note that WinDbg detects this corruption automatically during the **!analyze -v** command (there may be a delay while symbols are being copied from the Microsoft symbol server) but is not able to get its stack trace:

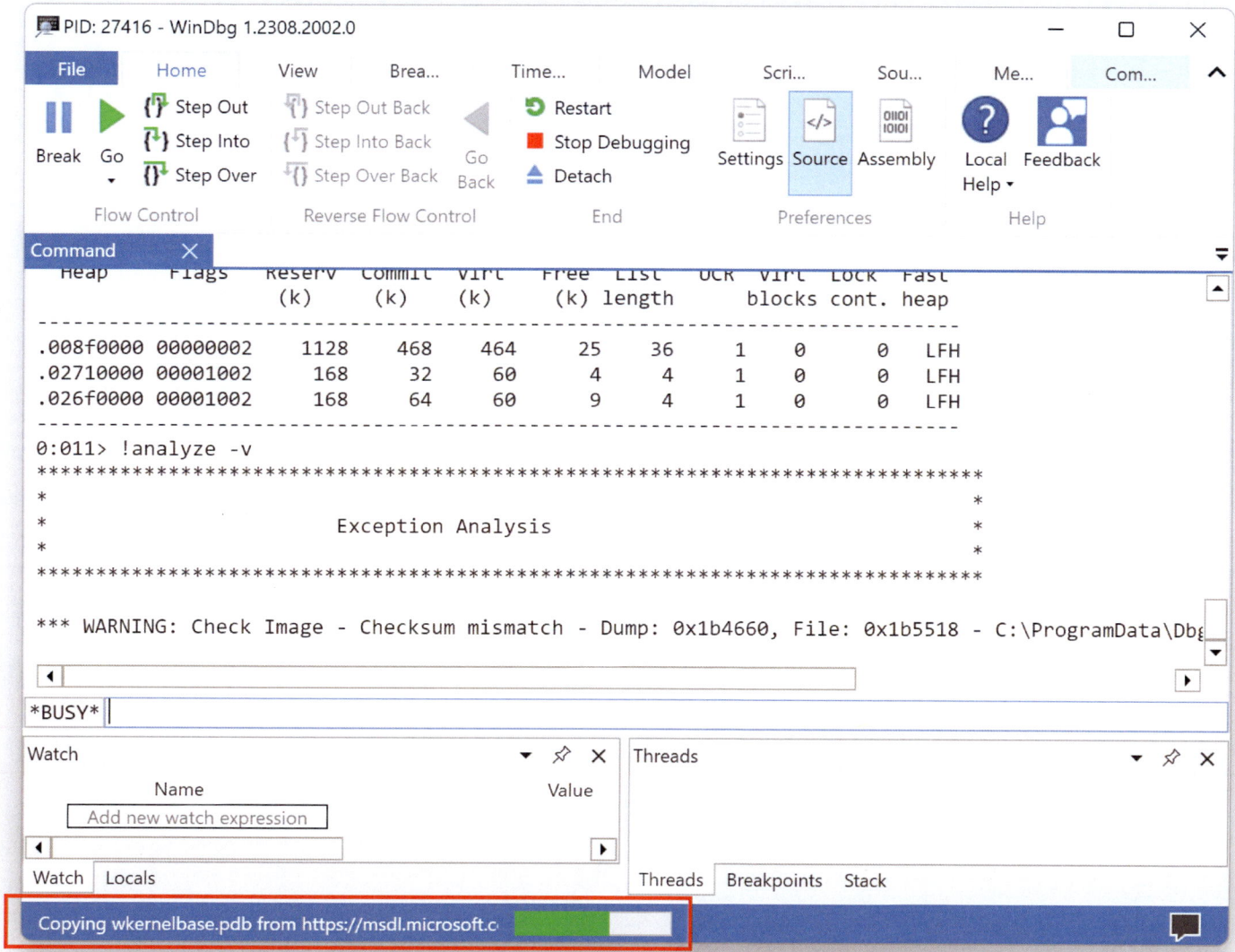

```
0:011> !analyze -v
*************************************************************************
*                                                                       *
*                        Exception Analysis                             *
*                                                                       *
*************************************************************************

*** WARNING: Check Image - Checksum mismatch - Dump: 0x1b4660, File: 0x1b5518 -
C:\ProgramData\Dbg\sym\ntdll.dll\FC3ED07C1b1000\ntdll.dll

KEY_VALUES_STRING: 1

    Key  : Analysis.CPU.mSec
    Value: 2296

    Key  : Analysis.Elapsed.mSec
    Value: 11606

    Key  : Analysis.IO.Other.Mb
    Value: 14

    Key  : Analysis.IO.Read.Mb
    Value: 23
```

```
    Key  : Analysis.IO.Write.Mb
    Value: 81

    Key  : Analysis.Init.CPU.mSec
    Value: 1827

    Key  : Analysis.Init.Elapsed.mSec
    Value: 210227

    Key  : Analysis.Memory.CommitPeak.Mb
    Value: 86

    Key  : Failure.Bucket
    Value: BREAKPOINT_ACTIONABLE_InvalidArgument_80000003_heap_corruption!AppD8.exe

    Key  : Failure.Hash
    Value: {a541cc46-fec3-5595-68bb-9b9b9b201a8c}

    Key  : Timeline.OS.Boot.DeltaSec
    Value: 243896

    Key  : Timeline.Process.Start.DeltaSec
    Value: 257

    Key  : WER.OS.Branch
    Value: ni_release

    Key  : WER.OS.Version
    Value: 10.0.22621.1


NTGLOBALFLAG:  400

PROCESS_BAM_CURRENT_THROTTLED: 0

PROCESS_BAM_PREVIOUS_THROTTLED: 0

APPLICATION_VERIFIER_FLAGS:  0

EXCEPTION_RECORD:  (.exr -1)
ExceptionAddress: 77618b80 (ntdll!DbgBreakPoint)
   ExceptionCode: 80000003 (Break instruction exception)
  ExceptionFlags: 00000000
NumberParameters: 1
   Parameter[0]: 00000000

FAULTING_THREAD:  00007670

PROCESS_NAME:  AppD8.exe

ERROR_CODE: (NTSTATUS) 0x80000003 - {EXCEPTION}  Breakpoint  A breakpoint has been reached.

EXCEPTION_CODE_STR:  80000003

EXCEPTION_PARAMETER1:  00000000

ADDITIONAL_DEBUG_TEXT:  Followup set based on attribute [Is_ChosenCrashFollowupThread] from
Frame:[0] on thread:[PSEUDO_THREAD]
```

STACK_TEXT:
00000000 00000000 heap_corruption!AppD8.exe+0x0

STACK_COMMAND: !heap ; ** Pseudo Context ** ManagedPseudo ** Value: ffffffff ** ; kb

SYMBOL_NAME: heap_corruption!AppD8.exe

MODULE_NAME: heap_corruption

IMAGE_NAME: heap_corruption

FAILURE_BUCKET_ID: BREAKPOINT_ACTIONABLE_InvalidArgument_80000003_heap_corruption!AppD8.exe

OS_VERSION: 10.0.22621.1

BUILDLAB_STR: ni_release

OSPLATFORM_TYPE: x86

OSNAME: Windows 10

FAILURE_ID_HASH: {a541cc46-fec3-5595-68bb-9b9b9b201a8c}

Followup: MachineOwner

Note: Let's examine the *RtlpHeapFailureInfo* variable:

```
0:011> dps ntdll!RtlpHeapFailureInfo
776cb918  00000002
776cb91c  000003d0
776cb920  00000009
776cb924  008f0000
776cb928  0095a05a
776cb92c  00000000
776cb930  00000000
776cb934  00000000
776cb938  00000000
776cb93c  00000000
776cb940  00000000
776cb944  00000000
776cb948  7769ce9b ntdll!RtlpLogHeapFailure+0x43
776cb94c  7762fe53 ntdll!RtlpFreeHeapInternal+0x10c
776cb950  775ef036 ntdll!RtlFreeHeap+0x46
776cb954  004e39cd AppD8!_free_base+0x1c [d:\th\minkernel\crts\ucrt\src\appcrt\heap\free_base.cpp @ 107]
776cb958  004e134d AppD8!StartModeling+0x1d [c:\awd3\appd8\appd8\appd8.cpp @ 195]
776cb95c  004e121a AppD8!WndProc+0x7a [c:\awd3\appd8\appd8\appd8.cpp @ 146]
776cb960  77412e53 USER32!_InternalCallWinProc+0x2b
776cb964  77403c26 USER32!UserCallWinProcCheckWow+0x4c6
776cb968  774024e5 USER32!DispatchMessageWorker+0x4a5
776cb96c  77402030 USER32!DispatchMessageW+0x10
776cb970  004e109d AppD8!wWinMain+0x9d [c:\awd3\appd8\appd8\appd8.cpp @ 57]
776cb974  004e1519 AppD8!__scrt_common_main_seh+0xf6 [f:\dd\vctools\crt\vcstartup\src\startup\exe_common.inl @ 253]
776cb978  77307ba9 KERNEL32!BaseThreadInitThunk+0x19
776cb97c  7760bd2b ntdll!__RtlUserThreadStart+0x2b
776cb980  7760bcaf ntdll!_RtlUserThreadStart+0x1b
776cb984  00000000
776cb988  00000000
776cb98c  00000000
776cb990  00000000
776cb994  00000000
```

5.   Heap termination on corruption is enabled by default on the x64 platform (and we have also found that since Visual C++ 2017, it is also enabled by default for x86 targets). If we launch under WinDbg the \AWD4\AppD8\x64\Release\AppD8.exe executable, continue, and choose *File \ Start,* we immediately catch the corruption:

```
Microsoft (R) Windows Debugger Version 10.0.25921.1001 AMD64
Copyright (c) Microsoft Corporation. All rights reserved.

CommandLine: C:\AWD4\AppD8\x64\Release\AppD8.exe

************* Path validation summary **************
Response                        Time (ms)    Location
Deferred                                     srv*
Symbol search path is: srv*
Executable search path is:
ModLoad: 00007ff7`26b50000 00007ff7`26b70000   AppD8.exe
ModLoad: 00007ff9`55530000 00007ff9`55747000   ntdll.dll
ModLoad: 00007ff9`55030000 00007ff9`550f4000   C:\WINDOWS\System32\KERNEL32.DLL
ModLoad: 00007ff9`52870000 00007ff9`52c16000   C:\WINDOWS\System32\KERNELBASE.dll
ModLoad: 00007ff9`4f780000 00007ff9`4f817000   C:\WINDOWS\SYSTEM32\apphelp.dll
ModLoad: 00007ff9`54130000 00007ff9`542de000   C:\WINDOWS\System32\USER32.dll
ModLoad: 00007ff9`53190000 00007ff9`531b6000   C:\WINDOWS\System32\win32u.dll
ModLoad: 00007ff9`542e0000 00007ff9`54309000   C:\WINDOWS\System32\GDI32.dll
ModLoad: 00007ff9`52c20000 00007ff9`52d38000   C:\WINDOWS\System32\gdi32full.dll
ModLoad: 00007ff9`52f30000 00007ff9`52fca000   C:\WINDOWS\System32\msvcp_win.dll
ModLoad: 00007ff9`53000000 00007ff9`53111000   C:\WINDOWS\System32\ucrtbase.dll
(7034.3dc): Break instruction exception - code 80000003 (first chance)
ntdll!LdrpDoDebuggerBreak+0x30:
00007ff9`5560b784 int     3
```

```
0:000> .logappend c:\AWD4\D8.log
Opened log file 'c:\AWD4\D8.log'
```

```
0:000> g
ModLoad: 00007ff9`53ef0000 00007ff9`53f21000   C:\WINDOWS\System32\IMM32.DLL
ModLoad: 00007ff9`4f920000 00007ff9`4f9cb000   C:\WINDOWS\system32\uxtheme.dll
ModLoad: 00007ff9`53b60000 00007ff9`53ee9000   C:\WINDOWS\System32\combase.dll
ModLoad: 00007ff9`543d0000 00007ff9`544e7000   C:\WINDOWS\System32\RPCRT4.dll
ModLoad: 00007ff9`54a40000 00007ff9`54b90000   C:\WINDOWS\System32\MSCTF.dll
ModLoad: 00007ff9`55100000 00007ff9`551a7000   C:\WINDOWS\System32\msvcrt.dll
ModLoad: 00007ff9`20a30000 00007ff9`20ae0000   C:\WINDOWS\SYSTEM32\TextShaping.dll
ModLoad: 00007ff9`51860000 00007ff9`51878000   C:\WINDOWS\SYSTEM32\kernel.appcore.dll
ModLoad: 00007ff9`52eb0000 00007ff9`52f2a000   C:\WINDOWS\System32\bcryptPrimitives.dll
clientcore\windows\advcore\ctf\uim\tim.cpp(800)\MSCTF.dll!00007FF954A565D9: (caller:
00007FF954A5720C) LogHr(1) tid(3dc) 8007029C An assertion failure has occurred.
clientcore\windows\advcore\ctf\uim\tim.cpp(800)\MSCTF.dll!00007FF954A565D9: (caller:
00007FF954A5720C) LogHr(2) tid(3dc) 8007029C An assertion failure has occurred.
ModLoad: 00007ff9`54e20000 00007ff9`54ec8000   C:\WINDOWS\System32\sechost.dll
ModLoad: 00007ff9`52fd0000 00007ff9`52ff8000   C:\WINDOWS\System32\bcrypt.dll
ModLoad: 00007ff9`54b90000 00007ff9`54c67000   C:\WINDOWS\System32\OLEAUT32.dll
ModLoad: 00007ff9`3fba0000 00007ff9`3fcea000   C:\WINDOWS\SYSTEM32\textinputframework.dll
ModLoad: 00007ff9`2b3e0000 00007ff9`2b449000   C:\WINDOWS\system32\Oleacc.dll
ModLoad: 00007ff9`54510000 00007ff9`545c0000   C:\WINDOWS\System32\clbcatq.dll
ModLoad: 00007ff9`20ae0000 00007ff9`20b2b000
C:\WINDOWS\system32\ApplicationTargetedFeatureDatabase.dll
ModLoad: 00007ff9`47160000 00007ff9`473e5000   C:\Windows\System32\twinapi.appcore.dll
ModLoad: 00007ff9`50f30000 00007ff9`5106e000   C:\Windows\System32\WinTypes.dll
ModLoad: 00007ff9`12ff0000 00007ff9`13435000   C:\Windows\System32\uiautomationcore.dll
```

```
ModLoad: 00007ff9`4f470000 00007ff9`4f5a4000   C:\WINDOWS\SYSTEM32\CoreMessaging.dll
ModLoad: 00007ff9`49070000 00007ff9`493dc000   C:\WINDOWS\SYSTEM32\CoreUIComponents.dll
ModLoad: 00007ff9`54310000 00007ff9`543c3000   C:\WINDOWS\System32\advapi32.dll
ModLoad: 00007ff9`51ed0000 00007ff9`51edc000   C:\WINDOWS\SYSTEM32\CRYPTBASE.DLL
ModLoad: 00007ff9`4fb50000 00007ff9`4fb7b000   C:\WINDOWS\system32\dwmapi.dll
ModLoad: 00007ff9`1e070000 00007ff9`1e085000   C:\Windows\System32\threadpoolwinrt.dll
(7034.5510): C++ EH exception - code e06d7363 (first chance)
(7034.5510): C++ EH exception - code e06d7363 (first chance)
(7034.5510): C++ EH exception - code e06d7363 (first chance)
(7034.5510): C++ EH exception - code e06d7363 (first chance)
(7034.5510): C++ EH exception - code e06d7363 (first chance)
(7034.5510): C++ EH exception - code e06d7363 (first chance)
```
Critical error detected c0000374
(7034.3dc): Break instruction exception - code 80000003 (first chance)
```
ntdll!RtlReportCriticalFailure+0x56:
00007ff9`5563c732 int     3
```

```
0:000> kL
 # Child-SP          RetAddr               Call Site
00 00000043`36faf630 00007ff9`5564580a     ntdll!RtlReportCriticalFailure+0x56
01 00000043`36faf720 00007ff9`55645aea     ntdll!RtlpHeapHandleError+0x12
02 00000043`36faf750 00007ff9`55651ae5     ntdll!RtlpHpHeapHandleError+0x7a
03 00000043`36faf780 00007ff9`5556bdfd     ntdll!RtlpLogHeapFailure+0x45
04 00000043`36faf7b0 00007ff9`5556ab11     ntdll!RtlpFreeHeapInternal+0x77d
*** WARNING: Unable to verify checksum for AppD8.exe
05 00000043`36faf870 00007ff7`26b568d8     ntdll!RtlFreeHeap+0x51
06 00000043`36faf8b0 00007ff7`26b51494     AppD8!_free_base+0x1c
07 00000043`36faf8e0 00007ff7`26b51301     AppD8!StartModeling+0x24
08 00000043`36faf920 00007ff9`54148241     AppD8!WndProc+0xb1
09 00000043`36faf9e0 00007ff9`54147d01     USER32!UserCallWinProcCheckWow+0x2d1
0a 00000043`36fafb40 00007ff7`26b510d0     USER32!DispatchMessageWorker+0x1f1
0b 00000043`36fafbc0 00007ff7`26b516ba     AppD8!wWinMain+0xd0
0c (Inline Function) --------`--------     AppD8!invoke_main+0x21
0d 00000043`36fafc30 00007ff9`5504257d     AppD8!__scrt_common_main_seh+0x106
0e 00000043`36fafc70 00007ff9`5558aa58     KERNEL32!BaseThreadInitThunk+0x1d
0f 00000043`36fafca0 00000000`00000000     ntdll!RtlUserThreadStart+0x28
```

```
0:000> g
(7034.3dc): Unknown exception - code c0000374 (first chance)
(7034.3dc): Unknown exception - code c0000374 (!!! second chance !!!)
ntdll!RtlReportFatalFailure+0x9:
00007ff9`5563c7a9 jmp     ntdll!RtlReportFatalFailure+0xb (00007ff9`5563c7ab)
```

```
0:000> kL
 # Child-SP          RetAddr               Call Site
00 00000043`36faf5e0 00007ff9`5563c773     ntdll!RtlReportFatalFailure+0x9
01 00000043`36faf630 00007ff9`5564580a     ntdll!RtlReportCriticalFailure+0x97
02 00000043`36faf720 00007ff9`55645aea     ntdll!RtlpHeapHandleError+0x12
03 00000043`36faf750 00007ff9`55651ae5     ntdll!RtlpHpHeapHandleError+0x7a
04 00000043`36faf780 00007ff9`5556bdfd     ntdll!RtlpLogHeapFailure+0x45
05 00000043`36faf7b0 00007ff9`5556ab11     ntdll!RtlpFreeHeapInternal+0x77d
06 00000043`36faf870 00007ff7`26b568d8     ntdll!RtlFreeHeap+0x51
07 00000043`36faf8b0 00007ff7`26b51494     AppD8!_free_base+0x1c
08 00000043`36faf8e0 00007ff7`26b51301     AppD8!StartModeling+0x24
09 00000043`36faf920 00007ff9`54148241     AppD8!WndProc+0xb1
0a 00000043`36faf9e0 00007ff9`54147d01     USER32!UserCallWinProcCheckWow+0x2d1
0b 00000043`36fafb40 00007ff7`26b510d0     USER32!DispatchMessageWorker+0x1f1
0c 00000043`36fafbc0 00007ff7`26b516ba     AppD8!wWinMain+0xd0
0d (Inline Function) --------`--------     AppD8!invoke_main+0x21
```

```
0e 00000043`36fafc30 00007ff9`5504257d     AppD8!__scrt_common_main_seh+0x106
0f 00000043`36fafc70 00007ff9`5558aa58     KERNEL32!BaseThreadInitThunk+0x1d
10 00000043`36fafca0 00000000`00000000     ntdll!RtlUserThreadStart+0x28
```

`0:000> !heap -s -v`

```
****************************************************************************************
                               NT HEAP STATS BELOW
****************************************************************************************
*******************************************************************
*                                                                 *
*                      HEAP ERROR DETECTED                        *
*                                                                 *
*******************************************************************
```

Details:

Heap address: 0000021b39940000
Error address: 0000021b399d9822
Error type: HEAP_FAILURE_INVALID_ARGUMENT
Details: The caller tried to a free a block at an invalid
**   (unaligned) address.**
Follow-up: Check the error's stack trace to find the culprit.

Stack trace:
Stack trace at 0x00007ff9556b38f8
    00007ff955651ae5: ntdll!RtlpLogHeapFailure+0x45
    00007ff95556bdfd: ntdll!RtlpFreeHeapInternal+0x77d
    00007ff95556ab11: ntdll!RtlFreeHeap+0x51
    00007ff726b568d8: AppD8!_free_base+0x1c
    00007ff726b51494: AppD8!StartModeling+0x24
    00007ff726b51301: AppD8!WndProc+0xb1
    00007ff954148241: USER32!UserCallWinProcCheckWow+0x2d1
    00007ff954147d01: USER32!DispatchMessageWorker+0x1f1
    00007ff726b510d0: AppD8!wWinMain+0xd0
    00007ff726b516ba: AppD8!__scrt_common_main_seh+0x106
    00007ff95504257d: KERNEL32!BaseThreadInitThunk+0x1d
    00007ff95558aa58: ntdll!RtlUserThreadStart+0x28
```

**NtGlobalFlag enables following debugging aids for new heaps:**
    **tail checking**
    **free checking**
    **validate parameters**
LFH Key                   : 0xcdded598b3974cf8
Termination on corruption : ENABLED

| Heap | Flags | Reserv (k) | Commit (k) | Virt (k) | Free (k) | List length | UCR | Virt blocks | Lock cont. | Fast heap |
|------|-------|--------|--------|------|------|--------|-----|--------|--------|------|
| .0000021b39940000 | 40000062 | 1020 | 628 | 1020 | 15 | 113 | 1 | 0 | 3 | |
| .0000021b39750000 | 40008060 | 64 | 4 | 64 | 2 | 1 | 1 | 0 | 0 | |
| .0000021b3b2c0000 | 40001062 | 60 | 24 | 60 | 1 | 10 | 1 | 0 | 0 | |
| ..0000021b3b270000 | 40001062 | 1080 | 76 | 1080 | 18 | 9 | 2 | 0 | 0 | |

6.      We now close both WinDbg sessions (the log should close automatically).
```

Kernel Mode Debugging

Exercises KD6, KD9, KD10

I use Windows 11 x64 as a Hyper-V Guest VM to run applications compiled under Visual Studio 2022. The host WinDbg from Debugging Tools for Windows runs under Windows 11 x64.

Exercise KD0

- **Goal:** Set up Hyper-V or VMware kernel debugging environment

- \AWD4\Exercise-KD0-Kernel-Debugging-Setup.pdf

Goal: Set up Hyper-V or VMware kernel debugging environment.

1.   You should have already set up Hyper-V or VMware Workstation with Windows 11. For these book edition exercises, we use Hyper-V Windows 11 dev environment (but keep VMware workstation setup as optional):

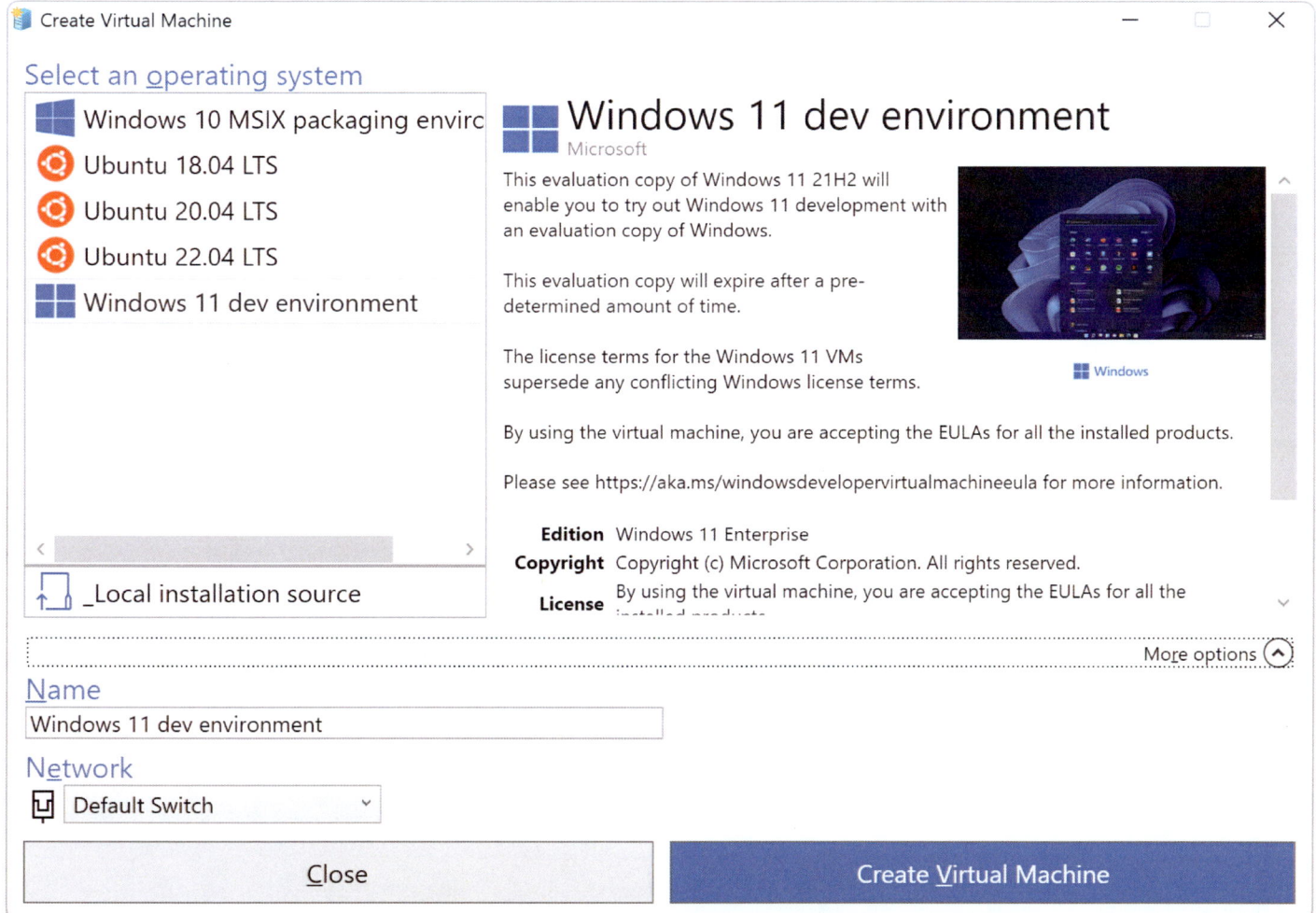

2.   For Hyper-V, we use network debugging via KDNET[13]. For Windows 11 dev environment and Windows 11 Pro host, we found that with the *Default Switch* network, everything works fine with WinDbg. Below are the steps that were required on my Windows 11 laptop.

---

[13] https://learn.microsoft.com/en-us/windows-hardware/drivers/debugger/setting-up-network-debugging-of-a-virtual-machine-host

3.   After creating a Windows 11 dev environment VM, disable Secure Boot in Security Settings in VM properties:

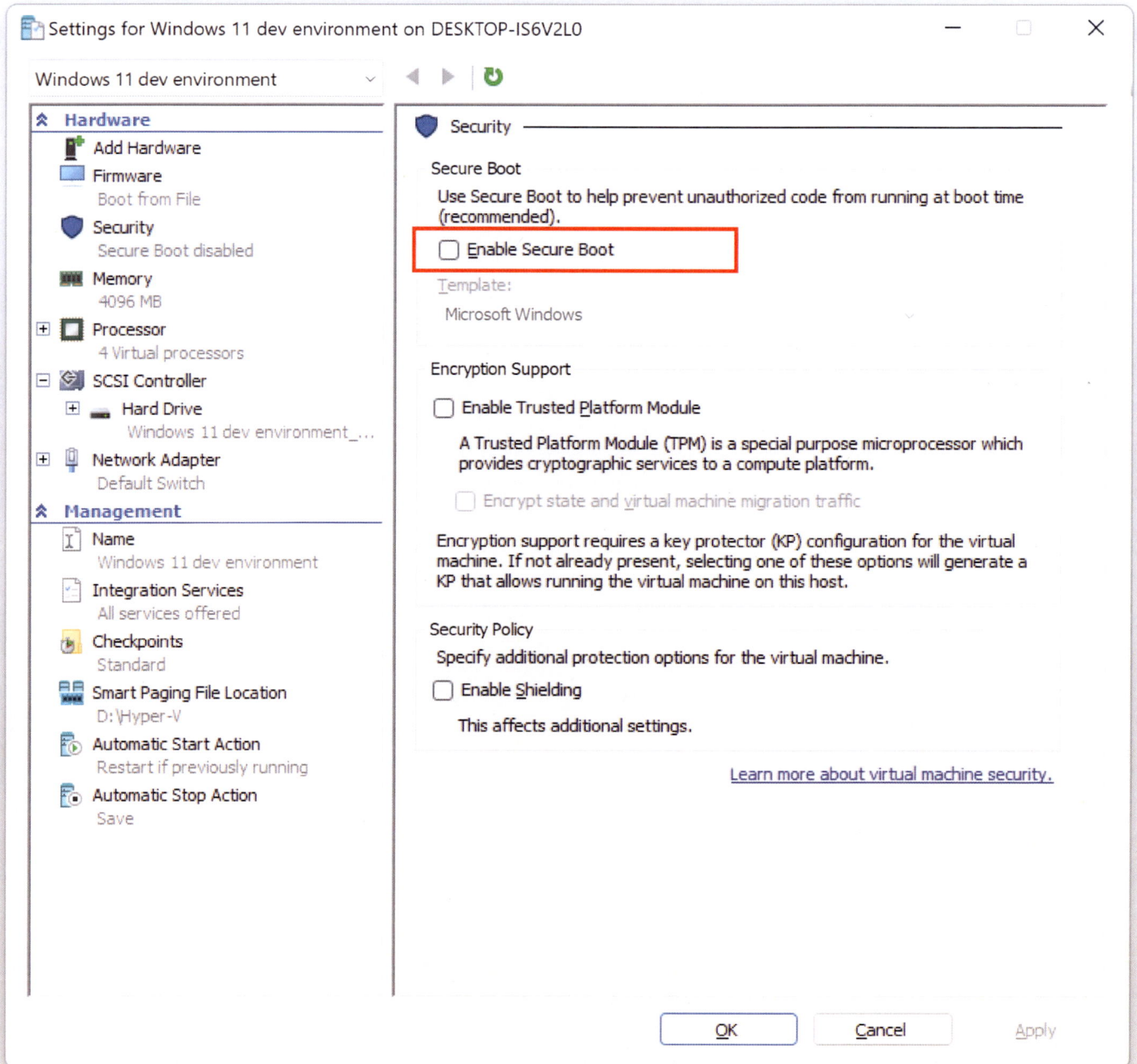

4.   Install Debugging Tools for Windows as a standalone toolset on the Guest VM[14].

Note: The version of WinDbg Preview we used in the previous edition had problems using KDNET when connecting to Hyper-V Guest VM, and we used WinDbg Classic from SDK on the host. In this edition, we use WinDbg on the host instead of WinDbg Classic.

---

[14] https://learn.microsoft.com/en-gb/windows-hardware/drivers/debugger/debugger-download-tools

5.   On the Host computer, run Command Prompt and note the IP4 address of the *Default Switch* (it may be different and change with every new Hyper-V start after the Host restart):

```
C:\Users\user>ipconfig
Windows IP Configuration
[...]
Ethernet adapter vEthernet (Default Switch):
   Connection-specific DNS Suffix  . :
   Link-local IPv6 Address . . . . . : [...]
   IPv4 Address. . . . . . . . . . . : 172.31.80.1
   Subnet Mask . . . . . . . . . . . : 255.255.240.0
   Default Gateway . . . . . . . . . :
[...]
```

6.   On the Guest VM, create the *C:\KDNET* folder and copy *kdnet.exe* and *VerifiedNICList.xml* files from your Debugging Tools for Windows installation folder (for example, *C:\Program Files (x86)\Windows Kits\10\Debuggers\x64*) to it.

7.   On the Guest VM, run Command Prompt as Administrator and get the debugging key after specifying the host address and port (your key should be different):

```
c:\KDNET>kdnet
```

Network debugging is supported by this Microsoft Hypervisor Virtual Machine

```
c:\KDNET>kdnet 172.31.80.1 50005
```

Enabling network debugging on Network debugging is supported by this Microsoft Hypervisor Virtual Machine.

To debug this vm, run the following command on your debugger host machine.
windbg -k net:port=50005,key=32ukpvnlc4og1.pfmgb9l0kzwo.2tohb1pajmuis.1gt40au5vdzb3

Then restart this VM by running shutdown -r -t 0 from this command prompt.

```
c:\KDNET>shutdown -r -t 0
```

Note: We do not reconnect to the guest VM on the host when we see the Virtual Machine Connection message box:

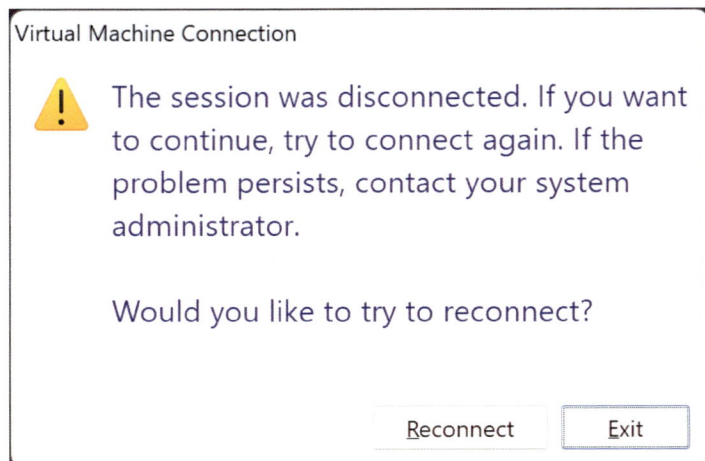

Virtual Machine Connection

⚠ The session was disconnected. If you want to continue, try to connect again. If the problem persists, contact your system administrator.

Would you like to try to reconnect?

[Reconnect]   [Exit]

8. On the Host computer, launch WinDbg and choose *File \ Attach to kernel* option:

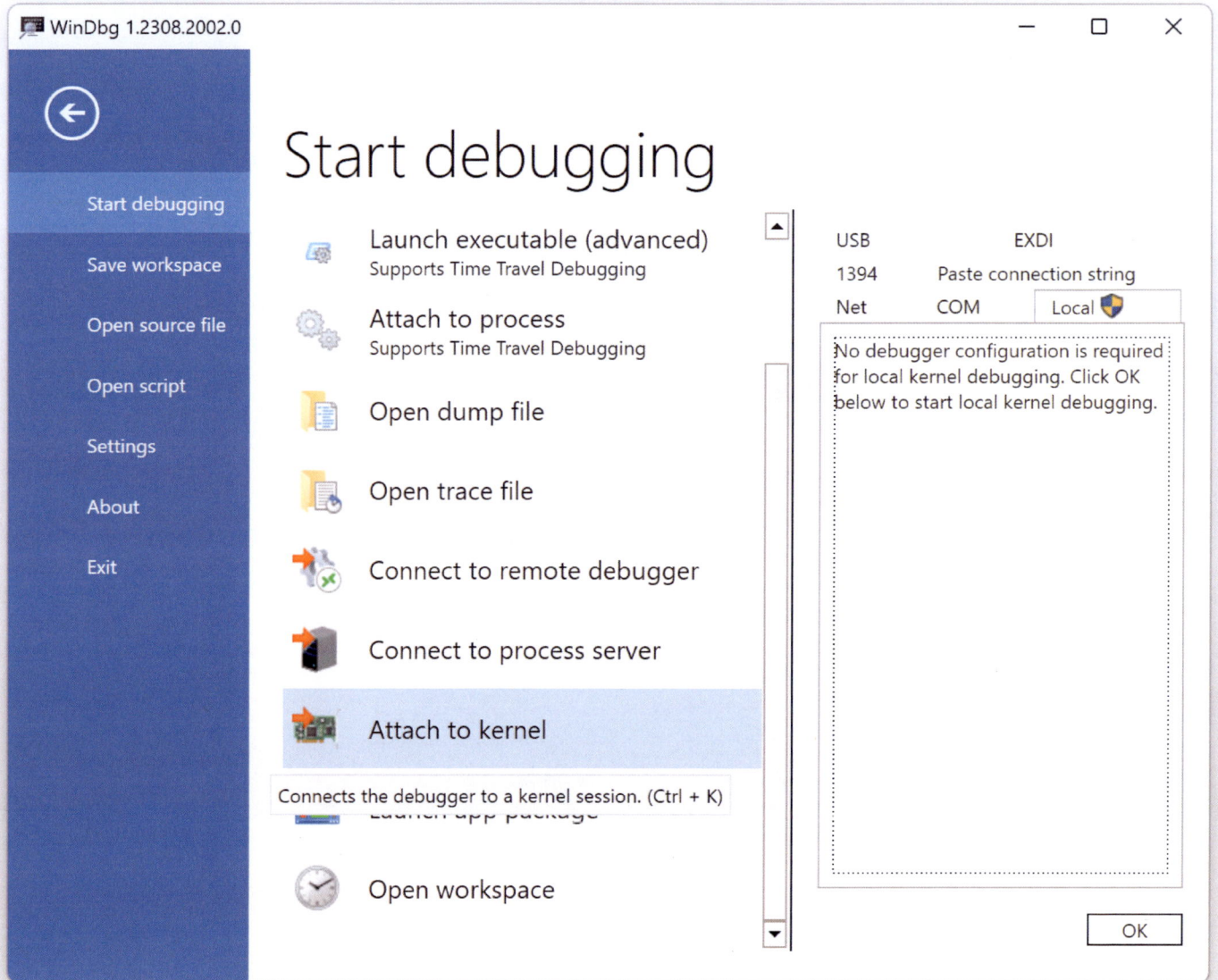

WinDbg 1.2308.2002.0

Start debugging

Start debugging

Save workspace

Open source file

Open script

Settings

About

Exit

Launch executable (advanced)
Supports Time Travel Debugging

Attach to process
Supports Time Travel Debugging

Open dump file

Open trace file

Connect to remote debugger

Connect to process server

Attach to kernel

Connects the debugger to a kernel session. (Ctrl + K)

~~Launch app package~~

Open workspace

USB	EXDI
1394	Paste connection string
Net	COM	Local

No debugger configuration is required for local kernel debugging. Click OK below to start local kernel debugging.

OK

9. Specify the *Port number* and *Key* obtained from the Guest VM in the *Net* tab:

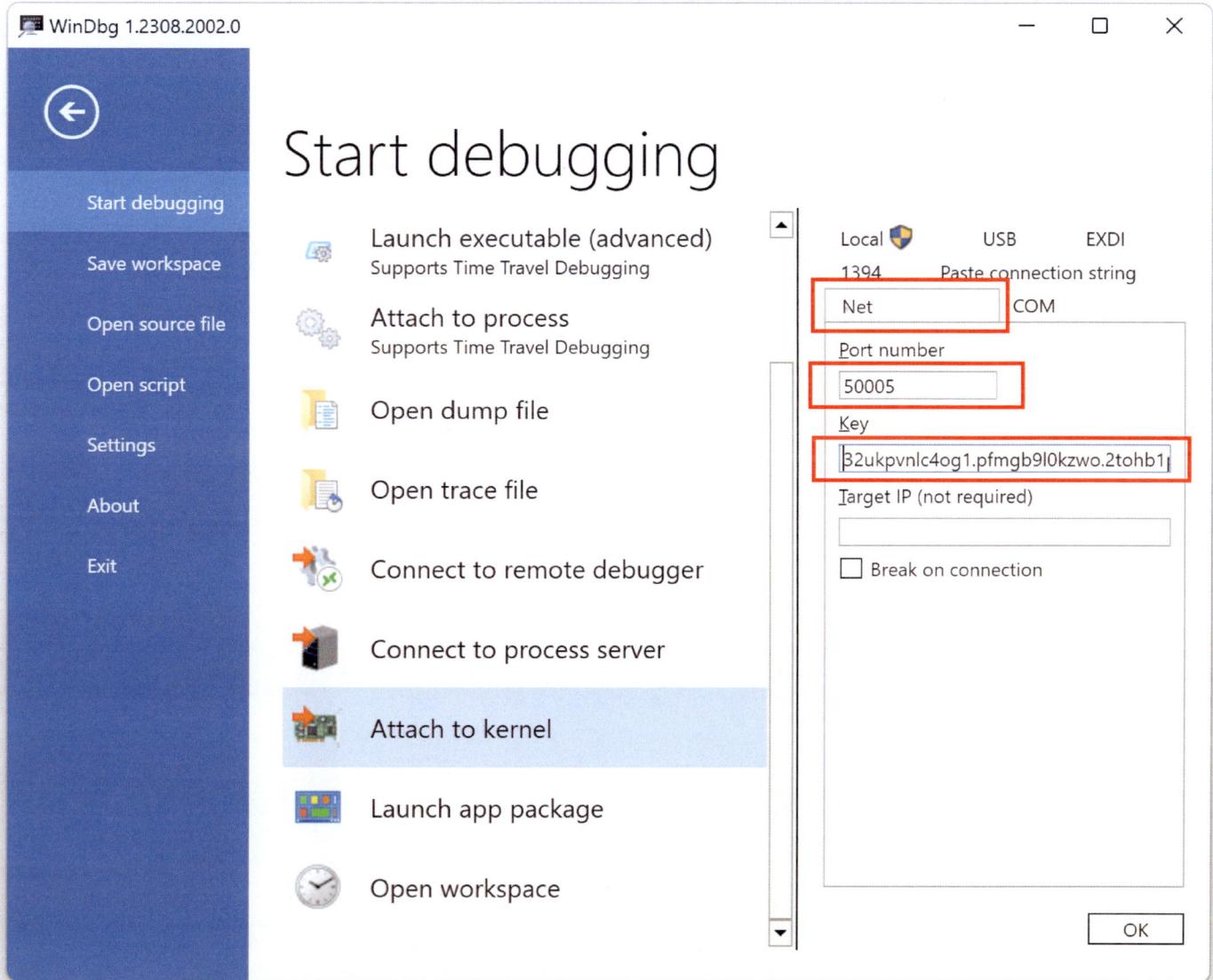

10. WinDbg is now connected to the Guest VM:

11. Use *the Break* button and wait. After some time, we get this output:

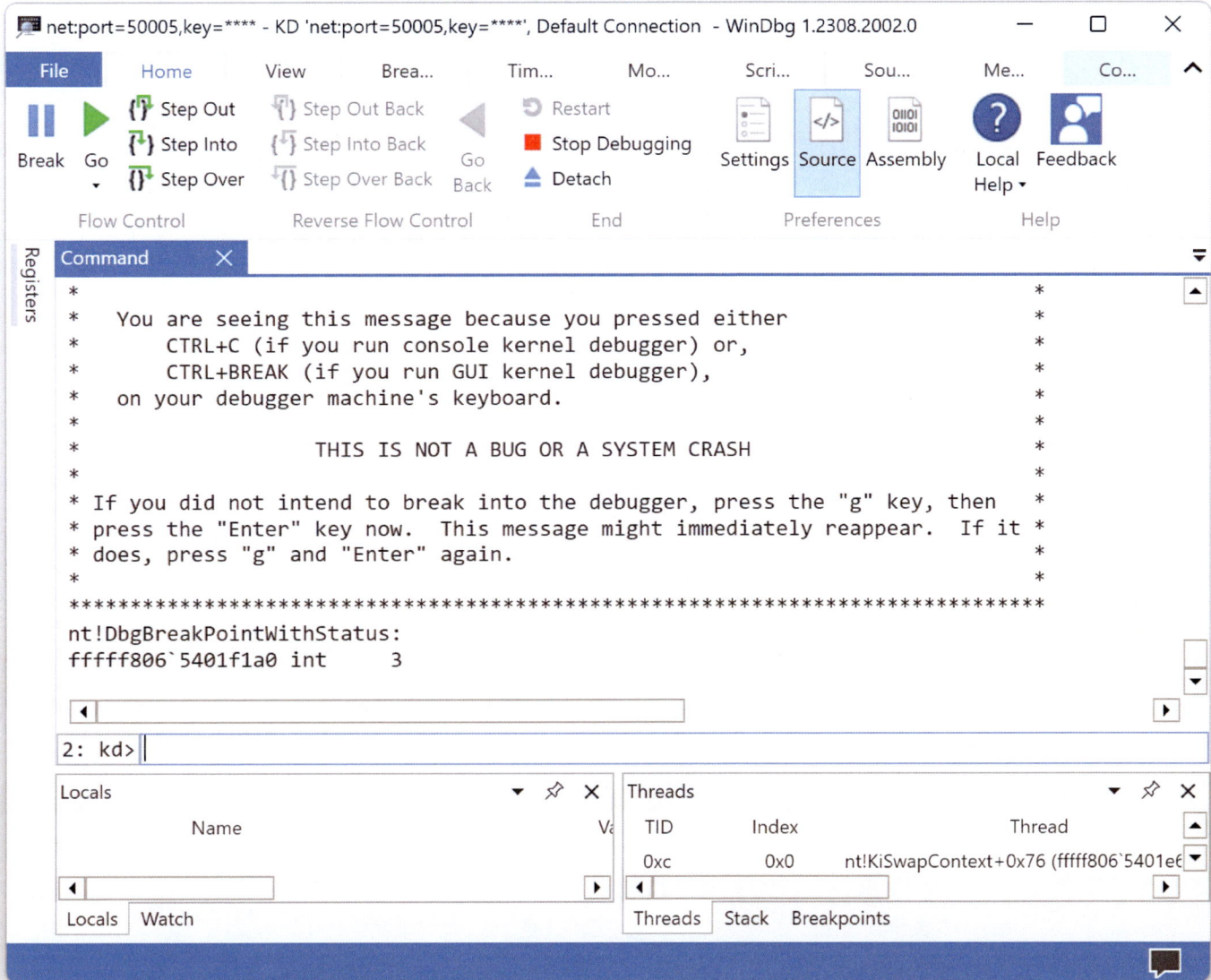

```
net:port=50005,key=**** - KD 'net:port=50005,key=****', Default Connection  - WinDbg 1.2308.2002.0

File    Home    View    Brea...    Tim...    Mo...    Scri...    Sou...    Me...    Co...

Break  Go   Step Out   Step Out Back   Go   Restart              Settings Source Assembly   Local  Feedback
             Step Into  Step Into Back  Back  Stop Debugging                                 Help
             Step Over  Step Over Back         Detach
       Flow Control      Reverse Flow Control         End              Preferences              Help
```

```
*                                                               *
*    You are seeing this message because you pressed either     *
*        CTRL+C (if you run console kernel debugger) or,        *
*        CTRL+BREAK (if you run GUI kernel debugger),           *
*    on your debugger machine's keyboard.                       *
*                                                               *
*                  THIS IS NOT A BUG OR A SYSTEM CRASH          *
*                                                               *
* If you did not intend to break into the debugger, press the "g" key, then *
* press the "Enter" key now.  This message might immediately reappear.  If it *
* does, press "g" and "Enter" again.                            *
*                                                               *
***************************************************************
nt!DbgBreakPointWithStatus:
fffff806`5401f1a0 int     3
```

```
2: kd>
```

Locals
Name	Va

Locals | Watch

Threads
TID	Index	Thread
0xc	0x0	nt!KiSwapContext+0x76 (fffff806`5401e6

Threads | Stack | Breakpoints

12.   We now check the stack trace of the current thread using the **k** command (the output may vary depending on when you broke into the system):

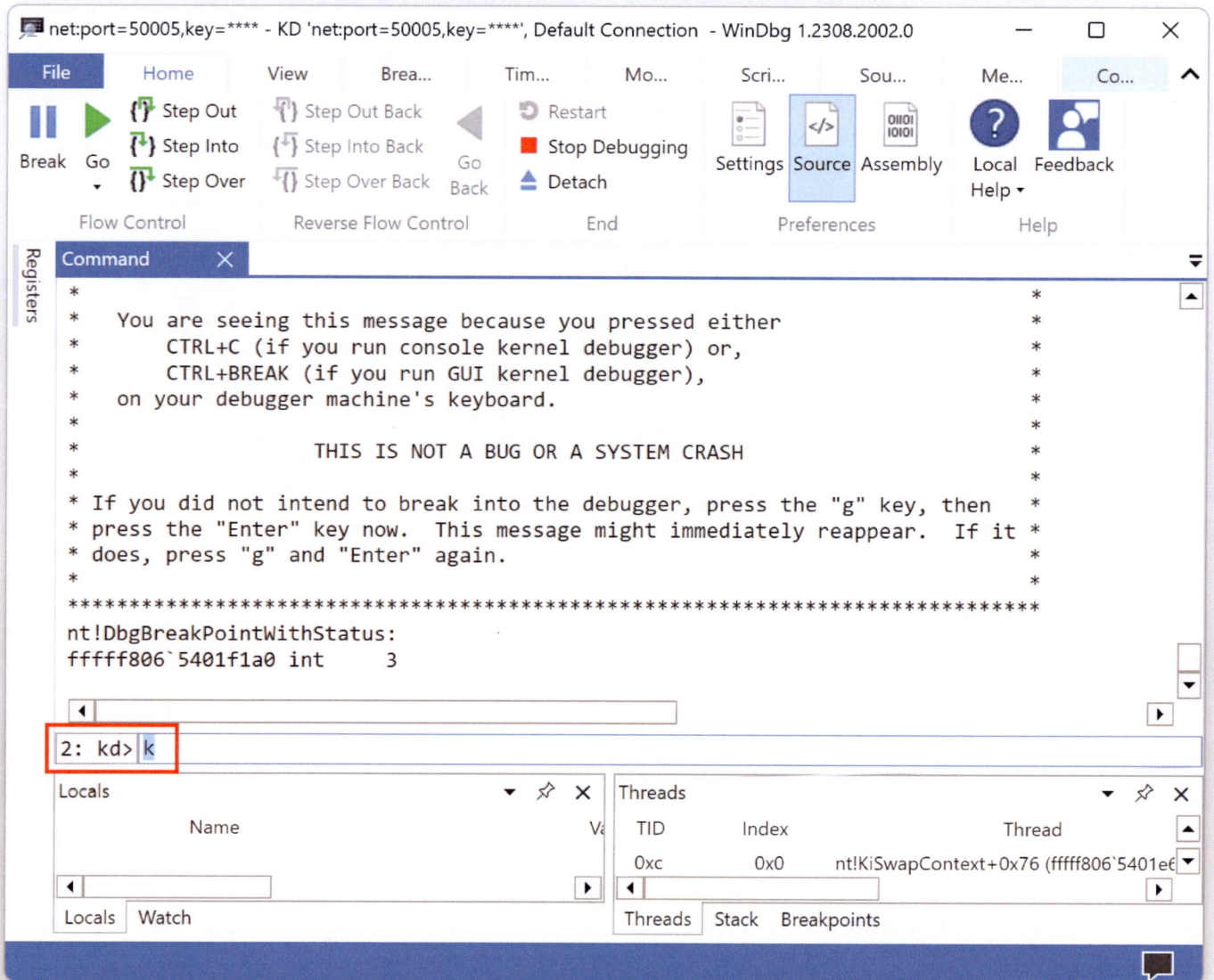

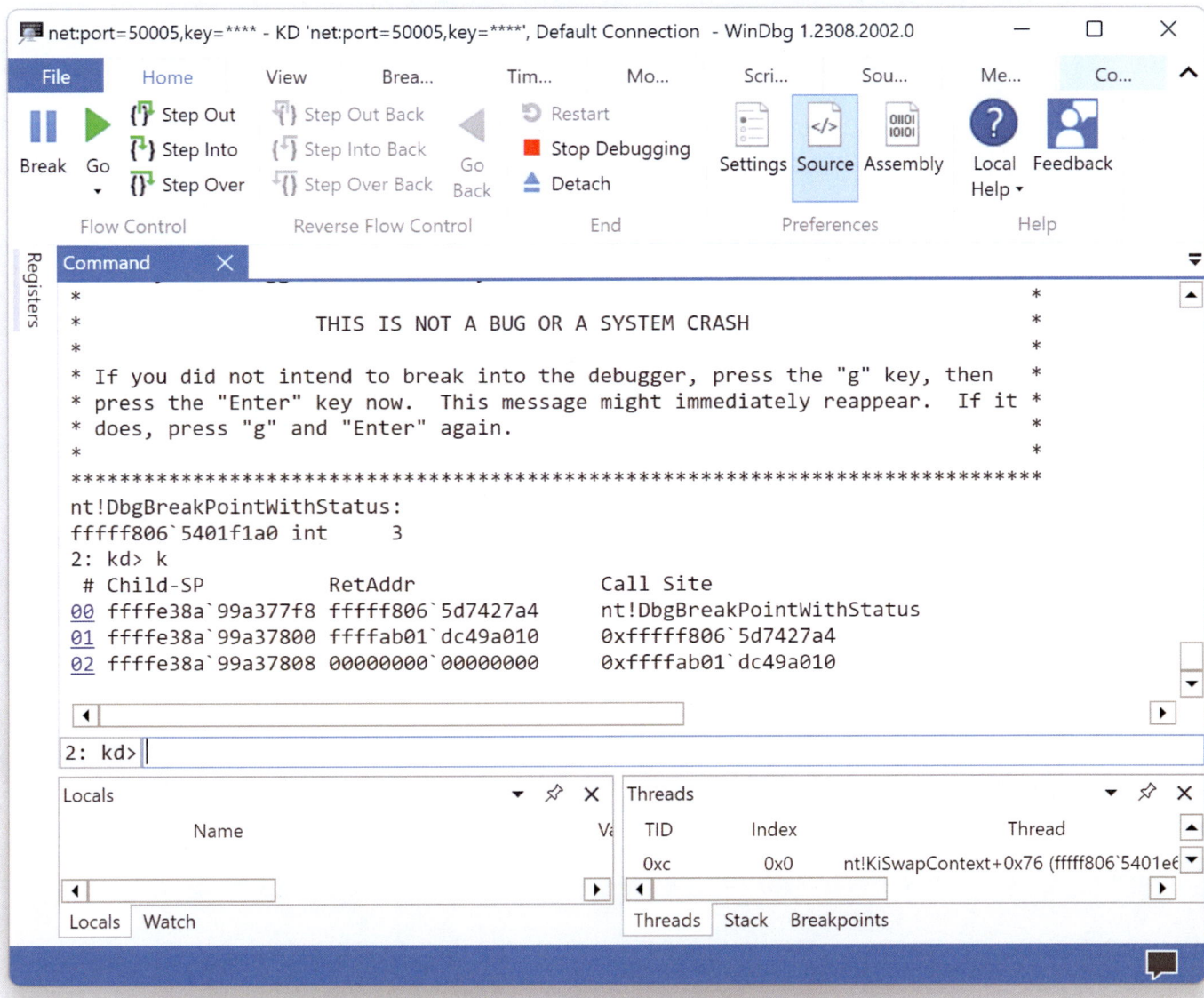

```
*                                                              *
*              THIS IS NOT A BUG OR A SYSTEM CRASH             *
*                                                              *
* If you did not intend to break into the debugger, press the "g" key, then *
* press the "Enter" key now.  This message might immediately reappear.  If it *
* does, press "g" and "Enter" again.                          *
*                                                              *
****************************************************************************
nt!DbgBreakPointWithStatus:
fffff806`5401f1a0 int       3
2: kd> k
 # Child-SP          RetAddr               Call Site
00 ffffe38a`99a377f8 fffff806`5d7427a4     nt!DbgBreakPointWithStatus
01 ffffe38a`99a37800 ffffab01`dc49a010     0xfffff806`5d7427a4
02 ffffe38a`99a37808 00000000`00000000     0xffffab01`dc49a010
```

Locals

Name	Va

Locals Watch

Threads

TID	Index	Thread
0xc	0x0	nt!KiSwapContext+0x76 (fffff806`5401e6

Threads Stack Breakpoints

13.   Here's the full command window content:

```
Microsoft (R) Windows Debugger Version 10.0.25921.1001 AMD64
Copyright (c) Microsoft Corporation. All rights reserved.

Using NET for debugging
Opened WinSock 2.0
Waiting to reconnect...
Connected to target 172.31.85.238 on port 50005 on local IP 172.31.80.1.
You can get the target MAC address by running .kdtargetmac command.
Connected to Windows 10 22000 x64 target at (Sat Feb  3 12:50:47.442 2024 (UTC + 0:00)), ptr64
TRUE
Kernel Debugger connection established.

************* Path validation summary **************
Response                        Time (ms)     Location
Deferred                                      srv*
Symbol search path is: srv*
Executable search path is:
Windows 10 Kernel Version 22000 MP (4 procs) Free x64
```

```
Product: WinNt, suite: TerminalServer SingleUserTS
Edition build lab: 22000.1.amd64fre.co_release.210604-1628
Kernel base = 0xfffff806`53c00000 PsLoadedModuleList = 0xfffff806`54829b90
Debug session time: Sat Feb  3 12:50:47.305 2024 (UTC + 0:00)
System Uptime: 0 days 0:05:13.041
Break instruction exception - code 80000003 (first chance)
*****************************************************************************
*                                                                           *
*    You are seeing this message because you pressed either                 *
*        CTRL+C (if you run console kernel debugger) or,                     *
*        CTRL+BREAK (if you run GUI kernel debugger),                        *
*    on your debugger machine's keyboard.                                    *
*                                                                           *
*                    THIS IS NOT A BUG OR A SYSTEM CRASH                     *
*                                                                           *
* If you did not intend to break into the debugger, press the "g" key, then  *
* press the "Enter" key now.  This message might immediately reappear.  If it *
* does, press "g" and "Enter" again.                                        *
*                                                                           *
*****************************************************************************
nt!DbgBreakPointWithStatus:
fffff806`5401f1a0 int     3
```

```
2: kd> k
 # Child-SP          RetAddr               Call Site
00 ffffe38a`99a377f8 fffff806`5d7427a4     nt!DbgBreakPointWithStatus
01 ffffe38a`99a37800 ffffab01`dc49a010     0xfffff806`5d7427a4
02 ffffe38a`99a37808 00000000`00000000     0xffffab01`dc49a010
```

14.   The stack trace doesn't have current symbols applied, so we load them using the **.reload** command:

```
2: kd> .reload
Connected to Windows 10 22000 x64 target at (Sat Feb  3 13:00:09.299 2024 (UTC + 0:00)), ptr64
TRUE
Loading Kernel Symbols
...............................................................
...............................................................
...................................
Loading User Symbols

Loading unloaded module list
..........
```

15.   Now the **k** command should produce the correct stack trace (the output may vary depending on when you broke into the system):

```
0: kd> k
 # Child-SP          RetAddr               Call Site
00 ffffe38a`99a377f8 fffff806`5d7427a4     nt!DbgBreakPointWithStatus
01 ffffe38a`99a37800 fffff806`53e7b284     kdnic!RxReceiveIndicateDpc+0x74
02 ffffe38a`99a37860 fffff806`53e79874     nt!KiProcessExpiredTimerList+0x204
03 ffffe38a`99a37990 fffff806`5401aa8e     nt!KiRetireDpcList+0x714
04 ffffe38a`99a37c40 00000000`00000000     nt!KiIdleLoop+0x9e
```

16.   Type the **g** command, and you may continue using the Guest VM after connecting to it.

196

17.   Quit WinDbg. We recommend exiting WinDbg after each exercise to avoid possible confusion and glitches. Your Guest VM should continue working.

18.   [Optional] If you choose to use VMware Workstation, here are optional instructions for Windows 11 and VMware Workstation Pro (we used version 15).

19.   For your x64 guest Windows OS, set up a pipe as a serial port (you may need to add it) with the following parameters:

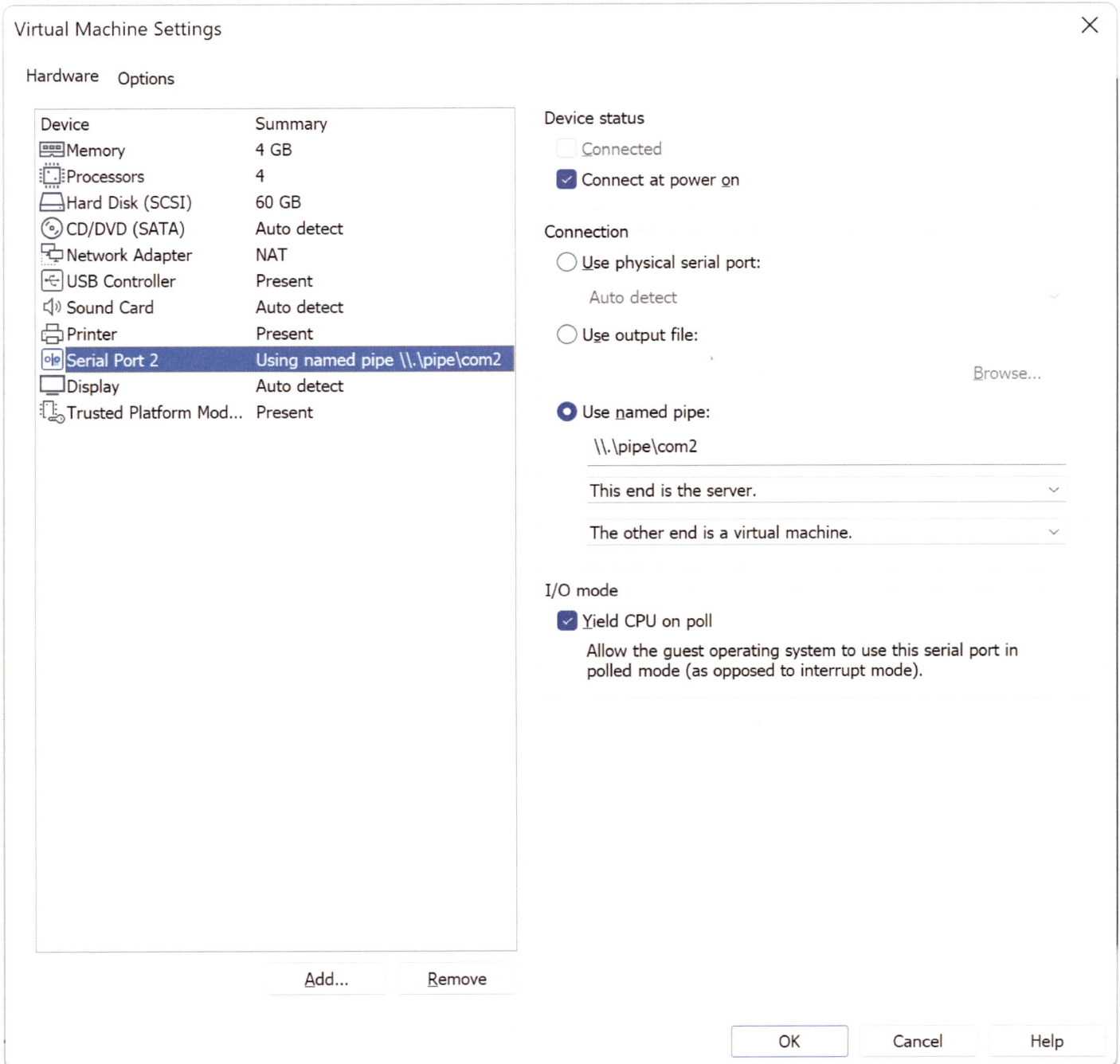

Virtual Machine Settings   ✕

Hardware   Options

Device	Summary
Memory	4 GB
Processors	4
Hard Disk (SCSI)	60 GB
CD/DVD (SATA)	Auto detect
Network Adapter	NAT
USB Controller	Present
Sound Card	Auto detect
Printer	Present
Serial Port 2	Using named pipe \\.\pipe\com2
Display	Auto detect
Trusted Platform Mod...	Present

Device status

☐ Connected
☑ Connect at power on

Connection

◯ Use physical serial port:
    Auto detect

◯ Use output file:
                                              Browse...

⦿ Use named pipe:
    \\.\pipe\com2

    This end is the server.   ⌄

    The other end is a virtual machine.   ⌄

I/O mode

☑ Yield CPU on poll
    Allow the guest operating system to use this serial port in polled mode (as opposed to interrupt mode).

Add...   Remove

OK   Cancel   Help

20.   When you power on your Guest VM, the device status should be shown as *Connected*:

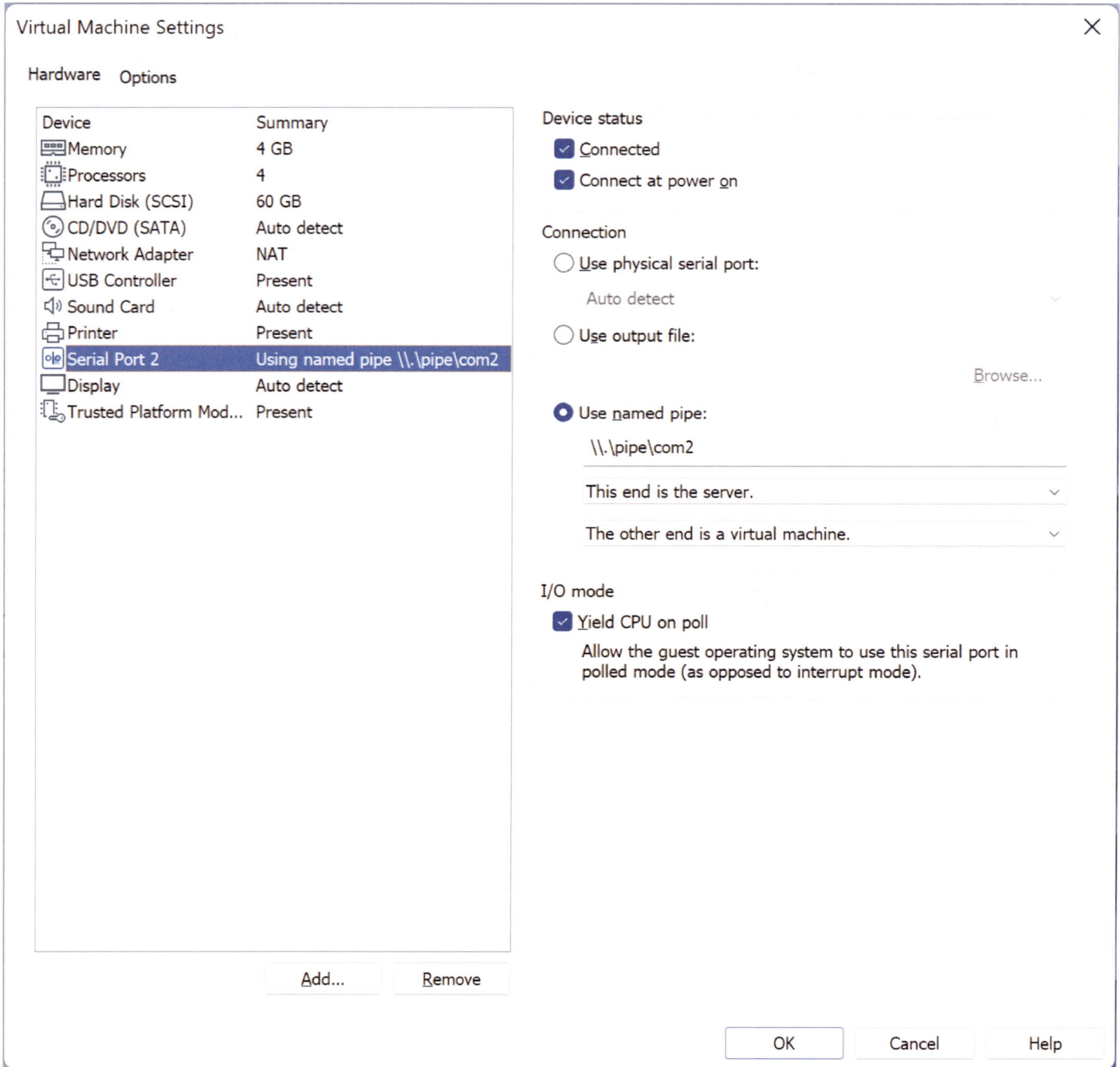

Virtual Machine Settings   ✕

Hardware   Options

Device	Summary
🖵 Memory	4 GB
⬚ Processors	4
🖴 Hard Disk (SCSI)	60 GB
⊙ CD/DVD (SATA)	Auto detect
🖧 Network Adapter	NAT
⊟ USB Controller	Present
🔊 Sound Card	Auto detect
🖶 Printer	Present
📟 Serial Port 2	Using named pipe \\.\pipe\com2
🖵 Display	Auto detect
🔐 Trusted Platform Mod...	Present

Device status
- ☑ Connected
- ☑ Connect at power on

Connection
- ○ Use physical serial port:
    Auto detect   ⌄
- ○ Use output file:
                                                         Browse...
- ◉ Use named pipe:
    \\.\pipe\com2
    This end is the server.   ⌄
    The other end is a virtual machine.   ⌄

I/O mode
- ☑ Yield CPU on poll
    Allow the guest operating system to use this serial port in
    polled mode (as opposed to interrupt mode).

Add...   Remove

OK   Cancel   Help

21.   Disable *Secure Boot* in the *Options* tab:

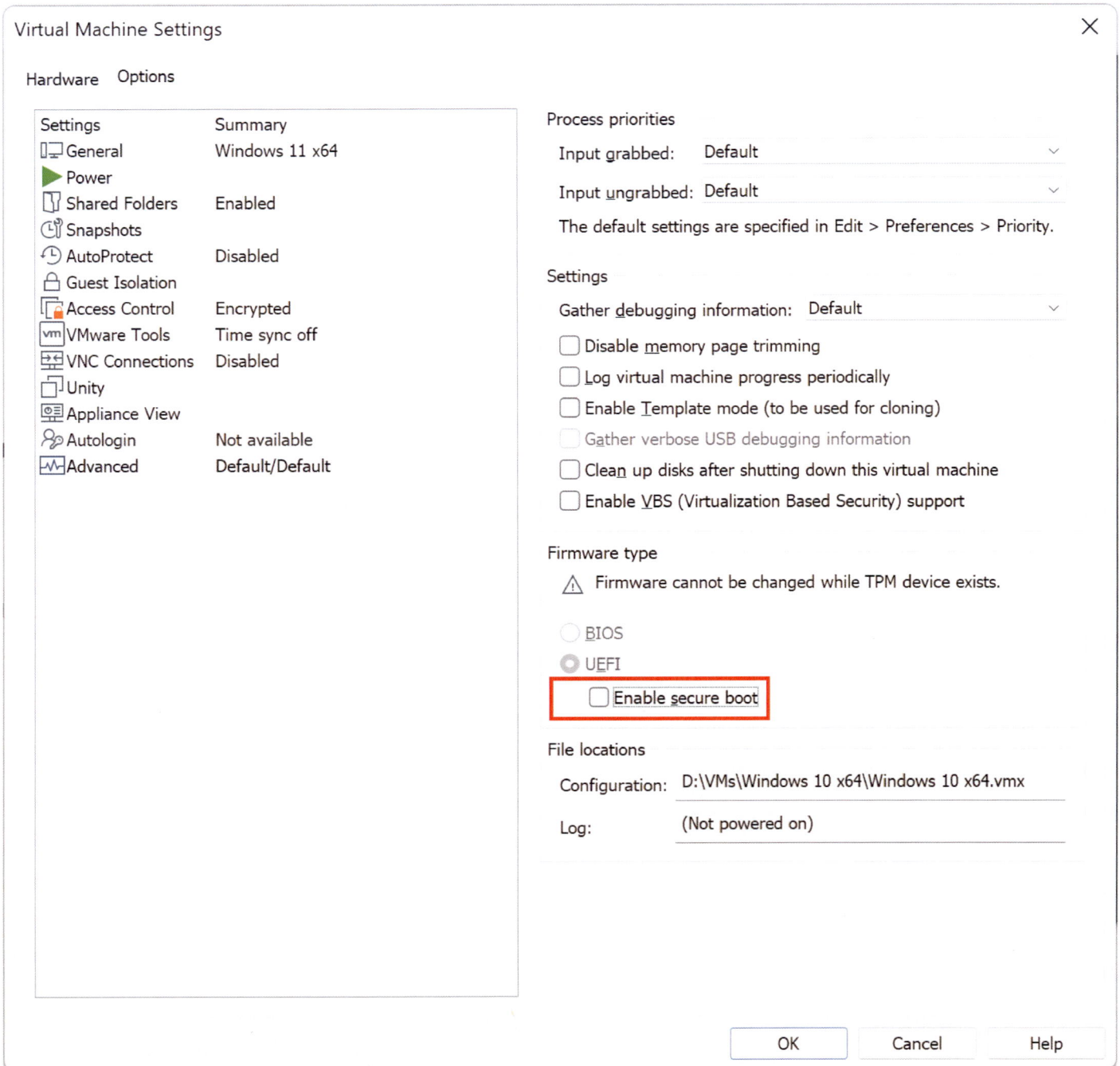

Virtual Machine Settings   ✕

Hardware   Options

Settings	Summary
🖥 General	Windows 11 x64
▶ Power	
🗋 Shared Folders	Enabled
🕒 Snapshots	
🕐 AutoProtect	Disabled
🔒 Guest Isolation	
🔒 Access Control	Encrypted
vm VMware Tools	Time sync off
🖧 VNC Connections	Disabled
🗔 Unity	
🖼 Appliance View	
👥 Autologin	Not available
〽 Advanced	Default/Default

Process priorities

Input grabbed: Default   ⌄

Input ungrabbed: Default   ⌄

The default settings are specified in Edit > Preferences > Priority.

Settings

Gather debugging information: Default   ⌄

☐ Disable memory page trimming

☐ Log virtual machine progress periodically

☐ Enable Template mode (to be used for cloning)

☐ Gather verbose USB debugging information

☐ Clean up disks after shutting down this virtual machine

☐ Enable VBS (Virtualization Based Security) support

Firmware type

⚠ Firmware cannot be changed while TPM device exists.

◯ BIOS

◉ UEFI

    ☐ Enable secure boot

File locations

Configuration: D:\VMs\Windows 10 x64\Windows 10 x64.vmx

Log: (Not powered on)

                                   OK   Cancel   Help

199

22.   In your running Guest VM, run the **msconfig** from the command prompt and set *Advanced options…* in the *Boot* tab:

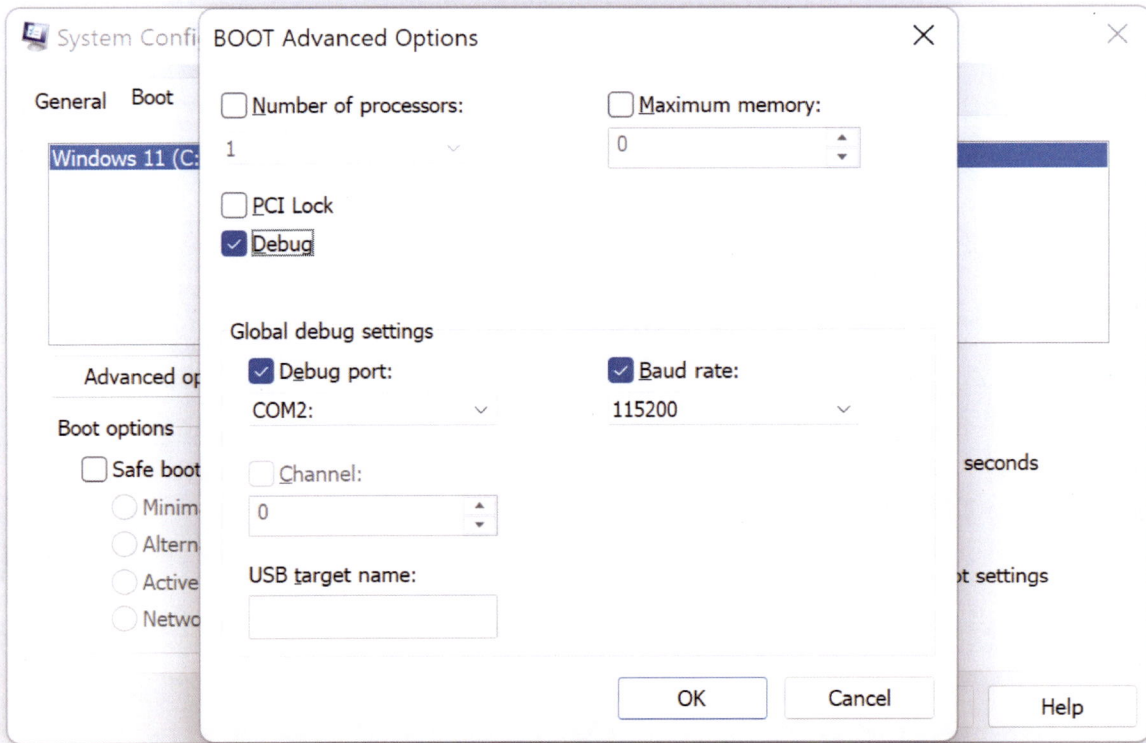

| System Confi | BOOT Advanced Options | ✕ | ✕ |

General   Boot

Windows 11 (C:

☐ Number of processors: ☐ Maximum memory:
1   0

☐ PCI Lock
☑ Debug

Advanced op

Boot options

Global debug settings
☑ Debug port: ☑ Baud rate:
COM2:   115200

☐ Safe boot   ☐ Channel: seconds
  ◯ Minim   0
  ◯ Altern
  ◯ Active   USB target name: t settings
  ◯ Netwo

                                 OK   Cancel   Help

23.   Reboot the Guest VM.

24.   Launch WinDbg from the Host computer and choose *File \ Attach to kernel*. Setup the pipe parameters in the COM tab:

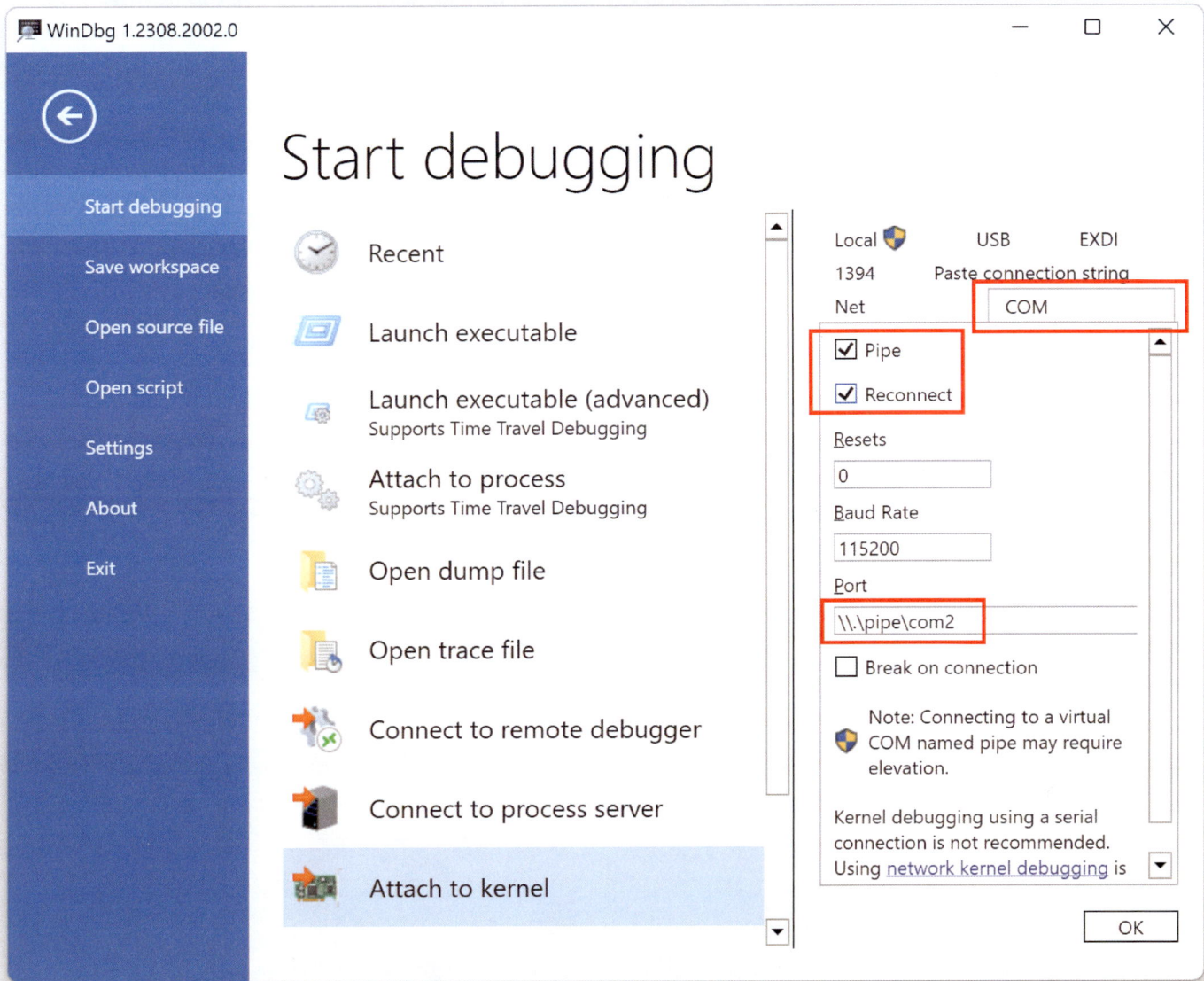

We should get the following output in the WinDbg command window:

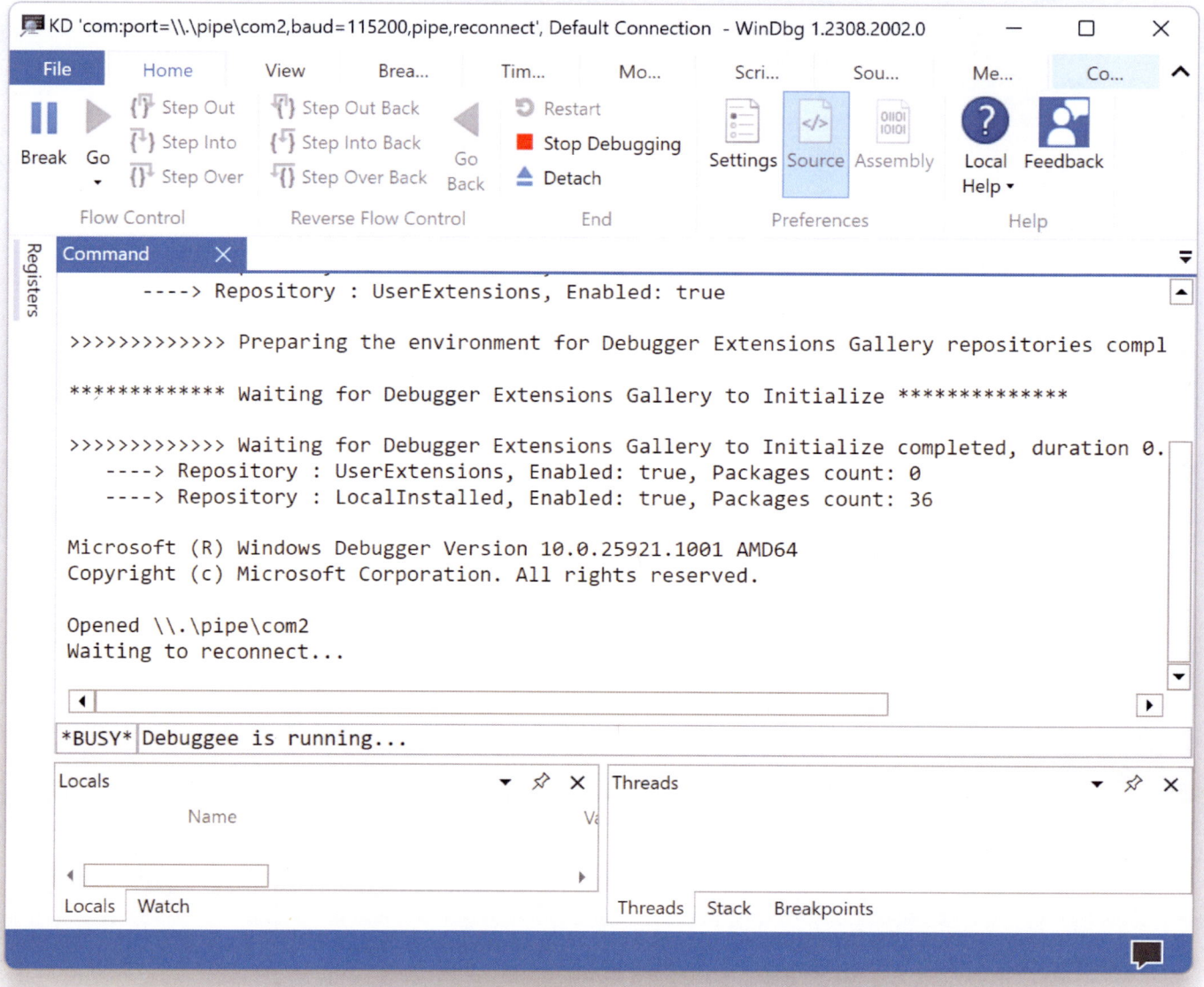

25.   Use the *Break* button and wait for a similar output:

```
Microsoft (R) Windows Debugger Version 10.0.25921.1001 AMD64
Copyright (c) Microsoft Corporation. All rights reserved.

Opened \\.\pipe\com2
Waiting to reconnect...
Connected to Windows 10 22000 x64 target at (Sat Feb  3 13:53:37.033 2024 (UTC + 0:00)), ptr64
TRUE
Kernel Debugger connection established.

************* Path validation summary **************
Response                      Time (ms)      Location
Deferred                                     srv*
Symbol search path is: srv*
Executable search path is:
Windows 10 Kernel Version 22000 MP (2 procs) Free x64
```

```
Product: WinNt, suite: TerminalServer SingleUserTS Personal
Edition build lab: 22000.1.amd64fre.co_release.210604-1628
Kernel base = 0xfffff805`54e00000 PsLoadedModuleList = 0xfffff805`55a29bc0
Debug session time: Wed Jul 26 20:56:07.201 2023 (UTC + 0:00)
System Uptime: 0 days 0:38:25.563
Break instruction exception - code 80000003 (first chance)
****************************************************************************
*                                                                        *
*    You are seeing this message because you pressed either              *
*        CTRL+C (if you run console kernel debugger) or,                  *
*        CTRL+BREAK (if you run GUI kernel debugger),                     *
*    on your debugger machine's keyboard.                                 *
*                                                                        *
*                   THIS IS NOT A BUG OR A SYSTEM CRASH                   *
*                                                                        *
* If you did not intend to break into the debugger, press the "g" key, then *
* press the "Enter" key now.  This message might immediately reappear.  If it *
* does, press "g" and "Enter" again.                                     *
*                                                                        *
****************************************************************************
nt!DbgBreakPointWithStatus:
fffff805`5521e880 int     3
```

26.   Reload symbols:

```
1: kd> .reload
Connected to Windows 10 22000 x64 target at (Sat Feb  3 13:55:42.169 2024 (UTC + 0:00)), ptr64
TRUE
Loading Kernel Symbols
...........

Press ctrl-c (cdb, kd, ntsd) or ctrl-break (windbg) to abort symbol loads that take too long.
Run !sym noisy before .reload to track down problems loading symbols.

.................................................
...................................................
...................................................
.
Loading User Symbols

Loading unloaded module list
................
```

27.   Type the **k** command to verify the correctness of the current CPU thread stack trace (the output may vary
depending on when you broke into the system):

```
1: kd> k
 # Child-SP          RetAddr             Call Site
00 ffffe281`11efada8 fffff805`5525ca8a   nt!DbgBreakPointWithStatus
01 ffffe281`11efadb0 fffff805`550db578   nt!KdCheckForDebugBreak+0x249942
02 ffffe281`11efade0 fffff805`550db211   nt!KeAccumulateTicks+0x188
03 ffffe281`11efae50 fffff805`550d93fa   nt!KiUpdateRunTime+0x61
04 ffffe281`11efaeb0 fffff805`550d91e6   nt!KeClockInterruptNotify+0x11a
05 ffffe281`11efaf40 fffff805`5508d720   nt!HalpTimerClockIpiRoutine+0x16
06 ffffe281`11efaf70 fffff805`55217e2a   nt!KiCallInterruptServiceRoutine+0xa0
07 ffffe281`11efafb0 fffff805`552183f7   nt!KiInterruptSubDispatchNoLockNoEtw+0xfa
08 ffff940f`85b937b0 fffff805`55196097   nt!KiInterruptDispatchNoLockNoEtw+0x37
```

```
09 ffff940f`85b93940  fffff805`55196199    nt!HvlGetReferenceTimeUsingTscPage+0x37
0a ffff940f`85b93970  fffff805`550d6938    nt!HalpHvCounterQueryCounter+0x19
0b ffff940f`85b939a0  fffff805`59a0b63b    nt!KeQueryPerformanceCounter+0x58
0c ffff940f`85b939e0  fffff805`5a681926    FLTMGR!FltSendMessage+0x41b
0d ffff940f`85b93b30  fffff805`5a681bf3    WdFilter!MpAsyncpSendMessage+0x5a
0e ffff940f`85b93b80  fffff805`550478f5    WdFilter!MpAsyncpWorkerThread+0x273
0f ffff940f`85b93bf0  fffff805`5521a2d4    nt!PspSystemThreadStartup+0x55
10 ffff940f`85b93c40  00000000`00000000    nt!KiStartSystemThread+0x34
```

28.   Type the **g** command, and you may continue using Guest VM.

29.   Quit WinDbg. We recommend exiting WinDbg after each exercise to avoid possible confusion and glitches. Your Guest OS should continue working.

Space Review (x86)

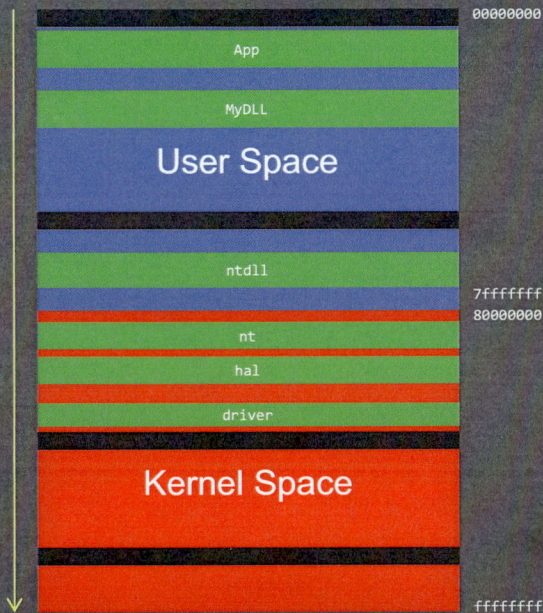

```
0: kd> lmk
start     end       module name
80200000 8020a000  BATTC
8020a000 8020c900  compbatt
8020d000 80215000  msisadrv
80215000 8021e000  WMILIB
8021e000 8022b000  WDFLDR
8022b000 80266000  CLFS
80266000 8026e000  BOOTVID
[...]
81800000 81ba1000  nt
81ba1000 81bd5000  hal
[...]
87eb3000 87ed6000  ndiswan
87ed6000 87ee1000  ndistapi
87ee1000 87ef8000  rasl2tp
87ef8000 87f03000  TDI
[...]
937b4000 93800000  srv
9446d000 94480000  dump_LSI_SCSI
96ca1000 96cc9000  fastfat
```

Similar to the user space slide shown previously, I just briefly repeat that when the operating system is booted, its executable file is loaded into memory together with additional modules such as **hal.** This OS executable file can be found as **nt** module. During the driver loading stage, they are loaded dynamically like DLLs, and if they reference other DLLs, they are loaded too. There may be gaps between modules and other space regions like black regions in this picture. Some memory is also allocated for additional working regions needed for system execution. Kernel space usually has a 2 GB range (but can be 1 GB for /3GB boot option), and we see addresses where modules are loaded using the **lm** or **lmk** command.

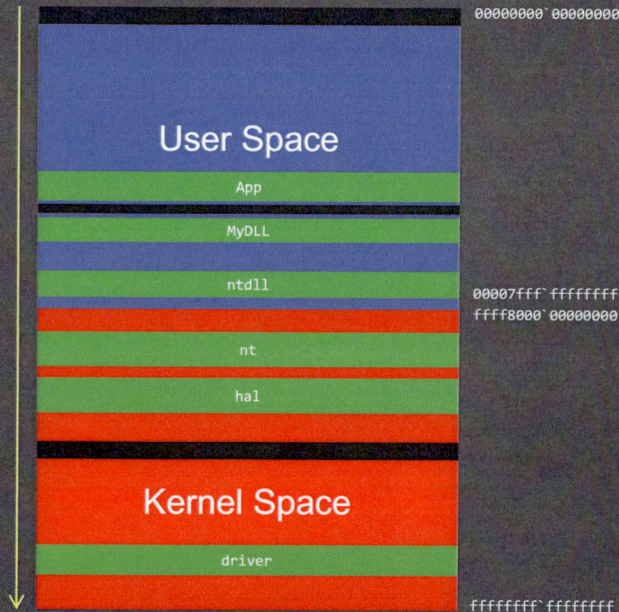

Here, we provide a picture of process space in 64-bit Windows. You see, kernel space is no longer restricted to 2 or 1 GB.

Space Review

```
0: kd> !process <address> 3f

0: kd> .process /r /p <address>

0: kd> !thread <address> 3f

0: kd> .thread /r /p <address>

0: kd> .thread /w <address>
```

Complete stack traces (x64 + x86)

© 2024 Software Diagnostics Services

When we do kernel debugging, we have access to physical space where there are several user spaces but only one kernel space. When navigating between processes, we need to make sure that we change to the correct user space and reload symbols. Also, for x64 systems, we may have running 32-bit processes, and if we use a command to list that process thread stack traces, we won't find 32-bit thread stacks in the output. In this presentation, I provided the link to a small WinDbg script that dumps both types of stack traces (also available in the Appendix).

Complete stack traces (x64 + x86)

https://www.dumpanalysis.org/blog/index.php/2010/02/09/complete-stack-traces-from-x64-system/

Context Switch

We always see the current process space

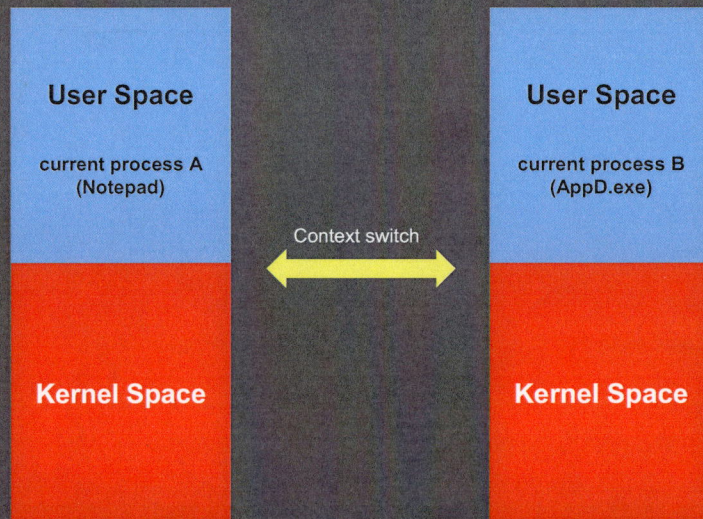

This diagram is another illustration of the current process context.

Common Commands

- **.logopen \<file\>**

  Opens a log file to save all subsequent output

- **View commands**

  Dump everything or selected processes and threads (context changes automatically)

- **Switch commands**

  Switch to a specific process or thread

View Commands

- **!process 0 0**
  Lists all processes

- **!process <address> 3f**
  Lists process information including CPU times, environment, modules and its thread stack traces

- **!thread <address> 1f**
  Shows thread information and stack trace

Switch Commands

⊙ **.process /r /p <address>**

Switches to a specified process. Its context becomes current. Reloads symbol files for user space.
Now we can use commands like !cs

```
0: kd> .process /r /p fffffa80044d8b30
Implicit process is now fffffa80`044d8b30
Loading User Symbols
...............................
```

⊙ **.thread <address>**

Switches to a specified thread. Assumes the current process context.

Now we can use commands like k*

⊙ **.thread /r /p <address>**

The same as the previous command but makes the thread process context current and reloads
symbol files for user space:

```
0: kd> .thread /r /p fffffa80051b7060
Implicit thread is now fffffa80`051b7060
Implicit process is now fffffa80`044d8b30
Loading User Symbols
...............................
```

Exercise KD6

- **Goal:** Learn how to use kernel level debugging to catch corruption caused by a driver or other process

- **Elementary Diagnostics Patterns:** Hang; Counter Value

- **Memory Analysis Patterns:** Abnormal Value (*from trace analysis patterns*); Spiking Thread

- **Debugging Implementation Patterns:** Code Breakpoint; Data Breakpoint; Code Trace

- \AWD4\Exercise-KD6.pdf

Goal: Learn how to use kernel level debugging to catch corruption caused by a driver or other process.

Elementary Diagnostics Patterns: Hang; Counter Value.

Memory Analysis Patterns: Abnormal Value (*from trace analysis patterns*); Spiking Thread.

Debugging Implementation Patterns: Code Breakpoint; Data Breakpoint; Code Trace.

1.   We use the same processes from Exercise UD6. Power your Guest OS VM and copy \AWD4\AppD6 and \AWD4\DriverEmulator folders to your VM to the same location (C:\AWD4\).

2.   Run WinDbg on your host and set up a kernel debugging connection as recommended in Exercise KD0. We get this output in WinDbg:

```
Microsoft (R) Windows Debugger Version 10.0.25921.1001 AMD64
Copyright (c) Microsoft Corporation. All rights reserved.

Using NET for debugging
Opened WinSock 2.0
Waiting to reconnect...
Connected to target 172.20.109.118 on port 50005 on local IP 172.20.96.1.
You can get the target MAC address by running .kdtargetmac command.
```

3.   Launch \AWD4\DriverEmulator\x64\Release\DriverEmulator.exe and \AWD4\AppD6\x64\Release\AppD6.exe executables in Guest VM.

4.   Break in via the *Break* button. We should get this output:

```
Connected to Windows 10 22000 x64 target at (Wed Feb  7 13:07:33.913 2024 (UTC + 0:00)), ptr64
TRUE
Kernel Debugger connection established.

************ Path validation summary **************
Response                      Time (ms)     Location
Deferred                                    srv*
Symbol search path is: srv*
Executable search path is:
Windows 10 Kernel Version 22000 MP (4 procs) Free x64
Product: WinNt, suite: TerminalServer SingleUserTS
Edition build lab: 22000.1.amd64fre.co_release.210604-1628
Kernel base = 0xfffff807`08200000 PsLoadedModuleList = 0xfffff807`08e297b0
Debug session time: Wed Feb  7 13:07:33.660 2024 (UTC + 0:00)
System Uptime: 0 days 0:05:48.666
Break instruction exception - code 80000003 (first chance)
*******************************************************************************
*                                                                           *
*    You are seeing this message because you pressed either                 *
*        CTRL+C (if you run console kernel debugger) or,                     *
*        CTRL+BREAK (if you run GUI kernel debugger),                        *
*    on your debugger machine's keyboard.                                    *
*                                                                           *
```

```
*                   THIS IS NOT A BUG OR A SYSTEM CRASH                    *
*                                                                          *
* If you did not intend to break into the debugger, press the "g" key, then *
* press the "Enter" key now.  This message might immediately reappear.  If it *
* does, press "g" and "Enter" again.                                       *
*                                                                          *
****************************************************************************
nt!DbgBreakPointWithStatus:
fffff807`086279f0 int     3
```

5.   Open a log file and reload symbols:

```
0: kd> .logopen c:\AWD4\KD6.log
Opened log file 'c:\AWD4\KD6.log'
```

```
0: kd> .reload
Connected to Windows 10 22000 x64 target at (Wed Feb  7 13:10:42.993 2024 (UTC + 0:00)), ptr64
TRUE
Loading Kernel Symbols
...........................................................
...........................................................
.........................................
Loading User Symbols

Loading unloaded module list
..........
```

6.   We now inspect processes on the Guest VM using the **!process** command:

```
0: kd> !process 0 0
**** NT ACTIVE PROCESS DUMP ****
PROCESS ffffa68795ab4040
    SessionId: none  Cid: 0004    Peb: 00000000  ParentCid: 0000
    DirBase: 007d5002  ObjectTable: ffff9480e9024e80  HandleCount: 3137.
    Image: System

PROCESS ffffa68795c02080
    SessionId: none  Cid: 0048    Peb: 00000000  ParentCid: 0004
    DirBase: f3cd2002  ObjectTable: ffff9480e902b340  HandleCount:    0.
    Image: Secure System

PROCESS ffffa68795b2d080
    SessionId: none  Cid: 007c    Peb: 00000000  ParentCid: 0004
    DirBase: 03168002  ObjectTable: ffff9480e906cb80  HandleCount:    0.
    Image: Registry

PROCESS ffffa68796a02080
    SessionId: none  Cid: 01d4    Peb: d035f09000  ParentCid: 0004
    DirBase: 0593f002  ObjectTable: ffff9480e954c500  HandleCount:   60.
    Image: smss.exe

PROCESS ffffa687999c1140
    SessionId: 0 Cid: 0258    Peb: 8242a9e000  ParentCid: 0250
    DirBase: 31129002  ObjectTable: ffff9480ec8ef380  HandleCount:  489.
    Image: csrss.exe

PROCESS ffffa68799cf60c0
    SessionId: 0 Cid: 02a0    Peb: 7e09968000  ParentCid: 0250
    DirBase: 345c6002  ObjectTable: ffff9480ec8f0b00  HandleCount:  159.
    Image: wininit.exe

PROCESS ffffa68799aa7140
    SessionId: 1 Cid: 02b4    Peb: 878d794000  ParentCid: 0298
    DirBase: 3c2d0002  ObjectTable: ffff9480ec8f07c0  HandleCount:  287.
```

```
   Image: csrss.exe

PROCESS ffffa68799aed0c0
    SessionId: 1  Cid: 0308    Peb: e864ab2000  ParentCid: 0298
    DirBase: 2af4c002  ObjectTable: ffff9480ec8ef6c0  HandleCount: 275.
    Image: winlogon.exe

PROCESS ffffa68799af71c0
    SessionId: 0  Cid: 0330    Peb: 1e1e3d9000  ParentCid: 02a0
    DirBase: 2aee8002  ObjectTable: ffff9480ec8ef9c0  HandleCount: 686.
    Image: services.exe

PROCESS ffffa68799aaa0c0
    SessionId: 0  Cid: 034c    Peb: 4d42b17000  ParentCid: 02a0
    DirBase: 32bd4002  ObjectTable: ffff9480ec9a6380  HandleCount:  54.
    Image: LsaIso.exe

PROCESS ffffa68799a880c0
    SessionId: 0  Cid: 0354    Peb: ac32753000  ParentCid: 02a0
    DirBase: 2c0ce002  ObjectTable: ffff9480ec9a6080  HandleCount: 1183.
    Image: lsass.exe

PROCESS ffffa68799b81080
    SessionId: 0  Cid: 03c4    Peb: d5d8be0000  ParentCid: 0330
    DirBase: 3c489002  ObjectTable: ffff9480ec9a7640  HandleCount: 1450.
    Image: svchost.exe

PROCESS ffffa68799bb20c0
    SessionId: 1  Cid: 03e0    Peb: 7244dc000  ParentCid: 0308
    DirBase: 3347d002  ObjectTable: ffff9480ec9a77c0  HandleCount:  37.
    Image: fontdrvhost.exe

PROCESS ffffa68799ba10c0
    SessionId: 0  Cid: 03e8    Peb: bbbb0fa000  ParentCid: 02a0
    DirBase: 33460002  ObjectTable: ffff9480ec9a7e00  HandleCount:  37.
    Image: fontdrvhost.exe

PROCESS ffffa68799bc1080
    SessionId: 0  Cid: 02b8    Peb: e2edb99000  ParentCid: 0330
    DirBase: 382d0002  ObjectTable: ffff9480ecac4080  HandleCount: 1131.
    Image: svchost.exe

PROCESS ffffa6879aa31080
    SessionId: 0  Cid: 0368    Peb: c8ab7dd000  ParentCid: 0330
    DirBase: 30d32002  ObjectTable: ffff9480ecac4840  HandleCount: 399.
    Image: svchost.exe

PROCESS ffffa6879ab17100
    SessionId: 1  Cid: 0450    Peb: e973828000  ParentCid: 0308
    DirBase: e6324002  ObjectTable: ffff9480ecc0be00  HandleCount: 1063.
    Image: dwm.exe

PROCESS ffffa6879ab63080
    SessionId: 0  Cid: 0494    Peb: 6b637a1000  ParentCid: 0330
    DirBase: 3c049002  ObjectTable: ffff9480ecbfe7c0  HandleCount: 184.
    Image: svchost.exe

PROCESS ffffa6879ab6b080
    SessionId: 0  Cid: 04a4    Peb: 19075c8000  ParentCid: 0330
    DirBase: 3c1f5002  ObjectTable: ffff9480eccee080  HandleCount: 790.
    Image: svchost.exe

PROCESS ffffa6879aba5080
    SessionId: 0  Cid: 04fc    Peb: e999a87000  ParentCid: 0330
    DirBase: 3a485002  ObjectTable: ffff9480eccef340  HandleCount: 123.
    Image: svchost.exe

PROCESS ffffa6879abad0c0
    SessionId: 0  Cid: 0504    Peb: d5d8947000  ParentCid: 0330
    DirBase: 3a464002  ObjectTable: ffff9480eccef180  HandleCount: 174.
    Image: svchost.exe

PROCESS ffffa6879abca080
    SessionId: 0  Cid: 0548    Peb: 1727746000  ParentCid: 0330
```

```
        DirBase: 3eec0002  ObjectTable: ffff9480eccee200  HandleCount: 139.
        Image: svchost.exe

    PROCESS ffffa6879abd3080
        SessionId: 0  Cid: 0570    Peb: c3d02ce000  ParentCid: 0330
        DirBase: 3f0d9002  ObjectTable: ffff9480eccee500  HandleCount: 399.
        Image: svchost.exe

    PROCESS ffffa6879abe9080
        SessionId: 0  Cid: 0588    Peb: 26c807d000  ParentCid: 0330
        DirBase: 3f089002  ObjectTable: ffff9480eccee6c0  HandleCount: 276.
        Image: svchost.exe

    PROCESS ffffa6879abee080
        SessionId: 0  Cid: 0590    Peb: d41bfbb000  ParentCid: 0330
        DirBase: 3f1c7002  ObjectTable: ffff9480eccee840  HandleCount: 214.
        Image: svchost.exe

    PROCESS ffffa6879ac74080
        SessionId: 0  Cid: 05e4    Peb: a588cb8000  ParentCid: 0330
        DirBase: 379cc002  ObjectTable: ffff9480ecde67c0  HandleCount: 795.
        Image: svchost.exe

    PROCESS ffffa6879ac87080
        SessionId: 0  Cid: 05f4    Peb: e94f3c000  ParentCid: 0330
        DirBase: 37b48002  ObjectTable: ffff9480ecde6e00  HandleCount: 190.
        Image: svchost.exe

    PROCESS ffffa6879acca080
        SessionId: 0  Cid: 064c    Peb: b333930000  ParentCid: 0330
        DirBase: 3b109002  ObjectTable: ffff9480ecde5200  HandleCount: 271.
        Image: svchost.exe

    PROCESS ffffa6879acd4080
        SessionId: 0  Cid: 066c    Peb: eb10a96000  ParentCid: 0330
        DirBase: 39206002  ObjectTable: ffff9480ecde5380  HandleCount: 131.
        Image: svchost.exe

    PROCESS ffffa6879ad29080
        SessionId: 0  Cid: 06a8    Peb: 346132000  ParentCid: 0330
        DirBase: 0fa77002  ObjectTable: ffff9480ecde5840  HandleCount: 237.
        Image: svchost.exe

    PROCESS ffffa6879ad5e080
        SessionId: 0  Cid: 070c    Peb: 5ccc607000  ParentCid: 0330
        DirBase: 39ab4002  ObjectTable: ffff9480ecde59c0  HandleCount: 193.
        Image: svchost.exe

    PROCESS ffffa6879ad570c0
        SessionId: 0  Cid: 0788    Peb: 2574fca000  ParentCid: 0330
        DirBase: c2a72002  ObjectTable: ffff9480ecde6980  HandleCount: 114.
        Image: svchost.exe

    PROCESS ffffa6879ada30c0
        SessionId: 0  Cid: 07a4    Peb: d237c81000  ParentCid: 0330
        DirBase: c2d66002  ObjectTable: ffff9480ecde6b00  HandleCount: 184.
        Image: svchost.exe

    PROCESS ffffa6879ada7080
        SessionId: 0  Cid: 07ac    Peb: a07a066000  ParentCid: 0330
        DirBase: c2ccf002  ObjectTable: ffff9480ecde56c0  HandleCount: 144.
        Image: svchost.exe

    PROCESS ffffa6879adaa080
        SessionId: 0  Cid: 07b4    Peb: 1a0046000  ParentCid: 0330
        DirBase: c2d3d002  ObjectTable: ffff9480ecde5b40  HandleCount: 272.
        Image: svchost.exe

    PROCESS ffffa68795bb5080
        SessionId: 0  Cid: 07c0    Peb: 5fb12ef000  ParentCid: 0330
        DirBase: 3d08b002  ObjectTable: ffff9480ecde5d00  HandleCount: 128.
        Image: svchost.exe

    PROCESS ffffa68795ba2080
```

```
    SessionId: 0  Cid: 07d4    Peb: 6ddaeb6000  ParentCid: 0330
    DirBase: 3c447002  ObjectTable: ffff9480ecde6340  HandleCount: 237.
    Image: svchost.exe

PROCESS ffffa68795b64080
    SessionId: 0  Cid: 05d8    Peb: 700af23000  ParentCid: 0330
    DirBase: c321e002  ObjectTable: ffff9480ec8ef200  HandleCount: 114.
    Image: svchost.exe

PROCESS ffffa68795b53080
    SessionId: 0  Cid: 06d4    Peb: 9d7a51c000  ParentCid: 0330
    DirBase: c0b37002  ObjectTable: ffff9480ecde6640  HandleCount: 140.
    Image: svchost.exe

PROCESS ffffa68795b4b080
    SessionId: 0  Cid: 0438    Peb: 181e8e6000  ParentCid: 0330
    DirBase: 3b5e7002  ObjectTable: ffff9480eccef4c0  HandleCount: 121.
    Image: svchost.exe

PROCESS ffffa6879ae890c0
    SessionId: 0  Cid: 08ec    Peb: 2b1ce0a000  ParentCid: 0330
    DirBase: ca9d2002  ObjectTable: ffff9480ed0b8480  HandleCount: 167.
    Image: VSSVC.exe

PROCESS ffffa6879adb1080
    SessionId: 0  Cid: 08f4    Peb: a0a3471000  ParentCid: 0330
    DirBase: 3e60d002  ObjectTable: ffff9480ed0b6380  HandleCount: 218.
    Image: svchost.exe

PROCESS ffffa6879ae70080
    SessionId: 0  Cid: 0940    Peb: 665a6e0000  ParentCid: 0330
    DirBase: c0373002  ObjectTable: ffff9480ed0b7800  HandleCount: 385.
    Image: svchost.exe

PROCESS ffffa6879ae96080
    SessionId: 0  Cid: 0988    Peb: 52ce9f4000  ParentCid: 0330
    DirBase: c2839002  ObjectTable: ffff9480ed0b8c40  HandleCount: 236.
    Image: svchost.exe

PROCESS ffffa6879aec1080
    SessionId: 0  Cid: 09ac    Peb: 41e84dd000  ParentCid: 0330
    DirBase: c29d6002  ObjectTable: ffff9480ed0b82c0  HandleCount: 200.
    Image: svchost.exe

PROCESS ffffa6879aed70c0
    SessionId: 0  Cid: 09c8    Peb: 9238d00000  ParentCid: 0330
    DirBase: c4ee0002  ObjectTable: ffff9480ed0b66c0  HandleCount: 180.
    Image: svchost.exe

PROCESS ffffa6879aed8080
    SessionId: 0  Cid: 09d0    Peb: 7232560000  ParentCid: 0330
    DirBase: 3f244002  ObjectTable: ffff9480ed0b6080  HandleCount: 236.
    Image: svchost.exe

PROCESS ffffa6879af53040
    SessionId: none  Cid: 0a78    Peb: 00000000  ParentCid: 0004
    DirBase: c0d6b002  ObjectTable: ffff9480ed0b7e40  HandleCount:   0.
    Image: MemCompression

PROCESS ffffa6879af59080
    SessionId: 0  Cid: 0a90    Peb: cbe7223000  ParentCid: 0330
    DirBase: 30498002  ObjectTable: ffff9480ed0b71c0  HandleCount: 287.
    Image: svchost.exe

PROCESS ffffa6879afad080
    SessionId: 0  Cid: 0ae4    Peb: 3eefdcd000  ParentCid: 0330
    DirBase: c9395002  ObjectTable: ffff9480ed0b7640  HandleCount: 191.
    Image: svchost.exe

PROCESS ffffa6879afb3080
    SessionId: 0  Cid: 0b10    Peb: 81fed38000  ParentCid: 0330
    DirBase: 04595002  ObjectTable: ffff9480ed0b6540  HandleCount: 182.
    Image: svchost.exe
```

```
PROCESS ffffa6879afef080
    SessionId: 0  Cid: 0b3c    Peb: f99defb000  ParentCid: 0330
    DirBase: c0080002  ObjectTable: ffff9480ed0b7340  HandleCount: 169.
    Image: svchost.exe

PROCESS ffffa6879aff2080
    SessionId: 0  Cid: 0b44    Peb: b5b3727000  ParentCid: 0330
    DirBase: c00a7002  ObjectTable: ffff9480ed0b7b00  HandleCount: 133.
    Image: svchost.exe

PROCESS ffffa6879b008080
    SessionId: 0  Cid: 0b5c    Peb: a3b8390000  ParentCid: 0330
    DirBase: c247b002  ObjectTable: ffff9480ed0b8dc0  HandleCount: 173.
    Image: svchost.exe

PROCESS ffffa6879b0240c0
    SessionId: 0  Cid: 0be0    Peb: ae7432b000  ParentCid: 0330
    DirBase: 2fe84002  ObjectTable: ffff9480ed0b6d00  HandleCount: 290.
    Image: svchost.exe

PROCESS ffffa6879b0af080
    SessionId: 0  Cid: 09e4    Peb: b51a1a1000  ParentCid: 0330
    DirBase: 3f9f2002  ObjectTable: ffff9480ed0b6b80  HandleCount: 427.
    Image: svchost.exe

PROCESS ffffa6879b16c080
    SessionId: 0  Cid: 0954    Peb: 583c92e000  ParentCid: 0330
    DirBase: c394e002  ObjectTable: ffff9480ed0b9740  HandleCount: 148.
    Image: svchost.exe

PROCESS ffffa6879b16b080
    SessionId: 0  Cid: 0ba0    Peb: ba866c2000  ParentCid: 0330
    DirBase: c163d002  ObjectTable: ffff9480ed0b9400  HandleCount: 386.
    Image: svchost.exe

PROCESS ffffa6879b17f080
    SessionId: 0  Cid: 0c08    Peb: 26deb9c000  ParentCid: 0330
    DirBase: c9360002  ObjectTable: ffff9480ed0b9580  HandleCount: 212.
    Image: svchost.exe

PROCESS ffffa6879b2020c0
    SessionId: 0  Cid: 0c7c    Peb: 00c72000  ParentCid: 0330
    DirBase: c1c9b002  ObjectTable: ffff9480ed6a5900  HandleCount: 620.
    Image: spoolsv.exe

PROCESS ffffa6879b49b0c0
    SessionId: 0  Cid: 0cf8    Peb: 28e5d15000  ParentCid: 0330
    DirBase: c471f002  ObjectTable: ffff9480ed6a3840  HandleCount: 140.
    Image: svchost.exe

PROCESS ffffa6879b5020c0
    SessionId: 0  Cid: 0d00    Peb: 3144e1000  ParentCid: 0330
    DirBase: cb281002  ObjectTable: ffff9480ed6a6100  HandleCount: 607.
    Image: svchost.exe

PROCESS ffffa6879b5350c0
    SessionId: 0  Cid: 0d0c    Peb: ba5429e000  ParentCid: 0330
    DirBase: cb2bc002  ObjectTable: ffff9480ed6a3200  HandleCount: 219.
    Image: svchost.exe

PROCESS ffffa6879b19f080
    SessionId: 0  Cid: 0d24    Peb: 4986f0e000  ParentCid: 0330
    DirBase: cb37f002  ObjectTable: ffff9480ed6a52c0  HandleCount: 351.
    Image: svchost.exe

PROCESS ffffa6879b3ec080
    SessionId: 0  Cid: 0d3c    Peb: 5204dd000  ParentCid: 0330
    DirBase: 00f67002  ObjectTable: ffff9480ed6a3540  HandleCount: 368.
    Image: svchost.exe

PROCESS ffffa6879b522080
    SessionId: 0  Cid: 0d64    Peb: ba096ff000  ParentCid: 0330
    DirBase: c73d3002  ObjectTable: ffff9480ed6a36c0  HandleCount: 436.
    Image: MpDefenderCoreService.exe
```

```
PROCESS ffffa6879b264080
    SessionId: 0  Cid: 0d84    Peb: d2a513f000  ParentCid: 0330
    DirBase: c7375002  ObjectTable: ffff9480ed6a4980  HandleCount: 145.
    Image: sqlwriter.exe

PROCESS ffffa6879b255080
    SessionId: 0  Cid: 0da0    Peb: 70d8438000  ParentCid: 0330
    DirBase: c13ba002  ObjectTable: ffff9480ed6a44c0  HandleCount: 305.
    Image: svchost.exe

PROCESS ffffa6879b2cc080
    SessionId: 0  Cid: 0db8    Peb: 34c0498000  ParentCid: 0330
    DirBase: c149c002  ObjectTable: ffff9480ed6a5140  HandleCount: 143.
    Image: svchost.exe

PROCESS ffffa6879b2dd080
    SessionId: 0  Cid: 0db4    Peb: f8c24a0000  ParentCid: 0330
    DirBase: c15f9002  ObjectTable: ffff9480ed6a4800  HandleCount: 211.
    Image: svchost.exe

PROCESS ffffa6879b3b9080
    SessionId: 0  Cid: 0dd0    Peb: 4162f40000  ParentCid: 0330
    DirBase: c1582002  ObjectTable: ffff9480ed6a41c0  HandleCount:  68.
    Image: wlms.exe

PROCESS ffffa6879b2ed080
    SessionId: 0  Cid: 0dd8    Peb: 4f1cc04000  ParentCid: 0330
    DirBase: c5aba002  ObjectTable: ffff9480ed6a5480  HandleCount: 881.
    Image: MsMpEng.exe

PROCESS ffffa6879b2ee080
    SessionId: 0  Cid: 0de0    Peb: c76b6b2000  ParentCid: 0330
    DirBase: 2a525002  ObjectTable: ffff9480ed6a5600  HandleCount: 150.
    Image: svchost.exe

PROCESS ffffa6879b3dd080
    SessionId: 0  Cid: 0dec    Peb: f3e5025000  ParentCid: 0330
    DirBase: 2db89002  ObjectTable: ffff9480ed6a3080  HandleCount: 368.
    Image: svchost.exe

PROCESS ffffa6879b1f2080
    SessionId: 0  Cid: 0f10    Peb: e92742000  ParentCid: 0330
    DirBase: cbaa4002  ObjectTable: ffff9480ed6a6280  HandleCount: 270.
    Image: sppsvc.exe

PROCESS ffffa6879b8e90c0
    SessionId: 0  Cid: 0fe0    Peb: bea3870000  ParentCid: 0d00
    DirBase: c8b55002  ObjectTable: ffff9480edbf39c0  HandleCount: 105.
    Image: AggregatorHost.exe

PROCESS ffffa6879b9cb080
    SessionId: 0  Cid: 03a0    Peb: deae41a000  ParentCid: 03c4
    DirBase: c9bd0002  ObjectTable: ffff9480edbf6100  HandleCount: 206.
    Image: dllhost.exe

PROCESS ffffa6879bbb3080
    SessionId: 0  Cid: 134c    Peb: 2078198000  ParentCid: 0330
    DirBase: 01a32002  ObjectTable: ffff9480ee81a080  HandleCount: 235.
    Image: svchost.exe

PROCESS ffffa6879c254080
    SessionId: 1  Cid: 091c    Peb: 4818ad5000  ParentCid: 06a8
    DirBase: 0916c002  ObjectTable: ffff9480ee9cd500  HandleCount: 578.
    Image: sihost.exe

PROCESS ffffa6879c317080
    SessionId: 1  Cid: 1304    Peb: d56064b000  ParentCid: 0330
    DirBase: 16213002  ObjectTable: ffff9480ee9cc6c0  HandleCount: 332.
    Image: svchost.exe

PROCESS ffffa6879c32f080
    SessionId: 1  Cid: 1188    Peb: e547bb1000  ParentCid: 0330
    DirBase: d4533002  ObjectTable: ffff9480ee9cd980  HandleCount: 399.
```

```
    Image: svchost.exe

PROCESS ffffa6879c4650c0
    SessionId: 1  Cid: 140c    Peb: 80a2aa5000  ParentCid: 0570
    DirBase: dd98b002  ObjectTable: 00000000  HandleCount:   0.
    Image: taskhostw.exe

PROCESS ffffa6879c461080
    SessionId: 1  Cid: 1440    Peb: 85086bf000  ParentCid: 0570
    DirBase: dbb65002  ObjectTable: ffff9480ee9cb740  HandleCount: 267.
    Image: taskhostw.exe

PROCESS ffffa6879c460080
    SessionId: 0  Cid: 1458    Peb: 935871f000  ParentCid: 0330
    DirBase: dda9b002  ObjectTable: ffff9480ee9cbc00  HandleCount: 239.
    Image: svchost.exe

PROCESS ffffa6879c2450c0
    SessionId: 0  Cid: 1560    Peb: e2027aa000  ParentCid: 0330
    DirBase: 3ee41002  ObjectTable: ffff9480eecf3680  HandleCount: 205.
    Image: svchost.exe

PROCESS ffffa6879c45e080
    SessionId: 0  Cid: 156c    Peb: f08a65a000  ParentCid: 0330
    DirBase: d938e002  ObjectTable: ffff9480eecf4dc0  HandleCount: 187.
    Image: svchost.exe

PROCESS ffffa6879c45d080
    SessionId: 1  Cid: 15c4    Peb: 4919f41000  ParentCid: 156c
    DirBase: ddeb7002  ObjectTable: ffff9480eecf3040  HandleCount: 447.
    Image: ctfmon.exe

PROCESS ffffa6879c45c080
    SessionId: 1  Cid: 15f8    Peb: 938c9c000  ParentCid: 0308
    DirBase: e49bc002  ObjectTable: 00000000  HandleCount:   0.
    Image: userinit.exe

PROCESS ffffa6879c45b080
    SessionId: 1  Cid: 1644    Peb: 00fbf000  ParentCid: 15f8
    DirBase: e0e54002  ObjectTable: ffff9480eecf3340  HandleCount: 3693.
    Image: explorer.exe

PROCESS ffffa6879c45a080
    SessionId: 0  Cid: 1650    Peb: cec9c19000  ParentCid: 0330
    DirBase: 51dec002  ObjectTable: ffff9480eecf2540  HandleCount: 312.
    Image: svchost.exe

PROCESS ffffa6879c458080
    SessionId: 0  Cid: 17a0    Peb: d4612ce000  ParentCid: 03c4
    DirBase: e6c65002  ObjectTable: ffff9480eecf3e40  HandleCount: 160.
    Image: SppExtComObj.Exe

PROCESS ffffa6879c463080
    SessionId: 0  Cid: 1510    Peb: 2cdf472000  ParentCid: 0330
    DirBase: d53d8002  ObjectTable: ffff9480eecf4940  HandleCount: 289.
    Image: svchost.exe

PROCESS ffffa6879c452080
    SessionId: 0  Cid: 16b0    Peb: f374859000  ParentCid: 0330
    DirBase: 3de50002  ObjectTable: ffff9480eecf2d00  HandleCount: 556.
    Image: svchost.exe

PROCESS ffffa6879c459080
    SessionId: 0  Cid: 04f0    Peb: 255bc38000  ParentCid: 0330
    DirBase: e2219002  ObjectTable: ffff9480eecf7980  HandleCount: 200.
    Image: svchost.exe

PROCESS ffffa6879c77d080
    SessionId: 0  Cid: 1874    Peb: f13a2ac000  ParentCid: 0330
    DirBase: e2ef4002  ObjectTable: ffff9480eecf55c0  HandleCount: 392.
    Image: svchost.exe

PROCESS ffffa6879c75d080
    SessionId: 0  Cid: 18dc    Peb: 4e9b14b000  ParentCid: 0330
```

```
      DirBase: ee024002  ObjectTable: ffff9480eecf5740  HandleCount: 233.
      Image: svchost.exe

PROCESS ffffa6879c75c080
    SessionId: 1  Cid: 1948    Peb: 549440e000  ParentCid: 0330
    DirBase: 32598002  ObjectTable: ffff9480eecf5c00  HandleCount: 274.
    Image: svchost.exe

PROCESS ffffa6879c759080
    SessionId: 0  Cid: 19d0    Peb: 5c6c3fd000  ParentCid: 0330
    DirBase: d5e00002  ObjectTable: ffff9480eecf8180  HandleCount: 121.
    Image: svchost.exe

PROCESS ffffa6879c758080
    SessionId: 0  Cid: 1a44    Peb: 3004e9e000  ParentCid: 0330
    DirBase: ec4ef002  ObjectTable: ffff9480eecf8300  HandleCount: 128.
    Image: svchost.exe

PROCESS ffffa6879c74f080
    SessionId: 0  Cid: 1a64    Peb: c1b09a2000  ParentCid: 0330
    DirBase: 60bd2002  ObjectTable: ffff9480eecf7e40  HandleCount: 278.
    Image: svchost.exe

PROCESS ffffa6879c9d60c0
    SessionId: 1  Cid: 1bac    Peb: 4cf52e3000  ParentCid: 03c4
DeepFreeze
    DirBase: f75f7002  ObjectTable: ffff9480eecf5d80  HandleCount: 1454.
    Image: SearchHost.exe

PROCESS ffffa6879ca020c0
    SessionId: 1  Cid: 1bd8    Peb: f9de0f7000  ParentCid: 03c4
    DirBase: f755c002  ObjectTable: ffff9480eecf6b80  HandleCount: 674.
    Image: StartMenuExperienceHost.exe

PROCESS ffffa6879ca3b080
    SessionId: 1  Cid: 1a24    Peb: 4e3cda1000  ParentCid: 03c4
    DirBase: 1673c002  ObjectTable: ffff9480eecf6240  HandleCount: 276.
    Image: RuntimeBroker.exe

PROCESS ffffa6879caec0c0
    SessionId: 1  Cid: 1b64    Peb: c50ebeb000  ParentCid: 03c4
    DirBase: 41fb1002  ObjectTable: ffff9480eecf7340  HandleCount: 367.
    Image: RuntimeBroker.exe

PROCESS ffffa6879caf6080
    SessionId: 1  Cid: 1c1c    Peb: 8d6c289000  ParentCid: 0330
    DirBase: 40210002  ObjectTable: ffff9480ee9cbd80  HandleCount: 134.
    Image: svchost.exe

PROCESS ffffa6879ccb1080
    SessionId: 1  Cid: 1ce8    Peb: f98fe4e000  ParentCid: 03c4
    DirBase: 6903b002  ObjectTable: ffff9480eecf71c0  HandleCount: 261.
    Image: dllhost.exe

PROCESS ffffa6879cda9080
    SessionId: 1  Cid: 1df8    Peb: e335e7a000  ParentCid: 03c4
DeepFreeze
    DirBase: 3a030002  ObjectTable: ffff9480eecf87c0  HandleCount: 637.
    Image: ShellExperienceHost.exe

PROCESS ffffa6879d0020c0
    SessionId: 0  Cid: 1f54    Peb: 988c5e6000  ParentCid: 0330
    DirBase: 16289002  ObjectTable: ffff9480eecf6880  HandleCount: 682.
    Image: SearchIndexer.exe

PROCESS ffffa6879d193080
    SessionId: 0  Cid: 1a0c    Peb: de1d998000  ParentCid: 0330
    DirBase: 40f1d002  ObjectTable: ffff9480efdb9140  HandleCount: 226.
    Image: NisSrv.exe

PROCESS ffffa6879d4750c0
    SessionId: 0  Cid: 20e8    Peb: 70f06d2000  ParentCid: 0330
    DirBase: 67701002  ObjectTable: ffff9480efdba100  HandleCount: 179.
    Image: svchost.exe
```

```
PROCESS ffffa6879d3990c0
    SessionId: 1  Cid: 21b8    Peb: e8eb4b2000  ParentCid: 1644
    DirBase: 672bb002  ObjectTable: ffff9480efdb9600  HandleCount: 182.
    Image: SecurityHealthSystray.exe

PROCESS ffffa6879d3880c0
    SessionId: 0  Cid: 21d4    Peb: 1ec86d8000  ParentCid: 0330
    DirBase: 697ea002  ObjectTable: ffff9480efdb7840  HandleCount: 377.
    Image: SecurityHealthService.exe

PROCESS ffffa6879d2f9080
    SessionId: 1  Cid: 2218    Peb: 33dd9bd000  ParentCid: 1644
    DirBase: 034ff002  ObjectTable: ffff9480efdb8340  HandleCount: 894.
    Image: OneDrive.exe

PROCESS ffffa6879d85b0c0
    SessionId: 1  Cid: 23b0    Peb: 66a0c9000  ParentCid: 0330
    DirBase: 2f12d002  ObjectTable: ffff9480efdba8c0  HandleCount: 432.
    Image: svchost.exe

PROCESS ffffa6879d29b0c0
    SessionId: 0  Cid: 07f0    Peb: e08caa6000  ParentCid: 0330
    DirBase: 31c1e002  ObjectTable: ffff9480efdbb080  HandleCount: 119.
    Image: SgrmBroker.exe

PROCESS ffffa6879d3610c0
    SessionId: 0  Cid: 087c    Peb: b0ca6b9000  ParentCid: 0330
    DirBase: 39eca002  ObjectTable: ffff9480efdbe5c0  HandleCount: 121.
    Image: uhssvc.exe

PROCESS ffffa6879d4710c0
    SessionId: 0  Cid: 0a14    Peb: 67addb8000  ParentCid: 0330
    DirBase: 1686a002  ObjectTable: ffff9480efdbe100  HandleCount: 182.
    Image: svchost.exe

PROCESS ffffa6879d2f00c0
    SessionId: 0  Cid: 0d2c    Peb: 706bc32000  ParentCid: 0330
    DirBase: 06872002  ObjectTable: ffff9480edbf6bc0  HandleCount: 196.
    Image: svchost.exe

PROCESS ffffa6879d5660c0
    SessionId: 0  Cid: 0e38    Peb: ab4b358000  ParentCid: 0330
    DirBase: 06bd9002  ObjectTable: ffff9480eecf9100  HandleCount: 225.
    Image: svchost.exe

PROCESS ffffa6879cd130c0
    SessionId: 0  Cid: 1750    Peb: d4f298e000  ParentCid: 03c4
    DirBase: dd769002  ObjectTable: ffff9480eecf4300  HandleCount: 173.
    Image: WmiPrvSE.exe

PROCESS ffffa6879c4540c0
    SessionId: 1  Cid: 14b4    Peb: dc66db6000  ParentCid: 03c4
    DirBase: 6e872002  ObjectTable: ffff9480f14f9dc0  HandleCount: 294.
    Image: RuntimeBroker.exe

PROCESS ffffa6879d3bd0c0
    SessionId: 0  Cid: 0c24    Peb: 1750f3d000  ParentCid: 0330
    DirBase: e412b002  ObjectTable: ffff9480f14f7b80  HandleCount: 153.
    Image: svchost.exe

PROCESS ffffa6879d5570c0
    SessionId: 3  Cid: 0ba4    Peb: cd987b1000  ParentCid: 0af8
    DirBase: 10178c002  ObjectTable: ffff9480f14f7e80  HandleCount: 157.
    Image: csrss.exe

PROCESS ffffa6879cc020c0
    SessionId: 3  Cid: 0bf4    Peb: 2084aec000  ParentCid: 0af8
    DirBase: e41ad002  ObjectTable: ffff9480f14f8800  HandleCount: 213.
    Image: winlogon.exe

PROCESS ffffa6879d2c90c0
    SessionId: 3  Cid: 2364    Peb: 3fcdb9c000  ParentCid: 0bf4
    DirBase: 42fa1002  ObjectTable: ffff9480efdbad80  HandleCount:  37.
```

```
        Image: fontdrvhost.exe

PROCESS ffffa6879cf570c0
    SessionId: 3  Cid: 1988    Peb: 7f89dc8000  ParentCid: 0bf4
    DirBase: 42f90002  ObjectTable: ffff9480f14f8980  HandleCount: 645.
    Image: LogonUI.exe

PROCESS ffffa6879d3130c0
    SessionId: 3  Cid: 1f6c    Peb: 32eb56a000  ParentCid: 0bf4
    DirBase: c8d72002  ObjectTable: ffff9480f14fcb40  HandleCount: 784.
    Image: dwm.exe

PROCESS ffffa6879d2ac0c0
    SessionId: 0  Cid: 0bac    Peb: 4052139000  ParentCid: 0330
    DirBase: 2e655002  ObjectTable: ffff9480f14fce40  HandleCount: 441.
    Image: svchost.exe

PROCESS ffffa6879d3430c0
    SessionId: 0  Cid: 1140    Peb: 6076db9000  ParentCid: 0330
    DirBase: 2d7e5002  ObjectTable: ffff9480f14fb6c0  HandleCount: 349.
    Image: WUDFHost.exe

PROCESS ffffa6879d3550c0
    SessionId: 1  Cid: 1528    Peb: 223ec20000  ParentCid: 04a4
    DirBase: 2b92d002  ObjectTable: ffff9480f14fc040  HandleCount: 470.
    Image: rdpclip.exe

PROCESS ffffa6879b48a0c0
    SessionId: 0  Cid: 1978    Peb: ab33744000  ParentCid: 0330
    DirBase: 4329b002  ObjectTable: ffff9480eecf9440  HandleCount: 152.
    Image: svchost.exe

PROCESS ffffa6879cd020c0
    SessionId: 0  Cid: 0a4c    Peb: c60e420000  ParentCid: 0330
    DirBase: 2680f002  ObjectTable: ffff9480ee81ae80  HandleCount: 506.
    Image: svchost.exe

PROCESS ffffa6879d2a10c0
    SessionId: 1  Cid: 0f04    Peb: a9a0e29000  ParentCid: 1528
    DirBase: 23fb5002  ObjectTable: ffff9480efdb76c0  HandleCount: 143.
    Image: rdpinput.exe

PROCESS ffffa6879d4790c0
    SessionId: 1  Cid: 176c    Peb: ed40191000  ParentCid: 156c
    DirBase: 1304a002  ObjectTable: ffff9480f14fa100  HandleCount: 311.
    Image: TabTip.exe

PROCESS ffffa6879b7dd140
    SessionId: 1  Cid: 0994    Peb: 93be9be000  ParentCid: 03c4
    DirBase: 363a5002  ObjectTable: ffff9480f14fa740  HandleCount: 706.
    Image: TextInputHost.exe

PROCESS ffffa6879cb610c0
    SessionId: 1  Cid: 0598    Peb: e95a908000  ParentCid: 03c4
    DirBase: 2d532002  ObjectTable: ffff9480f14f9940  HandleCount: 420.
    Image: smartscreen.exe

PROCESS ffffa6879d3720c0
    SessionId: 1  Cid: 081c    Peb: c5c4b43000  ParentCid: 1644
    DirBase: c3633002  ObjectTable: ffff9480f14fba00  HandleCount: 145.
    Image: DriverEmulator.exe

PROCESS ffffa6879b9780c0
    SessionId: 1  Cid: 1020    Peb: c99835a000  ParentCid: 1644
    DirBase: 47e45002  ObjectTable: ffff9480f14f9780  HandleCount: 144.
    Image: AppD6.exe
```

7.   Let's check the *AppD6* stack trace (**!process** command with **3f** flag)

```
0: kd> !process ffffa6879b9780c0 3f
PROCESS ffffa6879b9780c0
    SessionId: 1  Cid: 1020    Peb: c99835a000  ParentCid: 1644
```

```
        DirBase: 47e45002  ObjectTable: ffff9480f14f9780  HandleCount: 144.
        Image: AppD6.exe
        VadRoot ffffa6879cf87300 Vads 75 Clone 0 Private 361. Modified 2. Locked 0.
        DeviceMap ffff9480ee9bd8b0
        Token                            ffff9480ef728060
        ElapsedTime                      00:00:13.572
        UserTime                         00:00:00.000
        KernelTime                       00:00:00.000
        QuotaPoolUsage[PagedPool]        169768
        QuotaPoolUsage[NonPagedPool]     10528
        Working Set Sizes (now,min,max)  (2854, 50, 345) (11416KB, 200KB, 1380KB)
        PeakWorkingSetSize               2781
        VirtualSize                      4223 Mb
        PeakVirtualSize                  4235 Mb
        PageFaultCount                   2898
        MemoryPriority                   FOREGROUND
        BasePriority                     8
        CommitCharge                     409
        Job                              ffffa68799b13060


        PEB at 000000c99835a000
        InheritedAddressSpace:     No
        ReadImageFileExecOptions:  No
        BeingDebugged:             No
        ImageBaseAddress:          00007ff7e0230000
        NtGlobalFlag:              0
        NtGlobalFlag2:             0
        Ldr                        00007ffc752fa140
        Ldr.Initialized:           Yes
        Ldr.InInitializationOrderModuleList: 000001d0b3131fc0 . 000001d0b31769f0
        Ldr.InLoadOrderModuleList:           000001d0b3132140 . 000001d0b31769d0
        Ldr.InMemoryOrderModuleList:         000001d0b3132150 . 000001d0b31769e0
                    Base TimeStamp                     Module
            7ff7e0230000 6269b830 Apr 27 22:40:00 2022 C:\AWD4\AppD6\x64\Release\AppD6.exe
            7ffc75180000 5179e735 Apr 26 03:32:21 2013 C:\WINDOWS\SYSTEM32\ntdll.dll
            7ffc73f50000 399db95d Aug 18 23:31:57 2000 C:\WINDOWS\System32\KERNEL32.DLL
            7ffc72b30000 4412095c Mar 10 23:18:52 2006 C:\WINDOWS\System32\KERNELBASE.dll
            7ffc74a30000 42176440 Feb 19 16:07:28 2005 C:\WINDOWS\System32\USER32.dll
            7ffc72f80000 73c2c6b2 Jul 18 13:38:10 2031 C:\WINDOWS\System32\win32u.dll
            7ffc73620000 47353a16 Nov 10 04:56:54 2007 C:\WINDOWS\System32\GDI32.dll
            7ffc728f0000 4982aa9b Jan 30 07:22:03 2009 C:\WINDOWS\System32\gdi32full.dll
            7ffc72850000 1fb7fd57 Nov 12 03:53:59 1986 C:\WINDOWS\System32\msvcp_win.dll
            7ffc72a10000 00e78ce9 Jun 25 16:14:49 1970 C:\WINDOWS\System32\ucrtbase.dll
            7ffc73650000 a830d784 Jun 02 10:53:08 2059 C:\WINDOWS\System32\IMM32.DLL
            7ffc6fc60000 23788864 Nov 09 18:03:16 1988 C:\WINDOWS\system32\uxtheme.dll
            7ffc73080000 e6e0bfef Sep 29 02:07:59 2092 C:\WINDOWS\System32\combase.dll
            7ffc747e0000 4acc643c Oct 07 10:49:48 2009 C:\WINDOWS\System32\RPCRT4.dll
            7ffc74910000 d1eb1709 Aug 08 03:16:41 2081 C:\WINDOWS\System32\MSCTF.dll
            7ffc74010000 90483ed2 Sep 15 20:49:38 2046 C:\WINDOWS\System32\msvcrt.dll
            7ffc61480000 4aed9582 Nov 01 14:04:50 2009 C:\WINDOWS\SYSTEM32\TextShaping.dll
            7ffc71620000 90a828d2 Nov 27 13:53:22 2046 C:\WINDOWS\SYSTEM32\kernel.appcore.dll
            7ffc725f0000 a6f742a6 Oct 07 14:18:30 2058 C:\WINDOWS\System32\bcryptPrimitives.dll
            7ffc74d50000 529a8d7f Dec 01 01:14:39 2013 C:\WINDOWS\System32\sechost.dll
            7ffc725c0000 d4036918 Sep 18 22:41:44 2082 C:\WINDOWS\System32\bcrypt.dll
            7ffc60d60000 13ce190b Jul 12 19:18:51 1980 C:\WINDOWS\SYSTEM32\textinputframework.dll
            7ffc74e00000 75801aeb Jun 20 08:36:11 2032 C:\WINDOWS\System32\OLEAUT32.dll
            7ffc6f6f0000 0a8a231e Aug 09 15:05:18 1975 C:\WINDOWS\SYSTEM32\CoreMessaging.dll
            7ffc6d860000 578e8f6c Jul 19 21:37:00 2016 C:\WINDOWS\SYSTEM32\CoreUIComponents.dll
            7ffc70510000 3259a5f0 Oct 08 01:53:04 1996 C:\WINDOWS\SYSTEM32\wintypes.dll
            7ffc740c0000 47b39254 Feb 14 00:59:00 2008 C:\WINDOWS\System32\advapi32.dll
            7ffc71ca0000 14759998 Nov 16 19:35:52 1980 C:\WINDOWS\SYSTEM32\CRYPTBASE.DLL
            7ffc56f20000 d4726d59 Dec 12 02:41:29 2082 C:\WINDOWS\system32\Oleacc.dll
        SubSystemData:      0000000000000000
        ProcessHeap:        000001d0b3130000
        ProcessParameters:  000001d0b31364c0
        CurrentDirectory:   'C:\AWD4\AppD6\x64\Release\'
        WindowTitle:  'C:\AWD4\AppD6\x64\Release\AppD6.exe'
        ImageFile:    'C:\AWD4\AppD6\x64\Release\AppD6.exe'
        CommandLine:  '"C:\AWD4\AppD6\x64\Release\AppD6.exe" '
        DllPath:      '< Name not readable >'
        Environment:  000001d0b31311f0
            =::=::\
            ALLUSERSPROFILE=C:\ProgramData
            APPDATA=C:\Users\User\AppData\Roaming
```

```
CommonProgramFiles=C:\Program Files\Common Files
CommonProgramFiles(x86)=C:\Program Files (x86)\Common Files
CommonProgramW6432=C:\Program Files\Common Files
COMPUTERNAME=WINDEV2204EVAL
ComSpec=C:\WINDOWS\system32\cmd.exe
DriverData=C:\Windows\System32\Drivers\DriverData
HOMEDRIVE=C:
HOMEPATH=\Users\User
LOCALAPPDATA=C:\Users\User\AppData\Local
LOGONSERVER=\\WINDEV2204EVAL
NUMBER_OF_PROCESSORS=4
OneDrive=C:\Users\User\OneDrive
OS=Windows_NT

Path=C:\Windows\system32;C:\Windows;C:\Windows\System32\Wbem;C:\Windows\System32\WindowsPowerShell\v1.0\;C:\Windows\Sy
stem32\OpenSSH\;C:\Program Files\Microsoft SQL Server\150\Tools\Binn\;C:\Program Files\Microsoft SQL Server\Client
SDK\ODBC\170\Tools\Binn\;C:\Program
Files\dotnet\;C:\Users\User\AppData\Local\Microsoft\WindowsApps;C:\Users\User\.dotnet\tools
PATHEXT=.COM;.EXE;.BAT;.CMD;.VBS;.VBE;.JS;.JSE;.WSF;.WSH;.MSC
PROCESSOR_ARCHITECTURE=AMD64
PROCESSOR_IDENTIFIER=Intel64 Family 6 Model 142 Stepping 10, GenuineIntel
PROCESSOR_LEVEL=6
PROCESSOR_REVISION=8e0a
ProgramData=C:\ProgramData
ProgramFiles=C:\Program Files
ProgramFiles(x86)=C:\Program Files (x86)
ProgramW6432=C:\Program Files
PSModulePath=C:\Program Files\WindowsPowerShell\Modules;C:\WINDOWS\system32\WindowsPowerShell\v1.0\Modules
PUBLIC=C:\Users\Public
SESSIONNAME=Console
SystemDrive=C:
SystemRoot=C:\WINDOWS
TEMP=C:\Users\User\AppData\Local\Temp
TMP=C:\Users\User\AppData\Local\Temp
USERDOMAIN=WINDEV2204EVAL
USERDOMAIN_ROAMINGPROFILE=WINDEV2204EVAL
USERNAME=User
USERPROFILE=C:\Users\User
windir=C:\WINDOWS


    THREAD ffffa6879ba5a080  Cid 1020.1ad0  Teb: 000000c99835b000 Win32Thread: ffffa6879cf87350 WAIT:
(WrUserRequest) UserMode Non-Alertable
        ffffa6879c617cc0  QueueObject
    Not impersonating
    DeviceMap                 ffff9480ee9bd8b0
    Owning Process            ffffa6879b9780c0      Image:        AppD6.exe
    Attached Process          N/A        Image:        N/A
    Wait Start TickCount      41096      Ticks: 650 (0:00:00:10.156)
    Context Switch Count      399        IdealProcessor: 2
    UserTime                  00:00:00.031
    KernelTime                00:00:00.000
*** WARNING: Unable to verify checksum for AppD6.exe
    Win32 Start Address AppD6!wWinMainCRTStartup (0x00007ff7e0231818)
    Stack Init ffffc786f141bc70 Current ffffc786f141b140
    Base ffffc786f141c000 Limit ffffc786f1416000 Call 0000000000000000
    Priority 12 BasePriority 8 PriorityDecrement 2 IoPriority 2 PagePriority 5
    Child-SP          RetAddr               Call Site
    ffffc786`f141b180 fffff807`08542277     nt!KiSwapContext+0x76
    ffffc786`f141b2c0 fffff807`08544129     nt!KiSwapThread+0x3a7
    ffffc786`f141b3a0 fffff807`0853e044     nt!KiCommitThreadWait+0x159
    ffffc786`f141b440 fffff807`084f7490     nt!KeWaitForSingleObject+0x234
    ffffc786`f141b530 ffffcc94`a3dadf66     nt!KeWaitForMultipleObjects+0x540
    ffffc786`f141b630 ffffcc94`a3dadbcf     win32kfull!xxxRealSleepThread+0x2c6
    ffffc786`f141b750 ffffcc94`a3db13bb     win32kfull!xxxSleepThread2+0xb3
    ffffc786`f141b7a0 ffffcc94`a3e0511c     win32kfull!xxxRealInternalGetMessage+0x117b
    ffffc786`f141ba10 ffffcc94`a437645a     win32kfull!NtUserGetMessage+0x8c
    ffffc786`f141baa0 fffff807`08632485     win32k!NtUserGetMessage+0x16
    ffffc786`f141bae0 00007ffc`72f81414     nt!KiSystemServiceCopyEnd+0x25 (TrapFrame @ ffffc786`f141bae0)
    000000c9`981ff6d8 00007ffc`74a5472e     win32u!NtUserGetMessage+0x14
    000000c9`981ff6e0 00007ff7`e023109d     USER32!GetMessageW+0x2e
    000000c9`981ff740 00000000`00000000     AppD6!wWinMain+0x9d [C:\AWD3\AppD6\AppD6\AppD6.cpp @ 50]
```

225

```
        THREAD ffffa6879cef6080  Cid 1020.0794  Teb: 000000c99835d000 Win32Thread: 0000000000000000 WAIT: (WrQueue)
UserMode Alertable
            ffffa6879c615640  QueueObject
        Not impersonating
        DeviceMap                 ffff9480ee9bd8b0
        Owning Process            ffffa6879b9780c0        Image:          AppD6.exe
        Attached Process          N/A             Image:          N/A
        Wait Start TickCount      40881           Ticks: 865 (0:00:00:13.515)
        Context Switch Count      7               IdealProcessor: 1
        UserTime                  00:00:00.000
        KernelTime                00:00:00.000
        Win32 Start Address ntdll!TppWorkerThread (0x00007ffc75196a00)
        Stack Init ffffc786f1502c70 Current ffffc786f1502370
        Base ffffc786f1503000 Limit ffffc786f14fd000 Call 0000000000000000
        Priority 10 BasePriority 8 PriorityDecrement 2 IoPriority 2 PagePriority 5
        Child-SP          RetAddr               Call Site
        ffffc786`f15023b0 fffff807`08542277     nt!KiSwapContext+0x76
        ffffc786`f15024f0 fffff807`08544129     nt!KiSwapThread+0x3a7
        ffffc786`f15025d0 fffff807`08546fe6     nt!KiCommitThreadWait+0x159
        ffffc786`f1502670 fffff807`085469f8     nt!KeRemoveQueueEx+0x2b6
        ffffc786`f1502720 fffff807`08549cb4     nt!IoRemoveIoCompletion+0x98
        ffffc786`f1502840 fffff807`08632485     nt!NtWaitForWorkViaWorkerFactory+0xdf4
        ffffc786`f1502a70 00007ffc`75227824     nt!KiSystemServiceCopyEnd+0x25 (TrapFrame @ ffffc786`f1502ae0)
        000000c9`984ff838 00007ffc`75196cdf     ntdll!NtWaitForWorkViaWorkerFactory+0x14
        000000c9`984ff840 00007ffc`73f653e0     ntdll!TppWorkerThread+0x2df
        000000c9`984ffb30 00007ffc`7518485b     KERNEL32!BaseThreadInitThunk+0x10
        000000c9`984ffb60 00000000`00000000     ntdll!RtlUserThreadStart+0x2b

        THREAD ffffa6879d175080  Cid 1020.13d0  Teb: 000000c99835f000 Win32Thread: 0000000000000000 WAIT: (WrQueue)
UserMode Alertable
            ffffa6879c615640  QueueObject
        Not impersonating
        DeviceMap                 ffff9480ee9bd8b0
        Owning Process            ffffa6879b9780c0        Image:          AppD6.exe
        Attached Process          N/A             Image:          N/A
        Wait Start TickCount      40881           Ticks: 865 (0:00:00:13.515)
        Context Switch Count      16              IdealProcessor: 3
        UserTime                  00:00:00.000
        KernelTime                00:00:00.000
        Win32 Start Address ntdll!TppWorkerThread (0x00007ffc75196a00)
        Stack Init ffffc786f1509c70 Current ffffc786f1509370
        Base ffffc786f150a000 Limit ffffc786f1504000 Call 0000000000000000
        Priority 10 BasePriority 8 PriorityDecrement 2 IoPriority 2 PagePriority 5
        Child-SP          RetAddr               Call Site
        ffffc786`f15093b0 fffff807`08542277     nt!KiSwapContext+0x76
        ffffc786`f15094f0 fffff807`08544129     nt!KiSwapThread+0x3a7
        ffffc786`f15095d0 fffff807`08546fe6     nt!KiCommitThreadWait+0x159
        ffffc786`f1509670 fffff807`085469f8     nt!KeRemoveQueueEx+0x2b6
        ffffc786`f1509720 fffff807`08549cb4     nt!IoRemoveIoCompletion+0x98
        ffffc786`f1509840 fffff807`08632485     nt!NtWaitForWorkViaWorkerFactory+0xdf4
        ffffc786`f1509a70 00007ffc`75227824     nt!KiSystemServiceCopyEnd+0x25 (TrapFrame @ ffffc786`f1509ae0)
        000000c9`985ff728 00007ffc`75196cdf     ntdll!NtWaitForWorkViaWorkerFactory+0x14
        000000c9`985ff730 00007ffc`73f653e0     ntdll!TppWorkerThread+0x2df
        000000c9`985ffa20 00007ffc`7518485b     KERNEL32!BaseThreadInitThunk+0x10
        000000c9`985ffa50 00000000`00000000     ntdll!RtlUserThreadStart+0x2b

        THREAD ffffa6879d29d080  Cid 1020.14e4  Teb: 000000c998361000 Win32Thread: 0000000000000000 WAIT: (WrQueue)
UserMode Alertable
            ffffa6879c615640  QueueObject
        Not impersonating
        DeviceMap                 ffff9480ee9bd8b0
        Owning Process            ffffa6879b9780c0        Image:          AppD6.exe
        Attached Process          N/A             Image:          N/A
        Wait Start TickCount      40878           Ticks: 868 (0:00:00:13.562)
        Context Switch Count      1               IdealProcessor: 0
        UserTime                  00:00:00.000
        KernelTime                00:00:00.000
        Win32 Start Address ntdll!TppWorkerThread (0x00007ffc75196a00)
        Stack Init ffffc786f151ec70 Current ffffc786f151e370
        Base ffffc786f151f000 Limit ffffc786f1519000 Call 0000000000000000
        Priority 8 BasePriority 8 PriorityDecrement 0 IoPriority 2 PagePriority 5
        Child-SP          RetAddr               Call Site
        ffffc786`f151e3b0 fffff807`08542277     nt!KiSwapContext+0x76
        ffffc786`f151e4f0 fffff807`08544129     nt!KiSwapThread+0x3a7
```

```
ffffc786`f151e5d0 fffff807`08546fe6   nt!KiCommitThreadWait+0x159
ffffc786`f151e670 fffff807`085469f8   nt!KeRemoveQueueEx+0x2b6
ffffc786`f151e720 fffff807`08549cb4   nt!IoRemoveIoCompletion+0x98
ffffc786`f151e840 fffff807`08632485   nt!NtWaitForWorkViaWorkerFactory+0xdf4
ffffc786`f151ea70 00007ffc`75227824   nt!KiSystemServiceCopyEnd+0x25 (TrapFrame @ ffffc786`f151eae0)
000000c9`986ff868 00007ffc`75196cdf   ntdll!NtWaitForWorkViaWorkerFactory+0x14
000000c9`986ff870 00007ffc`73f653e0   ntdll!TppWorkerThread+0x2df
000000c9`986ffb60 00007ffc`7518485b   KERNEL32!BaseThreadInitThunk+0x10
000000c9`986ffb90 00000000`00000000   ntdll!RtlUserThreadStart+0x2b
```

Note: I highlighted kernel space stack trace parts in red color and user space stack trace parts in blue color.

8.   We now switch to that process in WinDbg (**.process /r /p**) and put a hardware code execution breakpoint on the *AppD6!StartModeling* function (the **ba** command) limited to the process **ffffa6879b9780c0**:

```
0: kd> .process /r /p ffffa6879b9780c0
Implicit process is now ffffa687`9b9780c0
.cache forcedecodeuser done
Loading User Symbols
..........................
```

```
0: kd> ba e 1 /p ffffa6879b9780c0 AppD6!StartModeling
*** WARNING: Unable to verify checksum for AppD6.exe
0: kd> bl
     0 e Disable Clear  00007ff7`e0231470 e 1 0001 (0001) AppD6!StartModeling
     Match process data ffffa687`9b9780c0
```

9.   We now set the source code location, resume the Guest VM (the **g** command), reconnect to the Guest VM if necessary, switch to the *AppD6* window, and choose *File\ Start*. We then switch to host WinDbg, and the breakpoint hit (you should also see the source code window):

```
0: kd> .srcpath C:\AWD4\AppD6\AppD6
Source search path is: C:\AWD4\AppD6\AppD6

************* Path validation summary **************
Response                    Time (ms)     Location
OK                                        C:\AWD4\AppD6\AppD6
```

```
0: kd> g
Breakpoint 0 hit
AppD6!StartModeling:
0033:00007ff7`e0231470 sub      rsp,38h
```

10.   We now step through source code lines (**p** command) until the *pint* variable line is highlighted:

```
3: kd> p
AppD6!StartModeling+0x4:
0033:00007ff7`e0231474 mov      qword ptr [rsp+20h],0
```

```
3: kd> p
AppD6!StartModeling+0xd:
0033:00007ff7`e023147d lea      rcx,[rsp+20h]
```

```
3: kd> p
AppD6!StartModeling+0x17:
0033:00007ff7`e0231487 mov      rax,qword ptr [rsp+20h]
```

```
AppD6.cpp                                              ▼ □ ✕
      192  void DeAllocateStorage(volatile unsigned int *);
      193
      194  void StartModeling(void)
  ●   195  {
      196      volatile unsigned int *pint = NULL;
      197
      198      AllocateStorage(&pint); // allocates a memory for pint
      199
  ⇨   200      *pint = 5000;
      201
      202      Sleep(30000);
      203
      204      while (--(*pint))
      205      {
      206          Sleep(0); // do some work
      207      }
```

11.   We now put a hardware data breakpoint on an address that *pint* variable points to (**ba** command):

```
3: kd> ?? pint
unsigned int * 0x00000000`12340000
```

```
3: kd> ba w 4 0x00000000`12340000
```

```
3: kd> bl
     0 e Disable Clear  00007ff7`e0231470 e 1 0001 (0001) AppD6!StartModeling
     Match process data ffffa687`9b9780c0
     1 e Disable Clear  00000000`12340000 w 4 0001 (0001)
```

12.   We now resume VM in WinDbg, and we should get the first hit over an assignment of 5000:

```
3: kd> g
Breakpoint 1 hit
AppD6!StartModeling+0x22:
0033:00007ff7`e0231492 mov        ecx,7530h
```

```
3: kd> ?? *pint
unsigned int 0x1388
```

```
3: kd> dx *pint
*pint            : 0x1388 [Type: unsigned int]
```

```
3: kd> ? 0x1388
Evaluate expression: 5000 = 00000000`00001388
```

13.   We then resume the VM, reconnect if necessary, inside it, switch to the *DriverEmulator* window, and choose *File \ Start* (we have no more than 30 seconds to do that!). We then should get a second breakpoint hit in WinDbg:

```
3: kd> g
Breakpoint 1 hit
0033:00007ff6`414014df mov        rcx,qword ptr [rsp+38h]
```

228

14. We then inspect the current process, which did a write to the *pint* location (**-1** is for a current process, and the **3f** flag is needed for its context and symbols):

```
3: kd> !process -1 3f
PROCESS ffffa6879d3720c0
    SessionId: 1  Cid: 081c    Peb: c5c4b43000  ParentCid: 1644
    DirBase: c3633002  ObjectTable: ffff9480f14fba00  HandleCount: 146.
    Image: DriverEmulator.exe
    VadRoot ffffa6879cbe0100 Vads 79 Clone 0 Private 372. Modified 2139. Locked 0.
    DeviceMap ffff9480ee9bd8b0
    Token                             ffff9480efc46060
    ElapsedTime                       00:54:47.746
    UserTime                          00:00:00.000
    KernelTime                        00:00:00.000
    QuotaPoolUsage[PagedPool]         169792
    QuotaPoolUsage[NonPagedPool]      11072
    Working Set Sizes (now,min,max)  (2996, 50, 345) (11984KB, 200KB, 1380KB)
    PeakWorkingSetSize                3254
    VirtualSize                       4223 Mb
    PeakVirtualSize                   4237 Mb
    PageFaultCount                    7174
    MemoryPriority                    FOREGROUND
    BasePriority                      8
    CommitCharge                      424
    Job                               ffffa6879ce14060

    PEB at 000000c5c4b43000
    InheritedAddressSpace:    No
    ReadImageFileExecOptions: No
    BeingDebugged:            No
    ImageBaseAddress:         00007ff641400000
    NtGlobalFlag:             0
    NtGlobalFlag2:            0
    Ldr                       00007ffc752fa140
    Ldr.Initialized:          Yes
    Ldr.InInitializationOrderModuleList: 00000201e05e1fc0 . 00000201e06252d0
    Ldr.InLoadOrderModuleList:           00000201e05e2140 . 00000201e06252b0
    Ldr.InMemoryOrderModuleList:         00000201e05e2150 . 00000201e06252c0
            Base TimeStamp                     Module
        7ff641400000 626b07fe Apr 28 22:32:46 2022 C:\AWD4\DriverEmulator\x64\Release\DriverEmulator.exe
        7ffc75180000 5179e735 Apr 26 03:32:21 2013 C:\WINDOWS\SYSTEM32\ntdll.dll
        7ffc73f50000 399db95d Aug 18 23:31:57 2000 C:\WINDOWS\System32\KERNEL32.DLL
        7ffc72b30000 4412095c Mar 10 23:18:52 2006 C:\WINDOWS\System32\KERNELBASE.dll
        7ffc74a30000 42176440 Feb 19 16:07:28 2005 C:\WINDOWS\System32\USER32.dll
        7ffc72f80000 73c2c6b2 Jul 18 13:38:10 2031 C:\WINDOWS\System32\win32u.dll
        7ffc73620000 47353a16 Nov 10 04:56:54 2007 C:\WINDOWS\System32\GDI32.dll
        7ffc728f0000 4982aa9b Jan 30 07:22:03 2009 C:\WINDOWS\System32\gdi32full.dll
        7ffc72850000 1fb7fd57 Nov 12 03:53:59 1986 C:\WINDOWS\System32\msvcp_win.dll
        7ffc72a10000 00e78ce9 Jun 25 16:14:49 1970 C:\WINDOWS\System32\ucrtbase.dll
        7ffc73650000 a830d784 Jun 02 10:53:08 2059 C:\WINDOWS\System32\IMM32.DLL
        7ffc6fc60000 23788864 Nov 09 18:03:16 1988 C:\WINDOWS\system32\uxtheme.dll
        7ffc73080000 e6e0bfef Sep 29 02:07:59 2092 C:\WINDOWS\System32\combase.dll
        7ffc747e0000 4acc643c Oct 07 10:49:48 2009 C:\WINDOWS\System32\RPCRT4.dll
        7ffc74910000 d1eb1709 Aug 08 03:16:41 2081 C:\WINDOWS\System32\MSCTF.dll
        7ffc74010000 90483ed2 Sep 15 20:49:38 2046 C:\WINDOWS\System32\msvcrt.dll
        7ffc61480000 4aed9582 Nov 01 14:04:50 2009 C:\WINDOWS\SYSTEM32\TextShaping.dll
        7ffc71620000 90a828d2 Nov 27 13:53:22 2046 C:\WINDOWS\SYSTEM32\kernel.appcore.dll
        7ffc725f0000 a6f742a6 Oct 07 14:18:30 2058 C:\WINDOWS\System32\bcryptPrimitives.dll
        7ffc74d50000 529a8d7f Dec 01 01:14:39 2013 C:\WINDOWS\System32\sechost.dll
        7ffc725c0000 d4036918 Sep 18 22:41:44 2082 C:\WINDOWS\System32\bcrypt.dll
        7ffc60d60000 13ce190b Jul 12 19:18:51 1980 C:\WINDOWS\SYSTEM32\textinputframework.dll
        7ffc74e00000 75801aeb Jun 20 08:36:11 2032 C:\WINDOWS\System32\OLEAUT32.dll
        7ffc6f6f0000 0a8a231e Aug 09 15:05:18 1975 C:\WINDOWS\SYSTEM32\CoreMessaging.dll
        7ffc6d860000 578e8f6c Jul 19 21:37:00 2016 C:\WINDOWS\SYSTEM32\CoreUIComponents.dll
        7ffc70510000 3259a5f0 Oct 08 01:53:04 1996 C:\WINDOWS\System32\wintypes.dll
        7ffc740c0000 47b39254 Feb 14 00:59:00 2008 C:\WINDOWS\System32\advapi32.dll
        7ffc71ca0000 14759998 Nov 16 19:35:52 1980 C:\WINDOWS\SYSTEM32\CRYPTBASE.DLL
        7ffc56f20000 d4726d59 Dec 12 02:41:29 2082 C:\WINDOWS\system32\Oleacc.dll
        7ffc6ff00000 f5060712 Apr 07 21:29:06 2100 C:\WINDOWS\system32\dwmapi.dll
    SubSystemData:      0000000000000000
    ProcessHeap:        00000201e05e0000
```

229

```
     ProcessParameters: 00000201e05e64c0
     CurrentDirectory:  'C:\AWD4\DriverEmulator\x64\Release\'
     WindowTitle:   'C:\AWD4\DriverEmulator\x64\Release\DriverEmulator.exe'
     ImageFile:     'C:\AWD4\DriverEmulator\x64\Release\DriverEmulator.exe'
     CommandLine:   '"C:\AWD4\DriverEmulator\x64\Release\DriverEmulator.exe" '
     DllPath:       '< Name not readable >'
     Environment:   00000201e05e11f0
        =::=::\
        ALLUSERSPROFILE=C:\ProgramData
        APPDATA=C:\Users\User\AppData\Roaming
        CommonProgramFiles=C:\Program Files\Common Files
        CommonProgramFiles(x86)=C:\Program Files (x86)\Common Files
        CommonProgramW6432=C:\Program Files\Common Files
        COMPUTERNAME=WINDEV2204EVAL
        ComSpec=C:\WINDOWS\system32\cmd.exe
        DriverData=C:\Windows\System32\Drivers\DriverData
        HOMEDRIVE=C:
        HOMEPATH=\Users\User
        LOCALAPPDATA=C:\Users\User\AppData\Local
        LOGONSERVER=\\WINDEV2204EVAL
        NUMBER_OF_PROCESSORS=4
        OneDrive=C:\Users\User\OneDrive
        OS=Windows_NT

Path=C:\Windows\system32;C:\Windows;C:\Windows\System32\Wbem;C:\Windows\System32\WindowsPowerShell\v1.0\;C:\Windows\Sy
stem32\OpenSSH\;C:\Program Files\Microsoft SQL Server\150\Tools\Binn\;C:\Program Files\Microsoft SQL Server\Client
SDK\ODBC\170\Tools\Binn\;C:\Program
Files\dotnet\;C:\Users\User\AppData\Local\Microsoft\WindowsApps;C:\Users\User\.dotnet\tools
        PATHEXT=.COM;.EXE;.BAT;.CMD;.VBS;.VBE;.JS;.JSE;.WSF;.WSH;.MSC
        PROCESSOR_ARCHITECTURE=AMD64
        PROCESSOR_IDENTIFIER=Intel64 Family 6 Model 142 Stepping 10, GenuineIntel
        PROCESSOR_LEVEL=6
        PROCESSOR_REVISION=8e0a
        ProgramData=C:\ProgramData
        ProgramFiles=C:\Program Files
        ProgramFiles(x86)=C:\Program Files (x86)
        ProgramW6432=C:\Program Files
        PSModulePath=C:\Program Files\WindowsPowerShell\Modules;C:\WINDOWS\system32\WindowsPowerShell\v1.0\Modules
        PUBLIC=C:\Users\Public
        SESSIONNAME=Console
        SystemDrive=C:
        SystemRoot=C:\WINDOWS
        TEMP=C:\Users\User\AppData\Local\Temp
        TMP=C:\Users\User\AppData\Local\Temp
        USERDOMAIN=WINDEV2204EVAL
        USERDOMAIN_ROAMINGPROFILE=WINDEV2204EVAL
        USERNAME=User
        USERPROFILE=C:\Users\User
        windir=C:\WINDOWS


     THREAD ffffa6879ad65080  Cid 081c.0ba8  Teb: 000000c5c4b44000 Win32Thread: ffffa6879c8d1b10 RUNNING on
processor 2
        Not impersonating
        DeviceMap                 ffff9480ee9bd8b0
        Owning Process            ffffa6879d3720c0      Image:         DriverEmulator.exe
        Attached Process          N/A           Image:        N/A
        Wait Start TickCount      46013         Ticks: 1 (0:00:00.015)
        Context Switch Count      5714          IdealProcessor: 2
        UserTime                  00:00:00.078
        KernelTime                00:00:00.203
*** WARNING: Unable to verify checksum for DriverEmulator.exe
        Win32 Start Address DriverEmulator (0x00007ff641401788)
        Stack Init ffffc786f204cc70 Current ffffc786f204c3c0
        Base ffffc786f204d000 Limit ffffc786f2047000 Call 0000000000000000
        Priority 12 BasePriority 8 PriorityDecrement 2 IoPriority 2 PagePriority 5
        Child-SP          RetAddr               Call Site
        000000c5`c4cff4f0 00007ff6`41401301     DriverEmulator+0x14df
        000000c5`c4cff540 00007ffc`74a41cac     DriverEmulator+0x1301
        000000c5`c4cff600 00007ffc`74a40f06     USER32!UserCallWinProcCheckWow+0x33c
        000000c5`c4cff770 00007ff6`414010d0     USER32!DispatchMessageWorker+0x2a6
        000000c5`c4cff7f0 00007ff6`4140171a     DriverEmulator+0x10d0
        000000c5`c4cff860 00007ffc`73f653e0     DriverEmulator+0x171a
        000000c5`c4cff8a0 00007ffc`7518485b     KERNEL32!BaseThreadInitThunk+0x10
```

```
         000000c5`c4cff8d0  00000000`00000000    ntdll!RtlUserThreadStart+0x2b

      THREAD ffffa6879b957040  Cid 081c.1678  Teb: 000000c5c4b50000 Win32Thread: 0000000000000000 WAIT: (WrQueue)
UserMode Alertable
         ffffa6879b716a80  QueueObject
      Not impersonating
      DeviceMap                ffff9480ee9bd8b0
      Owning Process           ffffa6879d3720c0       Image:          DriverEmulator.exe
      Attached Process         N/A            Image:       N/A
      Wait Start TickCount     44580          Ticks: 1434 (0:00:00:22.406)
      Context Switch Count     4              IdealProcessor: 3
      UserTime                 00:00:00.000
      KernelTime               00:00:00.000
      Win32 Start Address ntdll!TppWorkerThread (0x00007ffc75196a00)
      Stack Init ffffc786f245ac70 Current ffffc786f245a370
      Base ffffc786f245b000 Limit ffffc786f2455000 Call 0000000000000000
      Priority 8 BasePriority 8 PriorityDecrement 0 IoPriority 2 PagePriority 5

      Child-SP          RetAddr           Call Site
      ffffc786`f245a3b0 fffff807`08542277 nt!KiSwapContext+0x76
      ffffc786`f245a4f0 fffff807`08544129 nt!KiSwapThread+0x3a7
      ffffc786`f245a5d0 fffff807`08546fe6 nt!KiCommitThreadWait+0x159
      ffffc786`f245a670 fffff807`085469f8 nt!KeRemoveQueueEx+0x2b6
      ffffc786`f245a720 fffff807`08549cb4 nt!IoRemoveIoCompletion+0x98
      ffffc786`f245a840 fffff807`08632485 nt!NtWaitForWorkViaWorkerFactory+0xdf4
      ffffc786`f245aa70 00007ffc`75227824 nt!KiSystemServiceCopyEnd+0x25 (TrapFrame @ ffffc786`f245aae0)
      000000c5`c4dff538 00007ffc`75196cdf ntdll!NtWaitForWorkViaWorkerFactory+0x14
      000000c5`c4dff540 00007ffc`73f653e0 ntdll!TppWorkerThread+0x2df
      000000c5`c4dff830 00007ffc`7518485b KERNEL32!BaseThreadInitThunk+0x10
      000000c5`c4dff860 00000000`00000000 ntdll!RtlUserThreadStart+0x2b

...
...
...
```

Note: So, we could catch data corruption that we could not do using just process debugging in the UD6 exercise.

15.   We now resume VM in WinDbg and get another hit for the *pint* variable. We reload user space symbols for the current process (**.reload /user**), and we see it is now the loop in *AppD6* with the corrupted value of **pint*:

```
2: kd> g
Breakpoint 1 hit
0033:00007ff7`e02314ad mov      rax,qword ptr [rsp+20h]

2: kd> .reload /user
Loading User Symbols
...........................
*** WARNING: Unable to verify checksum for AppD6.exe

2: kd> kL
 # Child-SP          RetAddr           Call Site
00 000000c9`981ff450 00000000`00000001 AppD6!StartModeling+0x3d
01 000000c9`981ff458 00000000`00000000 0x1

2: kd> ?? *pint
unsigned int 0xfffffffe

2: kd> dx *pint
*pint            : 0xfffffffe [Type: unsigned int]
```

Note: We may also get the full stack trace, for example (from a different debugging session):

```
2: kd> kL
 # Child-SP          RetAddr           Call Site
```

```
00 000000d0`bc4ff730 00007ff7`0e531301    AppD6!StartModeling+0x3d
01 000000d0`bc4ff770 00007ffc`6a731cac    AppD6!WndProc+0xb1
02 000000d0`bc4ff830 00007ffc`6a730f06    USER32!UserCallWinProcCheckWow+0x33c
03 000000d0`bc4ff9a0 00007ff7`0e5310d0    USER32!DispatchMessageWorker+0x2a6
04 000000d0`bc4ffa20 00007ff7`0e5317aa    AppD6!wWinMain+0xd0
05 (Inline Function) --------`--------    AppD6!invoke_main+0x21
06 000000d0`bc4ffa90 00007ffc`6a6753e0    AppD6!__scrt_common_main_seh+0x106
07 000000d0`bc4ffad0 00007ffc`6b18485b    KERNEL32!BaseThreadInitThunk+0x10
08 000000d0`bc4ffb00 00000000`00000000    ntdll!RtlUserThreadStart+0x2b
```

16.   We now clear all breakpoints and resume seeing CPU consumption in the VM:

```
2: kd> bc *
```

```
2: kd> bl
```

```
2: kd> g
```

17.   We break in again to inspect the *AppD6* thread (we get its address, ffffbb8b95d18080, from the output of the !process command we did previously):

```
Break instruction exception - code 80000003 (first chance)
***************************************************************************
*                                                                         *
*     You are seeing this message because you pressed either              *
*         CTRL+C (if you run console kernel debugger) or,                  *
*         CTRL+BREAK (if you run GUI kernel debugger),                     *
*     on your debugger machine's keyboard.                                 *
*                                                                         *
*                    THIS IS NOT A BUG OR A SYSTEM CRASH                   *
*                                                                         *
* If you did not intend to break into the debugger, press the "g" key, then *
* press the "Enter" key now.  This message might immediately reappear.  If it *
* does, press "g" and "Enter" again.                                       *
*                                                                         *
***************************************************************************
nt!DbgBreakPointWithStatus:
fffff807`086279f0 int     3
```

```
0: kd> !thread ffffa6879ba5a080 1f
THREAD ffffa6879ba5a080  Cid 1020.1ad0  Teb: 000000c99835b000 Win32Thread: ffffa6879cf87350 RUNNING on processor 3
Not impersonating
DeviceMap                 ffff9480ee9bd8b0
Owning Process            ffffa6879b9780c0        Image:         AppD6.exe
Attached Process          N/A               Image:         N/A
Wait Start TickCount      51579             Ticks: 12 (0:00:00.187)
Context Switch Count      47321             IdealProcessor: 2
UserTime                  00:00:39.546
KernelTime                00:00:27.921
*** WARNING: Unable to verify checksum for AppD6.exe
Win32 Start Address AppD6!wWinMainCRTStartup (0x00007ff7e0231818)
Stack Init ffffc786f141bc70 Current ffffc786f141b680
Base ffffc786f141c000 Limit ffffc786f1416000 Call 0000000000000000
Priority 8 BasePriority 8 PriorityDecrement 0 IoPriority 2 PagePriority 5
Child-SP          RetAddr           Call Site
00000000`00000000 00000000`00000000   nt!KiKernelSysretExit+0x56
```

Note: We see this thread accumulated user and kernel times.

18.   We now resume (**g** command) and quit WinDbg.

Exercise KD9

◎ **Goal:** Learn how to debug a 32-bit process under x64 Windows

◎ **Elementary Diagnostics Patterns:** Hang

◎ **Memory Analysis Patterns:** Virtualized Process; Debugger Bug; Execution Residue (Unmanaged Space, User); Rough Stack Trace (Unmanaged Space); Message Box; String Parameter; Near Exception

◎ **Debugging Implementation Patterns:** Break-in

◎ \AWD4\Exercise-KD9.pdf

Goal: Learn how to debug a 32-bit process under x64 Windows.

Elementary Diagnostics Patterns: Hang.

Memory Analysis Patterns: Virtualized Process (WOW64); Debugger Bug; Execution Residue (Unmanaged Space, User); Rough Stack Trace (Unmanaged Space); Message Box; String Parameter; Near Exception.

Debugging Implementation Patterns: Break-in.

1.   Power your Guest OS VM and copy the \AWD4\AppD9 folder to your VM to the same location (C:\AWD4\).

2.   Run WinDbg on your host and set up a kernel debugging connection as recommended in Exercise KD0. We get this output in WinDbg:

```
Microsoft (R) Windows Debugger Version 10.0.25921.1001 AMD64
Copyright (c) Microsoft Corporation. All rights reserved.

Using NET for debugging
Opened WinSock 2.0
Waiting to reconnect...
Connected to target 172.30.30.138 on port 50005 on local IP 172.30.16.1.
You can get the target MAC address by running .kdtargetmac command.
```

3.   Switch to the Guest VM, Launch \AWD4\AppD9\Release\AppD9.exe executable, and choose *File \ Start* menu. The application should hang. Mute Guest VM sound if you hear beeps.

4.   Break in via the *Break* button. We should get this output:

```
Kernel Debugger connection established.

************ Path validation summary **************
Response                     Time (ms)     Location
Deferred                                   srv*
Symbol search path is: srv*
Executable search path is:
Windows 10 Kernel Version 22000 MP (4 procs) Free x64
Product: WinNt, suite: TerminalServer SingleUserTS
Edition build lab: 22000.1.amd64fre.co_release.210604-1628
Kernel base = 0xfffff802`5f400000 PsLoadedModuleList = 0xfffff802`600297b0
Debug session time: Fri Feb  9 11:59:35.507 2024 (UTC + 0:00)
System Uptime: 0 days 0:02:24.469
Break instruction exception - code 80000003 (first chance)
*******************************************************************************
*                                                                             *
*    You are seeing this message because you pressed either                   *
*        CTRL+C (if you run console kernel debugger) or,                       *
*        CTRL+BREAK (if you run GUI kernel debugger),                          *
*    on your debugger machine's keyboard.                                      *
*                                                                             *
*                    THIS IS NOT A BUG OR A SYSTEM CRASH                       *
*                                                                             *
```

```
* If you did not intend to break into the debugger, press the "g" key, then   *
* press the "Enter" key now.  This message might immediately reappear.  If it *
* does, press "g" and "Enter" again.                                          *
*                                                                             *
*******************************************************************************
nt!DbgBreakPointWithStatus:
fffff802`5f8279f0 int     3
```

5.   Open a log file and set up symbols:

```
0: kd> .logopen c:\AWD4\KD9.log
Opened log file 'c:\AWD4\KD9.log'
```

```
0: kd> .reload
Connected to Windows 10 22000 x64 target at (Fri Feb  9 12:08:40.993 2024 (UTC + 0:00)), ptr64
TRUE
Loading Kernel Symbols
.............................................................
.............................................................
.........................................
Loading User Symbols

Loading unloaded module list
...........
```

6.   We now find the *AppD9.exe* process using the **!process** command:

```
0: kd> !process 0 0 AppD9.exe
PROCESS ffffc0834b2d60c0
    SessionId: 1  Cid: 1f44    Peb: 006bb000  ParentCid: 0da4
    DirBase: c2f60002  ObjectTable: ffff800c3b703cc0  HandleCount: 165.
    Image: AppD9.exe
```

7.   Let's check *AppD9* thread stack traces:

```
0: kd> !process ffffc0834b2d60c0 3f
PROCESS ffffc0834b2d60c0
    SessionId: 1  Cid: 1f44    Peb: 006bb000  ParentCid: 0da4
    DirBase: c2f60002  ObjectTable: ffff800c3b703cc0  HandleCount: 165.
    Image: AppD9.exe
    VadRoot ffffc08345baeaa0 Vads 97 Clone 0 Private 372. Modified 66. Locked 0.
    DeviceMap ffff800c3a104af0
    Token                             ffff800c3d464060
    ElapsedTime                       00:00:22.838
    UserTime                          00:00:00.000
    KernelTime                        00:00:00.000
    QuotaPoolUsage[PagedPool]         189328
    QuotaPoolUsage[NonPagedPool]      13448
    Working Set Sizes (now,min,max)  (3058, 50, 345) (12232KB, 200KB, 1380KB)
    PeakWorkingSetSize                3001
    VirtualSize                       102 Mb
    PeakVirtualSize                   103 Mb
    PageFaultCount                    3125
    MemoryPriority                    FOREGROUND
    BasePriority                      8
    CommitCharge                      464
    Job                               ffffc0834a9e66b0

    PEB at 00000000006bb000
    InheritedAddressSpace:    No
    ReadImageFileExecOptions: No
```

```
     BeingDebugged:                No
     ImageBaseAddress:             00000000001d0000
     NtGlobalFlag:                 0
     NtGlobalFlag2:                0
     Ldr                           00007ffb45d1a140
     Ldr.Initialized:              Yes
     Ldr.InInitializationOrderModuleList: 00000000009e1fc0 . 00000000009e76d0
     Ldr.InLoadOrderModuleList:            00000000009e2140 . 00000000009e76b0
     Ldr.InMemoryOrderModuleList:          00000000009e2150 . 00000000009e76c0
           Base TimeStamp                        Module
         1d0000 6280bdc1 May 15 09:45:53 2022 C:\AWD4\AppD9\Release\AppD9.exe
     7ffb45ba0000 5179e735 Apr 26 03:32:21 2013 C:\WINDOWS\SYSTEM32\ntdll.dll
     7ffb456d0000 11c42f91 Jun 12 22:11:45 1979 C:\WINDOWS\System32\wow64.dll
     7ffb45340000 6bee9450 May 20 08:20:48 2027 C:\WINDOWS\System32\wow64base.dll
     7ffb44ea0000 65371bce Oct 24 02:20:14 2023 C:\WINDOWS\System32\wow64win.dll
     7ffb452b0000 4ef46b95 Dec 23 11:52:53 2011 C:\WINDOWS\System32\wow64con.dll
         775f0000 99d19ede Oct 11 16:42:22 2051 C:\WINDOWS\System32\wow64cpu.dll
     SubSystemData:      0000000000000000
     ProcessHeap:        00000000009e0000
     ProcessParameters:  00000000009e64c0
     CurrentDirectory:   'C:\WINDOWS\'
     WindowTitle:   'C:\AWD4\AppD9\Release\AppD9.exe'
     ImageFile:     'C:\AWD4\AppD9\Release\AppD9.exe'
     CommandLine:   '"C:\AWD4\AppD9\Release\AppD9.exe" '
     DllPath:       '< Name not readable >'
     Environment:   00000000009e11f0
         =::=::\
         ALLUSERSPROFILE=C:\ProgramData
         APPDATA=C:\Users\User\AppData\Roaming
         CommonProgramFiles=C:\Program Files\Common Files
         CommonProgramFiles(x86)=C:\Program Files (x86)\Common Files
         CommonProgramW6432=C:\Program Files\Common Files
         COMPUTERNAME=WINDEV2204EVAL
         ComSpec=C:\WINDOWS\system32\cmd.exe
         DriverData=C:\Windows\System32\Drivers\DriverData
         HOMEDRIVE=C:
         HOMEPATH=\Users\User
         LOCALAPPDATA=C:\Users\User\AppData\Local
         LOGONSERVER=\\WINDEV2204EVAL
         NUMBER_OF_PROCESSORS=4
         OneDrive=C:\Users\User\OneDrive
         OS=Windows_NT
Path=C:\Windows\system32;C:\Windows;C:\Windows\System32\Wbem;C:\Windows\System32\WindowsPowerShell\v1.0\;C:\Windows\Sy
stem32\OpenSSH\;C:\Program Files\Microsoft SQL Server\150\Tools\Binn\;C:\Program Files\Microsoft SQL Server\Client
SDK\ODBC\170\Tools\Binn\;C:\Program
Files\dotnet\;C:\Users\User\AppData\Local\Microsoft\WindowsApps;C:\Users\User\.dotnet\tools
         PATHEXT=.COM;.EXE;.BAT;.CMD;.VBS;.VBE;.JS;.JSE;.WSF;.WSH;.MSC
         PROCESSOR_ARCHITECTURE=AMD64
         PROCESSOR_IDENTIFIER=Intel64 Family 6 Model 142 Stepping 10, GenuineIntel
         PROCESSOR_LEVEL=6
         PROCESSOR_REVISION=8e0a
         ProgramData=C:\ProgramData
         ProgramFiles=C:\Program Files
         ProgramFiles(x86)=C:\Program Files (x86)
         ProgramW6432=C:\Program Files
         PSModulePath=C:\Program Files\WindowsPowerShell\Modules;C:\WINDOWS\system32\WindowsPowerShell\v1.0\Modules
         PUBLIC=C:\Users\Public
         SESSIONNAME=Console
         SystemDrive=C:
         SystemRoot=C:\WINDOWS
         TEMP=C:\Users\User\AppData\Local\Temp
         TMP=C:\Users\User\AppData\Local\Temp
         USERDOMAIN=WINDEV2204EVAL
         USERDOMAIN_ROAMINGPROFILE=WINDEV2204EVAL
         USERNAME=User
         USERPROFILE=C:\Users\User
         windir=C:\WINDOWS


     THREAD ffffc0834aee2080  Cid 1f44.1b10  Teb: 00000000006bd000 Win32Thread: ffffc0834aabeb40 WAIT:
(DelayExecution) UserMode Non-Alertable
             ffffffffffffffff  NotificationEvent
         Not impersonating
```

```
        DeviceMap                     ffff800c3a104af0
        Owning Process                ffffc0834b2d60c0          Image:          AppD9.exe
        Attached Process              N/A          Image:          N/A
        Wait Start TickCount          15632        Ticks: 14 (0:00:00:00.218)
        Context Switch Count          1480         IdealProcessor: 2
        UserTime                      00:00:00.031
        KernelTime                    00:00:00.140
*** WARNING: Unable to verify checksum for AppD9.exe
        Win32 Start Address AppD9 (0x00000000001d15e1)
        Stack Init ffffac07ac5bfc70 Current ffffac07ac5bf720
        Base ffffac07ac5c0000 Limit ffffac07ac5ba000 Call 0000000000000000
        Priority 12 BasePriority 8 PriorityDecrement 2 IoPriority 2 PagePriority 5

        Child-SP          RetAddr               Call Site
        ffffac07`ac5bf760 fffff802`5f742277     nt!KiSwapContext+0x76
        ffffac07`ac5bf8a0 fffff802`5f744129     nt!KiSwapThread+0x3a7
        ffffac07`ac5bf980 fffff802`5f748246     nt!KiCommitThreadWait+0x159
        ffffac07`ac5bfa20 fffff802`5fbad48f     nt!KeDelayExecutionThread+0x416
        ffffac07`ac5bfab0 fffff802`5f832485     nt!NtDelayExecution+0x5f
        ffffac07`ac5bfae0 00000000`775f1cf3     nt!KiSystemServiceCopyEnd+0x25 (TrapFrame @ ffffac07`ac5bfae0)
        00000000`0085e678 00000000`775f1bd2     wow64cpu!CpupSyscallStub+0x13
        00000000`0085e680 00000000`775f1d75     wow64cpu!Thunk2ArgNSpNSpReloadState+0xc
        00000000`0085e730 00007ffb`456de06d     wow64cpu!BTCpuSimulate+0xbb5
        00000000`0085e770 00007ffb`456dd8ad     wow64!RunCpuSimulation+0xd
        00000000`0085e7a0 00007ffb`45c7f7ae     wow64!Wow64LdrpInitialize+0x12d
        00000000`0085ea50 00007ffb`45c6d706     ntdll!LdrpInitializeProcess+0x16c2
        00000000`0085ee10 00007ffb`45c1ae53     ntdll!_LdrpInitialize+0x5287a
        00000000`0085ee90 00007ffb`45c1ad7e     ntdll!LdrpInitializeInternal+0x6b
        00000000`0085f110 00000000`00000000     ntdll!LdrInitializeThunk+0xe

        THREAD ffffc0834474e080  Cid 1f44.1fa0  Teb: 00000000006c1000 Win32Thread: 0000000000000000 WAIT: (WrQueue)
UserMode Alertable
            ffffc08345a17340  QueueObject
        Not impersonating
        DeviceMap                     ffff800c3a104af0
        Owning Process                ffffc0834b2d60c0          Image:          AppD9.exe
        Attached Process              N/A          Image:          N/A
        Wait Start TickCount          14342        Ticks: 1304 (0:00:00:20.375)
        Context Switch Count          17           IdealProcessor: 1
        UserTime                      00:00:00.000
        KernelTime                    00:00:00.000
        Win32 Start Address 0x00000000776317b0
        Stack Init ffffac07aa53ac70 Current ffffac07aa53a370
        Base ffffac07aa53b000 Limit ffffac07aa535000 Call 0000000000000000
        Priority 10 BasePriority 8 PriorityDecrement 2 IoPriority 2 PagePriority 5
        Child-SP          RetAddr               Call Site
        ffffac07`aa53a3b0 fffff802`5f742277     nt!KiSwapContext+0x76
        ffffac07`aa53a4f0 fffff802`5f744129     nt!KiSwapThread+0x3a7
        ffffac07`aa53a5d0 fffff802`5f746fe6     nt!KiCommitThreadWait+0x159
        ffffac07`aa53a670 fffff802`5f7469f8     nt!KeRemoveQueueEx+0x2b6
        ffffac07`aa53a720 fffff802`5f749cb4     nt!IoRemoveIoCompletion+0x98
        ffffac07`aa53a840 fffff802`5f832485     nt!NtWaitForWorkViaWorkerFactory+0xdf4
        ffffac07`aa53aa70 00007ffb`45c47824     nt!KiSystemServiceCopyEnd+0x25 (TrapFrame @ ffffac07`aa53aae0)
        00000000`00c9e5f8 00007ffb`456da76a     ntdll!NtWaitForWorkViaWorkerFactory+0x14
        00000000`00c9e600 00007ffb`456d77ca     wow64!whNtWaitForWorkViaWorkerFactory+0x11a
        00000000`00c9e690 00000000`775f17ba     wow64!Wow64SystemServiceEx+0x15a
        00000000`00c9ef50 00000000`775f1d75     wow64cpu!ServiceNoTurbo+0xb
        00000000`00c9f000 00007ffb`456de06d     wow64cpu!BTCpuSimulate+0xbb5
        00000000`00c9f040 00007ffb`456dd8ad     wow64!RunCpuSimulation+0xd
        00000000`00c9f070 00007ffb`45c1af68     wow64!Wow64LdrpInitialize+0x12d
        00000000`00c9f320 00007ffb`45c1ae53     ntdll!_LdrpInitialize+0xdc
        00000000`00c9f3a0 00007ffb`45c1ad7e     ntdll!LdrpInitializeInternal+0x6b
        00000000`00c9f620 00000000`00000000     ntdll!LdrInitializeThunk+0xe

        THREAD ffffc0834777f080  Cid 1f44.05c4  Teb: 00000000006c5000 Win32Thread: 0000000000000000 WAIT: (WrQueue)
UserMode Alertable
            ffffc08345a17340  QueueObject
        Not impersonating
        DeviceMap                     ffff800c3a104af0
        Owning Process                ffffc0834b2d60c0          Image:          AppD9.exe
        Attached Process              N/A          Image:          N/A
        Wait Start TickCount          14197        Ticks: 1449 (0:00:00:22.640)
        Context Switch Count          9            IdealProcessor: 3
        UserTime                      00:00:00.000
```

```
        KernelTime                    00:00:00.000
        Win32 Start Address 0x00000000776317b0
        Stack Init ffffac07aa556c70 Current ffffac07aa556370
        Base ffffac07aa557000 Limit ffffac07aa551000 Call 0000000000000000
        Priority 10 BasePriority 8 PriorityDecrement 2 IoPriority 2 PagePriority 5
        Child-SP          RetAddr           Call Site
        ffffac07`aa5563b0 fffff802`5f742277 nt!KiSwapContext+0x76
        ffffac07`aa5564f0 fffff802`5f744129 nt!KiSwapThread+0x3a7
        ffffac07`aa5565d0 fffff802`5f746fe6 nt!KiCommitThreadWait+0x159
        ffffac07`aa556670 fffff802`5f7469f8 nt!KeRemoveQueueEx+0x2b6
        ffffac07`aa556720 fffff802`5f749cb4 nt!IoRemoveIoCompletion+0x98
        ffffac07`aa556840 fffff802`5f832485 nt!NtWaitForWorkViaWorkerFactory+0xdf4
        ffffac07`aa556a70 00007ffb`45c47824 nt!KiSystemServiceCopyEnd+0x25 (TrapFrame @ ffffac07`aa556ae0)
        00000000`00dde2b8 00007ffb`456da76a ntdll!NtWaitForWorkViaWorkerFactory+0x14
        00000000`00dde2c0 00007ffb`456d77ca wow64!whNtWaitForWorkViaWorkerFactory+0x11a
        00000000`00dde350 00007ffb`775f17ba wow64!Wow64SystemServiceEx+0x15a
        00000000`00ddec10 00000000`775f1d75 wow64cpu!ServiceNoTurbo+0xb
        00000000`00ddecc0 00007ffb`456de06d wow64cpu!BTCpuSimulate+0xbb5
        00000000`00dded00 00007ffb`456dd8ad wow64!RunCpuSimulation+0xd
        00000000`00dded30 00007ffb`45c1af68 wow64!Wow64LdrpInitialize+0x12d
        00000000`00ddefe0 00007ffb`45c1ae53 ntdll!_LdrpInitialize+0xdc
        00000000`00ddf060 00007ffb`45c1ad7e ntdll!LdrpInitializeInternal+0x6b
        00000000`00ddf2e0 00000000`00000000 ntdll!LdrInitializeThunk+0xe

        THREAD ffffc0834a150080  Cid 1f44.1fcc  Teb: 00000000006c9000 Win32Thread: 0000000000000000 WAIT: (WrQueue)
UserMode Alertable
          ffffc08345a17340   QueueObject
        Not impersonating
        DeviceMap                     ffff800c3a104af0
        Owning Process                ffffc0834b2d60c0      Image:          AppD9.exe
        Attached Process     N/A                  Image:         N/A
        Wait Start TickCount 14197                Ticks: 1449 (0:00:00:22.640)
        Context Switch Count 2                    IdealProcessor: 0
        UserTime             00:00:00.000
        KernelTime           00:00:00.000
        Win32 Start Address 0x00000000776317b0
        Stack Init ffffac07aa572c70 Current ffffac07aa572370
        Base ffffac07aa573000 Limit ffffac07aa56d000 Call 0000000000000000
        Priority 10 BasePriority 8 PriorityDecrement 2 IoPriority 2 PagePriority 5

        Child-SP          RetAddr           Call Site
        ffffac07`aa5723b0 fffff802`5f742277 nt!KiSwapContext+0x76
        ffffac07`aa5724f0 fffff802`5f744129 nt!KiSwapThread+0x3a7
        ffffac07`aa5725d0 fffff802`5f746fe6 nt!KiCommitThreadWait+0x159
        ffffac07`aa572670 fffff802`5f7469f8 nt!KeRemoveQueueEx+0x2b6
        ffffac07`aa572720 fffff802`5f749cb4 nt!IoRemoveIoCompletion+0x98
        ffffac07`aa572840 fffff802`5f832485 nt!NtWaitForWorkViaWorkerFactory+0xdf4
        ffffac07`aa572a70 00007ffb`45c47824 nt!KiSystemServiceCopyEnd+0x25 (TrapFrame @ ffffac07`aa572ae0)
        00000000`00f1e088 00007ffb`456da76a ntdll!NtWaitForWorkViaWorkerFactory+0x14
        00000000`00f1e090 00007ffb`456d77ca wow64!whNtWaitForWorkViaWorkerFactory+0x11a
        00000000`00f1e120 00000000`775f17ba wow64!Wow64SystemServiceEx+0x15a
        00000000`00f1e9e0 00000000`775f1d75 wow64cpu!ServiceNoTurbo+0xb
        00000000`00f1ea90 00007ffb`456de06d wow64cpu!BTCpuSimulate+0xbb5
        00000000`00f1ead0 00007ffb`456dd8ad wow64!RunCpuSimulation+0xd
        00000000`00f1eb00 00007ffb`45c1af68 wow64!Wow64LdrpInitialize+0x12d
        00000000`00f1edb0 00007ffb`45c1ae53 ntdll!_LdrpInitialize+0xdc
        00000000`00f1ee30 00007ffb`45c1ad7e ntdll!LdrpInitializeInternal+0x6b
        00000000`00f1f0b0 00000000`00000000 ntdll!LdrInitializeThunk+0xe
```

Note: We only see the WOW64 modules and not our actual *AppD9* module because the process is 32-bit.

8.   If we switch to our thread **ffffc0834aee2080** in x86 mode (**.thread /w** command) and reload user space symbols, we won't see stack traces due to a possible bug in the current WinDbg engine implementation:

```
0: kd> .thread /w ffffc0834aee2080
Implicit thread is now ffffc083`4aee2080
WARNING: WOW context retrieval requires
switching to the thread's process context.
Use .process /p ffffc083`43ae2040 to switch back.
```

```
Implicit process is now ffffc083`4b2d60c0
.cache forcedecodeuser done
The context is partially valid. Only x86 user-mode context is available.
x86 context set
```

```
0: kd:x86> .reload /user
Loading User Symbols
.......
Loading Wow64 Symbols
..........................
```

```
0: kd:x86> k
  *** Stack trace for last set context - .thread/.cxr resets it
 # ChildEBP          RetAddr
WARNING: Frame IP not in any known module. Following frames may be wrong.
00 ac5bf919 00000000      0x5f826c96
```

9.   In the previous versions of WinDbg, we could see a long recursion of *MessageBox* calls:

```
0: kd:x86> k 0xfff
 # ChildEBP          RetAddr
00 006f5794 75f1350b ntdll_77b50000!NtDelayExecution+0xc
01 006f57fc 75f1345f KERNELBASE!SleepEx+0x9b
02 006f580c 0097138e KERNELBASE!Sleep+0xf
03 006f5818 00971338 AppD9!ConnectDB+0xe [c:\awd3\appd9\appd9\connectdb.cpp @ 6]
04 006f5820 0097121a AppD9!StartModeling+0x8 [c:\awd3\appd9\appd9\appd9.cpp @ 193]
05 006f5880 75cabe6b AppD9!WndProc+0x7a [c:\awd3\appd9\appd9\appd9.cpp @ 146]
06 006f58ac 75ca833a USER32!_InternalCallWinProc+0x2b
07 006f5994 75ca7bee USER32!UserCallWinProcCheckWow+0x3aa
08 006f5a10 75c89085 USER32!DispatchMessageWorker+0x20e
09 006f5a50 75c84b0a USER32!DialogBox2+0x184
0a 006f5a80 75ce8a17 USER32!InternalDialogBox+0xdf
0b 006f5b54 75ce78a0 USER32!SoftModalMessageBox+0x727
0c 006f5cb8 75ce8295 USER32!MessageBoxWorker+0x2a8
0d 006f5d40 75ce82da USER32!MessageBoxTimeoutW+0x165
0e 006f5d60 00971371 USER32!MessageBoxW+0x1a
0f 006f5d78 0097121a AppD9!StartModeling+0x41 [c:\awd3\appd9\appd9\appd9.cpp @ 198]
10 006f5dd8 75cabe6b AppD9!WndProc+0x7a [c:\awd3\appd9\appd9\appd9.cpp @ 146]
11 006f5e04 75ca833a USER32!_InternalCallWinProc+0x2b
12 006f5eec 75ca7bee USER32!UserCallWinProcCheckWow+0x3aa
13 006f5f68 75c89085 USER32!DispatchMessageWorker+0x20e
14 006f5fa8 75c84b0a USER32!DialogBox2+0x184
15 006f5fd8 75ce8a17 USER32!InternalDialogBox+0xdf
16 006f60ac 75ce78a0 USER32!SoftModalMessageBox+0x727
17 006f6210 75ce8295 USER32!MessageBoxWorker+0x2a8
18 006f6298 75ce82da USER32!MessageBoxTimeoutW+0x165
19 006f62b8 00971371 USER32!MessageBoxW+0x1a
1a 006f62d0 0097121a AppD9!StartModeling+0x41 [c:\awd3\appd9\appd9\appd9.cpp @ 198]
1b 006f6330 75cabe6b AppD9!WndProc+0x7a [c:\awd3\appd9\appd9\appd9.cpp @ 146]
1c 006f635c 75ca833a USER32!_InternalCallWinProc+0x2b
1d 006f6444 75ca7bee USER32!UserCallWinProcCheckWow+0x3aa
1e 006f64c0 75c89085 USER32!DispatchMessageWorker+0x20e
1f 006f6500 75c84b0a USER32!DialogBox2+0x184
20 006f6530 75ce8a17 USER32!InternalDialogBox+0xdf
21 006f6604 75ce78a0 USER32!SoftModalMessageBox+0x727
22 006f6768 75ce8295 USER32!MessageBoxWorker+0x2a8
23 006f67f0 75ce82da USER32!MessageBoxTimeoutW+0x165
24 006f6810 00971371 USER32!MessageBoxW+0x1a
25 006f6828 0097121a AppD9!StartModeling+0x41 [c:\awd3\appd9\appd9\appd9.cpp @ 198]
26 006f6888 75cabe6b AppD9!WndProc+0x7a [c:\awd3\appd9\appd9\appd9.cpp @ 146]
27 006f68b4 75ca833a USER32!_InternalCallWinProc+0x2b
28 006f699c 75ca7bee USER32!UserCallWinProcCheckWow+0x3aa
29 006f6a18 75c89085 USER32!DispatchMessageWorker+0x20e
2a 006f6a58 75c84b0a USER32!DialogBox2+0x184
2b 006f6a88 75ce8a17 USER32!InternalDialogBox+0xdf
2c 006f6b5c 75ce78a0 USER32!SoftModalMessageBox+0x727
2d 006f6cc0 75ce8295 USER32!MessageBoxWorker+0x2a8
2e 006f6d48 75ce82da USER32!MessageBoxTimeoutW+0x165
```

```
2f 006f6d68 00971371 USER32!MessageBoxW+0x1a
30 006f6d80 0097121a AppD9!StartModeling+0x41 [c:\awd3\appd9\appd9\appd9.cpp @ 198]
31 006f6de0 75cabe6b AppD9!WndProc+0x7a [c:\awd3\appd9\appd9\appd9.cpp @ 146]
32 006f6e0c 75ca833a USER32!_InternalCallWinProc+0x2b
33 006f6ef4 75ca7bee USER32!UserCallWinProcCheckWow+0x3aa
34 006f6f70 75c89085 USER32!DispatchMessageWorker+0x20e
35 006f6fb0 75c84b0a USER32!DialogBox2+0x184
36 006f6fe0 75ce8a17 USER32!InternalDialogBox+0xdf
37 006f70b4 75ce78a0 USER32!SoftModalMessageBox+0x727
38 006f7218 75ce8295 USER32!MessageBoxWorker+0x2a8
39 006f72a0 75ce82da USER32!MessageBoxTimeoutW+0x165
3a 006f72c0 00971371 USER32!MessageBoxW+0x1a
3b 006f72d8 0097121a AppD9!StartModeling+0x41 [c:\awd3\appd9\appd9\appd9.cpp @ 198]
3c 006f7338 75cabe6b AppD9!WndProc+0x7a [c:\awd3\appd9\appd9\appd9.cpp @ 146]
3d 006f7364 75ca833a USER32!_InternalCallWinProc+0x2b
3e 006f744c 75ca7bee USER32!UserCallWinProcCheckWow+0x3aa
3f 006f74c8 75c89085 USER32!DispatchMessageWorker+0x20e
40 006f7508 75c84b0a USER32!DialogBox2+0x184
41 006f7538 75ce8a17 USER32!InternalDialogBox+0xdf
42 006f760c 75ce78a0 USER32!SoftModalMessageBox+0x727
43 006f7770 75ce8295 USER32!MessageBoxWorker+0x2a8
44 006f77f8 75ce82da USER32!MessageBoxTimeoutW+0x165
45 006f7818 00971371 USER32!MessageBoxW+0x1a
46 006f7830 0097121a AppD9!StartModeling+0x41 [c:\awd3\appd9\appd9\appd9.cpp @ 198]
47 006f7890 75cabe6b AppD9!WndProc+0x7a [c:\awd3\appd9\appd9\appd9.cpp @ 146]
48 006f78bc 75ca833a USER32!_InternalCallWinProc+0x2b
49 006f79a4 75ca7bee USER32!UserCallWinProcCheckWow+0x3aa
4a 006f7a20 75c89085 USER32!DispatchMessageWorker+0x20e
4b 006f7a60 75c84b0a USER32!DialogBox2+0x184
4c 006f7a90 75ce8a17 USER32!InternalDialogBox+0xdf
4d 006f7b64 75ce78a0 USER32!SoftModalMessageBox+0x727
4e 006f7cc8 75ce8295 USER32!MessageBoxWorker+0x2a8
4f 006f7d50 75ce82da USER32!MessageBoxTimeoutW+0x165
50 006f7d70 00971371 USER32!MessageBoxW+0x1a
51 006f7d88 0097121a AppD9!StartModeling+0x41 [c:\awd3\appd9\appd9\appd9.cpp @ 198]
52 006f7de8 75cabe6b AppD9!WndProc+0x7a [c:\awd3\appd9\appd9\appd9.cpp @ 146]
53 006f7e14 75ca833a USER32!_InternalCallWinProc+0x2b
54 006f7efc 75ca7bee USER32!UserCallWinProcCheckWow+0x3aa
55 006f7f78 75c89085 USER32!DispatchMessageWorker+0x20e
56 006f7fb8 75c84b0a USER32!DialogBox2+0x184
57 006f7fe8 75ce8a17 USER32!InternalDialogBox+0xdf
58 006f80bc 75ce78a0 USER32!SoftModalMessageBox+0x727
59 006f8220 75ce8295 USER32!MessageBoxWorker+0x2a8
5a 006f82a8 75ce82da USER32!MessageBoxTimeoutW+0x165
5b 006f82c8 00971371 USER32!MessageBoxW+0x1a
5c 006f82e0 0097121a AppD9!StartModeling+0x41 [c:\awd3\appd9\appd9\appd9.cpp @ 198]
5d 006f8340 75cabe6b AppD9!WndProc+0x7a [c:\awd3\appd9\appd9\appd9.cpp @ 146]
5e 006f836c 75ca833a USER32!_InternalCallWinProc+0x2b
5f 006f8454 75ca7bee USER32!UserCallWinProcCheckWow+0x3aa
60 006f84d0 75c89085 USER32!DispatchMessageWorker+0x20e
61 006f8510 75c84b0a USER32!DialogBox2+0x184
62 006f8540 75ce8a17 USER32!InternalDialogBox+0xdf
63 006f8614 75ce78a0 USER32!SoftModalMessageBox+0x727
64 006f8778 75ce8295 USER32!MessageBoxWorker+0x2a8
65 006f8800 75ce82da USER32!MessageBoxTimeoutW+0x165
66 006f8820 00971371 USER32!MessageBoxW+0x1a
67 006f8838 0097121a AppD9!StartModeling+0x41 [c:\awd3\appd9\appd9\appd9.cpp @ 198]
68 006f8898 75cabe6b AppD9!WndProc+0x7a [c:\awd3\appd9\appd9\appd9.cpp @ 146]
69 006f88c4 75ca833a USER32!_InternalCallWinProc+0x2b
6a 006f89ac 75ca7bee USER32!UserCallWinProcCheckWow+0x3aa
6b 006f8a28 75c89085 USER32!DispatchMessageWorker+0x20e
6c 006f8a68 75c84b0a USER32!DialogBox2+0x184
6d 006f8a98 75ce8a17 USER32!InternalDialogBox+0xdf
6e 006f8b6c 75ce78a0 USER32!SoftModalMessageBox+0x727
6f 006f8cd0 75ce8295 USER32!MessageBoxWorker+0x2a8
70 006f8d58 75ce82da USER32!MessageBoxTimeoutW+0x165
71 006f8d78 00971371 USER32!MessageBoxW+0x1a
72 006f8d90 0097121a AppD9!StartModeling+0x41 [c:\awd3\appd9\appd9\appd9.cpp @ 198]
73 006f8df0 75cabe6b AppD9!WndProc+0x7a [c:\awd3\appd9\appd9\appd9.cpp @ 146]
74 006f8e1c 75ca833a USER32!_InternalCallWinProc+0x2b
75 006f8f04 75ca7bee USER32!UserCallWinProcCheckWow+0x3aa
76 006f8f80 75c89085 USER32!DispatchMessageWorker+0x20e
77 006f8fc0 75c84b0a USER32!DialogBox2+0x184
78 006f8ff0 75ce8a17 USER32!InternalDialogBox+0xdf
```

```
79 006f90c4 75ce78a0 USER32!SoftModalMessageBox+0x727
7a 006f9228 75ce8295 USER32!MessageBoxWorker+0x2a8
7b 006f92b0 75ce82da USER32!MessageBoxTimeoutW+0x165
7c 006f92d0 00971371 USER32!MessageBoxW+0x1a
7d 006f92e8 0097121a AppD9!StartModeling+0x41 [c:\awd3\appd9\appd9\appd9.cpp @ 198]
7e 006f9348 75cabe6b AppD9!WndProc+0x7a [c:\awd3\appd9\appd9\appd9.cpp @ 146]
7f 006f9374 75ca833a USER32!_InternalCallWinProc+0x2b
80 006f945c 75ca7bee USER32!UserCallWinProcCheckWow+0x3aa
81 006f94d8 75c89085 USER32!DispatchMessageWorker+0x20e
82 006f9518 75c84b0a USER32!DialogBox2+0x184
83 006f9548 75ce8a17 USER32!InternalDialogBox+0xdf
84 006f961c 75ce78a0 USER32!SoftModalMessageBox+0x727
85 006f9780 75ce8295 USER32!MessageBoxWorker+0x2a8
86 006f9808 75ce82da USER32!MessageBoxTimeoutW+0x165
87 006f9828 00971371 USER32!MessageBoxW+0x1a
88 006f9840 0097121a AppD9!StartModeling+0x41 [c:\awd3\appd9\appd9\appd9.cpp @ 198]
89 006f98a0 75cabe6b AppD9!WndProc+0x7a [c:\awd3\appd9\appd9\appd9.cpp @ 146]
8a 006f98cc 75ca833a USER32!_InternalCallWinProc+0x2b
8b 006f99b4 75ca7bee USER32!UserCallWinProcCheckWow+0x3aa
8c 006f9a30 75c89085 USER32!DispatchMessageWorker+0x20e
8d 006f9a70 75c84b0a USER32!DialogBox2+0x184
8e 006f9aa0 75ce8a17 USER32!InternalDialogBox+0xdf
8f 006f9b74 75ce78a0 USER32!SoftModalMessageBox+0x727
90 006f9cd8 75ce8295 USER32!MessageBoxWorker+0x2a8
91 006f9d60 75ce82da USER32!MessageBoxTimeoutW+0x165
92 006f9d80 00971371 USER32!MessageBoxW+0x1a
93 006f9d98 0097121a AppD9!StartModeling+0x41 [c:\awd3\appd9\appd9\appd9.cpp @ 198]
94 006f9df8 75cabe6b AppD9!WndProc+0x7a [c:\awd3\appd9\appd9\appd9.cpp @ 146]
95 006f9e24 75ca833a USER32!_InternalCallWinProc+0x2b
96 006f9f0c 75ca7bee USER32!UserCallWinProcCheckWow+0x3aa
97 006f9f88 75c89085 USER32!DispatchMessageWorker+0x20e
98 006f9fc8 75c84b0a USER32!DialogBox2+0x184
99 006f9ff8 75ce8a17 USER32!InternalDialogBox+0xdf
9a 006fa0cc 75ce78a0 USER32!SoftModalMessageBox+0x727
9b 006fa230 75ce8295 USER32!MessageBoxWorker+0x2a8
9c 006fa2b8 75ce82da USER32!MessageBoxTimeoutW+0x165
9d 006fa2d8 00971371 USER32!MessageBoxW+0x1a
9e 006fa2f0 0097121a AppD9!StartModeling+0x41 [c:\awd3\appd9\appd9\appd9.cpp @ 198]
9f 006fa350 75cabe6b AppD9!WndProc+0x7a [c:\awd3\appd9\appd9\appd9.cpp @ 146]
a0 006fa37c 75ca833a USER32!_InternalCallWinProc+0x2b
a1 006fa464 75ca7bee USER32!UserCallWinProcCheckWow+0x3aa
a2 006fa4e0 75c89085 USER32!DispatchMessageWorker+0x20e
a3 006fa520 75c84b0a USER32!DialogBox2+0x184
a4 006fa550 75ce8a17 USER32!InternalDialogBox+0xdf
a5 006fa624 75ce78a0 USER32!SoftModalMessageBox+0x727
a6 006fa788 75ce8295 USER32!MessageBoxWorker+0x2a8
a7 006fa810 75ce82da USER32!MessageBoxTimeoutW+0x165
a8 006fa830 00971371 USER32!MessageBoxW+0x1a
a9 006fa848 0097121a AppD9!StartModeling+0x41 [c:\awd3\appd9\appd9\appd9.cpp @ 198]
aa 006fa8a8 75cabe6b AppD9!WndProc+0x7a [c:\awd3\appd9\appd9\appd9.cpp @ 146]
ab 006fa8d4 75ca833a USER32!_InternalCallWinProc+0x2b
ac 006fa9bc 75ca7bee USER32!UserCallWinProcCheckWow+0x3aa
ad 006faa38 75c89085 USER32!DispatchMessageWorker+0x20e
ae 006faa78 75c84b0a USER32!DialogBox2+0x184
af 006faaa8 75ce8a17 USER32!InternalDialogBox+0xdf
b0 006fab7c 75ce78a0 USER32!SoftModalMessageBox+0x727
b1 006face0 75ce8295 USER32!MessageBoxWorker+0x2a8
b2 006fad68 75ce82da USER32!MessageBoxTimeoutW+0x165
b3 006fad88 00971371 USER32!MessageBoxW+0x1a
b4 006fada0 0097121a AppD9!StartModeling+0x41 [c:\awd3\appd9\appd9\appd9.cpp @ 198]
b5 006fae00 75cabe6b AppD9!WndProc+0x7a [c:\awd3\appd9\appd9\appd9.cpp @ 146]
b6 006fae2c 75ca833a USER32!_InternalCallWinProc+0x2b
b7 006faf14 75ca7bee USER32!UserCallWinProcCheckWow+0x3aa
b8 006faf90 75c89085 USER32!DispatchMessageWorker+0x20e
b9 006fafd0 75c84b0a USER32!DialogBox2+0x184
ba 006fb000 75ce8a17 USER32!InternalDialogBox+0xdf
bb 006fb0d4 75ce78a0 USER32!SoftModalMessageBox+0x727
bc 006fb238 75ce8295 USER32!MessageBoxWorker+0x2a8
bd 006fb2c0 75ce82da USER32!MessageBoxTimeoutW+0x165
be 006fb2e0 00971371 USER32!MessageBoxW+0x1a
bf 006fb2f8 0097121a AppD9!StartModeling+0x41 [c:\awd3\appd9\appd9\appd9.cpp @ 198]
c0 006fb358 75cabe6b AppD9!WndProc+0x7a [c:\awd3\appd9\appd9\appd9.cpp @ 146]
c1 006fb384 75ca833a USER32!_InternalCallWinProc+0x2b
c2 006fb46c 75ca7bee USER32!UserCallWinProcCheckWow+0x3aa
```

```
c3  006fb4e8 75c89085 USER32!DispatchMessageWorker+0x20e
c4  006fb528 75c84b0a USER32!DialogBox2+0x184
c5  006fb558 75ce8a17 USER32!InternalDialogBox+0xdf
c6  006fb62c 75ce78a0 USER32!SoftModalMessageBox+0x727
c7  006fb790 75ce8295 USER32!MessageBoxWorker+0x2a8
c8  006fb818 75ce82da USER32!MessageBoxTimeoutW+0x165
c9  006fb838 00971371 USER32!MessageBoxW+0x1a
ca  006fb850 0097121a AppD9!StartModeling+0x41 [c:\awd3\appd9\appd9\appd9.cpp @ 198]
cb  006fb8b0 75cabe6b AppD9!WndProc+0x7a [c:\awd3\appd9\appd9\appd9.cpp @ 146]
cc  006fb8dc 75ca833a USER32!_InternalCallWinProc+0x2b
cd  006fb9c4 75ca7bee USER32!UserCallWinProcCheckWow+0x3aa
ce  006fba40 75c89085 USER32!DispatchMessageWorker+0x20e
cf  006fba80 75c84b0a USER32!DialogBox2+0x184
d0  006fbab0 75ce8a17 USER32!InternalDialogBox+0xdf
d1  006fbb84 75ce78a0 USER32!SoftModalMessageBox+0x727
d2  006fbce8 75ce8295 USER32!MessageBoxWorker+0x2a8
d3  006fbd70 75ce82da USER32!MessageBoxTimeoutW+0x165
d4  006fbd90 00971371 USER32!MessageBoxW+0x1a
d5  006fbda8 0097121a AppD9!StartModeling+0x41 [c:\awd3\appd9\appd9\appd9.cpp @ 198]
d6  006fbe08 75cabe6b AppD9!WndProc+0x7a [c:\awd3\appd9\appd9\appd9.cpp @ 146]
d7  006fbe34 75ca833a USER32!_InternalCallWinProc+0x2b
d8  006fbf1c 75ca7bee USER32!UserCallWinProcCheckWow+0x3aa
d9  006fbf98 75c89085 USER32!DispatchMessageWorker+0x20e
da  006fbfd8 75c84b0a USER32!DialogBox2+0x184
db  006fc008 75ce8a17 USER32!InternalDialogBox+0xdf
dc  006fc0dc 75ce78a0 USER32!SoftModalMessageBox+0x727
dd  006fc240 75ce8295 USER32!MessageBoxWorker+0x2a8
de  006fc2c8 75ce82da USER32!MessageBoxTimeoutW+0x165
df  006fc2e8 00971371 USER32!MessageBoxW+0x1a
e0  006fc300 0097121a AppD9!StartModeling+0x41 [c:\awd3\appd9\appd9\appd9.cpp @ 198]
e1  006fc360 75cabe6b AppD9!WndProc+0x7a [c:\awd3\appd9\appd9\appd9.cpp @ 146]
e2  006fc38c 75ca833a USER32!_InternalCallWinProc+0x2b
e3  006fc474 75ca7bee USER32!UserCallWinProcCheckWow+0x3aa
e4  006fc4f0 75c89085 USER32!DispatchMessageWorker+0x20e
e5  006fc530 75c84b0a USER32!DialogBox2+0x184
e6  006fc560 75ce8a17 USER32!InternalDialogBox+0xdf
e7  006fc634 75ce78a0 USER32!SoftModalMessageBox+0x727
e8  006fc798 75ce8295 USER32!MessageBoxWorker+0x2a8
e9  006fc820 75ce82da USER32!MessageBoxTimeoutW+0x165
ea  006fc840 00971371 USER32!MessageBoxW+0x1a
eb  006fc858 0097121a AppD9!StartModeling+0x41 [c:\awd3\appd9\appd9\appd9.cpp @ 198]
ec  006fc8b8 75cabe6b AppD9!WndProc+0x7a [c:\awd3\appd9\appd9\appd9.cpp @ 146]
ed  006fc8e4 75ca833a USER32!_InternalCallWinProc+0x2b
ee  006fc9cc 75ca7bee USER32!UserCallWinProcCheckWow+0x3aa
ef  006fca48 75c89085 USER32!DispatchMessageWorker+0x20e
f0  006fca88 75c84b0a USER32!DialogBox2+0x184
f1  006fcab8 75ce8a17 USER32!InternalDialogBox+0xdf
f2  006fcb8c 75ce78a0 USER32!SoftModalMessageBox+0x727
f3  006fccf0 75ce8295 USER32!MessageBoxWorker+0x2a8
f4  006fcd78 75ce82da USER32!MessageBoxTimeoutW+0x165
f5  006fcd98 00971371 USER32!MessageBoxW+0x1a
f6  006fcdb0 0097121a AppD9!StartModeling+0x41 [c:\awd3\appd9\appd9\appd9.cpp @ 198]
f7  006fce10 75cabe6b AppD9!WndProc+0x7a [c:\awd3\appd9\appd9\appd9.cpp @ 146]
f8  006fce3c 75ca833a USER32!_InternalCallWinProc+0x2b
f9  006fcf24 75ca7bee USER32!UserCallWinProcCheckWow+0x3aa
fa  006fcfa0 75c89085 USER32!DispatchMessageWorker+0x20e
fb  006fcfe0 75c84b0a USER32!DialogBox2+0x184
fc  006fd010 75ce8a17 USER32!InternalDialogBox+0xdf
fd  006fd0e4 75ce78a0 USER32!SoftModalMessageBox+0x727
fe  006fd248 75ce8295 USER32!MessageBoxWorker+0x2a8
ff  006fd2d0 75ce82da USER32!MessageBoxTimeoutW+0x165
100 006fd2f0 00971371 USER32!MessageBoxW+0x1a
101 006fd308 0097121a AppD9!StartModeling+0x41 [c:\awd3\appd9\appd9\appd9.cpp @ 198]
102 006fd368 75cabe6b AppD9!WndProc+0x7a [c:\awd3\appd9\appd9\appd9.cpp @ 146]
103 006fd394 75ca833a USER32!_InternalCallWinProc+0x2b
104 006fd47c 75ca7bee USER32!UserCallWinProcCheckWow+0x3aa
105 006fd4f8 75c89085 USER32!DispatchMessageWorker+0x20e
106 006fd538 75c84b0a USER32!DialogBox2+0x184
107 006fd568 75ce8a17 USER32!InternalDialogBox+0xdf
108 006fd63c 75ce78a0 USER32!SoftModalMessageBox+0x727
109 006fd7a0 75ce8295 USER32!MessageBoxWorker+0x2a8
10a 006fd828 75ce82da USER32!MessageBoxTimeoutW+0x165
10b 006fd848 00971371 USER32!MessageBoxW+0x1a
10c 006fd860 0097121a AppD9!StartModeling+0x41 [c:\awd3\appd9\appd9\appd9.cpp @ 198]
```

```
10d 006fd8c0 75cabe6b AppD9!WndProc+0x7a [c:\awd3\appd9\appd9\appd9.cpp @ 146]
10e 006fd8ec 75ca833a USER32!_InternalCallWinProc+0x2b
10f 006fd9d4 75ca7bee USER32!UserCallWinProcCheckWow+0x3aa
110 006fda50 75c89085 USER32!DispatchMessageWorker+0x20e
111 006fda90 75c84b0a USER32!DialogBox2+0x184
112 006fdac0 75ce8a17 USER32!InternalDialogBox+0xdf
113 006fdb94 75ce78a0 USER32!SoftModalMessageBox+0x727
114 006fdcf8 75ce8295 USER32!MessageBoxWorker+0x2a8
115 006fdd80 75ce82da USER32!MessageBoxTimeoutW+0x165
116 006fdda0 00971371 USER32!MessageBoxW+0x1a
117 006fddb8 0097121a AppD9!StartModeling+0x41 [c:\awd3\appd9\appd9\appd9.cpp @ 198]
118 006fde18 75cabe6b AppD9!WndProc+0x7a [c:\awd3\appd9\appd9\appd9.cpp @ 146]
119 006fde44 75ca833a USER32!_InternalCallWinProc+0x2b
11a 006fdf2c 75ca7bee USER32!UserCallWinProcCheckWow+0x3aa
11b 006fdfa8 75c89085 USER32!DispatchMessageWorker+0x20e
11c 006fdfe8 75c84b0a USER32!DialogBox2+0x184
11d 006fe018 75ce8a17 USER32!InternalDialogBox+0xdf
11e 006fe0ec 75ce78a0 USER32!SoftModalMessageBox+0x727
11f 006fe250 75ce8295 USER32!MessageBoxWorker+0x2a8
120 006fe2d8 75ce82da USER32!MessageBoxTimeoutW+0x165
121 006fe2f8 00971371 USER32!MessageBoxW+0x1a
122 006fe310 0097121a AppD9!StartModeling+0x41 [c:\awd3\appd9\appd9\appd9.cpp @ 198]
123 006fe370 75cabe6b AppD9!WndProc+0x7a [c:\awd3\appd9\appd9\appd9.cpp @ 146]
124 006fe39c 75ca833a USER32!_InternalCallWinProc+0x2b
125 006fe484 75ca7bee USER32!UserCallWinProcCheckWow+0x3aa
126 006fe500 75c89085 USER32!DispatchMessageWorker+0x20e
127 006fe540 75c84b0a USER32!DialogBox2+0x184
128 006fe570 75ce8a17 USER32!InternalDialogBox+0xdf
129 006fe644 75ce78a0 USER32!SoftModalMessageBox+0x727
12a 006fe7a8 75ce8295 USER32!MessageBoxWorker+0x2a8
12b 006fe830 75ce82da USER32!MessageBoxTimeoutW+0x165
12c 006fe850 00971371 USER32!MessageBoxW+0x1a
12d 006fe868 0097121a AppD9!StartModeling+0x41 [c:\awd3\appd9\appd9\appd9.cpp @ 198]
12e 006fe8c8 75cabe6b AppD9!WndProc+0x7a [c:\awd3\appd9\appd9\appd9.cpp @ 146]
12f 006fe8f4 75ca833a USER32!_InternalCallWinProc+0x2b
130 006fe9dc 75ca7bee USER32!UserCallWinProcCheckWow+0x3aa
131 006fea58 75c89085 USER32!DispatchMessageWorker+0x20e
132 006fea98 75c84b0a USER32!DialogBox2+0x184
133 006feac8 75ce8a17 USER32!InternalDialogBox+0xdf
134 006feb9c 75ce78a0 USER32!SoftModalMessageBox+0x727
135 006fed00 75ce8295 USER32!MessageBoxWorker+0x2a8
136 006fed88 75ce82da USER32!MessageBoxTimeoutW+0x165
137 006feda8 00971371 USER32!MessageBoxW+0x1a
138 006fedc0 0097121a AppD9!StartModeling+0x41 [c:\awd3\appd9\appd9\appd9.cpp @ 198]
139 006fee20 75cabe6b AppD9!WndProc+0x7a [c:\awd3\appd9\appd9\appd9.cpp @ 146]
13a 006fee4c 75ca833a USER32!_InternalCallWinProc+0x2b
13b 006fef34 75ca7bee USER32!UserCallWinProcCheckWow+0x3aa
13c 006fefb0 75c89085 USER32!DispatchMessageWorker+0x20e
13d 006feff0 75c84b0a USER32!DialogBox2+0x184
13e 006ff020 75ce8a17 USER32!InternalDialogBox+0xdf
13f 006ff0f4 75ce78a0 USER32!SoftModalMessageBox+0x727
140 006ff258 75ce8295 USER32!MessageBoxWorker+0x2a8
141 006ff2e0 75ce82da USER32!MessageBoxTimeoutW+0x165
142 006ff300 00971371 USER32!MessageBoxW+0x1a
143 006ff318 0097121a AppD9!StartModeling+0x41 [c:\awd3\appd9\appd9\appd9.cpp @ 198]
144 006ff378 75cabe6b AppD9!WndProc+0x7a [c:\awd3\appd9\appd9\appd9.cpp @ 146]
145 006ff3a4 75ca833a USER32!_InternalCallWinProc+0x2b
146 006ff48c 75ca7bee USER32!UserCallWinProcCheckWow+0x3aa
147 006ff508 75c89085 USER32!DispatchMessageWorker+0x20e
148 006ff548 75c84b0a USER32!DialogBox2+0x184
149 006ff578 75ce8a17 USER32!InternalDialogBox+0xdf
14a 006ff64c 75ce78a0 USER32!SoftModalMessageBox+0x727
14b 006ff7b0 75ce8295 USER32!MessageBoxWorker+0x2a8
14c 006ff83c 75ce82da USER32!MessageBoxTimeoutW+0x165
14d 006ff85c 00971371 USER32!MessageBoxW+0x1a
14e 006ff874 0097121a AppD9!StartModeling+0x41 [c:\awd3\appd9\appd9\appd9.cpp @ 198]
14f 006ff8d4 75cabe6b AppD9!WndProc+0x7a [c:\awd3\appd9\appd9\appd9.cpp @ 146]
150 006ff900 75ca833a USER32!_InternalCallWinProc+0x2b
151 006ff9e8 75ca7bee USER32!UserCallWinProcCheckWow+0x3aa
152 006ffa64 75ca79d0 USER32!DispatchMessageWorker+0x20e
153 006ffa70 0097109d USER32!DispatchMessageW+0x10
154 006ffa9c 00971560 AppD9!wWinMain+0x9d [c:\awd3\appd9\appd9\appd9.cpp @ 59]
155 (Inline) -------- AppD9!invoke_main+0x1a [f:\dd\vctools\crt\vcstartup\src\startup\exe_common.inl @ 118]
156 006ffae8 777f8484 AppD9!__scrt_common_main_seh+0xf8 [f:\dd\vctools\crt\vcstartup\src\startup\exe_common.inl @ 288]
```

```
157 006ffafc 77bb2fea KERNEL32!BaseThreadInitThunk+0x24
158 006ffb44 77bb2fba ntdll_77b50000!__RtlUserThreadStart+0x2f
159 006ffb54 00000000 ntdll_77b50000!_RtlUserThreadStart+0x1b
```

10.   In our case, we try to reconstruct the 32-bit stack trace after checking 32-bit raw stack data:

```
0: kd:x86> !teb
Wow64 TEB32 at 006bf000
    ExceptionList:        0095969c
    StackBase:            00960000
    StackLimit:           00957000
    SubSystemTib:         00000000
    FiberData:            00001e00
    ArbitraryUserPointer: 00000000
    Self:                 006bf000
    EnvironmentPointer:   00000000
    ClientId:             00001f44 . 00001b10
    RpcHandle:            00000000
    Tls Storage:          00b46750
    PEB Address:          006bc000
    LastErrorValue:       0
    LastStatusValue:      c0000034
    Count Owned Locks:    0
    HardErrorMode:        0


Wow64 TEB at 006bd000
    ExceptionList:        006bf000
    StackBase:            0085fd20
    StackLimit:           00857000
    SubSystemTib:         00000000
    FiberData:            00001e00
    ArbitraryUserPointer: 00000000
    Self:                 006bd000
    EnvironmentPointer:   00000000
    ClientId:             00001f44 . 00001b10
    RpcHandle:            00000000
    Tls Storage:          00000000
    PEB Address:          006bb000
    LastErrorValue:       0
    LastStatusValue:      c0000008
    Count Owned Locks:    0
    HardErrorMode:        0
```

```
0: kd:x86> .sympath+ C:\AWD4\AppD9\Release
Symbol search path is: srv*; C:\AWD4\AppD9\Release
Expanded Symbol search path is: cache*;SRV*https://msdl.microsoft.com/download/symbols;
c:\awd4\appd9\release

************ Path validation summary **************
Response                      Time (ms)    Location
Deferred                                   srv*
OK                                         C:\AWD4\AppD9\Release
```

```
0: kd:x86> dpS 00957000 00960000
7765b3f9 ntdll_77600000!RtlSetLastWin32Error+0x39
76d3082b KERNELBASE!FlsGetValue+0x1b
772bc8d0 msvcrt!write_string+0x3d
772bd439 msvcrt!_output_l+0xb39
772bd4d2 msvcrt!_output_l+0xbd2
```

```
772f7078 msvcrt!__initiallocinfo
76e8d04c MSCTF!`string'
772b846a msvcrt!_vsnprintf_l+0x8a
76e8d008 MSCTF!`string'
772b83c8 msvcrt!_vsnprintf+0x18
76e8d008 MSCTF!`string'
76eeaa2b MSCTF!StringVPrintfWorkerA+0x1d
76e8d008 MSCTF!`string'
76eea9a2 MSCTF!StringCchVPrintfA+0x1d
76e8d008 MSCTF!`string'
76edb7c1 MSCTF!CicTrace+0x5e
76edb7f9 MSCTF!CicTrace+0x96
77202c32 IMM32!api-ms-win-core-com-private-l1-1-0_NULL_THUNK_DATA_DLA <PERF> (IMM32+0x22c32)
7539dff7 USER32!_GETPTI+0x10
75374d4a USER32!_GetWindowLong+0x9a
75374c46 USER32!GetWindowLongW+0x86
7539a600 USER32!_except_handler4
76eaffe7 MSCTF!CIMEUIWindowHandler::ImeUINotifyHandler+0x37
76eafcac MSCTF!CIMEUIWindowHandler::ImeUIWndProcWorker+0x18c
76eafb00 MSCTF!UIWndProc
7763edec ntdll_77600000!RtlDeactivateActivationContextUnsafeFast+0x9c
76e8d04c MSCTF!`string'
7763f080 ntdll_77600000!RtlActivateActivationContextUnsafeFast+0x70
76eafb16 MSCTF!UIWndProc+0x16
75397c12 USER32!_InternalCallWinProc+0x2a
76eafb00 MSCTF!UIWndProc
76eafb00 MSCTF!UIWndProc
7537700a USER32!UserCallWinProcCheckWow+0x4aa
753771e9 USER32!UserCallWinProcCheckWow+0x689
75377096 USER32!UserCallWinProcCheckWow+0x536
75376ce3 USER32!UserCallWinProcCheckWow+0x183
753771e9 USER32!UserCallWinProcCheckWow+0x689
7536cc40 USER32!RealGetSystemMetricsForDpi
752e23a2 uxtheme!ThemeGetSystemMetricsForDpi+0xd2
76eafb00 MSCTF!UIWndProc
76eafb00 MSCTF!UIWndProc
7539a600 USER32!_except_handler4
75376712 USER32!SendMessageWorker+0x842
76eafb00 MSCTF!UIWndProc
76eafb00 MSCTF!UIWndProc
75377f1c USER32!SendMessageToUI+0x5d
7537a6f0 USER32!ImeNotifyHandler+0x4e
771e4bc0 IMM32!CtfImmDispatchDefImeMessage
75377cd2 USER32!ImeWndProcWorker+0x182
75377b10 USER32!ImeWndProcW
7763edec ntdll_77600000!RtlDeactivateActivationContextUnsafeFast+0x9c
75377b35 USER32!ImeWndProcW+0x25
75397c12 USER32!_InternalCallWinProc+0x2a
75377b10 USER32!ImeWndProcW
75377b10 USER32!ImeWndProcW
7537700a USER32!UserCallWinProcCheckWow+0x4aa
753771e9 USER32!UserCallWinProcCheckWow+0x689
75377096 USER32!UserCallWinProcCheckWow+0x536
75376ce3 USER32!UserCallWinProcCheckWow+0x183
753771e9 USER32!UserCallWinProcCheckWow+0x689
75377b10 USER32!ImeWndProcW
75377b10 USER32!ImeWndProcW
7539a600 USER32!_except_handler4
75376712 USER32!SendMessageWorker+0x842
771e36f0 IMM32!ImmGetContext
771e36f0 IMM32!ImmGetContext
75372416 USER32!RealDefWindowProcWorker+0x1116
75372424 USER32!RealDefWindowProcWorker+0x1124
75375d46 USER32!HMValidateHandle+0x56
75371193 USER32!RealDefWindowProcW+0x53
753ff038 USER32!grgbDwpLiteHookMsg
753712b7 USER32!DefWindowProcW+0x107
753712ed USER32!DefWindowProcW+0x13d
753712c8 USER32!DefWindowProcW+0x118
7539a600 USER32!_except_handler4
753701c9 USER32!DefWindowProcWorker+0x39
753b6910 USER32!ButtonWndProcW
7763edec ntdll_77600000!RtlDeactivateActivationContextUnsafeFast+0x9c
753b6974 USER32!ButtonWndProcW+0x64
```

```
753b6910 USER32!ButtonWndProcW
75397c12 USER32!_InternalCallWinProc+0x2a
753b6910 USER32!ButtonWndProcW
753b6910 USER32!ButtonWndProcW
7537700a USER32!UserCallWinProcCheckWow+0x4aa
753771e9 USER32!UserCallWinProcCheckWow+0x689
75377096 USER32!UserCallWinProcCheckWow+0x536
75376ce3 USER32!UserCallWinProcCheckWow+0x183
753771e9 USER32!UserCallWinProcCheckWow+0x689
75376ce3 USER32!UserCallWinProcCheckWow+0x183
753771e9 USER32!UserCallWinProcCheckWow+0x689
753b6910 USER32!ButtonWndProcW
753b6910 USER32!ButtonWndProcW
76eafb00 MSCTF!UIWndProc
7539a600 USER32!_except_handler4
75376712 USER32!SendMessageWorker+0x842
7539e15c USER32!SendMessageInternal+0x2d
75375b56 USER32!SendMessageW+0x46
7537bd9e USER32!SendOpenStatusNotify+0x54
75564bac win32u!NtUserCheckImeShowStatusInThread+0xc
753781ed USER32!ImeSetContextHandler+0x2bb
7537826e USER32!ImeSetContextHandler+0x33c
76ea9a65 MSCTF!CtfImeDispatchDefImeMessage+0xb5
771e4bc0 IMM32!CtfImmDispatchDefImeMessage
777262e8 ntdll_77600000!LdrpLoaderLock
75377c7e USER32!ImeWndProcWorker+0x12e
75377b10 USER32!ImeWndProcW
7763edec ntdll_77600000!RtlDeactivateActivationContextUnsafeFast+0x9c
7539a600 USER32!_except_handler4
75377b35 USER32!ImeWndProcW+0x25
75397c12 USER32!_InternalCallWinProc+0x2a
75377b10 USER32!ImeWndProcW
75377b10 USER32!ImeWndProcW
7537700a USER32!UserCallWinProcCheckWow+0x4aa
753771e9 USER32!UserCallWinProcCheckWow+0x689
75377096 USER32!UserCallWinProcCheckWow+0x536
75376ce3 USER32!UserCallWinProcCheckWow+0x183
753771e9 USER32!UserCallWinProcCheckWow+0x689
772b846a msvcrt!_vsnprintf_l+0x8a
76e8c198 MSCTF!`string'
75377b10 USER32!ImeWndProcW
75377b10 USER32!ImeWndProcW
7539a600 USER32!_except_handler4
75376712 USER32!SendMessageWorker+0x842
76300b20 KERNEL32!SortCompareString+0x320
76300800 KERNEL32!SortCompareString
76300b31 KERNEL32!SortCompareString+0x331
74c35d00 Oleacc!`string'+0x34
76d33968 KERNELBASE!GetSortNode+0x78
74c35d00 Oleacc!`string'+0x34
74c35d00 Oleacc!`string'+0x34
76d338c8 KERNELBASE!CompareStringW+0x228
74c35d00 Oleacc!`string'+0x34
76d338d9 KERNELBASE!CompareStringW+0x239
7539a600 USER32!_except_handler4
753701c9 USER32!DefWindowProcWorker+0x39
753b6910 USER32!ButtonWndProcW
753b6974 USER32!ButtonWndProcW+0x64
753b6910 USER32!ButtonWndProcW
755610dc win32u!NtUserMessageCall+0xc
753713d0 USER32!RealDefWindowProcWorker+0xd0
755610dc win32u!NtUserMessageCall+0xc
753713d0 USER32!RealDefWindowProcWorker+0xd0
753713de USER32!RealDefWindowProcWorker+0xde
755617cc win32u!NtUserGetClassName+0xc
75371193 USER32!RealDefWindowProcW+0x53
75371193 USER32!RealDefWindowProcW+0x53
753ff038 USER32!grgbDwpLiteHookMsg
753712b7 USER32!DefWindowProcW+0x107
753712ed USER32!DefWindowProcW+0x13d
753712c8 USER32!DefWindowProcW+0x118
7539a600 USER32!_except_handler4
753701c9 USER32!DefWindowProcWorker+0x39
7538c4d6 USER32!StaticRepaint+0x15
```

```
7538c4b2 USER32!StaticWndProcWorker+0x3d2
77698260 ntdll_77600000!NtdllStaticWndProc_W
7538c217 USER32!StaticWndProcWorker+0x137
76d338c8 KERNELBASE!CompareStringW+0x228
76e8a228 MSCTF!`string'
77698260 ntdll_77600000!NtdllStaticWndProc_W
7763edec ntdll_77600000!RtlDeactivateActivationContextUnsafeFast+0x9c
753df1d9 USER32!StaticWndProcW+0x29
75397c12 USER32!_InternalCallWinProc+0x2a
77698260 ntdll_77600000!NtdllStaticWndProc_W
77698260 ntdll_77600000!NtdllStaticWndProc_W
7537700a USER32!UserCallWinProcCheckWow+0x4aa
77698260 ntdll_77600000!NtdllStaticWndProc_W
753771e9 USER32!UserCallWinProcCheckWow+0x689
75377096 USER32!UserCallWinProcCheckWow+0x536
75376ce3 USER32!UserCallWinProcCheckWow+0x183
753771e9 USER32!UserCallWinProcCheckWow+0x689
772cd313 msvcrt!_VEC_memzero+0x36
77647810 ntdll_77600000!RtlLeaveCriticalSection
772cd35f msvcrt!_VEC_memzero+0x82
755617cc win32u!NtUserGetClassName+0xc
75381505 USER32!RealGetWindowClassW+0x25
77698260 ntdll_77600000!NtdllStaticWndProc_W
77698260 ntdll_77600000!NtdllStaticWndProc_W
7539a600 USER32!_except_handler4
75376a9a USER32!DispatchClientMessage+0xea
77698260 ntdll_77600000!NtdllStaticWndProc_W
77698340 ntdll_77600000!NtdllDispatchMessage_W
7539a600 USER32!_except_handler4
7537f98f USER32!__fnDWORD+0x3f
77674c0c ntdll_77600000!NtCallbackReturn+0xc
7537f9a7 USER32!__fnDWORD+0x57
753996f0 USER32!NtUserMessageCall
7767718c ntdll_77600000!KiUserCallbackDispatcher+0x4c
776770c0 ntdll_77600000!KiUserCallbackExceptionHandler
77698260 ntdll_77600000!NtdllStaticWndProc_W
77698340 ntdll_77600000!NtdllDispatchMessage_W
755610dc win32u!NtUserMessageCall+0xc
753713d0 USER32!RealDefWindowProcWorker+0xd0
753713de USER32!RealDefWindowProcWorker+0xde
753739d1 USER32!UserCallDlgProcCheckWow+0x321
75375d46 USER32!HMValidateHandle+0x56
75371193 USER32!RealDefWindowProcW+0x53
753ff038 USER32!grgbDwpLiteHookMsg
753712b7 USER32!DefWindowProcW+0x107
753712ed USER32!DefWindowProcW+0x13d
753712c8 USER32!DefWindowProcW+0x118
7539a600 USER32!_except_handler4
75373459 USER32!DefDlgProcWorker+0x939
75372b7a USER32!DefDlgProcWorker+0x5a
76d338d9 KERNELBASE!CompareStringW+0x239
75372ab0 USER32!DefDlgProcW
7763edec ntdll_77600000!RtlDeactivateActivationContextUnsafeFast+0x9c
75372af8 USER32!DefDlgProcW+0x48
75372ab0 USER32!DefDlgProcW
75397c12 USER32!_InternalCallWinProc+0x2a
75372ab0 USER32!DefDlgProcW
75372ab0 USER32!DefDlgProcW
7537700a USER32!UserCallWinProcCheckWow+0x4aa
753771e9 USER32!UserCallWinProcCheckWow+0x689
75377096 USER32!UserCallWinProcCheckWow+0x536
75376ce3 USER32!UserCallWinProcCheckWow+0x183
753771e9 USER32!UserCallWinProcCheckWow+0x689
755617cc win32u!NtUserGetClassName+0xc
7539a600 USER32!_except_handler4
75374677 USER32!_MapWindowPoints+0x197
75372ab0 USER32!DefDlgProcW
75372ab0 USER32!DefDlgProcW
7539a600 USER32!_except_handler4
75376712 USER32!SendMessageWorker+0x842
7763edec ntdll_77600000!RtlDeactivateActivationContextUnsafeFast+0x9c
752e30d0 uxtheme!OnDdpPostInitDialog
753720ad USER32!RealDefWindowProcWorker+0xdad
753720bb USER32!RealDefWindowProcWorker+0xdbb
```

```
753739d1 USER32!UserCallDlgProcCheckWow+0x321
75375d46 USER32!HMValidateHandle+0x56
75371193 USER32!RealDefWindowProcW+0x53
753ff038 USER32!grgbDwpLiteHookMsg
753712b7 USER32!DefWindowProcW+0x107
753712ed USER32!DefWindowProcW+0x13d
753712c8 USER32!DefWindowProcW+0x118
7763edec ntdll_77600000!RtlDeactivateActivationContextUnsafeFast+0x9c
7763f080 ntdll_77600000!RtlActivateActivationContextUnsafeFast+0x70
753d92f0 USER32!MB_DlgProc
75397c12 USER32!_InternalCallWinProc+0x2a
75371668 USER32!RealDefWindowProcWorker+0x368
753739d1 USER32!UserCallDlgProcCheckWow+0x321
77674f1c ntdll_77600000!NtDelayExecution+0xc
7768ea99 ntdll_77600000!RtlDelayExecution+0xe9
76d4c7bf KERNELBASE!SleepEx+0x5f
*** WARNING: Unable to verify checksum for AppD9.exe
001d11a0 AppD9!WndProc [C:\AWD3\AppD9\AppD9\AppD9.cpp @ 131]
76d698e0 KERNELBASE!_except_handler4
76d4c74f KERNELBASE!Sleep+0xf
001d138e AppD9!ConnectDB+0xe [C:\AWD3\AppD9\AppD9\ConnectDB.cpp @ 6]
001d1338 AppD9!StartModeling+0x8 [C:\AWD3\AppD9\AppD9\AppD9.cpp @ 193]
001d121a AppD9!WndProc+0x7a [C:\AWD3\AppD9\AppD9\AppD9.cpp @ 146]
7765b3f9 ntdll_77600000!RtlSetLastWin32Error+0x39
752db450 uxtheme!ThemePostWndProc
7763edec ntdll_77600000!RtlDeactivateActivationContextUnsafeFast+0x9c
752db61d uxtheme!ThemePostWndProc+0x1cd
7763f080 ntdll_77600000!RtlActivateActivationContextUnsafeFast+0x70
752db450 uxtheme!ThemePostWndProc
75397c12 USER32!_InternalCallWinProc+0x2a
001d11a0 AppD9!WndProc [C:\AWD3\AppD9\AppD9\AppD9.cpp @ 131]
001d11a0 AppD9!WndProc [C:\AWD3\AppD9\AppD9\AppD9.cpp @ 131]
7537700a USER32!UserCallWinProcCheckWow+0x4aa
001d11a0 AppD9!WndProc [C:\AWD3\AppD9\AppD9\AppD9.cpp @ 131]
75376ce3 USER32!UserCallWinProcCheckWow+0x183
75373c86 USER32!HMValidateHandleNoSecure+0x46
7537a62f USER32!InternalCreateDialog+0x137f
001d11a0 AppD9!WndProc [C:\AWD3\AppD9\AppD9\AppD9.cpp @ 131]
001d11a0 AppD9!WndProc [C:\AWD3\AppD9\AppD9\AppD9.cpp @ 131]
7539a600 USER32!_except_handler4
75375938 USER32!DispatchMessageWorker+0x4b8
001d11a0 AppD9!WndProc [C:\AWD3\AppD9\AppD9\AppD9.cpp @ 131]
75378a15 USER32!IsDialogMessageW+0x105
001d11a0 AppD9!WndProc [C:\AWD3\AppD9\AppD9\AppD9.cpp @ 131]
7539a600 USER32!_except_handler4
7538e738 USER32!DialogBox2+0x189
7767718c ntdll_77600000!KiUserCallbackDispatcher+0x4c
7538e585 USER32!InternalDialogBox+0xc4
7538e598 USER32!InternalDialogBox+0xd7
753daeec USER32!SoftModalMessageBox+0x6bc
75350000 USER32!pfnClientA <PERF> (USER32+0x0)
753daf48 USER32!SoftModalMessageBox+0x718
753d92f0 USER32!MB_DlgProc
001e2cca AppD9!type_info::`vftable'+0x1e
7539a600 USER32!_except_handler4
7556202c win32u!NtUserModifyUserStartupInfoFlags+0xc
753d9cb0 USER32!MessageBoxWorker+0x314
001e2cc8 AppD9!type_info::`vftable'+0x1c
001e2cbc AppD9!type_info::`vftable'+0x10
7535701c USER32!SEBbuttons+0x4
753720ad USER32!RealDefWindowProcWorker+0xdad
753720bb USER32!RealDefWindowProcWorker+0xdbb
753739d1 USER32!UserCallDlgProcCheckWow+0x321
75375d46 USER32!HMValidateHandle+0x56
75371193 USER32!RealDefWindowProcW+0x53
753ff038 USER32!grgbDwpLiteHookMsg
753712b7 USER32!DefWindowProcW+0x107
753712ed USER32!DefWindowProcW+0x13d
753712c8 USER32!DefWindowProcW+0x118
7763edec ntdll_77600000!RtlDeactivateActivationContextUnsafeFast+0x9c
7763f080 ntdll_77600000!RtlActivateActivationContextUnsafeFast+0x70
753d92f0 USER32!MB_DlgProc
75397c12 USER32!_InternalCallWinProc+0x2a
75371668 USER32!RealDefWindowProcWorker+0x368
```

```
001e2cc8 AppD9!type_info::`vftable'+0x1c
753da660 USER32!MessageBoxTimeoutW+0x30
753da7b7 USER32!MessageBoxTimeoutW+0x187
001d11a0 AppD9!WndProc [C:\AWD3\AppD9\AppD9\AppD9.cpp @ 131]
7768ea99 ntdll_77600000!RtlDelayExecution+0xe9
001e2cc8 AppD9!type_info::`vftable'+0x1c
001e2cbc AppD9!type_info::`vftable'+0x10
753da825 USER32!MessageBoxW+0x45
001e2cc8 AppD9!type_info::`vftable'+0x1c
001e2cbc AppD9!type_info::`vftable'+0x10
001d1371 AppD9!StartModeling+0x41 [C:\AWD3\AppD9\AppD9\AppD9.cpp @ 198]
001e2cc8 AppD9!type_info::`vftable'+0x1c
001e2cbc AppD9!type_info::`vftable'+0x10
001d121a AppD9!WndProc+0x7a [C:\AWD3\AppD9\AppD9\AppD9.cpp @ 146]
7765b3f9 ntdll_77600000!RtlSetLastWin32Error+0x39
752db450 uxtheme!ThemePostWndProc
7763edec ntdll_77600000!RtlDeactivateActivationContextUnsafeFast+0x9c
752db61d uxtheme!ThemePostWndProc+0x1cd
7763f080 ntdll_77600000!RtlActivateActivationContextUnsafeFast+0x70
752db450 uxtheme!ThemePostWndProc
75397c12 USER32!_InternalCallWinProc+0x2a
001d11a0 AppD9!WndProc [C:\AWD3\AppD9\AppD9\AppD9.cpp @ 131]
001d11a0 AppD9!WndProc [C:\AWD3\AppD9\AppD9\AppD9.cpp @ 131]
7537700a USER32!UserCallWinProcCheckWow+0x4aa
001d11a0 AppD9!WndProc [C:\AWD3\AppD9\AppD9\AppD9.cpp @ 131]
75376ce3 USER32!UserCallWinProcCheckWow+0x183
75373c86 USER32!HMValidateHandleNoSecure+0x46
7537a62f USER32!InternalCreateDialog+0x137f
001d11a0 AppD9!WndProc [C:\AWD3\AppD9\AppD9\AppD9.cpp @ 131]
001d11a0 AppD9!WndProc [C:\AWD3\AppD9\AppD9\AppD9.cpp @ 131]
7539a600 USER32!_except_handler4
75375938 USER32!DispatchMessageWorker+0x4b8
001d11a0 AppD9!WndProc [C:\AWD3\AppD9\AppD9\AppD9.cpp @ 131]
75378a15 USER32!IsDialogMessageW+0x105
001d11a0 AppD9!WndProc [C:\AWD3\AppD9\AppD9\AppD9.cpp @ 131]
7539a600 USER32!_except_handler4
7538e738 USER32!DialogBox2+0x189
7767718c ntdll_77600000!KiUserCallbackDispatcher+0x4c
7538e585 USER32!InternalDialogBox+0xc4
7538e598 USER32!InternalDialogBox+0xd7
753daeec USER32!SoftModalMessageBox+0x6bc
75350000 USER32!pfnClientA <PERF> (USER32+0x0)
753daf48 USER32!SoftModalMessageBox+0x718
753d92f0 USER32!MB_DlgProc
001e2cca AppD9!type_info::`vftable'+0x1e
7539a600 USER32!_except_handler4
7556202c win32u!NtUserModifyUserStartupInfoFlags+0xc
753d9cb0 USER32!MessageBoxWorker+0x314
001e2cc8 AppD9!type_info::`vftable'+0x1c
001e2cbc AppD9!type_info::`vftable'+0x10
7535701c USER32!SEBbuttons+0x4
753720ad USER32!RealDefWindowProcWorker+0xdad
753720bb USER32!RealDefWindowProcWorker+0xdbb
753739d1 USER32!UserCallDlgProcCheckWow+0x321
75375d46 USER32!HMValidateHandle+0x56
75371193 USER32!RealDefWindowProcW+0x53
753ff038 USER32!grgbDwpLiteHookMsg
753712b7 USER32!DefWindowProcW+0x107
753712ed USER32!DefWindowProcW+0x13d
753712c8 USER32!DefWindowProcW+0x118
7763edec ntdll_77600000!RtlDeactivateActivationContextUnsafeFast+0x9c
7763f080 ntdll_77600000!RtlActivateActivationContextUnsafeFast+0x70
753d92f0 USER32!MB_DlgProc
75397c12 USER32!_InternalCallWinProc+0x2a
75371668 USER32!RealDefWindowProcWorker+0x368
001e2cc8 AppD9!type_info::`vftable'+0x1c
753da660 USER32!MessageBoxTimeoutW+0x30
753da7b7 USER32!MessageBoxTimeoutW+0x187
001d11a0 AppD9!WndProc [C:\AWD3\AppD9\AppD9\AppD9.cpp @ 131]
7768ea99 ntdll_77600000!RtlDelayExecution+0xe9
001e2cc8 AppD9!type_info::`vftable'+0x1c
001e2cbc AppD9!type_info::`vftable'+0x10
753da825 USER32!MessageBoxW+0x45
001e2cc8 AppD9!type_info::`vftable'+0x1c
```

250

```
001e2cbc AppD9!type_info::`vftable'+0x10
001d1371 AppD9!StartModeling+0x41 [C:\AWD3\AppD9\AppD9\AppD9.cpp @ 198]
001e2cc8 AppD9!type_info::`vftable'+0x1c
001e2cbc AppD9!type_info::`vftable'+0x10
001d121a AppD9!WndProc+0x7a [C:\AWD3\AppD9\AppD9\AppD9.cpp @ 146]
7765b3f9 ntdll_77600000!RtlSetLastWin32Error+0x39
752db450 uxtheme!ThemePostWndProc
7763edec ntdll_77600000!RtlDeactivateActivationContextUnsafeFast+0x9c
752db61d uxtheme!ThemePostWndProc+0x1cd
7763f080 ntdll_77600000!RtlActivateActivationContextUnsafeFast+0x70
752db450 uxtheme!ThemePostWndProc
75397c12 USER32!_InternalCallWinProc+0x2a
001d11a0 AppD9!WndProc [C:\AWD3\AppD9\AppD9\AppD9.cpp @ 131]
001d11a0 AppD9!WndProc [C:\AWD3\AppD9\AppD9\AppD9.cpp @ 131]
7537700a USER32!UserCallWinProcCheckWow+0x4aa
001d11a0 AppD9!WndProc [C:\AWD3\AppD9\AppD9\AppD9.cpp @ 131]
75376ce3 USER32!UserCallWinProcCheckWow+0x183
75373c86 USER32!HMValidateHandleNoSecure+0x46
7537a62f USER32!InternalCreateDialog+0x137f
001d11a0 AppD9!WndProc [C:\AWD3\AppD9\AppD9\AppD9.cpp @ 131]
001d11a0 AppD9!WndProc [C:\AWD3\AppD9\AppD9\AppD9.cpp @ 131]
7539a600 USER32!_except_handler4
75375938 USER32!DispatchMessageWorker+0x4b8
001d11a0 AppD9!WndProc [C:\AWD3\AppD9\AppD9\AppD9.cpp @ 131]
75378a15 USER32!IsDialogMessageW+0x105
001d11a0 AppD9!WndProc [C:\AWD3\AppD9\AppD9\AppD9.cpp @ 131]
7539a600 USER32!_except_handler4
7538e738 USER32!DialogBox2+0x189
7767718c ntdll_77600000!KiUserCallbackDispatcher+0x4c
7538e585 USER32!InternalDialogBox+0xc4
7538e598 USER32!InternalDialogBox+0xd7
753daeec USER32!SoftModalMessageBox+0x6bc
75350000 USER32!pfnClientA <PERF> (USER32+0x0)
753daf48 USER32!SoftModalMessageBox+0x718
753d92f0 USER32!MB_DlgProc
001e2cca AppD9!type_info::`vftable'+0x1e
7539a600 USER32!_except_handler4
7556202c win32u!NtUserModifyUserStartupInfoFlags+0xc
753d9cb0 USER32!MessageBoxWorker+0x314
001e2cc8 AppD9!type_info::`vftable'+0x1c
001e2cbc AppD9!type_info::`vftable'+0x10
7535701c USER32!SEBbuttons+0x4
753720ad USER32!RealDefWindowProcWorker+0xdad
753720bb USER32!RealDefWindowProcWorker+0xdbb
753739d1 USER32!UserCallDlgProcCheckWow+0x321
75375d46 USER32!HMValidateHandle+0x56
75371193 USER32!RealDefWindowProcW+0x53
753ff038 USER32!grgbDwpLiteHookMsg
753712b7 USER32!DefWindowProcW+0x107
753712ed USER32!DefWindowProcW+0x13d
753712c8 USER32!DefWindowProcW+0x118
7763edec ntdll_77600000!RtlDeactivateActivationContextUnsafeFast+0x9c
7763f080 ntdll_77600000!RtlActivateActivationContextUnsafeFast+0x70
753d92f0 USER32!MB_DlgProc
75397c12 USER32!_InternalCallWinProc+0x2a
75371668 USER32!RealDefWindowProcWorker+0x368
001e2cc8 AppD9!type_info::`vftable'+0x1c
753da660 USER32!MessageBoxTimeoutW+0x30
753da7b7 USER32!MessageBoxTimeoutW+0x187
001d11a0 AppD9!WndProc [C:\AWD3\AppD9\AppD9\AppD9.cpp @ 131]
7768ea99 ntdll_77600000!RtlDelayExecution+0xe9
001e2cc8 AppD9!type_info::`vftable'+0x1c
001e2cbc AppD9!type_info::`vftable'+0x10
753da825 USER32!MessageBoxW+0x45
001e2cc8 AppD9!type_info::`vftable'+0x1c
001e2cbc AppD9!type_info::`vftable'+0x10
001d1371 AppD9!StartModeling+0x41 [C:\AWD3\AppD9\AppD9\AppD9.cpp @ 198]
001e2cc8 AppD9!type_info::`vftable'+0x1c
001e2cbc AppD9!type_info::`vftable'+0x10
001d121a AppD9!WndProc+0x7a [C:\AWD3\AppD9\AppD9\AppD9.cpp @ 146]
7765b3f9 ntdll_77600000!RtlSetLastWin32Error+0x39
752db450 uxtheme!ThemePostWndProc
7763edec ntdll_77600000!RtlDeactivateActivationContextUnsafeFast+0x9c
752db61d uxtheme!ThemePostWndProc+0x1cd
```

251

```
7763f080 ntdll_77600000!RtlActivateActivationContextUnsafeFast+0x70
752db450 uxtheme!ThemePostWndProc
75397c12 USER32!_InternalCallWinProc+0x2a
001d11a0 AppD9!WndProc [C:\AWD3\AppD9\AppD9\AppD9.cpp @ 131]
001d11a0 AppD9!WndProc [C:\AWD3\AppD9\AppD9\AppD9.cpp @ 131]
7537700a USER32!UserCallWinProcCheckWow+0x4aa
001d11a0 AppD9!WndProc [C:\AWD3\AppD9\AppD9\AppD9.cpp @ 131]
75376ce3 USER32!UserCallWinProcCheckWow+0x183
75373c86 USER32!HMValidateHandleNoSecure+0x46
7537a62f USER32!InternalCreateDialog+0x137f
001d11a0 AppD9!WndProc [C:\AWD3\AppD9\AppD9\AppD9.cpp @ 131]
001d11a0 AppD9!WndProc [C:\AWD3\AppD9\AppD9\AppD9.cpp @ 131]
7539a600 USER32!_except_handler4
75375938 USER32!DispatchMessageWorker+0x4b8
001d11a0 AppD9!WndProc [C:\AWD3\AppD9\AppD9\AppD9.cpp @ 131]
75378a15 USER32!IsDialogMessageW+0x105
001d11a0 AppD9!WndProc [C:\AWD3\AppD9\AppD9\AppD9.cpp @ 131]
7539a600 USER32!_except_handler4
7538e738 USER32!DialogBox2+0x189
7767718c ntdll_77600000!KiUserCallbackDispatcher+0x4c
7538e585 USER32!InternalDialogBox+0xc4
7538e598 USER32!InternalDialogBox+0xd7
753daeec USER32!SoftModalMessageBox+0x6bc
75350000 USER32!pfnClientA <PERF> (USER32+0x0)
753daf48 USER32!SoftModalMessageBox+0x718
753d92f0 USER32!MB_DlgProc
001e2cca AppD9!type_info::`vftable'+0x1e
7539a600 USER32!_except_handler4
7556202c win32u!NtUserModifyUserStartupInfoFlags+0xc
753d9cb0 USER32!MessageBoxWorker+0x314
001e2cc8 AppD9!type_info::`vftable'+0x1c
001e2cbc AppD9!type_info::`vftable'+0x10
7535701c USER32!SEBbuttons+0x4
753720ad USER32!RealDefWindowProcWorker+0xdad
753720bb USER32!RealDefWindowProcWorker+0xdbb
753739d1 USER32!UserCallDlgProcCheckWow+0x321
75375d46 USER32!HMValidateHandle+0x56
75371193 USER32!RealDefWindowProcW+0x53
753ff038 USER32!grgbDwpLiteHookMsg
753712b7 USER32!DefWindowProcW+0x107
753712ed USER32!DefWindowProcW+0x13d
753712c8 USER32!DefWindowProcW+0x118
7763edec ntdll_77600000!RtlDeactivateActivationContextUnsafeFast+0x9c
7763f080 ntdll_77600000!RtlActivateActivationContextUnsafeFast+0x70
753d92f0 USER32!MB_DlgProc
75397c12 USER32!_InternalCallWinProc+0x2a
75371668 USER32!RealDefWindowProcWorker+0x368
001e2cc8 AppD9!type_info::`vftable'+0x1c
753da660 USER32!MessageBoxTimeoutW+0x30
753da7b7 USER32!MessageBoxTimeoutW+0x187
001d11a0 AppD9!WndProc [C:\AWD3\AppD9\AppD9\AppD9.cpp @ 131]
7768ea99 ntdll_77600000!RtlDelayExecution+0xe9
001e2cc8 AppD9!type_info::`vftable'+0x1c
001e2cbc AppD9!type_info::`vftable'+0x10
753da825 USER32!MessageBoxW+0x45
001e2cc8 AppD9!type_info::`vftable'+0x1c
001e2cbc AppD9!type_info::`vftable'+0x10
001d1371 AppD9!StartModeling+0x41 [C:\AWD3\AppD9\AppD9\AppD9.cpp @ 198]
001e2cc8 AppD9!type_info::`vftable'+0x1c
001e2cbc AppD9!type_info::`vftable'+0x10
001d121a AppD9!WndProc+0x7a [C:\AWD3\AppD9\AppD9\AppD9.cpp @ 146]
7765b3f9 ntdll_77600000!RtlSetLastWin32Error+0x39
752db450 uxtheme!ThemePostWndProc
7763edec ntdll_77600000!RtlDeactivateActivationContextUnsafeFast+0x9c
752db61d uxtheme!ThemePostWndProc+0x1cd
7763f080 ntdll_77600000!RtlActivateActivationContextUnsafeFast+0x70
752db450 uxtheme!ThemePostWndProc
75397c12 USER32!_InternalCallWinProc+0x2a
001d11a0 AppD9!WndProc [C:\AWD3\AppD9\AppD9\AppD9.cpp @ 131]
001d11a0 AppD9!WndProc [C:\AWD3\AppD9\AppD9\AppD9.cpp @ 131]
7537700a USER32!UserCallWinProcCheckWow+0x4aa
001d11a0 AppD9!WndProc [C:\AWD3\AppD9\AppD9\AppD9.cpp @ 131]
75376ce3 USER32!UserCallWinProcCheckWow+0x183
75373c86 USER32!HMValidateHandleNoSecure+0x46
```

```
7537a62f USER32!InternalCreateDialog+0x137f
001d11a0 AppD9!WndProc [C:\AWD3\AppD9\AppD9\AppD9.cpp @ 131]
001d11a0 AppD9!WndProc [C:\AWD3\AppD9\AppD9\AppD9.cpp @ 131]
7539a600 USER32!_except_handler4
75375938 USER32!DispatchMessageWorker+0x4b8
001d11a0 AppD9!WndProc [C:\AWD3\AppD9\AppD9\AppD9.cpp @ 131]
75378a15 USER32!IsDialogMessageW+0x105
001d11a0 AppD9!WndProc [C:\AWD3\AppD9\AppD9\AppD9.cpp @ 131]
7539a600 USER32!_except_handler4
7538e738 USER32!DialogBox2+0x189
7767718c ntdll_77600000!KiUserCallbackDispatcher+0x4c
7538e585 USER32!InternalDialogBox+0xc4
7538e598 USER32!InternalDialogBox+0xd7
753daeec USER32!SoftModalMessageBox+0x6bc
75350000 USER32!pfnClientA <PERF> (USER32+0x0)
753daf48 USER32!SoftModalMessageBox+0x718
753d92f0 USER32!MB_DlgProc
001e2cca AppD9!type_info::`vftable'+0x1e
7539a600 USER32!_except_handler4
7556202c win32u!NtUserModifyUserStartupInfoFlags+0xc
753d9cb0 USER32!MessageBoxWorker+0x314
001e2cc8 AppD9!type_info::`vftable'+0x1c
001e2cbc AppD9!type_info::`vftable'+0x10
7535701c USER32!SEBbuttons+0x4
753720ad USER32!RealDefWindowProcWorker+0xdad
753720bb USER32!RealDefWindowProcWorker+0xdbb
753739d1 USER32!UserCallDlgProcCheckWow+0x321
75375d46 USER32!HMValidateHandle+0x56
75371193 USER32!RealDefWindowProcW+0x53
753ff038 USER32!grgbDwpLiteHookMsg
753712b7 USER32!DefWindowProcW+0x107
753712ed USER32!DefWindowProcW+0x13d
753712c8 USER32!DefWindowProcW+0x118
7763edec ntdll_77600000!RtlDeactivateActivationContextUnsafeFast+0x9c
7763f080 ntdll_77600000!RtlActivateActivationContextUnsafeFast+0x70
753d92f0 USER32!MB_DlgProc
75397c12 USER32!_InternalCallWinProc+0x2a
75371668 USER32!RealDefWindowProcWorker+0x368
001e2cc8 AppD9!type_info::`vftable'+0x1c
753da660 USER32!MessageBoxTimeoutW+0x30
753da7b7 USER32!MessageBoxTimeoutW+0x187
001d11a0 AppD9!WndProc [C:\AWD3\AppD9\AppD9\AppD9.cpp @ 131]
7768ea99 ntdll_77600000!RtlDelayExecution+0xe9
001e2cc8 AppD9!type_info::`vftable'+0x1c
001e2cbc AppD9!type_info::`vftable'+0x10
753da825 USER32!MessageBoxW+0x45
001e2cc8 AppD9!type_info::`vftable'+0x1c
001e2cbc AppD9!type_info::`vftable'+0x10
001d1371 AppD9!StartModeling+0x41 [C:\AWD3\AppD9\AppD9\AppD9.cpp @ 198]
001e2cc8 AppD9!type_info::`vftable'+0x1c
001e2cbc AppD9!type_info::`vftable'+0x10
001d121a AppD9!WndProc+0x7a [C:\AWD3\AppD9\AppD9\AppD9.cpp @ 146]
7765b3f9 ntdll_77600000!RtlSetLastWin32Error+0x39
752db450 uxtheme!ThemePostWndProc
7763edec ntdll_77600000!RtlDeactivateActivationContextUnsafeFast+0x9c
752db61d uxtheme!ThemePostWndProc+0x1cd
7763f080 ntdll_77600000!RtlActivateActivationContextUnsafeFast+0x70
752db450 uxtheme!ThemePostWndProc
75397c12 USER32!_InternalCallWinProc+0x2a
001d11a0 AppD9!WndProc [C:\AWD3\AppD9\AppD9\AppD9.cpp @ 131]
001d11a0 AppD9!WndProc [C:\AWD3\AppD9\AppD9\AppD9.cpp @ 131]
7537700a USER32!UserCallWinProcCheckWow+0x4aa
001d11a0 AppD9!WndProc [C:\AWD3\AppD9\AppD9\AppD9.cpp @ 131]
75376ce3 USER32!UserCallWinProcCheckWow+0x183
75373c86 USER32!HMValidateHandleNoSecure+0x46
7537a62f USER32!InternalCreateDialog+0x137f
001d11a0 AppD9!WndProc [C:\AWD3\AppD9\AppD9\AppD9.cpp @ 131]
001d11a0 AppD9!WndProc [C:\AWD3\AppD9\AppD9\AppD9.cpp @ 131]
7539a600 USER32!_except_handler4
75375938 USER32!DispatchMessageWorker+0x4b8
001d11a0 AppD9!WndProc [C:\AWD3\AppD9\AppD9\AppD9.cpp @ 131]
75378a15 USER32!IsDialogMessageW+0x105
001d11a0 AppD9!WndProc [C:\AWD3\AppD9\AppD9\AppD9.cpp @ 131]
7539a600 USER32!_except_handler4
```

```
7538e738 USER32!DialogBox2+0x189
7767718c ntdll_77600000!KiUserCallbackDispatcher+0x4c
7538e585 USER32!InternalDialogBox+0xc4
7538e598 USER32!InternalDialogBox+0xd7
753daeec USER32!SoftModalMessageBox+0x6bc
75350000 USER32!pfnClientA <PERF> (USER32+0x0)
753daf48 USER32!SoftModalMessageBox+0x718
753d92f0 USER32!MB_DlgProc
001e2cca AppD9!type_info::`vftable'+0x1e
7539a600 USER32!_except_handler4
7556202c win32u!NtUserModifyUserStartupInfoFlags+0xc
753d9cb0 USER32!MessageBoxWorker+0x314
001e2cc8 AppD9!type_info::`vftable'+0x1c
001e2cbc AppD9!type_info::`vftable'+0x10
7535701c USER32!SEBbuttons+0x4
753720ad USER32!RealDefWindowProcWorker+0xdad
753720bb USER32!RealDefWindowProcWorker+0xdbb
753739d1 USER32!UserCallDlgProcCheckWow+0x321
75375d46 USER32!HMValidateHandle+0x56
75371193 USER32!RealDefWindowProcW+0x53
753ff038 USER32!grgbDwpLiteHookMsg
753712b7 USER32!DefWindowProcW+0x107
753712ed USER32!DefWindowProcW+0x13d
753712c8 USER32!DefWindowProcW+0x118
7763edec ntdll_77600000!RtlDeactivateActivationContextUnsafeFast+0x9c
7763f080 ntdll_77600000!RtlActivateActivationContextUnsafeFast+0x70
753d92f0 USER32!MB_DlgProc
75397c12 USER32!_InternalCallWinProc+0x2a
75371668 USER32!RealDefWindowProcWorker+0x368
001e2cc8 AppD9!type_info::`vftable'+0x1c
753da660 USER32!MessageBoxTimeoutW+0x30
753da7b7 USER32!MessageBoxTimeoutW+0x187
001d11a0 AppD9!WndProc [C:\AWD3\AppD9\AppD9\AppD9.cpp @ 131]
7768ea99 ntdll_77600000!RtlDelayExecution+0xe9
001e2cc8 AppD9!type_info::`vftable'+0x1c
001e2cbc AppD9!type_info::`vftable'+0x10
```
753da825 USER32!MessageBoxW+0x45
```
001e2cc8 AppD9!type_info::`vftable'+0x1c
001e2cbc AppD9!type_info::`vftable'+0x10
001d1371 AppD9!StartModeling+0x41 [C:\AWD3\AppD9\AppD9\AppD9.cpp @ 198]
001e2cc8 AppD9!type_info::`vftable'+0x1c
001e2cbc AppD9!type_info::`vftable'+0x10
001d121a AppD9!WndProc+0x7a [C:\AWD3\AppD9\AppD9\AppD9.cpp @ 146]
7765b3f9 ntdll_77600000!RtlSetLastWin32Error+0x39
752db450 uxtheme!ThemePostWndProc
7763edec ntdll_77600000!RtlDeactivateActivationContextUnsafeFast+0x9c
752db61d uxtheme!ThemePostWndProc+0x1cd
7763f080 ntdll_77600000!RtlActivateActivationContextUnsafeFast+0x70
752db450 uxtheme!ThemePostWndProc
75397c12 USER32!_InternalCallWinProc+0x2a
001d11a0 AppD9!WndProc [C:\AWD3\AppD9\AppD9\AppD9.cpp @ 131]
001d11a0 AppD9!WndProc [C:\AWD3\AppD9\AppD9\AppD9.cpp @ 131]
7537700a USER32!UserCallWinProcCheckWow+0x4aa
001d11a0 AppD9!WndProc [C:\AWD3\AppD9\AppD9\AppD9.cpp @ 131]
75376ce3 USER32!UserCallWinProcCheckWow+0x183
75373c86 USER32!HMValidateHandleNoSecure+0x46
7537a62f USER32!InternalCreateDialog+0x137f
001d11a0 AppD9!WndProc [C:\AWD3\AppD9\AppD9\AppD9.cpp @ 131]
001d11a0 AppD9!WndProc [C:\AWD3\AppD9\AppD9\AppD9.cpp @ 131]
7539a600 USER32!_except_handler4
75375938 USER32!DispatchMessageWorker+0x4b8
001d11a0 AppD9!WndProc [C:\AWD3\AppD9\AppD9\AppD9.cpp @ 131]
75378a15 USER32!IsDialogMessageW+0x105
001d11a0 AppD9!WndProc [C:\AWD3\AppD9\AppD9\AppD9.cpp @ 131]
7539a600 USER32!_except_handler4
7538e738 USER32!DialogBox2+0x189
7767718c ntdll_77600000!KiUserCallbackDispatcher+0x4c
7538e585 USER32!InternalDialogBox+0xc4
7538e598 USER32!InternalDialogBox+0xd7
753daeec USER32!SoftModalMessageBox+0x6bc
75350000 USER32!pfnClientA <PERF> (USER32+0x0)
753daf48 USER32!SoftModalMessageBox+0x718
753d92f0 USER32!MB_DlgProc
001e2cca AppD9!type_info::`vftable'+0x1e
```

```
7539a600 USER32!_except_handler4
7556202c win32u!NtUserModifyUserStartupInfoFlags+0xc
753d9cb0 USER32!MessageBoxWorker+0x314
001e2cc8 AppD9!type_info::`vftable'+0x1c
001e2cbc AppD9!type_info::`vftable'+0x10
7535701c USER32!SEBbuttons+0x4
753720ad USER32!RealDefWindowProcWorker+0xdad
753720bb USER32!RealDefWindowProcWorker+0xdbb
753739d1 USER32!UserCallDlgProcCheckWow+0x321
75375d46 USER32!HMValidateHandle+0x56
75371193 USER32!RealDefWindowProcW+0x53
753ff038 USER32!grgbDwpLiteHookMsg
753712b7 USER32!DefWindowProcW+0x107
753712ed USER32!DefWindowProcW+0x13d
753712c8 USER32!DefWindowProcW+0x118
7763edec ntdll_77600000!RtlDeactivateActivationContextUnsafeFast+0x9c
7763f080 ntdll_77600000!RtlActivateActivationContextUnsafeFast+0x70
753d92f0 USER32!MB_DlgProc
75397c12 USER32!_InternalCallWinProc+0x2a
75371668 USER32!RealDefWindowProcWorker+0x368
001e2cc8 AppD9!type_info::`vftable'+0x1c
753da660 USER32!MessageBoxTimeoutW+0x30
753da7b7 USER32!MessageBoxTimeoutW+0x187
001d11a0 AppD9!WndProc [C:\AWD3\AppD9\AppD9\AppD9.cpp @ 131]
7768ea99 ntdll_77600000!RtlDelayExecution+0xe9
001e2cc8 AppD9!type_info::`vftable'+0x1c
001e2cbc AppD9!type_info::`vftable'+0x10
753da825 USER32!MessageBoxW+0x45
001e2cc8 AppD9!type_info::`vftable'+0x1c
001e2cbc AppD9!type_info::`vftable'+0x10
001d1371 AppD9!StartModeling+0x41 [C:\AWD3\AppD9\AppD9\AppD9.cpp @ 198]
001e2cc8 AppD9!type_info::`vftable'+0x1c
001e2cbc AppD9!type_info::`vftable'+0x10
001d121a AppD9!WndProc+0x7a [C:\AWD3\AppD9\AppD9\AppD9.cpp @ 146]
7765b3f9 ntdll_77600000!RtlSetLastWin32Error+0x39
752db450 uxtheme!ThemePostWndProc
7763edec ntdll_77600000!RtlDeactivateActivationContextUnsafeFast+0x9c
752db61d uxtheme!ThemePostWndProc+0x1cd
7763f080 ntdll_77600000!RtlActivateActivationContextUnsafeFast+0x70
752db450 uxtheme!ThemePostWndProc
75397c12 USER32!_InternalCallWinProc+0x2a
001d11a0 AppD9!WndProc [C:\AWD3\AppD9\AppD9\AppD9.cpp @ 131]
001d11a0 AppD9!WndProc [C:\AWD3\AppD9\AppD9\AppD9.cpp @ 131]
7537700a USER32!UserCallWinProcCheckWow+0x4aa
001d11a0 AppD9!WndProc [C:\AWD3\AppD9\AppD9\AppD9.cpp @ 131]
75376ce3 USER32!UserCallWinProcCheckWow+0x183
75373c86 USER32!HMValidateHandleNoSecure+0x46
7537a62f USER32!InternalCreateDialog+0x137f
001d11a0 AppD9!WndProc [C:\AWD3\AppD9\AppD9\AppD9.cpp @ 131]
001d11a0 AppD9!WndProc [C:\AWD3\AppD9\AppD9\AppD9.cpp @ 131]
7539a600 USER32!_except_handler4
75375938 USER32!DispatchMessageWorker+0x4b8
001d11a0 AppD9!WndProc [C:\AWD3\AppD9\AppD9\AppD9.cpp @ 131]
75378a15 USER32!IsDialogMessageW+0x105
001d11a0 AppD9!WndProc [C:\AWD3\AppD9\AppD9\AppD9.cpp @ 131]
7539a600 USER32!_except_handler4
7538e738 USER32!DialogBox2+0x189
7767718c ntdll_77600000!KiUserCallbackDispatcher+0x4c
7538e585 USER32!InternalDialogBox+0xc4
7538e598 USER32!InternalDialogBox+0xd7
753daeec USER32!SoftModalMessageBox+0x6bc
75350000 USER32!pfnClientA <PERF> (USER32+0x0)
753daf48 USER32!SoftModalMessageBox+0x718
753d92f0 USER32!MB_DlgProc
001e2cca AppD9!type_info::`vftable'+0x1e
7539a600 USER32!_except_handler4
7556202c win32u!NtUserModifyUserStartupInfoFlags+0xc
753d9cb0 USER32!MessageBoxWorker+0x314
001e2cc8 AppD9!type_info::`vftable'+0x1c
001e2cbc AppD9!type_info::`vftable'+0x10
7535701c USER32!SEBbuttons+0x4
753720ad USER32!RealDefWindowProcWorker+0xdad
753720bb USER32!RealDefWindowProcWorker+0xdbb
753739d1 USER32!UserCallDlgProcCheckWow+0x321
```

```
75375d46 USER32!HMValidateHandle+0x56
75371193 USER32!RealDefWindowProcW+0x53
753ff038 USER32!grgbDwpLiteHookMsg
753712b7 USER32!DefWindowProcW+0x107
753712ed USER32!DefWindowProcW+0x13d
753712c8 USER32!DefWindowProcW+0x118
7763edec ntdll_77600000!RtlDeactivateActivationContextUnsafeFast+0x9c
7763f080 ntdll_77600000!RtlActivateActivationContextUnsafeFast+0x70
753d92f0 USER32!MB_DlgProc
75397c12 USER32!_InternalCallWinProc+0x2a
75371668 USER32!RealDefWindowProcWorker+0x368
001e2cc8 AppD9!type_info::`vftable'+0x1c
753da660 USER32!MessageBoxTimeoutW+0x30
753da7b7 USER32!MessageBoxTimeoutW+0x187
001d11a0 AppD9!WndProc [C:\AWD3\AppD9\AppD9\AppD9.cpp @ 131]
7768ea99 ntdll_77600000!RtlDelayExecution+0xe9
001e2cc8 AppD9!type_info::`vftable'+0x1c
001e2cbc AppD9!type_info::`vftable'+0x10
753da825 USER32!MessageBoxW+0x45
001e2cc8 AppD9!type_info::`vftable'+0x1c
001e2cbc AppD9!type_info::`vftable'+0x10
001d1371 AppD9!StartModeling+0x41 [C:\AWD3\AppD9\AppD9\AppD9.cpp @ 198]
001e2cc8 AppD9!type_info::`vftable'+0x1c
001e2cbc AppD9!type_info::`vftable'+0x10
001d121a AppD9!WndProc+0x7a [C:\AWD3\AppD9\AppD9\AppD9.cpp @ 146]
7765b3f9 ntdll_77600000!RtlSetLastWin32Error+0x39
752db450 uxtheme!ThemePostWndProc
7763edec ntdll_77600000!RtlDeactivateActivationContextUnsafeFast+0x9c
752db61d uxtheme!ThemePostWndProc+0x1cd
7763f080 ntdll_77600000!RtlActivateActivationContextUnsafeFast+0x70
752db450 uxtheme!ThemePostWndProc
75397c12 USER32!_InternalCallWinProc+0x2a
001d11a0 AppD9!WndProc [C:\AWD3\AppD9\AppD9\AppD9.cpp @ 131]
001d11a0 AppD9!WndProc [C:\AWD3\AppD9\AppD9\AppD9.cpp @ 131]
7537700a USER32!UserCallWinProcCheckWow+0x4aa
001d11a0 AppD9!WndProc [C:\AWD3\AppD9\AppD9\AppD9.cpp @ 131]
75376ce3 USER32!UserCallWinProcCheckWow+0x183
75373c86 USER32!HMValidateHandleNoSecure+0x46
7537a62f USER32!InternalCreateDialog+0x137f
001d11a0 AppD9!WndProc [C:\AWD3\AppD9\AppD9\AppD9.cpp @ 131]
001d11a0 AppD9!WndProc [C:\AWD3\AppD9\AppD9\AppD9.cpp @ 131]
7539a600 USER32!_except_handler4
75375938 USER32!DispatchMessageWorker+0x4b8
001d11a0 AppD9!WndProc [C:\AWD3\AppD9\AppD9\AppD9.cpp @ 131]
75378a15 USER32!IsDialogMessageW+0x105
001d11a0 AppD9!WndProc [C:\AWD3\AppD9\AppD9\AppD9.cpp @ 131]
7539a600 USER32!_except_handler4
7538e738 USER32!DialogBox2+0x189
7767718c ntdll_77600000!KiUserCallbackDispatcher+0x4c
7538e585 USER32!InternalDialogBox+0xc4
7538e598 USER32!InternalDialogBox+0xd7
753daeec USER32!SoftModalMessageBox+0x6bc
75350000 USER32!pfnClientA <PERF> (USER32+0x0)
753daf48 USER32!SoftModalMessageBox+0x718
753d92f0 USER32!MB_DlgProc
001e2cca AppD9!type_info::`vftable'+0x1e
7539a600 USER32!_except_handler4
7556202c win32u!NtUserModifyUserStartupInfoFlags+0xc
753d9cb0 USER32!MessageBoxWorker+0x314
001e2cc8 AppD9!type_info::`vftable'+0x1c
001e2cbc AppD9!type_info::`vftable'+0x10
7535701c USER32!SEBbuttons+0x4
753720ad USER32!RealDefWindowProcWorker+0xdad
753720bb USER32!RealDefWindowProcWorker+0xdbb
753739d1 USER32!UserCallDlgProcCheckWow+0x321
75375d46 USER32!HMValidateHandle+0x56
75371193 USER32!RealDefWindowProcW+0x53
753ff038 USER32!grgbDwpLiteHookMsg
753712b7 USER32!DefWindowProcW+0x107
753712ed USER32!DefWindowProcW+0x13d
753712c8 USER32!DefWindowProcW+0x118
7763edec ntdll_77600000!RtlDeactivateActivationContextUnsafeFast+0x9c
7763f080 ntdll_77600000!RtlActivateActivationContextUnsafeFast+0x70
753d92f0 USER32!MB_DlgProc
```

```
75397c12 USER32!_InternalCallWinProc+0x2a
75371668 USER32!RealDefWindowProcWorker+0x368
001e2cc8 AppD9!type_info::`vftable'+0x1c
753da660 USER32!MessageBoxTimeoutW+0x30
753da7b7 USER32!MessageBoxTimeoutW+0x187
001d11a0 AppD9!WndProc [C:\AWD3\AppD9\AppD9\AppD9.cpp @ 131]
7768ea99 ntdll_77600000!RtlDelayExecution+0xe9
001e2cc8 AppD9!type_info::`vftable'+0x1c
001e2cbc AppD9!type_info::`vftable'+0x10
753da825 USER32!MessageBoxW+0x45
001e2cc8 AppD9!type_info::`vftable'+0x1c
001e2cbc AppD9!type_info::`vftable'+0x10
001d1371 AppD9!StartModeling+0x41 [C:\AWD3\AppD9\AppD9\AppD9.cpp @ 198]
001e2cc8 AppD9!type_info::`vftable'+0x1c
001e2cbc AppD9!type_info::`vftable'+0x10
001d121a AppD9!WndProc+0x7a [C:\AWD3\AppD9\AppD9\AppD9.cpp @ 146]
7765b3f9 ntdll_77600000!RtlSetLastWin32Error+0x39
752db450 uxtheme!ThemePostWndProc
7763edec ntdll_77600000!RtlDeactivateActivationContextUnsafeFast+0x9c
752db61d uxtheme!ThemePostWndProc+0x1cd
7763f080 ntdll_77600000!RtlActivateActivationContextUnsafeFast+0x70
752db450 uxtheme!ThemePostWndProc
75397c12 USER32!_InternalCallWinProc+0x2a
001d11a0 AppD9!WndProc [C:\AWD3\AppD9\AppD9\AppD9.cpp @ 131]
001d11a0 AppD9!WndProc [C:\AWD3\AppD9\AppD9\AppD9.cpp @ 131]
7537700a USER32!UserCallWinProcCheckWow+0x4aa
001d11a0 AppD9!WndProc [C:\AWD3\AppD9\AppD9\AppD9.cpp @ 131]
75376ce3 USER32!UserCallWinProcCheckWow+0x183
75373c86 USER32!HMValidateHandleNoSecure+0x46
7537a62f USER32!InternalCreateDialog+0x137f
001d11a0 AppD9!WndProc [C:\AWD3\AppD9\AppD9\AppD9.cpp @ 131]
001d11a0 AppD9!WndProc [C:\AWD3\AppD9\AppD9\AppD9.cpp @ 131]
7539a600 USER32!_except_handler4
75375938 USER32!DispatchMessageWorker+0x4b8
001d11a0 AppD9!WndProc [C:\AWD3\AppD9\AppD9\AppD9.cpp @ 131]
75378a15 USER32!IsDialogMessageW+0x105
001d11a0 AppD9!WndProc [C:\AWD3\AppD9\AppD9\AppD9.cpp @ 131]
7539a600 USER32!_except_handler4
7538e738 USER32!DialogBox2+0x189
7767718c ntdll_77600000!KiUserCallbackDispatcher+0x4c
7538e585 USER32!InternalDialogBox+0xc4
7538e598 USER32!InternalDialogBox+0xd7
753daeec USER32!SoftModalMessageBox+0x6bc
75350000 USER32!pfnClientA <PERF> (USER32+0x0)
753daf48 USER32!SoftModalMessageBox+0x718
753d92f0 USER32!MB_DlgProc
001e2cca AppD9!type_info::`vftable'+0x1e
7539a600 USER32!_except_handler4
7556202c win32u!NtUserModifyUserStartupInfoFlags+0xc
753d9cb0 USER32!MessageBoxWorker+0x314
001e2cc8 AppD9!type_info::`vftable'+0x1c
001e2cbc AppD9!type_info::`vftable'+0x10
7535701c USER32!SEBbuttons+0x4
753720ad USER32!RealDefWindowProcWorker+0xdad
753720bb USER32!RealDefWindowProcWorker+0xdbb
753739d1 USER32!UserCallDlgProcCheckWow+0x321
75375d46 USER32!HMValidateHandle+0x56
75371193 USER32!RealDefWindowProcW+0x53
753ff038 USER32!grgbDwpLiteHookMsg
753712b7 USER32!DefWindowProcW+0x107
753712ed USER32!DefWindowProcW+0x13d
753712c8 USER32!DefWindowProcW+0x118
7763edec ntdll_77600000!RtlDeactivateActivationContextUnsafeFast+0x9c
7763f080 ntdll_77600000!RtlActivateActivationContextUnsafeFast+0x70
753d92f0 USER32!MB_DlgProc
75397c12 USER32!_InternalCallWinProc+0x2a
75371668 USER32!RealDefWindowProcWorker+0x368
001e2cc8 AppD9!type_info::`vftable'+0x1c
753da660 USER32!MessageBoxTimeoutW+0x30
753da7b7 USER32!MessageBoxTimeoutW+0x187
001d11a0 AppD9!WndProc [C:\AWD3\AppD9\AppD9\AppD9.cpp @ 131]
7768ea99 ntdll_77600000!RtlDelayExecution+0xe9
001e2cc8 AppD9!type_info::`vftable'+0x1c
001e2cbc AppD9!type_info::`vftable'+0x10
```

```
753da825 USER32!MessageBoxW+0x45
001e2cc8 AppD9!type_info::`vftable'+0x1c
001e2cbc AppD9!type_info::`vftable'+0x10
001d1371 AppD9!StartModeling+0x41 [C:\AWD3\AppD9\AppD9\AppD9.cpp @ 198]
001e2cc8 AppD9!type_info::`vftable'+0x1c
001e2cbc AppD9!type_info::`vftable'+0x10
001d121a AppD9!WndProc+0x7a [C:\AWD3\AppD9\AppD9\AppD9.cpp @ 146]
7765b3f9 ntdll_77600000!RtlSetLastWin32Error+0x39
752db450 uxtheme!ThemePostWndProc
7763edec ntdll_77600000!RtlDeactivateActivationContextUnsafeFast+0x9c
752db61d uxtheme!ThemePostWndProc+0x1cd
7763f080 ntdll_77600000!RtlActivateActivationContextUnsafeFast+0x70
752db450 uxtheme!ThemePostWndProc
75397c12 USER32!_InternalCallWinProc+0x2a
001d11a0 AppD9!WndProc [C:\AWD3\AppD9\AppD9\AppD9.cpp @ 131]
001d11a0 AppD9!WndProc [C:\AWD3\AppD9\AppD9\AppD9.cpp @ 131]
7537700a USER32!UserCallWinProcCheckWow+0x4aa
001d11a0 AppD9!WndProc [C:\AWD3\AppD9\AppD9\AppD9.cpp @ 131]
75376ce3 USER32!UserCallWinProcCheckWow+0x183
75373c86 USER32!HMValidateHandleNoSecure+0x46
7537a62f USER32!InternalCreateDialog+0x137f
001d11a0 AppD9!WndProc [C:\AWD3\AppD9\AppD9\AppD9.cpp @ 131]
001d11a0 AppD9!WndProc [C:\AWD3\AppD9\AppD9\AppD9.cpp @ 131]
7539a600 USER32!_except_handler4
75375938 USER32!DispatchMessageWorker+0x4b8
001d11a0 AppD9!WndProc [C:\AWD3\AppD9\AppD9\AppD9.cpp @ 131]
75378a15 USER32!IsDialogMessageW+0x105
001d11a0 AppD9!WndProc [C:\AWD3\AppD9\AppD9\AppD9.cpp @ 131]
7539a600 USER32!_except_handler4
7538e738 USER32!DialogBox2+0x189
7767718c ntdll_77600000!KiUserCallbackDispatcher+0x4c
7538e585 USER32!InternalDialogBox+0xc4
7538e598 USER32!InternalDialogBox+0xd7
753daeec USER32!SoftModalMessageBox+0x6bc
75350000 USER32!pfnClientA <PERF> (USER32+0x0)
753daf48 USER32!SoftModalMessageBox+0x718
753d92f0 USER32!MB_DlgProc
001e2cca AppD9!type_info::`vftable'+0x1e
7539a600 USER32!_except_handler4
7556202c win32u!NtUserModifyUserStartupInfoFlags+0xc
753d9cb0 USER32!MessageBoxWorker+0x314
001e2cc8 AppD9!type_info::`vftable'+0x1c
001e2cbc AppD9!type_info::`vftable'+0x10
7535701c USER32!SEBbuttons+0x4
753720ad USER32!RealDefWindowProcWorker+0xdad
753720bb USER32!RealDefWindowProcWorker+0xdbb
753739d1 USER32!UserCallDlgProcCheckWow+0x321
75375d46 USER32!HMValidateHandle+0x56
75371193 USER32!RealDefWindowProcW+0x53
753ff038 USER32!grgbDwpLiteHookMsg
753712b7 USER32!DefWindowProcW+0x107
753712ed USER32!DefWindowProcW+0x13d
753712c8 USER32!DefWindowProcW+0x118
7763edec ntdll_77600000!RtlDeactivateActivationContextUnsafeFast+0x9c
7763f080 ntdll_77600000!RtlActivateActivationContextUnsafeFast+0x70
753d92f0 USER32!MB_DlgProc
75397c12 USER32!_InternalCallWinProc+0x2a
75371668 USER32!RealDefWindowProcWorker+0x368
001e2cc8 AppD9!type_info::`vftable'+0x1c
753da660 USER32!MessageBoxTimeoutW+0x30
753da7b7 USER32!MessageBoxTimeoutW+0x187
001d11a0 AppD9!WndProc [C:\AWD3\AppD9\AppD9\AppD9.cpp @ 131]
7768ea99 ntdll_77600000!RtlDelayExecution+0xe9
001e2cc8 AppD9!type_info::`vftable'+0x1c
001e2cbc AppD9!type_info::`vftable'+0x10
753da825 USER32!MessageBoxW+0x45
001e2cc8 AppD9!type_info::`vftable'+0x1c
001e2cbc AppD9!type_info::`vftable'+0x10
001d1371 AppD9!StartModeling+0x41 [C:\AWD3\AppD9\AppD9\AppD9.cpp @ 198]
001e2cc8 AppD9!type_info::`vftable'+0x1c
001e2cbc AppD9!type_info::`vftable'+0x10
001d121a AppD9!WndProc+0x7a [C:\AWD3\AppD9\AppD9\AppD9.cpp @ 146]
7765b3f9 ntdll_77600000!RtlSetLastWin32Error+0x39
752db450 uxtheme!ThemePostWndProc
```

```
7763edec ntdll_77600000!RtlDeactivateActivationContextUnsafeFast+0x9c
752db61d uxtheme!ThemePostWndProc+0x1cd
7763f080 ntdll_77600000!RtlActivateActivationContextUnsafeFast+0x70
752db450 uxtheme!ThemePostWndProc
75397c12 USER32!_InternalCallWinProc+0x2a
001d11a0 AppD9!WndProc [C:\AWD3\AppD9\AppD9\AppD9.cpp @ 131]
001d11a0 AppD9!WndProc [C:\AWD3\AppD9\AppD9\AppD9.cpp @ 131]
7537700a USER32!UserCallWinProcCheckWow+0x4aa
001d11a0 AppD9!WndProc [C:\AWD3\AppD9\AppD9\AppD9.cpp @ 131]
75376ce3 USER32!UserCallWinProcCheckWow+0x183
75373c86 USER32!HMValidateHandleNoSecure+0x46
7537a62f USER32!InternalCreateDialog+0x137f
001d11a0 AppD9!WndProc [C:\AWD3\AppD9\AppD9\AppD9.cpp @ 131]
001d11a0 AppD9!WndProc [C:\AWD3\AppD9\AppD9\AppD9.cpp @ 131]
7539a600 USER32!_except_handler4
75375938 USER32!DispatchMessageWorker+0x4b8
001d11a0 AppD9!WndProc [C:\AWD3\AppD9\AppD9\AppD9.cpp @ 131]
75378a15 USER32!IsDialogMessageW+0x105
001d11a0 AppD9!WndProc [C:\AWD3\AppD9\AppD9\AppD9.cpp @ 131]
7539a600 USER32!_except_handler4
7538e738 USER32!DialogBox2+0x189
7767718c ntdll_77600000!KiUserCallbackDispatcher+0x4c
7538e585 USER32!InternalDialogBox+0xc4
7538e598 USER32!InternalDialogBox+0xd7
753daeec USER32!SoftModalMessageBox+0x6bc
75350000 USER32!pfnClientA <PERF> (USER32+0x0)
753daf48 USER32!SoftModalMessageBox+0x718
753d92f0 USER32!MB_DlgProc
001e2cca AppD9!type_info::`vftable'+0x1e
7539a600 USER32!_except_handler4
7556202c win32u!NtUserModifyUserStartupInfoFlags+0xc
753d9cb0 USER32!MessageBoxWorker+0x314
001e2cc8 AppD9!type_info::`vftable'+0x1c
001e2cbc AppD9!type_info::`vftable'+0x10
7535701c USER32!SEBbuttons+0x4
753720ad USER32!RealDefWindowProcWorker+0xdad
753720bb USER32!RealDefWindowProcWorker+0xdbb
753739d1 USER32!UserCallDlgProcCheckWow+0x321
75375d46 USER32!HMValidateHandle+0x56
75371193 USER32!RealDefWindowProcW+0x53
753ff038 USER32!grgbDwpLiteHookMsg
753712b7 USER32!DefWindowProcW+0x107
753712ed USER32!DefWindowProcW+0x13d
753712c8 USER32!DefWindowProcW+0x118
7763edec ntdll_77600000!RtlDeactivateActivationContextUnsafeFast+0x9c
7763f080 ntdll_77600000!RtlActivateActivationContextUnsafeFast+0x70
753d92f0 USER32!MB_DlgProc
75397c12 USER32!_InternalCallWinProc+0x2a
75371668 USER32!RealDefWindowProcWorker+0x368
001e2cc8 AppD9!type_info::`vftable'+0x1c
753da660 USER32!MessageBoxTimeoutW+0x30
753da7b7 USER32!MessageBoxTimeoutW+0x187
001d11a0 AppD9!WndProc [C:\AWD3\AppD9\AppD9\AppD9.cpp @ 131]
7768ea99 ntdll_77600000!RtlDelayExecution+0xe9
001e2cc8 AppD9!type_info::`vftable'+0x1c
001e2cbc AppD9!type_info::`vftable'+0x10
753da825 USER32!MessageBoxW+0x45
001e2cc8 AppD9!type_info::`vftable'+0x1c
001e2cbc AppD9!type_info::`vftable'+0x10
001d1371 AppD9!StartModeling+0x41 [C:\AWD3\AppD9\AppD9\AppD9.cpp @ 198]
001e2cc8 AppD9!type_info::`vftable'+0x1c
001e2cbc AppD9!type_info::`vftable'+0x10
001d121a AppD9!WndProc+0x7a [C:\AWD3\AppD9\AppD9\AppD9.cpp @ 146]
7765b3f9 ntdll_77600000!RtlSetLastWin32Error+0x39
752db450 uxtheme!ThemePostWndProc
7763edec ntdll_77600000!RtlDeactivateActivationContextUnsafeFast+0x9c
752db61d uxtheme!ThemePostWndProc+0x1cd
7763f080 ntdll_77600000!RtlActivateActivationContextUnsafeFast+0x70
752db450 uxtheme!ThemePostWndProc
75397c12 USER32!_InternalCallWinProc+0x2a
001d11a0 AppD9!WndProc [C:\AWD3\AppD9\AppD9\AppD9.cpp @ 131]
001d11a0 AppD9!WndProc [C:\AWD3\AppD9\AppD9\AppD9.cpp @ 131]
7537700a USER32!UserCallWinProcCheckWow+0x4aa
001d11a0 AppD9!WndProc [C:\AWD3\AppD9\AppD9\AppD9.cpp @ 131]
```

```
75376ce3 USER32!UserCallWinProcCheckWow+0x183
75373c86 USER32!HMValidateHandleNoSecure+0x46
7537a62f USER32!InternalCreateDialog+0x137f
001d11a0 AppD9!WndProc [C:\AWD3\AppD9\AppD9\AppD9.cpp @ 131]
001d11a0 AppD9!WndProc [C:\AWD3\AppD9\AppD9\AppD9.cpp @ 131]
7539a600 USER32!_except_handler4
75375938 USER32!DispatchMessageWorker+0x4b8
001d11a0 AppD9!WndProc [C:\AWD3\AppD9\AppD9\AppD9.cpp @ 131]
75378a15 USER32!IsDialogMessageW+0x105
001d11a0 AppD9!WndProc [C:\AWD3\AppD9\AppD9\AppD9.cpp @ 131]
7539a600 USER32!_except_handler4
7538e738 USER32!DialogBox2+0x189
7767718c ntdll_77600000!KiUserCallbackDispatcher+0x4c
7538e585 USER32!InternalDialogBox+0xc4
7538e598 USER32!InternalDialogBox+0xd7
753daeec USER32!SoftModalMessageBox+0x6bc
75350000 USER32!pfnClientA <PERF> (USER32+0x0)
753daf48 USER32!SoftModalMessageBox+0x718
753d92f0 USER32!MB_DlgProc
001e2cca AppD9!type_info::`vftable'+0x1e
7539a600 USER32!_except_handler4
7556202c win32u!NtUserModifyUserStartupInfoFlags+0xc
753d9cb0 USER32!MessageBoxWorker+0x314
001e2cc8 AppD9!type_info::`vftable'+0x1c
001e2cbc AppD9!type_info::`vftable'+0x10
7535701c USER32!SEBbuttons+0x4
753720ad USER32!RealDefWindowProcWorker+0xdad
753720bb USER32!RealDefWindowProcWorker+0xdbb
753739d1 USER32!UserCallDlgProcCheckWow+0x321
75375d46 USER32!HMValidateHandle+0x56
75371193 USER32!RealDefWindowProcW+0x53
753ff038 USER32!grgbDwpLiteHookMsg
753712b7 USER32!DefWindowProcW+0x107
753712ed USER32!DefWindowProcW+0x13d
753712c8 USER32!DefWindowProcW+0x118
7763edec ntdll_77600000!RtlDeactivateActivationContextUnsafeFast+0x9c
7763f080 ntdll_77600000!RtlActivateActivationContextUnsafeFast+0x70
753d92f0 USER32!MB_DlgProc
75397c12 USER32!_InternalCallWinProc+0x2a
75371668 USER32!RealDefWindowProcWorker+0x368
001e2cc8 AppD9!type_info::`vftable'+0x1c
753da660 USER32!MessageBoxTimeoutW+0x30
753da7b7 USER32!MessageBoxTimeoutW+0x187
001d11a0 AppD9!WndProc [C:\AWD3\AppD9\AppD9\AppD9.cpp @ 131]
7768ea99 ntdll_77600000!RtlDelayExecution+0xe9
001e2cc8 AppD9!type_info::`vftable'+0x1c
001e2cbc AppD9!type_info::`vftable'+0x10
753da825 USER32!MessageBoxW+0x45
001e2cc8 AppD9!type_info::`vftable'+0x1c
001e2cbc AppD9!type_info::`vftable'+0x10
001d1371 AppD9!StartModeling+0x41 [C:\AWD3\AppD9\AppD9\AppD9.cpp @ 198]
001e2cc8 AppD9!type_info::`vftable'+0x1c
001e2cbc AppD9!type_info::`vftable'+0x10
001d121a AppD9!WndProc+0x7a [C:\AWD3\AppD9\AppD9\AppD9.cpp @ 146]
7765b3f9 ntdll_77600000!RtlSetLastWin32Error+0x39
752db450 uxtheme!ThemePostWndProc
7763edec ntdll_77600000!RtlDeactivateActivationContextUnsafeFast+0x9c
752db61d uxtheme!ThemePostWndProc+0x1cd
7763f080 ntdll_77600000!RtlActivateActivationContextUnsafeFast+0x70
752db450 uxtheme!ThemePostWndProc
75397c12 USER32!_InternalCallWinProc+0x2a
001d11a0 AppD9!WndProc [C:\AWD3\AppD9\AppD9\AppD9.cpp @ 131]
001d11a0 AppD9!WndProc [C:\AWD3\AppD9\AppD9\AppD9.cpp @ 131]
7537700a USER32!UserCallWinProcCheckWow+0x4aa
001d11a0 AppD9!WndProc [C:\AWD3\AppD9\AppD9\AppD9.cpp @ 131]
75376ce3 USER32!UserCallWinProcCheckWow+0x183
75373c86 USER32!HMValidateHandleNoSecure+0x46
7537a62f USER32!InternalCreateDialog+0x137f
001d11a0 AppD9!WndProc [C:\AWD3\AppD9\AppD9\AppD9.cpp @ 131]
001d11a0 AppD9!WndProc [C:\AWD3\AppD9\AppD9\AppD9.cpp @ 131]
7539a600 USER32!_except_handler4
75375938 USER32!DispatchMessageWorker+0x4b8
001d11a0 AppD9!WndProc [C:\AWD3\AppD9\AppD9\AppD9.cpp @ 131]
75378a15 USER32!IsDialogMessageW+0x105
```

```
001d11a0 AppD9!WndProc [C:\AWD3\AppD9\AppD9\AppD9.cpp @ 131]
7539a600 USER32!_except_handler4
7538e738 USER32!DialogBox2+0x189
7767718c ntdll_77600000!KiUserCallbackDispatcher+0x4c
7538e585 USER32!InternalDialogBox+0xc4
7538e598 USER32!InternalDialogBox+0xd7
753daeec USER32!SoftModalMessageBox+0x6bc
75350000 USER32!pfnClientA <PERF> (USER32+0x0)
753daf48 USER32!SoftModalMessageBox+0x718
753d92f0 USER32!MB_DlgProc
001e2cca AppD9!type_info::`vftable'+0x1e
7539a600 USER32!_except_handler4
7556202c win32u!NtUserModifyUserStartupInfoFlags+0xc
753d9cb0 USER32!MessageBoxWorker+0x314
001e2cc8 AppD9!type_info::`vftable'+0x1c
001e2cbc AppD9!type_info::`vftable'+0x10
7535701c USER32!SEBbuttons+0x4
753720ad USER32!RealDefWindowProcWorker+0xdad
753720bb USER32!RealDefWindowProcWorker+0xdbb
753739d1 USER32!UserCallDlgProcCheckWow+0x321
75375d46 USER32!HMValidateHandle+0x56
75371193 USER32!RealDefWindowProcW+0x53
753ff038 USER32!grgbDwpLiteHookMsg
753712b7 USER32!DefWindowProcW+0x107
753712ed USER32!DefWindowProcW+0x13d
753712c8 USER32!DefWindowProcW+0x118
7763edec ntdll_77600000!RtlDeactivateActivationContextUnsafeFast+0x9c
7763f080 ntdll_77600000!RtlActivateActivationContextUnsafeFast+0x70
753d92f0 USER32!MB_DlgProc
75397c12 USER32!_InternalCallWinProc+0x2a
75371668 USER32!RealDefWindowProcWorker+0x368
001e2cc8 AppD9!type_info::`vftable'+0x1c
753da660 USER32!MessageBoxTimeoutW+0x30
753da7b7 USER32!MessageBoxTimeoutW+0x187
001d11a0 AppD9!WndProc [C:\AWD3\AppD9\AppD9\AppD9.cpp @ 131]
7768ea99 ntdll_77600000!RtlDelayExecution+0xe9
001e2cc8 AppD9!type_info::`vftable'+0x1c
001e2cbc AppD9!type_info::`vftable'+0x10
```
753da825 USER32!MessageBoxW+0x45
```
001e2cc8 AppD9!type_info::`vftable'+0x1c
001e2cbc AppD9!type_info::`vftable'+0x10
001d1371 AppD9!StartModeling+0x41 [C:\AWD3\AppD9\AppD9\AppD9.cpp @ 198]
001e2cc8 AppD9!type_info::`vftable'+0x1c
001e2cbc AppD9!type_info::`vftable'+0x10
001d121a AppD9!WndProc+0x7a [C:\AWD3\AppD9\AppD9\AppD9.cpp @ 146]
7765b3f9 ntdll_77600000!RtlSetLastWin32Error+0x39
752db450 uxtheme!ThemePostWndProc
7763edec ntdll_77600000!RtlDeactivateActivationContextUnsafeFast+0x9c
752db61d uxtheme!ThemePostWndProc+0x1cd
7763f080 ntdll_77600000!RtlActivateActivationContextUnsafeFast+0x70
752db450 uxtheme!ThemePostWndProc
75397c12 USER32!_InternalCallWinProc+0x2a
001d11a0 AppD9!WndProc [C:\AWD3\AppD9\AppD9\AppD9.cpp @ 131]
001d11a0 AppD9!WndProc [C:\AWD3\AppD9\AppD9\AppD9.cpp @ 131]
7537700a USER32!UserCallWinProcCheckWow+0x4aa
001d11a0 AppD9!WndProc [C:\AWD3\AppD9\AppD9\AppD9.cpp @ 131]
75376ce3 USER32!UserCallWinProcCheckWow+0x183
75373c86 USER32!HMValidateHandleNoSecure+0x46
7537a62f USER32!InternalCreateDialog+0x137f
001d11a0 AppD9!WndProc [C:\AWD3\AppD9\AppD9\AppD9.cpp @ 131]
001d11a0 AppD9!WndProc [C:\AWD3\AppD9\AppD9\AppD9.cpp @ 131]
7539a600 USER32!_except_handler4
75375938 USER32!DispatchMessageWorker+0x4b8
001d11a0 AppD9!WndProc [C:\AWD3\AppD9\AppD9\AppD9.cpp @ 131]
75378a15 USER32!IsDialogMessageW+0x105
001d11a0 AppD9!WndProc [C:\AWD3\AppD9\AppD9\AppD9.cpp @ 131]
7539a600 USER32!_except_handler4
7538e738 USER32!DialogBox2+0x189
7767718c ntdll_77600000!KiUserCallbackDispatcher+0x4c
7538e585 USER32!InternalDialogBox+0xc4
7538e598 USER32!InternalDialogBox+0xd7
753daeec USER32!SoftModalMessageBox+0x6bc
75350000 USER32!pfnClientA <PERF> (USER32+0x0)
753daf48 USER32!SoftModalMessageBox+0x718
```

```
753d92f0 USER32!MB_DlgProc
750c694b CoreMessaging!__guard_check_icall_thunk+0x30b
001e2cca AppD9!type_info::`vftable'+0x1e
750d1a72 CoreMessaging!__guard_check_icall_thunk+0xb432
7539a600 USER32!_except_handler4
7556202c win32u!NtUserModifyUserStartupInfoFlags+0xc
753d9cb0 USER32!MessageBoxWorker+0x314
001e2cc8 AppD9!type_info::`vftable'+0x1c
001e2cbc AppD9!type_info::`vftable'+0x10
7535701c USER32!SEBbuttons+0x4
76d461d0 KERNELBASE!FlsSetValue
7768c45e ntdll_77600000!RtlFlsSetValue+0x1e
76d461d0 KERNELBASE!FlsSetValue
76d461e1 KERNELBASE!FlsSetValue+0x11
77349545 ucrtbase!__crt_state_management::leave_os_call+0xe5
77349680 ucrtbase!free
773a0680 ucrtbase!_XMMI_FP_Emulation+0x132d
77349391 ucrtbase!__crt_state_management::wrapped_invoke<void (__cdecl*)(void *),void *,void>+0x91
7734935f ucrtbase!__crt_state_management::wrapped_invoke<void (__cdecl*)(void *),void *,void>+0x5f
750ab0e0 CoreMessaging!Microsoft::CoreUI::Dispatch::DeferredUserDispatcher::DeferredScheduleDispatchCallback
773888e0 ucrtbase!_except_handler4
7504513b CoreMessaging!Cn::Com::DeferredRelease::NoContext_Callback_ProcessItems+0x48
75054796
CoreMessaging!CFlat::ComExportAdapter<IExportDispatcherQueueInterop,Microsoft::CoreUI::IExportDispatcherQueueInterop>:
:Release+0x66
75054730
CoreMessaging!CFlat::ComExportAdapter<IExportDispatcherQueueInterop,Microsoft::CoreUI::IExportDispatcherQueueInterop>:
:Release
750c689b CoreMessaging!__guard_check_icall_thunk+0x25b
75054796
CoreMessaging!CFlat::ComExportAdapter<IExportDispatcherQueueInterop,Microsoft::CoreUI::IExportDispatcherQueueInterop>:
:Release+0x66
7508dd7a CoreMessaging!Microsoft::CoreUI::Dispatch::UserAdapter::DoWork+0x7c
7508dd7f CoreMessaging!Microsoft::CoreUI::Dispatch::UserAdapter::DoWork+0x81
750cdfab CoreMessaging!__guard_check_icall_thunk+0x796b
7508dd7f CoreMessaging!Microsoft::CoreUI::Dispatch::UserAdapter::DoWork+0x81
75088ac8 CoreMessaging!Microsoft::CoreUI::Dispatch::UserAdapter::HandleDispatchNotifyMessage+0x33
75088ad3 CoreMessaging!Microsoft::CoreUI::Dispatch::UserAdapter::HandleDispatchNotifyMessage+0x3e
7508dc90 CoreMessaging!Microsoft::CoreUI::Dispatch::UserAdapter::WindowProc
7763edec ntdll_77600000!RtlDeactivateActivationContextUnsafeFast+0x9c
001e2cc8 AppD9!type_info::`vftable'+0x1c
753da660 USER32!MessageBoxTimeoutW+0x30
753da7b7 USER32!MessageBoxTimeoutW+0x187
001d11a0 AppD9!WndProc [C:\AWD3\AppD9\AppD9\AppD9.cpp @ 131]
7768ea99 ntdll_77600000!RtlDelayExecution+0xe9
001e2cc8 AppD9!type_info::`vftable'+0x1c
001e2cbc AppD9!type_info::`vftable'+0x10
753da825 USER32!MessageBoxW+0x45
001e2cc8 AppD9!type_info::`vftable'+0x1c
001e2cbc AppD9!type_info::`vftable'+0x10
001d1371 AppD9!StartModeling+0x41 [C:\AWD3\AppD9\AppD9\AppD9.cpp @ 198]
001e2cc8 AppD9!type_info::`vftable'+0x1c
001e2cbc AppD9!type_info::`vftable'+0x10
001d121a AppD9!WndProc+0x7a [C:\AWD3\AppD9\AppD9\AppD9.cpp @ 146]
7508dc90 CoreMessaging!Microsoft::CoreUI::Dispatch::UserAdapter::WindowProc
7763edec ntdll_77600000!RtlDeactivateActivationContextUnsafeFast+0x9c
7508dc90 CoreMessaging!Microsoft::CoreUI::Dispatch::UserAdapter::WindowProc
7763f080 ntdll_77600000!RtlActivateActivationContextUnsafeFast+0x70
752db450 uxtheme!ThemePostWndProc
7508dcf6 CoreMessaging!Microsoft::CoreUI::Dispatch::UserAdapter::WindowProc+0x66
7508dc90 CoreMessaging!Microsoft::CoreUI::Dispatch::UserAdapter::WindowProc
75397c12 USER32!_InternalCallWinProc+0x2a
001d11a0 AppD9!WndProc [C:\AWD3\AppD9\AppD9\AppD9.cpp @ 131]
001d11a0 AppD9!WndProc [C:\AWD3\AppD9\AppD9\AppD9.cpp @ 131]
7537700a USER32!UserCallWinProcCheckWow+0x4aa
001d11a0 AppD9!WndProc [C:\AWD3\AppD9\AppD9\AppD9.cpp @ 131]
75376ce3 USER32!UserCallWinProcCheckWow+0x183
7537f98f USER32!__fnDWORD+0x3f
77674c0c ntdll_77600000!NtCallbackReturn+0xc
7537f9a7 USER32!__fnDWORD+0x57
7537a62f USER32!InternalCreateDialog+0x137f
001d11a0 AppD9!WndProc [C:\AWD3\AppD9\AppD9\AppD9.cpp @ 131]
001d11a0 AppD9!WndProc [C:\AWD3\AppD9\AppD9\AppD9.cpp @ 131]
77698340 ntdll_77600000!NtdllDispatchMessage_W
```

```
7539a600 USER32!_except_handler4
...
753da7b7 USER32!MessageBoxTimeoutW+0x187
001d11a0 AppD9!WndProc [C:\AWD3\AppD9\AppD9\AppD9.cpp @ 131]
7768ea99 ntdll_77600000!RtlDelayExecution+0xe9
001e2cc8 AppD9!type_info::`vftable'+0x1c
001e2cbc AppD9!type_info::`vftable'+0x10
753da825 USER32!MessageBoxW+0x45
001e2cc8 AppD9!type_info::`vftable'+0x1c
001e2cbc AppD9!type_info::`vftable'+0x10
001d1371 AppD9!StartModeling+0x41 [C:\AWD3\AppD9\AppD9\AppD9.cpp @ 198]
001e2cc8 AppD9!type_info::`vftable'+0x1c
001e2cbc AppD9!type_info::`vftable'+0x10
001d121a AppD9!WndProc+0x7a [C:\AWD3\AppD9\AppD9\AppD9.cpp @ 146]
7765b3f9 ntdll_77600000!RtlSetLastWin32Error+0x39
752db450 uxtheme!ThemePostWndProc
7763edec ntdll_77600000!RtlDeactivateActivationContextUnsafeFast+0x9c
752db61d uxtheme!ThemePostWndProc+0x1cd
7763f080 ntdll_77600000!RtlActivateActivationContextUnsafeFast+0x70
752db450 uxtheme!ThemePostWndProc
75397c12 USER32!_InternalCallWinProc+0x2a
001d11a0 AppD9!WndProc [C:\AWD3\AppD9\AppD9\AppD9.cpp @ 131]
001d11a0 AppD9!WndProc [C:\AWD3\AppD9\AppD9\AppD9.cpp @ 131]
7537700a USER32!UserCallWinProcCheckWow+0x4aa
001d11a0 AppD9!WndProc [C:\AWD3\AppD9\AppD9\AppD9.cpp @ 131]
75376ce3 USER32!UserCallWinProcCheckWow+0x183
75373c86 USER32!HMValidateHandleNoSecure+0x46
7537a62f USER32!InternalCreateDialog+0x137f
001d11a0 AppD9!WndProc [C:\AWD3\AppD9\AppD9\AppD9.cpp @ 131]
001d11a0 AppD9!WndProc [C:\AWD3\AppD9\AppD9\AppD9.cpp @ 131]
7539a600 USER32!_except_handler4
75375938 USER32!DispatchMessageWorker+0x4b8
001d11a0 AppD9!WndProc [C:\AWD3\AppD9\AppD9\AppD9.cpp @ 131]
75378a15 USER32!IsDialogMessageW+0x105
001d11a0 AppD9!WndProc [C:\AWD3\AppD9\AppD9\AppD9.cpp @ 131]
7539a600 USER32!_except_handler4
7538e738 USER32!DialogBox2+0x189
7767718c ntdll_77600000!KiUserCallbackDispatcher+0x4c
7538e585 USER32!InternalDialogBox+0xc4
7538e598 USER32!InternalDialogBox+0xd7
753daeec USER32!SoftModalMessageBox+0x6bc
75350000 USER32!pfnClientA <PERF> (USER32+0x0)
753daf48 USER32!SoftModalMessageBox+0x718
753d92f0 USER32!MB_DlgProc
001e2cca AppD9!type_info::`vftable'+0x1e
7539a600 USER32!_except_handler4
7556202c win32u!NtUserModifyUserStartupInfoFlags+0xc
753d9cb0 USER32!MessageBoxWorker+0x314
001e2cc8 AppD9!type_info::`vftable'+0x1c
001e2cbc AppD9!type_info::`vftable'+0x10
7535701c USER32!SEBbuttons+0x4
753720ad USER32!RealDefWindowProcWorker+0xdad
753720bb USER32!RealDefWindowProcWorker+0xdbb
753739d1 USER32!UserCallDlgProcCheckWow+0x321
75375d46 USER32!HMValidateHandle+0x56
75371193 USER32!RealDefWindowProcW+0x53
753ff038 USER32!grgbDwpLiteHookMsg
753712b7 USER32!DefWindowProcW+0x107
753712ed USER32!DefWindowProcW+0x13d
753712c8 USER32!DefWindowProcW+0x118
7539a600 USER32!_except_handler4
75373459 USER32!DefDlgProcWorker+0x939
75372b7a USER32!DefDlgProcWorker+0x5a
001e2cc8 AppD9!type_info::`vftable'+0x1c
753da660 USER32!MessageBoxTimeoutW+0x30
753da7b7 USER32!MessageBoxTimeoutW+0x187
001d11a0 AppD9!WndProc [C:\AWD3\AppD9\AppD9\AppD9.cpp @ 131]
7768ea99 ntdll_77600000!RtlDelayExecution+0xe9
001e2cc8 AppD9!type_info::`vftable'+0x1c
001e2cbc AppD9!type_info::`vftable'+0x10
753da825 USER32!MessageBoxW+0x45
001e2cc8 AppD9!type_info::`vftable'+0x1c
001e2cbc AppD9!type_info::`vftable'+0x10
001d1371 AppD9!StartModeling+0x41 [C:\AWD3\AppD9\AppD9\AppD9.cpp @ 198]
```

```
001e2cc8 AppD9!type_info::`vftable'+0x1c
001e2cbc AppD9!type_info::`vftable'+0x10
001d121a AppD9!WndProc+0x7a [C:\AWD3\AppD9\AppD9\AppD9.cpp @ 146]
753df1b0 USER32!StaticWndProcW
753df1b0 USER32!StaticWndProcW
7763f080 ntdll_77600000!RtlActivateActivationContextUnsafeFast+0x70
75397c12 USER32!_InternalCallWinProc+0x2a
001d11a0 AppD9!WndProc [C:\AWD3\AppD9\AppD9\AppD9.cpp @ 131]
001d11a0 AppD9!WndProc [C:\AWD3\AppD9\AppD9\AppD9.cpp @ 131]
7537700a USER32!UserCallWinProcCheckWow+0x4aa
001d11a0 AppD9!WndProc [C:\AWD3\AppD9\AppD9\AppD9.cpp @ 131]
75376ce3 USER32!UserCallWinProcCheckWow+0x183
75373c86 USER32!HMValidateHandleNoSecure+0x46
7537a62f USER32!InternalCreateDialog+0x137f
001d11a0 AppD9!WndProc [C:\AWD3\AppD9\AppD9\AppD9.cpp @ 131]
001d11a0 AppD9!WndProc [C:\AWD3\AppD9\AppD9\AppD9.cpp @ 131]
7539a600 USER32!_except_handler4
75375938 USER32!DispatchMessageWorker+0x4b8
001d11a0 AppD9!WndProc [C:\AWD3\AppD9\AppD9\AppD9.cpp @ 131]
75378a15 USER32!IsDialogMessageW+0x105
001d11a0 AppD9!WndProc [C:\AWD3\AppD9\AppD9\AppD9.cpp @ 131]
7539a600 USER32!_except_handler4
7538e738 USER32!DialogBox2+0x189
7767718c ntdll_77600000!KiUserCallbackDispatcher+0x4c
7538e585 USER32!InternalDialogBox+0xc4
7538e598 USER32!InternalDialogBox+0xd7
753daeec USER32!SoftModalMessageBox+0x6bc
75350000 USER32!pfnClientA <PERF> (USER32+0x0)
753daf48 USER32!SoftModalMessageBox+0x718
753d92f0 USER32!MB_DlgProc
001e2cca AppD9!type_info::`vftable'+0x1e
7539a600 USER32!_except_handler4
7556202c win32u!NtUserModifyUserStartupInfoFlags+0xc
753d9cb0 USER32!MessageBoxWorker+0x314
001e2cc8 AppD9!type_info::`vftable'+0x1c
001e2cbc AppD9!type_info::`vftable'+0x10
7537f9a7 USER32!__fnDWORD+0x57
7535701c USER32!SEBbuttons+0x4
752dc03f uxtheme!_ThemeDefWindowProc+0x5af
7767718c ntdll_77600000!KiUserCallbackDispatcher+0x4c
776770c0 ntdll_77600000!KiUserCallbackExceptionHandler
001d11a0 AppD9!WndProc [C:\AWD3\AppD9\AppD9\AppD9.cpp @ 131]
77698340 ntdll_77600000!NtdllDispatchMessage_W
755610dc win32u!NtUserMessageCall+0xc
753713d0 USER32!RealDefWindowProcWorker+0xd0
753713de USER32!RealDefWindowProcWorker+0xde
75375d46 USER32!HMValidateHandle+0x56
75375d46 USER32!HMValidateHandle+0x56
75371193 USER32!RealDefWindowProcW+0x53
75371140 USER32!RealDefWindowProcW
75371140 USER32!RealDefWindowProcW
752d9b5c uxtheme!DoMsgDefault+0x2c
752eacd6 uxtheme!OnDwpNcLButtonDown+0x66
752dc2b2 uxtheme!_ThemeDefWindowProc+0x822
001e2cc8 AppD9!type_info::`vftable'+0x1c
753da660 USER32!MessageBoxTimeoutW+0x30
753da7b7 USER32!MessageBoxTimeoutW+0x187
001d11a0 AppD9!WndProc [C:\AWD3\AppD9\AppD9\AppD9.cpp @ 131]
001e2cc8 AppD9!type_info::`vftable'+0x1c
001e2cbc AppD9!type_info::`vftable'+0x10
753da825 USER32!MessageBoxW+0x45
001e2cc8 AppD9!type_info::`vftable'+0x1c
001e2cbc AppD9!type_info::`vftable'+0x10
...
77698340 ntdll_77600000!NtdllDispatchMessage_W
755610cc win32u!NtUserGetMessage+0xc
7537ffa0 USER32!GetMessageW+0x30
001d11a0 AppD9!WndProc [C:\AWD3\AppD9\AppD9\AppD9.cpp @ 131]
7539a600 USER32!_except_handler4
75375470 USER32!DispatchMessageW+0x10
001d109d AppD9!wWinMain+0x9d [C:\AWD3\AppD9\AppD9\AppD9.cpp @ 59]
001d155d AppD9!__scrt_common_main_seh+0xf8 [d:\a01\_work\38\s\src\vctools\crt\vcstartup\src\startup\exe_common.inl @
288]
001d0000 AppD9!_LNan_C
```

```
001d15e1 AppD9!wWinMainCRTStartup [d:\a01\_work\38\s\src\vctools\crt\vcstartup\src\startup\exe_wwinmain.cpp @ 15]
001d15e1 AppD9!wWinMainCRTStartup [d:\a01\_work\38\s\src\vctools\crt\vcstartup\src\startup\exe_wwinmain.cpp @ 15]
001d1f40 AppD9!_except_handler4 [d:\a01\_work\38\s\src\vctools\crt\vcruntime\src\eh\i386\chandler4.c @ 316]
76306839 KERNEL32!BaseThreadInitThunk+0x19
76306820 KERNEL32!BaseThreadInitThunk
7766901f ntdll_77600000!__RtlUserThreadStart+0x2b
7767d260 ntdll_77600000!_except_handler4
77668fed ntdll_77600000!_RtlUserThreadStart+0x1b
77698e12 ntdll_77600000!FinalExceptionHandlerPad2
001d15e1 AppD9!wWinMainCRTStartup [d:\a01\_work\38\s\src\vctools\crt\vcstartup\src\startup\exe_wwinmain.cpp @ 15]
```

```
0: kd:x86> ub 753da825
USER32!MessageBoxW+0x26:
00000000`753da806 mov        dword ptr [USER32!gpReturnAddr (753fed30)],1
00000000`753da810 push       0FFFFFFFFh
00000000`753da812 push       0
00000000`753da814 push       dword ptr [ebp+14h]
00000000`753da817 push       dword ptr [ebp+10h]
00000000`753da81a push       dword ptr [ebp+0Ch]
00000000`753da81d push       dword ptr [ebp+8]
00000000`753da820 call       USER32!MessageBoxTimeoutW (753da630)
```

```
0: kd:x86> .effmach AMD64
Effective machine: x64 (AMD64)
```

```
0: kd> !teb
Wow64 TEB32 at 00000000006bf000
    ExceptionList:          000000000095969c
    StackBase:              0000000000960000
    StackLimit:             0000000000957000
    SubSystemTib:           0000000000000000
    FiberData:              0000000000001e00
    ArbitraryUserPointer:   0000000000000000
    Self:                   00000000006bf000
    EnvironmentPointer:     0000000000000000
    ClientId:               0000000000001f44 . 0000000000001b10
    RpcHandle:              0000000000000000
    Tls Storage:            0000000000b46750
    PEB Address:            00000000006bc000
    LastErrorValue:         0
    LastStatusValue:        c0000034
    Count Owned Locks:      0
    HardErrorMode:          0


Wow64 TEB at 00000000006bd000
    ExceptionList:          00000000006bf000
    StackBase:              000000000085fd20
    StackLimit:             0000000000857000
    SubSystemTib:           0000000000000000
    FiberData:              0000000000001e00
    ArbitraryUserPointer:   0000000000000000
    Self:                   00000000006bd000
    EnvironmentPointer:     0000000000000000
    ClientId:               0000000000001f44 . 0000000000001b10
    RpcHandle:              0000000000000000
    Tls Storage:            0000000000000000
    PEB Address:            00000000006bb000
    LastErrorValue:         0
    LastStatusValue:        c0000008
    Count Owned Locks:      0
```

```
         HardErrorMode:           0

0: kd> dt ntdll!_TEB   00000000006bd000
    +0x000 NtTib            : _NT_TIB
    +0x038 EnvironmentPointer : (null)
    +0x040 ClientId         : _CLIENT_ID
    +0x050 ActiveRpcHandle  : (null)
    +0x058 ThreadLocalStoragePointer : (null)
    +0x060 ProcessEnvironmentBlock : 0x00000000`006bb000 _PEB
    +0x068 LastErrorValue   : 0
    +0x06c CountOfOwnedCriticalSections : 0
    +0x070 CsrClientThread  : (null)
    +0x078 Win32ThreadInfo  : 0x00000000`00001b10 Void
    +0x080 User32Reserved   : [26] 0
    +0x0e8 UserReserved     : [5] 0
    +0x100 WOW32Reserved    : (null)
    +0x108 CurrentLocale    : 0x409
    +0x10c FpSoftwareStatusRegister : 0
    +0x110 ReservedForDebuggerInstrumentation : [16] (null)
    +0x190 SystemReserved1  : [30] (null)
    +0x280 PlaceholderCompatibilityMode : 0 ''
    +0x281 PlaceholderHydrationAlwaysExplicit : 0 ''
    +0x282 PlaceholderReserved : [10]   ""
    +0x28c ProxiedProcessId : 0
    +0x290 _ActivationStack : _ACTIVATION_CONTEXT_STACK
    +0x2b8 WorkingOnBehalfTicket : [8]   ""
    +0x2c0 ExceptionCode    : 0n0
    +0x2c4 Padding0         : [4]   ""
    +0x2c8 ActivationContextStackPointer : 0x00000000`006bd290 _ACTIVATION_CONTEXT_STACK
    +0x2d0 InstrumentationCallbackSp : 0
    +0x2d8 InstrumentationCallbackPreviousPc : 0
    +0x2e0 InstrumentationCallbackPreviousSp : 0
    +0x2e8 TxFsContext      : 0xfffe
    +0x2ec InstrumentationCallbackDisabled : 0 ''
    +0x2ed UnalignedLoadStoreExceptions : 0 ''
    +0x2ee Padding1         : [2]   ""
    +0x2f0 GdiTebBatch      : _GDI_TEB_BATCH
    +0x7d8 RealClientId     : _CLIENT_ID
    +0x7e8 GdiCachedProcessHandle : (null)
    +0x7f0 GdiClientPID     : 0
    +0x7f4 GdiClientTID     : 0
    +0x7f8 GdiThreadLocalInfo : (null)
    +0x800 Win32ClientInfo  : [62] 0x1388
    +0x9f0 glDispatchTable  : [233] (null)
    +0x1138 glReserved1     : [29] 0
    +0x1220 glReserved2     : (null)
    +0x1228 glSectionInfo   : (null)
    +0x1230 glSection       : (null)
    +0x1238 glTable         : (null)
    +0x1240 glCurrentRC     : (null)
    +0x1248 glContext       : (null)
    +0x1250 LastStatusValue : 0xc0000008
    +0x1254 Padding2        : [4]   ""
    +0x1258 StaticUnicodeString : _UNICODE_STRING ""
    +0x1268 StaticUnicodeBuffer : [261]   ""
    +0x1472 Padding3        : [6]   ""
    +0x1478 DeallocationStack : 0x00000000`00820000 Void
    +0x1480 TlsSlots         : [64] (null)
    +0x1680 TlsLinks         : _LIST_ENTRY [ 0x00000000`00000000 - 0x00000000`00000000 ]
```

```
+0x1690 Vdm                    : (null)
+0x1698 ReservedForNtRpc       : (null)
+0x16a0 DbgSsReserved          : [2] (null)
+0x16b0 HardErrorMode          : 0
+0x16b4 Padding4               : [4]   ""
+0x16b8 Instrumentation        : [11] (null)
+0x1710 ActivityId             : _GUID {00000000-0000-0000-0000-000000000000}
+0x1720 SubProcessTag          : (null)
+0x1728 PerflibData            : (null)
+0x1730 EtwTraceData           : (null)
+0x1738 WinSockData            : (null)
+0x1740 GdiBatchCount          : 0
+0x1744 CurrentIdealProcessor : _PROCESSOR_NUMBER
+0x1744 IdealProcessorValue : 0x2020000
+0x1744 ReservedPad0           : 0 ''
+0x1745 ReservedPad1           : 0 ''
+0x1746 ReservedPad2           : 0x2 ''
+0x1747 IdealProcessor         : 0x2 ''
+0x1748 GuaranteedStackBytes : 0
+0x174c Padding5               : [4]   ""
+0x1750 ReservedForPerf        : (null)
+0x1758 ReservedForOle         : (null)
+0x1760 WaitingOnLoaderLock : 0
+0x1764 Padding6               : [4]   ""
+0x1768 SavedPriorityState : (null)
+0x1770 ReservedForCodeCoverage : 0
+0x1778 ThreadPoolData         : (null)
+0x1780 TlsExpansionSlots      : (null)
+0x1788 ChpeV2CpuAreaInfo      : (null)
+0x1790 Unused                 : (null)
+0x1798 MuiGeneration          : 0
+0x179c IsImpersonating        : 0
+0x17a0 NlsCache               : (null)
+0x17a8 pShimData              : (null)
+0x17b0 HeapData               : 0x7cb30000
+0x17b4 Padding7               : [4]   ""
+0x17b8 CurrentTransactionHandle : (null)
+0x17c0 ActiveFrame            : (null)
+0x17c8 FlsData                : (null)
+0x17d0 PreferredLanguages : (null)
+0x17d8 UserPrefLanguages : (null)
+0x17e0 MergedPrefLanguages : (null)
+0x17e8 MuiImpersonation : 1
+0x17ec CrossTebFlags          : 0
+0x17ec SpareCrossTebBits : 0y0000000000000000 (0)
+0x17ee SameTebFlags           : 0x420
+0x17ee SafeThunkCall          : 0y0
+0x17ee InDebugPrint           : 0y0
+0x17ee HasFiberData           : 0y0
+0x17ee SkipThreadAttach       : 0y0
+0x17ee WerInShipAssertCode : 0y0
+0x17ee RanProcessInit         : 0y1
+0x17ee ClonedThread           : 0y0
+0x17ee SuppressDebugMsg : 0y0
+0x17ee DisableUserStackWalk : 0y0
+0x17ee RtlExceptionAttached : 0y0
+0x17ee InitialThread          : 0y1
+0x17ee SessionAware           : 0y0
+0x17ee LoadOwner              : 0y0
```

```
         +0x17ee LoaderWorker      : 0y0
         +0x17ee SkipLoaderInit    : 0y0
         +0x17ee SkipFileAPIBrokering : 0y0
         +0x17f0 TxnScopeEnterCallback : (null)
         +0x17f8 TxnScopeExitCallback : (null)
         +0x1800 TxnScopeContext   : (null)
         +0x1808 LockCount         : 0
         +0x180c WowTebOffset      : 0n8192
         +0x1810 ResourceRetValue  : (null)
         +0x1818 ReservedForWdf    : (null)
         +0x1820 ReservedForCrt    : 0
         +0x1828 EffectiveContainerId : _GUID {00000000-0000-0000-0000-000000000000}
         +0x1838 LastSleepCounter  : 0
         +0x1840 SpinCallCount     : 0
         +0x1844 Padding8          : [4]  ""
         +0x1848 ExtendedFeatureDisableMask : 0
```

```
0: kd> dp 00000000006bd000+0x1480+8
00000000`006be488  00000000`0085fd20 00000000`00000000
00000000`006be498  00000000`00000000 00000000`00000000
00000000`006be4a8  00000000`00000000 00000000`00000000
00000000`006be4b8  00000000`00000000 00000000`00000000
00000000`006be4c8  00000000`00000000 00000000`006bc488
00000000`006be4d8  00000000`00000000 00000000`00000000
00000000`006be4e8  00000000`00000000 00000000`00000000
00000000`006be4f8  00000000`00000000 00000000`00000000
```

```
0: kd> dd 00000000`0085fd20
00000000`0085fd20  014c0002 0001003f 00000000 00000000
00000000`0085fd30  00000000 00000000 00000000 00000000
00000000`0085fd40  0000027f 00000000 0000ffff 00000000
00000000`0085fd50  00000000 00000000 00000000 009591d0
00000000`0085fd60  00000000 77677140 00000000 00000000
00000000`0085fd70  00000000 00000000 00000000 00000000
00000000`0085fd80  00000000 00000000 00000000 00000000
00000000`0085fd90  00000000 00000000 00000000 00000000
```

```
0: kd> lmi m ntdll*
Browse full module list
start            end                     module name
00000000`77600000 00000000`777aa000  ntdll_77600000 # (pdb symbols)        ntdll.dll
00007ffb`45ba0000 00007ffb`45da9000  ntdll       (pdb symbols)          ntdll.dll
```

```
0: kd> dt ntdll_77600000!_CONTEXT 00000000`0085fd20+4
   +0x000 ContextFlags     : 0x1003f
   +0x004 Dr0              : 0
   +0x008 Dr1              : 0
   +0x00c Dr2              : 0
   +0x010 Dr3              : 0
   +0x014 Dr6              : 0
   +0x018 Dr7              : 0
   +0x01c FloatSave        : _FLOATING_SAVE_AREA
   +0x08c SegGs            : 0x2b
   +0x090 SegFs            : 0x53
   +0x094 SegEs            : 0x2b
   +0x098 SegDs            : 0x2b
   +0x09c Edi              : 0x959688
   +0x0a0 Esi              : 0x6bf000
   +0x0a4 Ebx              : 0x30406
```

```
  +0x0a8 Edx              : 0
  +0x0ac Ecx              : 0
  +0x0b0 Eax              : 1
  +0x0b4 Ebp              : 0x959644
  +0x0b8 Eip              : 0x77674f1c
  +0x0bc SegCs            : 0x23
  +0x0c0 EFlags           : 0x206
  +0x0c4 Esp              : 0x959624
  +0x0c8 SegSs            : 0x2b
  +0x0cc ExtendedRegisters : [512]   "???"

0: kd> .effmach x86
Effective machine: x86 compatible (x86)

0: kd:x86> .reload
Connected to Windows 10 22000 x64 target at (Fri Feb  9 12:38:40.924 2024 (UTC + 0:00)), ptr64
TRUE
Loading Kernel Symbols
...............................................................
...............................................................
..........................................
Loading User Symbols
.......
Loading unloaded module list
...........
Loading Wow64 Symbols
............................

0: kd:x86> k=0x959644 0x959624 0x77674f1c
 # ChildEBP          RetAddr
00 00959620 7768ea99    ntdll_77600000!NtDelayExecution+0xc
01 00959644 76d4c7bf    ntdll_77600000!RtlDelayExecution+0xe9
02 009596ac 76d4c74f    KERNELBASE!SleepEx+0x5f
*** WARNING: Unable to verify checksum for AppD9.exe
03 009596bc 001d138e    KERNELBASE!Sleep+0xf
04 009596c8 001d1338    AppD9!ConnectDB+0xe [C:\AWD3\AppD9\AppD9\ConnectDB.cpp @ 6]
05 009596d0 001d121a    AppD9!StartModeling+0x8 [C:\AWD3\AppD9\AppD9\AppD9.cpp @ 193]
06 00959730 75397c12    AppD9!WndProc+0x7a [C:\AWD3\AppD9\AppD9\AppD9.cpp @ 146]
07 0095975c 7537700a    USER32!_InternalCallWinProc+0x2a
08 0095984c 75375938    USER32!UserCallWinProcCheckWow+0x4aa
09 009598c8 7538e738    USER32!DispatchMessageWorker+0x4b8
0a 00959910 7538e598    USER32!DialogBox2+0x189
0b 00959940 753daf48    USER32!InternalDialogBox+0xd7
0c 00959a0c 753d9cb0    USER32!SoftModalMessageBox+0x718
0d 00959b68 753da7b7    USER32!MessageBoxWorker+0x314
0e 00959bf0 753da825    USER32!MessageBoxTimeoutW+0x187
0f 00959c10 001d1371    USER32!MessageBoxW+0x45
10 00959c28 001d121a    AppD9!StartModeling+0x41 [C:\AWD3\AppD9\AppD9\AppD9.cpp @ 198]
11 00959c88 75397c12    AppD9!WndProc+0x7a [C:\AWD3\AppD9\AppD9\AppD9.cpp @ 146]
12 00959cb4 7537700a    USER32!_InternalCallWinProc+0x2a
13 00959da4 75375938    USER32!UserCallWinProcCheckWow+0x4aa
14 00959e20 7538e738    USER32!DispatchMessageWorker+0x4b8
15 00959e68 7538e598    USER32!DialogBox2+0x189
16 00959e98 753daf48    USER32!InternalDialogBox+0xd7
17 00959f64 753d9cb0    USER32!SoftModalMessageBox+0x718
18 0095a0c0 753da7b7    USER32!MessageBoxWorker+0x314
19 0095a148 753da825    USER32!MessageBoxTimeoutW+0x187
1a 0095a168 001d1371    USER32!MessageBoxW+0x45
1b 0095a180 001d121a    AppD9!StartModeling+0x41 [C:\AWD3\AppD9\AppD9\AppD9.cpp @ 198]
1c 0095a1e0 75397c12    AppD9!WndProc+0x7a [C:\AWD3\AppD9\AppD9\AppD9.cpp @ 146]
1d 0095a20c 7537700a    USER32!_InternalCallWinProc+0x2a
1e 0095a2fc 75375938    USER32!UserCallWinProcCheckWow+0x4aa
1f 0095a378 7538e738    USER32!DispatchMessageWorker+0x4b8
20 0095a3c0 7538e598    USER32!DialogBox2+0x189
21 0095a3f0 753daf48    USER32!InternalDialogBox+0xd7
22 0095a4bc 753d9cb0    USER32!SoftModalMessageBox+0x718
```

```
23 0095a618 753da7b7    USER32!MessageBoxWorker+0x314
24 0095a6a0 753da825    USER32!MessageBoxTimeoutW+0x187
25 0095a6c0 001d1371    USER32!MessageBoxW+0x45
26 0095a6d8 001d121a    AppD9!StartModeling+0x41 [C:\AWD3\AppD9\AppD9\AppD9.cpp @ 198]
27 0095a738 75397c12    AppD9!WndProc+0x7a [C:\AWD3\AppD9\AppD9\AppD9.cpp @ 146]
28 0095a764 7537700a    USER32!_InternalCallWinProc+0x2a
29 0095a854 75375938    USER32!UserCallWinProcCheckWow+0x4aa
2a 0095a8d0 7538e738    USER32!DispatchMessageWorker+0x4b8
2b 0095a918 7538e598    USER32!DialogBox2+0x189
2c 0095a948 753daf48    USER32!InternalDialogBox+0xd7
2d 0095aa14 753d9cb0    USER32!SoftModalMessageBox+0x718
2e 0095ab70 753da7b7    USER32!MessageBoxWorker+0x314
2f 0095abf8 753da825    USER32!MessageBoxTimeoutW+0x187
30 0095ac18 001d1371    USER32!MessageBoxW+0x45
31 0095ac30 001d121a    AppD9!StartModeling+0x41 [C:\AWD3\AppD9\AppD9\AppD9.cpp @ 198]
32 0095ac90 75397c12    AppD9!WndProc+0x7a [C:\AWD3\AppD9\AppD9\AppD9.cpp @ 146]
33 0095acbc 7537700a    USER32!_InternalCallWinProc+0x2a
34 0095adac 75375938    USER32!UserCallWinProcCheckWow+0x4aa
35 0095ae28 7538e738    USER32!DispatchMessageWorker+0x4b8
36 0095ae70 7538e598    USER32!DialogBox2+0x189
37 0095aea0 753daf48    USER32!InternalDialogBox+0xd7
38 0095af6c 753d9cb0    USER32!SoftModalMessageBox+0x718
39 0095b0c8 753da7b7    USER32!MessageBoxWorker+0x314
3a 0095b150 753da825    USER32!MessageBoxTimeoutW+0x187
3b 0095b170 001d1371    USER32!MessageBoxW+0x45
3c 0095b188 001d121a    AppD9!StartModeling+0x41 [C:\AWD3\AppD9\AppD9\AppD9.cpp @ 198]
3d 0095b1e8 75397c12    AppD9!WndProc+0x7a [C:\AWD3\AppD9\AppD9\AppD9.cpp @ 146]
3e 0095b214 7537700a    USER32!_InternalCallWinProc+0x2a
3f 0095b304 75375938    USER32!UserCallWinProcCheckWow+0x4aa
40 0095b380 7538e738    USER32!DispatchMessageWorker+0x4b8
41 0095b3c8 7538e598    USER32!DialogBox2+0x189
42 0095b3f8 753daf48    USER32!InternalDialogBox+0xd7
43 0095b4c4 753d9cb0    USER32!SoftModalMessageBox+0x718
44 0095b620 753da7b7    USER32!MessageBoxWorker+0x314
45 0095b6a8 753da825    USER32!MessageBoxTimeoutW+0x187
46 0095b6c8 001d1371    USER32!MessageBoxW+0x45
47 0095b6e0 001d121a    AppD9!StartModeling+0x41 [C:\AWD3\AppD9\AppD9\AppD9.cpp @ 198]
48 0095b740 75397c12    AppD9!WndProc+0x7a [C:\AWD3\AppD9\AppD9\AppD9.cpp @ 146]
49 0095b76c 7537700a    USER32!_InternalCallWinProc+0x2a
4a 0095b85c 75375938    USER32!UserCallWinProcCheckWow+0x4aa
4b 0095b8d8 7538e738    USER32!DispatchMessageWorker+0x4b8
4c 0095b920 7538e598    USER32!DialogBox2+0x189
4d 0095b950 753daf48    USER32!InternalDialogBox+0xd7
4e 0095ba1c 753d9cb0    USER32!SoftModalMessageBox+0x718
4f 0095bb78 753da7b7    USER32!MessageBoxWorker+0x314
50 0095bc00 753da825    USER32!MessageBoxTimeoutW+0x187
51 0095bc20 001d1371    USER32!MessageBoxW+0x45
52 0095bc38 001d121a    AppD9!StartModeling+0x41 [C:\AWD3\AppD9\AppD9\AppD9.cpp @ 198]
53 0095bc98 75397c12    AppD9!WndProc+0x7a [C:\AWD3\AppD9\AppD9\AppD9.cpp @ 146]
54 0095bcc4 7537700a    USER32!_InternalCallWinProc+0x2a
55 0095bdb4 75375938    USER32!UserCallWinProcCheckWow+0x4aa
56 0095be30 7538e738    USER32!DispatchMessageWorker+0x4b8
57 0095be78 7538e598    USER32!DialogBox2+0x189
58 0095bea8 753daf48    USER32!InternalDialogBox+0xd7
59 0095bf74 753d9cb0    USER32!SoftModalMessageBox+0x718
5a 0095c0d0 753da7b7    USER32!MessageBoxWorker+0x314
5b 0095c158 753da825    USER32!MessageBoxTimeoutW+0x187
5c 0095c178 001d1371    USER32!MessageBoxW+0x45
5d 0095c190 001d121a    AppD9!StartModeling+0x41 [C:\AWD3\AppD9\AppD9\AppD9.cpp @ 198]
5e 0095c1f0 75397c12    AppD9!WndProc+0x7a [C:\AWD3\AppD9\AppD9\AppD9.cpp @ 146]
5f 0095c21c 7537700a    USER32!_InternalCallWinProc+0x2a
60 0095c30c 75375938    USER32!UserCallWinProcCheckWow+0x4aa
61 0095c388 7538e738    USER32!DispatchMessageWorker+0x4b8
62 0095c3d0 7538e598    USER32!DialogBox2+0x189
63 0095c400 753daf48    USER32!InternalDialogBox+0xd7
64 0095c4cc 753d9cb0    USER32!SoftModalMessageBox+0x718
65 0095c628 753da7b7    USER32!MessageBoxWorker+0x314
66 0095c6b0 753da825    USER32!MessageBoxTimeoutW+0x187
67 0095c6d0 001d1371    USER32!MessageBoxW+0x45
68 0095c6e8 001d121a    AppD9!StartModeling+0x41 [C:\AWD3\AppD9\AppD9\AppD9.cpp @ 198]
69 0095c748 75397c12    AppD9!WndProc+0x7a [C:\AWD3\AppD9\AppD9\AppD9.cpp @ 146]
6a 0095c774 7537700a    USER32!_InternalCallWinProc+0x2a
6b 0095c864 75375938    USER32!UserCallWinProcCheckWow+0x4aa
6c 0095c8e0 7538e738    USER32!DispatchMessageWorker+0x4b8
```

```
6d 0095c928 7538e598    USER32!DialogBox2+0x189
6e 0095c958 753daf48    USER32!InternalDialogBox+0xd7
6f 0095ca24 753d9cb0    USER32!SoftModalMessageBox+0x718
70 0095cb80 753da7b7    USER32!MessageBoxWorker+0x314
71 0095cc08 753da825    USER32!MessageBoxTimeoutW+0x187
72 0095cc28 001d1371    USER32!MessageBoxW+0x45
73 0095cc40 001d121a    AppD9!StartModeling+0x41 [C:\AWD3\AppD9\AppD9\AppD9.cpp @ 198]
74 0095cca0 75397c12    AppD9!WndProc+0x7a [C:\AWD3\AppD9\AppD9\AppD9.cpp @ 146]
75 0095cccc 7537700a    USER32!_InternalCallWinProc+0x2a
76 0095cdbc 75375938    USER32!UserCallWinProcCheckWow+0x4aa
77 0095ce38 7538e738    USER32!DispatchMessageWorker+0x4b8
78 0095ce80 7538e598    USER32!DialogBox2+0x189
79 0095ceb0 753daf48    USER32!InternalDialogBox+0xd7
7a 0095cf7c 753d9cb0    USER32!SoftModalMessageBox+0x718
7b 0095d0d8 753da7b7    USER32!MessageBoxWorker+0x314
7c 0095d160 753da825    USER32!MessageBoxTimeoutW+0x187
7d 0095d180 001d1371    USER32!MessageBoxW+0x45
7e 0095d198 001d121a    AppD9!StartModeling+0x41 [C:\AWD3\AppD9\AppD9\AppD9.cpp @ 198]
7f 0095d1f8 75397c12    AppD9!WndProc+0x7a [C:\AWD3\AppD9\AppD9\AppD9.cpp @ 146]
80 0095d224 7537700a    USER32!_InternalCallWinProc+0x2a
81 0095d314 75375938    USER32!UserCallWinProcCheckWow+0x4aa
82 0095d390 7538e738    USER32!DispatchMessageWorker+0x4b8
83 0095d3d8 7538e598    USER32!DialogBox2+0x189
84 0095d408 753daf48    USER32!InternalDialogBox+0xd7
85 0095d4d4 753d9cb0    USER32!SoftModalMessageBox+0x718
86 0095d630 753da7b7    USER32!MessageBoxWorker+0x314
87 0095d6b8 753da825    USER32!MessageBoxTimeoutW+0x187
88 0095d6d8 001d1371    USER32!MessageBoxW+0x45
89 0095d6f0 001d121a    AppD9!StartModeling+0x41 [C:\AWD3\AppD9\AppD9\AppD9.cpp @ 198]
8a 0095d750 75397c12    AppD9!WndProc+0x7a [C:\AWD3\AppD9\AppD9\AppD9.cpp @ 146]
8b 0095d77c 7537700a    USER32!_InternalCallWinProc+0x2a
8c 0095d86c 75375938    USER32!UserCallWinProcCheckWow+0x4aa
8d 0095d8e8 7538e738    USER32!DispatchMessageWorker+0x4b8
8e 0095d930 7538e598    USER32!DialogBox2+0x189
8f 0095d960 753daf48    USER32!InternalDialogBox+0xd7
90 0095da2c 753d9cb0    USER32!SoftModalMessageBox+0x718
91 0095db88 753da7b7    USER32!MessageBoxWorker+0x314
92 0095dc10 753da825    USER32!MessageBoxTimeoutW+0x187
93 0095dc30 001d1371    USER32!MessageBoxW+0x45
94 0095dc48 001d121a    AppD9!StartModeling+0x41 [C:\AWD3\AppD9\AppD9\AppD9.cpp @ 198]
95 0095dca8 75397c12    AppD9!WndProc+0x7a [C:\AWD3\AppD9\AppD9\AppD9.cpp @ 146]
96 0095dcd4 7537700a    USER32!_InternalCallWinProc+0x2a
97 0095ddc4 75375938    USER32!UserCallWinProcCheckWow+0x4aa
98 0095de40 7538e738    USER32!DispatchMessageWorker+0x4b8
99 0095de88 7538e598    USER32!DialogBox2+0x189
9a 0095deb8 753daf48    USER32!InternalDialogBox+0xd7
9b 0095df84 753d9cb0    USER32!SoftModalMessageBox+0x718
9c 0095e0e0 753da7b7    USER32!MessageBoxWorker+0x314
9d 0095e168 753da825    USER32!MessageBoxTimeoutW+0x187
9e 0095e188 001d1371    USER32!MessageBoxW+0x45
9f 0095e1a0 001d121a    AppD9!StartModeling+0x41 [C:\AWD3\AppD9\AppD9\AppD9.cpp @ 198]
a0 0095e200 75397c12    AppD9!WndProc+0x7a [C:\AWD3\AppD9\AppD9\AppD9.cpp @ 146]
a1 0095e22c 7537700a    USER32!_InternalCallWinProc+0x2a
a2 0095e31c 75375938    USER32!UserCallWinProcCheckWow+0x4aa
a3 0095e398 7538e738    USER32!DispatchMessageWorker+0x4b8
a4 0095e3e0 7538e598    USER32!DialogBox2+0x189
a5 0095e410 753daf48    USER32!InternalDialogBox+0xd7
a6 0095e4dc 753d9cb0    USER32!SoftModalMessageBox+0x718
a7 0095e638 753da7b7    USER32!MessageBoxWorker+0x314
a8 0095e6c0 753da825    USER32!MessageBoxTimeoutW+0x187
a9 0095e6e0 001d1371    USER32!MessageBoxW+0x45
aa 0095e6f8 001d121a    AppD9!StartModeling+0x41 [C:\AWD3\AppD9\AppD9\AppD9.cpp @ 198]
ab 0095e758 75397c12    AppD9!WndProc+0x7a [C:\AWD3\AppD9\AppD9\AppD9.cpp @ 146]
ac 0095e784 7537700a    USER32!_InternalCallWinProc+0x2a
ad 0095e874 75375938    USER32!UserCallWinProcCheckWow+0x4aa
ae 0095e8f0 7538e738    USER32!DispatchMessageWorker+0x4b8
af 0095e938 7538e598    USER32!DialogBox2+0x189
b0 0095e968 753daf48    USER32!InternalDialogBox+0xd7
b1 0095ea34 753d9cb0    USER32!SoftModalMessageBox+0x718
b2 0095eb90 753da7b7    USER32!MessageBoxWorker+0x314
b3 0095ec18 753da825    USER32!MessageBoxTimeoutW+0x187
b4 0095ec38 001d1371    USER32!MessageBoxW+0x45
b5 0095ec50 001d121a    AppD9!StartModeling+0x41 [C:\AWD3\AppD9\AppD9\AppD9.cpp @ 198]
b6 0095ecb0 75397c12    AppD9!WndProc+0x7a [C:\AWD3\AppD9\AppD9\AppD9.cpp @ 146]
```

```
b7 0095ecdc 7537700a    USER32!_InternalCallWinProc+0x2a
b8 0095edcc 75375938    USER32!UserCallWinProcCheckWow+0x4aa
b9 0095ee48 7538e738    USER32!DispatchMessageWorker+0x4b8
ba 0095ee90 7538e598    USER32!DialogBox2+0x189
bb 0095eec0 753daf48    USER32!InternalDialogBox+0xd7
bc 0095ef8c 753d9cb0    USER32!SoftModalMessageBox+0x718
bd 0095f0e8 753da7b7    USER32!MessageBoxWorker+0x314
be 0095f170 753da825    USER32!MessageBoxTimeoutW+0x187
bf 0095f190 001d1371    USER32!MessageBoxW+0x45
c0 0095f1a8 001d121a    AppD9!StartModeling+0x41 [C:\AWD3\AppD9\AppD9\AppD9.cpp @ 198]
c1 0095f208 75397c12    AppD9!WndProc+0x7a [C:\AWD3\AppD9\AppD9\AppD9.cpp @ 146]
c2 0095f234 7537700a    USER32!_InternalCallWinProc+0x2a
c3 0095f324 75375938    USER32!UserCallWinProcCheckWow+0x4aa
c4 0095f3a0 7538e738    USER32!DispatchMessageWorker+0x4b8
c5 0095f3e8 7538e598    USER32!DialogBox2+0x189
c6 0095f418 753daf48    USER32!InternalDialogBox+0xd7
c7 0095f4e4 753d9cb0    USER32!SoftModalMessageBox+0x718
c8 0095f640 753da7b7    USER32!MessageBoxWorker+0x314
c9 0095f6cc 753da825    USER32!MessageBoxTimeoutW+0x187
ca 0095f6ec 001d1371    USER32!MessageBoxW+0x45
cb 0095f704 001d121a    AppD9!StartModeling+0x41 [C:\AWD3\AppD9\AppD9\AppD9.cpp @ 198]
cc 0095f764 75397c12    AppD9!WndProc+0x7a [C:\AWD3\AppD9\AppD9\AppD9.cpp @ 146]
cd 0095f790 7537700a    USER32!_InternalCallWinProc+0x2a
ce 0095f880 75375938    USER32!UserCallWinProcCheckWow+0x4aa
cf 0095f8fc 75375470    USER32!DispatchMessageWorker+0x4b8
d0 0095f908 001d109d    USER32!DispatchMessageW+0x10
d1 0095f934 001d155d    AppD9!wWinMain+0x9d [C:\AWD3\AppD9\AppD9\AppD9.cpp @ 59]
d2 (Inline) --------    AppD9!invoke_main+0x1a
[d:\a01\_work\38\s\src\vctools\crt\vcstartup\src\startup\exe_common.inl @ 118]
d3 0095f980 76306839    AppD9!__scrt_common_main_seh+0xf8
[d:\a01\_work\38\s\src\vctools\crt\vcstartup\src\startup\exe_common.inl @ 288]
d4 0095f990 7766901f    KERNEL32!BaseThreadInitThunk+0x19
d5 0095f9e8 77668fed    ntdll_77600000!__RtlUserThreadStart+0x2b
d6 0095f9f8 00000000    ntdll_77600000!_RtlUserThreadStart+0x1b
```

11.   With the previous WinDbg versions could dump the first 16 stack trace lines with parameters (the **kv** command) and inspect *MessageBoxW* parameters (2nd and 3rd parameters) using the **du** command (because the function is a UNICODE variant of *MessageBox*, use the **da** command for ASCII variant such as *MessageBoxA*):

```
1: kd:x86> kv 20
# ChildEBP        RetAddr            Args to Child
00 012fc468 77e4ed89    00000000 012fc4d0 012fc4d0 ntdll_77dc0000!NtDelayExecution+0xc (FPO: [2,0,0])
01 012fc48c 75daa46f    00000000 012fc4d0 d1007752 ntdll_77dc0000!RtlDelayExecution+0xe9 (FPO: [2,2,0])
02 012fc4f4 75daa3ff    000003e8 00000000 012fc510 KERNELBASE!SleepEx+0x5f (FPO: [SEH])
03 012fc504 0099138e    000003e8 012fc518 00991338 KERNELBASE!Sleep+0xf (FPO: [Non-Fpo])
04 012fc510 00991338    012fc578 0099121a 00030732 AppD9!ConnectDB+0xe (FPO: [Non-Fpo]) (CONV: cdecl)
05 012fc518 0099121a    00030732 00000000 00008003 AppD9!StartModeling+0x8 (FPO: [Non-Fpo]) (CONV: cdecl)
06 012fc578 76b17c92    0009044c 00000111 00008003 AppD9!WndProc+0x7a (FPO: [Non-Fpo]) (CONV: stdcall)
07 012fc5a4 76af714a    009911a0 0009044c 00000111 USER32!_InternalCallWinProc+0x2a
08 012fc694 76af5a78    009911a0 00000000 00000111 USER32!UserCallWinProcCheckWow+0x4aa (FPO: [Non-Fpo])
09 012fc710 76b0e7b8    0009044c 00000000 00000008 USER32!DispatchMessageWorker+0x4b8 (FPO: [Non-Fpo])
0a 012fc758 76b0e618    00000008 00000000 00000000 USER32!DialogBox2+0x189 (FPO: [Non-Fpo])
0b 012fc788 76b5b008    0009044c 76b593b0 012fc9c8 USER32!InternalDialogBox+0xd7 (FPO: [Non-Fpo])
0c 012fc854 76b59d70    012fc9c8 009a2cc8 00000000 USER32!SoftModalMessageBox+0x718 (FPO: [1,41,4])
0d 012fc9b0 76b5a877    0025d24f 76b5a8a0 00000000 USER32!MessageBoxWorker+0x314 (FPO: [Non-Fpo])
0e 012fca38 76b5a8e5    0009044c 009a2cc8 009a2cbc USER32!MessageBoxTimeoutW+0x187 (FPO: [6,29,4])
0f 012fca58 75b21c8a    0009044c 009a2cc8 009a2cbc USER32!MessageBoxW+0x45 (FPO: [Non-Fpo])
```

```
1: kd:x86> du 009a2cc8
00000000`009a2cc8  "Connection Error"
```

```
1: kd:x86> du 009a2cbc
00000000`009a2cbc  "AppD9"
```

In our reconstruction case, we can inspect raw stack data memory instead:

```
0: kd:x86> dps 00959bf0
00000000`00959bf0  00959c10
00000000`00959bf4  753da825 USER32!MessageBoxW+0x45
00000000`00959bf8  00030406
00000000`00959bfc  001e2cc8 AppD9!type_info::`vftable'+0x1c
00000000`00959c00  001e2cbc AppD9!type_info::`vftable'+0x10
00000000`00959c04  00000000
00000000`00959c08  00000000
00000000`00959c0c  ffffffff
00000000`00959c10  00959c28
00000000`00959c14  001d1371 AppD9!StartModeling+0x41 [C:\AWD3\AppD9\AppD9\AppD9.cpp @ 198]
00000000`00959c18  00030406
00000000`00959c1c  001e2cc8 AppD9!type_info::`vftable'+0x1c
00000000`00959c20  001e2cbc AppD9!type_info::`vftable'+0x10
00000000`00959c24  00000000
00000000`00959c28  00959c88
00000000`00959c2c  001d121a AppD9!WndProc+0x7a [C:\AWD3\AppD9\AppD9\AppD9.cpp @ 146]
00000000`00959c30  0001047e
00000000`00959c34  00000000
00000000`00959c38  00008003
00000000`00959c3c  00008003
00000000`00959c40  00000111
00000000`00959c44  7765b3f9 ntdll_77600000!RtlSetLastWin32Error+0x39
00000000`00959c48  0001047e
00000000`00959c4c  0287a880
00000000`00959c50  0000031f
00000000`00959c54  752db450 uxtheme!ThemePostWndProc
00000000`00959c58  7763edec ntdll_77600000!RtlDeactivateActivationContextUnsafeFast+0x9c
00000000`00959c5c  01969a67
00000000`00959c60  00959cb0
```

```
0: kd:x86> du 001e2cc8
00000000`001e2cc8  "Connection Error"
```

```
0: kd:x86> du 001e2cbc
00000000`001e2cbc  "AppD9"
```

12.   If we examine the source code, we would see that the *StartModeling* function posts a message to the application window to repeat the *StartModeling* call again in case of connection error, but *MessageBox* has its own message processing, and it calls the main application window procedure triggering recursion:

```
void StartModeling (void)
{
      if (!ConnectDB())
      {
            PostMessage(hWndMain, WM_COMMAND, ID_FILE_START, 0);
            MessageBox(hWndMain, L"Connection Error", L"AppD9", MB_OK);
      }
}
```

Note: if you leave the application running for some time, it should crash with a stack overflow exception.

13.   We now continue with the **g** command, exit WinDbg, switch to Guest OS, and kill *AppD9* there.

Exercise KD10

- **Goal:** Learn how to debug handle leaks in user and kernel mode debugging

- **Elementary Diagnostics Patterns:** Counter Value

- **Memory Analysis Patterns:** Handle Leak; Historical Information

- **Debugging Implementation Patterns:** Break-in; Usage Trace

- \AWD4\Exercise-KD10.pdf

Goal: Learn how to debug handle leaks in user and kernel mode debugging.

Elementary Diagnostics Patterns: Counter Value.

Memory Analysis Patterns: Handle Leak; Historical Information.

Debugging Implementation Patterns: Break-in; Usage Trace.

1.   Launch \AWD4\AppD10\x64\Release\AppD10.exe executable from your host PC, Choose *File \ Start,* and run Task Manager. Choose the *Details* tab and add the Handles column (right-click on the grid header). Find *AppD10*. The number of handles is constantly increasing:

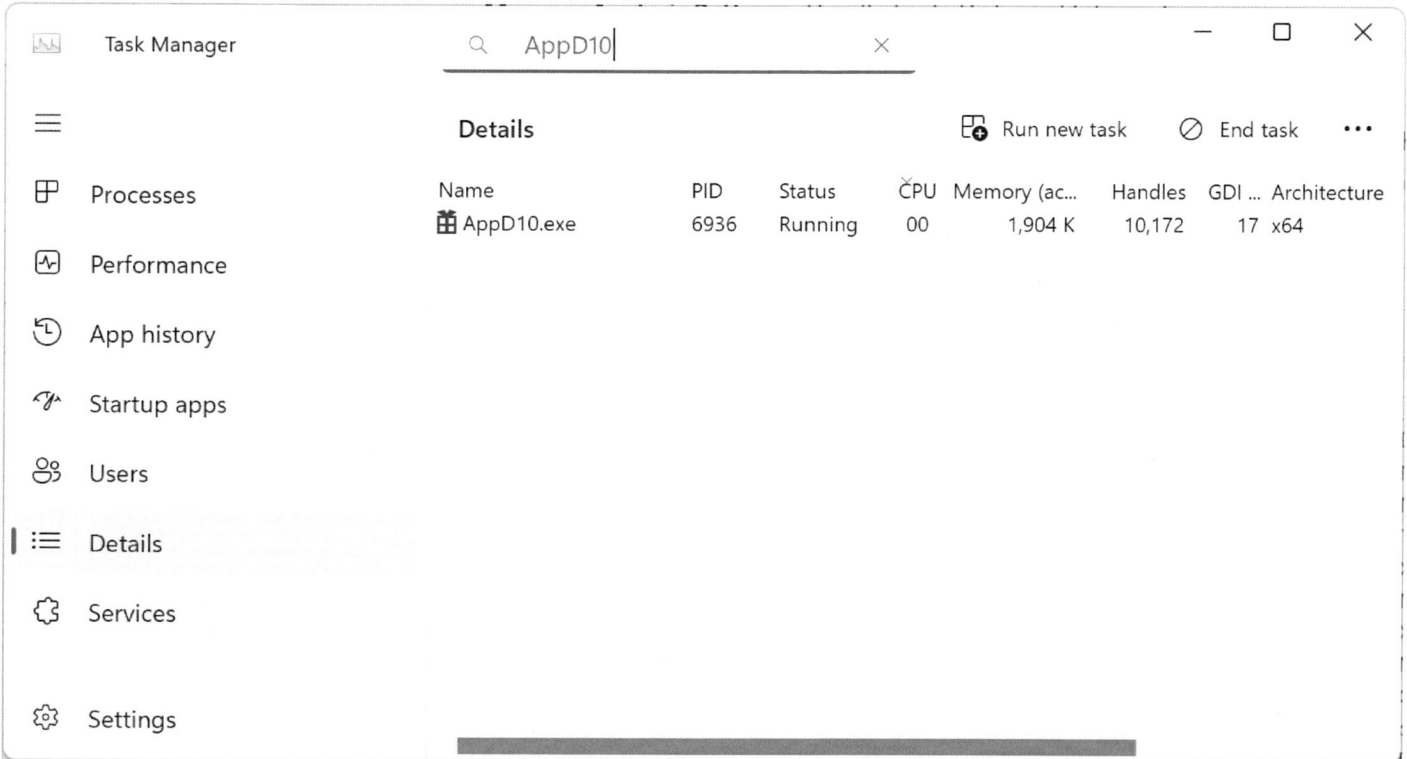

	Task Manager		Q AppD10|		×	— □	×

≡			**Details**			🔂 Run new task	⊘ End task	⋯

Ⓟ Processes	Name	PID	Status	CPU	Memory (ac…	Handles	GDI …	Architecture
	🔠 AppD10.exe	6936	Running	00	1,904 K	10,172	17	x64

Ⓐ	Performance
🕙	App history
⤺	Startup apps
😂	Users
☰	Details
⛭	Services
⚙	Settings

Note: We have a handle leak here.

2.   Launch WinDbg, attach it to the *App10* process, and open a log file:

```
Microsoft (R) Windows Debugger Version 10.0.25921.1001 AMD64
Copyright (c) Microsoft Corporation. All rights reserved.

*** wait with pending attach

************* Path validation summary **************
Response                       Time (ms)     Location
Deferred                                     srv*
OK                                           C:\AWD4\AppD9\Release
Symbol search path is: srv*;C:\AWD4\AppD9\Release
Executable search path is:
ModLoad: 00007ff7`ad360000 00007ff7`ad380000   C:\AWD4\AppD10\x64\Release\AppD10.exe
```

```
ModLoad: 00007ffb`36990000 00007ffb`36ba7000     C:\WINDOWS\SYSTEM32\ntdll.dll
ModLoad: 00007ffb`34760000 00007ffb`34824000     C:\WINDOWS\System32\KERNEL32.DLL
ModLoad: 00007ffb`34300000 00007ffb`346a6000     C:\WINDOWS\System32\KERNELBASE.dll
ModLoad: 00007ffb`2d980000 00007ffb`2da17000     C:\WINDOWS\SYSTEM32\apphelp.dll
ModLoad: 00007ffb`366d0000 00007ffb`3687e000     C:\WINDOWS\System32\USER32.dll
ModLoad: 00007ffb`33cd0000 00007ffb`33cf6000     C:\WINDOWS\System32\win32u.dll
ModLoad: 00007ffb`35600000 00007ffb`35629000     C:\WINDOWS\System32\GDI32.dll
ModLoad: 00007ffb`33d00000 00007ffb`33e18000     C:\WINDOWS\System32\gdi32full.dll
ModLoad: 00007ffb`34260000 00007ffb`342fa000     C:\WINDOWS\System32\msvcp_win.dll
ModLoad: 00007ffb`33fd0000 00007ffb`340e1000     C:\WINDOWS\System32\ucrtbase.dll
ModLoad: 00007ffb`35660000 00007ffb`35691000     C:\WINDOWS\System32\IMM32.DLL
ModLoad: 00007ffb`30ba0000 00007ffb`30c4b000     C:\WINDOWS\system32\uxtheme.dll
ModLoad: 00007ffb`34d90000 00007ffb`35119000     C:\WINDOWS\System32\combase.dll
ModLoad: 00007ffb`35700000 00007ffb`35817000     C:\WINDOWS\System32\RPCRT4.dll
ModLoad: 00007ffb`354b0000 00007ffb`35600000     C:\WINDOWS\System32\MSCTF.dll
ModLoad: 00007ffb`34ce0000 00007ffb`34d87000     C:\WINDOWS\System32\msvcrt.dll
ModLoad: 00007ffb`1a920000 00007ffb`1a9d0000     C:\WINDOWS\SYSTEM32\TextShaping.dll
ModLoad: 00007ffb`32cc0000 00007ffb`32cd8000     C:\WINDOWS\System32\kernel.appcore.dll
ModLoad: 00007ffb`33f50000 00007ffb`33fca000     C:\WINDOWS\System32\bcryptPrimitives.dll
ModLoad: 00007ffb`34c30000 00007ffb`34cd8000     C:\WINDOWS\System32\sechost.dll
ModLoad: 00007ffb`346b0000 00007ffb`346d8000     C:\WINDOWS\System32\bcrypt.dll
ModLoad: 00007ffb`21110000 00007ffb`2125a000     C:\WINDOWS\SYSTEM32\textinputframework.dll
ModLoad: 00007ffb`35120000 00007ffb`351f7000     C:\WINDOWS\System32\OLEAUT32.dll
ModLoad: 00007ffb`2d590000 00007ffb`2d6c4000     C:\WINDOWS\SYSTEM32\CoreMessaging.dll
ModLoad: 00007ffb`2a070000 00007ffb`2a3dc000     C:\WINDOWS\SYSTEM32\CoreUIComponents.dll
ModLoad: 00007ffb`31a90000 00007ffb`31bce000     C:\WINDOWS\SYSTEM32\wintypes.dll
ModLoad: 00007ffb`353d0000 00007ffb`35483000     C:\WINDOWS\System32\advapi32.dll
ModLoad: 00007ffb`33330000 00007ffb`3333c000     C:\WINDOWS\SYSTEM32\CRYPTBASE.DLL
ModLoad: 00007ffb`0cbf0000 00007ffb`0cc59000     C:\WINDOWS\system32\Oleacc.dll
ModLoad: 00007ffb`35310000 00007ffb`353c0000     C:\WINDOWS\System32\clbcatq.dll
ModLoad: 00007ffb`1a4c0000 00007ffb`1a50b000
C:\WINDOWS\system32\ApplicationTargetedFeatureDatabase.dll
ModLoad: 00007ffb`28410000 00007ffb`28695000     C:\Windows\System32\twinapi.appcore.dll
ModLoad: 00007ffb`00cb0000 00007ffb`010f5000     C:\Windows\System32\uiautomationcore.dll
ModLoad: 00007ffb`30fe0000 00007ffb`3100b000     C:\Windows\System32\dwmapi.dll
ModLoad: 00007ffb`0e8d0000 00007ffb`0e8e5000     C:\Windows\System32\threadpoolwinrt.dll
(1b18.11950): Break instruction exception - code 80000003 (first chance)
ntdll!DbgBreakPoint:
00007ffb`36a33060 int     3
```

```
0:012> .logopen c:\AWD4\D10.log
Opened log file 'c:\AWD4\D10.log'
```

3.   We examine the handle table using the **!handle** command (the output is long – this is why we need the log file):

```
0:012> !handle
Handle 4
  Type            Event
Handle 8
  Type            Event
Handle c
  Type            Event
Handle 10
  Type            WaitCompletionPacket
Handle 14
  Type            IoCompletion
Handle 18
```

```
    Type            TpWorkerFactory
Handle 1c
    Type            IRTimer
Handle 20
    Type            WaitCompletionPacket
Handle 24
    Type            IRTimer
Handle 28
    Type            WaitCompletionPacket
Handle 40
    Type            Directory
Handle 44
    Type            Event
Handle 48
    Type            Event
Handle 4c
    Type            File
Handle 58
    Type            ALPC Port
Handle 5c
    Type            Mutant
Handle 60
    Type            Directory
Handle 64
    Type            Semaphore
Handle 68
    Type            Semaphore
Handle 90
    Type            WaitCompletionPacket
Handle 94
    Type            IRTimer
Handle 98
    Type            TpWorkerFactory
Handle 9c
    Type            IoCompletion
Handle a0
    Type            IRTimer
Handle a4
    Type            WaitCompletionPacket
Handle a8
    Type            Key
Handle ac
    Type            Event
Handle b0
    Type            WaitCompletionPacket
Handle c0
    Type            Key
Handle c4
    Type            Event
Handle c8
    Type            IoCompletion
Handle cc
    Type            WindowStation
Handle d0
    Type            Desktop
Handle d4
    Type            WindowStation
Handle d8
    Type            Key
```

277

```
Handle dc
    Type                Key
Handle e0
    Type                Key
Handle e4
    Type                Event
Handle e8
    Type                Key
Handle ec
    Type                Key
Handle f0
    Type                Event
Handle 100
    Type                Event
Handle 104
    Type                Event
Handle 108
    Type                Event
Handle 10c
    Type                Event
Handle 110
    Type                Event
Handle 114
    Type                Event
Handle 138
    Type                ALPC Port
Handle 148
    Type                TpWorkerFactory
Handle 14c
    Type                IoCompletion
Handle 150
    Type                File
Handle 154
    Type                Section
Handle 158
    Type                Section
Handle 15c
    Type                Section
Handle 160
    Type                Key
Handle 164
    Type                Event
Handle 168
    Type                Event
Handle 170
    Type                Mutant
Handle 174
    Type                Event
Handle 180
    Type                Event
Handle 184
    Type                File
Handle 194
    Type                Semaphore
Handle 198
    Type                Semaphore
Handle 1ac
    Type                Semaphore
Handle 1b0
```

```
     Type                Semaphore
Handle 1b4
     Type                Event
Handle 1b8
     Type                File
Handle 1c8
     Type                Event
Handle 1d8
     Type                Event
Handle 1dc
     Type                Thread
Handle 1e0
     Type                Thread
Handle 1e4
     Type                IRTimer
Handle 1e8
     Type                WaitCompletionPacket
Handle 1ec
     Type                IRTimer
Handle 1f0
     Type                WaitCompletionPacket
Handle 1f4
     Type                ALPC Port
Handle 204
     Type                Key
Handle 210
     Type                ALPC Port
Handle 214
     Type                Event
Handle 218
     Type                Event
Handle 21c
     Type                WaitCompletionPacket
Handle 220
     Type                Event
Handle 224
     Type                Thread
Handle 228
     Type                WaitCompletionPacket
Handle 22c
     Type                Event
Handle 230
     Type                IoCompletionReserve
Handle 234
     Type                WaitCompletionPacket
Handle 248
     Type                Thread
Handle 24c
     Type                ALPC Port
Handle 250
     Type                WaitCompletionPacket
Handle 254
     Type                ALPC Port
Handle 258
     Type                WaitCompletionPacket
Handle 268
     Type                File
Handle 270
     Type                WaitCompletionPacket
```

279

```
Handle 280
    Type            Key
Handle 284
    Type            Mutant
Handle 288
    Type            Event
Handle 28c
    Type            Event
Handle 290
    Type            Event
Handle 294
    Type            Event
Handle 298
    Type            Event
Handle 29c
    Type            Section
Handle 2a0
    Type            Key
Handle 2a8
    Type            Event
Handle 2ac
    Type            Key
Handle 2b0
    Type            Key
Handle 2b4
    Type            Event
Handle 2b8
    Type            Key
Handle 2d8
    Type            Event
Handle 2dc
    Type            Event
Handle 2e0
    Type            Event
Handle 2e4
    Type            Event
Handle 2e8
    Type            Mutant
Handle 2ec
    Type            Event
Handle 2f0
    Type            Mutant
Handle 2f4
    Type            Mutant
Handle 2f8
    Type            Thread
Handle 2fc
    Type            Event
Handle 300
    Type            Event
Handle 304
    Type            IoCompletion
Handle 308
    Type            Event
Handle 30c
    Type            Thread
Handle 310
    Type            ALPC Port
Handle 314
```

```
    Type              Key
Handle 318
    Type              ALPC Port
Handle 31c
    Type              Event
Handle 320
    Type              Event
Handle 324
    Type              Thread
Handle 328
    Type              IoCompletion
Handle 32c
    Type              Section
Handle 330
    Type              Thread
Handle 334
    Type              Event
Handle 338
    Type              Thread
Handle 33c
    Type              ALPC Port
Handle 340
    Type              Event
Handle 34c
    Type              Thread
Handle 350
    Type              IoCompletion
Handle 354
    Type              File
Handle 358
    Type              Section
Handle 35c
    Type              IRTimer
Handle 360
    Type              TpWorkerFactory
Handle 364
    Type              ALPC Port
Handle 368
    Type              WaitCompletionPacket
Handle 36c
    Type              IRTimer
Handle 370
    Type              WaitCompletionPacket
Handle 374
    Type              Event
Handle 378
    Type              File
Handle 37c
    Type              Mutant
Handle 380
    Type              Event
Handle 384
    Type              Event
Handle 394
    Type              IoCompletion
Handle 39c
    Type              Event
Handle 3a0
    Type              Event
```

```
Handle 3a4
    Type                Thread
Handle 3a8
    Type                IoCompletion
Handle 3ac
    Type                TpWorkerFactory
Handle 3b0
    Type                IRTimer
Handle 3b4
    Type                WaitCompletionPacket
Handle 3b8
    Type                IRTimer
Handle 3bc
    Type                WaitCompletionPacket
Handle 3c0
    Type                File
Handle 3c4
    Type                Thread
Handle 3c8
    Type                File
Handle 3cc
    Type                Thread
Handle 3d0
    Type                Thread
Handle 3d4
    Type                Thread
Handle 3d8
    Type                Thread
Handle 3dc
    Type                Thread
Handle 3e0
    Type                Thread
Handle 3e4
    Type                Thread
Handle 3e8
    Type                Thread
Handle 3ec
    Type                Thread
Handle 3f0
    Type                Thread
Handle 3f4
    Type                Thread
[...]
Handle cbf8
    Type                Thread
Handle cbfc
    Type                Thread
Handle cc04
    Type                Thread
Handle cc08
    Type                Thread
Handle cc0c
    Type                Thread
Handle cc10
    Type                Thread
Handle cc14
    Type                Thread
Handle cc18
    Type                Thread
```

```
Handle cc1c
   Type              Thread
Handle cc20
   Type              Thread
Handle cc24
   Type              Thread
Handle cc28
   Type              Thread
Handle cc2c
   Type              Thread
Handle cc30
   Type              Thread
Handle cc34
   Type              Thread
Handle cc38
   Type              Thread
Handle cc3c
   Type              Thread
Handle cc40
   Type              Thread
Handle cc44
   Type              Thread
Handle cc48
   Type              Thread
Handle cc4c
   Type              Thread
Handle cc50
   Type              Thread
Handle cc54
   Type              Thread
Handle cc58
   Type              Thread
Handle cc5c
   Type              Thread
Handle cc60
   Type              Thread
Handle cc64
   Type              Thread
Handle cc68
   Type              Thread
Handle cc6c
   Type              Thread
Handle cc70
   Type              Thread
Handle cc74
   Type              Thread
Handle cc78
   Type              Thread
Handle cc7c
   Type              Thread
Handle cc80
   Type              Thread
Handle cc84
   Type              Thread
Handle cc88
   Type              Thread
Handle cc8c
   Type              Thread
Handle cc90
```

```
     Type              Thread
Handle cc94
     Type              Thread
Handle cc98
     Type              Thread
Handle cc9c
     Type              Thread
Handle cca0
     Type              Thread
Handle cca4
     Type              Thread
Handle cca8
     Type              Thread
Handle ccac
     Type              Thread
Handle ccb0
     Type              Thread
Handle ccb4
     Type              Thread
Handle ccb8
     Type              Thread
Handle ccbc
     Type              Thread
Handle ccc0
     Type              Thread
Handle ccc4
     Type              Thread
Handle ccc8
     Type              Thread
Handle cccc
     Type              Thread
Handle ccd0
     Type              Thread
12978 Handles
Type               Count
None               11
Event              50
Section            6
File               9
Directory          2
Mutant             7
WindowStation      2
Semaphore          6
Key                15
Thread             12827
Desktop            1
IoCompletion       9
TpWorkerFactory    5
ALPC Port          10
WaitCompletionPacket      18
```

Note: So we have a thread handle leak here.

4.   We now try to get as much info as we can from the handle table:

```
0:012> !handle -?
!handle [<handle>] [<flags>] [<type>]
  <handle> - Handle to get information about
```

```
                0 or -1 means all handles
   <flags> - Output control flags
                1   - Get type information (default)
                2   - Get basic information
                4   - Get name information
                8   - Get object specific info (where available) (space-delimited, 32-bit
                max)
   <type> - Limit query to handles of the given type
Display information about open handles
```

```
0:012> !handle 0 8 Thread
[...]
Handle cc98
  Object Specific Information
    Thread Id   1b18.11908
    Priority    8
    Base Priority 0
    Start Address ad361570 AppD10!ThreadWorkProc
Handle cc9c
  Object Specific Information
    Thread Id   1b18.1190c
    Priority    8
    Base Priority 0
    Start Address ad361570 AppD10!ThreadWorkProc
Handle cca0
  Object Specific Information
    Thread Id   1b18.11910
    Priority    8
    Base Priority 0
    Start Address ad361570 AppD10!ThreadWorkProc
Handle cca4
  Object Specific Information
    Thread Id   1b18.11914
    Priority    8
    Base Priority 0
    Start Address ad361570 AppD10!ThreadWorkProc
Handle cca8
  Object Specific Information
    Thread Id   1b18.11918
    Priority    8
    Base Priority 0
    Start Address ad361570 AppD10!ThreadWorkProc
Handle ccac
  Object Specific Information
    Thread Id   1b18.1191c
    Priority    9
    Base Priority 0
    Start Address ad361570 AppD10!ThreadWorkProc
Handle ccb0
  Object Specific Information
    Thread Id   1b18.11920
    Priority    8
    Base Priority 0
    Start Address ad361570 AppD10!ThreadWorkProc
Handle ccb4
  Object Specific Information
    Thread Id   1b18.11924
    Priority    8
    Base Priority 0
```

```
    Start Address ad361570 AppD10!ThreadWorkProc
Handle ccb8
  Object Specific Information
    Thread Id   1b18.11928
    Priority    8
    Base Priority 0
    Start Address ad361570 AppD10!ThreadWorkProc
Handle ccbc
  Object Specific Information
    Thread Id   1b18.1192c
    Priority    8
    Base Priority 0
    Start Address ad361570 AppD10!ThreadWorkProc
Handle ccc0
  Object Specific Information
    Thread Id   1b18.11930
    Priority    8
    Base Priority 0
    Start Address ad361570 AppD10!ThreadWorkProc
Handle ccc4
  Object Specific Information
    Thread Id   1b18.11934
    Priority    8
    Base Priority 0
    Start Address ad361570 AppD10!ThreadWorkProc
Handle ccc8
  Object Specific Information
    Thread Id   1b18.11938
    Priority    8
    Base Priority 0
    Start Address ad361570 AppD10!ThreadWorkProc
Handle cccc
  Object Specific Information
    Thread Id   1b18.11940
    Priority    10
    Base Priority 0
    Start Address ad361570 AppD10!ThreadWorkProc
Handle ccd0
  Object Specific Information
    Thread Id   1b18.11958
    Priority    8
    Base Priority 0
    Start Address ad361570 AppD10!ThreadWorkProc
12827 handles of type Thread
```

Note: We see the thread procedure (start address) but not function names where handles were created.

5.   To track thread creation, we need to enable handle trace (the **!htrace** command):

```
0:012> !htrace -?
!htrace [handle [max_traces]]
!htrace -enable [max_traces]
!htrace -disable
!htrace -snapshot
!htrace -diff

0:012> !htrace -enable
Handle tracing enabled.
```

```
Handle tracing information snapshot successfully taken.
```

6.   We then resume execution for a few seconds and then break in again (*Break* button on the *Home* tab):

```
0:012> g
(1b18.121d8): Break instruction exception - code 80000003 (first chance)
ntdll!DbgBreakPoint:
00007ffb`36a33060 int      3
```

7.   We can now check stack traces for the recently opened handles:

```
0:014> !htrace 0
[...]
---------------------------------------
Handle = 0x000000000000cce4 - OPEN
Thread ID = 0x0000000000005bb8, Process ID = 0x0000000000001b18

0x00007ffb36a30c44: ntdll!NtCreateThreadEx+0x0000000000000014
0x00007ffb3433f24f: KERNELBASE!CreateRemoteThreadEx+0x000000000000029f
0x00007ffb347744ed: KERNEL32!CreateThreadStub+0x000000000000003d
0x00007ff7ad361564: AppD10!DoWork+0x0000000000000034
0x00007ff7ad361525: AppD10!ThreadProcB+0x0000000000000015
0x00007ffb3477257d: KERNEL32!BaseThreadInitThunk+0x000000000000001d
0x00007ffb369eaa58: ntdll!RtlUserThreadStart+0x0000000000000028
---------------------------------------
Handle = 0x000000000000cce0 - OPEN
Thread ID = 0x0000000000005bb8, Process ID = 0x0000000000001b18

0x00007ffb36a30c44: ntdll!NtCreateThreadEx+0x0000000000000014
0x00007ffb3433f24f: KERNELBASE!CreateRemoteThreadEx+0x000000000000029f
0x00007ffb347744ed: KERNEL32!CreateThreadStub+0x000000000000003d
0x00007ff7ad361564: AppD10!DoWork+0x0000000000000034
0x00007ff7ad361525: AppD10!ThreadProcB+0x0000000000000015
0x00007ffb3477257d: KERNEL32!BaseThreadInitThunk+0x000000000000001d
0x00007ffb369eaa58: ntdll!RtlUserThreadStart+0x0000000000000028
---------------------------------------
Handle = 0x000000000000ccdc - OPEN
Thread ID = 0x0000000000005bb8, Process ID = 0x0000000000001b18

0x00007ffb36a30c44: ntdll!NtCreateThreadEx+0x0000000000000014
0x00007ffb3433f24f: KERNELBASE!CreateRemoteThreadEx+0x000000000000029f
0x00007ffb347744ed: KERNEL32!CreateThreadStub+0x000000000000003d
0x00007ff7ad361564: AppD10!DoWork+0x0000000000000034
0x00007ff7ad361525: AppD10!ThreadProcB+0x0000000000000015
0x00007ffb3477257d: KERNEL32!BaseThreadInitThunk+0x000000000000001d
0x00007ffb369eaa58: ntdll!RtlUserThreadStart+0x0000000000000028
---------------------------------------
Handle = 0x000000000000ccd8 - OPEN
Thread ID = 0x0000000000005bb8, Process ID = 0x0000000000001b18

0x00007ffb36a30c44: ntdll!NtCreateThreadEx+0x0000000000000014
0x00007ffb3433f24f: KERNELBASE!CreateRemoteThreadEx+0x000000000000029f
0x00007ffb347744ed: KERNEL32!CreateThreadStub+0x000000000000003d
0x00007ff7ad361564: AppD10!DoWork+0x0000000000000034
0x00007ff7ad361525: AppD10!ThreadProcB+0x0000000000000015
0x00007ffb3477257d: KERNEL32!BaseThreadInitThunk+0x000000000000001d
0x00007ffb369eaa58: ntdll!RtlUserThreadStart+0x0000000000000028
---------------------------------------
```

```
Handle = 0x000000000000ccd4 - OPEN
Thread ID = 0x0000000000005bb8, Process ID = 0x0000000000001b18

0x00007ffb36a30c44: ntdll!NtCreateThreadEx+0x0000000000000014
0x00007ffb3433f24f: KERNELBASE!CreateRemoteThreadEx+0x000000000000029f
0x00007ffb347744ed: KERNEL32!CreateThreadStub+0x000000000000003d
0x00007ff7ad361564: AppD10!DoWork+0x0000000000000034
0x00007ff7ad361525: AppD10!ThreadProcB+0x0000000000000015
0x00007ffb3477257d: KERNEL32!BaseThreadInitThunk+0x000000000000001d
0x00007ffb369eaa58: ntdll!RtlUserThreadStart+0x0000000000000028

----------------------------------------
Parsed 0xE8 stack traces.
Dumped 0xE8 stack traces.
```

Note: We see that all these allocations come from *ThreadProcB* and *DoWork* functions. If we inspect the source code of the *DoWork* function in *Work.cpp,* we see that a thread is created, but its handle is never stored for subsequent release:

```
void DoWork (void)
{
     Sleep(10);
     CreateThread(NULL, 0, ThreadWorkProc, NULL, 0, NULL);
}
```

8.   We now close WinDbg. This action terminates the *AppD10* process.

9.   We now debug the same process using kernel mode debugging. Power your Guest OS VM and copy the *\AWD4\AppD10* folder to your VM to the same location (C:\AWD4\).

10.   Run WinDbg on your host and set up a kernel debugging connection as recommended in Exercise KD0. We get this output in WinDbg:

```
Microsoft (R) Windows Debugger Version 10.0.25921.1001 AMD64
Copyright (c) Microsoft Corporation. All rights reserved.

Using NET for debugging
Opened WinSock 2.0
Waiting to reconnect...
Connected to target 172.30.30.138 on port 50005 on local IP 172.30.16.1.
You can get the target MAC address by running .kdtargetmac command.
Connected to Windows 10 22000 x64 target at (Fri Feb  9 17:22:20.053 2024 (UTC + 0:00)), ptr64
TRUE
Kernel Debugger connection established.

************* Path validation summary **************
Response                      Time (ms)     Location
Deferred                                    srv*
OK                                          C:\AWD4\AppD9\Release
Symbol search path is: srv*;C:\AWD4\AppD9\Release
Executable search path is:
Windows 10 Kernel Version 22000 MP (1 procs) Free x64
Edition build lab: 22000.1.amd64fre.co_release.210604-1628
Kernel base = 0xfffff804`76000000 PsLoadedModuleList = 0xfffff804`76c297b0
System Uptime: 0 days 0:00:00.397
```

11.　　　Break in via the *Break* button. We should get this output:

```
KDTARGET: Refreshing KD connection
DriverEntry failed 0xc00000bb for driver \REGISTRY\MACHINE\SYSTEM\ControlSet001\Services\vmbusr
Capacity:5000, FullChargedCapacity:5000, Voltage:5000, Rate:0
Break instruction exception - code 80000003 (first chance)
*************************************************************************
*                                                                       *
*    You are seeing this message because you pressed either             *
*        CTRL+C (if you run console kernel debugger) or,                 *
*        CTRL+BREAK (if you run GUI kernel debugger),                    *
*    on your debugger machine's keyboard.                                *
*                                                                       *
*                  THIS IS NOT A BUG OR A SYSTEM CRASH                    *
*                                                                       *
* If you did not intend to break into the debugger, press the "g" key, then  *
* press the "Enter" key now.  This message might immediately reappear.  If it *
* does, press "g" and "Enter" again.                                     *
*                                                                       *
*************************************************************************
nt!DbgBreakPointWithStatus:
fffff804`764279f0 int     3
```

12.　　　Open a log file and reload symbols:

```
0: kd> .logopen c:\AWD4\KD10.log
Opened log file 'c:\AWD4\KD10.log'
```

```
0: kd> .reload
Connected to Windows 10 22000 x64 target at (Fri Feb  9 17:26:03.630 2024 (UTC + 0:00)), ptr64
TRUE
Loading Kernel Symbols
............................................................
............................................................
.........................................
Loading User Symbols

Loading unloaded module list
...........
```

13.　　　We now inspect the non-paged pool (a kind of dynamic memory used to allocate structures such as for threads) using the **!poolused 3** command (**3** means sort by non-paged pool consumed):

```
0: kd> !poolused 3
Using a machine size of ffbf9 pages to configure the kd cache

*** CacheSize too low - increasing to 64 MB

Max cache size is      : 67108864 bytes (0x10000 KB)
Total memory in cache  : 735059 bytes (0x2ce KB)
Number of regions cached: 3481
15271 full reads broken into 16331 partial reads
    counts: 12325 cached/4006 uncached, 75.47% cached
    bytes : 466761 cached/512299 uncached, 47.67% cached
** Transition PTEs are implicitly decoded
** Prototype PTEs are implicitly decoded
....
 Sorting by NonPaged Pool Consumed
```

		NonPaged					Paged		
Tag	Allocs	Frees	Diff	Used	Allocs	Frees	Diff	Used

```
EtwB       234       15      219   15704320         15        6        9     208896   Etw Buffer , Binary: nt!etw
Thre      3192     1218     1974    5305088          0        0        0          0   Thread objects , Binary: nt!ps
EtwR     17307     5354    11953    2626592          0        0        0          0   Etw KM RegEntry , Binary: nt!etw
File     95948    89673     6275    2493136          0        0        0          0   File objects
[...]
```

Note: We see only 1974 currently allocated thread objects.

14.   We now resume, then switch to Guest OS, reconnect if necessary, launch
\AWD4\AppD10\x64\Release\AppD10.exe executable, choose *File \ Start*, then wait for a minute or so, and then
switch to WinDbg and break in:

```
0: kd> g
Break instruction exception - code 80000003 (first chance)
*****************************************************************************
*                                                                           *
*     You are seeing this message because you pressed either                *
*         CTRL+C (if you run console kernel debugger) or,                    *
*         CTRL+BREAK (if you run GUI kernel debugger),                       *
*     on your debugger machine's keyboard.                                   *
*                                                                           *
*                     THIS IS NOT A BUG OR A SYSTEM CRASH                    *
*                                                                           *
* If you did not intend to break into the debugger, press the "g" key, then  *
* press the "Enter" key now.  This message might immediately reappear.  If it *
* does, press "g" and "Enter" again.                                         *
*                                                                           *
*****************************************************************************
nt!DbgBreakPointWithStatus:
fffff804`764279f0 int       3
```

15.   If we examine the non-paged pool, we see that the **Thre** pool tag is the top non-paged pool memory
consumer with 9147 structures allocated:

```
0: kd> !poolused 3
Using a machine size of f7bf9 pages to configure the kd cache
....
 Sorting by NonPaged Pool Consumed

                    NonPaged                              Paged
 Tag     Allocs    Frees     Diff        Used      Allocs    Frees    Diff       Used
 Thre     11827     2680     9147    24586112          0        0        0          0   Thread objects , Binary: nt!ps
 EtwB       245       26      219     6906112         18        9        9     208896   Etw Buffer , Binary: nt!etw
 File    148799   141478     7321     2911472          0        0        0          0   File objects
 EtwR     22848    10366    12482     2745088          0        0        0          0   Etw KM RegEntry , Binary: nt!etw
[...]
```

16.   We now inspect processes on the Guest VM using the **!process** command:

```
0: kd> !process 0 0
**** NT ACTIVE PROCESS DUMP ****
PROCESS ffff800fd06e2040
    SessionId: none  Cid: 0004    Peb: 00000000  ParentCid: 0000
    DirBase: 007d5002  ObjectTable: ffffc887c5424e80  HandleCount: 3272.
    Image: System

PROCESS ffff800fd0745080
    SessionId: none  Cid: 0048    Peb: 00000000  ParentCid: 0004
    DirBase: 0284d002  ObjectTable: ffffc887c542b340  HandleCount:   0.
    Image: Secure System

PROCESS ffff800fd074f080
    SessionId: none  Cid: 007c    Peb: 00000000  ParentCid: 0004
```

```
    DirBase: 02862002  ObjectTable: ffffc887c546c180  HandleCount:    0.
    Image: Registry

PROCESS ffff800fd365c080
    SessionId: none  Cid: 01d4    Peb: 5e9d845000  ParentCid: 0004
    DirBase: 01082002  ObjectTable: ffffc887c594fc80  HandleCount: 60.
    Image: smss.exe

PROCESS ffff800fd498b140
    SessionId: 0  Cid: 0258    Peb: 53fcb85000  ParentCid: 024c
    DirBase: 33400002  ObjectTable: ffffc887c8cee7c0  HandleCount: 552.
    Image: csrss.exe

PROCESS ffff800fd4bed080
    SessionId: 0  Cid: 02a0    Peb: 4bc39e5000  ParentCid: 024c
    DirBase: 3f98c002  ObjectTable: ffffc887c8cede80  HandleCount: 155.
    Image: wininit.exe

PROCESS ffff800fd58020c0
    SessionId: 1  Cid: 02b4    Peb: 249b785000  ParentCid: 0298
    DirBase: 334a6002  ObjectTable: ffffc887c8cee640  HandleCount: 351.
    Image: csrss.exe

PROCESS ffff800fd5826080
    SessionId: 1  Cid: 02f0    Peb: 15f8bcf000  ParentCid: 0298
    DirBase: 34250002  ObjectTable: ffffc887c5ef17c0  HandleCount: 271.
    Image: winlogon.exe

PROCESS ffff800fd4be71c0
    SessionId: 0  Cid: 0334    Peb: 465f7d3000  ParentCid: 02a0
    DirBase: ce8d0002  ObjectTable: ffffc887c8ced9c0  HandleCount: 690.
    Image: services.exe

PROCESS ffff800fd5851080
    SessionId: 0  Cid: 034c    Peb: 1da598e000  ParentCid: 02a0
    DirBase: 380e9002  ObjectTable: ffffc887c8d95e80  HandleCount: 54.
    Image: LsaIso.exe

PROCESS ffff800fd5853180
    SessionId: 0  Cid: 0354    Peb: 18f44e2000  ParentCid: 02a0
    DirBase: 380b4002  ObjectTable: ffffc887c8d96980  HandleCount: 1181.
    Image: lsass.exe

PROCESS ffff800fd58c5080
    SessionId: 0  Cid: 03c8    Peb: e6fcd47000  ParentCid: 0334
    DirBase: 35a38002  ObjectTable: ffffc887c8d96180  HandleCount: 1526.
    Image: svchost.exe

PROCESS ffff800fd58c9080
    SessionId: 1  Cid: 03e4    Peb: 2cc13a000  ParentCid: 02f0
    DirBase: 3539f002  ObjectTable: ffffc887c8d96e00  HandleCount: 37.
    Image: fontdrvhost.exe

PROCESS ffff800fd58d30c0
    SessionId: 0  Cid: 03ec    Peb: 5991dac000  ParentCid: 02a0
    DirBase: 352cc002  ObjectTable: ffffc887c8d96b00  HandleCount: 37.
    Image: fontdrvhost.exe

PROCESS ffff800fd598d0c0
    SessionId: 0  Cid: 02b8    Peb: 7dc48f7000  ParentCid: 0334
    DirBase: 313ac002  ObjectTable: ffffc887c8ef8080  HandleCount: 1181.
    Image: svchost.exe

PROCESS ffff800fd59a9080
    SessionId: 0  Cid: 0318    Peb: 86b62d3000  ParentCid: 0334
    DirBase: 32750002  ObjectTable: ffffc887c8ef8b40  HandleCount: 417.
    Image: svchost.exe

PROCESS ffff800fd5a51100
    SessionId: 1  Cid: 0450    Peb: c720085000  ParentCid: 02f0
    DirBase: 3d6c0002  ObjectTable: ffffc887c901ec80  HandleCount: 1047.
    Image: dwm.exe

PROCESS ffff800fd5aad0c0
```

```
    SessionId: 0  Cid: 0494     Peb: bdbf520000  ParentCid: 0334
    DirBase: 3d56d002  ObjectTable: ffffc887c90eb500  HandleCount: 184.
    Image: svchost.exe

PROCESS ffff800fd5aaf080
    SessionId: 0  Cid: 04ac     Peb: 6c3f9db000  ParentCid: 0334
    DirBase: cbc7a002  ObjectTable: ffffc887c90ec7c0  HandleCount: 779.
    Image: svchost.exe

PROCESS ffff800fd5ae6080
    SessionId: 0  Cid: 0508     Peb: 9fe9922000  ParentCid: 0334
    DirBase: 3dbe2002  ObjectTable: ffffc887c90eb080  HandleCount: 123.
    Image: svchost.exe

PROCESS ffff800fd5b020c0
    SessionId: 0  Cid: 0510     Peb: 89725f8000  ParentCid: 0334
    DirBase: c7f89002  ObjectTable: ffffc887c90ec4c0  HandleCount: 175.
    Image: svchost.exe

PROCESS ffff800fd5b21080
    SessionId: 0  Cid: 054c     Peb: 225bc6a000  ParentCid: 0334
    DirBase: d0a6a002  ObjectTable: ffffc887c90eb6c0  HandleCount: 219.
    Image: svchost.exe

PROCESS ffff800fd5b25080
    SessionId: 0  Cid: 0560     Peb: 6424b36000  ParentCid: 0334
    DirBase: d0af4002  ObjectTable: ffffc887c90eb840  HandleCount: 296.
    Image: svchost.exe

PROCESS ffff800fd5b28080
    SessionId: 0  Cid: 0570     Peb: 112573b000  ParentCid: 0334
    DirBase: 3e232002  ObjectTable: ffffc887c90eb9c0  HandleCount: 144.
    Image: svchost.exe

PROCESS ffff800fd5b5d080
    SessionId: 0  Cid: 05b4     Peb: cc79e0a000  ParentCid: 0334
    DirBase: d0a8e002  ObjectTable: ffffc887c90ebb40  HandleCount: 401.
    Image: svchost.exe

PROCESS ffff800fd5b96080
    SessionId: 0  Cid: 05e0     Peb: deb8a1000  ParentCid: 0334
    DirBase: d13c8002  ObjectTable: ffffc887c9224200  HandleCount: 788.
    Image: svchost.exe

PROCESS ffff800fd335d080
    SessionId: 0  Cid: 0610     Peb: fc38f44000  ParentCid: 0334
    DirBase: d129b002  ObjectTable: ffffc887c9225180  HandleCount: 190.
    Image: svchost.exe

PROCESS ffff800fd5c70080
    SessionId: 0  Cid: 067c     Peb: 1af6414000  ParentCid: 0334
    DirBase: c4520002  ObjectTable: ffffc887c9224380  HandleCount: 270.
    Image: svchost.exe

PROCESS ffff800fd5c73080
    SessionId: 0  Cid: 06a4     Peb: d83b31e000  ParentCid: 0334
    DirBase: d35b2002  ObjectTable: ffffc887c9225640  HandleCount: 129.
    Image: svchost.exe

PROCESS ffff800fd5c880c0
    SessionId: 0  Cid: 06b0     Peb: c0492ab000  ParentCid: 0334
    DirBase: 179c7002  ObjectTable: ffffc887c9224840  HandleCount: 245.
    Image: svchost.exe

PROCESS ffff800fd5cf2080
    SessionId: 0  Cid: 076c     Peb: 266fd43000  ParentCid: 0334
    DirBase: c11e4002  ObjectTable: ffffc887c92257c0  HandleCount: 193.
    Image: svchost.exe

PROCESS ffff800fd5ca7080
    SessionId: 0  Cid: 07a4     Peb: 35fbd30000  ParentCid: 0334
    DirBase: c1543002  ObjectTable: ffffc887c9225340  HandleCount: 268.
    Image: svchost.exe
```

```
PROCESS ffff800fd5d90080
    SessionId: 0  Cid: 07d8    Peb: b3d18cb000  ParentCid: 0334
    DirBase: d4ecf002  ObjectTable: ffffc887c9224b40  HandleCount: 114.
    Image: svchost.exe

PROCESS ffff800fd076a080
    SessionId: 0  Cid: 07f0    Peb: 5d7e5b7000  ParentCid: 0334
    DirBase: c1a4f002  ObjectTable: ffffc887c8ced6c0  HandleCount: 145.
    Image: svchost.exe

PROCESS ffff800fd075d080
    SessionId: 0  Cid: 07fc    Peb: da5177e000  ParentCid: 0334
    DirBase: c41e0002  ObjectTable: ffffc887c9225e00  HandleCount: 128.
    Image: svchost.exe

PROCESS ffff800fd0752080
    SessionId: 0  Cid: 0428    Peb: d9eb115000  ParentCid: 0334
    DirBase: c6ed5002  ObjectTable: ffffc887c9224080  HandleCount: 237.
    Image: svchost.exe

PROCESS ffff800fd0750080
    SessionId: 0  Cid: 0500    Peb: a736bbc000  ParentCid: 0334
    DirBase: d0e57002  ObjectTable: ffffc887c92254c0  HandleCount: 114.
    Image: svchost.exe

PROCESS ffff800fd0748080
    SessionId: 0  Cid: 05c8    Peb: b75043f000  ParentCid: 0334
    DirBase: d0f0c002  ObjectTable: ffffc887c9224d00  HandleCount: 182.
    Image: svchost.exe

PROCESS ffff800fd06b8080
    SessionId: 0  Cid: 0818    Peb: 7c377ec000  ParentCid: 0334
    DirBase: d57f8002  ObjectTable: ffffc887c9225980  HandleCount: 121.
    Image: svchost.exe

PROCESS ffff800fd07e1080
    SessionId: 0  Cid: 0848    Peb: 49092bf000  ParentCid: 0334
    DirBase: c8c9b002  ObjectTable: ffffc887c94dae80  HandleCount: 140.
    Image: svchost.exe

PROCESS ffff800fd5d98080
    SessionId: 0  Cid: 0920    Peb: 70e4e4c000  ParentCid: 0334
    DirBase: c50be002  ObjectTable: ffffc887c94dc2c0  HandleCount: 236.
    Image: svchost.exe

PROCESS ffff800fd5d5a080
    SessionId: 0  Cid: 0970    Peb: 53cb4ab000  ParentCid: 0334
    DirBase: c3730002  ObjectTable: ffffc887c94dab80  HandleCount: 382.
    Image: svchost.exe

PROCESS ffff800fd5e11080
    SessionId: 0  Cid: 097c    Peb: 4bd9bab000  ParentCid: 0334
    DirBase: d78c5002  ObjectTable: ffffc887c94dc140  HandleCount: 214.
    Image: svchost.exe

PROCESS ffff800fd5e18080
    SessionId: 0  Cid: 0988    Peb: 4721629000  ParentCid: 0334
    DirBase: d781a002  ObjectTable: ffffc887c94dd100  HandleCount: 157.
    Image: VSSVC.exe

PROCESS ffff800fd5e31080
    SessionId: 0  Cid: 09e8    Peb: e1046ff000  ParentCid: 0334
    DirBase: d9a02002  ObjectTable: ffffc887c94dc600  HandleCount: 287.
    Image: svchost.exe

PROCESS ffff800fd5e3d0c0
    SessionId: 0  Cid: 09f0    Peb: e9bf1a6000  ParentCid: 0334
    DirBase: d9be4002  ObjectTable: ffffc887c94dad00  HandleCount: 197.
    Image: svchost.exe

PROCESS ffff800fd5e40080
    SessionId: 0  Cid: 0a10    Peb: 23d68bd000  ParentCid: 0334
    DirBase: d9af6002  ObjectTable: ffffc887c94dc780  HandleCount: 190.
    Image: svchost.exe
```

```
PROCESS ffff800fd5e41080
    SessionId: 0  Cid: 0a18    Peb: fac0c1b000  ParentCid: 0334
    DirBase: d9a36002  ObjectTable: ffffc887c94db4c0  HandleCount: 186.
    Image: svchost.exe

PROCESS ffff800fd5f0e040
    SessionId: none Cid: 0aa8    Peb: 00000000  ParentCid: 0004
    DirBase: c739a002  ObjectTable: ffffc887c94da6c0  HandleCount:   0.
    Image: MemCompression

PROCESS ffff800fd5f340c0
    SessionId: 0  Cid: 0ae0    Peb: 32af758000  ParentCid: 0334
    DirBase: c36bd002  ObjectTable: ffffc887c94da9c0  HandleCount: 186.
    Image: svchost.exe

PROCESS ffff800fd5f39080
    SessionId: 0  Cid: 0af8    Peb: 94720c9000  ParentCid: 0334
    DirBase: c54a3002  ObjectTable: ffffc887c94dc900  HandleCount: 189.
    Image: svchost.exe

PROCESS ffff800fd5f5a080
    SessionId: 0  Cid: 0b24    Peb: 4314209000  ParentCid: 0334
    DirBase: d89a5002  ObjectTable: ffffc887c94db980  HandleCount: 156.
    Image: svchost.exe

PROCESS ffff800fd5f87080
    SessionId: 0  Cid: 0b80    Peb: d16a396000  ParentCid: 0334
    DirBase: c3dac002  ObjectTable: ffffc887c94dcac0  HandleCount: 165.
    Image: svchost.exe

PROCESS ffff800fd600e080
    SessionId: 0  Cid: 0ba0    Peb: 429d8b7000  ParentCid: 0334
    DirBase: d7014002  ObjectTable: ffffc887c94db340  HandleCount: 172.
    Image: svchost.exe

PROCESS ffff800fd6011080
    SessionId: 0  Cid: 0ba8    Peb: c10c9cc000  ParentCid: 0334
    DirBase: c6371002  ObjectTable: ffffc887c94dcc40  HandleCount: 133.
    Image: svchost.exe

PROCESS ffff800fd60350c0
    SessionId: 0  Cid: 0b1c    Peb: 2e987b1000  ParentCid: 0334
    DirBase: cd38e002  ObjectTable: ffffc887c94dcdc0  HandleCount: 261.
    Image: svchost.exe

PROCESS ffff800fd60e7080
    SessionId: 0  Cid: 0c2c    Peb: c2c770e000  ParentCid: 0334
    DirBase: d153b002  ObjectTable: ffffc887c94dda40  HandleCount: 425.
    Image: svchost.exe

PROCESS ffff800fd6158080
    SessionId: 0  Cid: 0c34    Peb: 359b152000  ParentCid: 0334
    DirBase: d15d8002  ObjectTable: ffffc887c9225b00  HandleCount: 144.
    Image: svchost.exe

PROCESS ffff800fd615e080
    SessionId: 0  Cid: 0c4c    Peb: ad45490000  ParentCid: 0334
    DirBase: d1582002  ObjectTable: ffffc887c92249c0  HandleCount: 386.
    Image: svchost.exe

PROCESS ffff800fd61b3080
    SessionId: 0  Cid: 0c98    Peb: a10ccdf000  ParentCid: 0334
    DirBase: c7d1f002  ObjectTable: ffffc887c9b23900  HandleCount: 212.
    Image: svchost.exe

PROCESS ffff800fd62680c0
    SessionId: 0  Cid: 0d04    Peb: 0073f000  ParentCid: 0334
    DirBase: cf5b3002  ObjectTable: ffffc887c9b21200  HandleCount: 613.
    Image: spoolsv.exe

PROCESS ffff800fd6566080
    SessionId: 0  Cid: 0d88    Peb: 22907a9000  ParentCid: 0334
    DirBase: c559d002  ObjectTable: ffffc887c9b221c0  HandleCount: 140.
```

```
    Image: svchost.exe

PROCESS ffff800fd6575080
    SessionId: 0  Cid: 0d94    Peb: b89251b000  ParentCid: 0334
    DirBase: 31912002  ObjectTable: ffffc887c9b21540  HandleCount: 647.
    Image: svchost.exe

PROCESS ffff800fd6576080
    SessionId: 0  Cid: 0d9c    Peb: 3df7857000  ParentCid: 0334
    DirBase: d1949002  ObjectTable: ffffc887c9b216c0  HandleCount: 361.
    Image: svchost.exe

PROCESS ffff800fd630f080
    SessionId: 0  Cid: 0db4    Peb: 7d9deac000  ParentCid: 0334
    DirBase: d1986002  ObjectTable: ffffc887c9b22340  HandleCount: 346.
    Image: svchost.exe

PROCESS ffff800fd6310080
    SessionId: 0  Cid: 0dcc    Peb: 515ba2d000  ParentCid: 0334
    DirBase: d973c002  ObjectTable: ffffc887c9b219c0  HandleCount: 363.
    Image: svchost.exe

PROCESS ffff800fd6443080
    SessionId: 0  Cid: 0e28    Peb: 1343de1000  ParentCid: 0334
    DirBase: d59a8002  ObjectTable: ffffc887c9b22b00  HandleCount: 318.
    Image: svchost.exe

PROCESS ffff800fd6454080
    SessionId: 0  Cid: 0e3c    Peb: acef717000  ParentCid: 0334
    DirBase: d3ba1002  ObjectTable: ffffc887c9b224c0  HandleCount: 143.
    Image: svchost.exe

PROCESS ffff800fd6433080
    SessionId: 0  Cid: 0e48    Peb: 4c2f51b000  ParentCid: 0334
    DirBase: d3ab9002  ObjectTable: ffffc887c9b24580  HandleCount: 820.
    Image: MsMpEng.exe

PROCESS ffff800fd6455080
    SessionId: 0  Cid: 0e54    Peb: 1cebcd9000  ParentCid: 0334
    DirBase: cd91b002  ObjectTable: ffffc887c9b24740  HandleCount: 372.
    Image: svchost.exe

PROCESS ffff800fd6466080
    SessionId: 0  Cid: 0e5c    Peb: 59c0489000  ParentCid: 0334
    DirBase: c96c3002  ObjectTable: ffffc887c9b248c0  HandleCount: 145.
    Image: sqlwriter.exe

PROCESS ffff800fd65111c0
    SessionId: 0  Cid: 0e6c    Peb: 8c8802b000  ParentCid: 0334
    DirBase: cd985002  ObjectTable: ffffc887c9b24d80  HandleCount: 207.
    Image: svchost.exe

PROCESS ffff800fd6588080
    SessionId: 0  Cid: 0e84    Peb: 4cad0d9000  ParentCid: 0334
    DirBase: cbaab002  ObjectTable: ffffc887c9b24a40  HandleCount:  68.
    Image: wlms.exe

PROCESS ffff800fd6599080
    SessionId: 0  Cid: 0e8c    Peb: a83f748000  ParentCid: 0334
    DirBase: e2384002  ObjectTable: ffffc887c9b24bc0  HandleCount: 147.
    Image: svchost.exe

PROCESS ffff800fd6366080
    SessionId: 0  Cid: 0ee8    Peb: ce53db000  ParentCid: 0334
    DirBase: d4b79002  ObjectTable: ffffc887c9b24280  HandleCount: 437.
    Image: MpDefenderCoreService.exe

PROCESS ffff800fd672e080
    SessionId: 0  Cid: 0f58    Peb: 2178c62000  ParentCid: 0334
    DirBase: db83f002  ObjectTable: ffffc887c9ee86c0  HandleCount: 273.
    Image: sppsvc.exe

PROCESS ffff800fd67a90c0
    SessionId: 0  Cid: 1014    Peb: 49a61de000  ParentCid: 0d94
```

```
    DirBase: d7cb2002  ObjectTable: ffffc887c9ee9980  HandleCount: 99.
    Image: AggregatorHost.exe

PROCESS ffff800fd6954080
    SessionId: 0  Cid: 11f0    Peb: 523e141000  ParentCid: 03c8
    DirBase: d42cb002  ObjectTable: ffffc887c9eeb400  HandleCount: 205.
    Image: dllhost.exe

PROCESS ffff800fd696a080
    SessionId: 0  Cid: 11f8    Peb: 8bc6a51000  ParentCid: 0334
    DirBase: d42dd002  ObjectTable: ffffc887c9eeb580  HandleCount: 159.
    Image: svchost.exe

PROCESS ffff800fd7082080
    SessionId: 0  Cid: 1334    Peb: 8dc2d81000  ParentCid: 03c8
    DirBase: eee1d002  ObjectTable: ffffc887ca2f8200  HandleCount: 161.
    Image: SppExtComObj.Exe

PROCESS ffff800fd7110080
    SessionId: 0  Cid: 13f4    Peb: 28dfa88000  ParentCid: 0334
    DirBase: e16a9002  ObjectTable: ffffc887ca2f8380  HandleCount: 235.
    Image: svchost.exe

PROCESS ffff800fd71a3080
    SessionId: 0  Cid: 107c    Peb: d793a13000  ParentCid: 0334
    DirBase: e2739002  ObjectTable: ffffc887cad49740  HandleCount: 308.
    Image: svchost.exe

PROCESS ffff800fd71ea0c0
    SessionId: 0  Cid: 1390    Peb: 70130cf000  ParentCid: 0334
    DirBase: 1884b002  ObjectTable: ffffc887cad49c00  HandleCount: 147.
    Image: svchost.exe

PROCESS ffff800fd7267080
    SessionId: 0  Cid: 0c60    Peb: 4f59d53000  ParentCid: 0334
    DirBase: 13303002  ObjectTable: ffffc887cad4b1c0  HandleCount: 339.
    Image: svchost.exe

PROCESS ffff800fd5d59080
    SessionId: 0  Cid: 14fc    Peb: 31eadb5000  ParentCid: 0334
    DirBase: d8c65002  ObjectTable: ffffc887cad4be40  HandleCount: 331.
    Image: svchost.exe

PROCESS ffff800fd72640c0
    SessionId: 0  Cid: 158c    Peb: 93b48f1000  ParentCid: 0334
    DirBase: 2ee6c002  ObjectTable: ffffc887ca2f94c0  HandleCount: 237.
    Image: svchost.exe

PROCESS ffff800fd71f9080
    SessionId: 0  Cid: 160c    Peb: b227f0b000  ParentCid: 0334
    DirBase: 3ff09002  ObjectTable: ffffc887cad4bcc0  HandleCount: 219.
    Image: svchost.exe

PROCESS ffff800fd71f7080
    SessionId: 1  Cid: 1660    Peb: 546addc000  ParentCid: 06b0
    DirBase: 1d537002  ObjectTable: ffffc887cad4aa00  HandleCount: 541.
    Image: sihost.exe

PROCESS ffff800fd71f6080
    SessionId: 1  Cid: 1680    Peb: 9ed35a3000  ParentCid: 0334
    DirBase: dd56e002  ObjectTable: ffffc887cad4cac0  HandleCount: 331.
    Image: svchost.exe

PROCESS ffff800fd70ad080
    SessionId: 1  Cid: 1704    Peb: b40d915000  ParentCid: 0334
    DirBase: 06a61002  ObjectTable: ffffc887cad4d280  HandleCount: 489.
    Image: svchost.exe

PROCESS ffff800fd71f0080
    SessionId: 1  Cid: 17d0    Peb: 4ca1590000  ParentCid: 05b4
    DirBase: f3251002  ObjectTable: ffffc887cad4d5c0  HandleCount: 269.
    Image: taskhostw.exe

PROCESS ffff800fd71ef080
```

```
      SessionId: 0  Cid: 17fc      Peb: ce4ab98000  ParentCid: 0334
      DirBase: e6da6002  ObjectTable: ffffc887cad4d8c0  HandleCount: 254.
      Image: svchost.exe

PROCESS ffff800fd71ee080
      SessionId: 0  Cid: 0d84      Peb: da683d5000  ParentCid: 0334
      DirBase: e49c4002  ObjectTable: ffffc887ca2faac0  HandleCount: 186.
      Image: svchost.exe

PROCESS ffff800fd70b3080
      SessionId: 1  Cid: 154c      Peb: eb1926a000  ParentCid: 0d84
      DirBase: e4212002  ObjectTable: ffffc887cb2f5780  HandleCount: 430.
      Image: ctfmon.exe

PROCESS ffff800fd7562080
      SessionId: 1  Cid: 1730      Peb: 94cceaa000  ParentCid: 02f0
      DirBase: e6b80002  ObjectTable: 00000000  HandleCount:   0.
      Image: userinit.exe

PROCESS ffff800fd7561080
      SessionId: 0  Cid: 18d4      Peb: 5e2779f000  ParentCid: 0334
      DirBase: 0ad35002  ObjectTable: ffffc887cb2f8e40  HandleCount: 297.
      Image: svchost.exe

PROCESS ffff800fd7560080
      SessionId: 1  Cid: 18dc      Peb: 0036f000  ParentCid: 1730
      DirBase: eeb74002  ObjectTable: ffffc887cb2f9180  HandleCount: 3335.
      Image: explorer.exe

PROCESS ffff800fd750e080
      SessionId: 0  Cid: 1ae8      Peb: e07cfd7000  ParentCid: 0334
      DirBase: e5078002  ObjectTable: ffffc887cb2f7540  HandleCount: 215.
      Image: svchost.exe

PROCESS ffff800fd71f2080
      SessionId: 0  Cid: 1b70      Peb: 81d1378000  ParentCid: 0334
      DirBase: 41b54002  ObjectTable: ffffc887cb2f6280  HandleCount: 128.
      Image: svchost.exe

PROCESS ffff800fd71f3080
      SessionId: 1  Cid: 1b94      Peb: 79c886d000  ParentCid: 0334
      DirBase: f1cb6002  ObjectTable: ffffc887cb2f7080  HandleCount: 284.
      Image: svchost.exe

PROCESS ffff800fd77ea080
      SessionId: 0  Cid: 1be4      Peb: 325ab8e000  ParentCid: 0334
      DirBase: 44a1d002  ObjectTable: ffffc887cad4ab80  HandleCount: 282.
      Image: svchost.exe

PROCESS ffff800fd78b5080
      SessionId: 0  Cid: 15e8      Peb: cac9380000  ParentCid: 0334
      DirBase: 43712002  ObjectTable: ffffc887cb2f7880  HandleCount: 121.
      Image: svchost.exe

PROCESS ffff800fd78eb080
      SessionId: 0  Cid: 1470      Peb: d4371ac000  ParentCid: 0334
      DirBase: 422f8002  ObjectTable: ffffc887cb2f6400  HandleCount: 673.
      Image: SearchIndexer.exe

PROCESS ffff800fd78f2080
      SessionId: 0  Cid: 1668      Peb: a503992000  ParentCid: 0334
      DirBase: 4d377002  ObjectTable: ffffc887cb2f65c0  HandleCount: 146.
      Image: TrustedInstaller.exe

PROCESS ffff800fd7970080
      SessionId: 0  Cid: 1934      Peb: 86231fe000  ParentCid: 1668
      DirBase: 159fd002  ObjectTable: ffffc887cb2f8b40  HandleCount: 248.
      Image: GenValObj.exe

PROCESS ffff800fd7974080
      SessionId: 1  Cid: 1c20      Peb: 3232534000  ParentCid: 03c8
      DirBase: 4dbf1002  ObjectTable: ffffc887cb2f8cc0  HandleCount: 229.
      Image: Widgets.exe
```

297

```
PROCESS ffff800fd7a760c0
    SessionId: 1  Cid: 1c88    Peb: 59a213f000  ParentCid: 03c8
    DirBase: 4c128002  ObjectTable: ffffc887cb2fa280  HandleCount: 668.
    Image: StartMenuExperienceHost.exe

PROCESS ffff800fd7a8f0c0
    SessionId: 1  Cid: 1ca0    Peb: 3ed802000  ParentCid: 03c8
DeepFreeze
    DirBase: 513b6002  ObjectTable: ffffc887cb2faa80  HandleCount: 1560.
    Image: SearchHost.exe

PROCESS ffff800fd7e2e0c0
    SessionId: 1  Cid: 1ce0    Peb: c4049d000  ParentCid: 03c8
    DirBase: 4e14f002  ObjectTable: ffffc887cb2fa440  HandleCount: 293.
    Image: RuntimeBroker.exe

PROCESS ffff800fd7e130c0
    SessionId: 1  Cid: 1d38    Peb: 56a740c000  ParentCid: 03c8
    DirBase: 6a52d002  ObjectTable: ffffc887cb2f9c40  HandleCount: 376.
    Image: RuntimeBroker.exe

PROCESS ffff800fd81020c0
    SessionId: 1  Cid: 1d8c    Peb: 18b8865000  ParentCid: 0334
    DirBase: 50759002  ObjectTable: ffffc887cb2f9480  HandleCount: 134.
    Image: svchost.exe

PROCESS ffff800fd7db5080
    SessionId: 1  Cid: 1e90    Peb: 1002e3000  ParentCid: 03c8
    DirBase: 511af002  ObjectTable: ffffc887cb2fad80  HandleCount: 270.
    Image: dllhost.exe

PROCESS ffff800fd78b00c0
    SessionId: 0  Cid: 20a0    Peb: b7b4127000  ParentCid: 0334
    DirBase: 5dcdf002  ObjectTable: ffffc887cbff4040  HandleCount: 232.
    Image: NisSrv.exe

PROCESS ffff800fd4513080
    SessionId: 0  Cid: 20ac    Peb: 5fea755000  ParentCid: 0334
    DirBase: 5ddeb002  ObjectTable: ffffc887cbff5dc0  HandleCount: 382.
    Image: svchost.exe

PROCESS ffff800fd580f080
    SessionId: 3  Cid: 2130    Peb: 916295c000  ParentCid: 210c
    DirBase: dd9b7002  ObjectTable: ffffc887cbff76c0  HandleCount: 154.
    Image: csrss.exe

PROCESS ffff800fd7663080
    SessionId: 3  Cid: 2174    Peb: 18d714d000  ParentCid: 210c
    DirBase: 5ad19002  ObjectTable: ffffc887cbff6400  HandleCount: 209.
    Image: winlogon.exe

PROCESS ffff800fd7664080
    SessionId: 3  Cid: 2210    Peb: 6e27b4e000  ParentCid: 2174
    DirBase: dc32a002  ObjectTable: ffffc887cbff8b40  HandleCount:  37.
    Image: fontdrvhost.exe

PROCESS ffff800fd68f7080
    SessionId: 3  Cid: 2244    Peb: 16f8baf000  ParentCid: 2174
    DirBase: d27b5002  ObjectTable: ffffc887c901d6c0  HandleCount: 624.
    Image: LogonUI.exe

PROCESS ffff800fd8273080
    SessionId: 3  Cid: 224c    Peb: 6eed92b000  ParentCid: 2174
    DirBase: e8d4b002  ObjectTable: ffffc887cad4c7c0  HandleCount: 775.
    Image: dwm.exe

PROCESS ffff800fd7b92080
    SessionId: 1  Cid: 22a4    Peb: 38fd932000  ParentCid: 04ac
    DirBase: 63b59002  ObjectTable: ffffc887cbff7080  HandleCount: 469.
    Image: rdpclip.exe

PROCESS ffff800fd7aeb080
    SessionId: 0  Cid: 22ac    Peb: 2c33647000  ParentCid: 0334
    DirBase: 624da002  ObjectTable: ffffc887c900b740  HandleCount. 571.
```

```
    Image: svchost.exe

PROCESS ffff800fd495c080
    SessionId: 1  Cid: 1328    Peb: 608c636000  ParentCid: 22a4
    DirBase: 2344b002  ObjectTable: ffffc887cbff33c0  HandleCount: 157.
    Image: rdpinput.exe

PROCESS ffff800fd495f080
    SessionId: 1  Cid: 1850    Peb: 6637233000  ParentCid: 0d84
    DirBase: 6d691002  ObjectTable: ffffc887cbff3e80  HandleCount: 314.
    Image: TabTip.exe

PROCESS ffff800fd83440c0
    SessionId: 1  Cid: 1960    Peb: ee340ae000  ParentCid: 03c8
    DirBase: 77eea002  ObjectTable: ffffc887c9ee9b00  HandleCount: 1260.
    Image: PhoneExperienceHost.exe

PROCESS ffff800fd7dc90c0
    SessionId: 1  Cid: 21a0    Peb: a950916000  ParentCid: 03c8
    DirBase: cc7a6002  ObjectTable: ffffc887c9ee9800  HandleCount: 401.
    Image: smartscreen.exe

PROCESS ffff800fd7cc40c0
    SessionId: 1  Cid: 10dc    Peb: fa54699000  ParentCid: 18dc
    DirBase: 7e7ec002  ObjectTable: ffffc887cbff8e40  HandleCount: 186.
    Image: SecurityHealthSystray.exe

PROCESS ffff800fd81860c0
    SessionId: 0  Cid: 0620    Peb: 626b5c7000  ParentCid: 0334
    DirBase: 7c78f002  ObjectTable: ffffc887cbff6c00  HandleCount: 389.
    Image: SecurityHealthService.exe

PROCESS ffff800fd7510080
    SessionId: 1  Cid: 1aa8    Peb: a6736e5000  ParentCid: 18dc
    DirBase: 6f113002  ObjectTable: ffffc887cbff7d00  HandleCount: 938.
    Image: OneDrive.exe

PROCESS ffff800fd7b6b140
    SessionId: 0  Cid: 226c    Peb: 3880d00000  ParentCid: 0334
    DirBase: 7ee73002  ObjectTable: ffffc887c9eea600  HandleCount: 178.
    Image: svchost.exe

PROCESS ffff800fd83f6080
    SessionId: 1  Cid: 244c    Peb: 9999dc000  ParentCid: 03c8
    DirBase: 7d1aa002  ObjectTable: ffffc887cbff7a00  HandleCount: 332.
    Image: WidgetService.exe

PROCESS ffff800fd818b0c0
    SessionId: 1  Cid: 24b0    Peb: c1f492f000  ParentCid: 03c8
    DirBase: 803fa002  ObjectTable: ffffc887c9eea900  HandleCount: 207.
    Image: RuntimeBroker.exe

PROCESS ffff800fd7de80c0
    SessionId: 1  Cid: 25e0    Peb: d503942000  ParentCid: 03c8
    DirBase: 1ed4b002  ObjectTable: ffffc887cbff9940  HandleCount: 700.
    Image: TextInputHost.exe

PROCESS ffff800fd6de50c0
    SessionId: 0  Cid: 0b48    Peb: 6b0e9e9000  ParentCid: 0334
    DirBase: ce242002  ObjectTable: ffffc887cda7d780  HandleCount: 345.
    Image: WUDFHost.exe

PROCESS ffff800fd7fe50c0
    SessionId: 1  Cid: 1b3c    Peb: b8765fe000  ParentCid: 18dc
    DirBase: ce2d9002  ObjectTable: ffffc887cda7c340  HandleCount: 7753.
    Image: AppD10.exe

PROCESS ffff800fd334d080
    SessionId: 0  Cid: 28d4    Peb: 4ad22b2000  ParentCid: 0334
    DirBase: c04c5002  ObjectTable: ffffc887cda7d300  HandleCount: 119.
    Image: SgrmBroker.exe

PROCESS ffff800fd6de6080
    SessionId: 0  Cid: 2968    Peb: ebc120a000  ParentCid: 0334
```

```
        DirBase: 073ef002  ObjectTable: ffffc887cda7ce40  HandleCount: 123.
        Image: uhssvc.exe

PROCESS ffff800fd7c73080
    SessionId: 0  Cid: 29cc    Peb: ebec20f000  ParentCid: 0334
    DirBase: 105a84002  ObjectTable: ffffc887cda7b540  HandleCount: 184.
    Image: svchost.exe

PROCESS ffff800fd43c1080
    SessionId: 0  Cid: 2a88    Peb: 95dbfd4000  ParentCid: 0334
    DirBase: 7e9f6002  ObjectTable: ffffc887cda7d940  HandleCount: 196.
    Image: svchost.exe

PROCESS ffff800fd45330c0
    SessionId: 0  Cid: 2b40    Peb: bf2e841000  ParentCid: 0334
    DirBase: 629c5002  ObjectTable: ffffc887cda7c4c0  HandleCount: 232.
    Image: svchost.exe

PROCESS ffff800fd461a0c0
    SessionId: 1  Cid: 2bb8    Peb: 1c1f1b5000  ParentCid: 0334
    DirBase: 0d3d2002  ObjectTable: ffffc887cda7b840  HandleCount: 451.
    Image: svchost.exe

PROCESS ffff800fd479b080
    SessionId: 0  Cid: 2f38    Peb: b86eb5b000  ParentCid: 03c8
    DirBase: 33bcd002  ObjectTable: ffffc887cbff6100  HandleCount: 258.
    Image: TiWorker.exe

PROCESS ffff800fd427e080
    SessionId: 0  Cid: 35c0    Peb: 47237a7000  ParentCid: 03c8
    DirBase: 3aab5002  ObjectTable: ffffc887cb2f68c0  HandleCount: 277.
    Image: WmiPrvSE.exe

PROCESS ffff800fd10e90c0
    SessionId: 1  Cid: 3d4c    Peb: db1380a000  ParentCid: 03c8
    DirBase: 37475002  ObjectTable: ffffc887c9eebbc0  HandleCount: 211.
    Image: RuntimeBroker.exe

PROCESS ffff800fd1d020c0
    SessionId: 1  Cid: 6790    Peb: ff97e24000  ParentCid: 03c8
    DirBase: 1c842002  ObjectTable: ffffc887cbff5c40  HandleCount: 145.
    Image: RuntimeBroker.exe

PROCESS ffff800fd1cfe080
    SessionId: 1  Cid: 67f0    Peb: 109b132000  ParentCid: 03c8
    DirBase: 2239f002  ObjectTable: ffffc887cda7e740  HandleCount: 252.
    Image: RuntimeBroker.exe
```

Note: We see the possible leak from *App10.exe*.

17.   Let's now switch to that process and examine its handle table (we break it by the *Break* button as soon as we see a stream of *Thread* handles as the output is long):


```
0: kd> .process /r /p ffff800fd7fe50c0
Implicit process is now ffff800f`d7fe50c0
.cache forcedecodeuser done
Loading User Symbols
............................
```

```
0: kd> !handle
```

```
PROCESS ffff800fd7fe50c0
    SessionId: 1  Cid: 1b3c    Peb: b8765fe000  ParentCid: 18dc
    DirBase: ce2d9002  ObjectTable: ffffc887cda7c340  HandleCount: 7753.
    Image: AppD10.exe
```

Handle table at ffffc887cda7c340 with 7753 entries in use

[...]

02b4: Object: ffff800fd585d080 GrantedAccess: 001fffff (Protected) (Audit) Entry: ffffc887cbafcad0
Object: ffff800fd585d080 Type: (ffff800fd06e0a60) Thread
    ObjectHeader: ffff800fd585d050 (new version)
        HandleCount: 1 PointerCount: 1

02b8: Object: ffff800fd68c1080 GrantedAccess: 001fffff (Protected) (Audit) Entry: ffffc887cbafcae0
Object: ffff800fd68c1080 Type: (ffff800fd06e0a60) Thread
    ObjectHeader: ffff800fd68c1050 (new version)
        HandleCount: 1 PointerCount: 1

02bc: Object: ffff800fd715f080 GrantedAccess: 001fffff (Protected) (Audit) Entry: ffffc887cbafcaf0
Object: ffff800fd715f080 Type: (ffff800fd06e0a60) Thread
    ObjectHeader: ffff800fd715f050 (new version)
        HandleCount: 1 PointerCount: 1

02c0: Object: ffff800fd7ad5080 GrantedAccess: 001fffff (Protected) (Audit) Entry: ffffc887cbafcb00
Object: ffff800fd7ad5080 Type: (ffff800fd06e0a60) Thread
    ObjectHeader: ffff800fd7ad5050 (new version)
        HandleCount: 1 PointerCount: 1

02c4: Object: ffff800fd61af080 GrantedAccess: 001fffff (Protected) (Audit) Entry: ffffc887cbafcb10
Object: ffff800fd61af080 Type: (ffff800fd06e0a60) Thread
    ObjectHeader: ffff800fd61af050 (new version)
        HandleCount: 1 PointerCount: 1

02c8: Object: ffff800fd31f2080 GrantedAccess: 001fffff (Protected) (Audit) Entry: ffffc887cbafcb20
Object: ffff800fd31f2080 Type: (ffff800fd06e0a60) Thread
    ObjectHeader: ffff800fd31f2050 (new version)
        HandleCount: 1 PointerCount: 1

02cc: Object: ffff800fd78d7080 GrantedAccess: 001fffff (Protected) (Audit) Entry: ffffc887cbafcb30
Object: ffff800fd78d7080 Type: (ffff800fd06e0a60) Thread
    ObjectHeader: ffff800fd78d7050 (new version)
        HandleCount: 1 PointerCount: 1

02d0: Object: ffff800fd497f080 GrantedAccess: 001fffff (Protected) (Audit) Entry: ffffc887cbafcb40
Object: ffff800fd497f080 Type: (ffff800fd06e0a60) Thread
    ObjectHeader: ffff800fd497f050 (new version)
        HandleCount: 1 PointerCount: 1

02d4: Object: ffff800fd0732080 GrantedAccess: 001fffff (Protected) (Audit) Entry: ffffc887cbafcb50
Object: ffff800fd0732080 Type: (ffff800fd06e0a60) Thread
    ObjectHeader: ffff800fd0732050 (new version)
        HandleCount: 1 PointerCount: 1

```
02d8: Object: ffff800fd7670080  GrantedAccess: 001fffff (Protected) (Audit) Entry:
ffffc887cbafcb60
Object: ffff800fd7670080  Type: (ffff800fd06e0a60) Thread
    ObjectHeader: ffff800fd7670050 (new version)
        HandleCount: 1  PointerCount: 1

02dc: Object: ffff800fd7f89080  GrantedAccess: 001fffff (Protected) (Audit) Entry:
ffffc887cbafcb70
Object: ffff800fd7f89080  Type: (ffff800fd06e0a60) Thread
    ObjectHeader: ffff800fd7f89050 (new version)
        HandleCount: 1  PointerCount: 1

02e0: Object: ffff800fd5acc080  GrantedAccess: 001fffff (Protected) (Audit) Entry:
ffffc887cbafcb80
Object: ffff800fd5acc080  Type: (ffff800fd06e0a60) Thread
    ObjectHeader: ffff800fd5acc050 (new version)
        HandleCount: 1  PointerCount: 1

02e4: Object: ffff800fd693c080  GrantedAccess: 001fffff (Protected) (Audit) Entry:
ffffc887cbafcb90
Object: ffff800fd693c080  Type: (ffff800fd06e0a60) Thread
    ObjectHeader: ffff800fd693c050 (new version)
        HandleCount: 1  PointerCount: 1
```

[...]

18.   Since the object address here is also a thread structure address, we can use the **!thread** command to examine it in more detail:

```
0: kd> !thread ffff800fd693c080 1f
THREAD ffff800fd693c080  Cid 1b3c.1310  Teb: 0000000000000000 Win32Thread: 0000000000000000 TERMINATED
Not impersonating
DeviceMap                   ffffc887cad3e1f0
Owning Process              ffff800fd7fe50c0      Image:          AppD10.exe
Attached Process            N/A          Image:          N/A
Wait Start TickCount        9164         Ticks: 5812 (0:00:01:30.812)
Context Switch Count        2            IdealProcessor: 3
UserTime                    00:00:00.000
KernelTime                  00:00:00.000
*** WARNING: Unable to verify checksum for AppD10.exe
Win32 Start Address AppD10!ThreadWorkProc (0x00007ff7b9661570)
Stack Init 0000000000000000 Current ffffc70fe3bcd670
Base ffffc70fe3bce000 Limit ffffc70fe3bc8000 Call 0000000000000000
Priority 10 BasePriority 8 PriorityDecrement 2 IoPriority 2 PagePriority 5
```

Note: So we see that the thread leak comes from *AppD10.exe*.

19.   We now continue with the **g** command and exit WinDbg, switch to Guest OS, and exit *AppD10*.

Managed Debugging

Exercise MD11

Now, we have come to managed debugging. We cover a few techniques and commands here to give you a basic overview in the context of user process space debugging.

Modeling with LINQPad

http://www.linqpad.net/

We use LINQPad to model abnormal software behavior because it is a complex application with many threads, as in real .NET programs.

Download LINQPad: https://www.linqpad.net/

User / Managed Space

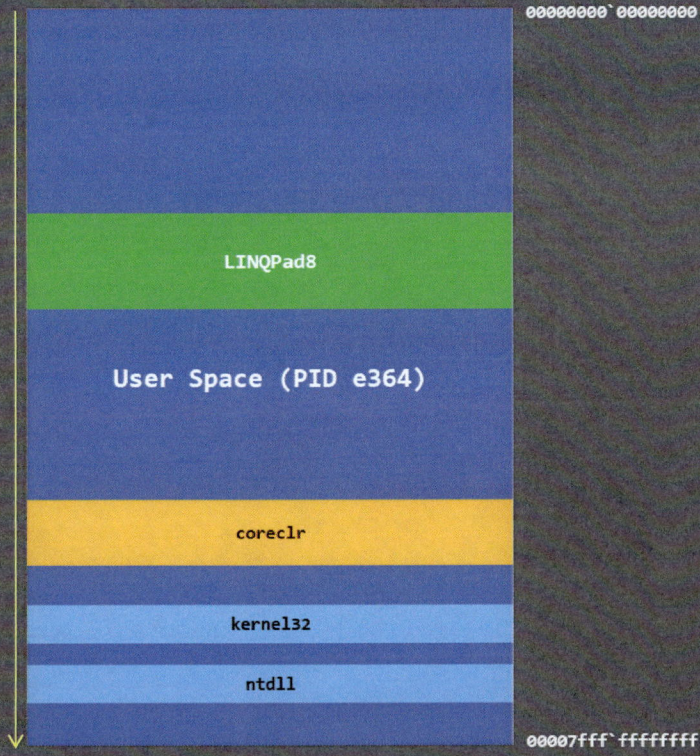

```
00000000`00000000
```

LINQPad8
User Space (PID e364)
coreclr
kernel32
ntdll

```
00007fff`ffffffff
```

Here's a typical .NET Core executable layout in memory.

Process Threads

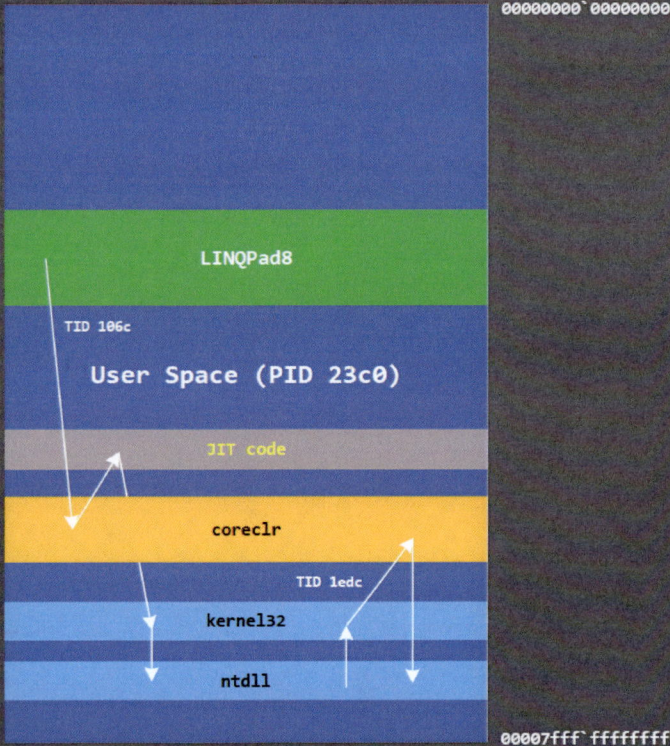

When a thread executes managed code, it is compiled into memory: the so-called JIT code. You need to load a WinDbg SOS extension to analyze it. It is named *sos.dll*, and it is loaded automatically by WinDbg.

Stack Trace Example

```
0:000> kL
 # Child-SP          RetAddr           Call Site
00 00000029`6e3add78 00007ffa`7eb90458 win32u!NtUserWaitMessage+0x14
01 00000029`6e3add80 00007ffa`d7244d61 0x00007ffa`7eb90458
02 00000029`6e3ade40 00007ffa`d7247486 System_Windows_Forms!...+0x581
03 00000029`6e3adf50 00007ffa`d7247026 System_Windows_Forms!...+0x416
04 00000029`6e3ae000 00007ffa`d6ef212b System_Windows_Forms!...+0x46
05 00000029`6e3ae060 00007ffa`7cb021e4 System_Windows_Forms!...+0x3b
06 00000029`6e3ae0a0 00007ffa`7cae2534 0x00007ffa`7cb021e4
07 00000029`6e3ae350 00007ffa`7c70a16d 0x00007ffa`7cae2534
08 00000029`6e3ae680 00007ffa`7c7015c2 0x00007ffa`7c70a16d
09 00000029`6e3ae6e0 00007ffa`dc226ce3 0x00007ffa`7c7015c2
0a 00000029`6e3ae7b0 00007ffa`dc1bcc42 coreclr!CallDescrWorkerInternal+0x83
0b (Inline Function) --------`-------- coreclr!CallDescrWorkerWithHandler+0x57
0c 00000029`6e3ae7f0 00007ffa`dc1c3c09 coreclr!MethodDescCallSite::...+0x196
0d (Inline Function) --------`-------- coreclr!MethodDescCallSite::Call+0xb
0e 00000029`6e3ae930 00007ffa`dc1c4097 coreclr!RunMain+0x1f5
0f 00000029`6e3aeb10 00007ffa`dc1c4841 coreclr!Assembly::ExecuteMainMethod+0x1cb
10 00000029`6e3aeea0 00007ffa`dc0e21c1 coreclr!CorHost2::ExecuteAssembly+0x221
11 00000029`6e3af030 00007ffb`2ef54e2d coreclr!coreclr_execute_assembly+0x101
12 00000029`6e3af0d0 00007ffb`2ef62e27 hostpolicy!coreclr_t::execute_assembly+0x2d
13 00000029`6e3af120 00007ffb`2ef62a36 hostpolicy!run_app_for_context+0x387
14 00000029`6e3af280 00007ffb`2ef64262 hostpolicy!run_app+0x46
15 00000029`6e3af2d0 00007ffb`36ff3a7e hostpolicy!corehost_main+0x132
16 00000029`6e3af480 00007ffb`36ff72d8 hostfxr!execute_app+0x1de
17 (Inline Function) --------`-------- hostfxr!?A0xd51c85dd::read_config...+0x10a
18 00000029`6e3af570 00007ffb`36ff5b5b hostfxr!fx_muxer_t::handle_exec_...+0x214
19 00000029`6e3af660 00007ffb`36ff2109 hostfxr!fx_muxer_t::execute+0x39b
1a 00000029`6e3af7a0 00007ff6`ea712361 hostfxr!hostfxr_main_startupinfo+0x89
1b 00000029`6e3af8a0 00007ff6`ea712758 LINQPad6!exe_start+0x651
1c 00000029`6e3afad0 00007ff6`ea714608 LINQPad6!wmain+0x88
1d (Inline Function) --------`-------- LINQPad6!invoke_main+0x22
1e 00000029`6e3afb00 00007ffb`58387034 LINQPad6!__scrt_common_main_seh+0x10c
1f 00000029`6e3afb40 00007ffb`5a002651 kernel32!BaseThreadInitThunk+0x14
20 00000029`6e3afb70 00000000`00000000 ntdll!RtlUserThreadStart+0x21
```

After .NET managed code is translated to machine code (the so-called JIT), the *coreclr* module calls it. You see this continuity when you look at a stack trace. This JIT code is shown in yellow color. There is also precompiled managed code you see in blue color.

Examining JIT Code

```
0:000> !IP2MD 0x00007ffa`7cae2534
MethodDesc:      00007ffa7c7f5aa0
Method Name:     LINQPad.UIProgram.Go(System.String[])
Class:           00007ffa7c803a28
MethodTable:     00007ffa7c7f7078
mdToken:         00000000060001A4
Module:          00007ffa7c79f798
IsJitted:        yes
Current CodeAddr:     00007ffa7cae1b90
Version History:
  ILCodeVersion:      0000000000000000
  ReJIT ID:           0
  IL Addr:            0000000000000000
     CodeAddr:           00007ffa7cae1b90  (MinOptJitted)
     NativeCodeVersion:  0000000000000000


0:000> !DumpModule 00007ffa7c79f798
Name: C:\Program Files\LINQPad6\LINQPad.GUI.dll
Attributes:             PEFile SupportsUpdateableMethods
Assembly:               00000177c5cdece0
BaseAddress:            00000177DFDE0000
PEFile:                 00000177C5CDE0E0
ModuleId:               00007FFA7C7D1860
ModuleIndex:            0000000000000001
LoaderHeap:             0000000000000000
TypeDefToMethodTableMap: 00007FFA7C7A0020
TypeRefToMethodTableMap: 00007FFA7C7A1860
MethodDefToDescMap:     00007FFA7C7A4138
FieldDefToDescMap:      00007FFA7C7AF300
MemberRefToDescMap:     0000000000000000
FileReferencesMap:      00007FFA7C7B7F78
AssemblyReferencesMap:  00007FFA7C7B7F80
MetaData start address: 00000177DFE887DC (719936 bytes)
```

Using SOS extension commands, we can examine this compiled code. For example, I used addresses taken from the previous slide's stack trace.

Exercise MD11

- **Goal:** Learn how to find problem modules, classes and methods, disassemble code, dump object references, recognize and analyze deadlocks

- **Elementary Diagnostics Patterns:** Crash; Hang

- **Memory Analysis Patterns:** Exception Stack Trace; NULL Pointer (Data); CLR Thread; JIT Code; Deadlock (Managed Space); Execution Residue (Managed Space); Hidden Exception (Managed Space)

- **Debugging Implementation Patterns:** Break-in

- \AWD4\Exercise-MD11.pdf

Exercise MD11

Goal: Learn how to find problem modules, classes, and methods, disassemble code, dump object references, and recognize and analyze deadlocks.

Elementary Diagnostics Patterns: Crash; Hang.

Memory Analysis Patterns: Exception Stack Trace; NULL Pointer (Data); CLR Thread; JIT Code; Deadlock (Managed Space); Execution Residue (Managed Space); Hidden Exception (Managed Space).

Debugging Implementation Patterns: Break-in.

1.   Launch LINQPad 8 (x64), open *\AWD4\AppMD11\AppMD11.linq (File \ Open* menu*)*, and remove Query 1 tab:

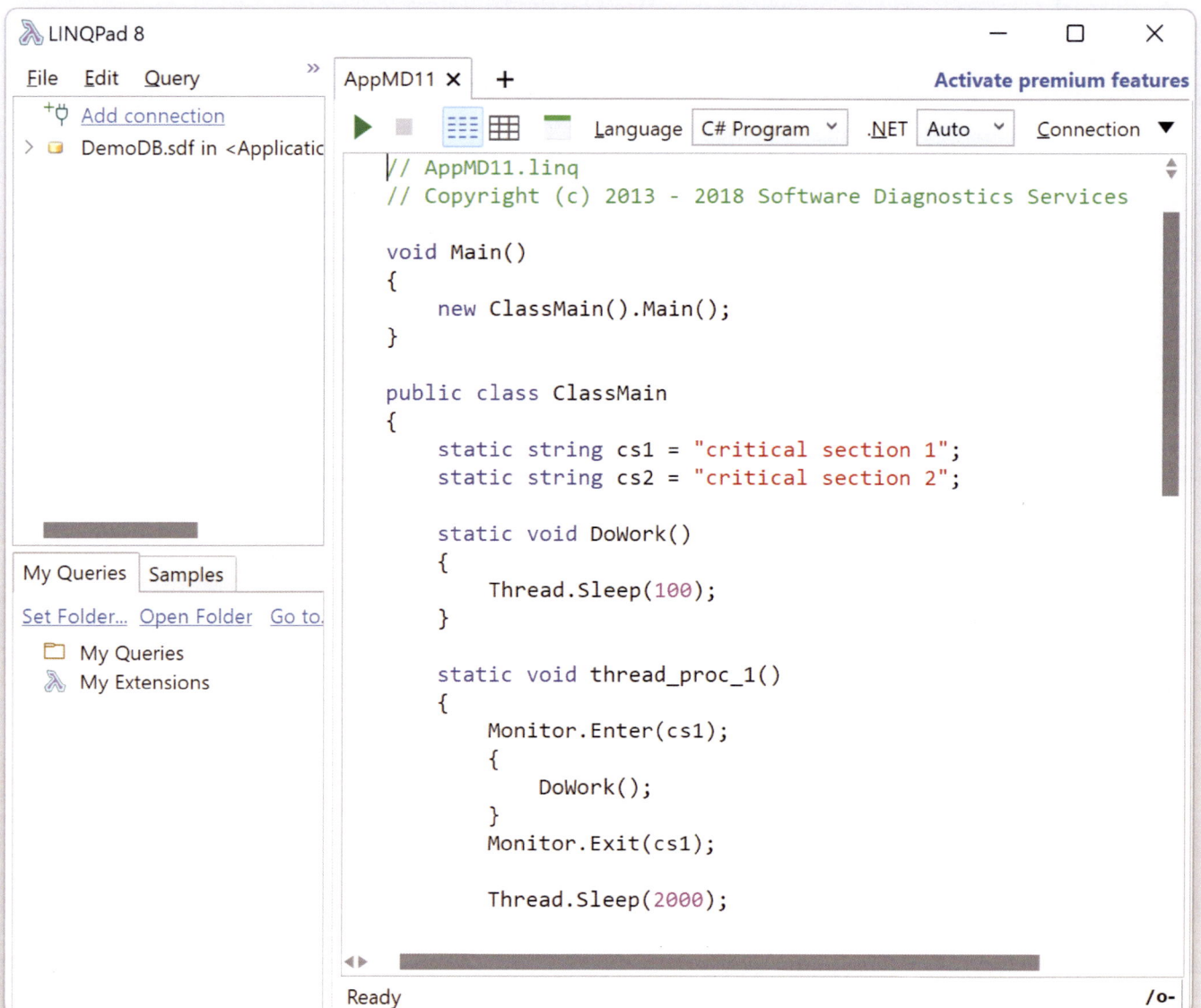

2. Execute the program (*Query \ Execute*). We get it finished in approx. 5 seconds with the following diagnostic output about finished threads:

3. The exercise is similar to *UD5*. We have a similar synchronization object: **Monitor,** which we enter and exit, similar to **Mutex** ownership. Here's the source code of 2 threads:

```
static void thread_proc_1()
{
        Monitor.Enter(cs1);
        {
                DoWork();
        }
        Monitor.Exit(cs1);

        Thread.Sleep(2000);

        Monitor.Enter(cs2);
        {
                DoWork();
        }
        Monitor.Exit(cs2);

        Console.WriteLine("Thread 1 has finished.");
}


static void thread_proc_2()
{
        Monitor.Enter(cs2);
        {
                DoWork();
                Monitor.Enter(cs1);
                {
                        DoWork();
                        Thread.Sleep(3000);
                        DoWork();
                }
                Monitor.Exit(cs1);
                DoWork();
        }
        Monitor.Exit(cs2);

        Console.WriteLine("Thread 2 has finished.");
}
```

4.　　　Open \AWD4\AppMD11\AppMD11V2.linq and close AppMD11 tab:

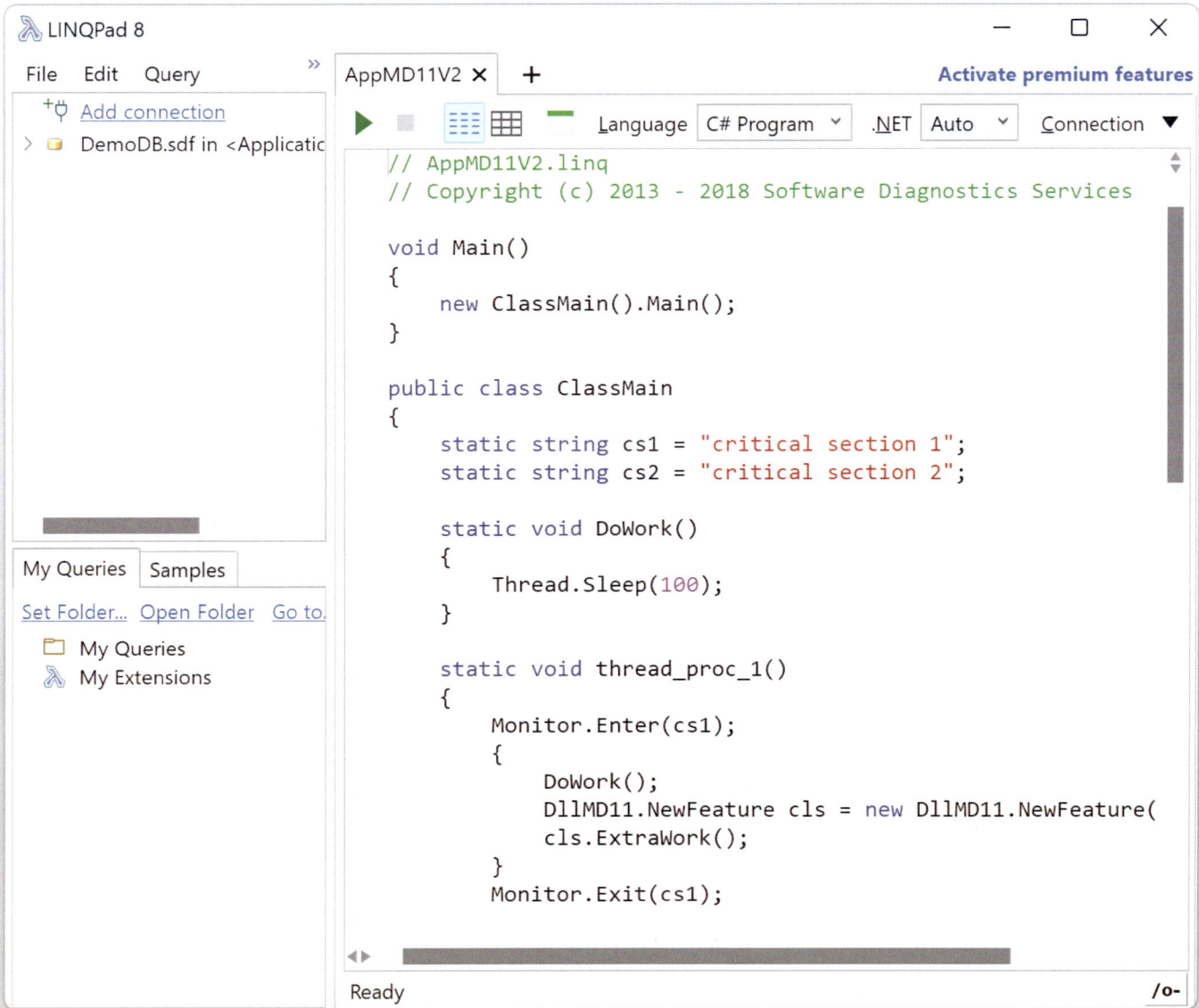

Note: Version 2 has a new feature added, implemented as a function *ExtraWork* in the *NewFeature* class in the *DllMD11* namespace (this is an assembly DLL name too). The new assembly module should be already referenced (*Query \ References and Properties*) – *Add... \ Browse...* if it is not added or you have it in a different folder:

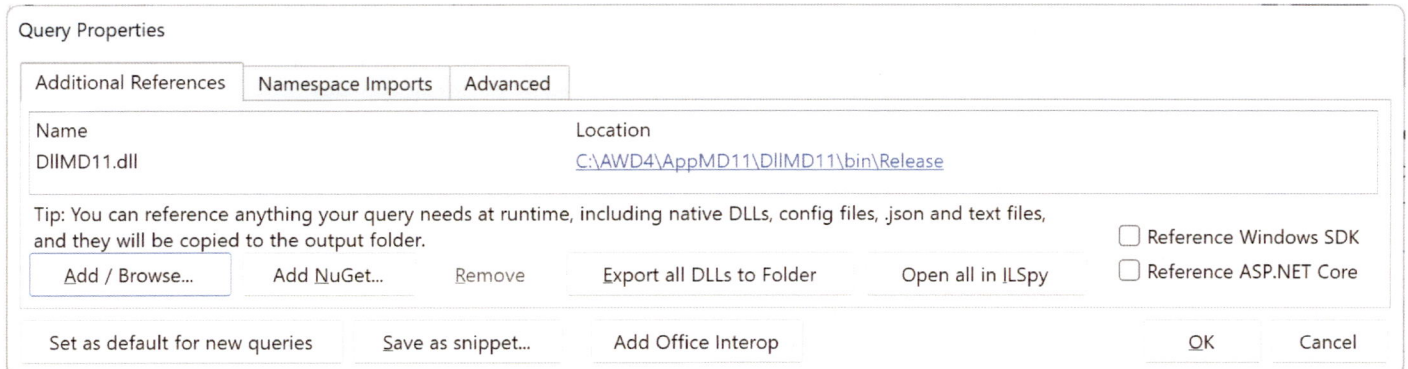

5.   If we run the program, we get *NullReferenceException*:

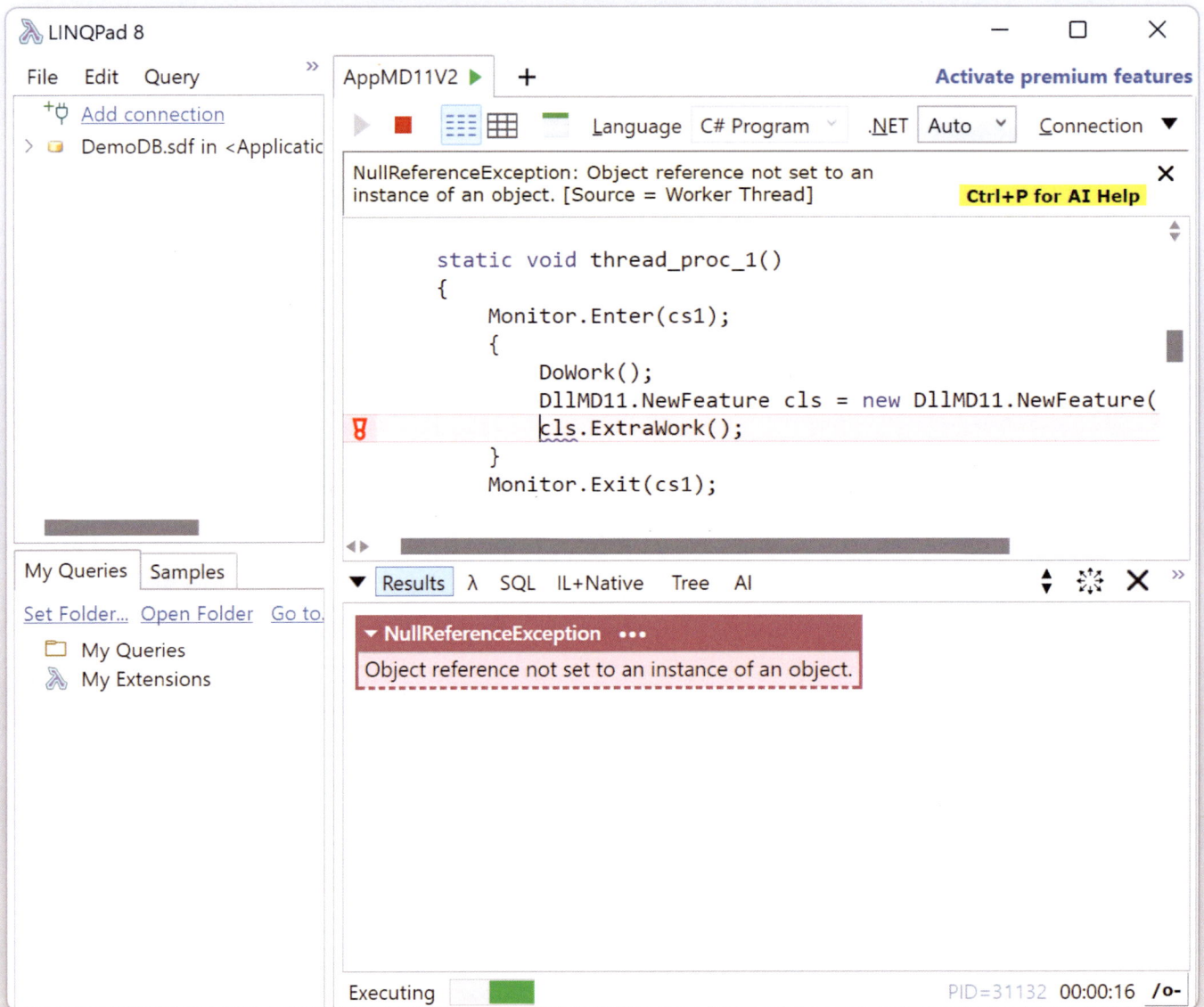

6.   Quit LINQPad. Run WinDbg and open *LINQPad8.exe* from your LINQPad 8 installation folder (for example, *C:\Program Files\LINQPad8\LINQPad8.exe*). We get this output:

```
Microsoft (R) Windows Debugger Version 10.0.25921.1001 AMD64
Copyright (c) Microsoft Corporation. All rights reserved.

CommandLine: C:\Program Files\LINQPad8\LINQPad8.exe

************* Path validation summary **************
Response                        Time (ms)     Location
Deferred                                      srv*
Symbol search path is: srv*
Executable search path is:
ModLoad: 00007ff7`ac4c0000 00007ff7`ac567000   CustomLauncher.exe
ModLoad: 00007ffb`36990000 00007ffb`36ba7000   ntdll.dll
ModLoad: 00007ffb`34760000 00007ffb`34824000   C:\WINDOWS\System32\KERNEL32.DLL
ModLoad: 00007ffb`34300000 00007ffb`346a6000   C:\WINDOWS\System32\KERNELBASE.dll
```

```
ModLoad: 00007ffb`33ee0000 00007ffb`33f4b000   C:\WINDOWS\System32\WINTRUST.dll
ModLoad: 00007ffb`1fde0000 00007ffb`1fdea000   C:\WINDOWS\SYSTEM32\VERSION.dll
ModLoad: 00007ffb`34ce0000 00007ffb`34d87000   C:\WINDOWS\System32\msvcrt.dll
ModLoad: 00007ffb`35700000 00007ffb`35817000   C:\WINDOWS\System32\RPCRT4.dll
ModLoad: 00007ffb`366d0000 00007ffb`3687e000   C:\WINDOWS\System32\USER32.dll
ModLoad: 00007ffb`33cd0000 00007ffb`33cf6000   C:\WINDOWS\System32\win32u.dll
ModLoad: 00007ffb`35600000 00007ffb`35629000   C:\WINDOWS\System32\GDI32.dll
ModLoad: 00007ffb`33d00000 00007ffb`33e18000   C:\WINDOWS\System32\gdi32full.dll
ModLoad: 00007ffb`34260000 00007ffb`342fa000   C:\WINDOWS\System32\msvcp_win.dll
ModLoad: 00007ffb`33fd0000 00007ffb`340e1000   C:\WINDOWS\System32\ucrtbase.dll
ModLoad: 00007ffb`353d0000 00007ffb`35483000   C:\WINDOWS\System32\ADVAPI32.dll
ModLoad: 00007ffb`34c30000 00007ffb`34cd8000   C:\WINDOWS\System32\sechost.dll
ModLoad: 00007ffb`346b0000 00007ffb`346d8000   C:\WINDOWS\System32\bcrypt.dll
ModLoad: 00007ffb`35cb0000 00007ffb`3650a000   C:\WINDOWS\System32\SHELL32.dll
ModLoad: 00007ffb`34930000 00007ffb`34ad0000   C:\WINDOWS\System32\ole32.dll
ModLoad: 00007ffb`34d90000 00007ffb`35119000   C:\WINDOWS\System32\combase.dll
ModLoad: 00007ffb`340f0000 00007ffb`34256000   C:\WINDOWS\System32\CRYPT32.dll
(11584.6648): Break instruction exception - code 80000003 (first chance)
ntdll!LdrpDoDebuggerBreak+0x30:
00007ffb`36a6b784 int     3
```

7.   Open a log file and then continue:

```
0:000> .logopen c:\AWD4\MD11.log
Opened log file 'c:\AWD4\MD11.log'
```

```
0:000> g
ModLoad: 00007ffb`33970000 00007ffb`33982000   C:\WINDOWS\SYSTEM32\MSASN1.dll
ModLoad: 00007ffb`35660000 00007ffb`35691000   C:\WINDOWS\System32\IMM32.DLL
ModLoad: 00007ffb`32cc0000 00007ffb`32cd8000   C:\WINDOWS\SYSTEM32\kernel.appcore.dll
ModLoad: 00007ffb`33f50000 00007ffb`33fca000   C:\WINDOWS\System32\bcryptPrimitives.dll
ModLoad: 00007ffb`30ba0000 00007ffb`30c4b000   C:\WINDOWS\system32\uxtheme.dll
ModLoad: 00007ffb`34830000 00007ffb`34923000   C:\WINDOWS\System32\shcore.dll
ModLoad: 00007ffb`31bd0000 00007ffb`324c6000   C:\WINDOWS\SYSTEM32\windows.storage.dll
ModLoad: 00007ffb`31a90000 00007ffb`31bce000   C:\WINDOWS\SYSTEM32\wintypes.dll
ModLoad: 00007ffb`356a0000 00007ffb`356fe000   C:\WINDOWS\System32\shlwapi.dll
ModLoad: 00007ffa`e6590000 00007ffa`e65e9000   C:\Program Files\dotnet\host\fxr\8.0.1\hostfxr.dll
ModLoad: 00007ffa`e5fa0000 00007ffa`e6004000   C:\Program Files\dotnet\shared\Microsoft.NETCore.App\8.0.1\hostpolicy.dll
ModLoad: 00007ffa`8d930000 00007ffa`8de19000   C:\Program Files\dotnet\shared\Microsoft.NETCore.App\8.0.1\coreclr.dll
ModLoad: 00007ffb`35120000 00007ffb`351f7000   C:\WINDOWS\System32\OLEAUT32.dll
(11584.6648): Unknown exception - code 04242420 (first chance)
ModLoad: 00007ffa`8cca0000 00007ffa`8d92d000   C:\Program Files\dotnet\shared\Microsoft.NETCore.App\8.0.1\System.Private.CoreLib.dll
ModLoad: 00007ffa`a5f70000 00007ffa`a6129000   C:\Program Files\dotnet\shared\Microsoft.NETCore.App\8.0.1\clrjit.dll
ModLoad: 00007ffb`0f020000 00007ffb`0f290000   C:\WINDOWS\SYSTEM32\icu.dll
ModLoad: 0000023a`a0af0000 0000023a`a1698000   C:\Program Files\LINQPad8\LINQPad.GUI.dll
ModLoad: 0000023a`a16a0000 0000023a`a16ae000   C:\Program Files\dotnet\shared\Microsoft.NETCore.App\8.0.1\System.Runtime.dll
ModLoad: 00007ffb`08820000 00007ffb`08835000   C:\Program Files\dotnet\shared\Microsoft.NETCore.App\8.0.1\System.Runtime.InteropServices.dll
ModLoad: 0000023a`a16b0000 0000023a`a16b8000   C:\Program
Files\dotnet\shared\Microsoft.NETCore.App\8.0.1\System.Runtime.InteropServices.RuntimeInformation.dll
ModLoad: 0000023a`a16c0000 0000023a`a3402000   C:\Program Files\LINQPad8\LINQPad.Runtime.dll
ModLoad: 0000023a`a3410000 0000023a`a3418000   C:\Program Files\dotnet\shared\Microsoft.NETCore.App\8.0.1\System.Runtime.Loader.dll
ModLoad: 0000023a`a3420000 0000023a`a3428000   C:\Program Files\dotnet\shared\Microsoft.NETCore.App\8.0.1\System.Runtime.Extensions.dll
ModLoad: 00007ffa`f4960000 00007ffa`f499d000   C:\Program Files\dotnet\shared\Microsoft.NETCore.App\8.0.1\System.Collections.dll
ModLoad: 00007ffb`06d10000 00007ffb`06d22000   C:\Program Files\dotnet\shared\Microsoft.NETCore.App\8.0.1\System.Threading.dll
ModLoad: 00007ffa`e5f10000 00007ffa`e5f92000   C:\Program Files\dotnet\shared\Microsoft.NETCore.App\8.0.1\System.Linq.dll
ModLoad: 0000023a`a3430000 0000023a`a3438000   C:\Program Files\dotnet\shared\Microsoft.NETCore.App\8.0.1\System.IO.FileSystem.dll
ModLoad: 00007ffa`ea0e0000 00007ffa`ea11e000   C:\Program Files\dotnet\shared\Microsoft.NETCore.App\8.0.1\System.IO.Compression.dll
ModLoad: 0000023a`a3440000 0000023a`a3448000   C:\Program Files\dotnet\shared\Microsoft.NETCore.App\8.0.1\System.Threading.Thread.dll
ModLoad: 00007ffa`e1520000 00007ffa`e15bf000   C:\Program Files\dotnet\shared\Microsoft.NETCore.App\8.0.1\System.Transactions.Local.dll
ModLoad: 00007ffa`86000000 00007ffa`86cec000   C:\Program Files\dotnet\shared\Microsoft.WindowsDesktop.App\8.0.1\System.Windows.Forms.dll
ModLoad: 00007ffa`fb8a0000 00007ffa`fb8c1000   C:\Program Files\dotnet\shared\Microsoft.NETCore.App\8.0.1\System.Diagnostics.TraceSource.dll
ModLoad: 00007ffb`14b90000 00007ffb`14b9e000   C:\Program Files\dotnet\shared\Microsoft.NETCore.App\8.0.1\System.Diagnostics.TextWriterTraceListener.dll
(11584.10da8): C++ EH exception - code e06d7363 (first chance)
(11584.10da8): C++ EH exception - code e06d7363 (first chance)
(11584.10da8): C++ EH exception - code e06d7363 (first chance)
ModLoad: 00007ffa`8c2a0000 00007ffa`8c4c4000   C:\Program Files\dotnet\shared\Microsoft.WindowsDesktop.App\8.0.1\WindowsBase.dll
ModLoad: 00007ffa`85d20000 00007ffa`85ffd000   C:\Program Files\dotnet\shared\Microsoft.WindowsDesktop.App\8.0.1\System.Windows.Forms.Primitives.dll
ModLoad: 00007ffb`04550000 00007ffb`04561000   C:\Program Files\dotnet\shared\Microsoft.NETCore.App\8.0.1\System.ComponentModel.Primitives.dll
ModLoad: 00007ffb`04340000 00007ffb`0435e000   C:\Program Files\dotnet\shared\Microsoft.NETCore.App\8.0.1\System.Drawing.Primitives.dll
ModLoad: 00007ffb`03d10000 00007ffb`03d27000   C:\Program Files\dotnet\shared\Microsoft.NETCore.App\8.0.1\System.Collections.Specialized.dll
ModLoad: 0000023a`a3450000 0000023a`a3458000   C:\Program Files\dotnet\shared\Microsoft.NETCore.App\8.0.1\Microsoft.Win32.Primitives.dll
(11584.10da8): C++ EH exception - code e06d7363 (first chance)
(11584.10da8): C++ EH exception - code e06d7363 (first chance)
(11584.10da8): C++ EH exception - code e06d7363 (first chance)
(11584.10da8): C++ EH exception - code e06d7363 (first chance)
...
(11584.268): C++ EH exception - code e06d7363 (first chance)
(11584.268): CLR exception - code e0434352 (first chance)
(11584.268): C++ EH exception - code e06d7363 (first chance)
```

```
(11584.268): CLR exception - code e0434352 (first chance)
(11584.268): C++ EH exception - code e06d7363 (first chance)
(11584.268): CLR exception - code e0434352 (first chance)
(11584.268): C++ EH exception - code e06d7363 (first chance)
(11584.268): CLR exception - code e0434352 (first chance)
(11584.268): C++ EH exception - code e06d7363 (first chance)
(11584.268): CLR exception - code e0434352 (first chance)
(11584.268): C++ EH exception - code e06d7363 (first chance)
(11584.268): CLR exception - code e0434352 (first chance)
(11584.268): C++ EH exception - code e06d7363 (first chance)
(11584.268): CLR exception - code e0434352 (first chance)
(11584.268): C++ EH exception - code e06d7363 (first chance)
(11584.268): CLR exception - code e0434352 (first chance)
(11584.268): C++ EH exception - code e06d7363 (first chance)
(11584.268): CLR exception - code e0434352 (first chance)
(11584.268): C++ EH exception - code e06d7363 (first chance)
(11584.268): CLR exception - code e0434352 (first chance)
(11584.268): C++ EH exception - code e06d7363 (first chance)
(11584.268): CLR exception - code e0434352 (first chance)
```

Note: We see a lot of first chance exceptions because they are ignored in WinDbg. You can always change such behavior. Break-in and then open *File \ Settings \ Events & exceptions* dialog to set *Break Status* to *Break* for C++ EH exception (*Break* means first chance in this dialog):

```
(11584.6f78): Break instruction exception - code 80000003 (first chance)
ntdll!DbgBreakPoint:
00007ffb`36a33060 int     3
```

316

Then WinDbg stops at each C++ EH exception. For this exercise, we assume that *Break Status* is set to *Second Chance Break* to avoid unnecessary break-ins.

8. We now resume again, switch to *LINQPad* 8 (x64) window, open *\AWD4\AppMD11\AppMD11V2.linq* and then execute it:

```
0:004> g
(11584.a73c): C++ EH exception - code e06d7363 (first chance)
(11584.a73c): CLR exception - code e0434352 (first chance)
(11584.a73c): C++ EH exception - code e06d7363 (first chance)
(11584.a73c): CLR exception - code e0434352 (first chance)
(11584.a73c): C++ EH exception - code e06d7363 (first chance)
(11584.a73c): CLR exception - code e0434352 (first chance)
(11584.a73c): C++ EH exception - code e06d7363 (first chance)
(11584.a73c): CLR exception - code e0434352 (first chance)
(11584.a73c): C++ EH exception - code e06d7363 (first chance)
(11584.a73c): CLR exception - code e0434352 (first chance)
```

Note: Unfortunately, WinDbg didn't stop when we had the exception in *LINQPad*. The reason for this is that *LINQPad* version 8 uses separate processes for the execution of queries. If we look at the list of processes in Task Manager, we see an additional *LINQPad8.exe* process:

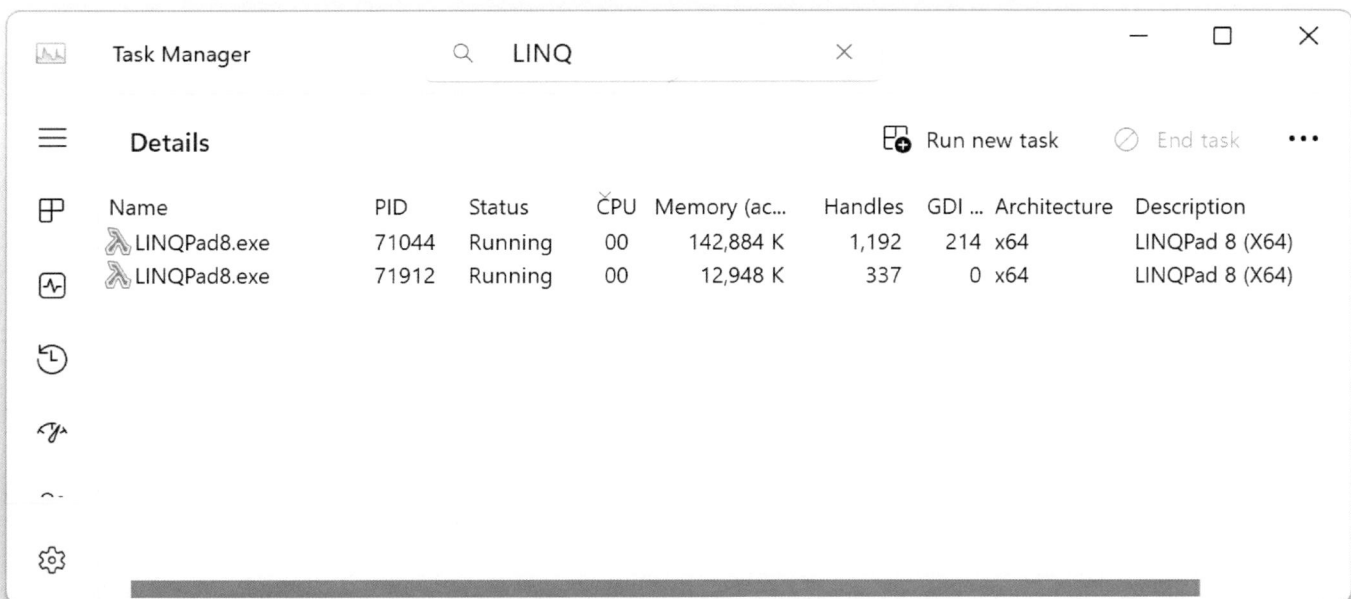

9. We break in and then restart the process.

```
(11584.52a0): Break instruction exception - code 80000003 (first chance)
ntdll!DbgBreakPoint:
00007ffb`36a33060 int     3
```

```
0:001> .restart
NatVis script unloaded from 'C:\Program
Files\WindowsApps\Microsoft.WinDbg_1.2308.2002.0_x64__8wekyb3d8bbwe\amd64\Visualizers\atlmfc.na
tvis'
```

```
NatVis script unloaded from 'C:\Program
Files\WindowsApps\Microsoft.WinDbg_1.2308.2002.0_x64__8wekyb3d8bbwe\amd64\Visualizers\Objective
C.natvis'
NatVis script unloaded from 'C:\Program
Files\WindowsApps\Microsoft.WinDbg_1.2308.2002.0_x64__8wekyb3d8bbwe\amd64\Visualizers\concurren
cy.natvis'
NatVis script unloaded from 'C:\Program
Files\WindowsApps\Microsoft.WinDbg_1.2308.2002.0_x64__8wekyb3d8bbwe\amd64\Visualizers\cpp_rest.
natvis'
NatVis script unloaded from 'C:\Program
Files\WindowsApps\Microsoft.WinDbg_1.2308.2002.0_x64__8wekyb3d8bbwe\amd64\Visualizers\stl.natvi
s'
NatVis script unloaded from 'C:\Program
Files\WindowsApps\Microsoft.WinDbg_1.2308.2002.0_x64__8wekyb3d8bbwe\amd64\Visualizers\Windows.D
ata.Json.natvis'
NatVis script unloaded from 'C:\Program
Files\WindowsApps\Microsoft.WinDbg_1.2308.2002.0_x64__8wekyb3d8bbwe\amd64\Visualizers\Windows.D
evices.Geolocation.natvis'
NatVis script unloaded from 'C:\Program
Files\WindowsApps\Microsoft.WinDbg_1.2308.2002.0_x64__8wekyb3d8bbwe\amd64\Visualizers\Windows.D
evices.Sensors.natvis'
NatVis script unloaded from 'C:\Program
Files\WindowsApps\Microsoft.WinDbg_1.2308.2002.0_x64__8wekyb3d8bbwe\amd64\Visualizers\Windows.M
edia.natvis'
NatVis script unloaded from 'C:\Program
Files\WindowsApps\Microsoft.WinDbg_1.2308.2002.0_x64__8wekyb3d8bbwe\amd64\Visualizers\windows.n
atvis'
NatVis script unloaded from 'C:\Program
Files\WindowsApps\Microsoft.WinDbg_1.2308.2002.0_x64__8wekyb3d8bbwe\amd64\Visualizers\winrt.nat
vis'


Microsoft (R) Windows Debugger Version 10.0.25921.1001 AMD64
Copyright (c) Microsoft Corporation. All rights reserved.

CommandLine: C:\Program Files\LINQPad8\LINQPad8.exe

************* Path validation summary **************
Response                        Time (ms)      Location
Deferred                                       srv*
Symbol search path is: srv*
Executable search path is:
ModLoad: 00007ff7`ac4c0000 00007ff7`ac567000   CustomLauncher.exe
ModLoad: 00007ffb`36990000 00007ffb`36ba7000   ntdll.dll
ModLoad: 00007ffb`34760000 00007ffb`34824000   C:\WINDOWS\System32\KERNEL32.DLL
ModLoad: 00007ffb`34300000 00007ffb`346a6000   C:\WINDOWS\System32\KERNELBASE.dll
ModLoad: 00007ffb`33ee0000 00007ffb`33f4b000   C:\WINDOWS\System32\WINTRUST.dll
ModLoad: 00007ffb`34ce0000 00007ffb`34d87000   C:\WINDOWS\System32\msvcrt.dll
ModLoad: 00007ffb`1fde0000 00007ffb`1fdea000   C:\WINDOWS\SYSTEM32\VERSION.dll
ModLoad: 00007ffb`35700000 00007ffb`35817000   C:\WINDOWS\System32\RPCRT4.dll
ModLoad: 00007ffb`366d0000 00007ffb`3687e000   C:\WINDOWS\System32\USER32.dll
ModLoad: 00007ffb`33cd0000 00007ffb`33cf6000   C:\WINDOWS\System32\win32u.dll
ModLoad: 00007ffb`35600000 00007ffb`35629000   C:\WINDOWS\System32\GDI32.dll
ModLoad: 00007ffb`33d00000 00007ffb`33e18000   C:\WINDOWS\System32\gdi32full.dll
ModLoad: 00007ffb`34260000 00007ffb`342fa000   C:\WINDOWS\System32\msvcp_win.dll
ModLoad: 00007ffb`33fd0000 00007ffb`340e1000   C:\WINDOWS\System32\ucrtbase.dll
ModLoad: 00007ffb`353d0000 00007ffb`35483000   C:\WINDOWS\System32\ADVAPI32.dll
ModLoad: 00007ffb`34c30000 00007ffb`34cd8000   C:\WINDOWS\System32\sechost.dll
ModLoad: 00007ffb`346b0000 00007ffb`346d8000   C:\WINDOWS\System32\bcrypt.dll
ModLoad: 00007ffb`35cb0000 00007ffb`3650a000   C:\WINDOWS\System32\SHELL32.dll
```

```
ModLoad: 00007ffb`34930000 00007ffb`34ad0000   C:\WINDOWS\System32\ole32.dll
ModLoad: 00007ffb`34d90000 00007ffb`35119000   C:\WINDOWS\System32\combase.dll
ModLoad: 00007ffb`340f0000 00007ffb`34256000   C:\WINDOWS\System32\CRYPT32.dll
(74e8.74c8): Break instruction exception - code 80000003 (first chance)
ntdll!LdrpDoDebuggerBreak+0x30:
00007ffb`36a6b784 int     3
```

We now see only one new process in Task Manager but no other processes:

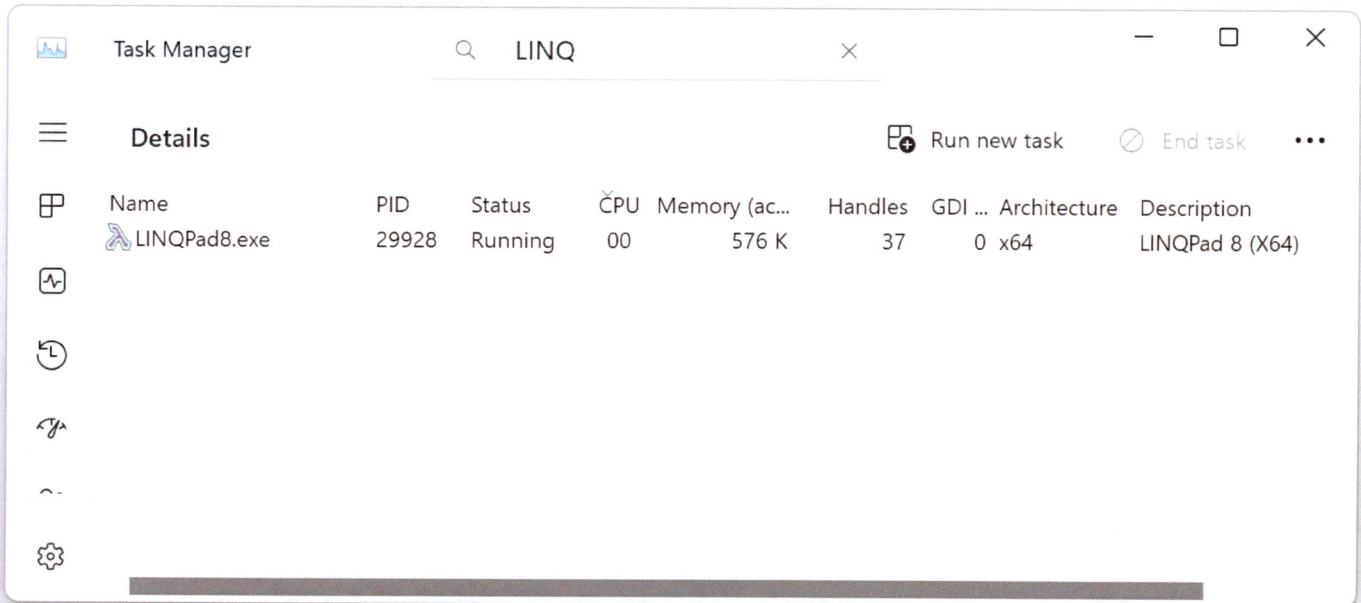

10.   When we continue (**g**), we see the additional process:

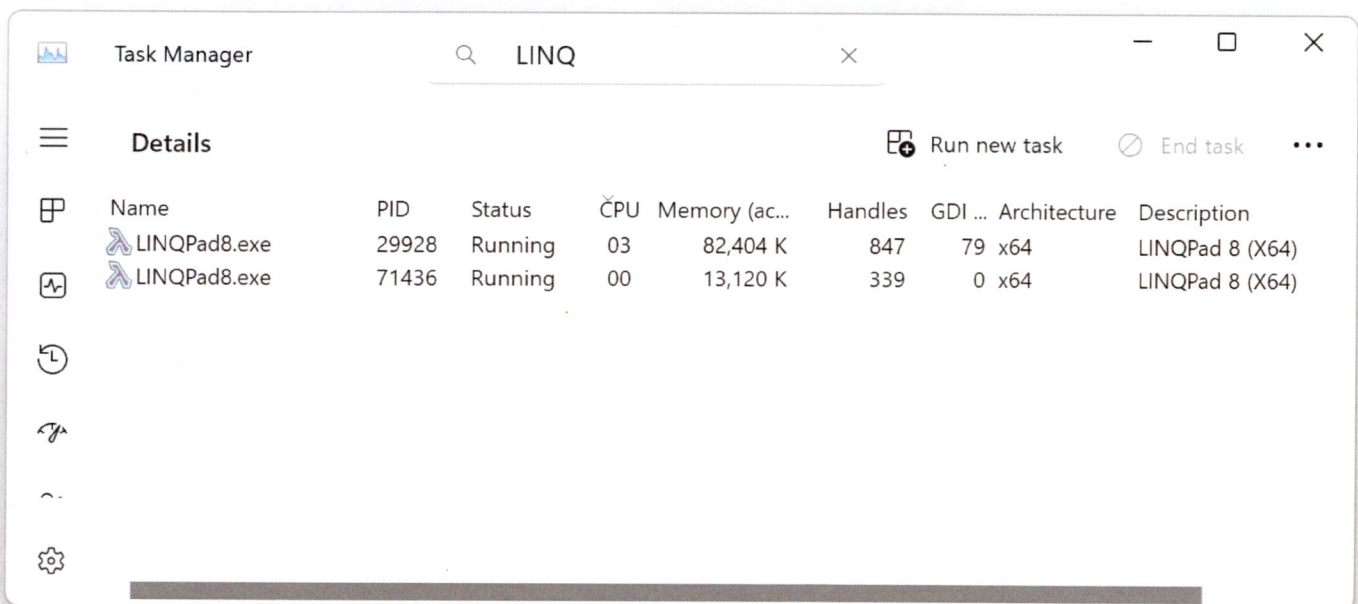

11.   When we reopen *AppMD11V2.linq* (and close the Query 1 tab), we don't see any new query processes, so we launch an instance of WinDbg and attach it to PID 71436:

```
Microsoft (R) Windows Debugger Version 10.0.25921.1001 AMD64
Copyright (c) Microsoft Corporation. All rights reserved.

*** wait with pending attach

************** Path validation summary **************
Response                        Time (ms)    Location
Deferred                                     srv*
OK                                           C:\AWD4\AppD9\Release
Symbol search path is: srv*;C:\AWD4\AppD9\Release
Executable search path is:
ModLoad: 00007ff7`ac4c0000 00007ff7`ac567000   C:\Program Files\LINQPad8\LINQPad8.exe
ModLoad: 00007ffb`36990000 00007ffb`36ba7000   C:\WINDOWS\SYSTEM32\ntdll.dll
ModLoad: 00007ffb`34760000 00007ffb`34824000   C:\WINDOWS\System32\KERNEL32.DLL
ModLoad: 00007ffb`34300000 00007ffb`346a6000   C:\WINDOWS\System32\KERNELBASE.dll
ModLoad: 00007ffb`33ee0000 00007ffb`33f4b000   C:\WINDOWS\System32\WINTRUST.dll
ModLoad: 00007ffb`34ce0000 00007ffb`34d87000   C:\WINDOWS\System32\msvcrt.dll
ModLoad: 00007ffb`1fde0000 00007ffb`1fdea000   C:\WINDOWS\SYSTEM32\VERSION.dll
ModLoad: 00007ffb`35700000 00007ffb`35817000   C:\WINDOWS\System32\RPCRT4.dll
ModLoad: 00007ffb`366d0000 00007ffb`3687e000   C:\WINDOWS\System32\USER32.dll
ModLoad: 00007ffb`33cd0000 00007ffb`33cf6000   C:\WINDOWS\System32\win32u.dll
ModLoad: 00007ffb`35600000 00007ffb`35629000   C:\WINDOWS\System32\GDI32.dll
ModLoad: 00007ffb`33d00000 00007ffb`33e18000   C:\WINDOWS\System32\gdi32full.dll
ModLoad: 00007ffb`34260000 00007ffb`342fa000   C:\WINDOWS\System32\msvcp_win.dll
ModLoad: 00007ffb`33fd0000 00007ffb`340e1000   C:\WINDOWS\System32\ucrtbase.dll
ModLoad: 00007ffb`353d0000 00007ffb`35483000   C:\WINDOWS\System32\ADVAPI32.dll
ModLoad: 00007ffb`34c30000 00007ffb`34cd8000   C:\WINDOWS\System32\sechost.dll
ModLoad: 00007ffb`346b0000 00007ffb`346d8000   C:\WINDOWS\System32\bcrypt.dll
ModLoad: 00007ffb`35cb0000 00007ffb`3650a000   C:\WINDOWS\System32\SHELL32.dll
ModLoad: 00007ffb`34930000 00007ffb`34ad0000   C:\WINDOWS\System32\ole32.dll
ModLoad: 00007ffb`34d90000 00007ffb`35119000   C:\WINDOWS\System32\combase.dll
ModLoad: 00007ffb`340f0000 00007ffb`34256000   C:\WINDOWS\System32\CRYPT32.dll
ModLoad: 00007ffb`33970000 00007ffb`33982000   C:\WINDOWS\SYSTEM32\MSASN1.dll
ModLoad: 00007ffb`35660000 00007ffb`35691000   C:\WINDOWS\SYSTEM32\IMM32.DLL
ModLoad: 00007ffb`32cc0000 00007ffb`32cd8000   C:\WINDOWS\SYSTEM32\kernel.appcore.dll
ModLoad: 00007ffb`33f50000 00007ffb`33fca000   C:\WINDOWS\System32\bcryptPrimitives.dll
ModLoad: 00007ffb`30ba0000 00007ffb`30c4b000   C:\WINDOWS\system32\uxtheme.dll
ModLoad: 00007ffb`34830000 00007ffb`34923000   C:\WINDOWS\System32\shcore.dll
ModLoad: 00007ffb`04c50000 00007ffb`04ca9000   C:\Program Files\dotnet\host\fxr\8.0.1\hostfxr.dll
ModLoad: 00007ffb`04be0000 00007ffb`04c44000   C:\Program Files\dotnet\shared\Microsoft.NETCore.App\8.0.1\hostpolicy.dll
ModLoad: 00007ffa`c9a00000 00007ffa`c9ee9000   C:\Program Files\dotnet\shared\Microsoft.NETCore.App\8.0.1\coreclr.dll
ModLoad: 00007ffb`35120000 00007ffb`351f7000   C:\WINDOWS\System32\OLEAUT32.dll
ModLoad: 00007ffa`8d190000 00007ffa`8de1d000   C:\Program Files\dotnet\shared\Microsoft.NETCore.App\8.0.1\System.Private.CoreLib.dll
ModLoad: 00007ffa`e12b0000 00007ffa`e1469000   C:\Program Files\dotnet\shared\Microsoft.NETCore.App\8.0.1\clrjit.dll
ModLoad: 000001d7`e5030000 000001d7`e5044000   C:\Users\dmitr\AppData\Local\LINQPad\8.1.6\ProcessServer\8.0.1\LINQPad.Query.dll
ModLoad: 000001d7`c5050000 000001d7`c505e000   C:\Program Files\dotnet\shared\Microsoft.NETCore.App\8.0.1\System.Runtime.dll
ModLoad: 00007ffa`86000000 00007ffa`86cec000   C:\Program Files\dotnet\shared\Microsoft.WindowsDesktop.App\8.0.1\System.Windows.Forms.dll
ModLoad: 000001d7`e6820000 000001d7`e6828000   C:\Program Files\dotnet\shared\Microsoft.NETCore.App\8.0.1\System.Runtime.Loader.dll
ModLoad: 00007ffa`f6f40000 00007ffa`f6f68000   C:\Program Files\dotnet\shared\Microsoft.NETCore.App\8.0.1\System.Console.dll
ModLoad: 000001d7`e6830000 000001d7`e6838000   C:\Program Files\dotnet\shared\Microsoft.NETCore.App\8.0.1\System.Runtime.Extensions.dll
ModLoad: 00007ffa`a6500000 00007ffa`a67dd000   C:\Program Files\dotnet\shared\Microsoft.WindowsDesktop.App\8.0.1\System.Windows.Forms.Primitives.dll
ModLoad: 00007ffb`15460000 00007ffb`15475000   C:\Program Files\dotnet\shared\Microsoft.NETCore.App\8.0.1\System.Runtime.InteropServices.dll
ModLoad: 00007ffb`093b0000 00007ffb`093c2000   C:\Program Files\dotnet\shared\Microsoft.NETCore.App\8.0.1\System.Threading.dll
ModLoad: 00007ffb`092a0000 00007ffb`092c1000   C:\Program Files\dotnet\shared\Microsoft.NETCore.App\8.0.1\System.Diagnostics.TraceSource.dll
ModLoad: 00007ffb`080e0000 00007ffb`0811d000   C:\Program Files\dotnet\shared\Microsoft.NETCore.App\8.0.1\System.Collections.dll
ModLoad: 00007ffb`08820000 00007ffb`08831000   C:\Program Files\dotnet\shared\Microsoft.NETCore.App\8.0.1\System.ComponentModel.Primitives.dll
ModLoad: 00007ffb`06d10000 00007ffb`06d2e000   C:\Program Files\dotnet\shared\Microsoft.NETCore.App\8.0.1\System.Drawing.Primitives.dll
ModLoad: 000001d7`e6860000 000001d7`e6868000   C:\Program Files\dotnet\shared\Microsoft.NETCore.App\8.0.1\System.IO.FileSystem.dll
ModLoad: 00007ffb`31bd0000 00007ffb`324c6000   C:\WINDOWS\SYSTEM32\windows.storage.dll
ModLoad: 00007ffb`31a90000 00007ffb`31bce000   C:\WINDOWS\SYSTEM32\wintypes.dll
ModLoad: 00007ffb`356a0000 00007ffb`356fe000   C:\WINDOWS\System32\shlwapi.dll
ModLoad: 00007ffa`a6220000 00007ffa`a6393000   C:\Program Files\dotnet\shared\Microsoft.WindowsDesktop.App\8.0.1\System.Drawing.Common.dll
ModLoad: 00000218`7b630000 00000218`7d372000   C:\Program Files\LINQPad8\LINQPad.Runtime.dll
ModLoad: 00007ffa`f5a90000 00007ffa`f5b12000   C:\Program Files\dotnet\shared\Microsoft.NETCore.App\8.0.1\System.Linq.dll
ModLoad: 00007ffb`04ba0000 00007ffb`04bde000   C:\Program Files\dotnet\shared\Microsoft.NETCore.App\8.0.1\System.IO.Compression.dll
ModLoad: 00007ffa`fbb60000 00007ffa`fbbb0000   C:\Program Files\dotnet\shared\Microsoft.NETCore.App\8.0.1\System.Diagnostics.Process.dll
ModLoad: 00007ffa`e57b0000 00007ffa`e584f000   C:\Program Files\dotnet\shared\Microsoft.NETCore.App\8.0.1\System.Transactions.Local.dll
ModLoad: 00007ffb`0f020000 00007ffb`0f290000   C:\WINDOWS\SYSTEM32\icu.dll
ModLoad: 000001d7`e68a0000 000001d7`e68a8000   C:\Program Files\dotnet\shared\Microsoft.NETCore.App\8.0.1\System.Threading.Tasks.dll
ModLoad: 00007ffb`03d10000 00007ffb`03d22000   C:\Program Files\dotnet\shared\Microsoft.NETCore.App\8.0.1\System.IO.MemoryMappedFiles.dll
ModLoad: 000001d7`e68d0000 000001d7`e68d8000   C:\Program Files\dotnet\shared\Microsoft.NETCore.App\8.0.1\System.Threading.ThreadPool.dll
ModLoad: 000001d7`e68e0000 000001d7`e68e8000   C:\Program Files\dotnet\shared\Microsoft.NETCore.App\8.0.1\System.Diagnostics.Debug.dll
ModLoad: 000001d7`e68f0000 000001d7`e68f8000   C:\Program Files\dotnet\shared\Microsoft.NETCore.App\8.0.1\System.Threading.Thread.dll
ModLoad: 00007ffb`33c00000 00007ffb`33c26000   C:\WINDOWS\SYSTEM32\profapi.dll
ModLoad: 000001d7`e6900000 000001d7`e6908000   C:\Program
Files\dotnet\shared\Microsoft.NETCore.App\8.0.1\System.Runtime.InteropServices.RuntimeInformation.dll
ModLoad: 00007ffb`044d0000 00007ffb`044f4000   C:\Program Files\dotnet\shared\Microsoft.NETCore.App\8.0.1\System.Memory.dll
ModLoad: 000001d7`e6a20000 000001d7`e6a28000   C:\Program Files\dotnet\shared\Microsoft.NETCore.App\8.0.1\Microsoft.Win32.Primitives.dll
ModLoad: 00007ffb`feea0000 00007ffa`feedd000   C:\Program Files\dotnet\shared\Microsoft.NETCore.App\8.0.1\System.Private.Uri.dll
ModLoad: 00007ffa`c9900000 00007ffa`c99f7000   C:\Program Files\dotnet\shared\Microsoft.NETCore.App\8.0.1\System.Text.RegularExpressions.dll
ModLoad: 000001d7`e6a30000 000001d7`e6a38000   C:\Program Files\dotnet\shared\Microsoft.NETCore.App\8.0.1\System.Reflection.Emit.Lightweight.dll
ModLoad: 000001d7`e6a40000 000001d7`e6a48000   C:\Program Files\dotnet\shared\Microsoft.NETCore.App\8.0.1\System.Reflection.Emit.ILGeneration.dll
ModLoad: 000001d7`e6a50000 000001d7`e6a58000   C:\Program Files\dotnet\shared\Microsoft.NETCore.App\8.0.1\System.Reflection.Primitives.dll
ModLoad: 000001d7`e6a60000 000001d7`e6a68000   C:\Program Files\dotnet\shared\Microsoft.NETCore.App\8.0.1\System.Xml.XDocument.dll
ModLoad: 00007ffa`e6590000 00007ffa`e65f0000   C:\Program Files\dotnet\shared\Microsoft.NETCore.App\8.0.1\System.Private.Xml.Linq.dll
ModLoad: 00007ffa`85860000 00007ffa`85ffc000   C:\Program Files\dotnet\shared\Microsoft.NETCore.App\8.0.1\System.Private.Xml.dll
ModLoad: 00007ffa`e9f00000 00007ffa`e9f41000   C:\Program Files\dotnet\shared\Microsoft.NETCore.App\8.0.1\System.Collections.Concurrent.dll
ModLoad: 00007ffa`8c210000 00007ffa`8c4c8000   C:\Program Files\dotnet\shared\Microsoft.NETCore.App\8.0.1\System.Data.Common.dll
ModLoad: 00007ffa`dab10000 00007ffa`dabc3000   C:\Program Files\dotnet\shared\Microsoft.NETCore.App\8.0.1\System.ComponentModel.TypeConverter.dll
ModLoad: 00007ffb`12f70000 00007ffb`12f75000   C:\Program Files\dotnet\shared\Microsoft.NETCore.App\8.0.1\System.ComponentModel.dll
ModLoad: 000001d7`e4fd0000 000001d7`e4fda000   C:\Program Files\dotnet\shared\Microsoft.NETCore.App\8.0.1\System.Xml.ReaderWriter.dll
ModLoad: 00007ffa`8ce10000 00007ffa`8d18f000   C:\Program Files\dotnet\shared\Microsoft.NETCore.App\8.0.1\System.Linq.Expressions.dll
```

```
ModLoad: 00007ffa`e14f0000 00007ffa`e15be000    C:\Program Files\dotnet\shared\Microsoft.NETCore.App\8.0.1\System.IO.Compression.Native.dll
ModLoad: 00007ffb`16970000 00007ffb`16979000    C:\Program Files\dotnet\shared\Microsoft.NETCore.App\8.0.1\System.Diagnostics.FileVersionInfo.dll
ModLoad: 00007ffa`db860000 00007ffa`db96e000    C:\Program Files\dotnet\shared\Microsoft.NETCore.App\8.0.1\System.Reflection.Metadata.dll
ModLoad: 00007ffa`dd6b0000 00007ffa`dd77a000    C:\Program Files\dotnet\shared\Microsoft.NETCore.App\8.0.1\System.Collections.Immutable.dll
ModLoad: 000001d7`e6a70000 000001d7`e6a78000    C:\Program Files\dotnet\shared\Microsoft.NETCore.App\8.0.1\System.Text.Encoding.Extensions.dll
ModLoad: 00007ffa`a60b0000 00007ffa`a621c000    C:\Program Files\dotnet\shared\Microsoft.NETCore.App\8.0.1\System.Text.Json.dll
ModLoad: 00007ffa`fee80000 00007ffa`fee91000    C:\Program Files\dotnet\shared\Microsoft.NETCore.App\8.0.1\System.ObjectModel.dll
ModLoad: 00007ffa`abb70000 00007ffa`abc63000    C:\Program Files\dotnet\shared\Microsoft.NETCore.App\8.0.1\Microsoft.CSharp.dll
ModLoad: 00007ffb`1da90000 00007ffb`1daad000    C:\WINDOWS\SYSTEM32\amsi.dll
ModLoad: 00007ffb`331d0000 00007ffb`331fc000    C:\WINDOWS\SYSTEM32\USERENV.dll
ModLoad: 00007ffb`1d690000 00007ffb`1d70c000    C:\ProgramData\Microsoft\Windows Defender\Platform\4.18.23110.3-0\MpOav.dll
ModLoad: 00007ffb`0f2d0000 00007ffb`0f409000    C:\ProgramData\Microsoft\Windows Defender\Platform\4.18.23110.3-0\MPCLIENT.DLL
ModLoad: 00007ffb`331a0000 00007ffb`331c6000    C:\WINDOWS\SYSTEM32\gpapi.dll
ModLoad: 000001d7`e6a80000 000001d7`e6a9c000    C:\Program Files\dotnet\shared\Microsoft.NETCore.App\8.0.1\netstandard.dll
(1170c.a628): Break instruction exception - code 80000003 (first chance)
ntdll!DbgBreakPoint:
00007ffb`36a33060 int     3
```

12.   We resume and execute the loaded query file in the *LINQPad 8 (x64)* window. We then see a NULL pointer access violation in *LINQPad8.exe*:

```
0:010> g
ModLoad: 00007ffa`daf70000 00007ffa`dafb9000    C:\Program Files\dotnet\shared\Microsoft.NETCore.App\8.0.1\System.Runtime.Serialization.Formatters.dll
(1170c.ff98): CLR exception - code e0434352 (first chance)
(1170c.ff98): CLR exception - code e0434352 (first chance)
ModLoad: 00007ffb`11d10000 00007ffb`11d19000    C:\Program Files\dotnet\shared\Microsoft.NETCore.App\8.0.1\System.Diagnostics.StackTrace.dll
ModLoad: 00007ffb`17120000 00007ffb`1712e000    C:\Program Files\dotnet\shared\Microsoft.NETCore.App\8.0.1\System.Diagnostics.TextWriterTraceListener.dll
ModLoad: 000001d7`e5010000 000001d7`e5016000    C:\Users\dmitr\AppData\Local\Temp\LINQPad8\_khrzlzag\mmszxo\LINQPadQuery.dll
ModLoad: 000001d7`e6850000 000001d7`e6858000    C:\Users\dmitr\AppData\Local\Temp\LINQPad8\_khrzlzag\shadow-1\DllMD11.dll
ModLoad: 000001d7`e6aa0000 000001d7`e6ab2000    C:\Program Files\dotnet\shared\Microsoft.NETCore.App\8.0.1\mscorlib.dll
(1170c.ac1c): Access violation - code c0000005 (first chance)
First chance exceptions are reported before any exception handling.
This exception may be expected and handled.
*** WARNING: Unable to verify checksum for C:\Users\dmitr\AppData\Local\Temp\LINQPad8\_khrzlzag\shadow-1\DllMD11.dll
*** WARNING: Unable to verify checksum for C:\Users\dmitr\AppData\Local\Temp\LINQPad8\_khrzlzag\mmszxo\LINQPadQuery.dll
DllMD11!DllMD11.NewFeature.ExtraWork+0x30:
00007ffa`6aa509a0 mov     dword ptr [rax],1        ds:00000000`00000000=????????
```

```
0:016> kL
 # Child-SP          RetAddr           Call Site
00 00000030`1343fad0 00007ffa`6aa507a3 DllMD11!DllMD11.NewFeature.ExtraWork+0x30
01 00000030`1343fb10 00007ffa`8d4b657d LINQPadQuery!UserQuery.ClassMain.thread_proc_1+0x83
02 00000030`1343fb50 00007ffa`c9b5a333 System_Private_CoreLib!System.Threading.ExecutionContext.RunInternal+0x7d
03 00000030`1343fbc0 00007ffa`c9a14cb4 coreclr!CallDescrWorkerInternal+0x83
04 00000030`1343fc00 00007ffa`c9b474f3 coreclr!DispatchCallSimple+0x60
05 00000030`1343fc90 00007ffa`c9ae89dd coreclr!ThreadNative::KickOffThread_Worker+0x63
06 (Inline Function) --------`-------- coreclr!ManagedThreadBase_DispatchInner+0xd
07 00000030`1343fcf0 00007ffa`c9ae88f3 coreclr!ManagedThreadBase_DispatchMiddle+0x85
08 00000030`1343fdd0 00007ffa`c9ae8a8e coreclr!ManagedThreadBase_DispatchOuter+0xab
09 (Inline Function) --------`-------- coreclr!ManagedThreadBase_FullTransition+0x28
0a (Inline Function) --------`-------- coreclr!ManagedThreadBase::KickOff+0x28
0b 00000030`1343fe70 00007ffb`3477257d coreclr!ThreadNative::KickOffThread+0x7e
0c 00000030`1343fed0 00007ffb`369eaa58 KERNEL32!BaseThreadInitThunk+0x1d
0d 00000030`1343ff00 00000000`00000000 ntdll!RtlUserThreadStart+0x28
```

Note: Since the thread runs through *coreclr* and *System_Private_CoreLib* DLLs, most likely, it is executing JIT-compiled .NET code.

13.   To find out more about .NET calls, we use the .NET SOS extension. It is automatically loaded when we start using SOS commands; for example, we see that there is still not yet any managed exception:

```
0:016> !pe
There is no current managed exception on this thread
```

14.   We can also inspect JIT translated code that caused the exception (note that we have source file location because we also have symbol files for DLL):

```
0:016> !IP2MD 00007ffa`6aa509a0
MethodDesc:     00007ffa6aa3c590
Method Name:        DllMD11.NewFeature.ExtraWork()
Class:          00007ffa6aad9a20
MethodTable:        00007ffa6aa3c5b8
```

```
mdToken:                0000000006000001
Module:                 00007ffa6aa3b948
IsJitted:               yes
Current CodeAddr:       00007ffa6aa50970
Version History:
  ILCodeVersion:        0000000000000000
  ReJIT ID:             0
  IL Addr:              000001d7e6852050
      CodeAddr:             00007ffa6aa50970  (MinOptJitted)
      NativeCodeVersion:  0000000000000000
```

Note: We can even disassemble it using the **!U** SOS extension command:

```
0:016> !U 00007ffa`6aa509a0
Normal JIT generated code
DllMD11.NewFeature.ExtraWork()
ilAddr is 000001D7E6852050 pImport is 000001A8225EA3A0
Begin 00007FFA6AA50970, size 3e
00007ffa`6aa50970 push    rbp
00007ffa`6aa50971 sub     rsp,30h
00007ffa`6aa50975 lea     rbp,[rsp+30h]
00007ffa`6aa5097a xor     eax,eax
00007ffa`6aa5097c mov     qword ptr [rbp-8],rax
00007ffa`6aa50980 mov     qword ptr [rbp+10h],rcx
00007ffa`6aa50984 cmp     dword ptr [00007ffa`6aa3bbd0],0
00007ffa`6aa5098b je      DllMD11!DllMD11.NewFeature.ExtraWork+0x22 (00007ffa`6aa50992)
00007ffa`6aa5098d call    coreclr!JIT_DbgIsJustMyCode (00007ffa`c9c7eb10)
00007ffa`6aa50992 nop
00007ffa`6aa50993 nop
00007ffa`6aa50994 xor     eax,eax
00007ffa`6aa50996 mov     eax,eax
00007ffa`6aa50998 mov     qword ptr [rbp-8],rax
00007ffa`6aa5099c mov     rax,qword ptr [rbp-8]
>>> 00007ffa`6aa509a0 mov     dword ptr [rax],1
00007ffa`6aa509a6 nop
00007ffa`6aa509a7 nop
00007ffa`6aa509a8 add     rsp,30h
00007ffa`6aa509ac pop     rbp
00007ffa`6aa509ad ret
```

Note: If we specify the symbol path, we can see source code lines:

```
0:016> .sympath+ C:\AWD4\AppMD11\DllMD11\bin\Release
Symbol search path is: srv*;C:\AWD4\AppMD11\DllMD11\bin\Release
Expanded Symbol search path is:
cache*;SRV*https://msdl.microsoft.com/download/symbols;c:\awd4\appmd11\dllmd11\bin\release

************* Path validation summary **************
Response                        Time (ms)      Location
Deferred                                       srv*
OK                                             C:\AWD4\AppMD11\DllMD11\bin\Release
*** WARNING: Unable to verify checksum for
C:\Users\dmitr\AppData\Local\Temp\LINQPad8\_khrzlzag\shadow-1\DllMD11.dll
*** WARNING: Unable to verify checksum for
C:\Users\dmitr\AppData\Local\Temp\LINQPad8\_khrzlzag\mmszxo\LINQPadQuery.dll
```

```
0:016> !IP2MD 00007ffa`6aa509a0
MethodDesc:     00007ffa6aa3c590
Method Name:        DllMD11.NewFeature.ExtraWork()
Class:              00007ffa6aad9a20
MethodTable:        00007ffa6aa3c5b8
mdToken:            0000000006000001
Module:             00007ffa6aa3b948
IsJitted:           yes
Current CodeAddr:   00007ffa6aa50970
Version History:
  ILCodeVersion:      0000000000000000
  ReJIT ID:           0
  IL Addr:            000001d7e6852050
     CodeAddr:            00007ffa6aa50970  (MinOptJitted)
     NativeCodeVersion:  0000000000000000
Source file:  C:\AWD3\AppMD11\DllMD11\Class1.cs @ 16


0:016> !U 00007ffa`6aa509a0
Normal JIT generated code
DllMD11.NewFeature.ExtraWork()
ilAddr is 000001D7E6852050 pImport is 000001A8213FEB40
Begin 00007FFA6AA50970, size 3e

C:\AWD3\AppMD11\DllMD11\Class1.cs @ 12:
00007ffa`6aa50970 push    rbp
00007ffa`6aa50971 sub     rsp,30h
00007ffa`6aa50975 lea     rbp,[rsp+30h]
00007ffa`6aa5097a xor     eax,eax
00007ffa`6aa5097c mov     qword ptr [rbp-8],rax
00007ffa`6aa50980 mov     qword ptr [rbp+10h],rcx
00007ffa`6aa50984 cmp     dword ptr [00007ffa`6aa3bbd0],0
00007ffa`6aa5098b je      DllMD11!DllMD11.NewFeature.ExtraWork+0x22 (00007ffa`6aa50992)
00007ffa`6aa5098d call    coreclr!JIT_DbgIsJustMyCode (00007ffa`c9c7eb10)
00007ffa`6aa50992 nop

C:\AWD3\AppMD11\DllMD11\Class1.cs @ 14:
00007ffa`6aa50993 nop

C:\AWD3\AppMD11\DllMD11\Class1.cs @ 15:
00007ffa`6aa50994 xor     eax,eax
00007ffa`6aa50996 mov     eax,eax
00007ffa`6aa50998 mov     qword ptr [rbp-8],rax

C:\AWD3\AppMD11\DllMD11\Class1.cs @ 16:
00007ffa`6aa5099c mov     rax,qword ptr [rbp-8]
>>> 00007ffa`6aa509a0 mov     dword ptr [rax],1

C:\AWD3\AppMD11\DllMD11\Class1.cs @ 17:
00007ffa`6aa509a6 nop

C:\AWD3\AppMD11\DllMD11\Class1.cs @ 18:
00007ffa`6aa509a7 nop
00007ffa`6aa509a8 add     rsp,30h
00007ffa`6aa509ac pop     rbp
00007ffa`6aa509ad ret
```

Note: We look at yet another return address from the stack trace (now with source code references since we loaded symbols):

```
0:016> !IP2MD 00007ffa`6aa507a3
MethodDesc:        00007ffa6aa33d50
Method Name:       UserQuery+ClassMain.thread_proc_1()
Class:             00007ffa6aa14248
MethodTable:       00007ffa6aa33db8
mdToken:           0000000006000007
Module:            00007ffa6a9e1100
IsJitted:          yes
Current CodeAddr:  00007ffa6aa50720
Version History:
  ILCodeVersion:   0000000000000000
  ReJIT ID:        0
  IL Addr:         000001d7e5012100
     CodeAddr:        00007ffa6aa50720  (MinOptJitted)
     NativeCodeVersion:  0000000000000000
Source file:  C:\Users\dmitr\AppData\Local\Temp\LINQPad8\_khrzlzag\mmszxo\LINQPadQuery @ 25
```

```
0:016> !U 00007ffa`6aa507a3
Normal JIT generated code
UserQuery+ClassMain.thread_proc_1()
ilAddr is 000001D7E5012100 pImport is 000001A8213FEB40
Begin 00007FFA6AA50720, size 127

C:\Users\dmitr\AppData\Local\Temp\LINQPad8\_khrzlzag\mmszxo\LINQPadQuery @ 20:
00007ffa`6aa50720 push    rbp
00007ffa`6aa50721 sub     rsp,30h
00007ffa`6aa50725 lea     rbp,[rsp+30h]
00007ffa`6aa5072a xor     eax,eax
00007ffa`6aa5072c mov     qword ptr [rbp-8],rax
00007ffa`6aa50730 mov     qword ptr [rbp-10h],rax
00007ffa`6aa50734 cmp     dword ptr [00007ffa`6a9e1388],0
00007ffa`6aa5073b je      LINQPadQuery!UserQuery.ClassMain.thread_proc_1+0x22
(00007ffa`6aa50742)
00007ffa`6aa5073d call    coreclr!JIT_DbgIsJustMyCode (00007ffa`c9c7eb10)
00007ffa`6aa50742 nop


C:\Users\dmitr\AppData\Local\Temp\LINQPad8\_khrzlzag\mmszxo\LINQPadQuery @ 21:
00007ffa`6aa50743 mov     rcx,7FFA6A9E14E8h
00007ffa`6aa5074d mov     edx,3
00007ffa`6aa50752 call    coreclr!JIT_GetSharedNonGCStaticBase_SingleAppDomain
(00007ffa`c9b5afe0)
00007ffa`6aa50757 mov     rcx,1D7E6C14010h
00007ffa`6aa50761 mov     rcx,qword ptr [rcx]
00007ffa`6aa50764 call    coreclr!JIT_MonEnter_Portable (00007ffa`c9b1dca0)
00007ffa`6aa50769 nop


C:\Users\dmitr\AppData\Local\Temp\LINQPad8\_khrzlzag\mmszxo\LINQPadQuery @ 22:
00007ffa`6aa5076a nop


C:\Users\dmitr\AppData\Local\Temp\LINQPad8\_khrzlzag\mmszxo\LINQPadQuery @ 23:
00007ffa`6aa5076b call    qword ptr [00007ffa`6a9def28]
00007ffa`6aa50771 nop


C:\Users\dmitr\AppData\Local\Temp\LINQPad8\_khrzlzag\mmszxo\LINQPadQuery @ 24:
00007ffa`6aa50772 mov     rcx,7FFA6AA3C5B8h
00007ffa`6aa5077c call    coreclr!JIT_TrialAllocSFastMP_InlineGetThread (00007ffa`c9b5ae10)
00007ffa`6aa50781 mov     qword ptr [rbp-10h],rax
00007ffa`6aa50785 mov     rcx,qword ptr [rbp-10h]
```

```
00007ffa`6aa50789 call     qword ptr [00007ffa`6aa457a0]
00007ffa`6aa5078f mov      rcx,qword ptr [rbp-10h]
00007ffa`6aa50793 mov      qword ptr [rbp-8],rcx

C:\Users\dmitr\AppData\Local\Temp\LINQPad8\_khrzlzag\mmszxo\LINQPadQuery @ 25:
00007ffa`6aa50797 mov      rcx,qword ptr [rbp-8]
00007ffa`6aa5079b cmp      dword ptr [rcx],ecx
00007ffa`6aa5079d call     qword ptr [00007ffa`6aa45788]
>>> 00007ffa`6aa507a3 nop

C:\Users\dmitr\AppData\Local\Temp\LINQPad8\_khrzlzag\mmszxo\LINQPadQuery @ 26:
00007ffa`6aa507a4 nop

C:\Users\dmitr\AppData\Local\Temp\LINQPad8\_khrzlzag\mmszxo\LINQPadQuery @ 27:
00007ffa`6aa507a5 mov      rcx,7FFA6A9E14E8h
00007ffa`6aa507af mov      edx,3
00007ffa`6aa507b4 call     coreclr!JIT_GetSharedNonGCStaticBase_SingleAppDomain
(00007ffa`c9b5afe0)
00007ffa`6aa507b9 mov      rcx,1D7E6C14010h
00007ffa`6aa507c3 mov      rcx,qword ptr [rcx]
00007ffa`6aa507c6 call     coreclr!JIT_MonExit_Portable (00007ffa`c9ae9790)
00007ffa`6aa507cb nop

C:\Users\dmitr\AppData\Local\Temp\LINQPad8\_khrzlzag\mmszxo\LINQPadQuery @ 29:
00007ffa`6aa507cc mov      ecx,7D0h
00007ffa`6aa507d1 call     qword ptr [00007ffa`69fed698]
00007ffa`6aa507d7 nop

C:\Users\dmitr\AppData\Local\Temp\LINQPad8\_khrzlzag\mmszxo\LINQPadQuery @ 31:
00007ffa`6aa507d8 mov      rcx,7FFA6A9E14E8h
00007ffa`6aa507e2 mov      edx,3
00007ffa`6aa507e7 call     coreclr!JIT_GetSharedNonGCStaticBase_SingleAppDomain
(00007ffa`c9b5afe0)
00007ffa`6aa507ec mov      rcx,1D7E6C14018h
00007ffa`6aa507f6 mov      rcx,qword ptr [rcx]
00007ffa`6aa507f9 call     coreclr!JIT_MonEnter_Portable (00007ffa`c9b1dca0)
00007ffa`6aa507fe nop

C:\Users\dmitr\AppData\Local\Temp\LINQPad8\_khrzlzag\mmszxo\LINQPadQuery @ 32:
00007ffa`6aa507ff nop

C:\Users\dmitr\AppData\Local\Temp\LINQPad8\_khrzlzag\mmszxo\LINQPadQuery @ 33:
00007ffa`6aa50800 call     qword ptr [00007ffa`6a9def28]
00007ffa`6aa50806 nop

C:\Users\dmitr\AppData\Local\Temp\LINQPad8\_khrzlzag\mmszxo\LINQPadQuery @ 34:
00007ffa`6aa50807 nop

C:\Users\dmitr\AppData\Local\Temp\LINQPad8\_khrzlzag\mmszxo\LINQPadQuery @ 35:
00007ffa`6aa50808 mov      rcx,7FFA6A9E14E8h
00007ffa`6aa50812 mov      edx,3
00007ffa`6aa50817 call     coreclr!JIT_GetSharedNonGCStaticBase_SingleAppDomain
(00007ffa`c9b5afe0)
00007ffa`6aa5081c mov      rcx,1D7E6C14018h
00007ffa`6aa50826 mov      rcx,qword ptr [rcx]
00007ffa`6aa50829 call     coreclr!JIT_MonExit_Portable (00007ffa`c9ae9790)
00007ffa`6aa5082e nop

C:\Users\dmitr\AppData\Local\Temp\LINQPad8\_khrzlzag\mmszxo\LINQPadQuery @ 37:
```

```
00007ffa`6aa5082f mov     rcx,1D780228E40h
00007ffa`6aa50839 call    qword ptr [00007ffa`6a0c5e30]
00007ffa`6aa5083f nop
```

C:\Users\dmitr\AppData\Local\Temp\LINQPad8_khrzlzag\mmszxo\LINQPadQuery @ 38:
```
00007ffa`6aa50840 nop
00007ffa`6aa50841 add     rsp,30h
00007ffa`6aa50845 pop     rbp
00007ffa`6aa50846 ret
```

`0:016> dps 00007ffa`6aa45788 L1`
```
00007ffa`6aa45788  00007ffa`6aa50970 DllMD11!DllMD11.NewFeature.ExtraWork
[C:\AWD3\AppMD11\DllMD11\Class1.cs @ 12]
```

15.   We can also check the CLR stack:

`0:016> !CLRStack`
```
OS Thread Id: 0xac1c (16)
        Child SP               IP Call Site
000000301343FAD0 00007ffa6aa509a0 DllMD11.NewFeature.ExtraWork() [C:\AWD3\AppMD11\DllMD11\Class1.cs @ 16]
000000301343FB10 00007ffa6aa507a3 UserQuery+ClassMain.thread_proc_1() [C:\Users\dmitr\AppData\Local\Temp\LINQPad8\_khrzlzag\mmszxo\LINQPadQuery @ 25]
000000301343FB50 00007ffa8d4b657d System.Threading.ExecutionContext.RunInternal(System.Threading.ExecutionContext, System.Threading.ContextCallback,
System.Object) [/_/src/libraries/System.Private.CoreLib/src/System/Threading/ExecutionContext.cs @ 179]
000000301343FE10 00007ffac9b5a333 [DebuggerU2MCatchHandlerFrame: 000000301343fe10]
```

16.   When we resume, we come to another exception – our original exception handled and rethrown by *coreclr*:

`0:016> g`
(1170c.ac1c): Access violation - code c0000005 (first chance)
First chance exceptions are reported before any exception handling.
This exception may be expected and handled.
KERNELBASE!RaiseException+0x6c:
```
00007ffb`3436567c nop     dword ptr [rax+rax]
```

`0:016> kL`
```
 # Child-SP          RetAddr           Call Site
00 00000030`1343e9a0 00007ffa`c9c1ecd2 KERNELBASE!RaiseException+0x6c
01 00000030`1343ea80 00007ffa`c9bf02d4 coreclr!HandleManagedFault+0xd2
02 00000030`1343f000 00007ffb`36a07a8a coreclr!CLRVectoredExceptionHandlerShim+0xc4b84
03 00000030`1343f050 00007ffb`369ae242 ntdll!RtlpCallVectoredHandlers+0x112
04 00000030`1343f0f0 00007ffb`36a3340e ntdll!RtlDispatchException+0x62
05 00000030`1343f340 00007ffa`6aa509a0 ntdll!KiUserExceptionDispatch+0x2e
06 00000030`1343fad0 00007ffa`6aa507a3 DllMD11!DllMD11.NewFeature.ExtraWork+0x30
07 00000030`1343fb10 00007ffa`8d4b657d LINQPadQuery!UserQuery.ClassMain.thread_proc_1+0x83
08 00000030`1343fb50 00007ffa`c9b5a333 System_Private_CoreLib!System.Threading.ExecutionContext.RunInternal+0x7d
09 00000030`1343fbc0 00007ffa`c9a14cb4 coreclr!CallDescrWorkerInternal+0x83
0a 00000030`1343fc00 00007ffa`c9b474f3 coreclr!DispatchCallSimple+0x60
0b 00000030`1343fc90 00007ffa`c9ae89dd coreclr!ThreadNative::KickOffThread_Worker+0x63
0c (Inline Function) --------`-------- coreclr!ManagedThreadBase_DispatchInner+0xd
0d 00000030`1343fcf0 00007ffa`c9ae88f3 coreclr!ManagedThreadBase_DispatchMiddle+0x85
0e 00000030`1343fdd0 00007ffa`c9ae8a8e coreclr!ManagedThreadBase_DispatchOuter+0xab
0f (Inline Function) --------`-------- coreclr!ManagedThreadBase_FullTransition+0x28
10 (Inline Function) --------`-------- coreclr!ManagedThreadBase::KickOff+0x28
11 00000030`1343fe70 00007ffb`3477257d coreclr!ThreadNative::KickOffThread+0x7e
12 00000030`1343fed0 00007ffb`369eaa58 KERNEL32!BaseThreadInitThunk+0x1d
13 00000030`1343ff00 00000000`00000000 ntdll!RtlUserThreadStart+0x28
```

17.   However, when we resume, we don't see any second chance exceptions, which means the process handled exceptions. We now quit both instances of WinDbg. *LINQPad8* processes should also disappear from Task Manager.

18.   We now launch *LINQPad 8 (x64)* again, open *\AWD4\AppMD11\AppMD11V3.linq*, and close other tabs in LINQPad, if any.

Note: The problem when calling the *ExtraWork* function was "fixed" by enclosing the call inside the try-catch block:

```
static void thread_proc_1()
{
        try
        {
                Monitor.Enter(cs1);
                {
                        DoWork();
                        DllMD11.NewFeature cls = new DllMD11.NewFeature();
                        cls.ExtraWork();
                }
                Monitor.Exit(cs1);
        }
        catch (Exception e)
        {
                Console.WriteLine("We caught an exception.");
        }

        Thread.Sleep(2000);

        Monitor.Enter(cs2);
        {
                DoWork();
        }
        Monitor.Exit(cs2);

        Console.WriteLine("Thread 1 has finished.");
}
```

19.   Before we execute the query, we note the PID 41632, which uses less memory:

Name	PID	Status	CPU	Memory (ac...	Handles	GDI ...	Architecture	Description
LINQPad8.exe	40948	Running	00	151,072 K	1,223	285	x64	LINQPad 8 (X64)
LINQPad8.exe	41632	Running	00	12,732 K	332	0	x64	LINQPad 8 (X64)

Task Manager — LINQ — Details — Run new task — End task

20. When we execute the query, we get a message: "We caught an exception." However, execution hangs:

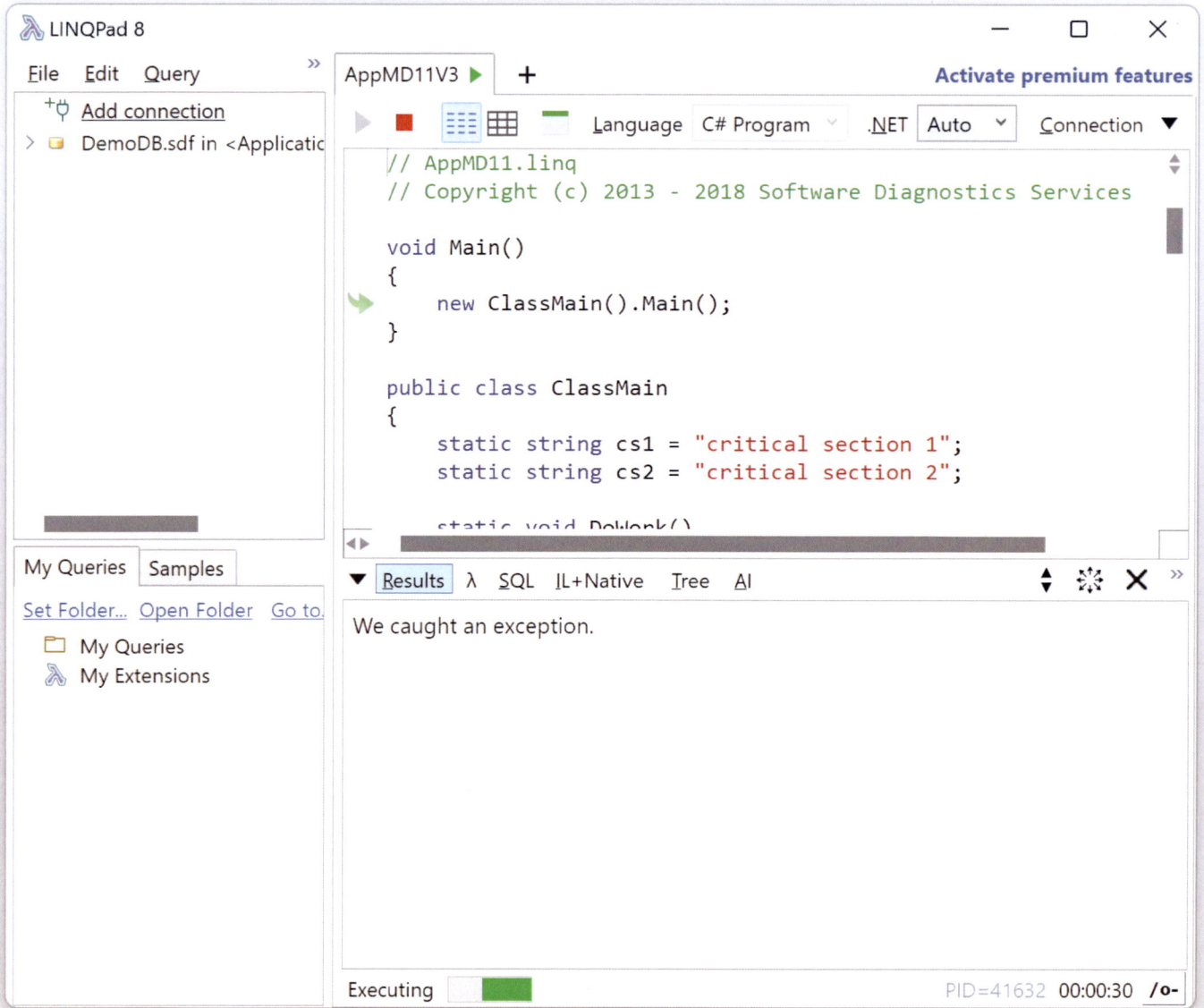

21. We now launch WinDbg, attach it to PID 41632, and open a log file in append mode (there may be another *LINQPad8.exe* process created after executing the query, but we ignore it):

```
Microsoft (R) Windows Debugger Version 10.0.25921.1001 AMD64
Copyright (c) Microsoft Corporation. All rights reserved.

*** wait with pending attach

************** Path validation summary **************
Response                     Time (ms)     Location
Deferred                                   srv*
Symbol search path is: srv*
Executable search path is:
ModLoad: 00007ff7`ac4c0000 00007ff7`ac567000   C:\Program Files\LINQPad8\LINQPad8.exe
ModLoad: 00007ffb`36990000 00007ffb`36ba7000   C:\WINDOWS\SYSTEM32\ntdll.dll
ModLoad: 00007ffb`34760000 00007ffb`34824000   C:\WINDOWS\System32\KERNEL32.DLL
ModLoad: 00007ffb`34300000 00007ffb`346a6000   C:\WINDOWS\System32\KERNELBASE.dll
ModLoad: 00007ffb`33ee0000 00007ffb`33f4b000   C:\WINDOWS\System32\WINTRUST.dll
ModLoad: 00007ffb`34ce0000 00007ffb`34d87000   C:\WINDOWS\System32\msvcrt.dll
ModLoad: 00007ffb`1fde0000 00007ffb`1fdea000   C:\WINDOWS\SYSTEM32\VERSION.dll
ModLoad: 00007ffb`35700000 00007ffb`35817000   C:\WINDOWS\System32\RPCRT4.dll
ModLoad: 00007ffb`366d0000 00007ffb`3687e000   C:\WINDOWS\System32\USER32.dll
ModLoad: 00007ffb`33cd0000 00007ffb`33cf6000   C:\WINDOWS\System32\win32u.dll
ModLoad: 00007ffb`35600000 00007ffb`35629000   C:\WINDOWS\System32\GDI32.dll
ModLoad: 00007ffb`33d00000 00007ffb`33e18000   C:\WINDOWS\System32\gdi32full.dll
ModLoad: 00007ffb`34260000 00007ffb`342fa000   C:\WINDOWS\System32\msvcp_win.dll
```

```
ModLoad: 00007ffb`33fd0000 00007ffb`340e1000   C:\WINDOWS\System32\ucrtbase.dll
ModLoad: 00007ffb`353d0000 00007ffb`35483000   C:\WINDOWS\System32\ADVAPI32.dll
ModLoad: 00007ffb`34c30000 00007ffb`34cd8000   C:\WINDOWS\System32\sechost.dll
ModLoad: 00007ffb`346b0000 00007ffb`346d8000   C:\WINDOWS\System32\bcrypt.dll
ModLoad: 00007ffb`35cb0000 00007ffb`3650a000   C:\WINDOWS\System32\SHELL32.dll
ModLoad: 00007ffb`34930000 00007ffb`34ad0000   C:\WINDOWS\System32\ole32.dll
ModLoad: 00007ffb`34d90000 00007ffb`35119000   C:\WINDOWS\System32\combase.dll
ModLoad: 00007ffb`340f0000 00007ffb`34256000   C:\WINDOWS\System32\CRYPT32.dll
ModLoad: 00007ffb`33970000 00007ffb`33982000   C:\WINDOWS\SYSTEM32\MSASN1.dll
ModLoad: 00007ffb`35660000 00007ffb`35691000   C:\WINDOWS\System32\IMM32.DLL
ModLoad: 00007ffb`32cc0000 00007ffb`32cd8000   C:\WINDOWS\SYSTEM32\kernel.appcore.dll
ModLoad: 00007ffb`33f50000 00007ffb`33fca000   C:\WINDOWS\System32\bcryptPrimitives.dll
ModLoad: 00007ffb`30ba0000 00007ffb`30c4b000   C:\WINDOWS\system32\uxtheme.dll
ModLoad: 00007ffb`34830000 00007ffb`34923000   C:\WINDOWS\System32\shcore.dll
ModLoad: 00007ffb`169f0000 00007ffb`16a49000   C:\Program Files\dotnet\host\fxr\8.0.1\hostfxr.dll
ModLoad: 00007ffb`11d30000 00007ffb`11d94000   C:\Program Files\dotnet\shared\Microsoft.NETCore.App\8.0.1\hostpolicy.dll
ModLoad: 00007ffa`e5820000 00007ffa`e5d09000   C:\Program Files\dotnet\shared\Microsoft.NETCore.App\8.0.1\coreclr.dll
ModLoad: 00007ffb`35120000 00007ffb`351f7000   C:\WINDOWS\System32\OLEAUT32.dll
ModLoad: 00007ffa`9b8a0000 00007ffa`9c52d000   C:\Program Files\dotnet\shared\Microsoft.NETCore.App\8.0.1\System.Private.CoreLib.dll
ModLoad: 00007ffa`ec340000 00007ffa`ec4f9000   C:\Program Files\dotnet\shared\Microsoft.NETCore.App\8.0.1\clrjit.dll
ModLoad: 00000226`fff90000 00000226`fffa4000   C:\Users\dmitr\AppData\Local\LINQPad\8.1.6\ProcessServer\8.0.1\LINQPad.Query.dll
ModLoad: 00000226`fffb0000 00000226`fffbe000   C:\Program Files\dotnet\shared\Microsoft.NETCore.App\8.0.1\System.Runtime.dll
ModLoad: 00007ffa`9abb0000 00007ffa`9b89c000   C:\Program Files\dotnet\shared\Microsoft.WindowsDesktop.App\8.0.1\System.Windows.Forms.dll
ModLoad: 00000226`fffc0000 00000226`fffc8000   C:\Program Files\dotnet\shared\Microsoft.NETCore.App\8.0.1\System.Runtime.Loader.dll
ModLoad: 00007ffb`14330000 00007ffb`14358000   C:\Program Files\dotnet\shared\Microsoft.NETCore.App\8.0.1\System.Console.dll
ModLoad: 00000226`fffd0000 00000226`fffd8000   C:\Program Files\dotnet\shared\Microsoft.NETCore.App\8.0.1\System.Runtime.Extensions.dll
ModLoad: 00007ffa`e9b60000 00007ffa`e9e3d000   C:\Program Files\dotnet\shared\Microsoft.WindowsDesktop.App\8.0.1\System.Windows.Forms.Primitives.dll
ModLoad: 00007ffb`170f0000 00007ffb`17105000   C:\Program Files\dotnet\shared\Microsoft.NETCore.App\8.0.1\System.Runtime.InteropServices.dll
ModLoad: 00007ffb`17060000 00007ffb`17072000   C:\Program Files\dotnet\shared\Microsoft.NETCore.App\8.0.1\System.Threading.dll
ModLoad: 00007ffb`15880000 00007ffb`158a1000   C:\Program Files\dotnet\shared\Microsoft.NETCore.App\8.0.1\System.Diagnostics.TraceSource.dll
ModLoad: 00007ffb`169b0000 00007ffb`169ed000   C:\Program Files\dotnet\shared\Microsoft.NETCore.App\8.0.1\System.Collections.dll
ModLoad: 00007ffb`16960000 00007ffb`16971000   C:\Program Files\dotnet\shared\Microsoft.NETCore.App\8.0.1\System.ComponentModel.Primitives.dll
ModLoad: 00007ffb`16860000 00007ffb`1687e000   C:\Program Files\dotnet\shared\Microsoft.NETCore.App\8.0.1\System.Drawing.Primitives.dll
ModLoad: 00000267`94b20000 00000267`94b28000   C:\Program Files\dotnet\shared\Microsoft.NETCore.App\8.0.1\System.IO.FileSystem.dll
ModLoad: 00007ffb`31bd0000 00007ffb`324c6000   C:\WINDOWS\SYSTEM32\windows.storage.dll
ModLoad: 00007ffb`31a90000 00007ffb`31bce000   C:\WINDOWS\SYSTEM32\wintypes.dll
ModLoad: 00007ffb`356a0000 00007ffb`356fe000   C:\WINDOWS\System32\shlwapi.dll
ModLoad: 00007ffa`e9f10000 00007ffa`ea083000   C:\Program Files\dotnet\shared\Microsoft.WindowsDesktop.App\8.0.1\System.Drawing.Common.dll
ModLoad: 00000267`94b30000 00000267`96872000   C:\Program Files\LINQPad8\LINQPad.Runtime.dll
ModLoad: 00007ffb`092d0000 00007ffb`09352000   C:\Program Files\dotnet\shared\Microsoft.NETCore.App\8.0.1\System.Linq.dll
ModLoad: 00007ffb`16880000 00007ffb`168be000   C:\Program Files\dotnet\shared\Microsoft.NETCore.App\8.0.1\System.IO.Compression.dll
ModLoad: 00007ffb`11c90000 00007ffb`11ce0000   C:\Program Files\dotnet\shared\Microsoft.NETCore.App\8.0.1\System.Diagnostics.Process.dll
ModLoad: 00007ffb`09230000 00007ffb`092cf000   C:\Program Files\dotnet\shared\Microsoft.NETCore.App\8.0.1\System.Transactions.Local.dll
ModLoad: 00007ffb`0f020000 00007ffb`0f290000   C:\WINDOWS\SYSTEM32\icu.dll
ModLoad: 00000267`96880000 00000267`96888000   C:\Program Files\dotnet\shared\Microsoft.NETCore.App\8.0.1\System.Threading.Tasks.dll
ModLoad: 00007ffb`14570000 00007ffb`14582000   C:\Program Files\dotnet\shared\Microsoft.NETCore.App\8.0.1\System.IO.MemoryMappedFiles.dll
ModLoad: 00000267`96890000 00000267`96898000   C:\Program Files\dotnet\shared\Microsoft.NETCore.App\8.0.1\System.Threading.ThreadPool.dll
ModLoad: 00000267`968a0000 00000267`968a8000   C:\Program Files\dotnet\shared\Microsoft.NETCore.App\8.0.1\System.Diagnostics.Debug.dll
ModLoad: 00000267`968b0000 00000267`968b8000   C:\Program Files\dotnet\shared\Microsoft.NETCore.App\8.0.1\System.Threading.Thread.dll
ModLoad: 00007ffb`33c00000 00007ffb`33c26000   C:\WINDOWS\SYSTEM32\profapi.dll
ModLoad: 00000267`968c0000 00000267`968c8000   C:\Program
Files\dotnet\shared\Microsoft.NETCore.App\8.0.1\System.Runtime.InteropServices.RuntimeInformation.dll
ModLoad: 00007ffb`15350000 00007ffb`15374000   C:\Program Files\dotnet\shared\Microsoft.NETCore.App\8.0.1\System.Memory.dll
ModLoad: 00000267`968d0000 00000267`968d8000   C:\Program Files\dotnet\shared\Microsoft.NETCore.App\8.0.1\Microsoft.Win32.Primitives.dll
ModLoad: 00007ffb`155e0000 00007ffb`1561d000   C:\Program Files\dotnet\shared\Microsoft.NETCore.App\8.0.1\System.Private.Uri.dll
ModLoad: 00007ffa`e75d0000 00007ffa`e76c7000   C:\Program Files\dotnet\shared\Microsoft.NETCore.App\8.0.1\System.Text.RegularExpressions.dll
ModLoad: 00000267`968e0000 00000267`968e8000   C:\Program Files\dotnet\shared\Microsoft.NETCore.App\8.0.1\System.Reflection.Emit.Lightweight.dll
ModLoad: 00000267`968f0000 00000267`968f8000   C:\Program Files\dotnet\shared\Microsoft.NETCore.App\8.0.1\System.Reflection.Emit.ILGeneration.dll
ModLoad: 00000267`96900000 00000267`96908000   C:\Program Files\dotnet\shared\Microsoft.NETCore.App\8.0.1\System.Reflection.Primitives.dll
ModLoad: 00000267`96910000 00000267`96918000   C:\Program Files\dotnet\shared\Microsoft.NETCore.App\8.0.1\System.Xml.XDocument.dll
ModLoad: 00007ffb`0ece0000 00007ffb`0ed40000   C:\Program Files\dotnet\shared\Microsoft.NETCore.App\8.0.1\System.Private.Xml.Linq.dll
ModLoad: 00007ffa`e1c90000 00007ffa`e242c000   C:\Program Files\dotnet\shared\Microsoft.NETCore.App\8.0.1\System.Private.Xml.dll
ModLoad: 00007ffb`11020000 00007ffb`11061000   C:\Program Files\dotnet\shared\Microsoft.NETCore.App\8.0.1\System.Collections.Concurrent.dll
ModLoad: 00007ffa`dbb70000 00007ffa`dbe28000   C:\Program Files\dotnet\shared\Microsoft.NETCore.App\8.0.1\System.Data.Common.dll
ModLoad: 00007ffa`f5a60000 00007ffa`f5b13000   C:\Program Files\dotnet\shared\Microsoft.NETCore.App\8.0.1\System.ComponentModel.TypeConverter.dll
ModLoad: 00007ffb`16fe0000 00007ffb`16fe5000   C:\Program Files\dotnet\shared\Microsoft.NETCore.App\8.0.1\System.ComponentModel.dll
ModLoad: 00000226`ffc30000 00000226`ffc3a000   C:\Program Files\dotnet\shared\Microsoft.NETCore.App\8.0.1\System.Xml.ReaderWriter.dll
ModLoad: 00007ffa`e1910000 00007ffa`e1c8f000   C:\Program Files\dotnet\shared\Microsoft.NETCore.App\8.0.1\System.Linq.Expressions.dll
ModLoad: 00007ffb`04aa0000 00007ffb`04b6e000   C:\Program Files\dotnet\shared\Microsoft.NETCore.App\8.0.1\System.IO.Compression.Native.dll
ModLoad: 00007ffb`18ff0000 00007ffb`18ff9000   C:\Program Files\dotnet\shared\Microsoft.NETCore.App\8.0.1\System.Diagnostics.FileVersionInfo.dll
ModLoad: 00007ffa`f8800000 00007ffa`f890e000   C:\Program Files\dotnet\shared\Microsoft.NETCore.App\8.0.1\System.Reflection.Metadata.dll
ModLoad: 00007ffa`fd9d0000 00007ffa`fda9a000   C:\Program Files\dotnet\shared\Microsoft.NETCore.App\8.0.1\System.Collections.Immutable.dll
ModLoad: 00000267`96920000 00000267`96928000   C:\Program Files\dotnet\shared\Microsoft.NETCore.App\8.0.1\System.Text.Encoding.Extensions.dll
ModLoad: 00007ffa`e6650000 00007ffa`e67bc000   C:\Program Files\dotnet\shared\Microsoft.NETCore.App\8.0.1\System.Text.Json.dll
ModLoad: 00007ffb`11c70000 00007ffb`11c81000   C:\Program Files\dotnet\shared\Microsoft.NETCore.App\8.0.1\System.ObjectModel.dll
ModLoad: 00007ffa`e5f10000 00007ffa`e6003000   C:\Program Files\dotnet\shared\Microsoft.NETCore.App\8.0.1\Microsoft.CSharp.dll
ModLoad: 00007ffb`1da90000 00007ffb`1daad000   C:\WINDOWS\SYSTEM32\amsi.dll
ModLoad: 00007ffb`331d0000 00007ffb`331fc000   C:\WINDOWS\SYSTEM32\USERENV.dll
ModLoad: 00007ffb`1d690000 00007ffb`1d70c000   C:\ProgramData\Microsoft\Windows Defender\Platform\4.18.23110.3-0\MpOav.dll
ModLoad: 00007ffb`0f2d0000 00007ffb`0f409000   C:\ProgramData\Microsoft\Windows Defender\Platform\4.18.23110.3-0\MPCLIENT.DLL
ModLoad: 00007ffb`331a0000 00007ffb`331c6000   C:\WINDOWS\SYSTEM32\gpapi.dll
ModLoad: 00000267`96930000 00000267`9694c000   C:\Program Files\dotnet\shared\Microsoft.NETCore.App\8.0.1\netstandard.dll
ModLoad: 00007ffa`f4590000 00007ffa`f45d9000   C:\Program Files\dotnet\shared\Microsoft.NETCore.App\8.0.1\System.Runtime.Serialization.Formatters.dll
ModLoad: 00007ffb`15870000 00007ffb`15879000   C:\Program Files\dotnet\shared\Microsoft.NETCore.App\8.0.1\System.Diagnostics.StackTrace.dll
ModLoad: 00007ffb`26a80000 00007ffb`26a8e000   C:\Program Files\dotnet\shared\Microsoft.NETCore.App\8.0.1\System.Diagnostics.TextWriterTraceListener.dll
ModLoad: 00000267`96950000 00000267`96956000   C:\Users\dmitr\AppData\Local\Temp\LINQPad8\_gvtxlrce\ayhdzk\LINQPadQuery.dll
ModLoad: 00000267`96960000 00000267`96968000   C:\Users\dmitr\AppData\Local\Temp\LINQPad8\_gvtxlrce\shadow-1\DllMD11.dll
ModLoad: 00000267`96970000 00000267`96982000   C:\Program Files\dotnet\shared\Microsoft.NETCore.App\8.0.1\mscorlib.dll
(a2a0.d7b0): Break instruction exception - code 80000003 (first chance)
ntdll!DbgBreakPoint:
00007ffb`36a33060 int     3
```

```
0:017> .logappend c:\AWD4\MD11.log
Opened log file 'c:\AWD4\MD11.log'
```

22.   Because the application is hanging, we check possible locks using the **!syncblk** SOS command:

```
0:017> !syncblk
Index         SyncBlock MonitorHeld Recursion Owning Thread Info          SyncBlock Owner
    2 000002268175F150           3         1 0000022683D4DFD0 b5a0   16   0000022681858f10 System.String
    3 000002268175F1A8           3         1 00000226817628F0 87d4   15   0000022681858ed0 System.String
-------------------------------
Total           4
CCW             0
RCW             0
ComClassFactory 0
Free            1
```

Note: What we see here is that thread **#16** holds a lock on the **000002268175F150** synchronization block that is owned by the **0000022681858f10** String object with the "**critical section 2**" value:

```
0:017> !DumpObj 0000022681858f10
Name:          System.String
MethodTable: 00007ffa85deec08
EEClass:       00007ffa85dca500
Tracked Type: false
Size:          58(0x3a) bytes
File:          C:\Program Files\dotnet\shared\Microsoft.NETCore.App\8.0.1\System.Private.CoreLib.dll
String:        critical section 2
Fields:
              MT    Field   Offset                 Type VT     Attr            Value Name
00007ffa85d71188  400033b        8         System.Int32  1 instance               18 _stringLength
00007ffa85d7b538  400033c        c         System.Char   1 instance               63 _firstChar
00007ffa85deec08  400033a       c8       System.String   0   static 0000022681830008 Empty
```

and that thread **#15** holds a lock on the **000002268175F1A8** block that is owned by the **0000022681858ed0** String object with the "**critical section 1**" value:

```
0:017> !DumpObj 0000022681858ed0
Name:          System.String
MethodTable: 00007ffa85deec08
EEClass:       00007ffa85dca500
Tracked Type: false
Size:          58(0x3a) bytes
File:          C:\Program Files\dotnet\shared\Microsoft.NETCore.App\8.0.1\System.Private.CoreLib.dll
String:        critical section 1
Fields:
              MT    Field   Offset                 Type VT     Attr            Value Name
00007ffa85d71188  400033b        8         System.Int32  1 instance               18 _stringLength
00007ffa85d7b538  400033c        c         System.Char   1 instance               63 _firstChar
00007ffa85deec08  400033a       c8       System.String   0   static 0000022681830008 Empty
```

23.   However, to verify whether thread **#15** is waiting for the sync block owner from thread **#16** and vice versa, we need to inspect execution residue on their thread stack regions to see if there are any value references there:

```
0:017> ~15kL 10
*** WARNING: Unable to verify checksum for
C:\Users\dmitr\AppData\Local\Temp\LINQPad8\_gvtxlrce\ayhdzk\LINQPadQuery.dll
 # Child-SP          RetAddr               Call Site
00 000000aa`54fff0d8 00007ffb`3435ffe9    ntdll!NtWaitForMultipleObjects+0x14
01 000000aa`54fff0e0 00007ffa`e590b54b    KERNELBASE!WaitForMultipleObjectsEx+0xe9
02 (Inline Function) --------`--------    coreclr!Thread::DoAppropriateAptStateWait+0x47
03 000000aa`54fff3c0 00007ffa`e590b395    coreclr!Thread::DoAppropriateWaitWorker+0x177
```

```
04 000000aa`54fff4a0 00007ffa`e590ab95      coreclr!Thread::DoAppropriateWait+0x85
05 (Inline Function) --------`--------      coreclr!CLREventBase::WaitEx+0x53
06 000000aa`54fff520 00007ffa`e590a8b4      coreclr!CLREventBase::Wait+0x59
07 000000aa`54fff570 00007ffa`e590a766      coreclr!AwareLock::EnterEpilogHelper+0x134
08 000000aa`54fff660 00007ffa`e590a6ed      coreclr!AwareLock::EnterEpilog+0x42
09 000000aa`54fff6b0 00007ffa`e5909f5b      coreclr!AwareLock::Enter+0x99
0a (Inline Function) --------`--------      coreclr!SyncBlock::EnterMonitor+0x8
0b (Inline Function) --------`--------      coreclr!ObjHeader::EnterObjMonitor+0xd
0c (Inline Function) --------`--------      coreclr!Object::EnterObjMonitor+0x16
0d 000000aa`54fff6e0 00007ffa`e593dde5      coreclr!JIT_MonEnter_Helper+0x103
0e 000000aa`54fff870 00007ffa`86860809      coreclr!JIT_MonEnter_Portable+0x145
0f 000000aa`54fff8b0 00007ffa`9bbc657d      LINQPadQuery!UserQuery.ClassMain.thread_proc_1+0xe9
```

```
0:017> !IP2MD 00007ffa`86860809
MethodDesc:          00007ffa86843d50
Method Name:         UserQuery+ClassMain.thread_proc_1()
Class:               00007ffa86824248
MethodTable:         00007ffa86843db8
mdToken:             0000000006000007
Module:              00007ffa867f1100
IsJitted:            yes
Current CodeAddr:    00007ffa86860720
Version History:
  ILCodeVersion:     0000000000000000
  ReJIT ID:          0
  IL Addr:           0000026796952100
     CodeAddr:          00007ffa86860720  (MinOptJitted)
     NativeCodeVersion: 0000000000000000
Source file:  C:\Users\dmitr\AppData\Local\Temp\LINQPad8\_gvtxlrce\ayhdzk\LINQPadQuery @ 38
```

```
0:017> dps 000000aa`54fff6b0 000000aa`54fff8b0
000000aa`54fff6b0  00000226`817628f0
000000aa`54fff6b8  00000000`00000000
000000aa`54fff6c0  00000000`00000000
000000aa`54fff6c8  00000227`0295b700
000000aa`54fff6d0  00000000`00000000
000000aa`54fff6d8  00007ffa`e5909f5b coreclr!JIT_MonEnter_Helper+0x103 [D:\a\_work\1\s\src\coreclr\vm\jithelpers.cpp @ 3794]
000000aa`54fff6e0  00007ffa`e593dca0 coreclr!JIT_MonEnter_Portable [D:\a\_work\1\s\src\coreclr\vm\jithelpers.cpp @ 3819]
000000aa`54fff6e8  00007ffa`e5caaaa0 coreclr!g_SyncBlockCacheInstance+0x10
000000aa`54fff6f0  00000226`8175f150
000000aa`54fff6f8  00007ffa`e593dca0 coreclr!JIT_MonEnter_Portable [D:\a\_work\1\s\src\coreclr\vm\jithelpers.cpp @ 3819]
000000aa`54fff700  00000000`00000000
000000aa`54fff708  00000226`81858f10
000000aa`54fff710  00000000`00000000
000000aa`54fff718  00000000`000007d0
000000aa`54fff720  00000000`00000000
000000aa`54fff728  00000226`817628f0
000000aa`54fff730  000000aa`54fff710
000000aa`54fff738  00000001`00000001
000000aa`54fff740  06000000`00000001
000000aa`54fff748  000000aa`54fff900
000000aa`54fff750  0000c510`210ccab0
000000aa`54fff758  00007ffa`e5c1cbb0 coreclr!HelperMethodFrame_1OBJ::`vftable'
000000aa`54fff760  000000aa`54fffbd0
000000aa`54fff768  00007ffa`85e824e8
000000aa`54fff770  00007ffa`00000030
000000aa`54fff778  00000226`817628f0
000000aa`54fff780  00007ffa`e593dca0 coreclr!JIT_MonEnter_Portable [D:\a\_work\1\s\src\coreclr\vm\jithelpers.cpp @ 3819]
000000aa`54fff788  00007ffa`86860809 LINQPadQuery!UserQuery.ClassMain.thread_proc_1+0xe9
000000aa`54fff790  000000aa`54fff8b0
000000aa`54fff798  00000227`0295aa00
000000aa`54fff7a0  00000227`0295b7d0
000000aa`54fff7a8  00007ffa`e593dca0 coreclr!JIT_MonEnter_Portable [D:\a\_work\1\s\src\coreclr\vm\jithelpers.cpp @ 3819]
000000aa`54fff7b0  000000aa`54fff900
000000aa`54fff7b8  00000000`00000000
000000aa`54fff7c0  00000000`00000000
000000aa`54fff7c8  00000000`00000000
000000aa`54fff7d0  00000000`00000000
000000aa`54fff7d8  000000aa`54fff850
000000aa`54fff7e0  000000aa`54fff858
000000aa`54fff7e8  000000aa`54fff8a0
```

```
000000aa`54fff7f0  000000aa`54fff7b0
000000aa`54fff7f8  000000aa`54fff7b8
000000aa`54fff800  000000aa`54fff7c0
000000aa`54fff808  000000aa`54fff7c8
000000aa`54fff810  000000aa`54fff7d0
000000aa`54fff818  000000aa`54fff788
000000aa`54fff820  00007ffa`e5909ec8 coreclr!JIT_MonEnter_Helper+0x70 [D:\a\_work\1\s\src\coreclr\vm\jithelpers.cpp @ 3781]
000000aa`54fff828  000000aa`54fff6d8
000000aa`54fff830  000000aa`54fff708
000000aa`54fff838  00000000`00000000
000000aa`54fff840  0000c5ba`77c9c178
000000aa`54fff848  00000000`00000000
000000aa`54fff850  00000227`04cd3118
000000aa`54fff858  00000227`04cd3220
000000aa`54fff860  00000226`81858f10
000000aa`54fff868  00007ffa`e593dde5 coreclr!JIT_MonEnter_Portable+0x145 [D:\a\_work\1\s\src\coreclr\vm\jithelpers.cpp @ 3828]
000000aa`54fff870  00000226`81858f10
000000aa`54fff878  000000aa`54fff900
000000aa`54fff880  00007ffa`e593dca0 coreclr!JIT_MonEnter_Portable [D:\a\_work\1\s\src\coreclr\vm\jithelpers.cpp @ 3819]
000000aa`54fff888  00000227`00000003
000000aa`54fff890  00000227`0295b7d0
000000aa`54fff898  00000227`0295aa00
000000aa`54fff8a0  00000227`02813740
000000aa`54fff8a8  00007ffa`86860809 LINQPadQuery!UserQuery.ClassMain.thread_proc_1+0xe9
000000aa`54fff8b0  00000227`02977ce0
```

Note: We can also see that from managed execution residue using the **!DumpStackObjects** (**!dso**) SOS command (you may need to remove backticks if the SOS extension command throws a parsing error):

```
0:017> !dso 000000aa54fff6b0 000000aa54fff8b0
OS Thread Id: 0xd7b0 (17)
        SP/REG        Object Name
    00aa54fff708    022681858f10 System.String
    00aa54fff850    022704cd3118 System.Threading.Thread+StartHelper
    00aa54fff858    022704cd3220 System.Threading.ContextCallback
    00aa54fff860    022681858f10 System.String
    00aa54fff870    022681858f10 System.String
```

24.   We repeat the same sequence of commands for thread **#16**:

```
0:017> ~16kL 10
 # Child-SP          RetAddr           Call Site
00 000000aa`554ff0d8 00007ffb`3435ffe9 ntdll!NtWaitForMultipleObjects+0x14
01 000000aa`554ff0e0 00007ffa`e590b54b KERNELBASE!WaitForMultipleObjectsEx+0xe9
02 (Inline Function) --------`-------- coreclr!Thread::DoAppropriateAptStateWait+0x47
03 000000aa`554ff3c0 00007ffa`e590b395 coreclr!Thread::DoAppropriateWaitWorker+0x177
04 000000aa`554ff4a0 00007ffa`e590ab95 coreclr!Thread::DoAppropriateWait+0x85
05 (Inline Function) --------`-------- coreclr!CLREventBase::WaitEx+0x53
06 000000aa`554ff520 00007ffa`e590a8b4 coreclr!CLREventBase::Wait+0x59
07 000000aa`554ff570 00007ffa`e590a766 coreclr!AwareLock::EnterEpilogHelper+0x134
08 000000aa`554ff660 00007ffa`e590a6ed coreclr!AwareLock::EnterEpilog+0x42
09 000000aa`554ff6b0 00007ffa`e5909f5b coreclr!AwareLock::Enter+0x99
0a (Inline Function) --------`-------- coreclr!SyncBlock::EnterMonitor+0x8
0b (Inline Function) --------`-------- coreclr!ObjHeader::EnterObjMonitor+0xd
0c (Inline Function) --------`-------- coreclr!Object::EnterObjMonitor+0x16
0d 000000aa`554ff6e0 00007ffa`e593dde5 coreclr!JIT_MonEnter_Helper+0x103
0e 000000aa`554ff870 00007ffa`86893846 coreclr!JIT_MonEnter_Portable+0x145
0f 000000aa`554ff8b0 00007ffa`9bbc657d LINQPadQuery!UserQuery.ClassMain.thread_proc_2+0x46
```

```
0:017> !IP2MD 00007ffa`86893846
MethodDesc:      00007ffa86843d68
Method Name:          UserQuery+ClassMain.thread_proc_2()
Class:                00007ffa86824248
MethodTable:          00007ffa86843db8
mdToken:              0000000006000008
```

```
Module:              00007ffa867f1100
IsJitted:            yes
Current CodeAddr:    00007ffa86893800
Version History:
   ILCodeVersion:    0000000000000000
   ReJIT ID:         0
   IL Addr:          0000026796952194
      CodeAddr:          00007ffa86893800  (MinOptJitted)
      NativeCodeVersion: 0000000000000000
Source file:  C:\Users\dmitr\AppData\Local\Temp\LINQPad8\_gvtxlrce\ayhdzk\LINQPadQuery @ 53
```

```
0:017> dps 000000aa`554ff6b0 000000aa`554ff8b0
000000aa`554ff6b0  00000226`83d4dfd0
000000aa`554ff6b8  00000000`00000000
000000aa`554ff6c0  00000000`00000000
000000aa`554ff6c8  00000227`0295b700
000000aa`554ff6d0  00000000`00000000
000000aa`554ff6d8  00007ffa`e5909f5b coreclr!JIT_MonEnter_Helper+0x103 [D:\a\_work\1\s\src\coreclr\vm\jithelpers.cpp @ 3794]
000000aa`554ff6e0  00007ffa`e593dca0 coreclr!JIT_MonEnter_Portable [D:\a\_work\1\s\src\coreclr\vm\jithelpers.cpp @ 3819]
000000aa`554ff6e8  00007ffa`e5caaaa0 coreclr!g_SyncBlockCacheInstance+0x10
000000aa`554ff6f0  00000226`8175f1a8
000000aa`554ff6f8  00007ffa`e593dca0 coreclr!JIT_MonEnter_Portable [D:\a\_work\1\s\src\coreclr\vm\jithelpers.cpp @ 3819]
000000aa`554ff700  06000000`00000001
000000aa`554ff708  00000226`81858ed0
000000aa`554ff710  00000000`00000000
000000aa`554ff718  000000aa`00000064
000000aa`554ff720  00000000`00000000
000000aa`554ff728  00000226`83d4dfd0
000000aa`554ff730  000000aa`554ff710
000000aa`554ff738  00000001`00000001
000000aa`554ff740  0000c510`210ccab0
000000aa`554ff748  00007ffa`e5c1cce0 coreclr!HelperMethodFrame::`vftable'
000000aa`554ff750  0000c510`210ccab0
000000aa`554ff758  00007ffa`e5c1cbb0 coreclr!HelperMethodFrame_1OBJ::`vftable'
000000aa`554ff760  000000aa`554ffba0
000000aa`554ff768  00007ffa`85e824e8
000000aa`554ff770  00007ffa`00000030
000000aa`554ff778  00000226`83d4dfd0
000000aa`554ff780  00007ffa`e593dca0 coreclr!JIT_MonEnter_Portable [D:\a\_work\1\s\src\coreclr\vm\jithelpers.cpp @ 3819]
000000aa`554ff788  00007ffa`86893846 LINQPadQuery!UserQuery.ClassMain.thread_proc_2+0x46
000000aa`554ff790  000000aa`554ff8b0
000000aa`554ff798  00000227`0295aac8
000000aa`554ff7a0  00000227`0295b7d0
000000aa`554ff7a8  00007ffa`e593dca0 coreclr!JIT_MonEnter_Portable [D:\a\_work\1\s\src\coreclr\vm\jithelpers.cpp @ 3819]
000000aa`554ff7b0  000000aa`554ff8d0
000000aa`554ff7b8  00000000`00000000
000000aa`554ff7c0  00000000`00000000
000000aa`554ff7c8  00000000`00000000
000000aa`554ff7d0  00000000`00000000
000000aa`554ff7d8  000000aa`554ff850
000000aa`554ff7e0  000000aa`554ff858
000000aa`554ff7e8  000000aa`554ff8a0
000000aa`554ff7f0  000000aa`554ff7b0
000000aa`554ff7f8  000000aa`554ff7b8
000000aa`554ff800  000000aa`554ff7c0
000000aa`554ff808  000000aa`554ff7c8
000000aa`554ff810  000000aa`554ff7d0
000000aa`554ff818  000000aa`554ff788
000000aa`554ff820  00007ffa`e5909ec8 coreclr!JIT_MonEnter_Helper+0x70 [D:\a\_work\1\s\src\coreclr\vm\jithelpers.cpp @ 3781]
000000aa`554ff828  000000aa`554ff6d8
000000aa`554ff830  000000aa`554ff708
000000aa`554ff838  00007ffa`9bbbe751 System_Private_CoreLib!System.Threading.Thread.Sleep+0x11
[/_/src/libraries/System.Private.CoreLib/src/System/Threading/Thread.cs @ 368]
000000aa`554ff840  0000c5ba`7679c178
000000aa`554ff848  00000000`00000000
000000aa`554ff850  00000227`04cd31e0
000000aa`554ff858  00000227`04cd3220
000000aa`554ff860  00000226`81858ed0
000000aa`554ff868  00007ffa`e593dde5 coreclr!JIT_MonEnter_Portable+0x145 [D:\a\_work\1\s\src\coreclr\vm\jithelpers.cpp @ 3828]
000000aa`554ff870  00000226`81858ed0
000000aa`554ff878  000000aa`554ff8d0
000000aa`554ff880  00007ffa`e593dca0 coreclr!JIT_MonEnter_Portable [D:\a\_work\1\s\src\coreclr\vm\jithelpers.cpp @ 3819]
000000aa`554ff888  00000000`00000003
000000aa`554ff890  00000227`0295aac8
000000aa`554ff898  00000227`0295aac8
000000aa`554ff8a0  00000227`02813740
000000aa`554ff8a8  00007ffa`86893846 LINQPadQuery!UserQuery.ClassMain.thread_proc_2+0x46
000000aa`554ff8b0  000000aa`554ff940
```

```
0:017> !dso 000000aa554ff6b0 000000aa554ff8b0
OS Thread Id: 0xd7b0 (17)
        SP/REG          Object Name
    00aa554ff708        022681858ed0 System.String
    00aa554ff850        022704cd31e0 System.Threading.Thread+StartHelper
    00aa554ff858        022704cd3220 System.Threading.ContextCallback
    00aa554ff860        022681858ed0 System.String
    00aa554ff870        022681858ed0 System.String
```

Note: We see that thread **#16** is waiting for the sync block owner (String) from thread **#15**. Since both threads are mutually waiting for each other, we consider them deadlocked.

25.   How did this deadlock happen? If we look at both threads' execution residue, we would see that in the case of thread **#15,** an exception was thrown (we use the **!DumpStackObjects** or **!dso** command to inspect raw stack data):

```
0:017> ~15s
ntdll!NtWaitForMultipleObjects+0x14:
00007ffb`36a2fec4 ret
```

```
0:015> !teb
TEB at 000000aa545da000
    ExceptionList:          0000000000000000
    StackBase:              000000aa55000000
    StackLimit:             000000aa54fef000
    SubSystemTib:           0000000000000000
    FiberData:              0000000000001e00
    ArbitraryUserPointer:   0000000000000000
    Self:                   000000aa545da000
    EnvironmentPointer:     0000000000000000
    ClientId:               000000000000a2a0 . 00000000000087d4
    RpcHandle:              0000000000000000
    Tls Storage:            0000022681741090
    PEB Address:            000000aa545a7000
    LastErrorValue:         0
    LastStatusValue:        c000003a
    Count Owned Locks:      0
    HardErrorMode:          0
```

```
0:015> !dso 000000aa54fef000 000000aa55000000
OS Thread Id: 0x87d4 (15)
        SP/REG          Object Name
    00aa54fff5c0        022681858f10 System.String
    00aa54fff708        022681858f10 System.String
    00aa54fff850        022704cd3118 System.Threading.Thread+StartHelper
    00aa54fff858        022704cd3220 System.Threading.ContextCallback
    00aa54fff860        022681858f10 System.String
    00aa54fff870        022681858f10 System.String
    00aa54fff8e0        022704ce5b70 System.NullReferenceException
    00aa54fff8e8        022704ce5b58 DllMD11.NewFeature
    00aa54fff8f0        022704ce5b70 System.NullReferenceException
    00aa54fff8f8        022704ce5b58 DllMD11.NewFeature
    00aa54fff950        022704cd30d0 System.Threading.Thread
```

```
0:015> ~16s
ntdll!NtWaitForMultipleObjects+0x14:
00007ffb`36a2fec4 ret
```

```
0:016> !teb
TEB at 000000aa545dc000
    ExceptionList:           0000000000000000
    StackBase:               000000aa55500000
    StackLimit:              000000aa554fc000
    SubSystemTib:            0000000000000000
    FiberData:               0000000000001e00
    ArbitraryUserPointer:    0000000000000000
    Self:                    000000aa545dc000
    EnvironmentPointer:      0000000000000000
    ClientId:                000000000000a2a0 . 000000000000b5a0
    RpcHandle:               0000000000000000
    Tls Storage:             000002268173f810
    PEB Address:             000000aa545a7000
    LastErrorValue:          0
    LastStatusValue:         c000000d
    Count Owned Locks:       0
    HardErrorMode:           0


0:016> !dso 000000aa554fc000 000000aa55500000
OS Thread Id: 0xb5a0 (16)
         SP/REG           Object Name
    00aa554fd108      022681858f10 System.String
    00aa554fd7c0      02268185adf0 System.String
    00aa554ff5c0      022681858ed0 System.String
    00aa554ff708      022681858ed0 System.String
    00aa554ff850      022704cd31e0 System.Threading.Thread+StartHelper
    00aa554ff858      022704cd3220 System.Threading.ContextCallback
    00aa554ff860      022681858ed0 System.String
    00aa554ff870      022681858ed0 System.String
    00aa554ff920      022704cd3198 System.Threading.Thread


0:016> !pe 022704ce5b70
Exception object: 0000022704ce5b70
Exception type:    System.NullReferenceException
Message:           Object reference not set to an instance of an object.
InnerException:    <none>
StackTrace (generated):
    SP                 IP                 Function
    000000AA54FFF870   00007FFA868644C0   DllMD11!DllMD11.NewFeature.ExtraWork()+0x30
    000000AA54FFF8B0   00007FFA868607AC   LINQPadQuery!UserQuery+ClassMain.thread_proc_1()+0x8c

StackTraceString: <none>
HResult: 80004003


0:016> !U 00007FFA868644C0
Normal JIT generated code
DllMD11.NewFeature.ExtraWork()
ilAddr is 0000026796962050 pImport is 00000162577FFB40
Begin 00007FFA86864490, size 3e
00007ffa`86864490 push    rbp
00007ffa`86864491 sub     rsp,30h
00007ffa`86864495 lea     rbp,[rsp+30h]
00007ffa`8686449a xor     eax,eax
00007ffa`8686449c mov     qword ptr [rbp-8],rax
00007ffa`868644a0 mov     qword ptr [rbp+10h],rcx
00007ffa`868644a4 cmp     dword ptr [00007ffa`8684bbd0],0
00007ffa`868644ab je      00007ffa`868644b2
00007ffa`868644ad call    coreclr!JIT_DbgIsJustMyCode (00007ffa`e5a9eb10)
```

```
00007ffa`868644b2 nop
00007ffa`868644b3 nop
00007ffa`868644b4 xor      eax,eax
00007ffa`868644b6 mov      eax,eax
00007ffa`868644b8 mov      qword ptr [rbp-8],rax
00007ffa`868644bc mov      rax,qword ptr [rbp-8]
>>> 00007ffa`868644c0 mov      dword ptr [rax],1
00007ffa`868644c6 nop
00007ffa`868644c7 nop
00007ffa`868644c8 add      rsp,30h
00007ffa`868644cc pop      rbp
00007ffa`868644cd ret
```

26.   We now close WinDbg and LINQPad 8 (x64).

Expected Behavior

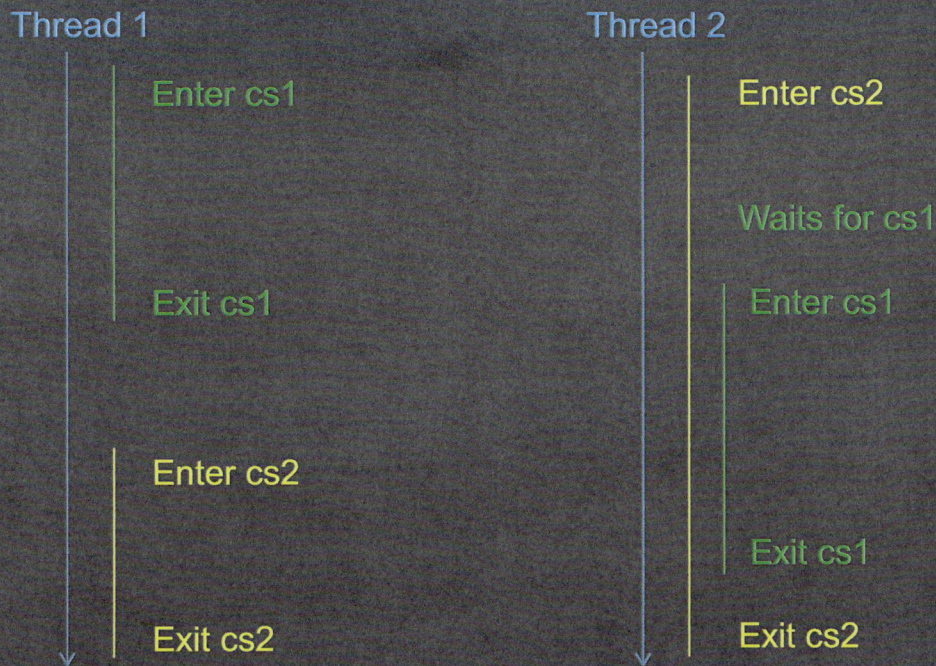

This diagram shows the expected behavior for the *AppMD11* program. The code is deadlock-free.

Deadlock

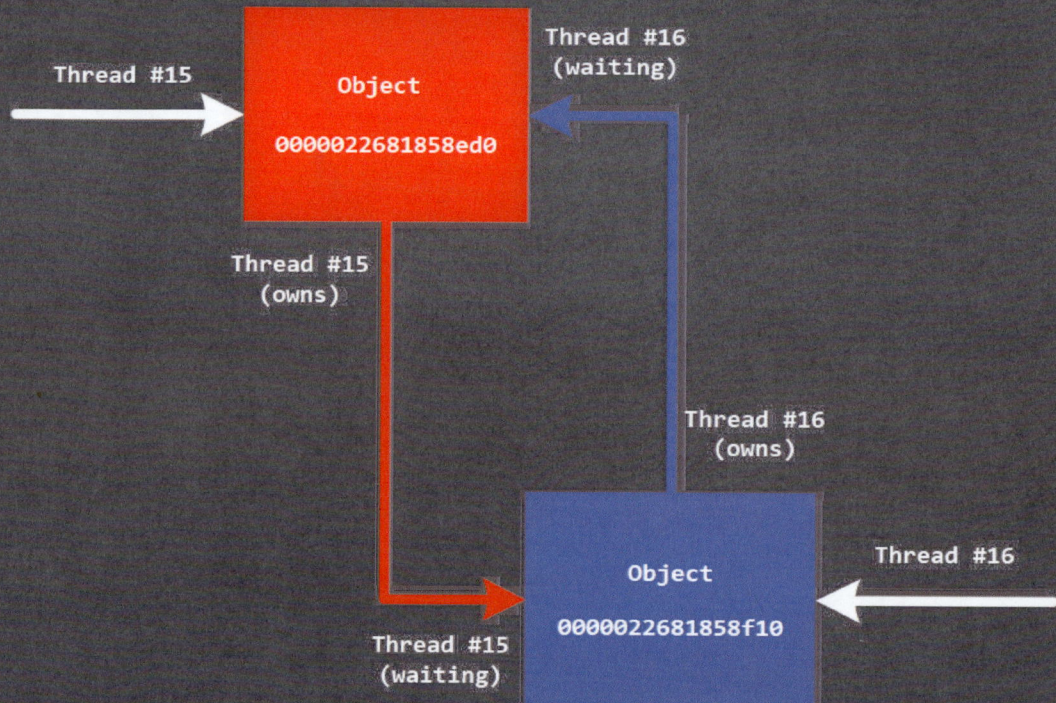

This diagram shows the abnormal behavior of *AppMD11V3* after a problem new feature was introduced in *AppMD11V2* and incorrectly fixed. The data on the diagram corresponds to the exercise transcript and may differ in your debugging system.

Time Travel Debugging

Exercise TD5

Exercise TD5

- **Goal:** Learn how to find hidden exceptions using Time Travel Debugging

- **Elementary Diagnostics Patterns:** Hang

- **Memory Analysis Patterns:** Hidden Exception (User Space)

- **Debugging Implementation Patterns:** Instruction Trace

- \AWD4\Exercise-TD5.pdf

Exercise TD5

Goal: Learn how to find hidden exceptions using Time Travel Debugging.

Elementary Diagnostics Patterns: Hang.

Memory Analysis Patterns: Hidden Exception (User Space).

Debugging Implementation Patterns: Instruction Trace.

1.   Launch WinDbg. Open *\AWD4\AppD5BV3\x64\Release\AppD5BV3.exe* executable by choosing *File \ Launch executable* menu option, selecting *Record with Time Travel Debugging*, and choosing *Configure and Record*:

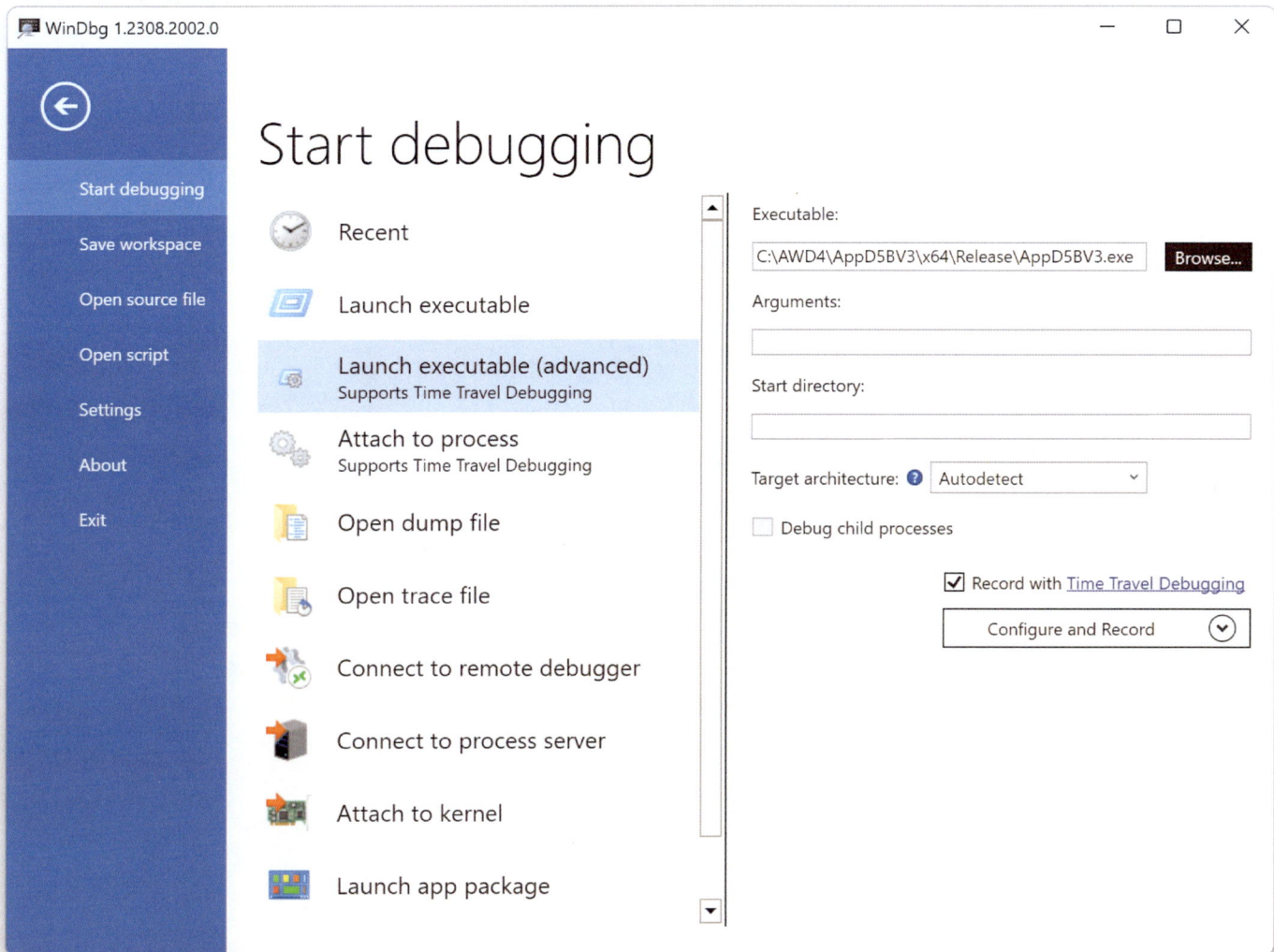

2.   Choose the folder to save the recording trace file and start recording:

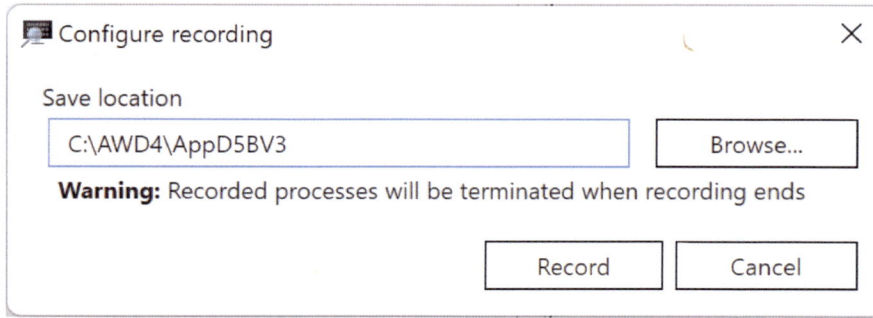

AppD5BV3 is launched, and the following dialog appears:

3.   Switch to *AppD5BV3* and choose *File \ Start*. The app hangs for 30 seconds but then becomes responsive again. Wait for a few minutes, and then close *AppD5BV3*.

4.   WinDbg now shows the *Timelines* dialog:

When you point at a rectangle, you see past exception information:

0xc0000005

Clock time:	11:00:37
Exception Type:	Hardware
Program Counter:	0x7ff7244f1510
Record Address:	0x0

5.   If we click on the red rectangle, WinDbg travels to that point in time:

```
Microsoft (R) Windows Debugger Version 10.0.25921.1001 AMD64
Copyright (c) Microsoft Corporation. All rights reserved.


Loading Dump File [C:\AWD4\AppD5BV3\AppD5BV302.run]
JavaScript script successfully loaded from 'C:\Program
Files\WindowsApps\Microsoft.WinDbg_1.2308.2002.0_x64__8wekyb3d8bbwe\amd64\TTD\Analyzers\HeapAnalysis.js'
JavaScript script successfully loaded from 'C:\Program
Files\WindowsApps\Microsoft.WinDbg_1.2308.2002.0_x64__8wekyb3d8bbwe\amd64\TTD\Analyzers\TtdAnalyze.js'

************* Path validation summary **************
Response                     Time (ms)       Location
Deferred                                     srv*
Symbol search path is: srv*
Executable search path is:
ModLoad: 00007ff7`244f0000 00007ff7`24513000   C:\AWD4\AppD5BV3\x64\Release\AppD5BV3.exe
ModLoad: 00007ffa`e9cc0000 00007ffa`e9e3f000
C:\Users\dmitr\AppData\Local\Microsoft\WindowsApps\Microsoft.WinDbg_8wekyb3d8bbwe\amd64\TTD\TTDRecordCPU.dll
ModLoad: 00007ffb`33cd0000 00007ffb`33cf6000   C:\WINDOWS\System32\win32u.dll
ModLoad: 00007ffb`33d00000 00007ffb`33e18000   C:\WINDOWS\System32\gdi32full.dll
ModLoad: 00007ffb`33fd0000 00007ffb`340e1000   C:\WINDOWS\System32\ucrtbase.dll
ModLoad: 00007ffb`34260000 00007ffb`342fa000   C:\WINDOWS\System32\msvcp_win.dll
ModLoad: 00007ffb`34300000 00007ffb`346a6000   C:\WINDOWS\System32\KERNELBASE.dll
ModLoad: 00007ffb`34760000 00007ffb`34824000   C:\WINDOWS\System32\KERNEL32.DLL
ModLoad: 00007ffb`35600000 00007ffb`35629000   C:\WINDOWS\System32\GDI32.dll
ModLoad: 00007ffb`35660000 00007ffb`35691000   C:\WINDOWS\System32\IMM32.DLL
ModLoad: 00007ffb`366d0000 00007ffb`3687e000   C:\WINDOWS\System32\USER32.dll
ModLoad: 00007ffb`36990000 00007ffb`36ba7000   C:\WINDOWS\SYSTEM32\ntdll.dll
...........
(c380.d078): Break instruction exception - code 80000003 (first/second chance not available)
Time Travel Position: 12:0 [Unindexed] Index
!index
Indexed 10/18 keyframes
Indexed 18/18 keyframes
Successfully created the index in 2361ms.

************* Preparing the environment for Debugger Extensions Gallery repositories **************
    ExtensionRepository : Implicit
    UseExperimentalFeatureForNugetShare : false
    AllowNugetExeUpdate : false
    AllowNugetMSCredentialProviderInstall : false
    AllowParallelInitializationOfLocalRepositories : true

    -- Configuring repositories
        ----> Repository : LocalInstalled, Enabled: true
        ----> Repository : UserExtensions, Enabled: true

>>>>>>>>>>>> Preparing the environment for Debugger Extensions Gallery repositories completed, duration 0.000 seconds

************* Waiting for Debugger Extensions Gallery to Initialize **************

>>>>>>>>>>>> Waiting for Debugger Extensions Gallery to Initialize completed, duration 0.047 seconds
```

```
----> Repository : UserExtensions, Enabled: true, Packages count: 0
----> Repository : LocalInstalled, Enabled: true, Packages count: 36

Microsoft (R) Windows Debugger Version 10.0.25921.1001 AMD64
Copyright (c) Microsoft Corporation. All rights reserved.


Loading Dump File [C:\AWD4\AppD5BV3\AppD5BV302.run]
JavaScript script successfully loaded from 'C:\Program
Files\WindowsApps\Microsoft.WinDbg_1.2308.2002.0_x64__8wekyb3d8bbwe\amd64\TTD\Analyzers\HeapAnalysis.js'
JavaScript script successfully loaded from 'C:\Program
Files\WindowsApps\Microsoft.WinDbg_1.2308.2002.0_x64__8wekyb3d8bbwe\amd64\TTD\Analyzers\TtdAnalyze.js'

************* Path validation summary **************
Response                        Time (ms)    Location
Deferred                                     srv*
Symbol search path is: srv*
Executable search path is:
ModLoad: 00007ff7`244f0000 00007ff7`24513000    C:\AWD4\AppD5BV3\x64\Release\AppD5BV3.exe
ModLoad: 00007ffa`e9cc0000 00007ffa`e9e3f000
C:\Users\dmitr\AppData\Local\Microsoft\WindowsApps\Microsoft.WinDbg_8wekyb3d8bbwe\amd64\TTD\TTDRecordCPU.dll
ModLoad: 00007ffb`33cd0000 00007ffb`33cf6000    C:\WINDOWS\System32\win32u.dll
ModLoad: 00007ffb`33d00000 00007ffb`33e18000    C:\WINDOWS\System32\gdi32full.dll
ModLoad: 00007ffb`33fd0000 00007ffb`340e1000    C:\WINDOWS\System32\ucrtbase.dll
ModLoad: 00007ffb`34260000 00007ffb`342fa000    C:\WINDOWS\System32\msvcp_win.dll
ModLoad: 00007ffb`34300000 00007ffb`346a6000    C:\WINDOWS\System32\KERNELBASE.dll
ModLoad: 00007ffb`34760000 00007ffb`34824000    C:\WINDOWS\System32\KERNEL32.DLL
ModLoad: 00007ffb`35600000 00007ffb`35629000    C:\WINDOWS\System32\GDI32.dll
ModLoad: 00007ffb`35660000 00007ffb`35691000    C:\WINDOWS\System32\IMM32.DLL
ModLoad: 00007ffb`366d0000 00007ffb`3687e000    C:\WINDOWS\System32\USER32.dll
ModLoad: 00007ffb`36990000 00007ffb`36ba7000    C:\WINDOWS\SYSTEM32\ntdll.dll
............
(c380.d078): Break instruction exception - code 80000003 (first/second chance not available)
Time Travel Position: 12:0
ntdll!LdrInitializeThunk:
00007ffb`36a03dd0 push    rbx

0:000> dx @$curprocess.TTD.Events.Where(t => t.Type == "Exception")[0x0].Position.SeekTo()
ModLoad: 00007ffb`35700000 00007ffb`35817000    C:\WINDOWS\System32\RPCRT4.dll
ModLoad: 00007ffb`34d90000 00007ffb`35119000    C:\WINDOWS\System32\combase.dll
ModLoad: 00007ffb`30ba0000 00007ffb`30c4b000    C:\WINDOWS\system32\uxtheme.dll
ModLoad: 00007ffb`34ce0000 00007ffb`34d87000    C:\WINDOWS\System32\msvcrt.dll
ModLoad: 00007ffb`354b0000 00007ffb`35600000    C:\WINDOWS\System32\MSCTF.dll
ModLoad: 00007ffb`1a920000 00007ffb`1a9d0000    C:\WINDOWS\SYSTEM32\TextShaping.dll
ModLoad: 00007ffb`32cc0000 00007ffb`32cd8000    C:\WINDOWS\SYSTEM32\kernel.appcore.dll
ModLoad: 00007ffb`33f50000 00007ffb`33fca000    C:\WINDOWS\System32\bcryptPrimitives.dll
ModLoad: 00007ffb`346b0000 00007ffb`346d8000    C:\WINDOWS\System32\bcrypt.dll
ModLoad: 00007ffb`34c30000 00007ffb`34cd8000    C:\WINDOWS\System32\sechost.dll
ModLoad: 00007ffb`35120000 00007ffb`351f7000    C:\WINDOWS\System32\OLEAUT32.dll
ModLoad: 00007ffb`21110000 00007ffb`2125a000    C:\WINDOWS\SYSTEM32\textinputframework.dll
ModLoad: 00007ffb`2d590000 00007ffb`2d6c4000    C:\WINDOWS\SYSTEM32\CoreMessaging.dll
ModLoad: 00007ffb`31a90000 00007ffb`31bce000    C:\WINDOWS\SYSTEM32\wintypes.dll
ModLoad: 00007ffb`2a070000 00007ffb`2a3dc000    C:\WINDOWS\SYSTEM32\CoreUIComponents.dll
ModLoad: 00007ffb`353d0000 00007ffb`35483000    C:\WINDOWS\System32\advapi32.dll
ModLoad: 00007ffb`33330000 00007ffb`3333c000    C:\WINDOWS\SYSTEM32\CRYPTBASE.DLL
ModLoad: 00007ffb`0cbf0000 00007ffb`0cc59000    C:\WINDOWS\system32\Oleacc.dll
ModLoad: 00007ffb`35310000 00007ffb`353c0000    C:\WINDOWS\system32\clbcatq.dll
ModLoad: 00007ffb`1a4c0000 00007ffb`1a50b000    C:\WINDOWS\system32\ApplicationTargetedFeatureDatabase.dll
ModLoad: 00007ffb`28410000 00007ffb`28695000    C:\Windows\System32\twinapi.appcore.dll
ModLoad: 00007ffb`30fe0000 00007ffb`3100b000    C:\WINDOWS\system32\dwmapi.dll
(c380.d078): Break instruction exception - code 80000003 (first/second chance not available)
Time Travel Position: 286E:0
@$curprocess.TTD.Events.Where(t => t.Type == "Exception")[0x0].Position.SeekTo()
*** WARNING: Unable to verify checksum for AppD5BV3.exe
```

6.   We can now inspect exception context and stack trace:

```
0:000> kL
 # Child-SP          RetAddr               Call Site
00 00000095`47bffa20 00007ff7`244f149e     AppD5BV3!NewFeature+0x10
01 00000095`47bffa40 00007ff7`244f1301     AppD5BV3!StartModeling+0x2e
```

```
02 00000095`47bffa80 00007ffb`366e8241     AppD5BV3!WndProc+0xb1
03 00000095`47bffb40 00007ffb`366e7d01     USER32!UserCallWinProcCheckWow+0x2d1
04 00000095`47bffca0 00007ff7`244f10d0     USER32!DispatchMessageWorker+0x1f1
05 00000095`47bffd20 00007ff7`244f173a     AppD5BV3!wWinMain+0xd0
06 (Inline Function) --------`--------     AppD5BV3!invoke_main+0x21
07 00000095`47bffd90 00007ffb`3477257d     AppD5BV3!__scrt_common_main_seh+0x106
08 00000095`47bffdd0 00007ffb`369eaa58     KERNEL32!BaseThreadInitThunk+0x1d
09 00000095`47bffe00 00000000`00000000     ntdll!RtlUserThreadStart+0x28


0:000> r
rax=0000000000000000 rbx=0000000000000000 rcx=0000000000000000
rdx=0000000000000000 rsi=0000000080006010 rdi=0000000000000001
rip=00007ff7244f1510 rsp=0000009547bffa20 rbp=0000000000000000
 r8=0000000000000000  r9=0000000000000000 r10=0000000000000000
r11=0000009547bffa30 r12=0000000000000000 r13=0000000000000000
r14=0000000000000111 r15=0000000000000000
iopl=0         nv up ei pl nz na pe nc
cs=0033  ss=002b  ds=002b  es=002b  fs=0053  gs=002b             efl=00000202
AppD5BV3!NewFeature+0x10:
00007ff7`244f1510 mov      dword ptr [rax],1        ds:00000000`00000000=????????
```

7.   If we set the source code path (if not set previously), we can even see the problem statement:

```
0:000> .srcpath+ C:\AWD4\AppD5BV3\AppD5BV3
Source search path is: SRV*;C:\AWD4\AppD5BV3\AppD5BV3

************* Path validation summary **************
Response                        Time (ms)       Location
Deferred                                        SRV*
OK                                              C:\AWD4\AppD5BV3\AppD5BV3
```

```
NewFeature.cpp                                              ▼ ☐ ✕
    1 #include "stdafx.h"
    2
    3 void NewFeature(void)
    4 {
    5     int *p = NULL;
    6
 ➡  7     *p = 1;
    8 }
```

8.   We now quit WinDbg.

9. Suppose three *AppD5BV301.** files (*.idx*, *.out*, and *.run*) were sent to us for analysis. We launch WinDbg and open *\AWD4\AppD5BV3\AppD5BV301.run* by choosing *File \ Open trace file*:

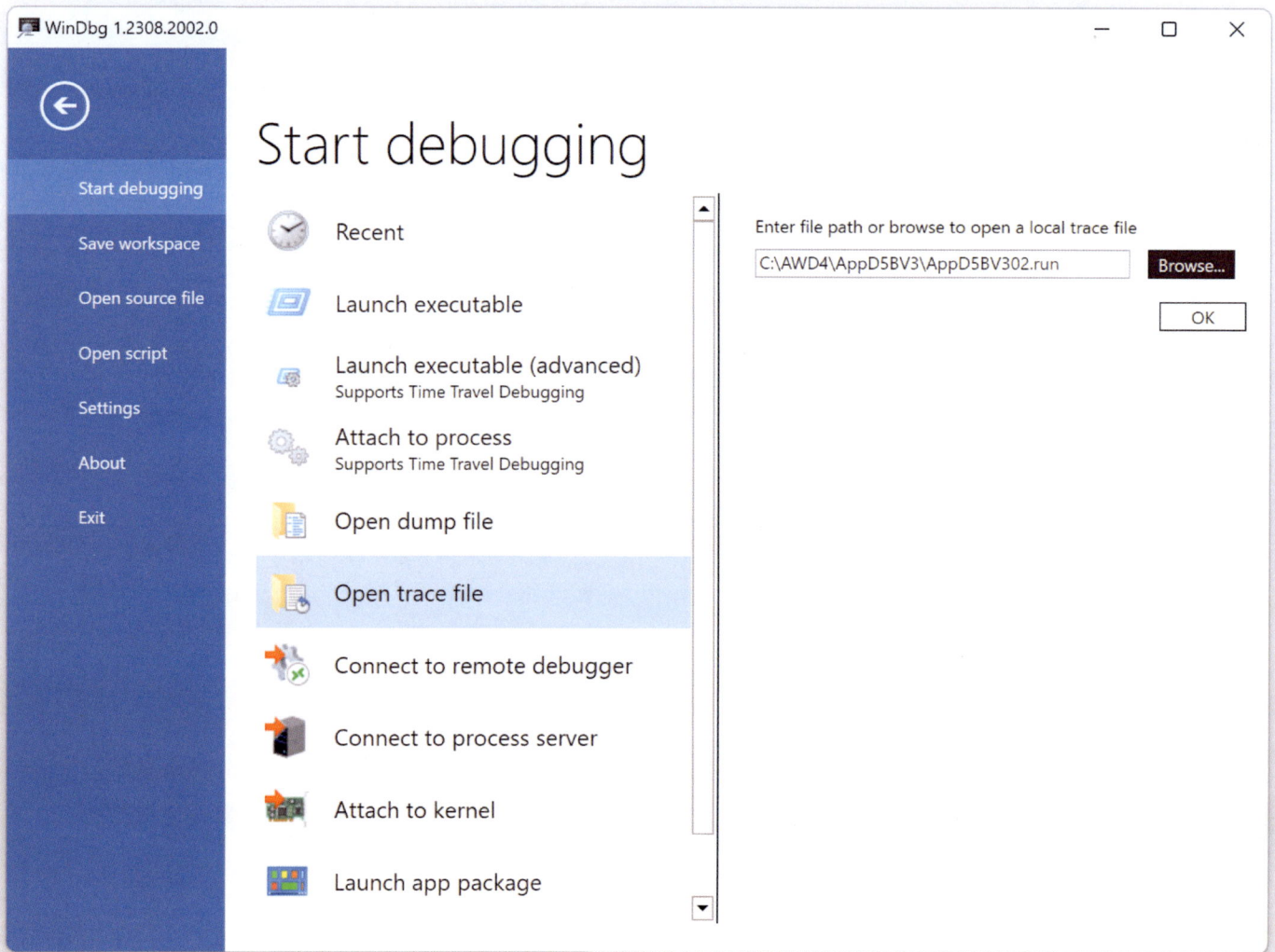

WinDbg 1.2308.2002.0 — □ ×

←

Start debugging

Start debugging

Save workspace

Open source file

Open script

Settings

About

Exit

🕐 Recent

▣ Launch executable

🖼 Launch executable (advanced)
Supports Time Travel Debugging

⚙ Attach to process
Supports Time Travel Debugging

📄 Open dump file

📁 Open trace file

Connect to remote debugger

Connect to process server

Attach to kernel

Launch app package

Enter file path or browse to open a local trace file

C:\AWD4\AppD5BV3\AppD5BV302.run   Browse...

OK

10.   We see the trace file loaded and the *Exceptions* timeline:

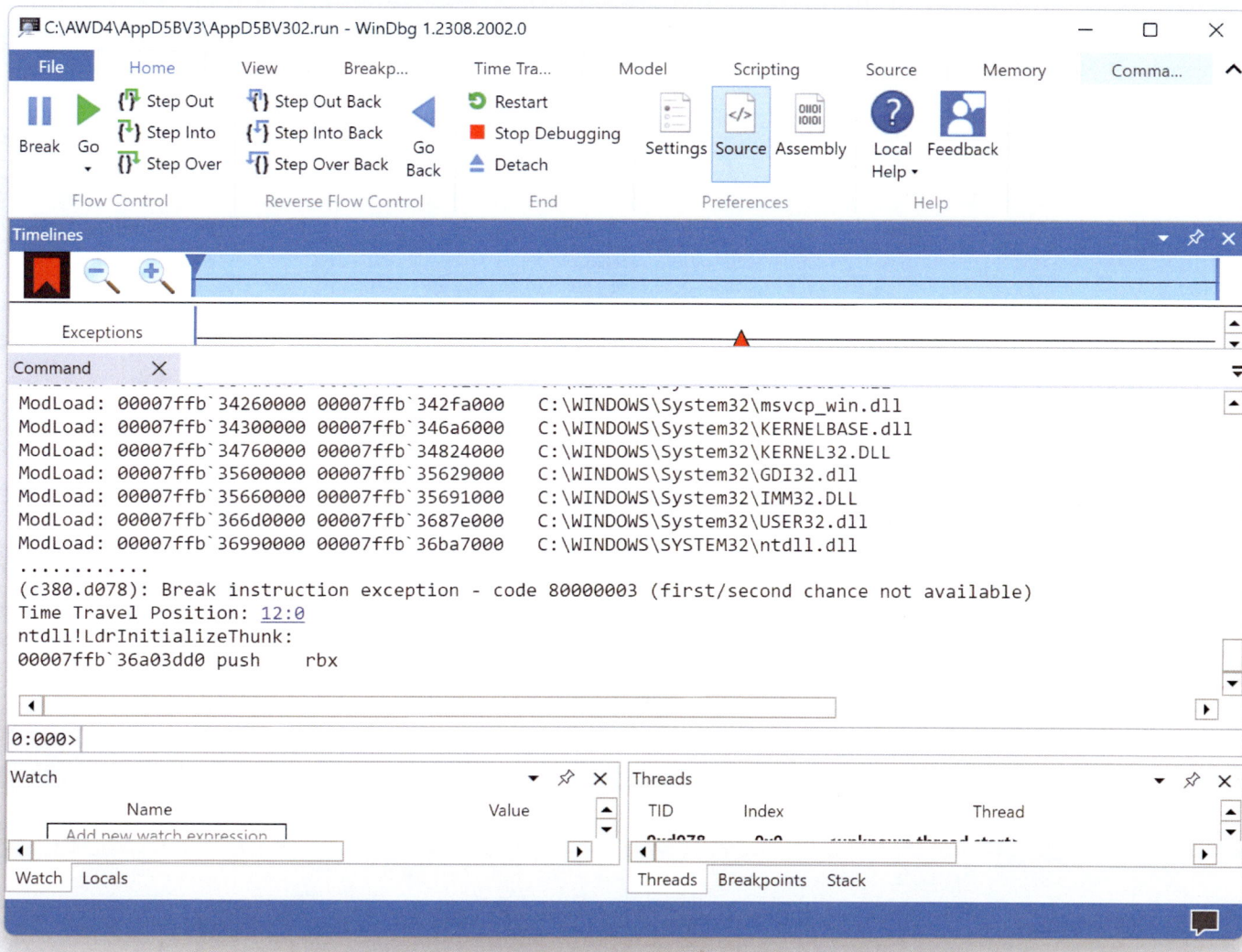

```
Microsoft (R) Windows Debugger Version 10.0.25921.1001 AMD64
Copyright (c) Microsoft Corporation. All rights reserved.


Loading Dump File [C:\AWD4\AppD5BV3\AppD5BV302.run]
JavaScript script successfully loaded from 'C:\Program
Files\WindowsApps\Microsoft.WinDbg_1.2308.2002.0_x64__8wekyb3d8bbwe\amd64\TTD\Analyzers\HeapAnalysis.js'
JavaScript script successfully loaded from 'C:\Program
Files\WindowsApps\Microsoft.WinDbg_1.2308.2002.0_x64__8wekyb3d8bbwe\amd64\TTD\Analyzers\TtdAnalyze.js'

************* Path validation summary **************
Response                      Time (ms)      Location
Deferred                                     srv*
Symbol search path is: srv*
Executable search path is:
ModLoad: 00007ff7`244f0000 00007ff7`24513000    C:\AWD4\AppD5BV3\x64\Release\AppD5BV3.exe
ModLoad: 00007ffa`e9cc0000 00007ffa`e9e3f000
C:\Users\dmitr\AppData\Local\Microsoft\WindowsApps\Microsoft.WinDbg_8wekyb3d8bbwe\amd64\TTD\TTDRecordCPU.dll
ModLoad: 00007ffb`33cd0000 00007ffb`33cf6000    C:\WINDOWS\System32\win32u.dll
ModLoad: 00007ffb`33d00000 00007ffb`33e18000    C:\WINDOWS\System32\gdi32full.dll
ModLoad: 00007ffb`33fd0000 00007ffb`340e1000    C:\WINDOWS\System32\ucrtbase.dll
ModLoad: 00007ffb`34260000 00007ffb`342fa000    C:\WINDOWS\System32\msvcp_win.dll
ModLoad: 00007ffb`34300000 00007ffb`346a6000    C:\WINDOWS\System32\KERNELBASE.dll
ModLoad: 00007ffb`34760000 00007ffb`34824000    C:\WINDOWS\System32\KERNEL32.DLL
ModLoad: 00007ffb`35600000 00007ffb`35629000    C:\WINDOWS\System32\GDI32.dll
ModLoad: 00007ffb`35660000 00007ffb`35691000    C:\WINDOWS\System32\IMM32.DLL
ModLoad: 00007ffb`366d0000 00007ffb`3687e000    C:\WINDOWS\System32\USER32.dll
```

```
ModLoad: 00007ffb`36990000 00007ffb`36ba7000   C:\WINDOWS\SYSTEM32\ntdll.dll
............
(c380.d078): Break instruction exception - code 80000003 (first/second chance not available)
Time Travel Position: 12:0
!index
Successfully created the index in 0ms.

************* Preparing the environment for Debugger Extensions Gallery repositories **************
    ExtensionRepository : Implicit
    UseExperimentalFeatureForNugetShare : false
    AllowNugetExeUpdate : false
    AllowNugetMSCredentialProviderInstall : false
    AllowParallelInitializationOfLocalRepositories : true

    -- Configuring repositories
        ----> Repository : LocalInstalled, Enabled: true
        ----> Repository : UserExtensions, Enabled: true

>>>>>>>>>>>> Preparing the environment for Debugger Extensions Gallery repositories completed, duration 0.000 seconds

************* Waiting for Debugger Extensions Gallery to Initialize **************

>>>>>>>>>>>> Waiting for Debugger Extensions Gallery to Initialize completed, duration 0.047 seconds
        ----> Repository : UserExtensions, Enabled: true, Packages count: 0
        ----> Repository : LocalInstalled, Enabled: true, Packages count: 36

Microsoft (R) Windows Debugger Version 10.0.25921.1001 AMD64
Copyright (c) Microsoft Corporation. All rights reserved.


Loading Dump File [C:\AWD4\AppD5BV3\AppD5BV302.run]
JavaScript script successfully loaded from 'C:\Program
Files\WindowsApps\Microsoft.WinDbg_1.2308.2002.0_x64__8wekyb3d8bbwe\amd64\TTD\Analyzers\HeapAnalysis.js'
JavaScript script successfully loaded from 'C:\Program
Files\WindowsApps\Microsoft.WinDbg_1.2308.2002.0_x64__8wekyb3d8bbwe\amd64\TTD\Analyzers\TtdAnalyze.js'

************* Path validation summary **************
Response                        Time (ms)    Location
Deferred                                     srv*
Symbol search path is: srv*
Executable search path is:
ModLoad: 00007ff7`244f0000 00007ff7`24513000   C:\AWD4\AppD5BV3\x64\Release\AppD5BV3.exe
ModLoad: 00007ffa`e9cc0000 00007ffa`e9e3f000
C:\Users\dmitr\AppData\Local\Microsoft\WindowsApps\Microsoft.WinDbg_8wekyb3d8bbwe\amd64\TTD\TTDRecordCPU.dll
ModLoad: 00007ffb`33cd0000 00007ffb`33cf6000   C:\WINDOWS\System32\win32u.dll
ModLoad: 00007ffb`33d00000 00007ffb`33e18000   C:\WINDOWS\System32\gdi32full.dll
ModLoad: 00007ffb`33fd0000 00007ffb`340e1000   C:\WINDOWS\System32\ucrtbase.dll
ModLoad: 00007ffb`34260000 00007ffb`342fa000   C:\WINDOWS\System32\msvcp_win.dll
ModLoad: 00007ffb`34300000 00007ffb`346a6000   C:\WINDOWS\System32\KERNELBASE.dll
ModLoad: 00007ffb`34760000 00007ffb`34824000   C:\WINDOWS\System32\KERNEL32.DLL
ModLoad: 00007ffb`35600000 00007ffb`35629000   C:\WINDOWS\System32\GDI32.dll
ModLoad: 00007ffb`35660000 00007ffb`35691000   C:\WINDOWS\System32\IMM32.DLL
ModLoad: 00007ffb`366d0000 00007ffb`3687e000   C:\WINDOWS\System32\USER32.dll
ModLoad: 00007ffb`36990000 00007ffb`36ba7000   C:\WINDOWS\SYSTEM32\ntdll.dll
............
(c380.d078): Break instruction exception - code 80000003 (first/second chance not available)
Time Travel Position: 12:0
ntdll!LdrInitializeThunk:
00007ffb`36a03dd0 push    rbx
```

11.   We travel to the exception point by clicking on the red rectangle:

```
0:000> dx @$curprocess.TTD.Events.Where(t => t.Type == "Exception")[0x0].Position.SeekTo()
ModLoad: 00007ffb`35700000 00007ffb`35817000   C:\WINDOWS\System32\RPCRT4.dll
ModLoad: 00007ffb`34d90000 00007ffb`35119000   C:\WINDOWS\System32\combase.dll
ModLoad: 00007ffb`30ba0000 00007ffb`30c4b000   C:\WINDOWS\system32\uxtheme.dll
ModLoad: 00007ffb`34ce0000 00007ffb`34d87000   C:\WINDOWS\System32\msvcrt.dll
ModLoad: 00007ffb`354b0000 00007ffb`35600000   C:\WINDOWS\System32\MSCTF.dll
ModLoad: 00007ffb`1a920000 00007ffb`1a9d0000   C:\WINDOWS\SYSTEM32\TextShaping.dll
ModLoad: 00007ffb`32cc0000 00007ffb`32cd8000   C:\WINDOWS\SYSTEM32\kernel.appcore.dll
ModLoad: 00007ffb`33f50000 00007ffb`33fca000   C:\WINDOWS\System32\bcryptPrimitives.dll
```

```
ModLoad: 00007ffb`346b0000 00007ffb`346d8000   C:\WINDOWS\System32\bcrypt.dll
ModLoad: 00007ffb`34c30000 00007ffb`34cd8000   C:\WINDOWS\System32\sechost.dll
ModLoad: 00007ffb`35120000 00007ffb`351f7000   C:\WINDOWS\System32\OLEAUT32.dll
ModLoad: 00007ffb`21110000 00007ffb`2125a000   C:\WINDOWS\SYSTEM32\textinputframework.dll
ModLoad: 00007ffb`2d590000 00007ffb`2d6c4000   C:\WINDOWS\SYSTEM32\CoreMessaging.dll
ModLoad: 00007ffb`31a90000 00007ffb`31bce000   C:\WINDOWS\SYSTEM32\wintypes.dll
ModLoad: 00007ffb`2a070000 00007ffb`2a3dc000   C:\WINDOWS\SYSTEM32\CoreUIComponents.dll
ModLoad: 00007ffb`353d0000 00007ffb`35483000   C:\WINDOWS\SYSTEM32\advapi32.dll
ModLoad: 00007ffb`33330000 00007ffb`3333c000   C:\WINDOWS\SYSTEM32\CRYPTBASE.DLL
ModLoad: 00007ffb`0cbf0000 00007ffb`0cc59000   C:\WINDOWS\system32\Oleacc.dll
ModLoad: 00007ffb`35310000 00007ffb`353c0000   C:\WINDOWS\System32\clbcatq.dll
ModLoad: 00007ffb`1a4c0000 00007ffb`1a50b000   C:\WINDOWS\system32\ApplicationTargetedFeatureDatabase.dll
ModLoad: 00007ffb`28410000 00007ffb`28695000   C:\Windows\System32\twinapi.appcore.dll
ModLoad: 00007ffb`30fe0000 00007ffb`3100b000   C:\WINDOWS\system32\dwmapi.dll
(c380.d078): Break instruction exception - code 80000003 (first/second chance not available)
Time Travel Position: 286E:0
@$curprocess.TTD.Events.Where(t => t.Type == "Exception")[0x0].Position.SeekTo()
*** WARNING: Unable to verify checksum for AppD5BV3.exe
```

12.   We can now trace backward in time (and forward if necessary) either using commands or GUI:

```
0:000> t-
Time Travel Position: 286D:1F
AppD5BV3!NewFeature+0x4:
00007ff7`244f1504 mov     qword ptr [rsp],0 ss:00000095`47bffa20=0000000000000000


0:000> g-u
Time Travel Position: 286D:1D
AppD5BV3!StartModeling+0x29:
00007ff7`244f1499 call    AppD5BV3!NewFeature (00007ff7`244f1500)


0:000> t-
Time Travel Position: 286D:1C
AppD5BV3!StartModeling+0x28:
00007ff7`244f1498 nop


0:000> t
Time Travel Position: 286D:1D
AppD5BV3!StartModeling+0x29:
00007ff7`244f1499 call    AppD5BV3!NewFeature (00007ff7`244f1500)


0:000> t
Time Travel Position: 286D:1E
AppD5BV3!NewFeature:
00007ff7`244f1500 sub     rsp,18h


0:000> t-
Time Travel Position: 286D:1D
AppD5BV3!StartModeling+0x29:
00007ff7`244f1499 call    AppD5BV3!NewFeature (00007ff7`244f1500)
```

The source code window is updated if the source code path is set:

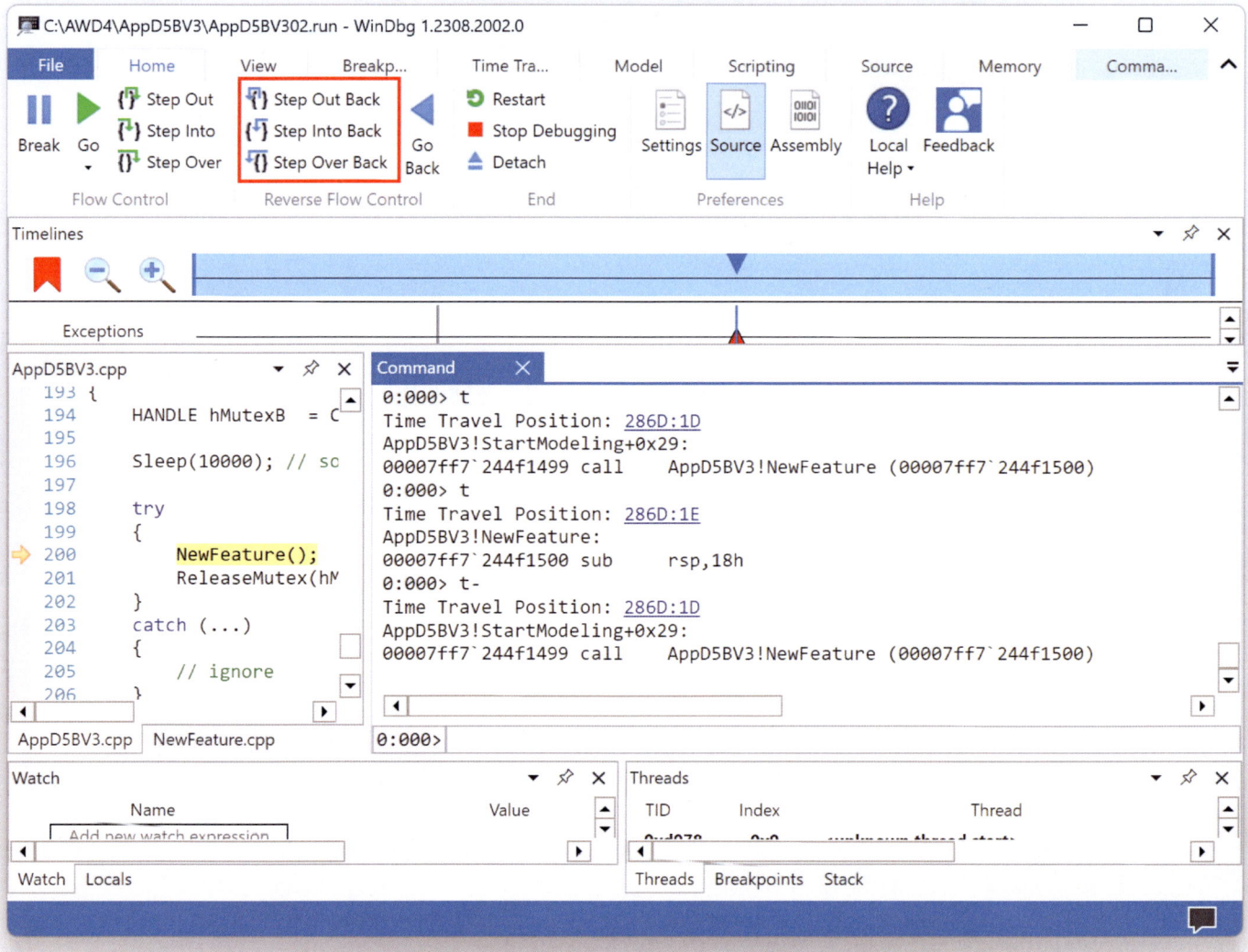

Note: We clearly see the advantage of Time Travel Debugging to preserve past exception information that could be overwritten by subsequent calls and not available later using traditional live and postmortem debugging techniques.

13.   We now quit WinDbg.

Rust Debugging

Exercise RD12

Exercise RD12

- **Goal:** Learn how WinDbg can be used to debug Rust applications

- **Elementary Diagnostics Patterns:** Error Message

- **Memory Analysis Patterns:** Stack Trace

- **Debugging Implementation Patterns:** Break-in; Code Breakpoint; Scope; Variable Value; Type Structure

- \AWD4\Exercise-RD12.pdf

Goal: Learn how WinDbg can be used to debug Rust applications.

Elementary Diagnostics Patterns: Error Message.

Memory Analysis Patterns: Stack Trace.

Debugging Implementation Patterns: Break-in; Code Breakpoint; Scope; Variable Value; Type Structure.

1.   Launch WinDbg. Choose *File \ Launch executable* and select *C:\AWD4\AppR12\target\release\appr12.exe*
executable.

2.   You get the following WinDbg output:

```
Microsoft (R) Windows Debugger Version 10.0.25921.1001 AMD64
Copyright (c) Microsoft Corporation. All rights reserved.

CommandLine: C:\AWD4\AppR12\target\release\appr12.exe

************* Path validation summary **************
Response                        Time (ms)       Location
Deferred                                        srv*
Symbol search path is: srv*
Executable search path is:
ModLoad: 00007ff7`094c0000 00007ff7`094ed000   appr12.exe
ModLoad: 00007ffb`36990000 00007ffb`36ba7000   ntdll.dll
ModLoad: 00007ffb`34760000 00007ffb`34824000   C:\WINDOWS\System32\KERNEL32.DLL
ModLoad: 00007ffb`34300000 00007ffb`346a6000   C:\WINDOWS\System32\KERNELBASE.dll
ModLoad: 00007ffb`366d0000 00007ffb`3687e000   C:\WINDOWS\System32\user32.dll
ModLoad: 00007ffb`33cd0000 00007ffb`33cf6000   C:\WINDOWS\System32\win32u.dll
ModLoad: 00007ffb`35600000 00007ffb`35629000   C:\WINDOWS\System32\GDI32.dll
ModLoad: 00007ffb`33d00000 00007ffb`33e18000   C:\WINDOWS\System32\gdi32full.dll
ModLoad: 00007ffb`34260000 00007ffb`342fa000   C:\WINDOWS\System32\msvcp_win.dll
ModLoad: 00007ffb`33fd0000 00007ffb`340e1000   C:\WINDOWS\System32\ucrtbase.dll
ModLoad: 00007ffb`35120000 00007ffb`351f7000   C:\WINDOWS\System32\oleaut32.dll
ModLoad: 00007ffb`34d90000 00007ffb`35119000   C:\WINDOWS\System32\combase.dll
ModLoad: 00007ffb`35700000 00007ffb`35817000   C:\WINDOWS\System32\RPCRT4.dll
ModLoad: 00007ffb`266b0000 00007ffb`266cb000   C:\WINDOWS\SYSTEM32\VCRUNTIME140.dll
(c1d0.cd08): Break instruction exception - code 80000003 (first chance)
ntdll!LdrpDoDebuggerBreak+0x30:
00007ffb`36a6b784 int     3
```

3.   Open a log file:

```
0:000> .logopen C:\AWD4\RD12.log
Opened log file 'C:\AWD4\RD12.log'
```

4.   Continue execution using the **g** command, switch to the *AppR12* window (there is also a console window with the full application path in its title), and choose *File \ Start*. After approx. 10 seconds we get an error message on the console. Every time we choose the *Start,* we get such a message. We want to know where in the code it is printed.

5.   We switch to WinDbg and break in.

```
0:000> g
ModLoad: 00007ffb`35660000 00007ffb`35691000   C:\WINDOWS\System32\IMM32.DLL
ModLoad: 00007ffb`30ba0000 00007ffb`30c4b000   C:\WINDOWS\system32\uxtheme.dll
ModLoad: 00007ffb`354b0000 00007ffb`35600000   C:\WINDOWS\System32\MSCTF.dll
ModLoad: 00007ffb`34ce0000 00007ffb`34d87000   C:\WINDOWS\System32\msvcrt.dll
ModLoad: 00007ffb`32cc0000 00007ffb`32cd0000   C:\WINDOWS\SYSTEM32\kernel.appcore.dll
ModLoad: 00007ffb`33f50000 00007ffb`33fca000   C:\WINDOWS\System32\bcryptPrimitives.dll
clientcore\windows\advcore\ctf\uim\tim.cpp(800)\MSCTF.dll!00007FFB354C65D9: (caller: 00007FFB354C720C) LogHr(1)
tid(cd08) 8007029C An assertion failure has occurred.
clientcore\windows\advcore\ctf\uim\tim.cpp(800)\MSCTF.dll!00007FFB354C65D9: (caller: 00007FFB354C720C) LogHr(2)
tid(cd08) 8007029C An assertion failure has occurred.
ModLoad: 00007ffb`34c30000 00007ffb`34cd8000   C:\WINDOWS\System32\sechost.dll
ModLoad: 00007ffb`346b0000 00007ffb`346d8000   C:\WINDOWS\System32\bcrypt.dll
ModLoad: 00007ffb`21110000 00007ffb`2125a000   C:\WINDOWS\SYSTEM32\textinputframework.dll
ModLoad: 00007ffb`2d590000 00007ffb`2d6c4000   C:\WINDOWS\SYSTEM32\CoreMessaging.dll
ModLoad: 00007ffb`2a070000 00007ffb`2a3dc000   C:\WINDOWS\SYSTEM32\CoreUIComponents.dll
ModLoad: 00007ffb`31a90000 00007ffb`31bce000   C:\WINDOWS\SYSTEM32\wintypes.dll
ModLoad: 00007ffb`353d0000 00007ffb`35483000   C:\WINDOWS\System32\advapi32.dll
ModLoad: 00007ffb`33330000 00007ffb`3333c000   C:\WINDOWS\SYSTEM32\CRYPTBASE.DLL
ModLoad: 00007ffb`0cbf0000 00007ffb`0cc59000   C:\WINDOWS\system32\Oleacc.dll
ModLoad: 00007ffb`1a920000 00007ffb`1a9d0000   C:\WINDOWS\SYSTEM32\TextShaping.dll
ModLoad: 00007ffb`35310000 00007ffb`353c0000   C:\WINDOWS\System32\clbcatq.dll
ModLoad: 00007ffb`1a4c0000 00007ffb`1a50b000   C:\WINDOWS\system32\ApplicationTargetedFeatureDatabase.dll
ModLoad: 00007ffb`28410000 00007ffb`28695000   C:\Windows\System32\twinapi.appcore.dll
ModLoad: 00007ffb`00cb0000 00007ffb`010f5000   C:\Windows\System32\uiautomationcore.dll
ModLoad: 00007ffb`30fe0000 00007ffb`3100b000   C:\Windows\System32\dwmapi.dll
ModLoad: 00007ffb`0e8d0000 00007ffb`0e8e5000   C:\Windows\System32\threadpoolwinrt.dll
(c1d0.381c): C++ EH exception - code e06d7363 (first chance)
(c1d0.381c): C++ EH exception - code e06d7363 (first chance)
(c1d0.381c): C++ EH exception - code e06d7363 (first chance)
(c1d0.381c): C++ EH exception - code e06d7363 (first chance)
(c1d0.381c): C++ EH exception - code e06d7363 (first chance)
(c1d0.381c): C++ EH exception - code e06d7363 (first chance)
(c1d0.381c): C++ EH exception - code e06d7363 (first chance)
(c1d0.381c): C++ EH exception - code e06d7363 (first chance)
(c1d0.381c): C++ EH exception - code e06d7363 (first chance)
(c1d0.381c): C++ EH exception - code e06d7363 (first chance)
(c1d0.381c): C++ EH exception - code e06d7363 (first chance)
(c1d0.381c): C++ EH exception - code e06d7363 (first chance)
(c1d0.381c): C++ EH exception - code e06d7363 (first chance)
(c1d0.381c): C++ EH exception - code e06d7363 (first chance)
(c1d0.381c): C++ EH exception - code e06d7363 (first chance)
(c1d0.381c): C++ EH exception - code e06d7363 (first chance)
(c1d0.381c): C++ EH exception - code e06d7363 (first chance)
(c1d0.381c): C++ EH exception - code e06d7363 (first chance)
(c1d0.381c): C++ EH exception - code e06d7363 (first chance)
(c1d0.381c): C++ EH exception - code e06d7363 (first chance)
(c1d0.381c): C++ EH exception - code e06d7363 (first chance)
(c1d0.381c): C++ EH exception - code e06d7363 (first chance)
(c1d0.381c): C++ EH exception - code e06d7363 (first chance)
(c1d0.381c): C++ EH exception - code e06d7363 (first chance)
(c1d0.381c): C++ EH exception - code e06d7363 (first chance)
(c1d0.7300): Break instruction exception - code 80000003 (first chance)
ntdll!DbgBreakPoint:
00007ffb`36a33060 int     3
```

6.   Because the error message is printed on the console we put a breakpoint on all possible *WriteConsole* functions:

```
0:001> bm *!*WriteConsole*
  0: 00007ffb`3433d668 @!"KERNELBASE!WriteConsoleInternal"
  1: 00007ffb`3433d640 @!"KERNELBASE!WriteConsoleW"
  2: 00007ffb`343b4114 @!"KERNELBASE!WriteConsoleOutputInternal"
```

```
 3: 00007ffb`343b5b90 @!"KERNELBASE!WriteConsoleOutputString"
 4: 00007ffb`343cf970 @!"KERNELBASE!WriteConsoleOutputCharacterA"
 5: 00007ffb`344475dc @!"KERNELBASE!WriteConsoleInputInternal"
 6: 00007ffb`344476e0 @!"KERNELBASE!WriteConsoleOutputAttribute"
 7: 00007ffb`343b5b60 @!"KERNELBASE!WriteConsoleOutputCharacterW"
 8: 00007ffb`344476b0 @!"KERNELBASE!WriteConsoleOutputA"
 9: 00007ffb`343b40f0 @!"KERNELBASE!WriteConsoleOutputW"
10: 00007ffb`34447690 @!"KERNELBASE!WriteConsoleInputW"
11: 00007ffb`344483d0 @!"KERNELBASE!WriteConsoleA"
12: 00007ffb`344475c0 @!"KERNELBASE!WriteConsoleInputA"
13: 00007ffb`34780f60 @!"KERNEL32!WriteConsoleOutputCharacterA"
14: 00007ffb`34780f50 @!"KERNEL32!WriteConsoleOutputAttribute"
15: 00007ffb`34780f70 @!"KERNEL32!WriteConsoleOutputCharacterW"
16: 00007ffb`34780f40 @!"KERNEL32!WriteConsoleOutputA"
17: 00007ffb`34780f80 @!"KERNEL32!WriteConsoleOutputW"
18: 00007ffb`34780f30 @!"KERNEL32!WriteConsoleInputW"
19: 00007ffb`34780d00 @!"KERNEL32!WriteConsoleA"
20: 00007ffb`34780f20 @!"KERNEL32!WriteConsoleInputA"
21: 00007ffb`34780d10 @!"KERNEL32!WriteConsoleW"
22: 00007ffb`347cb8e0 @!"KERNEL32!WriteConsoleInputVDMA"
23: 00007ffb`347cb970 @!"KERNEL32!WriteConsoleInputVDMW"
```

7.   We resume, switch to the *AppR12* window, and choose *File \ Start* again. After approx. 10 seconds, we see a breakpoint hit:

```
0:001> g
(c1d0.381c): C++ EH exception - code e06d7363 (first chance)
(c1d0.381c): C++ EH exception - code e06d7363 (first chance)
(c1d0.381c): C++ EH exception - code e06d7363 (first chance)
(c1d0.381c): C++ EH exception - code e06d7363 (first chance)
(c1d0.381c): C++ EH exception - code e06d7363 (first chance)
(c1d0.381c): C++ EH exception - code e06d7363 (first chance)
Breakpoint 21 hit
KERNEL32!WriteConsoleW:
00007ffb`34780d10 jmp      qword ptr [KERNEL32!_imp_WriteConsoleW (00007ffb`347e4020)]
ds:00007ffb`347e4020={KERNELBASE!WriteConsoleW (00007ffb`3433d640)}
```

8.   From the stack trace, we see where it was called from:

```
0:006> kL
 # Child-SP          RetAddr               Call Site
00 0000005a`730fd908 00007ff7`094cdd6b     KERNEL32!WriteConsoleW
01 (Inline Function) --------`--------     appr12!std::sys::windows::stdio::write_u16s+0x27
02 0000005a`730fd910 00007ff7`094cdb58     appr12!std::sys::windows::stdio::write_valid_utf8_to_console+0xbb
03 0000005a`730ff9b0 00007ff7`094c8201     appr12!std::sys::windows::stdio::write+0x1e8
04 (Inline Function) --------`--------     appr12!std::sys::windows::stdio::impl$5::write+0x18
05 0000005a`730ffa90 00007ff7`094c79f1     appr12!std::io::Write::write_all<std::sys::windows::stdio::Stdout>+0x71
06 0000005a`730ffb10 00007ff7`094c8afe     appr12!std::io::stdio::impl$13::write_all+0xf1
07 0000005a`730ffb90 00007ff7`094d8a13
appr12!std::io::Write::write_fmt::impl$0::write_str<std::io::stdio::StdoutLock>+0x1e
08 0000005a`730ffbe0 00007ff7`094c7825     appr12!core::fmt::write+0x1f3
09 (Inline Function) --------`--------     appr12!std::io::Write::write_fmt+0x1f
0a 0000005a`730ffc90 00007ff7`094c8083     appr12!std::io::stdio::impl$12::write_fmt+0xa5
0b (Inline Function) --------`--------     appr12!std::io::stdio::impl$11::write_fmt+0x10
0c (Inline Function) --------`--------     appr12!std::io::stdio::print_to+0x34
0d 0000005a`730ffcf0 00007ff7`094c1f93     appr12!std::io::stdio::_print+0x63
0e (Inline Function) --------`--------     appr12!appr12::foo+0x3f
0f (Inline Function) --------`--------     appr12!appr12::start_modeling::closure$0+0x3f
10 0000005a`730ffda0 00007ff7`094c1969
appr12!std::sys_common::backtrace::__rust_begin_short_backtrace<appr12::start_modeling::closure_env$0,tuple$<> >+0x43
11 (Inline Function) --------`--------     appr12!std::thread::impl$0::spawn_unchecked_::closure$1::closure$0+0x11
```

```
12 (Inline Function) --------`--------     appr12!core::panic::unwind_safe::impl$23::call_once+0x11
13 (Inline Function) --------`--------     appr12!std::panicking::try::do_call+0x11
14 (Inline Function) --------`--------     appr12!std::panicking::try+0x11
15 (Inline Function) --------`--------     appr12!std::panic::catch_unwind+0x11
16 (Inline Function) --------`--------     appr12!std::thread::impl$0::spawn_unchecked_::closure$1+0x88
17 0000005a`730ffe00 00007ff7`094ce10c
appr12!core::ops::function::FnOnce::call_once<std::thread::impl$0::spawn_unchecked_::closure_env$1<appr12::start_model
ing::closure_env$0,tuple$<> >,tuple$<> >+0xa9
18 0000005a`730ffea0 00007ffb`3477257d     appr12!std::sys::windows::thread::impl$0::new::thread_start+0x4c
19 0000005a`730fff30 00007ffb`369eaa58     KERNEL32!BaseThreadInitThunk+0x1d
1a 0000005a`730fff60 00000000`00000000     ntdll!RtlUserThreadStart+0x28
```

9.   We set the source code location and set the current stack trace frame to **0e**:

```
0:006> .srcpath+ C:\AWD4\AppR12\src
Source search path is: SRV*;C:\AWD4\AppR12\src

************* Path validation summary **************
Response                        Time (ms)      Location
Deferred                                       SRV*
OK                                             C:\AWD4\AppR12\src
```

```
0:006> .frame e
0e (Inline Function) --------`--------     appr12!appr12::foo+0x3f [C:\AWD4\AppR12\src\main.rs
@ 89]
```

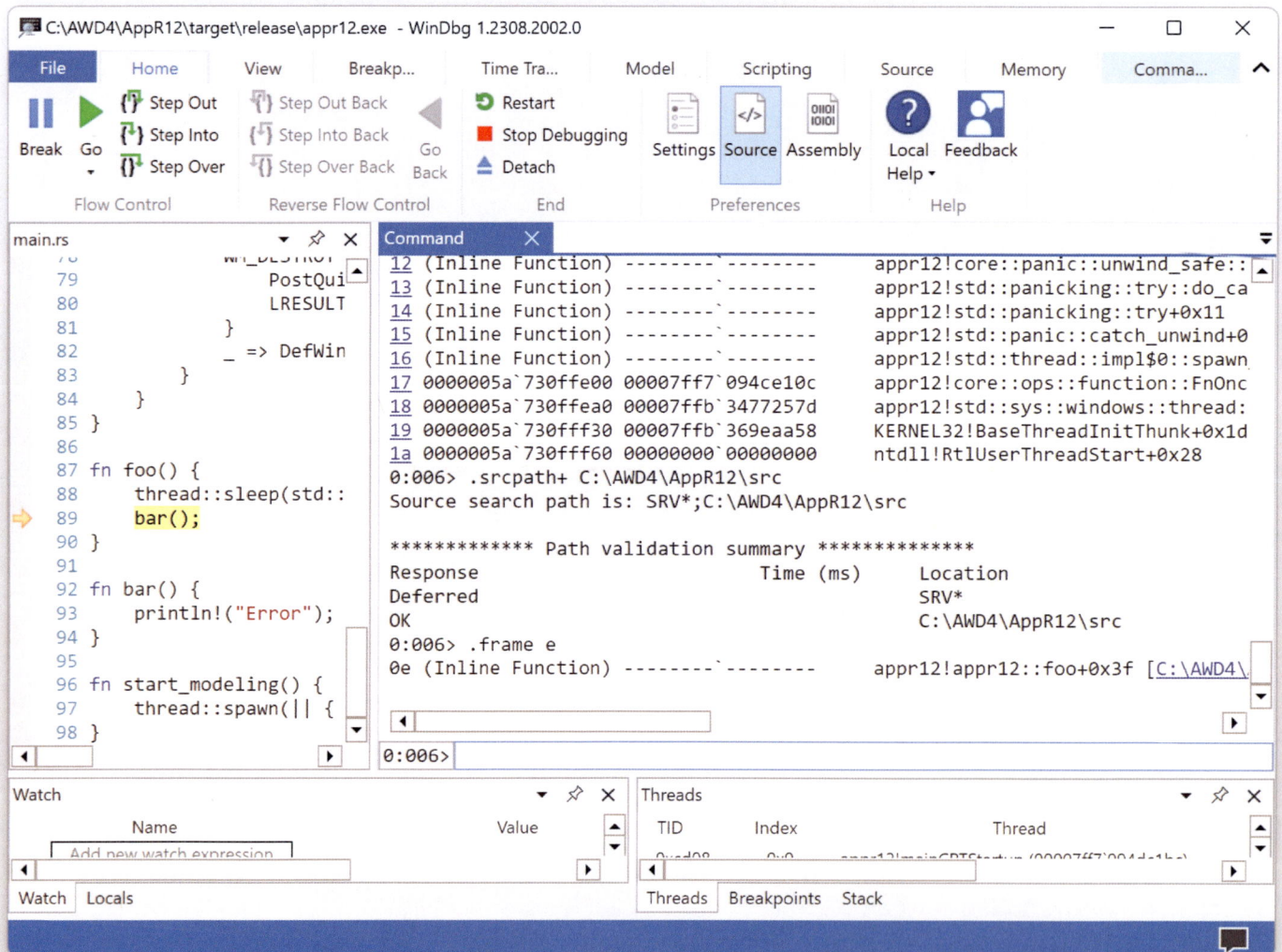

10. We navigate to the *main* function and put a breakpoint at the line 19:

11. We then restart:

```
0:006> .restart
NatVis script unloaded from 'C:\Program
Files\WindowsApps\Microsoft.WinDbg_1.2308.2002.0_x64__8wekyb3d8bbwe\amd64\Visualizers\atlmfc.natvis'
NatVis script unloaded from 'C:\Program
Files\WindowsApps\Microsoft.WinDbg_1.2308.2002.0_x64__8wekyb3d8bbwe\amd64\Visualizers\ObjectiveC.natvis'
NatVis script unloaded from 'C:\Program
Files\WindowsApps\Microsoft.WinDbg_1.2308.2002.0_x64__8wekyb3d8bbwe\amd64\Visualizers\concurrency.natvis'
NatVis script unloaded from 'C:\Program
Files\WindowsApps\Microsoft.WinDbg_1.2308.2002.0_x64__8wekyb3d8bbwe\amd64\Visualizers\cpp_rest.natvis'
NatVis script unloaded from 'C:\Program
Files\WindowsApps\Microsoft.WinDbg_1.2308.2002.0_x64__8wekyb3d8bbwe\amd64\Visualizers\stl.natvis'
NatVis script unloaded from 'C:\Program
Files\WindowsApps\Microsoft.WinDbg_1.2308.2002.0_x64__8wekyb3d8bbwe\amd64\Visualizers\Windows.Data.Json.natvis'
NatVis script unloaded from 'C:\Program
Files\WindowsApps\Microsoft.WinDbg_1.2308.2002.0_x64__8wekyb3d8bbwe\amd64\Visualizers\Windows.Devices.Geolocation.natv
is'
NatVis script unloaded from 'C:\Program
Files\WindowsApps\Microsoft.WinDbg_1.2308.2002.0_x64__8wekyb3d8bbwe\amd64\Visualizers\Windows.Devices.Sensors.natvis'
NatVis script unloaded from 'C:\Program
Files\WindowsApps\Microsoft.WinDbg_1.2308.2002.0_x64__8wekyb3d8bbwe\amd64\Visualizers\Windows.Media.natvis'
NatVis script unloaded from 'C:\Program
Files\WindowsApps\Microsoft.WinDbg_1.2308.2002.0_x64__8wekyb3d8bbwe\amd64\Visualizers\windows.natvis'
```

```
NatVis script unloaded from 'C:\Program
Files\WindowsApps\Microsoft.WinDbg_1.2308.2002.0_x64__8wekyb3d8bbwe\amd64\Visualizers\winrt.natvis'

************* Preparing the environment for Debugger Extensions Gallery repositories **************
   ExtensionRepository : Implicit
   UseExperimentalFeatureForNugetShare : false
   AllowNugetExeUpdate : false
   AllowNugetMSCredentialProviderInstall : false
   AllowParallelInitializationOfLocalRepositories : true

   -- Configuring repositories
      ----> Repository : LocalInstalled, Enabled: true
      ----> Repository : UserExtensions, Enabled: true

>>>>>>>>>>>>> Preparing the environment for Debugger Extensions Gallery repositories completed, duration 0.000 seconds

************* Waiting for Debugger Extensions Gallery to Initialize **************

>>>>>>>>>>>>> Waiting for Debugger Extensions Gallery to Initialize completed, duration 0.047 seconds
      ----> Repository : UserExtensions, Enabled: true, Packages count: 0
      ----> Repository : LocalInstalled, Enabled: true, Packages count: 36
```

Microsoft (R) Windows Debugger Version 10.0.25921.1001 AMD64
Copyright (c) Microsoft Corporation. All rights reserved.

CommandLine: C:\AWD4\AppR12\target\release\appr12.exe

************* Path validation summary **************
Response   Time (ms)   Location
Deferred   srv*
Symbol search path is: srv*
Executable search path is:
ModLoad: 00007ff7`094c0000 00007ff7`094ed000   appr12.exe
ModLoad: 00007ffb`36990000 00007ffb`36ba7000   ntdll.dll
ModLoad: 00007ffb`34760000 00007ffb`34824000   C:\WINDOWS\System32\KERNEL32.DLL
ModLoad: 00007ffb`34300000 00007ffb`346a6000   C:\WINDOWS\System32\KERNELBASE.dll
ModLoad: 00007ffb`366d0000 00007ffb`3687e000   C:\WINDOWS\System32\user32.dll
ModLoad: 00007ffb`33cd0000 00007ffb`33cf6000   C:\WINDOWS\System32\win32u.dll
ModLoad: 00007ffb`35600000 00007ffb`35629000   C:\WINDOWS\System32\GDI32.dll
ModLoad: 00007ffb`33d00000 00007ffb`33e18000   C:\WINDOWS\System32\gdi32full.dll
ModLoad: 00007ffb`34260000 00007ffb`342fa000   C:\WINDOWS\System32\msvcp_win.dll
ModLoad: 00007ffb`33fd0000 00007ffb`340e1000   C:\WINDOWS\System32\ucrtbase.dll
ModLoad: 00007ffb`35120000 00007ffb`351f7000   C:\WINDOWS\System32\oleaut32.dll
ModLoad: 00007ffb`34d90000 00007ffb`35119000   C:\WINDOWS\System32\combase.dll
ModLoad: 00007ffb`35700000 00007ffb`35817000   C:\WINDOWS\System32\RPCRT4.dll
ModLoad: 00007ffb`266b0000 00007ffb`266cb000   C:\WINDOWS\SYSTEM32\VCRUNTIME140.dll
(c954.cbfc): Break instruction exception - code 80000003 (first chance)
ntdll!LdrpDoDebuggerBreak+0x30:
00007ffb`36a6b784 int   3
```

12.      Then we resume execution, hit the breakpoint, and execute one line:

```
0:000> g
ModLoad: 00007ffb`35660000 00007ffb`35691000   C:\WINDOWS\System32\IMM32.DLL
Breakpoint 24 hit
appr12!appr12::main+0x4d:
00007ff7`094c260d mov       dword ptr [rsp+68h],3   ss:000000e7`5154f728=00000000

0:000> p
   could step in/over inline function frames ...
01 000000e7`5154f6c0 00007ff7`094c1f3a   appr12!appr12::main+0xb2 [C:\AWD4\AppR12\src\main.rs @ 28]
appr12!appr12::main+0xb2:
```
```

```
00007ff7`094c2672 call     qword ptr [appr12!_imp_RegisterClassW (00007ff7`094de348)]
ds:00007ff7`094de348={user32!RegisterClassW (00007ffb`366df130)}
```

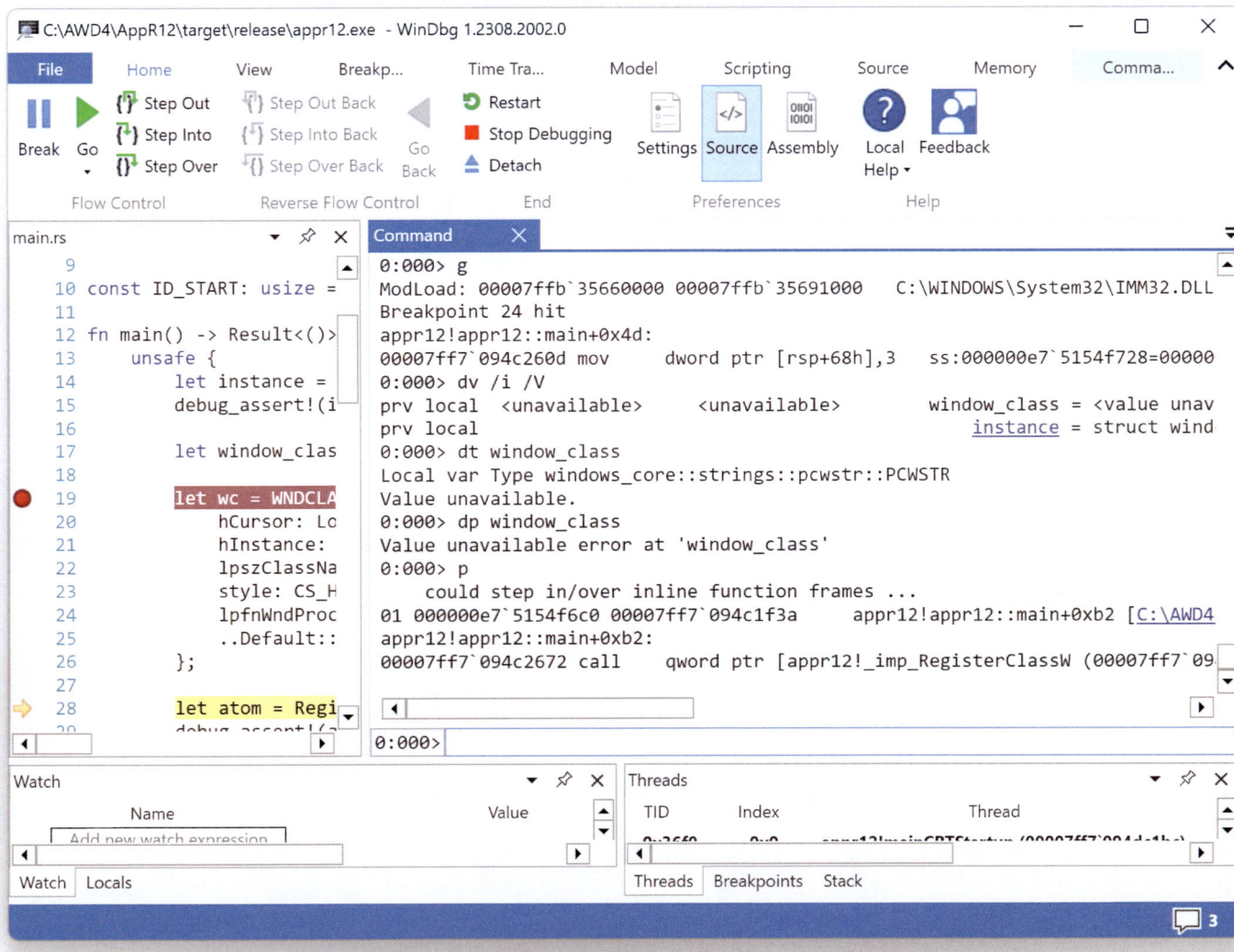

13.   We can also inspect local variables and their values:

```
0:000> dv /i /V
prv local   000000e7`5154f728 @rsp+0x0068            wc = struct windows::Win32::UI::WindowsAndMessaging::WNDCLASSW
prv local   <unavailable>     <unavailable>          window_class = <value unavailable>
prv local                                            instance = struct windows::Win32::Foundation::HMODULE
```

```
0:000> dt -r wc
Local var @ 0xe75154f728 Type windows::Win32::UI::WindowsAndMessaging::WNDCLASSW
   +0x000 style            : windows::Win32::UI::WindowsAndMessaging::WNDCLASS_STYLES
      +0x000 __0          : 3
   +0x008 lpfnWndProc      : enum2$<core::option::Option<windows::Win32::Foundation::LRESULT
(*)(windows::Win32::Foundation::HWND,u32,windows::Win32::Foundation::WPARAM,windows::Win32::Foundation::LPARAM)> >
      +0x000 variant0      : enum2$<core::option::Option<windows::Win32::Foundation::LRESULT
(*)(windows::Win32::Foundation::HWND,u32,windows::Win32::Foundation::WPARAM,windows::Win32::Foundation::LPARAM)>
>::Variant0
         +0x000 value      : enum2$<core::option::Option<windows::Win32::Foundation::LRESULT
(*)(windows::Win32::Foundation::HWND,u32,windows::Win32::Foundation::WPARAM,windows::Win32::Foundation::LPARAM)>
>::None
      +0x000 variant1      : enum2$<core::option::Option<windows::Win32::Foundation::LRESULT
(*)(windows::Win32::Foundation::HWND,u32,windows::Win32::Foundation::WPARAM,windows::Win32::Foundation::LPARAM)>
>::Variant1
```

```
       +0x000 value             : enum2$<core::option::Option<windows::Win32::Foundation::LRESULT
(*)(windows::Win32::Foundation::HWND,u32,windows::Win32::Foundation::WPARAM,windows::Win32::Foundation::LPARAM)>
>::Some
          +0x000 tag            : 0x00007ff7`094c27d0
    +0x010 cbClsExtra           : 0n0
    +0x014 cbWndExtra           : 0n0
    +0x018 hInstance            : windows::Win32::Foundation::HINSTANCE
       +0x000 __0               : 0n140698989625344
    +0x020 hIcon                : windows::Win32::UI::WindowsAndMessaging::HICON
       +0x000 __0               : 0n0
    +0x028 hCursor              : windows::Win32::UI::WindowsAndMessaging::HCURSOR
       +0x000 __0               : 0n65539
    +0x030 hbrBackground        : windows::Win32::Graphics::Gdi::HBRUSH
       +0x000 __0               : 0n0
    +0x038 lpszMenuName         : windows_core::strings::pcwstr::PCWSTR
       +0x000 __0               : (null)
    +0x040 lpszClassName        : windows_core::strings::pcwstr::PCWSTR
       +0x000 __0               : 0x00007ff7`094de6a8  -> 0x41
```

`0:000> ln 0x00007ff7`094c27d0`

Browse module
Set bu breakpoint

```
 [C:\AWD4\AppR12\src\main.rs @ 62] (00007ff7`094c27d0)    appr12!appr12::wndproc   |
(00007ff7`094c28b0)    appr12!main
Exact matches:
    appr12!appr12::wndproc (struct windows::Win32::Foundation::HWND, unsigned int, struct
windows::Win32::Foundation::WPARAM, struct windows::Win32::Foundation::LPARAM)
```

14.   We now quit WinDbg.

Postmortem Debugging

- ⊚ Memory dump collection

  - **.dump** / **.dumpcab** WinDbg commands
  - External methods

- ⊚ Training

  - Accelerated Windows Memory Dump Analysis
  - Advanced Windows Memory Dump Analysis
  - Accelerated .NET Core Memory Dump Analysis
  - Accelerated Rust Windows Memory Dump Analysis

A few words about postmortem debugging using crash dumps: most of the time, memory analysis patterns are the same. However, crash and hang memory dump analysis is also used to analyze abnormal software behavior when we don't have the source code, and we need to analyze multiple processes and services and their relations because we don't know who caused the problem. We can save a process memory dump from user mode WinDbg using the **.dump** command (please refer to its documentation. The **.dumpcab** command allows you to pack the dump with the current symbols), and also you can save a complete physical memory dump during kernel mode debugging using the same **.dump** command.

External methods
https://www.patterndiagnostics.com/files/LegacyWindowsDebugging.pdf

Accelerated Windows Memory Dump Analysis
https://www.patterndiagnostics.com/accelerated-windows-memory-dump-analysis-book

Advanced Windows Memory Dump Analysis
https://www.patterndiagnostics.com/advanced-windows-memory-dump-analysis-book

Accelerated .NET Core Memory Dump Analysis:

https://www.patterndiagnostics.com/accelerated-net-memory-dump-analysis-book

Accelerated Rust Windows Memory Dump Analysis:

https://www.patterndiagnostics.com/accelerated-rust-windows-memory-dump-analysis

Additional Training for Debugging

- Accelerated Windows API for Software Diagnostics

- Accelerated C & C++ for Windows Diagnostics

- Accelerated Disassembly, Reconstruction and Reversing

- Memory Thinking for Rust

Accelerated Windows API for Software Diagnostics

https://www.patterndiagnostics.com/accelerated-windows-api-book

Accelerated C & C++ for Windows Diagnostics

https://www.patterndiagnostics.com/accelerated-c-cpp-windows-diagnostics

Accelerated Disassembly, Reconstruction and Reversing

https://www.patterndiagnostics.com/accelerated-disassembly-reconstruction-reversing-book

Memory Thinking for Rust

https://www.patterndiagnostics.com/memory-thinking-rust

Analysis Pattern Links

Spiking Thread	CLR Thread
Debugger Bug	Exception Stack Trace
Hidden Exception (User Space)	Handled Exception (User Space)
Execution Residue (Managed Space)	Managed Code Exception
Managed Stack Trace	NULL Pointer (Data)
NULL Pointer (Code)	Dynamic Memory Corruption (Process Heap)
Stack Overflow (User Mode)	Rough Stack Trace (Unmanaged Space)
Deadlock (Objects, User Space)	Virtualized Process (WOW64)
Message Box	Memory Leak (Process Heap)
String Parameter	Wait Chain (Mutex Objects)
Handle Leak	Historical Information
Abnormal Value	Counter Value
Module Variable	Deadlock (Managed Space)
JIT Code	Hidden Exception (Managed Space)
Unloaded Module	Corrupt Structure
Main Thread	Execution Residue (Unmanaged Space, User)
Near Exception	

Here are links to pattern descriptions and additional examples from the memory analysis pattern catalog we used for software diagnostics (also available in **Memory Dump Analysis Anthology** volumes or **Encyclopedia of Crash Dump Analysis Patterns**).

Spiking Thread
https://www.dumpanalysis.org/blog/index.php/2007/05/11/crash-dump-analysis-patterns-part-14/

CLR Thread
https://www.dumpanalysis.org/blog/index.php/2009/12/07/crash-dump-analysis-patterns-part-95/

Debugger Bug
https://www.dumpanalysis.org/blog/index.php/2011/12/11/crash-dump-analysis-patterns-part-160/

Exception Stack Trace
https://www.dumpanalysis.org/blog/index.php/2010/08/05/crash-dump-analysis-patterns-part-105/

Hidden Exception (User Space)
https://www.dumpanalysis.org/blog/index.php/2007/02/02/crash-dump-analysis-patterns-part-8/

Handled Exception (User Space)
https://www.dumpanalysis.org/blog/index.php/2011/10/17/crash-dump-analysis-patterns-part-152a/

Execution Residue (Managed Space)
https://www.dumpanalysis.org/blog/index.php/2011/10/17/crash-dump-analysis-patterns-part-60b/

Managed Code Exception
https://www.dumpanalysis.org/blog/index.php/2007/07/20/crash-dump-analysis-patterns-part-17/

Managed Stack Trace
https://www.dumpanalysis.org/blog/index.php/2011/06/17/crash-dump-analysis-patterns-part-139/

NULL Pointer (Data)
https://www.dumpanalysis.org/blog/index.php/2009/04/14/crash-dump-analysis-patterns-part-6b/

NULL Pointer (Code)
https://www.dumpanalysis.org/blog/index.php/2008/04/28/crash-dump-analysis-patterns-part-6a/

Dynamic Memory Corruption (Process Heap)
https://www.dumpanalysis.org/blog/index.php/2006/10/31/crash-dump-analysis-patterns-part-2/

Stack Overflow (User Mode)
https://www.dumpanalysis.org/blog/index.php/2008/06/10/crash-dump-analysis-patterns-part-16b/

Rough Stack Trace (Unmanaged Space)
https://www.dumpanalysis.org/blog/index.php/2014/10/07/crash-dump-analysis-patterns-part-213/

Deadlock (Objects, User Space)
https://www.dumpanalysis.org/blog/index.php/2007/07/28/crash-dump-analysis-patterns-part-9c/

Virtualized Process (WOW64)
https://www.dumpanalysis.org/blog/index.php/2007/09/11/crash-dump-analysis-patterns-part-26/

Message Box
https://www.dumpanalysis.org/blog/index.php/2008/02/19/crash-dump-analysis-patterns-part-51/

Memory Leak (Process Heap)
https://www.dumpanalysis.org/blog/index.php/2007/08/06/crash-dump-analysis-patterns-part-20a/

String Parameter
https://www.dumpanalysis.org/blog/index.php/2010/12/02/crash-dump-analysis-patterns-part-118/

Handle Leak
https://www.dumpanalysis.org/blog/index.php/2012/12/23/crash-dump-analysis-patterns-part-189/

Historical Information
https://www.dumpanalysis.org/blog/index.php/2007/11/06/crash-dump-analysis-patterns-part-34/

Abnormal Value
https://www.dumpanalysis.org/blog/index.php/2013/03/23/trace-analysis-patterns-part-68/

Counter Value
https://www.dumpanalysis.org/blog/index.php/2012/06/23/trace-analysis-patterns-part-51/

Module Variable
https://www.dumpanalysis.org/blog/index.php/2011/12/03/crash-dump-analysis-patterns-part-157/

Deadlock (Managed Space)
https://www.dumpanalysis.org/blog/index.php/2011/10/17/crash-dump-analysis-patterns-part-9g/

JIT Code
https://www.dumpanalysis.org/blog/index.php/2009/05/15/crash-dump-analysis-patterns-part-84/

Hidden Exception (Managed Space)
https://www.dumpanalysis.org/blog/index.php/2018/08/11/crash-dump-analysis-patterns-part-8c/

Unloaded Module
https://www.dumpanalysis.org/blog/index.php/2012/06/27/crash-dump-analysis-patterns-part-178/

Corrupt Structure
https://www.dumpanalysis.org/blog/index.php/2015/02/21/crash-dump-analysis-patterns-part-221/

Main Thread
https://www.dumpanalysis.org/blog/index.php/2007/10/23/crash-dump-analysis-patterns-part-32/

Execution Residue (Unmanaged Space, User)
https://www.dumpanalysis.org/blog/index.php/2008/04/29/crash-dump-analysis-patterns-part-60/

Wait Chain (Mutex Objects)
https://www.dumpanalysis.org/blog/index.php/2011/10/13/crash-dump-analysis-part-42j/

Near Exception
https://www.dumpanalysis.org/blog/index.php/2024/02/11/crash-dump-analysis-patterns-part-287/

Resources

- ◉ WinDbg Help / WinDbg.org (quick links)
- ◉ DumpAnalysis.org / SoftwareDiagnostics.Institute / PatternDiagnostics.com
- ◉ Debugging.TV / YouTube.com/DebuggingTV / YouTube.com/PatternDiagnostics
- ◉ Practical Foundations of Windows Debugging, Disassembling, Reversing, Second Edition
- ◉ Windows Debugging Notebook: Essential User Space WinDbg Commands
- ◉ Software Diagnostics Library
- ◉ Pattern-Driven Software Problem Solving
- ◉ Memory Dump Analysis Anthology (Diagnomicon)

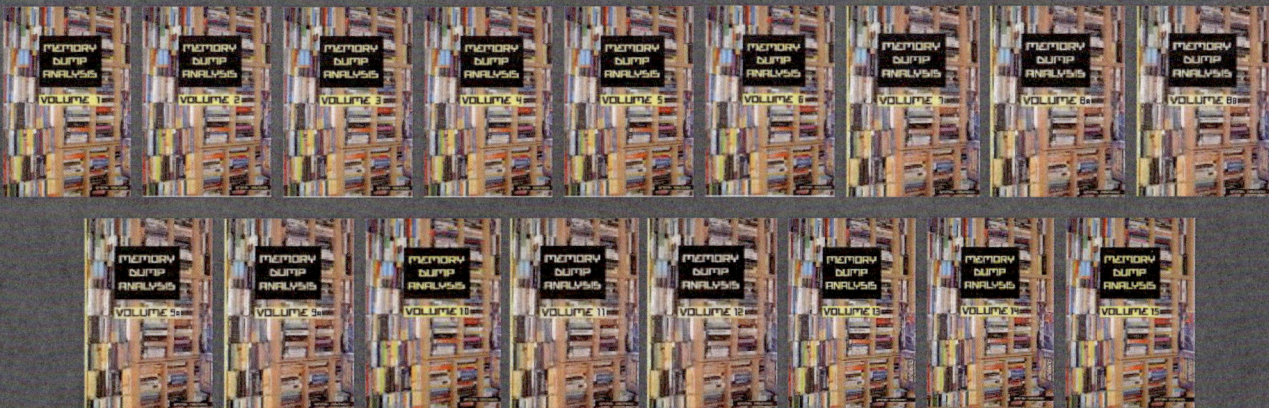

© 2024 Software Diagnostics Services

If you don't have experience with assembly language, then *Practical Foundations of Windows Debugging, Disassembling, Reversing, Second Edition* book teaches you assembly language from scratch in the context of WinDbg.

WinDbg Help / WinDbg.org (quick links)
http://www.windbg.org/

Software Diagnostics Institute
https://www.dumpanalysis.org/

Debugging.TV / DebuggingTV YouTube Channel
http://www.debugging.tv/
https://www.youtube.com/DebuggingTV

Practical Foundations of Windows Debugging, Disassembling, Reversing, Second Edition
https://www.patterndiagnostics.com/practical-foundations-windows-debugging-disassembling-reversing

Windows Debugging Notebook: Essential User Space WinDbg Commands
https://www.dumpanalysis.org/Forthcoming+Windows+Debugging+Notebook

Software Diagnostics Library

https://www.dumpanalysis.org/blog/

Pattern-Driven Software Problem Solving

https://www.dumpanalysis.org/pattern-driven-software-problem-solving

Memory Dump Analysis Anthology (Diagnomicon)

https://www.dumpanalysis.org/advanced-software-debugging-reference

Appendix

Complete Stack Traces from x64 System

Reprinted from Memory Dump Analysis Anthology, Volume 5, Revised Edition, pages 30 – 31[15]

Previously we wrote on how to get a 32-bit stack trace from a 32-bit process thread on an x64 system (**32-bit Stack Traces from x64 Complete Memory Dumps**, Volume 3, page 43). There are situations when we are interested in all such stack traces, for example, from a complete memory dump. We wrote a script that extracted both 64-bit and WOW64 32-bit stack traces:

```
.load wow64exts
!for_each_thread "!thread @#Thread 1f;.thread /w @#Thread; .reload; kb 256; .effmach
AMD64"
```

Here is WinDbg example output fragment for a thread fffffa801f3a3bb0 from a very long debugger log file:

```
[...]

Setting context for owner process...
.process /p /r fffffa8013177c10


THREAD fffffa801f3a3bb0  Cid 4b4c.5fec  Teb: 000000007efaa000 Win32Thread:
fffff900c1efad50 WAIT: (UserRequest) UserMode Non-Alertable
    fffffa8021ce4590  NotificationEvent
    fffffa801f3a3c68  NotificationTimer
Not impersonating
DeviceMap                  fffff8801b551720
Owning Process             fffffa8013177c10       Image:         application.exe
Attached Process           N/A            Image:         N/A
Wait Start TickCount       14066428       Ticks: 301 (0:00:04.695)
Context Switch Count       248                    LargeStack
UserTime                   00:00:00.000
KernelTime                 00:00:00.000
Win32 Start Address mscorwks!Thread::intermediateThreadProc (0x00000000733853b3)
Stack Init fffffa60190e5db0 Current fffffa60190e5940
Base fffffa60190e6000 Limit fffffa60190df000 Call 0
Priority 11 BasePriority 10 PriorityDecrement 0 IoPriority 2 PagePriority 5
Child-SP          RetAddr           Call Site
fffffa60`190e5980 fffff800`01cba0fa nt!KiSwapContext+0x7f
fffffa60`190e5ac0 fffff800`01caedab nt!KiSwapThread+0x13a
fffffa60`190e5b30 fffff800`01f1d608 nt!KeWaitForSingleObject+0x2cb
fffffa60`190e5bc0 fffff800`01cb7973 nt!NtWaitForSingleObject+0x98
fffffa60`190e5c20 00000000`75183d09 nt!KiSystemServiceCopyEnd+0x13 (TrapFrame @
fffffa60`190e5c20)
00000000`069ef118 00000000`75183b06 wow64cpu!CpupSyscallStub+0x9
00000000`069ef120 00000000`74f8ab46 wow64cpu!Thunk0ArgReloadState+0x1a
00000000`069ef190 00000000`74f8a14c wow64!RunCpuSimulation+0xa
00000000`069ef1c0 00000000`771605a8 wow64!Wow64LdrpInitialize+0x4b4
```

---

[15] Note from Software Diagnostics Library. With extra frame arguments:
```
!for_each_thread "!thread @#Thread 16;.thread /w @#Thread; .reload; kv 256; .effmach AMD64"
```

```
00000000`069ef720 00000000`771168de ntdll! ?? ::FNODOBFM::`string'+0x20aa1
00000000`069ef7d0 00000000`00000000 ntdll!LdrInitializeThunk+0xe


.process /p /r 0
Implicit thread is now fffffa80`1f3a3bb0
WARNING: WOW context retrieval requires
switching to the thread's process context.
Use .process /p fffffa80`1f6b2990 to switch back.
Implicit process is now fffffa80`13177c10
x86 context set
Loading Kernel Symbols
Loading User Symbols
Loading unloaded module list
Loading Wow64 Symbols
ChildEBP RetAddr
06aefc68 76921270 ntdll_772b0000!ZwWaitForSingleObject+0x15
06aefcd8 7328c639 kernel32!WaitForSingleObjectEx+0xbe
06aefd1c 7328c56f mscorwks!PEImage::LoadImage+0x1af
06aefd6c 7328c58e mscorwks!CLREvent::WaitEx+0x117
06aefd80 733770fb mscorwks!CLREvent::Wait+0x17
06aefe00 73377589 mscorwks!ThreadpoolMgr::SafeWait+0x73
06aefe64 733853f9 mscorwks!ThreadpoolMgr::WorkerThreadStart+0x11c
06aeff88 7699eccb mscorwks!Thread::intermediateThreadProc+0x49
06aeff94 7732d24d kernel32!BaseThreadInitThunk+0xe
06aeffd4 7732d45f ntdll_772b0000!__RtlUserThreadStart+0x23
06aeffec 00000000 ntdll_772b0000!_RtlUserThreadStart+0x1b
Effective machine: x64 (AMD64)


[...]
```

www.ingramcontent.com/pod-product-compliance
Lightning Source LLC
Chambersburg PA
CBRC091939210326
41598CB00012B/860